D1083090

A HISTORY OF

MODERN POETRY

Modernism and After

DAVID PERKINS

1 9 8 7

THE BELKNAP PRESS OF

HARVARD UNIVERSITY PRESS

Cambridge, Massachusetts, and London, England

Copyright © 1987 by the President and Fellows of Harvard College
All rights reserved
Printed in the United States of America
10 9 8 7 6 5 4 3 2 1

This book is printed on acid-free paper, and its binding materials have been chosen for strength and durability.

Library of Congress Cataloging in Publication Data

Perkins, David, 1928–
     A history of modern poetry.

     Includes index.
     1. American poetry—20th century—History and
criticism. 2. English poetry—20th century—History
and criticism. I. Title.
PS323.5.P46   1987   821'.91'09   86-14904
ISBN 0-674-39946-3 (alk. paper)

Acknowledgments begin on page 661.

PREFACE

THIS is the second of two volumes that together unfold the history of modern poetry from the 1890s to the present. The first volume ended in the mid-1920s. By this time major works of high Modernist poetry had been published—T. S. Eliot's *The Waste Land* (1922), Ezra Pound's *A Draft of XVI Cantos* (1925), Wallace Stevens' *Harmonium* (1923), D. H. Lawrence's *Birds, Beasts, and Flowers* (1923), and William Carlos Williams' *Spring and All* (1923)—and the critical hegemony of Eliot, which was to last for another twenty-five years, was already beginning in Great Britain. That volume traced the ways in which the Romantic, essentially popular style of poetry of the nineteenth century was abandoned or transformed, and in three phases. The Aesthetic-Impressionist-Symbolist poetry of the 1890s was followed, after a conservative reaction, by the phase of "Popular Modernism" that began approximately in 1910 and lasted until the end of the First World War. The latter style was widespread. It was briefly exemplified before the First World War in the poetry of Yeats, Pound, and Williams, and is also represented by, among many others, the Imagists, Carl Sandburg, and Robert Frost. The third phase was that of the "high Modernist style," which was fully mature in T. S. Eliot's *Poems* (1919) and Pound's *Hugh Selwyn Mauberley* (1920). Yeats was the major figure throughout the entire period covered in the first volume, which closed with a chapter on his career.

The principal theme of the present volume is the continuing effort of poets since the 1920s to modify or break away from the high Modernist style. We see this in the young English poets of the 1930s, such as Auden; in Dylan Thomas, Theodore Roethke, and other poets of the Romantic revival in England and the United States during the 1930s and 1940s; in the later careers of the high Modernist poets themselves; in Philip Larkin and the group of poets, known as the "Movement," that emerged in Great Britain in the 1950s; and in the several reactions in the United States during the 1950s and 1960s against the genteel codification of high Modernist values associated with the New Criticism.

Because of the scope, boldness, brilliance, and idiosyncrasy of the high Modernist poetry of the 1920s, no later poets could adopt the style without appearing to themselves, as well as to others, to dwindle in the comparison. After so great an achievement, poets felt that they had to develop a different style in order to exist. Moreover, from the 1930s to the present poets have been motivated to repudiate high Modernist style because they feared it might isolate their art. The difficulty of this style was such that it could, they felt, be understood only by an elite few. Its concrete presentation and ellipsis precluded reflective discourse and generalization in verse, the usual language of meditation and thoughtful conversation. The impersonality of the high Modernist style interposed itself as an emotional barrier between the poet and the reader, and a persistent irony tended to limit emotion expressed in poetry by qualifying it.

Yet though they felt that they could not continue as mere followers to write in the high Modernist style, poets have also been unable to reject it. For this style embodied a major access of reality, both in its subject matters and in the complexity of its perspectives, and it was also formally challenging and proficient in the highest degree. Therefore, to depart from this style has troubled the conscience. Poets have feared lest they seem sentimental and diluted in comparison. Whatever they have said in manifestoes, in their hearts they have been unable either to accept or to refuse the stylistic legacy of high Modernism.

A major hope, in writing these volumes, has been to widen the canon of modern poets. The aim is not a reevaluation that would displace some poets for the sake of others. But in the number and variety of poets worth serious attention our century is richer than most readers assume. In this volume I discuss approximately one hundred and sixty poets, and many more are mentioned in passing. Others are silently passed over for reasons of space, and in doing this, I have recollected the feelings of Little Father Time in Thomas Hardy's *Jude the Obscure,* who hanged himself and his brothers and sisters and left a note that said, "Done because we are too many."

To consider literary history within a perspective so inclusive makes it possible to stress the complex interrelations of movements, groups, and poets that are usually discussed only separately. Interconnection becomes a major theme and cross-reference a leading expository method. That the volume focuses on the poetry of both Great Britain and the United States is especially appropriate, since throughout the twentieth century the main influence on the poetry of each country has been that of the other. The breadth of perspective also fosters critical judgments that are many-sided, for in considering so many gifted poets, I cannot identify with only one or a few. Yet though I hope that my critical perceptions may be accurate, and that my distribution of attention among poets will seem reasonable and fair, the discussion of contemporary poetry is inherently and rightly controversial, and I expect to evoke dialogue more than agreement.

While concentrating on poets and their careers, I have tried also to present the contexts in which their styles were formed. Such contexts include the predecessors they responded to; the contemporaries they knew, admired, or regarded as rivals; the writings of critics; the audience and its expectations; the journals in which their work was accepted; developments in other arts; and events in political history, such as the Depression and the approaching war in the 1930s, the Socialist era in postwar England, and the protest against the war in Vietnam in the United States during the 1960s. Since a style always reflects general assumptions about poetry—what it is and how it should be written—I give prominence to these assumptions as they change over time.

In writing a history of literature, it is necessary, as we approach the present, to resist acute pressures to produce something resembling an annotated catalogue of names and titles, a featureless book with brief notices of every possible author. More works seem important, or possibly important, than can be discussed in any single book, however capacious. In chapters on contemporary poetry, therefore, I have concentrated on authors whose careers by the 1970s could be viewed as something of a whole and who were at the peak of their reputations. The cost paid for this is that less space is available for considering the middle generation of poets now in their forties, and in the pages that follow most of them can be noticed only briefly in a paragraph or two. That they are less discussed does not mean that they are less worth reading, but only that a choice had to be made, and it seemed more necessary to focus on poets who had written over a longer period of time. The same consideration applies even more drastically to the still younger generation of poets. Their careers will eventually be the subject of another historian or of a future installment of this history.

I am grateful for much kindly assistance. The Harvard administration and my colleagues in the English department released time from teaching. Quotations were checked by Sarah Bayliss, Kathy Cox, and Michael Gibson. John Brawner helped with research. Michael Gibson made the index. I owe special thanks to those who read the manuscript in whole or part: W. Jackson Bate, Ronald Bush, Walton Litz, James Richardson, and Alan Williamson.

CONTENTS

Part Three. Postmodernism

PART ONE

THE AGE OF HIGH MODERNISM

1

THE ASCENDANCY OF T. S. ELIOT,
1925–1950

FOR twenty-five years T. S. Eliot exercised an authority in the literary world not possessed by any writer before him for more than a century. By the end of the 1920s his poetry was an inescapable influence on younger poets, and his criticism shaped their work even more pervasively, if only because they read the authors he praised. Twenty years later *The Waste Land* was still widely regarded as the most radical and brilliant development of Modernist poetry. One must have lived through the 1940s and 1950s to grasp how frequently and respectfully Eliot's literary judgments were cited. By this time few poets were imitating him, for his elliptical style had severe disadvantages. Eliot felt this himself, and in the *Four Quartets* he partly reverted to a personal, meditative voice traditional in poetry. Moreover, except during and after the Second World War, his conservative, Christian ideology was unattractive to many intellectuals in England and the United States. Even without these grounds for rejection, the poets who came after Eliot would have been compelled to resist him in order to establish an identity of their own. Thus the future development of poetry did not proceed from Eliot, but both from and against him, and in both respects he was central.

"I do not know for certain how much of my own mind he

invented," William Empson wrote, "let alone how much of it is a reaction against him or indeed a consequence of misreading him." "To our generation," recalled Stephen Spender, "Eliot was the poet of poets." "*Are* there any better poems of their kind in English," Archibald MacLeish wistfully asked himself in 1925, having just read "Three Poems" in *Criterion* magazine (of which two became portions of "The Hollow Men"). In a letter to John Peale Bishop at this time MacLeish said that "after Eliot" it was impossible to write anything except "more Eliot," of which MacLeish felt personally incapable. When Allen Tate first read Eliot in 1922, he reported the "shock" in a letter to Hart Crane. Crane replied: "I have been facing him for *four* years . . . You see it is such a fearful temptation to imitate him that at times I have been distracted." But Crane hoped he had discovered a way "*through* [Eliot] toward a *different goal*." William Carlos Williams believed that with the publication of *The Waste Land* "the bottom had dropped out of everything" he cared about in poetry. Eliot's poem, Williams felt, was "the great catastrophe to our letters . . . I was defeated." The yearbook of Delmore Schwartz's high school remarked that "T. S. Eliot is God, and Delmore Schwartz is his prophet," so much had Schwartz extolled Eliot. In later years Schwartz sensed that he was living under a literary dictatorship, and he both submitted and rebelled. Eliot was equally an obsession for Karl Shapiro, who violently attacked him as a simulacrum. Stanley Kunitz later explained that "for more than three decades" before the Second World War "you could scarcely pick up a poem by a young writer without overhearing [Eliot] somewhere in the background . . . In the twenties and thirties one had to follow Eliot in order to win a reputation or an audience."

During the 1950s and 1960s it was frequently said that Eliot's ascendancy had deflected English and American poetry from its natural path. This view of literary history is represented by Philip Larkin's 1973 *Oxford Book of Twentieth-Century English Verse*, which emphasizes continuities between poetry before the First and after the Second World War. Eliot's poetry has always seemed alien—Franco-American—to many English readers. In the United States William Carlos Williams and his followers deplored Eliot's prestige on similar grounds. He had disseminated, they said, a formalism, a cosmopolitanism, and an academicism from which American poetry recovered only in the 1950s and 1960s, when it reattached itself to poets and traditions it had deserted in the 1920s. As Robert Lowell put it to Williams in a 1952 letter, Eliot's "personality and opinions" were "not at all what anyone in America or England [had] really wanted . . . I think the field was open, and that" Williams and his fellow poets had enjoyed "the more direct road." Eliot had dominated, Lowell bluntly told Williams, because of his superior "artistry and sincerity."

Eliot was not a better poet than Yeats or Frost, and the course of poetry after the Second World War showed that he was not inevitably a stronger influence than Pound, Williams, or Wallace Stevens. We may ask, therefore, why it was Eliot, so much more than these other poets, who loomed in the path of his immediate successors. During the first period of Pound's strong influence on modern poetry, roughly from 1912 to 1925, Pound and Eliot were a front, and Eliot's impact was augmented by this alliance. Their critical statements spread the demand that poetry should "modernize" its style, and their own poetry exemplified what was meant. Yeats, Hardy, and Frost did not seem comparably "modern" in the period when this adjective acquired a special cachet. Recognition of Wallace Stevens and William Carlos Williams was delayed by Eliot's ascendancy, and Pound's influence waned after 1921, when Pound left London. Living in Paris and, after 1924, in Italy, Pound could no longer be a personal force. Meanwhile in London Eliot founded and edited *Criterion* magazine and became an editor at the publishing firm of Faber and Faber. Most younger poets in England and the United States were published by Eliot or hoped to be.

Eliot's literary criticism enormously enhanced his prestige. The transformation of taste he effected is a commonplace of modern literature. I. A. Richards, William Empson, F. R. Leavis, Allen Tate, and others who also played important roles were themselves influenced by Eliot. "It is as much as one's life is worth nowadays, among young people," Edmund Wilson wrote in 1931, "to say an approving word for Shelley or a dubious one about Donne." When in 1923 Archibald MacLeish quit the law for literature, he thought he should prepare himself for his new vocation by a course of reading. Even at this early date his program reflected the critical perceptions of Eliot and Pound: he intended to learn "Italian with a view to reading Dante," to go through "pre-Chaucerian stuff," to "follow the trend from Anglo-Saxon and Provençal," and to study Laforgue in French, *The Golden Bough*, and "that line." Malcolm Cowley was also intimidated into learning Italian in order to read Dante, and as late as 1952 I knew numerous graduate students who began studying Italian under the same influences. Eliot was among the writers who led Hart Crane and Allen Tate to French *symbolisme*. Owing partly to Eliot, Dylan Thomas and William Empson were infatuated with "Metaphysical" conceits at the end of the 1920s, and so were numerous other English and American poets in the 1930s, while books and articles on the Metaphysical poetry of the seventeenth century poured from the universities.

The authority of Eliot never permeated the literary world completely, however, and it arrived at different times for different readers. With poets younger than Eliot it was at its height from 1922, when *The Waste Land* was published, into the 1930s. But with critics, editors, academic students of literature, and general readers the story is more complicated. Few persons older than Eliot were able to appreciate his poetry. The record is full of experienced readers—H. L. Mencken, Harriet Monroe, Van Wyck Brooks, Louis Untermeyer, Amy Lowell, Harold Monro, W. B. Yeats—who never understood why Eliot's poetry was so much admired, though some of them paid lip service. We may illustrate the generational situation by comparing the reactions of John Crowe Ransom with those of Allen Tate. When Tate began to praise Eliot, Ransom, who was eleven years older than Tate, had never read Eliot, and he did not much like Eliot's poetry when he did read it. Yet we do not suppose that Ransom was a less receptive or intelligent reader than Tate.

Most academic critics lagged a quarter-century behind. The first important book on Eliot by a university professor was by F. O. Matthiessen and came out in 1935. In 1949 UNESCO asked a group of American professors of English to name the twenty best American books. Their list included Robinson and Frost but not Eliot. Perhaps Eliot was viewed as English, but "The Best Books of Our Time," a list compiled from publications of library associations and other "expert" sources, affirmed in 1948 that the best poets were, in order of rank, Frost, Auden, and Sandburg, with Eliot in fourteenth place. In the same year

New Colophon: A Book Collector's Quarterly asked its readers to name living American writers most likely to be regarded as classics in A.D. 2000. The poets on this list were Frost, Sandburg, Eliot, and Millay, in third, fifth, seventh, and tenth place respectively. Ten years later, in 1958, a poll of graduate students in English at Columbia University placed Eliot first among living poets. With general readers and the professoriat, in other words, Eliot's reputation reached its height only after the Second World War, just when it was rapidly eroding among poets.

In later chapters I will have occasion to dwell on the relations between Eliot and this or that particular poet or group, but I here sketch the continuing dialectic of emulation and resistance as a whole. In following the order of chapters to come, this sketch also provides an overview of the course of modern poetry from the 1920s to the present. Needless to say, a great many older poets, such as Hardy, Frost, and Yeats, were active during this period, and Yeats rivaled Eliot in reputation. These poets, whose careers were described in the first volume of this history, are central in modern poetry, but owed nothing to Eliot, having formed their styles before he wrote. Our story concerns the successive generations of poets who emerged after the high Modernist revolution of 1917–22, and we begin with four Americans—E. E. Cummings, Archibald MacLeish, Robinson Jeffers, and Hart Crane—who first made their reputations in the 1920s. They illustrate different types of poetry that seemed "modern" at that time. Of these four only MacLeish and Crane were much influenced by Eliot, for Cummings and Jeffers, like Robert Graves in England, derived from earlier moments in the modern development. We shall see that in the 1920s and 1930s Eliot challenged the Whitmanian tradition—he is the great antagonist to Whitman in American poetry, even though his *Four Quartets* is full of Whitman—and that Crane conceived his epic *The Bridge* as a reply to *The Waste Land*. He hoped to carry Eliot's methods into a celebration, altogether in the spirit of Whitman, of American experience, and finally into mystical ecstasy.

Coming next to an international style, we observe what I call "the poetry of critical intelligence," a type of poetry that was created primarily by William Empson, John Crowe Ransom, and Allen Tate. So far as it descended from Eliot, this style was shaped more by his criticism than by his poetry. In other words, Empson and Tate followed Eliot more closely as critics than as poets, and their poetry reflected their critical ideals and tastes. Gradually their criticism, together with that of I. A. Richards, Richard Blackmur, Yvor Winters, Robert Penn Warren, and Cleanth Brooks, was perceived as forming a school, and in the United States this so-called New Criticism penetrated the university teaching of literature. Young poets began to write for the kind of "close reading" or "explication" they had been taught in the classroom. This was during the 1940s and 1950s, when symbolism, "organic" interconnection of images, formal meters and stanzas, and packed "wit" characterized an academic style in the United States. This style was adopted by, among many others, John Berryman, Robert Lowell, Richard Wilbur, and Adrienne Rich at the start of their careers. Thus there were two generations of New Critical poets, the older one that created the style in the 1920s and the younger one that received it in the classroom during the 1940s. The second generation, which eventually rebelled against this style, is the subject of a later chapter, "Breaking through the New Criticism."

In the 1930s intellectual life was preoccupied by political events—economic collapse, Fascism in Italy and Germany, the Italian invasion of Ethiopia, the Spanish Civil War, rearmament, and the growing threat of a second World War. The important new poets who emerged in the 1930s were English rather than American, for most poets of the same generation in the United States did not begin to publish until the 1940s. The thirties poets of England expressed the emotions evoked in them by the historical crises, and these emotions were widely shared. Moreover, many poets desired to engage their art directly in the historical crises by forwarding a political cause, and so they wrote to warn, to denounce, or to rally supporters. Such intentions presupposed a loosening of style, and one might have expected that their poetry would reach a large audience. The same type of reader who had responded to the Georgian poets and to Wilfred Owen and Siegfried Sassoon during the First World War, but had not been able to appreciate Eliot, Pound, and Yeats, might have been addressed by the gifted new generation of W. H. Auden, Stephen Spender, Louis MacNeice, and Cecil Day-Lewis.

Yet, on the whole, this did not happen, and the main reason

lies in the continuing grip of the difficult Modernist style on the young poets. This is the more remarkable because Modernism meant chiefly Eliot—his literary criticism and *The Waste Land*— and yet the social attitudes implied in *The Waste Land* were offensive to most poets in the 1930s. After 1934, when he published *After Strange Gods*, Eliot was suspected of Fascist sympathies. Nevertheless, the young poets could not surrender what Eliot had taught them about writing, for it represented to them the highest standards of contemporary poetic art. We should also keep in mind that even in relation to the public crises the poets' emotions were likely to be complex and ambivalent. If, for example, they hoped for a Communist revolution, they also dreaded it, for it would destroy the middle-class way of life to which they were fondly attached—the thatched, rural, private cottage, for example, in which Cecil Day-Lewis was living while he distributed Communist pamphlets. Modernist complexity and obscurity were necessary for a poet as self-divided and unclear about his position as Auden. Thus these poets could not readily adopt Modernist style, and neither could they reject it. They found themselves in a dilemma, one that has been prototypical for poets since.

Eliot's poetry overturned poetic conventions of the Romantic tradition, and his criticism attacked them. His anti-Romantic polemic was continued by most of the more important critics of the following generation—William Empson, F. R. Leavis, and the New Critics in the United States—and at least a third of the new poets subscribed to it in theory. Auden viewed Romanticism as leading to Fascism. Yet Romantic aspects and derivations have since been highlighted in both Eliot and Auden, not to mention other great Modernist poets such as Yeats, Williams, and Stevens. And though most poets after Eliot would have become irritable at any suggestion that they themselves were not modern, their hearts still melted when they read Romantic lyrics. They hungered for the melody and cadence, imagery of nature, strong personal emotion, idealism, and mysticism of poetry in the Romantic tradition. Cummings, MacLeish, Crane, Spender, Day-Lewis, Thomas, and Roethke, among many others, were modern poets of Romantic sensibility. Thus in practice the Modernist movement in poetry was much less anti-Romantic than is usually supposed. Despite conflicting cross-currents, the dominant impulse of poets in the twenty years after *The Waste Land* was not to carry the Modernist development further, but to modify it by combining it with the poetic traditions of the nineteenth century.

The English Romantic revival, which I describe in Chapter 8, expressed a definite restlessness with Eliot's hegemony. Dylan Thomas, the greatest of the neo-Romantic poets, combined *symboliste* technique with Metaphysical wit, but he also challenged the ethos of Eliot through biblical tones of prophecy and an imagery of quasi-mystical oneness with nature. The "True Confessions" of George Barker were the apotheosis of the un-Eliotic personal and unbuttoned. The Second World War fostered feelings of solidarity among classes and of continuity with the national past. In this atmosphere high Modernist style had little appeal, and neither the poets who described war experience nor those who expressed the religious emotions evoked by the war were much influenced by it. The chief exception is Eliot himself, whose "Little Gidding" is the great English poem of the war years.

In the United States, meanwhile, the poets who emerged in the 1930s, such as Stanley Kunitz, Richard Eberhart, Delmore Schwartz, and Karl Shapiro, felt themselves inhibited by the authority of Eliot, since it militated against the strong, direct emotional expression that was natural for them. Generally they opposed Eliot's influence as much as they dared, though, as I have mentioned, Schwartz was ambivalent. Theodore Roethke imitated Eliot at times, but in his finest poems he shared the Romantic ethos of Dylan Thomas.

After the Modernist revolution of 1912–22, the second major transition in the history of modern poetry was the revolt against Modernism, which took place between roughly 1954 and 1964. In England this second revolution was the work of Philip Larkin and other poets of the so-called Movement; they returned for inspiration to Hardy, the Georgian poets of the 1910s and 1920s, and the Augustan poets of the eighteenth century. English poets now wrote almost as though Eliot had never existed. In the United States the break with Modernism was less drastic but more explosive, as can be seen in Allen Ginsberg's *Howl* (1955), Robert Lowell's *Life Studies* (1959), and the many new disciples of William Carlos Williams at this time. The Beat movement, itself merely the visible tip of a much larger, deeper change in American culture and lifestyle, contributed to the dispelling of Modernism. So also did the protest in the 1960s against the war in Vietnam. But the history of Postmodernism in poetry, the subject of Part Three of this book, begins in the United States with the academic triumph of Modernism, that is, with the establishment of the New Criticism, and therefore of the authority of Eliot, as an orthodoxy within university English departments. At this point, when *The Waste Land* was routinely "explicated" to freshmen, a poet could be truly "modern" and "avant-garde" only by rejecting the New Criticism and Eliot. The style of poetry that had been fostered by the New Criticism now seemed lifeless and remote from reality, and young poets looked about for new ways of writing. The most visible sources of a poetic renewal were the great poets of Eliot's own generation—Pound, Williams, and Stevens—whom Eliot had more or less eclipsed. By 1950 they were authors of vastly impressive oeuvres, and they had recently published new work of major importance— Pound's *Pisan Cantos* (1948), Williams' *Paterson I* (1946), and Stevens' *Transport to Summer* (1947) and *Auroras of Autumn* (1950). Yet, except for Pound, these poets had never been adequately recognized, and Pound had been neglected after 1930. All were available, so to speak, to be discovered, championed, identified with, and learned from.

The first factor, then, in the reaction against Eliot and the New Criticism in the 1950s was the resurgence of Pound, Williams, and Stevens, which is described in Part Two of this book. The term "resurgence" refers both to their own splendid creativity after the Second World War and to their rising reputations and influence on younger poets at this time. But a poet could hardly draw inspiration from both Stevens, on the one hand, and Pound and Williams, on the other, for their styles were widely different, and hence the admirers of one generally lacked interest in the other, a situation still reflected in critical writing. The new admiration for Pound and Williams also focused attention on minor followers of theirs in earlier generations, and Basil Bunting and Louis Zukofsky found a small readership for the first time. This appreciation led Bunting, who had stopped writing poetry, to resume it, and at the age of sixty-six he produced his masterpiece, *Briggflatts* (1966). Meanwhile, David Jones, though not personally associated with Pound or influenced by him, also found new readers at this time, since the resurgence of Pound created a warmer acceptance for Jones's methods of allusive, fragmentary montage in *Anathemata* (1955) and other poems.

Since from the 1960s to the present Eliot has not been an important influence on poets, there is no reason to dwell here on the final chapters of this book. In them I shall be telling how American poets greatly modified or abandoned the New Critical style. I shall discuss the disciples of William Carlos Williams, the theories of open form propagated by Charles Olson, Robert Duncan, and others, the Beat ethos of Allen Ginsberg, and the Confessional poetry of Lowell and Berryman. Over the last twenty years poetry in Great Britain has been generally more conservative than in the United States. The chief figures are Thom Gunn, Ted Hughes, and Geoffrey Hill; and with them I discuss the contemporary poetry of Ireland, especially as this is represented in the achievement of Seamus Heaney. I look at the American poetry of black and women's experience, and in the poetry of Robert Bly, James Wright, W. S. Merwin, Gary Snyder, and others, I explore the emotional rejection of civilization evoked by materialistic glut, ecological pollution, extermination of animal species, and terror of nuclear war, together with the compensatory idealization of the primitive. After a discussion of A. R. Ammons, I conclude with substantial essays on the finest living American poets, John Ashbery and James Merrill.

2

ELIOT'S LATER CAREER

T. S. ELIOT (1888–1965) came of a genteel, middle-class family. As a child he lived in St. Louis and spent summers on the coast north of Boston. On a trip to Europe in 1910–11, after graduating from Harvard College, he completed his first important poems, "Portrait of a Lady" and "The Love Song of J. Alfred Prufrock." In London in 1914 he showed these to Ezra Pound, who arranged for "Prufrock" to be published. In 1915 Eliot married Vivien Haigh-Wood, an Englishwoman, and abandoned the academic career he had been intending. For a while he earned his living by teaching school, and then he found a job in a London bank. His marriage proved unhappy, but despite the emotional turmoil it produced, he continued his literary career, composing "Gerontion" and the famous poems in quatrains. After 1917 he was also writing the book reviews that were eventually to make him influential as a critic, and his first collection of critical essays, *The Sacred Wood*, was published in 1920. In 1921, his health temporarily broken, he went to a sanatorium in Switzerland, and there he completed *The Waste Land* (1922). A year later he founded *Criterion* magazine, an influential journal of literature and criticism, which he edited henceforth. I described Eliot's life to this point at length in the first volume of this history, paying particular attention to *The Waste Land* and its revolutionary methods of poetic expression.

In 1927 Eliot was baptized and confirmed as a member of the Anglican Church. The demon of doubt, with which he had wrestled since college, had not left him. Virtually all his poetry from this time forth presents the struggle for belief and faith in one who has already made a religious commitment. But intellectual and psychological needs—for tradition, order, belief, hope that his suffering had a purpose, for God as an object of his devotion, and for absolution—were overriding. To his mind, moreover, Christianity was less implausible than any other doctrine. Once he had joined the Church, he was punctilious in attendance and duties. His later poetry is saturated with the rhythm and diction of the Anglican liturgy, which he heard daily.

Eliot's conversion shocked many of his readers. The skepticism of *The Waste Land* had contributed to the impression of its modernity and hence to its prestige. Eliot's poem had displayed the modern mind saturated with history, possessing incongruous elements from different cultures in the past but no unified culture of its own. The poem had expressed the fascination of the modern intellectual with myths that had once embodied religious truth for a culture. It had dramatized the weakened will to live in the modern world, and had suggested to many readers that if the myths could again be believed, our culture and will would be restored to wholeness and vitality. Thus in *The Waste Land* Eliot had given concrete expression to ideas familiar in Nietzsche and several other diagnosers of the wounded modern spirit. That a bearer of this wound should actually join the Church could not be wholly unexpected, but it was viewed by some as another symptom of the illness.

Rereading *The Waste Land* after Eliot's conversion, one could find foretokenings of it. If the poem showed, as I. A. Richards said, that poetry could be written in the absence of all positive belief, it also testified to the woe of this state of mind. And Eliot had been moving toward conversion slowly over a period of time. He had never since his college years doubted the truth of Original Sin, the Christian doctrine that man's nature is fallen. Like many of the Aesthetes at the end of the nineteenth century, he felt, even during the years when he was not a Christian, that liberal optimism was shallow by comparison with the pessimistic insight of Christianity into the vanity of human life and the corruption of the heart. In 1919 Eliot was attentively reading sermons of John Donne and Lancelot Andrewes. He loved the churches of London, and would sometimes retreat into them for moments of peace. Though in his personal life and his poetry he had rebelled against tradition, a part of him had always believed in tradition and in the need for institutions that embody it. He was convinced that responsible thinking must lead to commitment. His relations with his wife, to which I shall come in a moment, left him with a sense of guilt and a disillusion with the possibilities of human love. By 1926 he was taking Anglican instruction and attending morning services, and on a trip to Rome he astonished his Unitarian relatives by kneeling before Michelangelo's *Pietà*.

Vivien Eliot was sensitive and vivacious, and she had unusual literary intelligence, appreciated Eliot's writing, and supported him in it. But she had a long history of nervous illnesses, and after her marriage these were exacerbated. While Eliot was working fifteen hours a day, Vivien had little to do. Their troubles were compounded by sexual failures. Vivien's symptoms were variable—headaches, stomach upsets, prostration, sleeplessness—and were made worse by the "cures," such as virtual starvation, to which the medical practice of the time condemned her. For long periods she required constant attendance. The Eliots' life together was dominated by the rhythm of collapse and partial recovery, the despair with flickers of hope, of chronic invalidism. Eliot felt responsible, helpless, and guilty, and the strain of caring for his wife undermined his own health. Vivien felt guilty for being a burden and for interfering with his work. To both their relationship could seem utterly empty. By 1925 they were spending much time apart, yet Vivien was showing signs of extreme dependence. Her mental states were increasingly alarming. Eliot tried to withdraw emotionally, wondered whether his presence might be harmful to her, and considered a separation. She sensed that he was withdrawing, and her resentment and fear vented themselves in hostility. At last he decided that he must leave her, and in 1933, while in the United States, he wrote his solicitors to prepare a deed of separation, enclosing a letter to be given to her. He did not see her again, for when he returned to England his home address was kept from her, and she was denied access to him at his office. In 1938 Vivien was committed to a mental institution, where she died in 1947.

Throughout these years of enormous unhappiness Eliot had been making his literary career. Through Bertrand Russell, who had taught him at Harvard, he met Lady Ottoline Morrell, a celebrated literary hostess, and through her he was introduced to other writers such as Aldous Huxley and Katherine Mansfield. Pound made him acquainted with Wyndham Lewis, and in 1918 he got to know Virginia Woolf and Edith and Osbert Sitwell. Personal contacts called the attention of these writers to his poetry. When Pound arranged to have *Prufrock and Other Observations,* Eliot's first collection of poems, published in 1917, reviewers ignored or dismissed the book, but the poems were already being discussed in drawing rooms that mattered. In the same year Eliot became assistant editor of *Egoist* magazine, where he began his career as a book reviewer. *Poems* (1919), which Leonard and Virginia Woolf published from the Hogarth Press, included Eliot's poems in quatrains, such as "Sweeney Among the Nightingales." Eliot started to contribute literary essays to Middleton Murry's *Athenaeum* and then to the *Times Literary Supplement,* for which he composed "Tradition and the Individual Talent" and other famous pieces. By 1920 his poems were beginning to find an enthusiastic audience among young literary academics, such as I. A. Richards, and in the same year the critical essays in *The Sacred Wood* augmented his reputation with this audience. *The Waste Land* came in 1922, and with *Criterion* he was editor of his own magazine. In 1925 Eliot joined the publishing firm of Faber and Gwyer (later Faber and Faber). "The Hollow Men" appeared in *Poems 1909–1925,* and *Ash Wednesday* was published in 1930. Meanwhile Eliot continued to turn out critical prose. He was invited to give the Clark Lectures at Cambridge in 1926 and the Norton Lectures at Harvard in 1932–33. These invitations show that his name would now attract an audience.

During the 1920s he stressed more forcibly than ever the virtues of the "classical" attitude. Like other modern thinkers of similar tendency, such as Irving Babbitt, Paul Elmer More, T. E. Hulme, and Charles Maurras (who all influenced him), Eliot advocated "classicism" in hostility to the modern world, which he viewed as Romantic, and his formulations were often harsh and intransigent. Emotion is naturally disordered and must be disciplined. External authority is necessary. Order is a principal ideal, and is to be achieved through intellectual awareness and control. Doubtless Eliot's "classicism" was, in part, a response to the emotional chaos of his own life. His baptism in 1927 and his naturalization as a British citizen were formal commitments expressing his resolve to put his life in order.

Eliot's literary tastes and ideals changed somewhat during the 1920s. Donne continued to fascinate him, but in the Clark lectures of 1926 he pronounced Donne to be personal, emotional, immature, and Romantic. Laforgue, with whom he had identified fifteen years before, he now criticized for lacking a coherent philosophy. Because of this, he argued Laforgue's emotion had little significance. He contrasted both Laforgue and Donne in this respect with Dante, whose *Vita Nuova* placed erotic feelings within a total order of thought. Eliot's ideals of poetic impersonality and objectivity now somewhat shifted their meaning. In his 1919 essay "Hamlet and His Problems" he had asserted that a poet can express emotion only through an "objective correlative," but he had assumed that by this method the writer would express personal emotion. By 1926, however, the ideal of impersonality might mean that the writer does not express his personal emotion at all; more exactly, he should express an emotion derived from and appropriate to whatever he contemplates. Thus Eliot praised Lancelot Andrewes because his emotion "is not personal, it is wholly evoked by the object of contemplation, to which it is adequate." Had he been able to emulate Andrewes, his poetry would have been a meditative discipline ordering the personal, emotional self.

Yet Eliot's poetic style did not become "classical," not, at least, if by that term we mean what Eliot did—"ordonnance," impersonality, continuous syntax, prose word order, and intellectual concentration and precision. Moreover, while rereading Dante, he also studied Mallarmé and Valéry, and he translated St.-John Perse's *Anabase* into English. These *symboliste* authors were also impersonal and intellectually deliberate, but they were scarcely "classical," if only because they liberated words from denotation and activated remote suggestions. The fusion of "classical" or

Augustan with *symboliste* verse that Eliot would achieve in the *Four Quartets* was preparing itself.

During the 1920s Eliot began to interpret his own life in a different way. Christianity teaches that the world moves on one plane and the spirit on another, and that the same event may have totally opposed meanings in these different realms. Thus Eliot's personal descent into humiliation and guilt might also be an ascent toward God. "The way up and the way down are one and the same," to quote the words of Heraclitus that Eliot later used as an epigraph to "Burnt Norton." As an epigraph to *Sweeney Agonistes*, the experimental drama he began in 1923, Eliot quoted St. John of the Cross: "Hence the soul cannot be possessed of the divine union, until it has divested itself of the love of created things"; and Eliot came to see such divestment as the purpose behind his marriage. He viewed himself as one of those exceptional persons, like Harry in *The Family Reunion* or Celia in *The Cocktail Party,* whose lives follow a spiritual pattern of which others are not aware. He accepted isolation and emotional aridity as the worldly side of a spiritual vocation.

"THE HOLLOW MEN" AND *ASH WEDNESDAY*

To its first readers "The Hollow Men" (1925) seemed to continue from *The Waste Land*. There is a similar imagery of a desert, and some images are almost identical. For example, "rats' feet over broken glass / In our dry cellar" at the start of "The Hollow Men" echos "a little low dry garret" with rats' feet in lines 194–5 of *The Waste Land*. The two poems employ similar methods of allusion and juxtaposition—in "The Hollow Men" the allusion, for example, in the epigraph to Joseph Conrad's *Heart of Darkness*. At the end of "The Hollow Men" a fragment of the Lord's Prayer ("For Thine is the Kingdom") is interwoven with a sigh of weariness ("Life is very long"); in technique this juxtaposition recalls lines 308–11 of *The Waste Land*. Above all, "The Hollow Men" resembles *The Waste Land* in mood. The opening and closing parts, especially, might almost fit into the earlier poem. Like *The Waste Land,* "The Hollow Men" begins with a chorus—

> We are the hollow men
> We are the stuffed men
> Leaning together

—expressing a collective death in life; it ends like *The Waste Land* with a mocking representation of the world going to smash. Hence in 1925 it was reasonable to see in "The Hollow Men" a further expression of the despair of *The Waste Land*—for *The Waste Land* was then understood to express only despair.

Yet after Eliot's conversion and the publication of *Ash Wednesday* a few years later, "The Hollow Men" could be read in a different way, as beginning a new development that *Ash Wednesday* extended. For amid the gestures and symbols that recalled *The Waste Land*, there is in "The Hollow Men" a much more explicit religiousness. The possibility of salvation is present, though the speakers either cannot or will not receive it, and this possibility is expressed in Christian symbols mediated through Dante: the "multifoliate rose" of part IV—"The hope only / Of empty men"—and the "eyes" the speaker dares not meet. The latter presumably belong to a composite figure including the Virgin Mary and Dante's Beatrice. "The Hollow Men" ends in a state of mind mingling disbelieving mockery, sorrow, weariness, and prayer, and cannot be simplified into affirmation, but as compared with *The Waste Land*, it registers a step of Eliot's mind toward conversion.

In style "The Hollow Men" differs strikingly from *The Waste Land* because, like every major poem of Eliot's henceforth, it lacks fragments of dramatic scenes and passages of extended narration. Such concrete vignettes as the conversation of Marie in *The Waste Land*, the session with the fortuneteller Madame Sosostris, and the description of the lovemaking of the typist and the real estate clerk are totally absent. This side of Eliot's genius went partly into making plays, but to a large extent it died. "The Hollow Men" still juxtaposed various styles, as *The Waste Land* had, but they were styles of abstraction. The stylistic virtue of

> Between the idea
> And the reality
> Between the motion
> And the act

lies in the precise philosophical terminology, in the "ordonnance" of the statement, and in the intellectual clarity to which these contribute, as well as in the chantlike rhythm.

The style of parts II–IV of "The Hollow Men" might also be characterized as abstract, but it is the abstraction of *symbolisme:*

> Eyes I dare not meet in dreams
> In death's dream kingdom
> These do not appear:
> There, the eyes are
> Sunlight on a broken column
> There, is a tree swinging
> And voices are
> In the wind's singing
> More distant and more solemn
> Than a fading star.

These lines can readily be interpreted. They express a state of consciousness in which presences (eyes, voices) that might possibly be salvific are not wholly withdrawn, but are distant, only reflected, and fading. Nevertheless, we are meant to be uncertain as to just where the eyes "do not appear," what and where "death's dream kingdom" may be, and what exactly the tree, voices, and star may symbolize. The images are precise—"Sunlight on a broken column"—but their meanings and emotional resonances are complicated and not fully determinable. The effect is of haunting vagueness with rich music.

"The Hollow Men" was created only gradually as a sequence, and part III originally belonged to an earlier sequence entitled "Doris's Dream Songs," while parts II and IV were composed for still another sequence, "Three Poems." Part I was first published as a separate lyric. Doris was a character in *Sweeney Agonistes,* and Eliot told Lady Ottoline Morrell that the poem arose as a byproduct of the play. The simple diction and the repetitions of "The Hollow Men" ("This is the dead land / This is cactus land") reflect his stylistic effort in the play, and so do the strong rhythms of some passages.

The first major poem Eliot published after he joined the Church, *Ash Wednesday* (1930) enacts the stress of the mind in the process of conversion. The image of turning dominates the first and final sections of the poem. Considered as the work of a recent convert, the poem strikingly lacks joyous belief. In fact, some passages are almost shockingly anguished, as Eliot speaks of those "who chose thee and oppose thee," who "affirm before the world and deny between the rocks." "Between" is the spiritual locus of the speaker throughout: he is between faith and doubt; between the order of nature and the order of grace; between the objects of desire of a natural creature, which are now lost, and those of religious faith, which are not yet wholly possessed. The speaker is in a "brief transit where the dreams cross" or intersect, "The dreamcrossed twilight between birth and dying" or between dying and birth. Like the characters in *The Waste Land* and "The Hollow Men," the protagonist is in a desert and can only wait. "Teach us to sit still," he says, "Even among these rocks"; but as these quotations show, the waiting in the desert has a different quality in *Ash Wednesday*, for it is filled with prayer, or with broken attempts at prayer.

Like "The Hollow Men," *Ash Wednesday* lacks the concrete, dramatic vignettes of *The Waste Land,* but in other respects it shows Eliot widening his stylistic resources. Some of his experiments were not to be repeated: the brilliant repetition of lines with variation of their terminal points—

> Because I do not hope to turn again
> Because I do not hope
> Because I do not hope to turn

—at the start of the poem; the allegorical imagery and the litany of part II; and the mannered repetitions and internal rhymes of part V. Other experiments had a future. Admirers of the impersonal concision of Eliot's earlier property must have been amazed to encounter these lines:

> Because I know that time is always time
> And place is always and only place
> And what is actual is actual only for one time
> And only for one place
> I rejoice that things are as they are.

For such writing is personal and ample, almost verbose. There would be similar passages in *Four Quartets.* If we contrast with this passage the lovely "reprise of Prufrock," as Ronald Bush describes it, from Part III of *Ash Wednesday*—"Blown hair is sweet, brown hair over the mouth blown, / Lilac and brown hair"—we see at once how much Eliot's style had changed. In other passages there is the emotional directness he had earlier deplored in the poetry of the nineteenth century:

> And the lost heart stiffens and rejoices
> In the lost lilac and the lost sea voices

> And the weak spirit quickens to rebel
> For the bent golden-rod and the lost sea smell
> Quickens to recover
> The cry of quail and the whirling plover.

In comparable passages in *Four Quartets,* Eliot uses this style for its own sake, but here it is thematic. It expresses an insurgent emotion of which he disapproves and against which he is struggling.

Eliot's reading of Dante shapes the poem, and two concepts are fundamental. In his depiction of Beatrice, Eliot believed, "Dante expresses the recrudescence of an ancient [erotic] passion in a new emotion, in a new situation, which comprehends, enlarges, and gives a meaning to it." If the general conception is familiar in Christian Platonism—erotic love can lead to religious love of God and find therein its meaning—Eliot's point of emphasis was not typical, for he stressed that the religious emotion not only contains but also revives the erotic one. Eliot's poetry never represented erotic attraction as happy. It was distasteful, or frustrated, or rejected through some failure of courage, or lost in the past, or was a temptation to be renounced. But when erotic feeling became a transfigured element in a religious experience or symbol, Eliot could rejoice in it without reserve, as he does in passages of *Ash Wednesday:*

> Here are the years that walk between, bearing
> Away the fiddles and the flutes, restoring
> One who moves in the time between sleep and waking, wearing
>
> White light folded, sheathed about her, folded.

Thus Dante's attitude to Beatrice unlocked a part of Eliot's sensibility.

In part II of *Ash Wednesday* the protagonist has been eaten by three white leopards, and exists only as dry bones. But the bones, "shining with brightness," are glad to be dead and scattered in the desert. Not because they are weary of life, like the characters of *The Waste Land,* but because they accept their condition as purgative. Eliot had been deeply impressed by a passage in Dante in which the souls in Purgatory crowd toward Dante "so far as they could, but ever watchful not to come so far that they should *not be in the fire.*" In his essay on Dante Eliot remarked, with the wonder of sudden insight, that "the souls in purgatory suffer because they *wish to suffer.*" This conception modifies the tone of feeling throughout *Ash Wednesday.* Darkness and anguish are present in the poem, but their quality is changed from *The Waste Land,* for the speaker knows that they may have a religious meaning, and they are shot through with waiting, hope, and prayer.

Eliot completed and published *Ash Wednesday* in 1930. In the academic year 1932–33 he was in the United States, lecturing at Harvard University and at the University of Virginia. These lectures were published as *The Use of Poetry and the Use of Criticism* (1933) and *After Strange Gods* (1934). While in the United States he took, as I mentioned earlier, the decisive step of formally separating from his wife. He renewed affections with his family and with Emily Hale, an American he had known before he met Vivien.

His poetry of the early thirties experimented in various directions. "Marina" (1930) is the most elusive poem Eliot ever wrote. It reflects his fascination at this time with Shakespeare's late plays, *Cymbeline, Pericles, The Winter's Tale,* and *The Tempest,* and conveys a nexus of emotions—fatigue, fear associated with old age, a feeling of shipwreck, discovery, wonder, and love. He started a new suite of poems, *Coriolan,* which he intended to be a political satire. But the poems soon began to reflect ambivalent personal emotions and the suite was never completed. In the United States he wrote poems evoking landscape in "Virginia" and "Cape Ann," and these poems slightly anticipated methods and emotions in the *Four Quarters.*

Returning to Great Britain, Eliot lived in drab accommodations in the presbytery of St. Stephen's in London, where he was to remain until the start of the second World War. Though Geoffrey Faber, Herbert Read, Frank Morley, and others were close friends, he was lonely. Eliot was one of those persons who take refuge from a bleak personal life in work, but of the work that filled his days, relatively little was composing poetry. He spent long hours on his editorial duties, and he accepted a great many chores—lectures, essays, poetry readings, committees, conferences—on behalf of worthy causes.

In the 1930s and thereafter Eliot's main effort as a writer went into poetic drama. Since dramas are not the subject of this history, I shall not discuss Eliot's. In general they wasted his creative energy, and as he moved from the unfinished *Sweeney Agonistes* (1932) to *Murder in the Cathedral* (1935), *The Family Reunion* (1939), *The Cocktail Party* (1950), *The Confidential Clerk* (1954), and *The Elder Statesman* (1958), each was less interesting than its predecessors. The time Eliot spent on these dramas counts among the notorious losses to English literature, like the twenty years Milton devoted to pamphleteering.

Eliot's political attitude throughout the 1930s was hand-wringing. He disliked all contemporary political systems and philosophies, including British democracy, and was rightly sure that no system of which he could approve would be established. When the Second World War began, however, he put such criticisms aside and felt a renewed identification with his adopted country. He became an air-raid warden, a job that required him to sit up two nights a week, and he increased his other activities.

FOUR QUARTETS

To my mind the *Four Quartets* is the greatest long poem yet written in English in the twentieth century. It is uneven. Some bits fail lamentably, and many passages seem to me set pieces, fine but contrived. But other passages are magnificent, and, what is more important, Eliot's formal procedures compensate for local inadequacies of imagination and phrasing. The context of the whole poem impends in every part, charging the language with resonance. Moreover, through long passages the poem combines concentrated meaning with direct emotional force and accessibility. Some of its rhythms are deeply moving, especially the legato of the final paragraph of "Burnt Norton" and the similar rhythms in "Little Gidding" III and V. The symbolism of the poem is inexhaustible, and so are its paradoxes: "In my end is my beginning"; "the way up is the way down"; "We die with the dying"; "the end of all our exploring / Will be to arrive where we started." Other passages impress by their austere truths wrung from the aridity of Eliot's daily life and the exacerbations of his conscience: the concluding lines of "Burnt Norton," the whole speech of the ghost in "Little Gidding" II, and the aphor-

ism that concludes the second movement of "East Coker"—
"The only wisdom we can hope to acquire / Is the wisdom of
humility." At its best the *Four Quartets* is more honest, more intelligent, more concerned with the essential in human experience, or more of all these in combination, than any other modern English or American poem.

"Burnt Norton," the first quartet in the sequence, had been
created as an independent poem in the mid-1930s. It had developed out of passages rejected from *Murder in the Cathedral*.
The three later quartets—"East Coker," "The Dry Salvages," and
"Little Gidding"—were written between 1940 and 1942. It was
only in 1940, while working on "East Coker," that Eliot had the
idea of making a suite of four poems.

In poetic form the *Four Quartets* withdraws from the high
Modernism of the 1920s, as can be seen from a quick comparison of the *Four Quartets* with *The Waste Land*. *The Waste Land* is
impersonal presentation; the *Four Quartets* is personal speech. In
it we overhear the poet exploring and reflecting upon personal
memories—memories of the rose garden at the manor house of
Burnt Norton, which Eliot had visited with Emily Hale in September 1935; of a 1937 trip to the village of East Coker, whence
his ancestor Andrew Eliot had emigrated to America; and of his
childhood in St. Louis and the sea and coast near Gloucester,
Massachusetts, where he had spent his summers as a boy. *The
Waste Land* is discontinuous and concrete, juxtaposing fragments
of actions and scenes. In passages the *Four Quartets* is continuous
and discursive; in other words, it employs the language of meditation and generalization. *The Waste Land* is laced with literary
allusions and uses a variety of contrasting, historical styles; both
these features are much softened in the *Four Quartets*. *The Waste
Land* interprets modern life within the perspective of ancient
myth, and it also parallels or contrasts the present with the historical past. The mythical dimension is less prominent in the
Four Quartets, and history is conceived in a different way, as a
past saturated with values, as a tradition to which the present is
or can be linked. And finally, *The Waste Land* exhibits the character and quality of life in the contemporary, urban world. Social
critique is largely absent from the *Four Quartets*, which is a poem
of Romantic metaphysical exploration. It presents the lonely
mind of the poet attempting to read ultimate mysteries.

Of these developments, unquestionably the most important was Eliot's return in the *Four Quartets* to the language of reflection and generalization, to the conceptual language in which most people think. At the start of his career Eliot had tried to shed his predilection for reflective verse, but now he returned to it as a mode deeply congenial to him. Instances of such language could already be found, as we noted, in "The Hollow Men," *Ash Wednesday*, and other poems of the same period. Eliot's success with such language in the *Four Quartets* followed long experiment, particularly in his plays. The same development had been taking place generally in modern poetry; in Chapter 6 of this history I discuss at some length the new poetry of discourse of the 1930s and its motivations. But the chief motivation, influencing Eliot as much as other poets, was simply that discursive thinking and generalization are as natural for a poet as for anyone else. To exclude them from poetry imposes an artificial limitation.

Yet if the *Four Quartets* returns to English poetic tradition, we cannot say precisely which tradition. Several passages in the poem, especially some of the briefer lyrics, recall verse of the seventeenth century. Some lines are partly modeled on prose. In *Ash Wednesday* V Eliot had experimented with the puns and repetitions of the seventeenth-century sermon, and he does this again, though in a different way, in "East Coker" III. Most readers associate Eliot's discursive passages with the Augustan mode. And since each of the quartets begins with a description or evocation of a place—the rose garden at Burnt Norton; the village of East Coker; the Mississippi River and the coast of Cape Ann; and the landscape along the way to the chapel at Little Gidding—the *Four Quartets* has a general affinity with the so-called descriptive-meditative poetry of the eighteenth century. In such poems, of which Gray's "Elegy in a Country Churchyard" is the most famous example, the poet renders the place where he is or the landscape before him, and then goes on to express thoughts the scene suggests to him.

The *Four Quartets* is a traditional type of poem in less definable ways, also: ways that have to do with the uses to which poetry is put or with notions of the "poetic." *The Waste Land* was sometimes read as satire, but the *Four Quartets* is undeviatingly serious. In fact, its tone is generally elegiac. Poems in the nineteenth century were, in contrast to novels, expected to soar above worldly dust. As the *Four Quartets* contemplates such large issues as art, death, time and eternity, it escapes from ordinary, humdrum reality. Moreover, its major symbols—the rose, fire, light, dark, the wheel, the sea, the river, the garden—are, as imagery, not emotionally disagreeable. In such respects the *Four Quartets* was in keeping with the Romantic conventions of the nineteenth century.

On the other hand, the *Four Quartets* is also the culmination of twentieth-century symbolism. The title proposes that the poem resembles music. Specific lines and passages activate the semantic suggestions and emotional overtones of words while precluding determinate meaning. Eliot impedes denotation by verbal contradiction, vagueness, ambiguous or incomplete grammar, failure of logical sequence, and paradox. In "Burnt Norton," for example, the opening episode in the rose garden is a memory of something that never happened—

> Footfalls echo in the memory
> Down the passage which we did not take
> Towards the door we never opened
> Into the rose-garden

—and most of what follows in this episode is similarly self-contradictory and indefinite. Later in the poem there are, to mention only a few illustrations, the vaguenesses of "Garlic and sapphires in the mud / Clot the bedded axle-tree," where the first line is adapted from one by Mallarmé; the paradoxes of "at the still point, there the dance is, / But neither arrest nor movement"; and the finely ominous mysteriousness of "Time and the bell have buried the day."

In *The Waste Land* Eliot had used recurrent images and actions as leitmotifs—for example, the desert, rain or water, and death by drowning. As the same images were repeated in different contexts, they associated these contexts, and thus tended to integrate the poem as a whole. At the same time, with each repetition the image acquired new connotations, until it became a densely suggestive nexus or symbol. To what degree Eliot had consciously intended these effects as he created *The Waste Land* is uncertain, but in writing the *Four Quartets* he was fully aware of their possibilities, and the *Four Quartets* is leitmotific, so to speak, to an unparalleled degree. As leitmotifs Eliot uses not only images and symbols—darkness, traveling, dancing, roses, fire—but also conceptual terms, such as "end," "beginning," "motion," "stillness," "word," and "pattern." By incremental, leitmotific repetition of such terms he gives intensity even to the abstract diction of the poem. Moreover, the poem returns in separate passages throughout to the same intellectual themes and existential concerns: to ways of conceiving time; to concepts of patterns; to the question of the relation of intense moments to the "waste sad time / Stretching before and after"; to experiences of psychological depression and religious darkness; and to fears of old age and death. Such themes should not be called leitmotifs, but the way they recur is analogous. The effective formal principles of the *Four Quartets,* making it a long poem rather than an assemblage of short ones, are cross-reference, increment, and reprise.

The word "end," to take an obvious example, occurs first in the tenth line of "Burnt Norton," where it means "termination" and "result":

> What might have been and what has been
> Point to one end.

Exactly the same words are repeated thirty-five lines later as the conclusion to the first part of "Burnt Norton." But now the statement has a changed emotional meaning. Coming after a brief, visionary experience of "reality," the lines represent a return to the realm of time, and thus carry an added emotional burden of regret. The word "end" recurs again in "Burnt Norton" V. Here the subject is art as form, but art is itself an analogy to reality as pattern, and Eliot illustrates his points by meditating on a Chinese jar. As one follows the pattern around the sides of the jar, each moment is both an end and a beginning.

> Or say that the end precedes the beginning,
> And the end and the beginning were always there
> Before the beginning and after the end.
> And all is always now.

And in the final paragraph of "Burnt Norton" we read that

> Desire itself is movement
> Not in itself desirable;

> Love is itself unmoving,
> Only the cause and end of movement.

In this context "end" clearly means not only "termination" but also "goal" or "final cause." With this meaning in mind, we may recall, as we read "And the end and the beginning were always there," the words of Revelation 12:6, "I am Alpha and Omega, the beginning and the end," and we realize that in the first occurrence of the word, near the start of the poem, this sense of "end" was already active:

> What might have been and what has been
> Point to one end, which is always present.

For a larger example of the kinds of echoing and cross-reference that integrate the *Four Quartets* we may briefly consider the concept of pattern as the poem explores it. The rose garden at the start of "Burnt Norton" is a formal one in which paths are laid out. As the protagonist moves through the garden, he follows, Eliot writes, a "formal pattern." "Burnt Norton" II introduces the idea, fundamental to the *Four Quartets,* of cyclic pattern, which is seen as governing existence from the circulation of the blood to that of the stars. When observed from a sufficient distance, strife—the boarhound pursuing the boar—is revealed as pattern. In these contexts the pattern is pervasive, unchanging, and always controlling though not always known. In "Burnt Norton" V Eliot meditates that "Only by the form, the pattern" can works of art "reach / The stillness"; the latter term is an evocative image for ultimate reality beyond the phenomenal. It refers to what earlier in the poem Eliot called "the still point of the turning world." In this context, then, Eliot is suggesting that pattern in the phenomenal, temporal world links to or impels toward the spiritual and eternal. But, significantly, in this same fifth section he conveys for the first time that the pattern is not automatically controlling, that things—in this instance, "words"—may fall out of the pattern: "Words strain, / Crack and sometimes break, under the burden"; and he links the "words" of a formal utterance, a poem or prayer, with Christ, the Logos or Word, assailed by temptations in the desert. In this passage the concept of a pattern is associated with moral and spiritual striving; one imposes pattern on oneself or one accepts it by will and faith.

Ideas of pattern are central to three of the five sections of "Burnt Norton" and continue to be developed in later quartets. The concept articulates Eliot's will to conform his being to a prior, external order, to express love as self-discipline, self-abnegation, and penitential acceptance of suffering. The pattern is not God, needless to say, but is created by God and is the way to Him. In the most powerful passage in the poem, the great second movement in "Little Gidding" II, the speaker contrasts mere onward, linear progression with patterned motion:

> From wrong to wrong the exasperated spirit
> Proceeds, unless restored by that refining fire
> Where you must move in measure, like a dancer.

And the concept of pattern is connected with Eliot's desire not to desire, with the "detachment" that in "Little Gidding" III he describes as a virtue (but which I suspect was his spiritual sin). For if one sees people and their lives as elements of a pattern, the sense of the pattern mitigates "Attachment"—to use Eliot's word—"to self and to things and to persons." "See, now they vanish," he writes,

> The faces and places, with the self which, as it could, loved them,
> To become renewed, transfigured, in another pattern.

Most of all, the idea of a pattern is related to Eliot's search for meaning in experience; to see a pattern, as opposed to incoherence or even to mere sequence, is to feel assured that meaning is present.

The major subject of the *Four Quartets* is life in time in relation to the eternal. Eliot dwells on different conceptions of time as a linear sequence of continual change, as cyclic, and as an infinite plane, like the ocean, on which one is adrift, and he ponders these conceptions in relation to the brief years of one's own life and the longer span of history. Unless time has meaning in relation to eternity, it is, in Eliot's experience, waste and empty. In rare moments, however, the eternal is incarnate within the realm of time. Within our personal lives, such moments are elusive. They are charged with a quality and significance we feel but cannot understand. The episode in the rose garden, at the start of "Burnt Norton," renders one such moment, and the rest of the *Four Quartets* might be described as a meditation on it, as an effort to recover it "in a different form" by approaching its meaning. But in the lives of others in the past such moments can be more clearly read. Here Eliot is thinking of the incarnation of the divine in Christ as the ultimate prototype, but he also has in mind other instances of suffering, self-sacrifice, and love. Finally, at the conclusion of the *Four Quartets* in "Little Gidding," the Church itself, which is temporal and historical and also supernatural and eternal, is also seen as a point where the timeless and time intersect and are reconciled.

After "Little Gidding" Eliot composed no more important poetry. His routine of life consisted of morning Mass, breakfast, writing, and, in the afternoon, work at Faber and Faber. Lunch was usually a social occasion and so was tea, but he often dined alone with a tray on his knees. In the evenings he would work or read. As the years passed he spent less time at Faber and Faber, chiefly because of dwindling health and energy. He made frequent visits to the United States and also lectured elsewhere. Illness and exhaustion compelled him to take many holidays. His closest personal attachments were with his family and old friends. Between 1946 and 1956 he shared an apartment with John Hayward, a literary scholar and critic. Since Hayward could not live alone—he suffered from muscular dystrophy and was confined to a wheelchair—Eliot was probably motivated by feelings of charity and duty, but also he was lonely and welcomed the companionship. Meanwhile, as I said, his fame flourished as never before in this postwar period. He received the Nobel Prize in 1948, and was treated by the media as a celebrity. When he lectured at the University of Minnesota in Minneapolis in 1956, 14,000 people attended, and the lecture was delivered in a stadium. Vivien Eliot having died in 1947, Eliot married for a second time in 1956. His wife, Valerie Fletcher, had been his secretary since 1949. Thanks to their marriage, his last years were his happiest since childhood. But he had been recurrently and increasingly ill over the last ten years with bronchitis and emphysema (he was a heavy smoker), and he also suffered bouts of tachycardia. Marriage altered his state of mind, but his physical decline continued, and he died in January 1965. By his wish, his body was cremated and his ashes interred in the church at East Coker.

3

MODES OF MODERN STYLE
IN THE UNITED STATES

MORE famous volumes of American poetry were published in the 1920s than in any decade since. They include Pound's *Hugh Selwyn Mauberly* (1920) and *A Draft of XVI Cantos* (1925), Eliot's *The Waste Land* (1922) and *Poems 1909–1925*, Stevens' *Harmonium* (1923), Williams' *Spring and All* (1923), Frost's *New Hampshire* (1923), Marianne Moore's *Poems* (1921) and *Observations* (1925), Cummings' *Tulips and Chimneys* (1923), Ransom's *Chills and Fever* (1924), Jeffers' *Roan Stallion, Tamar and Other Poems* (1924), and Crane's *White Buildings* (1926). The great development ended with Crane's *The Bridge* in 1930.

The variety of this poetry was as astonishing as its amount. Even if for the moment we ignore poets who mainly continued in the traditions of the nineteenth century, the modes of the modern differed as widely as Frost's "The Witch of Coos" from Stevens' "The Comedian as the Letter C," or as Ransom's "The Equilibrists" from Crane's "Voyages." The oldest of the poets who were then thought modern, Edward Arlington Robinson, produced ten volumes in the 1920s. Some of his earlier lyrics, such as "Reuben Bright" and "Richard Cory," had been revolutionary. Realistic in subject matter and colloquial in language, these lyrics had imported into poetry observations and methods typical of prose fiction—psychological complications within and between people, social milieu and its impact on character, the limited point of view of some onlooker. Robert Frost, the finest of the Georgian poets though an American, similarly located his poetry in New England, but he preferred the countryside and its pleasant imagery of nature to Robinson's small town. His art of the spoken idiom presented a Yankee character (an "I" as opposed to Robinson's "we" who speaks for the small-town community) whose tenderness, humor, and reflective wisdom were deeply attractive. Vachel Lindsay toured the nation with stage performances of his "Higher Vaudeville," and Sandburg, the celebrator of industrial workers in his innovative *Chicago Poems* (1917) and *Smoke and Steel* (1920), pursued his genial democratic observation of the people. These poets were now approaching middle age; their work represented the modern movement in early phases. So also did Imagism. The Imagists of the original 1913 and 1915 groups—Ezra Pound, Hilda Doolittle, Amy Lowell, William Carlos Williams, and John Gould Fletcher, among the Americans—were still publishing, though by the 1920s only Doolittle was still an Imagist. The mode was spreading, however, from *Poetry* magazine to graduation yearbooks, becoming less rigorous as it spread. Yvor Winters, not yet devoted to the terse classicism of Walter Savage Landor, was among the many younger poets who took it up. Conrad Aiken, one of the most sophisticated writers of the decade, was attempting in his "symphonies" to create poetic structures on principles derived from music. In and around New York City Wallace Stevens, William Carlos Williams, Marianne Moore, Mina Loy, and Alfred Kreymborg circulated in an avant garde that also included photographers, sculptors, painters, and musicians. Edna St. Vincent Millay, Elinor Wylie, Louise Bogan, and Mark Van Doren were also in the city. This was the flowering time of the Harlem Renaissance, when poetry by black Americans, such as James Weldon Johnson, Jean Toomer, and Langston Hughes, took a long leap in quality and asserted a more explicit and prouder racial identification. Almost all the poetry of John Crowe Ransom and of Laura Riding was published during the 1920s, and Allen Tate brought out his first volume then. In *Roan Stallion, Tamar and Other Poems* (1924) Robinson Jeffers cracked the shell of his earlier work in the genteel mode. The achievements of Pound and Eliot defy brief summary, but by the mid-1920s they were, as we said, strong influences on younger poets such as Hart Crane and Archibald MacLeish.

Throughout the 1920s a more traditional poetry also continued to be written. Lizette Reese and Sara Teasdale were the best of these poets, but Bliss Carman, the Benéts, Robert Hillyer, Arthur Ficke, and Witter Bynner were among the many others who enjoyed popularity or respectful reviews. And American sentimental and regional poetry poured forth as usual. The year of *The Waste Land*, 1922, also produced *Corn: Moods from Mid-America* by Harold Swanson, and the next year saw both Stevens' *Harmonium* and Rudolph Valentino's *Day Dreams*. While a few persons in 1925 shopped for Pound's *A Draft of XVI Cantos*, a less selective audience pocketed three volumes by Edgar Guest— *Mother, Home,* and *Friends.*

To account for the major new developments I should need again to tell the story of the Modernist revolution, as I did in the first volume of this history. From the 1890s on the premises and styles of the nineteenth century were increasingly rejected because they seemed false. Some writers and artists, such as the Futurists, sought to express the immediately contemporary. Art, they thought, must capture the sensations and feelings of men and women living now, the tempo and jag of nerves assailed with the shapes and sounds of machines, the speed of modern travel, cinema, radio, and so forth. Other poets believed they should express what was unique in America, such as its democracy, space, and newness. Yet on the whole, the Modernists sought a reality deeper than the contemporary or the local. The music of Schönberg, as Theodor Adorno pointed out, does not reflect sounds of the modern world—droning engines, klaxons, the rhythms of the production line—but, instead, the immediate reality of human suffering. If we do not enjoy this music, it at least reminds us that our heavens are not full of singing violins. This facing of reality—more exactly, this feeling of repossessing it after a period of sentimental evasion, or of seeing deeper than was possible in earlier ages—was a fundamental source of the Modernist achievement.

Moreover, the sense that one was breaking with the past and developing a new style engendered élan. Writers were fascinated by the new technical problems to be overcome in their art. Since the accepted styles at the end of the nineteenth century had been weak in some ways, it was easy for writers of the next generation to be confident that they had made an advance, that their work was more rapid, precise, economical, and bold than that of their predecessors. Developing a new type of poetry, one acquired a place within literary history, and this was also satisfying. In short, that the new styles expressed new visions of reality was the deepest justification for creating these styles, but there were strong additional motives also.

The Modernist revolution in poetry was mainly the work of American rather than English poets because in the United States the poetry of the previous generation presented a greater opportunity for a new development. A young poet in England in the 1910s had an avant-garde movement behind him—the aesthetic-symbolist-impressionist-decadent poetry of the 1890s—and, rejecting it, he might turn back to tradition, as the Georgian poets did. In the United States, however, most of the poems routinely published and admired at the turn of the century were negligibly Genteel. No wonder that Robinson, Pound, Eliot, Stevens, Frost, and so many others felt the need of something new. But what path to take?

The American Modernists created their poetry out of sources they themselves assembled. (Not, of course, at random, for they had preceptors, such as Arthur Symons on the Symbolist movement or Rossetti on Tuscan poets before Dante.) Pound studying world literature from Yeats and Remy de Gourmont to Provençal and ancient Chinese for examples of how to write is only the extreme instance that reveals the general case. Though others did not go so far afield as Pound, they nevertheless drew on very diverse sources and models—the formalism, impressionism, and Dandyism of the London avant-garde of the 1890s; the poetry of France, *symboliste* and otherwise, which had helped to form this earlier English modernism; the techniques of prose fiction, especially those of Flaubert, Henry James, and Joyce; Dante; the "wit" of the Metaphysical poets and the styles of Elizabethan and Jacobean dramatists; Whitman; Cubism and other schools of modern painting; cinematic montage; the Wagnerian leitmotif; Sir James Frazer's *The Golden Bough* and similar comparative studies of mythology; and psychological theories concerning the stream of consciousness, the unconscious mind, the significance and interpretation of dreams, the collective unconscious and the archetype. Not every poet, needless to say, reflected all these elements. Modernist style was, in fact, a highly variable synthesis, different in each poet and with some poets in each poem. And once a modern poet or school had developed a particular style, this style was itself an additional resource available to succeeding poets.

Just this variety of sources was another main reason for the great achievement of modern poetry in the 1920s. It forced comparisons, challenged assumptions, and activated critical awareness and debate in a way that was altogether healthy in the United States, where poetry and criticism had been gripped by limiting conventions. Moreover, the rich matrix of heterogeneous sources and models made it easy to make new combinations. Poets forged their own styles by amalgamating the dissimilar, and because their sources were dissimilar, their styles engaged complex perspectives. In their programs and exemplary poems Imagism and Dada, for example, had nothing in common, yet Cummings assimilated both and combined them. The expansive Whitman and constrictive Eliot merged in Crane's *The Bridge*. Ransom's ironic portraits of the genteel South owe much to Hardy and to Robinson's observations in New England; more surprisingly, they are also indebted to Laforgue. The possibility of such amalgamations did not absolutely depend on the lack of a vigorous national tradition in the poetry of the United States, for major moments of renewal in poetry always involve something analogous—the infusion of new, heterogeneous styles adapted from the past or imported from abroad. But psychologically speaking, it was easier to do this in the United States than in England.

The poetry of the 1920s is far too abundant and varied to be discussed in one chapter. Most of the poets and types I have mentioned were noticed in the first volume or will be elsewhere in this one. To illustrate the variety and interweaving of modern styles at this time, and the different lines of development that were possible, I here concentrate on E. E. Cummings, Archibald MacLeish, and Robinson Jeffers. Each produced his first important work in the mid-1920s (between 1923 and 1926), and Cummings and MacLeish created their styles by assimilating Modernist predecessors. The work of Jeffers was shaped more by rejecting American Modernism than by emulating it, but at his time of crisis, when he rejected it, he felt that his decision was desperate. His only chance of originality was to be found, as he then thought, in the Modernist modes. Thus even Jeffers witnesses to the intense attraction for poets of the Modernist development. Cummings and MacLeish show how quickly they picked it up.

The style of Cummings reflected the Imagist movement and types of Modernism centered, so far as the United States is concerned, in New York City and derived from modern painting and from theorizing about it. These influences gave Cummings affinities, somewhat masked by his distortions of grammar and typography, with Williams and Stevens in their moments of sophisticated frivolity and bright, painterly abstraction. He was intrigued by Dada and, more generally, caught from France his attitude of bohemian rebellion against the middle class. (This expressed itself in satires on propriety, praise of prostitutes, sexual plain speaking, and the like, all more or less at the level of the Folies Bergères and, additionally, out of date by the 1920s.) Pound also influenced Cummings' style, but only Pound's epigrams, *vers de société*, and Imagism—the early Pound of *Lustra* (1916). With Eliot Cummings' only point of contact was the *vers de société* Eliot composed in 1915. In general, then, Cummings built on earlier rather than later phases of Modernism. Though he started publishing in the 1920s, his styles derived from the 1910s.

MacLeish, on the other hand, created his style in the 1920s out of French poets of the nineteenth century and the high Modernism of Pound and Eliot. For the most part, he borrowed from Pound and Eliot with tact and selectivity. Though his famous "Ars Poetica" has been taken as a statement of Imagist poetics, he was not an Imagist except in the generalized but important respect that he practiced a clear, economical, concrete presentation, which he developed more from Pound's *Cantos* and Hemingway's prose than he did from the Imagist anthologies. At times in the 1920s he illustrated how vulnerable a poet could be if he emulated Modernist achievement too confidently. *The Hamlet of Archibald MacLeish* (1928) is a textbook example of high Modernist structure in a long poem. It suffers greatly in comparison with the greater works it derives from. According to the classifications of the time, MacLeish was a "cosmopolitan" in the 1920s, though in the 1930s he changed and became a leading "nativist."

The poetry of Jeffers is too colloquial and realistic to have been written in the United States in an earlier period. On the other hand, it is at times lavishly rhetorical in ways most Modernists would not have permitted themselves. But Jeffers, as I said, had weighed Symbolism, Impressionism, and Imagism and found them restrictive. His relation to the nativist tradition in modern American poetry is more complicated. The Californian setting of his narratives—his rendering of the dramatic landscape and the picturesque way of life—was in keeping with nativist prescription, but Jeffers was also inspired by Yeats and by Synge's book on the Aran islands. In their versification and their expansive, amplifying syntax his lyrics were modeled on Whitman, but what they express is antithetical to Whitman, for Jeffers' thoughts and moods made Schopenhauer seem a Pollyanna. Having begun as a poet in the Genteel tradition, Jeffers rejected it violently in his mature work. Nietzsche, Freud, the First World War, and doubtless more intimate experiences coalesced to impel his repudiation. In Freud he found the underworld of the unconscious that his poetry explores; he caught from Nietzsche his prophetic pose and his morality of unsparing truth. His implicit polemic against the falsely (as he viewed it) optimistic, uplifting, and ideal was typical of modern poetry, but no other poetry written in his generation was so ruthless and extreme in violating sexual and moral taboos.

E. E. CUMMINGS

In *i: six nonlectures* (1953) Cummings (1894–1962) recalled his beginnings. He voiced his first rhymes when three years old and kept on thereafter. With puberty his poems turned religious— his father was a Unitarian minister—and as an undergraduate at Harvard he went through a Keatsian and Pre-Raphaelite phase. But by 1915, when he graduated, he was studying the modern movements in painting and literature. He was also rebelling against the parental ethos, and in his speech at his commencement exercises he deliberately nettled respectable Massachusetts, embodied on the podium in President Lowell of

Harvard, by quoting from Lowell's embarrassing sister Amy the
lyric that begins, "Why do the lilies goggle their tongues at me."
   Cummings took a job with a publisher in New York, but quit
after two months, for regular office work from nine to five hin-
dered his painting and writing. He subsisted mainly on hand-
outs from his family and friends. In 1917 he joined an ambu-
lance corps in order to escape the draft. Incautious statements
in France made him suspected of treason, and he spent three
months in a concentration camp. (He described the camp brilliantly in *The Enormous Room,* 1923). Returned to the United
States, he was trained at Fort Devens until his discharge in 1919.
Back in New York he resumed the way of life he was to follow
thenceforth. He would rise around noon, hole up working, and
spend evenings convivially. In summers he returned to the family place in New Hampshire. A love affair with the wife of a close
friend (the friend approving and encouraging) led to the birth
of a daughter, marriage, and then a painful divorce.
   In college, France, Fort Devens, New Hampshire, and New
York, Cummings had never stopped writing. He placed his lyrics
in little magazines, but no publisher would bring out a volume.
For some of his poems shocked by their "obscenity"—for example, they were about prostitutes—and others by their distorted typography and logic:

> inthe,exquisite;
> morning   sure   lyHer eye s exactly sit . . .

Finally a selection was published as *Tulips and Chimneys* (1923)
and another as *XLI Poems* (1925). The poems that remained un-
published, including those rejected as obscene, Cummings himself published privately in *&* (1925). Thus each of his three early
volumes contained poems that had accumulated over many
years. The justly famous "All in green went my love riding," for
example, dates from his last year at college. Except in its versification, it is a Pre-Raphaelite ballad. "In Just- / spring," to mention another favorite, dates at least from 1916 and "Buffalo Bill's
/ defunct" from early in 1917.
   In 1927 Cummings' Expressionist and Dadaist play *Him* went
over well as an avant-garde event. A brief visit to Russia in 1931
lead to *Eimi* (1933), a book-length account of the trip, in which
the style was avant-garde but the emotions New Hampshire.

Cummings was an individualist unconformer and bitterly criticized the Soviet polity. Around this time he met Marion Morehouse, with whom he lived henceforth. After the Second World War he started to give public readings of his poetry more frequently, and these enlarged both his audience and his bank account. He suffered from health troubles, and these, with the schedule of public readings, slowed his productivity. He died suddenly in New Hampshire of a stroke in September 1962.

In conversation Cummings was ebullient. He told anecdotes, remembered bits of repartee, created picturesque images, and indulged in flights of imagination. He was vivid, light, humorous, surprising, and delighted, and he heightened his effects by expressive looks, tones, timing, and mimicry. His thoughts were always concrete, and he shunned intellectual generalization and argument, for which he had no aptitude. Nevertheless, his conversation was didactic; his comic skits, fancies, and images advocated his values, about which he felt defensive and militant. They illustrated, for example, how some child confounded a scientist, or a New Hampshire farmer a New Yorker, or Marianne Moore a critic, or Pound Eliot. He believed in living in the moment, like the lilies of the field, for most moments were good if only we concentrated on them. The simpler the thing—maybe an apple for dessert—the more his lyrical appreciation poured forth to enhance it. (In his poetry the difficult style with commonplace subjects—spring, roses—enforces the same morality; it makes us respond to the ordinary.) He trusted—indeed, had—no way of knowing except emotional intuition. Hence if someone disagreed with his views, it was not possible to bridge or even to explain the gap. With his individualist and Romantic feelings, he had little sympathy for or from the thirties ideologues and the New Critics, and he resented the fame of poets such as Auden, whose way of writing seemed to him too generalizing, argumentative, and professorial. With most matters that preoccupy conventional moralists, Cummings was not preoccupied, but spontaneity, imagination, asocial selfhood, integrity, outgoing responsiveness, vivid being—in short, his Romantic creed—formed a code by which he estimated others fiercely. Lovers, children, country people, and nature exemplified good ways of being; the bad ones had ampler illustration in scientists, philosophers, New Dealers, Cambridge ladies, Communists, fro-

zen-food gourmets, advertising agencies, the rich, the middle
class, and also the poor in their quality of "mostpeople" or un-
humanoids, conformists even in their dreams. In his early volumes many poems were amorous in medieval,
Renaissance, Victorian, biblical, or pastiche styles. "Thy whitest
feet crisply are straying" lilts one song; "Puella Mea" includes
the line "Her body is most beauteous"; and a sonnet begins, "a
connotation of infinity / sharpens the temporal splendor of this
night." Of course most poets born in the 1890s loved similarly
old-fashioned styles in adolescence. But in Cummings these
styles persisted beside or within his Modernist ones. A sonnet in
Xaipe (1950), for example, starts out,

> i thank You God for most this amazing
> day: for the leaping greenly spirits of trees
> and a blue true dream of sky; and for everything
> which is natural which is infinite which is yes.

The irregularities of meter, punctuation, typography, and word
order would not be found in a nineteenth-century poet, but in
diction, sentiment, and conception the stanza is traditional.

If such writing makes us eager for Imagism, we find it in Cummings, but it is Imagism of the 1925 style, by which time the
charged, compressed objectivity of Pound in 1912, at the start
of the Imagist movement, had somewhat loosened in lesser
hands. To most American poets Imagism meant a short, free-
verse impression of some object, scene, or happening. The impression would be conveyed in a few, carefully selected and vividly rendered details and metaphors, with understated emotion
and maybe a mute, musing implication of further meaning.
"Buffalo Bill's / defunct" is a poem of this kind. A somewhat less
familiar example is Cummings' variation on *Paradise Lost* IV,
268ff. Milton wrote in the famous passage:

> Not that fair field
> Of Enna, where Prosérpine gathering flowers,
> Herself a fairer flower, by gloomy Dis
> Was gathered . . .

Cummings' Imagist handling of this theme goes,

> Tumbling-hair
>   picker of buttercups
>   violets
>   dandelions

```
And the big bullying daisies
                    through the field wonderful
with eyes a little sorry
Another comes
            also picking flowers.
```

Other modern styles besides Imagism shaped Cummings' writing. The poem that begins "Paris; this April sunset . . ." might be 1890s Impressionism. "The Cambridge ladies who live in furnished souls" and many similar satires resemble the *vers de société* of Pound and Eliot—Pound's "Les Millwin," for example, or Eliot's "The *Boston Evening Transcript.*" Sandburg was another influence, though Cummings' attitude to Sandburgian materials—the "blueeyed Finn," McSorley's saloon, tellurian prostitutes with "kind large flesh," and so forth—was usually more complicated and fastidious than Sandburg's blowsy hurrah. Like Williams and Sandburg, Cummings used colloquial language effectively—"a woman with sticking out breasts / hanging clothes"—but also he imitated the colloquial humorously—

```
                    oo-oo.   dearie
    not so
    hard dear
    you're killing me
```

—and the low colloquial was to him always comic. His phonetic renderings of speech are deliberate puzzles:

```
yoozwidduhpoimnuntwaiv un duhyookuhsumpnruddur
givusuhtoonunduhphugnting.
```

Like Williams and Stevens, Cummings caught procedures and effects from modern painting. His early volumes have sequences entitled "Impressions," "Post Impressions," and "Portraits." Especially in these sequences he experimented with the ellipsis, distortion, fragmentation, and agrammatical juxtaposition that make some of his poetry difficult. He dismembered words into syllables and syllables into letters, and though this fragmentation activated rhymes and puns, the reasons for it were also typographical—the look of the poem on the page. Manipulating letters, syllables, punctuation, capitals, columns of print, indentation, line length, and white space as visual or spatial forms, Cummings arranged them in order to enact feeling and carry meaning.

In one simple example he breaks up the image of a jazz player
into toe, back, eyes, and hands.

```
        ta
        ppin
        g
        toe

        hip
        popot
        amus Back

        gen
        teel-ly
        lugu-
        bri ous

                eyes
        LOOPTHELOOP
        as

        fathandsbangrag.
```

The final stanza pictures exuberant syncopation. "Eyes" is emphasized by identation, "as" by white space and rhyme (with
"eyes"). The jammed words of the climactic line speed all the
faster because of the suspense collected in the space around "as."
The double O's in "LOOPTHELOOP" are eyes, and the sounds
of "fathandsbangrag" suggest the pounding chords of the
music.

Even in this exercise the spacing and other visual devices are
backed by more complicated ones of other kinds, such as fragmented grammar, juxtaposition, metaphor, and punning. A
poem from Cummings' W[Viva] (1931) illustrates his devices
more completely:

```
        twi-
            is -Light bird
        ful
        -ly dar
        kness eats

        a distance a
        c(h)luck
        (l)ing of just bells (touch)ing
        ?mind
```

(moon begins The
)
now,est hills er dream;new
.oh if

when:
&
a
nd O impercept i bl.

Almost every syllable and sign focuses attention by its surprise. Cummings' punctuation is obviously not grammatical but expressive. The question mark before "mind" does not complete an interrogatory sentence. Instead, it inserts a doubt as to the predication. The comma and semicolon in "now,est hills er dream;new" are notations of timing, not markers of syntactical units. (The suffixes "est" and "er" in this line float freely, without being attached to adverbs or adjectives, and indicate superlative and comparative degrees of feeling.) The period at the start of the next line— ".oh if"—prolongs the pause at the line break; the effect may be analogous to beginning a musical measure with a rest. The colon after "when" suggests a pause full of suspense. It anticipates the climax that follows.

No less obviously, Cummings distorts conventional word order. "Moon begins The" is not the same predication as "The moon begins," though it includes this. The reversed word order also changes the part of speech, making "The" into a noun. Cummings worked this device habitually, transforming verbs into nouns, adverbs into adjectives, and so forth.

Parenthesis, another favorite device, may stress a syllable— "(touch)ing." The parentheses enclosing the moon picture it. In "c(h)luck / (l)ing" the parentheses create a portmanteau word that unpacks into *cluck, clucking, chuck,* and *chuckling,* plus onomatopoeic bird and bell sounds in *chluck* and *ling.* Often in other poems parentheses dramatize simultaneity; in other words, they overcome the seriatim presentation inherent in language. In "Look! Pigeons flying and wheeling are sprinkling an instant with sunlight," the event takes place at once, but the words order attention sequentially from pigeons to flying, wheeling, and sunlight. So Cummings writes,

              l ook-
       pigeons fly ingand

whee(:are,SpRiN,k,LiNg an in-stant with sunLight
t h e n)l-
ing . . .

(The spaced "t h e n" within the parentheses begins the transition to another phase as the poem continues. The alternat-
ing capital and lower-case letters and the commas in
"SpRiN,k,LiNg" picture the action of the water drops; the capital *L* in "sunLight" dramatizes the sudden burst of light.) At
other times parentheses may indicate an interpolated thought
or an utterance in a different tone of voice or by a different
speaker.

Critics complained that Cummings' poetry did not develop,
and he was infuriated. Yet, on the whole, the critics were right.
He maintained a higher general level of performance in most
volumes after his first ones. His linguistic and typographical un-
conventionalities became more frequent and extreme and then,
later, less so. He acquired religious leanings. But all his volumes
contained the same types of poems and expressed similar attitudes. If, however, Cummings did not develop—why should he
have?—the critical perception of him changed startlingly. In the
1920s he was viewed as one of the Modernist avant-garde: experimental, Frenchified, and shocking. A critic might or might
not relish this, but the work of Cummings was damned or
praised with the Modernist movement in general. The foes or
partisans of Impressionism, Imagism, *vers de société*, sexual
frankness, realism, Cubism, Joyce, Pound, Eliot, and Edna St.
Vincent Millay could recognize these styles and influences in
Cummings. But for the next generation of critics, including the
New Critics, Modernism meant high Modernism especially, with
The Waste Land as the preeminent example and Eliot's critical
essays as scripture. For these critics Cummings was not a Modernist, for they thought his language imprecise, his feelings Romantic, his mind simplistic. On the other hand, they granted
him lyric freshness. By the time of his death in 1962 he was
largely ignored except by academic critics, who were then taking
him up. A weird, late phase of Cummings studies sees in him an

Emersonian-Taoist-Zen teacher, a mystic who was able to hold all life in this moment's grain of sand. Doubtless any simple utterance may be said to transcend life's complexities instead of falling short, but such assertions do not improve the poems in question.

Cummings had little capacity for self-criticism, and he published many poems that are trivial and a great many that are emotionally overinsistent. Some are offensive in their prejudices. Omitting all these from our personal Cummings selection, we face a more difficult judgment with the many poems in which his typographical and linguistic idiosyncrasies are extreme. As we puzzle our way through such writings, we are amused by Cummings the stunt performer and sometimes moved. Moreover, his devices extend the resources of language. Though his playful distortion of logic and language may have been influenced by Dada, Cummings was far from Dadaist, for he did not seek to destroy grammar, logic, or consciousness. Yet to many readers his devices seem a mannerism, a style with no function except to display itself. These readers are put off by the minimal interest or Romantic convention in what he presents—for example, "twi- / is -Light"—and with such subjects the stylistic difficulty seems external and irrelevant. Yet "twi- / is -Light" is a better poem—denser, newer, more arresting, with a more dramatic heave of feeling at the end—than it would have been if written in conventionally Romantic style. Nevertheless, Cummings' devices tend to make the poem something of a verbal game, and though this has its positive side, especially when the sentiment might otherwise seem exaggerated, the danger is aridity. In his best poems his devices are less obtrusive. Among his better poems are the deft and savage satire of a cakey world, "this little bride & groom," exhibiting the bride and groom on a wedding cake,

> protected by
> cellophane against anything(because
> nothing really exists.

Little Effie, "whose brains are made of gingerbread," and the heroic Olaf who says "there is some s. I will not eat," are unforgettable. We can add "in Just- / spring," "anyone lived in a pretty how town," and "my father moved through dooms of love."

These make a collection of finer artistry than we could assemble from Sandburg, Hilda Doolittle, or Edith Sitwell, though these are eminent names.

ARCHIBALD MACLEISH

Archibald MacLeish (1892–1982) had a Joseph nature, as Thomas Mann presents that character in *Joseph and His Brothers,* and, like Joseph, he may be said to have been doubly blessed, both by the sun from above and by the underworld from beneath. With his sunny nature he pursued the world's good things and obtained them by intelligence, drive, charm, courage, and power of working. And he deserved well of the world, for he managed its affairs with enormous goodwill. Yet the underworld whispered to him of cosmic space, devouring time, doomed effort, inevitable sorrow, loss, and death: in short, of the vanity of being. And so, while at Yale, he starred in courses, athletics, and society, but he also wrote poems, publishing his first volumes in 1917, two years after he graduated. Though married, he enlisted in the First World War and fought with the field artillery. Then came law school and practice until, by 1923, he found the conflict between law and poetry too acute, and, choosing poetry, moved with his family to Paris. Here for five years he lived in the expatriate community of writers that also included Ernest Hemingway, Gertrude Stein, James Joyce, and, briefly, Ezra Pound. *Streets in the Moon* (1926), a collection of lyrics, was followed by two long poems, *The Hamlet of Archibald Macleish* (1928) and *Einstein* (1929). The latter takes for its theme the scientist's heroic struggle for ultimate knowledge.

In 1928 financial uncertainties brought MacLeish back to the United States. He settled in an old farmhouse in Conway, Massachusetts. A year earlier he had started an epic of Cortez's conquest of Mexico, *Conquistador* (1932). The idiom of this poem, though MacLeish's own, is of the same school as Hemingway's prose and the simpler epic passages of Pound's *Cantos.* The story is told by a former soldier of Cortez, Bernal Diaz, who is now more than eighty years old. As Diaz remembers his youth, he is elegiac. Not only the Indian empire and the conquistadors, but hope, struggle, passion, and wonder are no more. Lawyers and businessmen have succeeded Montezuma and Cortez. We sympathize with the protagonists, cruel and violent though they are, because they are doomed. Picked out against a dark background of fate, their passion and courage move us by their splendor and pathos.

At the time he conceived *Conquistador* MacLeish must already have been attracted to the poetic aims he pursued during the 1930s. The subject matter is public, historical, and American. The point of view is that of a common soldier and is also collective, for the narrator thinks of himself as one of a group; he speaks of "we," not "I." In his next major work, *Frescoes for Mr. Rockefeller's City* (1933), MacLeish presented, evoked, and commented on the history of the United States in an even more popular style. According to this elegiac and satiric poem, the bounty of the land, the hopes and toil of the immigrants, and everything else in American history have served only to enrich financiers.

Constraint of purse led MacLeish to work part time during the Depression for *Fortune* magazine, for which he wrote over a hundred articles during the eight years (1930–38) he was associated with it. Journalism showed him life in the United States on many sides, and also brought him into contact with men of affairs. He acquired a wider acquaintance with the world of business and industry, politics and government, than any other poet of the time. This did little to assist or hinder the writing of poetry, for poetry depends much more on imagination, intelligence, and sensitivity to language than on personal experience. But his knowledge of the public world gave him insight into its crises and a feeling of responsibility toward them.

During the European crises of the 1930s, as one country after another became a dictatorship, MacLeish tried in speeches and poems to warn of the growing danger. He also wrote three experimental verse dramas for radio. MacLeish was trying to create new forms, forms that would address social and political issues and appeal to a very large audience. No other important poet tried more systematically to create a public art, or defended it more boldly, or found himself more embattled in the literary world because of it. For MacLeish attacked writers because they were less engaged than he was, and it was natural for them to attack him. His dislike of Communism and of Stalin also led to bitter exchanges with their partisans. And the principles of the

New Critics were antipathetic to his. To this day no influential critic has considered MacLeish's work of the 1930s with a general approach to literature that would be favorable to the attempt MacLeish was making, despite the fact that since the 1960s a substantial amount of criticism has paid ardent lip-service to analogous sociological and political intentions.

Meanwhile, MacLeish entered public service as Librarian of Congress (1939–44), aide and speechwriter for President Roosevelt, Director of the Office of Facts and Figures, Assistant Director of the Office of War Information, Assistant Secretary of State, and Chairman of the U.S. delegation to the UNESCO conference of 1945 and 1946. In 1949, at an age when many persons are looking forward to retirement, he began a new career as Boylston Professor of English at Harvard.

Of MacLeish's writings, only his lyrics will continue to be read. They unite the Romantic styles of the nineteenth century with the modern ones of his youth. On the one hand, he has the lovely melodies and cadences, the suggestive imagery, and the appreciative, elegiac, and ideal emotions of nineteenth-century poetry. Frequently his speakers gaze on nature or landscape, not the city, and take their metaphors from this traditional source. His phrasing is always accessible; it tends even to rhetorical repetition and emphasis. And so he writes in "The Silent Slain":

> We too, we too, descending once again
> The hills of our own land, we too have heard
> Far off—Ah, que ce cor a longue haleine—
> The horn of Roland in the passages of Spain,
> The first, the second blast, the failing third.

Though Roland's horn evokes many meanings in the poem (it is a warning of treachery, a summons to rescue and battle, and a reminder of heroic pride in defeat and death), the imaginative effect lies partly in the remote, exotic world the allusion brings to mind, the epic chivalry of the medieval *chansons de geste*. And in the poetry and music of the nineteenth century the distant horn was a stock image, saturated with nostalgia for the far mountain forest or valley from which the music calls. No other poet of the twentieth century, not even de la Mare, wrote this Romantic poetry of the far place so well as MacLeish—for example, in "You, Andrew Marvell":

> And strange at Ecbatan the trees
> Take leaf by leaf the evening strange
> The flooding dark about their knees
> The mountains over Persia change
>
> And now at Kermanshah the gate
> Dark empty . . .

When he wrote these lines, MacLeish was unfurling euphonious names and gathering Romantic associations, but he had also been to Ecbatan and Kermanshah, and had observed what his poem described. His poetry is full of things seen, heard, touched, tasted, and smelled with pleasure. His best images sympathize and cherish: "the sleeve-worn stone / Of casement ledges where the moss has grown"; and

> the thin
> Child's hand that opened to the moth
> And let the flutter of the moonlight in.

MacLeish is a contemplative, musing poet, too, and reflects that "the generations / Of man are a ripple of thin fire burning," or feels the "infinity sorrow" (as the Germans call it) that "Endless is unknown earth before a man." To ultimate questions he finds no answers, and he suspects that the final truth may be only meaninglessness. As "The End of the World" says, the reality is "nothing—nothing at all." But he goes on asking ultimate questions, and the tone of his unavailing quest is much closer to the philosophic pathos of Arnold's "Dover Beach" than to the stark fear of *The Waste Land*. Among his favorite words and images are love, beauty, girl, autumn, moon, rain, wind, sea, and night. They build a happy-sad, pleasurable world.

What MacLeish chiefly took from the Modernist movement was the necessity, in Pound's words, of "presenting an image, or enough images of concrete things arranged to stir the reader," of finding the "objective correlative," as Eliot put it, as opposed to naming emotions and stating general views. And he learned, in presenting concretely, not to present too much, since one image may suggest more than paragraphs can say. He saw that rapid syntax matters more than grammar. "You, Andrew Marvell" is, grammatically speaking, a sentence without a predicate. In "L'an trentiesme de mon eage" he employs a sequence of

memory fragments, specific yet unexplained, somewhat as Eliot
had in passages of "Gerontion" and Pound in his seventh Canto.

> And I have come upon this place
> By lost ways, by a nod, by words,
> By faces, by an old man's face
> At Morlaix lifted to the birds,
>
> By hands upon the table cloth
> At Aldebori's . . .

He advocates the method of the elliptical image in "Ars Poetica":
to express "all the history" of an experience that ends in grief,
a poet should not tell the story but give the suggestive image:

> An empty doorway and a maple leaf
>
> For love
> The leaning grasses and two lights above the sea.

Because MacLeish's lyrics amalgamate some of the best
strengths of both the Romantic and Modernist modes, they have
an unusually broad appeal. "After all the refinements of subtilty
and the dogmatism of learning," as Samuel Johnson said, "all
claim to poetical honours" is finally decided by the "common
sense of readers uncorrupted with literary prejudices." Concerning a few lyrics of MacLeish—"The Silent Slain," "L'an trentiesme . . . ," "Ars Poetica," "You, Andrew Marvell," "Immortal
Autumn," "Winter Is Another Country"—the "common reader"
has decided. The last-named poem, from *Act Five* (1948), is an
admirable example. It was at once singled out, at its first appearance, by popular reviews for quotation, and it has remained
a perennial favorite in poetry readings. It appeals through a
combination of large implication in subject, elegiac poignance,
suggestive and concrete imagery, and quasi-oratorical repetition:

> If the autumn would
> End! If the sweet season,
> The late light in the tall trees would
> End! If the fragrance, the odor of
> Fallen apples, dust on the road,
> Water somewhere near, the scent of
> Water touching me; if this would end
> I could endure the absence in the night,

The hands beyond the reach of hands, the name
Called out and never answered with my name:
The image seen but never seen with sight.
I could endure this all
If autumn ended and the cold light came.

ROBINSON JEFFERS

Jeffers (1887–1962) is forever associated with the California coast near Carmel, where he lived for almost fifty years. But in the earlier part of his life he was wafted about like thistledown, coming to rest briefly—though always changing houses and schools within these places—in Pennsylvania, Switzerland, and California, with summers and side excursions elsewhere. The restlessness was that of his valetudinarian father, a Presbyterian minister and professor of theology who kept uprooting the family in pursuit of health. The pessimistic, anti-Christian, and Nietzschean philosophy to which Jeffers committed himself in his mature years, and the emphasis with which he asserted it, doubtless owe much to reaction against his father. Perhaps his itinerant childhood and youth motivated his adult unwillingness to move. However these things may be, his growing up left Jeffers shy, moody, taciturn, generally uncomfortable with people, and uncertain what he wanted to do, though very well educated. He graduated from Occidental College in 1906 and continued to study at universities in California, Europe, and Washington, changing his field from literature to medicine and then to forestry. He was also writing poems. Meanwhile in 1906 he had met Una Kuster, but she was married, and so there were guilty tensions, emotional vicissitudes, and renunciations, which ended in Una's divorce and marriage to Jeffers in 1913. The couple moved to Carmel, where, Jeffers later said, in the "Monterey coast mountains . . . I could see people living—amid magnificent unspoiled scenery—essentially as they did in the Idyls or the Sagas, or in Homer's Ithaca. Here was life purged of its ephemeral accretions. Men were riding after cattle, or plowing the headland, hovered by white sea-gulls, as they have done for thousands of years, and will for thousands of years to come."

He and his wife built a home, Tor House, on a part of the

coast that was then relatively isolated. After the house was finished, Jeffers, having learned to work as a mason, constructed a tower from granite stones, which he hauled from the beach. He would write indoors in the morning, pacing about as he revolved words and cadences, and do his stonework in the afternoons, planning his poetic narratives as he hauled and mortared. To Carmelites and occasional visitors his way of life seemed at first eccentric and then, as his poetic fame spread, romantically independent and austere, until, in the imagination of some readers, Jeffers seems to have become an incarnation of the Carmel stones, surf, and hawky sky.

Jeffers' reclusive life passed mainly in the writing of poems. As his fame grew, he had many visitors, and he posted a signboard that read, "No Visitors Until After 4. O'Clock," by which time he and his wife would be away on their daily walk. In 1929 he traveled with his family in England, Scotland, and Ireland, returning with a huge stone from Yeats's tower in his luggage. He built garden walls and additional rooms for Tor House, visited several times with Mabel Dodge Luhan in New Mexico, and took another trip to Great Britain and Ireland. Toward the end of the 1930s he found it harder to write and, not writing, became depressed. And he was preoccupied by the approaching war. He foresaw the defeat of Hitler, but that did not make him hopeful, for he was sure that the world after the war would be even harsher and more dangerous than before. The United States, he thought, should stay out of the combat. In 1948 his adaptation of Euripides' *Medea*, with Judith Anderson in the title role, had a stage success and brought his name before a large public. But in the same year, on a third visit to Ireland, he became gravely ill with pleurisy and an embolism. Two years later his wife died of cancer. He felt, he said, "like a leafless tree waiting for the roots to rot and the trunk to fall." He lived on at Tor House, cared for by his son and daughter-in-law, and kept on writing, but by 1958 he was too weak and ailing for further work. He died in 1962.

In 1912 Jeffers published his first collection of poems, *Flagons and Apples*, at his own expense, and in 1916 a second collection, *Californians*, was brought out by Macmillan. These were mostly derivative, unremarkable verses in the Romantic tradition, and justly attracted little notice except in California. But between

1916 and 1924 Jeffers' poetry entered an incomparably bolder and more arresting phase.

The most obvious explanation for the immense change in his work is his feeling, as early as 1914, that as a poet he had reached a cul de sac. He was imitating the verses of "dead men"—Shelley, for example, and Milton—and this was "worthless." "I had imitated and imitated, and that was all." But what else could he do? The Modernist movement, which extended in his view from Mallarmé to Pound and beyond, was original, he recognized, but at an enormous cost. Every "advance" in the Modernist direction had involved a "narrowing" of poetry, a "renunciation" of reason and ideas, "substance and sense, and physical and psychological reality," breadth, intelligibility, and even meter. Followers on this path could only make further renunciations. He firmly decided "not to become a 'modern,'" but since "imitation" was the only alternative, he "was doomed to go on imitating." In his desperation he seems to have made a number of resolves. He would write in a capacious genre. Poetry had to reclaim for itself the possibilities of imaginative scope and serious relevance that were open to the novel. His first experiment, the unfinished *The Alpine Christ* of 1916, was a vast lyrical drama, its form influenced by Shelley's *Prometheus Unbound* and Hardy's *The Dynasts*. Soon Jeffers started to write long narrative poems. And he resolved also to "draw subjects from contemporary life; to present aspects of life that modern poetry has generally avoided; and to attempt the expression of philosophic and scientific ideas in verse." Still, poetry was not the same as prose, and one difference was that poetry concerned itself "chiefly with permanent things and the permanent aspects of life . . . poetry must deal with things that a reader two thousand years away could understand and be moved by. This excludes much of the circumstance of modern life, especially in the cities." It did not, however, exclude the landscape and ranch life of the Monterey peninsula, and Jeffers perfectly understood the advantage to his poetry of locating it within the vicinity of such images. As a final shaping resolve a saying of Nietzsche's welled up within him: "The poets? The poets lie too much." He was determined "Not to feign any emotion that I did not feel; not to pretend to believe in optimism or pessimism, or unreversible progress; not to say anything because it was popular, or generally accepted, or fashionable."

What beliefs, then, was Jeffers refusing to be silent about?

From the religious melancholy and pessimism of Swinburne, Hardy, and other late-nineteenth-century poets and novelists, and from the honey poisons of Schopenhauer and Nietzsche, on which he sucked deep, and from Freud, Jung, Havelock Ellis, and other modern exposers of fantasies, desires, and doings beneath the veils of civilization and consciousness, and from the World War, he had come to a conviction that the human race is utterly unimportant and unworthy. Humanism is unhealthy "introversion," and we must uncenter, as he said in a letter, the "human mind from itself"; we must break away from the human in order to love and identify with the whole inhuman universe. Jeffers' late work *The Double Axe* (1948) introduces a figure called the Inhumanist. This old man lives alone and converses with his axe. "Man," he says, "is no measure of anything," and the axe agrees; in fact, it wants to kill humanity. The positive theme of the Inhumanist's prophecy is the "transhuman" beauty of God, who is "rock, earth and water, and the beasts and stars; and the night that contains them"—everything except human beings.

Jeffers' first narrative poems were several times rejected by publishers, and finally he brought out a collection privately. Admirers from California interested two New York reviewers, Mark Van Doren and Babette Deutsch, in the book. They were enthusiastic—Mrs. Deutsch felt, she said, like Keats looking into Chapman's Homer—and their reviews influenced others. The book sold out, and Boni and Liveright published a new edition, *Roan Stallion, Tamar, and Other Poems* (1924). This won Jeffers recognition, fame, and readers. If we measure success in these terms, Jeffers' 1924 volume had perhaps the quickest large success of any collection of poems by an American in the twentieth century.

Plot summary is usually reductive, but few readers today are acquainted with these poems, and there is no more telling way to introduce the world of Jeffers' imagination. To state what happens conveys more than carloads of adjectives such as "intense," "lurid," "sensational," and "morbid." *Roan Stallion*, a relatively short poem of seventeen pages, is usually thought to be Jeffers' best. A woman named California lives on a lonely ranch with a man, Johnny, and her child, Christine. (In the symbolism of these names California is the still primitive region as well as a woman, Johnny ordinary mankind, and Christine an item in Jeffers' anti-Christian argument.) Johnny brings home a stallion, in which gradually California perceives an incarnation of sexual power, of clean, fierce, inhuman nature, and of the indifferent, unknowable other—in short, of God. At this point the reader has, needless to say, entered into her unconscious mind. Symbolically speaking, California copulates with it—or Him—twice, once on fording a river (she imagines that the water mounting up on her as she enters the river is the stallion) and for a second time on a wild night ride that culminates in a religious vision. She ends up prostrating herself before the stallion, while it appropriately pays no attention. The next night she finds Johnny even less to her taste than she usually does, and, conspiring with events, she enables the stallion to kill him. The murderousness of the stallion expresses inhuman nature or God rejecting mankind, and when it is all over Johnny's corpse makes a "smear on the moon-like earth"—a typical Jeffers image of the human in nature. Yet California, moved by some obscure human fidelity, uses the gun, which Christine has brought her, to shoot the horse. However we interpret the poem, California's attempt to "break away from" humanity has failed.

That such poems once appealed to readers like Van Doren tells much about the poetic milieu of the 1920s. Jeffers' intention in these poems was partly, of course, to expound and illustrate his beliefs. But also he wished to make a "valid study" in "morbid" psychology. And finally, he hoped to achieve in a modern setting the elevation and intensity of classical tragedy, which reveals, he said, "essential elements by the burning away through pain and ruin of inertia and the inessential." But these intentions conflict with each other. California is certainly unhappy (and very bad luck for whoever comes near her), but the peculiarly morbid development of her psychology deprives her of tragic greatness. She is shocking and grotesque, but as a case history. And if California is a psychological unfortunate, she cannot figure very convincingly as a Nietzschean Superman, casting off in existential freedom the trammels of conventional morality and religion.

How, then, do we explain the enthusiastic reception of Jeffers in the twenties and thirties, not only at a popular level and in California but also among critics who were of the Eastern establishment? For one thing, Jeffers was a discovery. He seemed promising. Whatever reviewers found lacking in his poems, they credited hopefully to his future ones. But the deeper reason is that readers such as Van Doren shared Jeffers' doubts about the directions poetry was taking in the twentieth century. In the 1920s, after all, the taste of most readers had been formed around the turn of the century. Even if they were rebelling against Tennyson and the high Victorians, they still hungered for the direct intelligibility, "philosophical" ambition, scope, seriousness, and emotional intensity of poetry in the nineteenth century from Wordsworth to Hardy. Much modern poetry—Impressionism, Imagism, Symbolism, the Georgian school, Dada— seemed conspicuously to lack these qualities. When a poet offered the traditional satisfactions and could also be thought "modern," a surprisingly eager welcome might await him. The "modern" elements in Jeffers' work were the use of Freudian and Jungian psychology; the sexual frankness and the large place of sexual feelings in his picture of life; the breaking of taboos (zooerastia, incest); the unflinching representation of suffering, violence, and cruelty; the assumption that these are intrinsic to human nature and life, in other words, the darkly pessimistic *Weltanschauung;* and the absence, given such materials, of sentimental impulses in the narrator, or more exactly, the replacement of the nineteenth-century sympathizing author with an unpitying, stoic, and Nietzschean one. Much of this could seem—was—honest and bold. To these considerations we must add the hope, strongly felt at this time, for a distinctively American poetic expression. And what could be more American than the landscape and ranchers of still unspoiled California?

Jeffers' imagery builds a world of simple, general things—sun, wind, redwoods, hills, ocean, light, dark—and these are presented in terms that are easy and familiar. Rain falls in "big, black drops"; leaves in a wood are "stirred faintly" by a "breath of wind" to a "gentle whispering." Jeffers was occasionally capable of a more exact, fresh, and surprising perception: the corpse of a shot deer is a "spongy, scarlet thing"—spongy! His vision is of giant shapes and immense energies, which are often antagonistic and cruel. "Bison-shaped hills" look "flayed"; the "glittering ocean fills the gorge-mouth," with a suggestion of drowning. Habitually Jeffers introduces the human after or amid the description of huge landscape forms or panoramas, or his syntax presents nature as an independent life, proceeding with its own activity while men and women carry on theirs: "the afternoon was . . . and Tamar dreamed"; "Cloud steered between; / Helen Thurso said . . ." Often the human figures are dramatically posed against nature and separate from it.

In the 1930s Jeffers gradually began to lose his following. Having found his genre in *Tamar* and *Roan Stallion,* he became prolific and published more than eight substantial narrative poems over the next twenty years. As he ceased to be new, reviewers saw his limitations more clearly or forgave them less easily. Moreover, there was some deterioration in his product. His political views were also a factor. He saw in history Nietzsche's eternal return and in contemporary America Spenglerian decline. "Hope," he wrote, "is not for the wise," an uncongenial sentiment in the age of the New Deal, especially since his hope was for life to perish utterly from the earth. As the Second World War approached, he saw a tragic grandeur in the mass Dionysian urge towards death—"the dance of the / Dream-led masses down the dark mountain"—and during the war he was contemptuous of the emotion it fostered. Meanwhile, the New Critics ignored him (except for Yvor Winters, who took to the warpath), and under their influence few younger poets or readers in the 1940s could sympathize with Jeffers' way of writing. He was too large a figure to be forgotten, but he was generally relegated to the horizon, vaguely looming but unnoticed. Thus his 1937 *Selected Poems* marked the high point of his reputation. In the 1960s, however, when readers of poetry might have thought the time come to which Milton had looked forward in *Areopagitica,* when all the Lord's people shall become prophets, the prophetic mode of Jeffers in his shorter poems moved some readers strongly.

Many of the shorter poems are brief narratives, which do not differ essentially from the longer ones already discussed. But most of Jeffers' shorter poems are in a reflective-declamatory mode. Among his better lyrics are "Birds," "Boats in the Fog," "Shine, Perishing Republic," "Tor House," "Shine Republic," and "Self-Criticism in February." In some obvious features they take after Whitman: the long, free-verse lines, the chantlike rhetoric, the direct, accessible idiom, the centrality of the first-person speaker, and the outrageousness of his assertions. In these poems Jeffers voices his prophecy of doom. Down vistas of time he sees first human and then all life fade from the earth. Or he looks on contemporary history from the point of view of the sea cliffs. Or he sees ominous and terrible revelations. "The Purse-Seine" describes sardines caught in a net at night, their phosphorescence making a pool of light as the net closes. The scene is beautiful, but it reminds the speaker of another occasion, when at night he saw the lights of Los Angeles shining amid the blackness. In the lyric mode his continuously intense emotion is acceptable, and the extreme pessimism that makes his plots incredible has a very different effect. When in "Hurt Hawks" the speaker affirms, "I'd sooner, except for the penalties, kill a man than a hawk," we half believe him. The shorter form compels Jeffers to convey his attitude through a single posed gesture or assertion, and this captures attention and lingers in memory. And the first-person convention brings before us a figure—we may call him Jeffers—who interests the imagination as a dramatic character.

4

HART CRANE

HAROLD Hart Crane was born in 1889 in Warren, Ohio. His temperament showed itself creative almost from infancy. He loved colors, and at the age of three he would play for hours with patches, buttons, feathers, and the like from his mother's sewing box, decorating and redecorating hats. A healthy child but high-strung, he was given to rages of thwarted will, fears, and obscure compunctions, which were accompanied by fevers, nausea, and facial welts. Both his well-to-do father, a candy merchant, and his mother were persons of strong and labile emotions, and his mother was prone to hysteria and nervous collapse. They quarreled fiercely. To the "avalanche" of domestic "bitterness and wailing" from the time he was seven years old Crane later attributed his own ruin. He took his mother's side in the family dramas, and she encouraged him to do so. She displayed her suffering, poured out her helpless resentment and protest. What emotions she thus activated in the child cannot be known, but when he was a grown man, the report from her of some new trouble—for the parade of her afflictions was endless—would arouse in him frantic anxiety and desperate wishes to help, until finally he rejected her in hatred.

At the age of nine, the marriage having temporarily collapsed, Crane was taken to his grandparents' home in Cleveland, where he spent most of his adolescence. (His mother also moved in, and before long his father.) He had rooms to himself on the third floor, including a sunny den in a tower, and a piano, books, photographs, and records. By the time he was sixteen he had published his first poem (in *Bruno's Bohemia*, a little magazine in New York). "I believe I have found my life's work," he said to a friend.

His father put him in touch with Mrs. William Vaughn Moody, the widow of a famous poet and patron of many others. She wrote him long, encouraging letters, full of news about the literary world. He discovered little magazines—*Poetry, The Pagan, Others, The Soil*—and took them home to read in his tower room, where he was also devouring Plato, Swinburne, Yeats, and the Georgian poets. Thanks to the little magazines, he was *au courant*, though possibly he had not yet read Shakespeare or Milton. Most of us are ushered into literature by teachers or friends, from whom we learn what to like and why, but Crane was reading on his own. The independence of mind and judgment he thus formed stayed with him in later life, so far, at least, as poetry was concerned. Though he was always painfully sensitive to criticism and praise, he would not modify his style, and his insights as a reviewer had the authority of the self-won.

From lonely absorptions in his Cleveland tower room Crane moved, at the age of seventeen, to New York City, where he rented a room on East 15th Street. Mrs. Moody was in the city, and Carl Schmitt, an artist from Ohio patronized by Crane's aunt. With Schmitt Crane spent long hours talking about painting and poetry, including his own poetry. Through Mrs. Moody he met the Irish poet Padraic Colum, Alfred Kreymborg, who was editor of *Others,* and Maxwell Bodenheim. His poems were getting into print. A "douche," as he called it, from Ezra Pound—"Beauty is a good enough egg," Pound wrote him, "but as far as I can see, you haven't the ghost of a setting hen or an incubator"—could in those circumstances be accepted bravely.

But his life was again overwhelmed by the emotional turmoil of his parents. His mother, now in New York herself, lay in a semi-coma, shocked by what she considered a new outrage from her former husband and blaming her son for her condition. As he sat by her bed in the darkened room, he felt himself trying to hold onto "sanity with both hands." Two years later maternal collapses drew him back to Cleveland for a while, where he worked in a munitions plant, as a riveter in a shipyard, and as a newspaper reporter, before returning to New York. Unable to find work, he was supported by friends and by his mother, but this naturally aggravated his already active feelings of guilt and inadequacy. He became even more touchy and prone to project his self-dislike onto others. Since solitude had made him egoistic, and since he was utterly unrestrained in expressing his feelings, whatever they might be, he was already a trial to his friends, though far less so than he later became. At the same time he could be immensely vital, considerate, and charming.

Unable to bear himself as a sponger, he went to work for his father in Akron, Ohio, tending a candy shop. Here he wrote two charming poems: "Porphyro in Akron," on the gap between poetry (as beauty, idealism, romance—as in Keats's "The Eve of St. Agnes") and Akron; and the gentle, subtle "My Grandmother's Love Letters." He also enjoyed his first homosexual love affair, at least the first he mentioned to his friends. Though this love soon went "down through lust to indifference," it caught up for a few months all his capacity of vivid idealization and his pathetically intense, scarcely believing gratitude that his devotion could be returned. For the next few years his loves had for him a religious and mystical dimension. Through love or the lover he was, he felt, led toward communion with the transcendent and the divine. He felt "like weeping most of the time . . . I have so much now to reverence, discovering more and more beauty every day,—beauty of character, manner, and body."

During this period Crane was reading Elizabethan dramatists and poets—Webster, Marlowe, Jonson, Shakespeare, Donne, Vaughan. Presumably he was led to these writers by T. S. Eliot's critical essays. Crane was, with Yvor Winters, the first American poet to owe his education largely to Modernist poetry and criticism. Elizabethan literature contributed to his emotional rhetoric, diction, and blank-verse rhythm:

> The earth may glide diaphanous to death;
> But if I lift my arms it is to bend
> To you who turned away once, Helen, knowing . . .

These lines, from Crane's "For the Marriage of Faustus and Helen," might almost be from Marlowe. In "Voyages II" we read, "The seal's wide spindrift gaze toward Paradise"; in "Voyages

IV," "The chancel port and portion of our June"; and in *The Bridge* of "pearls that whisper through the doge's hand," lost "Indian emperies," and "that violet wedge / of Adirondacks"—the last illustrating Crane's Marlovian-Miltonic use of proper names. A reinforcing influence on this bold rhetoric of line came from Melville, especially some of the great passages in *Moby-Dick*. Lesley Simpson recalls reading aloud with Crane, the year before Crane's death, "one of Captain Ahab's magnificent monologues. Hart took fire. 'By God!' he roared. 'That is poetry. If only I could write like that!'" He was also puzzling out French poets—Vildrac, Laforgue, Rimbaud—with the help of a dictionary, and he published three poems translated from Laforgue.

Crane's employment with his father terminated in mutual misunderstanding and rage. In April 1921 he was back in his grandmother's house in Cleveland, and he found work as a writer of advertising copy. Composing all day on behalf of water heaters and tires, he would write poetry half the night. As he worked in his tower room, the phonograph blared the same record over and over—maybe "that glorious Bolero"—a jug of red wine stood on the desk, and Crane paced the floor declaiming. He was forming and reforming his verses, now and again dropping to the desk to write one down. Swigging and exalting, he lived in his imagination, knowing "more and more that in the absolute sense the artist *identifies* himself with life." Yet all the while he subjected what he wrote to exacting scrutiny and stubborn revision. In states like this he composed, between April 1922 and February 1923, his first major poem, "For the Marriage of Faustus and Helen."

The setting and imagery of this poem are those of the contemporary urban world, of the office building, subway, nightclub, and jazz band. Such material had already been used by other poets in the United States, for example, by Sandburg in his *Chicago Poems* (1916) and by Lola Ridge in *The Ghetto and Other Poems* (1918). But these free-verse poems had been pictorial and anecdotal, large and easy, like billboards. Crane used the traditional poetic line, and with the variety and power of a master in rhythm and melody. In "For the Marriage of Faustus and Helen," moreover, he first developed the alogical language of packed associations—for example, "The abating shadows of our conscript dust"—for which he later became a byword, though he was not yet impenetrable. Thus Crane was almost the first American poet to combine the imagery of the modern city with intellectual and emotional intensity. Almost the first, because T. S. Eliot had preceded him.

Crane was aware of Eliot's work. In fact, Eliot's rhythms and diction emerge in Crane's poems occasionally. But, like most American poets at this time, Crane dissented from Eliot's pessimism. His reason was, in part, literary ambition. Eliot had "dug the ground and buried hope as deep and direfully as it can ever be done. . . . After this perfection of death—nothing is possible in motion but a resurrection of some kind." But deeper reasons lay in his character and experience. "For the Marriage of Faustus and Helen" includes among its materials picking up a woman in a subway, dancing to jazz music, and piloting a warplane. Eliot's onlooker (whether called Prufrock, Gerontion, or Tiresias) would have viewed these doings wearily. Crane's poem is not without ironic or critical perspectives on such experiences, but, nevertheless, they become in Crane ecstatic and almost mystical. On this desperate ground, the chance of ecstasy, Crane staked his justification of life. "Ecstasy" is not quite the right word, but no word puts precisely what Crane expressed with his suggestive power. Using many words, we could try to invoke feelings of delight, power, exaltation, reverence, ultimate communion, and transcendence. "I have known moments in eternity." Such moments came occasionally in the process of writing, in love affairs, in drinking, and once while a dentist was boring into his tooth. They were "spiritual events" as real, powerful, and possible in the modern world as "in the time of Blake." Crane wished, therefore, to apply as much of Eliot's technique as he could "absorb and assemble toward a more positive, or (if [I] must put it so in a sceptical age) ecstatic goal." After all, as he understated his case to Allen Tate, "one *does* have joys."

Hence though interpreters often speak (with some warrant from the poet) of Crane's Helen as "beauty" and his Faustus as the poet finding her in the modern world, this vocabulary is too limiting. She is the symbol of the possible moments of experience that for Crane redeem life. If, for shorthand, we call these "beauty," still Crane does not present the beautiful (Helen), but, instead, the dynamics of our subjective, emotional response to it.

Joyce was coalescing ancient myth and modern life in *Ulysses*.

Eliot also experimented with what he called the "mythical method," which consists, he said in his 1923 review of *Ulysses*, in "manipulating a continuous parallel between contemporaneity and antiquity," and so "giving shape and significance to the immense panorama of futility and anarchy which is contemporary history." Crane's poem does not manipulate a "continuous parallel," but nevertheless, Crane may have hoped for similar advantages from his allusions to myth. In 1925, two years after Eliot's remark, Crane explained that in "For the Marriage of Faustus and Helen" he was "building a bridge between so-called classic experience"—the sense of beauty, Dionysian acceptance of tragedy—and "many divergent realities of our seething, confused cosmos of today." With admirable common sense he added that "the importance of this scaffolding may easily be exaggerated, but it gave me a series of correspondences between two widely separated worlds on which to sound some major themes of human speculation—love, beauty, death, renascence."

Returning from Cleveland to New York, Crane made new friends—Waldo Frank, E. E. Cummings, Jean Toomer—and eventually found a job with an advertising firm. His situation was typical, he thought, "for the artist in America . . . If you make enough to live decently on, you have no time left for your real work,—and otherwise you are constantly liable to starve." He quit his job, moved for cheaper living to the country, missed the city and returned to it, and eventually found another job, writing little poetry amid the worries and upheavals. By April 1924 he was living in a room that overlooked the East River and the Brooklyn Bridge. "That window," he said in a letter, "is where I would be most remembered of all: the ships, the harbor, and the skyline of Manhattan, midnight, morning or evening,—rain, snow, or sun, it is everything from mountains to the walls of Jerusalem and Nineveh, and all related and in actual contact with the changelessness of the many waters that surround it. I think the sea has thrown itself upon me." That last sentence refers also to his being again deeply in love. "I have seen the Word made Flesh. . . . And I have been able to give freedom and life which was acknowledged in the ecstasy of walking hand in hand across the most beautiful bridge of the world, the cables enclosing us and pulling us upward in such a dance as I have never walked and never can walk with another." Thus inspired he com-

posed from the summer of 1924 to that of 1925 the four great
lyrics that, with introductory and concluding poems written earlier, made up his six "Voyages." The title alludes, among other
things, to the journeys and returns of his seagoing lover, who
sailed aboard ships as a printer and cargo checker. But of course
these are psychological and spiritual voyages.

"A PLATE OF VIBRANT MERCURY"

In "Voyages" and other lyrics of 1924 and 1925 and sporadically thereafter—in such lyrics as "Paraphrase," "Possessions,"
"Lachrymae Christi," and "At Melville's Tomb"—Crane wove a
poetic texture of incredible density. He did this by composing
slowly, thoughtfully, and deliberately, with a sense of joyous mastery as the multiple associations gathered and fused. At its best
such poetry justifies itself before it is understood. An example
is the famous third stanza of "Voyages II":

> And onward, as bells off San Salvador
> Salute the crocus lustres of the stars,
> In these poinsettia meadows of her tides,—
> Adagios of islands, O my Prodigal,
> Complete the dark confessions her veins spell.

The context tells us that "her" is the sea (and much else), but on
first encounter no reader attaches much meaning to "poinsettia
meadows," "Prodigal," or the whole last line. No matter. The
melody and emotional rhythm compel us to read the lines over
and over, until possibly meanings dawn. Possibly, because in
some lyrics they do not dawn. As Robert Lowell once put it, you
can analyze every phrase, but when you reread the poem, you
cannot keep your explications in mind; the text remains as
opaque as ever. Even Crane admitted that "Possessions" cannot
be explained. "It must rely (even to a large extent with myself)
on its organic impact on the imagination to successfully imply
its meaning." "A plate of vibrant mercury"—Crane's phrase
from "Recitative"—is his apt metaphor of his idiom or texture
in this phase of his career; the phrase suggests the reactivity and
amalgamating seamless fluidity of this style.

When he showed these obscure, alogical poems to his friends
or mailed them out to editors, Crane naturally found himself

embattled. Marianne Moore, as editor of the *Dial*, usually rejected his poems, sometimes published them, and occasionally infuriated Crane by excising and rewriting. Harriet Monroe of *Poetry* did not herself tinker with Crane's texts, but demanded revisions and also prose paraphrases, which in the case of "At Melville's Tomb" she published with the poem. Justifying his work, Crane repeated Mallarmé's dicta (though without mentioning Mallarmé) that a poem is or should be "a single, new *word*, never before spoken and impossible to actually enunciate," and that its terms are selected less for their denotative and logical values than for connotative and associative ones and for the "metaphorical inter-relationships" they activate. Language so used is a "field of added consciousness and increased perceptions ... fresh concepts, more inclusive evaluations." Thus though phrases such as "adagios of islands" may make "initial difficulties in understanding my poems," such a phrase "seems a much more direct and creative statement than any other more logical employment of words such as 'coasting slowly through the islands.'" It refers "to the motion of a boat through islands clustered thickly, the rhythm of the motion ... besides ushering in a whole world of music." And Crane took for granted the Modernist technique that renders experience through the medium of somebody's subjectivity. He presents, in other words, the sensations and feelings, the "physical-psychic experience," of a person immediately involved in the event, and he does not employ the "abstract tags," "formulations of experience in factual terms, etc.," which would orient a reader but which also would cause poetry to "lose its impact and become simply categorical." Since just what is "going on"—such as coasting slowly through the islands—is not said in so many words, readers must infer it. If they fail to do so, the text is for them a jumble. But an artist, Crane insists, has no choice. He must count on some "bases in the reader." "As long as poetry is written, an audience, however small, is implied, and there remains the question of an active or an inactive imagination as its characteristic."

In December 1925, Crane described his resourceless situation and his literary ambitions to Otto Kahn, a banker and patron of the arts, and received a loan of two thousand dollars. Elated, he joined Allen Tate and Tate's wife in the country, living in two rooms of a house they had rented. As winter settled down, he made plans and gathered materials for *The Bridge*. But he was unable to write much; he found Tate unsympathetic to the Whitmanian mood intended for *The Bridge;* for their part the Tates, both of them writers, suffered from Crane's restless exuberance. As they tried to work he came trampling and shouting in. The little tensions accumulated until a night in April when both Tates rose from bed, composed their versions of the last months with Crane, and shoved the letters under his door.

Crane left for the Isle of Pines, near Cuba, where his grandparents had a plantation. News that a publisher had at last accepted his first volume, *White Buildings* (Allen Tate generously contributed a foreword to it) helped him start composing again. In July and August 1926 he wrote much of *The Bridge;* more precisely, he substantially completed "Cutty Sark," "Powhattan's Daughter," and "The Tunnel," and revised the "Proem" and "Ave Maria." In this second and last of his great creative bursts words came to him even in dreams. He felt an "absolute music in the air" or "as though I were dancing on dynamite." With the whole poem in mind, he could "slip from one section to another" like a "girder-jack." Working day and night, he was by September exhausted. He hoped that a week's vacation in Havana would refresh him, but afterwards found himself still unable to write. At the end of October he returned to New York.

Writing had given Crane's life its meaning and hope. From now on, as composition became harder and rarer, he was more vulnerable to whatever guilts and inner panics destroyed him. Seeing what was happening to him, his friends were helpless and increasingly appalled. He was still, when sober or only half-drunk, animated, full of literary insight and knowledge, and charming. He had fits of writing, love affairs, plans for new poems, and schemes of amendment. He also appeared to have an inexhaustible capacity to recover from collapses. Neither was he doing anything he had not done before, except that he did it now more frequently and intensely. Nevertheless, the story of his final years dismays. He fled from the city to the country, from New York to Hollywood, Paris, Chagrin Falls, Ohio (where his father had a restaurant), and Mexico. His mother pursued him with letters and threatened visits, with complaints of illness, woes in her second marriage (it ended in divorce), fears of poverty, hysterias and breakdowns, until finally he developed a hatred and terror of her, and pleaded with his friends not to tell her where he was. He had money worries, and occasionally planned to become a plumber's or mechanic's helper. He was plagued by hangovers, indigestion, hay fever, hives, boils, toothaches, and attacks of delirium tremens. He was jailed for drunkenness in New York, Paris, and Mexico. He could not sleep, and when he did, his nightmares made him prefer insomnia. Though he had many friends, and always made new ones, he constantly suspected them of "betrayal." He was lonely, and sought (and sometimes found) affection from sailors he would pick up as he prowled the city parks and waterfront bars at night. Sometimes the police would find him drunk and beaten in an alley. He was arrested for soliciting. He feared blackmail. He drank habitually, enormously. In heroic desperation he forced himself, in the late summer and fall of 1929, to complete *The Bridge,* so far as he could complete it, composing "Cape Hatteras," "Quaker Hill," and "Indiana," and revising other sections. He called upon his friends at all hours, sometimes weeping, sometimes smashing things, sometimes exclaiming that he was dying. (But he always phoned apologies the next day.) Katherine Anne Porter, who knew him in Mexico, jotted down recollections that resemble those of many others:

The next evening, or rather some time after midnight, he arrived at our gate in a taxicab, and began the habitual dreary brawl with the driver, shouting that he had been cheated, robbed; calling for us to come and pay his fare, as he had been robbed in a cafe. . . . he broke into the monotonous obsessed dull obscenity which was the only language he knew after reaching a certain point of drunkenness, but this time he cursed things and elements as well as human beings. His voice at these times was intolerable; a steady harsh inhuman bellow which stunned the ears and shocked the nerves and caused the heart to contract. In this voice and with words so foul there is no question of repeating them, he cursed separately and by name the moon, and its light: the heliotrope, the heaven-tree, the sweet-by-night, the star jessamine, and their perfumes. . . . But those were not the things he hated. He did not even hate us, for we were nothing to him. He hated and feared himself.

On April 27, 1932, Crane walked to the stern of a boat returning from Mexico to New York, and jumped overboard. His body was never found.

THE BRIDGE

Crane's great poem has eight numbered sections and runs for about seventy-five pages. No narrative continues from one section to another, but there is a sequence of psychological and spiritual states from the emotions of dawn wonder, freshness, and hope in the opening three poems to the mystical climax of "The Dance." Thereafter the world of the poem gradually reaches a nadir of materialistic meaninglessness in "Quaker Hill." As if in heroic despair the following section, "The Tunnel," goes down deeper into the realm of death. This section is a subway ride under the East River from Manhattan to Brooklyn; the underworld transit is an opposite counterpart to the overarching vault of Brooklyn Bridge. The next and final poem, "Atlantis," concludes in religious ecstasy. The language of this and several other sections has the density of fused, ambiguous suggestions of Crane's lyrics; in fact, the context of a long work gives an immense reverberation to the images as they recur, interweave, and pick up more and more connotations. But in other sections of the poem the idiom is relatively traditional and directly accessible.

The Bridge united the two main directions in American poetry of its time. On the one hand, it descended from French poets of the nineteenth century—Baudelaire, Rimbaud, Mallarmé, Laforgue—and from the Elizabethan dramatists and the Metaphysical poets of the seventeenth century. Eliot fused these separate sources, and Crane completely absorbed Eliot's work. On the other hand, there was the optimistic, democratic, expansive, mystical tradition of Whitman, unfolding a vision of America as its main symbol and prophetic promise. The Bridge carried the legacy of Whitman into the urban, industrial world of the twentieth century.

Crane conceived The Bridge when he was completing "For the Marriage of Faustus and Helen." He planned to use, as Eliot had, interrelated and telescoped themes and symbols (Crane called this form "symphonic") and, again like Eliot, to juxtapose the present and the past. But in contrast to Eliot, his would not be a "poetry of negation." He hoped to go *through* [Eliot] toward a *different goal.* He was, he felt, "directly connected with Whitman." "A mystical synthesis of 'America'" gleamed vaguely but gloriously. "The initial impulses of 'our people,'" as he explained in a February 1923 letter to Gorham Munson, "will have to [be] gathered up toward the climax of the bridge, symbol of our constructive future, our unique identity, in which is included also our scientific hopes and achievements of the future." The imaginative possibilities were "positively awesome in their extent." If "I do succeed," he told Munson, "such a waving of banners, such ascent of towers, such dancing, etc. will never have been put down on paper."

So his subject was, at one level, America. The poem packs in an enormous amount of American landscape, history, and contemporary life, and steeps most of its vignettes and allusions in affirmative emotion. It includes monologues of Columbus voyaging back to Spain, a pioneer mother, and a drunken sailor in a modern bar; it participates in a subway ride, an Indian death dance, and an airplane battle; it sees Manhattan towers across the harbor, "Grey tepees tufting the blue knolls ahead," and, through Columbus' eyes, the new world at dawn: he "saw / The first palm chevron the first lighted hill"; it reports the sounds of foghorns, trains, bison, jukeboxes, and the speech of the people; and it is composed in blank verse, free verse, jazz rhythm, ballad meter, and blues. Like many other American poets, Crane feels the Romantic appeal in specifically American materials. How Sandburg must have envied the talk of Crane's hoboes ("Jesus! Oh I remember watermelon days!"); his montage of the Union Pacific trains and the lost world of the Indian:

> Trains sounding the long blizzards out—I heard
> Wail into distances I knew were hers.
> Papooses crying on the wind's long mane . . .

and the "airy regatta of phantom clipper ships seen from Brooklyn Bridge on the way home" (as Crane explained the following lines to Otto Kahn):

> Buntlines tusseling (91 days, 20 hours and anchored!)
> *Rainbow, Leander*
> (last trip a tragedy)—where can you be
> *Nimbus?* and you rivals two—
>
> a long tack keeping—
>
> *Taeping?*
> *Ariel?*

Yet other passages depict the doleful life of the contemporary city, the urban hell that is now one of the conventions of modern poetry. For Crane these sordid images did not express a final reality—they are only a stage in the pilgrimage of consciousness his poem enacts—but he presented them with a greater concentrated power than any other American poet, excepting only Eliot, his master in this vein.

But in the poem America is much more than a continent, a history, and a modern civilization; it is a nexus of emotions and spiritual experience. Like so many interpreters of the American character—Whitman, Lawrence, Williams—Crane expressed himself in his portrait of us. From Columbus on, his explorers, pioneers, sailors, hoboes, office workers, and moviegoers are en route in caravels and caravans, canoes, clippers, wagons, airplanes, automobiles, sternwheelers, trains, subways, daydreams, and afoot. People in the poem look at things far off or high up; they remember their childhood; they bend forward—a kind of motion—in movie houses toward the screen. In its thrusting and rising arc the bridge expresses this up, out, and awayness, and it also becomes a ship. (The bridge has, as Crane said, quite a "career" in the poem.) In the wide immensities of Crane's continent hardly anyone is settled down. The widowed mother in "Indiana" has a farm and children, but her monologue dwells on her *Wanderjahre* that went before. The son to whom she speaks is himself, typically, about to ship out for Rio. No one in the poem enjoys long or close relationships with other people. Their significant contacts are with the landscape or with strangers. The loners and journeyers are seeking Cathay, El Dorado, Thee. What they seek gleams in the distance, like the dawnlit "Indian emperies" of Columbus, or the morning star, or the "flashing scene" projected in the movies, or the cable strands "veering with light" above the bridge, or the remembered smile of the protagonist's mother that "flickered through the snow screen" as she walked home from church. In short, the poem shows the Romantic, isolated consciousness in its quest for ultimate communion.

Yet also the images of the poem present things making contact and entering into each other. The lovely proem "To Brooklyn Bridge"—

All afternoon the cloud-flown derricks turn . . .
Thy cables breathe the North Atlantic still

—brings together modern industrial construction with the sky
and the sea—brings together much else besides, if we sense the
resonance of these symbols throughout the poem. Such opposites as the primitive and the modern, the historical past and the
present, the Indian race and the white, the sacred and the pro-
fane are repeatedly both contrasted and also fused. Metamorphosis is the poem's rule of procedure. The pioneers become
the twentieth-century hoboes—similar, yet also different; Columbus gazing at the "crescent ring" of the sea's horizon reap-
pears as Columbus Circle with its ring of lights and refractions;
the "inviolate curve" of the seagull's flight turns into a bridge.
As we read, we ourselves build bridges between the widely scattered contexts. The "strange bird-wit" of the hoboes in "The
River" recalls the "bedlamite" in "To Brooklyn Bridge"; as the
bedlamite jumps from the bridge, his "ballooning" shirt resembles a sail, and thus his suicide is associated with the quest
motif. The transformations of the feminine figure into Poka-
hantus, the Southern Cross, a burlesque dancer, and so forth,
are an archetypal extravaganza. In climactic passages the fused
opposites include agony and love, sexuality and death, space and
time, the human and the divine. The symbol of a circle runs
through the poem, from the "white rings" of the seagull in its
flight at the third line to the "lariat sweep" of divine vision and
knowledge in the final stanzas. Ambiguous and many-faceted
like all the symbols in the poem, the circle is, among other
things, that which includes and contains. Within the "encinctur-
ing lariat sweep" at the end everything is present in timeless,
ecstatic being. This "Everpresence" or "Love" is the other shore,
so to speak, of this bridge that begins in modern Brooklyn; it is
the Cathay, America, or Atlantis of which the characters in the
poem are in quest. Brooklyn Bridge becomes a symbol of that
which expresses and aspires—"O harp and altar"—to the divine. And the Bridge is also *The Bridge*, a poem, a constructed
work of art and an act of imagination. The rapt descriptions of
the Bridge in the poem are hymns to the imagination.

5

THE POETRY OF CRITICAL INTELLIGENCE

A T Cambridge in 1928 William Empson was attacking God in formal, dense, ironic poems with complicated metaphors. "I thought it would be very nice to write beautiful things like the poet Donne," he later recalled. "I would sit by the fire trying to think of an interesting puzzle." A note to one of his poems explains, typically, "the point is to get puns." Another Cambridge student, Ronald Bottrall, saw himself as a Mauberley-Gerontion, a poet flypapered by the age. His polished stanzas said that the Romantic tradition is exhausted and no other exists. The imagery of our urban, industrial world is not "fused" with our feelings. And so forth. He was versifying the cultural views of Pound's poetry and Eliot's, but especially of literary criticism—modern culture and its plights as described in the prose of Eliot, I. A. Richards, and Edgell Rickword. Empson's style was shaped out of Hardy, Donne, Marvell; Bottrall's of these with Hopkins, Eliot, and Pound. He first saw in *Hugh Selwyn Mauberley*, Bottrall said, "how contemporary verse should be written." W. H. Auden, at Oxford, was discovering the poetry of Eliot and writing, Christopher Isherwood says, lines like, "Inexorable Rembrandt rays that stab . . ." These young writers were exploring especially the poetic possibilities of wit—Metaphysical, Augustan, or Laforguean—and so was an older American, John

Crowe Ransom, in brilliant volumes of 1924 and 1927. Ransom was at Vanderbilt University in Tennessee, where a group of young teachers and students, including Ransom and Allen Tate, were meeting regularly to go over each other's poems. When in 1922 they founded a little magazine, *The Fugitive*, they received in the mail and admired the poems of Laura Riding. Riding went to England in 1925 and two years later published with Robert Graves *A Survey of Modernist Poetry*. This bright book contained a now famous sixteen-page analysis of Shakespeare's Sonnet 129, "Th' expense of spirit in a waste of shame . . . ," showing how many different, interwoven meanings the text might activate. Excited by this, Empson went to work on other texts, illustrating the same point about poetic language, first for his director of studies, I. A. Richards, and then for the world in *Seven Types of Ambiguity* (1930).

SOURCES AND HISTORY OF THE STYLE

From sources such as these a new style of poetry developed—and in two stages. The poets I have mentioned—Ransom, Tate, Riding, Empson, Bottrall—may represent it in the 1920s and 1930s. These poets missed the Imagist phase of the modern movement. They never rivaled that earlier generation in concrete renderings of sights, motions, sensations—the marvelously vivid particularity of Pound, Marianne Moore, the early Stevens—nor did they seek to do so. They were not Symbolists in either French or Yeatsian ways. And they lacked the break-loose experimentalism that had helped to create the high Modernist style. Usually their thought processes were rational, their grammar *comme il faut*, their forms self-consciously studied and rigorous in meters and stanzas. Their texture of phrasing was dense and active, and as they telescoped images and associations, they also pondered the interwoven network they were making.

At length a second generation emerged. This was mainly in the United States and included, among others, John Berryman, Robert Lowell, Randall Jarrell, Robert Penn Warren, W. S. Merwin, Richard Wilbur, Adrienne Rich, Howard Nemerov, Melvin Tolson, and James Merrill, all of them just beginning in the 1940s. (In England "The Movement," associated in the 1950s with Kingsley Amis, Robert Conquest, Donald Davie, and Philip Larkin, promoted a somewhat similar type of poetry.) Patting each syllable diligently into place, these young writers composed formal, impersonal poems, suitable for close explication. The world to which their complexities were a response was kept at a distance. But great things were to come from some of them.

Throughout its whole career this style lived in intellectual symbiosis with a school of critics. Eliot's critical essays attacked Romantic emotionalism and self-expression and assumed that poetry at present must be complex, packed, and ironical. They praised neoclassical sophisticated awareness, colloquial ease, and clear outline and structure, as in Dryden. Eliot's discussion of Metaphysical wit was especially important for the young poets. Eliot pointed to the wit of Shakespeare, Donne, or Marvell as the central tradition for English poets, and added that it had been lost since the seventeenth century. He defined it in suggestive ways, and the examples he quoted in his essays had a finer, deeper resonance than the few that could be found in his own poetry.

The criticism of Coleridge was vividly present to this generation, having been rediscovered by the Edwardians. "So, then, there abide these three, Aristotle, Longinus, and Coleridge," proclaimed George Saintsbury in his huge *History of Criticism* (1900–04), and the Regius Professor went on to say that if all the chairs in literature were to be disestablished, and the proceeds applied to furnishing "everyone who goes up to the University with a copy of the *Biographia Literaria,* I should decline to be the person chosen to be heard against this revolution." Everyman republished *Biographia Literaria* in 1906, Arthur Symons echoing in his introduction that it was "the greatest book of criticism in English," and Oxford University Press brought it out in 1907 with a long, valuable introduction by John Shawcross exploring Coleridge's ideas. Newly attentive readers found Coleridge arguing that criticism did not have to be either relative and impressionistic or, as a worse alternative, objective in the sense that you measure a poem against external criteria. At every point a good poem contains within itself the reason why its text is so and not otherwise, for it is organized, "and what is organization, but the connection of parts to a whole." As we study and appreciate its organization, we form a critical judgment that is principled, analytic, and objective, yet wholly responsive to the particular poem. Insisting that the poetic imagination works by integrating the multiple and diverse, Coleridge illustrated his point in brilliant moments of what later was to be called "close reading." Thus he quoted a couplet from Shakespeare's *Venus and Adonis* describing "the flight of Adonis from the enamoured goddess in the dusk of the evening":

> Look! how a bright star shooteth from the sky;
> So glides he in the night from Venus' eye.

"How many images and feelings are here brought together," Coleridge commented, "without effort and without discord, in the beauty of Adonis, the rapidity of his flight, the yearning, yet hopelessness, of the enamoured gazer, and a shadowy ideal character is thrown over the whole." What makes one poem better than another, assuming that both are equally integrated compositions? Coleridge said that the greater the multiplicity (he called it "multëity") and diversity a poem subsumes, the greater its value. These and other Coleridgean positions were so influential from the 1920s to the 1940s that the impact of his critical ideas a hundred years after his death was greater than it had been in his own time.

In four theorizing books in the 1920s, I. A. Richards dismissed notions that poetry is feeling, the ideal, truth, revelation, the sense of infinitude, or some mysterious *je ne sais quoi,* and argued, instead, that a poem is an organization of meanings and as such can be rationally analyzed. At Cambridge University Richards had been exposed to the procedures in philosophical argument of G. E. Moore, who concentrated on problems of meaning in language. And in studying psychology Richards learned from Freud and others that texts express many meanings at once, including ones of which the writer is not conscious. Nevertheless, Richards' application of psychology to literary theory and criticism was not Freudian. Reviving a type of British criticism that had been brilliantly speculative in the eighteenth century, Richards tried to build the theory of literature out of empirical psychological study of the workings of the nervous system and brain—the processes by which the mind produces and organizes sensations, images, ideas, feelings, attitudes, and so forth. Later critics took over many of Richards' premises, but without the psychologizing in which he had grounded them. They learned from him that the acts of criticism are mainly "reading" and evaluating. "Reading" is the process of obtaining the "total meaning" of the poem; put with more complicated exactness, "reading" is having a mental experience that approximately resembles the relevant mental experience of the poet as he contemplates the finished poem. The psychological processes involved are complicated and perilously exposed to interferences and misadventures, and most persons lack ability or training for the enterprise. The latter point was unforgettably illustrated in *Practical Criticism* (1929), where Richards reproduced and commented on the sometimes grotesque misinterpretations of Cambridge students encountering poems. As a remedy he advocated vigilant and prolonged attention to the text. In my opinion, to know the "period" and the author will in most cases enrich the total meaning. But Richards felt that such knowledge is not usually necessary for successful reading, and he feared lest the study of authors and periods take precedence over close reading. We should make the poem "in all its minute particulars as intimately and as fully present to our minds as we can contrive." Critical evaluation ordinarily follows from this without hesitation. Nevertheless, the moment of evaluation is of supreme importance, for it involves not just our choice of a poem but "the form and order" of our "whole personality."

Thus by the end of the 1920s there was not only a brilliant Modernist poetry but also a challenging new criticism. This criticism helped the young poets to use the high Modernist achievement selectively and to combine it with other styles. Its development continued in F. R. Leavis' *New Bearings in English Poetry* (1932) and *Revaluation* (1936), in the magazine *Scrutiny*, which Leavis and his associates edited from 1932 to 1953, and in Richards' *Coleridge on Imagination* (1934). Meanwhile in the United States R. P. Blackmur's first book of criticism came out in 1935, Yvor Winters' in 1937, and Ransom's in 1938, though the views of these writers were already current through periodical essays. *Understanding Poetry* (1938), by Cleanth Brooks and Robert Penn Warren, was an almost universally used anthology for college students. The poems were provided with commentaries and study exercises. A poem, these authors explained, "should always be treated as an organic system of relationships," and their comments and questions illustrated the point concretely. They showed (or asked) just how some element of a poem—for example, the details about Michael's way of life in Wordsworth's poem—"works with all the [other] elements to create the effect intended by the poet." Though it was judiciously simplified for students, the book owed its enormous impact to the many teachers who read it themselves and found in it a purposeful, practical method to be followed in classroom instruction. In 1941 Ransom published a book about a few of the critics he wanted to argue with, and, as so often happens, solidified the sense of a school or movement by finding a name for it: *The New Criticism*.

The "New Critics" attacked each other as much as they did their common enemies. Each had his individualities of approach and taste. Nevertheless, they shared main assumptions, caught especially from Eliot, Richards, and Coleridge. Since most of them—though certainly not Ransom or Winters—desired to defend high Modernist literature, this also shaped their premises and methods. They held that the object of criticism is not the author—his life, psychology, class consciousness, ideas, *Weltanschauung*, works in general, predecessors, or influences—but the particular text. This was to be analyzed closely and objectively, as opposed to enthusiastic impressions or creative "misprision." Valuable states of mind, they argued, are always both integrated and inclusive; in other words, the greater the amount of diverse, relevant experience and feeling that is present and organized, the greater the contact with reality. Since good poems embody such states of mind, their language will be polysemous through metaphor, irony, paradox, ambiguity, and the like, and their total form will combine the multiple perspectives into a complex yet coherent pattern. Thus in practice these critics concentrated on the language of a text, seeking to bring all its relevant meanings and their interplay into consciousness. (This type of analysis was usually called "explication," the term borrowed from the rather different method of close reading in the university study of literature in France.) These meanings were not the lexical ones only, but included also the further range of meanings implicated in form and style, that is, in figures, syntax, rhythm, versification, and so forth.

These critics were and still are dismissed as "formalist," but this is not just. They paid much attention to form and style in

the texts they analyzed, but only because they were close interpreters of meaning and adhered to Coleridge's premise of organic form: the form is not external and separable from the
meaning, but further defines it. Most of them were moralists,
and the ultimate object of their evaluation, on which the worth
of the text finally depended, was the speaker's state of mind. Not
his ideas on social revolution, sex, God, or whatever, and not his
emotional disposition—uplifted? hopeful? benevolent? defeatist?—but the extent to which he was in touch with reality at all
relevant points. Did the text embody a mature awareness, a
many-sided, complex, yet integrated attitude and vision?

Naturally such minute examinations could best be addressed
to short poems. When these critics discussed dramas, novels, and
longer narrative poems, they tended still to focus on language—
for example, the patterns of imagery in a Shakespearean play—
and thus to deal inadequately with other major components,
such as plot and character. Given their methods, sources, and
criteria, it was also natural that gradually, despite many disagree-
ments with one another and themselves, they built up a canon
of approved authors, including Donne, Marvell, Dryden, Pope,
Hopkins, and Eliot. Since works in translation lacked the complex textures of their original phrasing, the New Critics wasted
no time writing about them. Thus where Eliot and Pound had
so much formed their style in reading foreign literatures from
ancient Greece to modern France, the New Critics presented an
exclusively English and American tradition, though it was no
longer that of the Romantic lyric, the common, accepted norm
of poetry up to the 1920s.

Let us imagine later poets encountering this school of criticism. This would have happened in college (almost all went to
college), but not, at first, in the classroom. Empson had Richards
for his teacher, and Tate was taught by Ransom, but Auden's
tutor was a Chaucerian, and his case was more typical. The New
Criticism, in the thirties, was rarely expounded within English
departments, which fed their hungry sheep on impressionistic
appreciation, philology, positivistic literary history, source hunting, *Geistesgeschichte*, and Arnoldian or New Humanism. Against
most of these the New Critics declared war, affording their student readers a delicious iconoclastic frisson and inspiring in
some of the Ph.D. candidates and junior faculty a range of emo-

tions from satiric relief to Young Turkishness. The professoriate felt the justified reproaches. Recognizing that the tastes of Eliot, Empson, Leavis, and the others were too restrictive, their arguments often uninformed and dogmatic, the English departments turned a blinder eye to their virtues than they should have. Neither did they at first offer jobs to followers of the New Critics.

By the later 1940s, however, much had changed. The New Critics were becoming established in English departments in the United States, both personally in many cases and intellectually in more. Hardly an English major graduated without having been exhorted to keep his eye on the text and to read closely. Explications were regularly undertaken as classroom exercises. I do not wish to imply that the New Criticism had taken over English departments, for this was far from the case. But it was accepted as one orthodoxy among others, and it was also penetrating the teaching of literature in secondary schools.

Kunst wird Kritik, "art is becoming criticism," as the devil notes in Mann's *Doctor Faustus*. Having been taught to explicate, the young poets were explicating for themselves their own poems in the process of writing them. They composed with the same kind and intensity of "reading" that their readers would in turn bring to bear. Wordsworth used to argue that every great poet must create the taste by which he is to be enjoyed, but Lowell, Berryman, Nemerov, and many another starting out were trying to create great poems to fit a taste that already existed. To the extent that they succeeded, recognition came instantly. This agreement between the producers and consumers of a style is a normal feature of the academic in art. As this state of affairs continued into the 1950s, the New Criticism established itself more firmly as an academic orthodoxy, and the desire to break with it became more intense.

"To think more simply is also a gift of God," as Konrad Adenauer used to say, and there were plenty of poets in the 1940s and 1950s to prove it. The poetry of New Critical complexity was never without an opposition from followers of Whitman and Williams, and from political poets in the Second World War and the 1950s and 1960s. Today, when conventions have so much changed, the poetry of New Critical intelligence appears so artificial, labored, and remote that its former enthusiastic accept-

ance seems hard to understand, in fact, one of the stranger episodes in literary history. We should keep in mind, however, that
if this poetry was academic, it so idealized and manifested intelligence that it remained admirable even when it ceased to be
interesting. If this poetry and criticism formed a new Genteel
tradition, analogous in some ways to that of the later nineteenth
century, nevertheless, in contrast to the period of Whitman, the
Genteel pole of American literature now attracted the strongest
talents. And the artistic discipline of that style persists to the
present moment as an essential element in the greater poetry
that has been written since, often by the same poets.

METAPHYSICAL WIT

"About the beginning of the seventeenth century," Samuel
Johnson explained in his *Life of Cowley*, "appeared a race of writers that may be termed the metaphysical poets," and he pro-
ceeded to give his remarkable critique of their style. Weary of so
much namby-pamby verse in his own generation, he praised
these poets because at least they exercised the intellect, though
in other respects he was less favorable to them. By 1780, when
Johnson was writing, the Metaphysical poets were very little
read. There was no revival of interest in the next century,
though Coleridge was aware of their virtues. Richard Garnett
and Edmund Gosse, in their *English Literature* (1903–04), typically complained of Donne's "tortured irregularities," "monstrous pedantries," and "alembicated verbiage": he is "the father
of all that is exasperating, affected, and 'metaphysical' in English
poetry"; "No one has injured English writing more than Donne,
not even Carlyle." As late as 1926 Emile Legouis and Louis Ca-
zamian could still speak in their *A History of English Literature* of
Donne's "bad taste and eccentricity, all pushed to such an extreme that the critic's head swims as he condemns." Yet before
the First World War young poets such as Isaac Rosenberg and
Herbert Read were reading Donne with pleasure, and after the
war he was advocated by Eliot, Graves, Richards, and so down
through all the critics I mentioned. The "Metaphysical revival"
was in full swing. One researcher has counted the number of
critical and scholarly writings on the Metaphysical poets pub-

lished each year; they rose from fourteen in 1900 to forty-one in 1923 to seventy-three at the peak in 1934, after which there was a gradual decline to fifteen in 1950. Meanwhile the young poets were reading this formerly neglected "race," and, since Metaphysical qualities and characteristics—whatever they might be—were being praised by so many authorities, the young poets tried to emulate them. By 1952 more than seventy living poets had been denominated Metaphysical by one critic or another. If some of these names—Yeats, Cummings, Frost, Rexroth—now surprise, they indicate to what extent "Metaphysical" had become a synonym for "modern." No less surprising are the older poets in whom Metaphysical affinities were found; this list includes Lucretius, Goethe, Blake, Wordsworth, and Emerson. Clearly there was no agreement on just what the "Metaphysical" qualities were.

To review what this criticism admired in the Metaphysical poets is to restate some of the values of the New Critics. Metaphysical poets, so the argument went, kept many and contrasting attitudes, experiences, and ideals in mind at the same time. They amalgamated thought (intellectual agility, logic, learning, awareness, generalization) with emotional intensity and strongly concrete imagery. Their unified sensibility had been lost in the eighteenth and nineteenth centuries, though this "dissociation of sensibility"—in Eliot's famous phrase—had set in earlier. According to this version of literary history, thought processes had become more abstract; divorced from intelligence, emotions had become self-indulgently sentimental; and language, as in Swinburne, had taken on a life of its own, separate from either thinking or feeling.

Trying to pinpoint the distinctive quality of Metaphysical poetry, Eliot resurrected the term "wit," which had also been central in Johnson's critique. Wit expressed complex insight and feeling with immediacy and surprise. It presupposed rapid thought and wide awareness brought to bear in a constant pressure of the mind on experience, the mind inquiring more deeply into or beyond the present moment. It showed itself especially in contiguities, puns, metaphors, paradoxes, and the like, where the things brought into relation would ordinarily have been considered remote from each other. Wit is "a kind of *discordia concors*," as Johnson put it, "a combination of dissimilar images, or discovery of occult resemblances in things apparently unlike." How are "Golden lads and girls" like chimney sweepers? or how is a photograph like the hand that holds it? or, still more surprising question, how is the church advantageously different from a hippopotamus? The answers are in Shakespeare:

> Golden lads and girls all must,
> As chimney-sweepers, come to dust;

in Robert Lowell translating Rilke:

> Oh quickly disappearing photograph
> in my more slowly disappearing hand;

and in Eliot:

> The hippopotamus's day
> Is passed in sleep; at night he hunts;
> God works in a mysterious way—
> The Church can sleep and feed at once.

The shock of surprise may be sustained through many lines in Metaphysical poetry, for example, in Donne's "The Relique":

> When my grave is broke up again
> Some second guest to entertain
> (For graves have learned that woman-head
> To be to more than one a bed) . . .

The first word, "When," is the first jolt, premising that graves will be disturbed and thus violating pious convention by fact. The comparison of the corpse to a transient guest and of the grave to a sexual bed and a faithless woman, the half-activated pun on breaking the maidenhead, the assumption that women are promiscuous in a poem that idealizes love and lovers' fidelity—no wonder Eliot, faced with such swift, complex recognitions, felt moved to say that Metaphysical wit "is not cynicism, though it has a kind of toughness which may be confused with cynicism by the tender-minded." And Eliot added, "it is confused with cynicism because it implies a constant inspection and criticism of experience. It involves, probably, a recognition, implicit in the expression of every experience, of other kinds of experience which are possible." For another example, there is Eliot's perception, in "Whispers of Immortality," that the Jacobean playwright John Webster, in sex, kept death in mind, and in imagining the skeletons underground, thought of sex in death, and not abstractly or generally, but with terrible concreteness: he saw the skeletons leaning back underground, grinning in the pose of sexual invitation:

> Webster was much possessed by death
> And saw the skull beneath the skin;
> And breastless creatures under ground
> Leaned backward with a lipless grin.

In Metaphysical wit there was an "alliance of levity and seriousness," as Eliot put it, "by which the seriousness is intensified."

SAMPLES OF THE STYLE

Empson's *Poems* (1935) includes a villanelle on the familiar theme of fatal beauty or love. The speaker's "stare" has drunk "deep beauty"; his heart "pumps yet the poison draught of you"; no "later purge from this deep toxin cures." A villanelle is so troublesome a form, especially in English, that the technical achievement always calls attention to itself. Usually, in fact, there is nothing else to notice and admire, for the complications of the form induce a vague, conventional content. When the first rhyme must repeat itself twelve times, the second six, and other rules are no less maddening, a prudent poet will not also burden himself with a particular meaning. Empson does. In his poem the required formal repetitions of a villanelle become expressive, enacting the almost frozen emotion, the pain going on and on. And despite its burden of obsessing feeling, his villanelle packs in generalizations, individualizing details, and one metaphor after another. Its speaker declares, explains, argues, questions, recalls, and narrates, working over his experience in continuously active thinking. Yet though it articulates the pain of lost love, the poem is interestingly not entitled something like "You," or "You Burn Through Me Like a Poison," or "The Pain of Love Endures," but "Villanelle," stressing the feat of versification. For whatever reasons of personal temperament or critical premise, the title asserts that the form, not the emotion, is what matters.

Here is the first stanza:

> It is the pain, it is the pain, endures.
> Your chemic beauty burned my muscles through.
> Poise of my hands reminded me of yours.

The first line states a discursive generalization, an emotionally weighted and brooding one. The third line is personal, intimate speech, imparting an expressive detail. The metaphor of the second line is concrete, shocking, and original. In contrast to the cobras, vampires, Medusas, and hothouse horrors that figured fatal beauty in the villanelle-writing nineties, here is a chemical reaction. The many other metaphors in the poem are similarly arresting and disagreeable. The sequence of sentences is relatively discontinuous, the phrases, as the poem goes on, frequently compressed and sometimes obscure. A hundred years earlier the poem would have seemed comparatively difficult, but not ten years earlier. It builds on the Modernism of the 1920s and on the critical development from Eliot to Empson himself, yet compared with the work of Eliot, Pound, Stevens, or Williams in that decade, it represents something of a return to tradition.

John Crowe Ransom's "Here Lies a Lady," published in 1924, is peculiarly and intentionally unpleasant. It begins,

> Here lies a lady of beauty and high degree.
> Of chills and fever she died, of fever and chills,
> The delight of her husband, her aunt, an infant of three,
> And of medicos marveling sweetly on her ills.

The poem is the more unpleasant because of its strict, old-fashioned form; we imagine that the speaker, expressing himself so carefully, must intend everything he suggests. He intends, for example, the implications of the chiasmus of line two, which makes of the lady's death an occasion for decorative display. The stanza does not end in proper pathos but in a joke—the delighted doctors, dismissively called medicos, marveling instead of curing. The speaker seems very like the medicos, "marveling sweetly" rather than grieving.

The last stanza reveals what lies behind this distancing elegance. "Was she not lucky," the speaker asks, to die so easily, with only "six little spaces of chill, and six of burning?" The question is ironic, of course—death is not lucky; we call a death lucky in order to deny its actual character—yet the speaker also means that she really is lucky. Fear of death's pain and horror, and the attempt to control fear, are the deep motivations behind the poem, and result in its almost mocking refusal to feel. If we ask ourselves where else we have encountered terror masking itself behind intellectual irony, emotional incapacity, and formal polish, one answer is Laforgue, and Laforgue was an influence on this poem.

So if we understand this poem completely, we shall not wish to identify with the speaker. But many a reader has enjoyed the poem partly because, with its irony and elegance, it gives a sensation of being in control. And since we also feel that its distant, slightly mocking attitude in the face of death is one that ordinary people would not share, the poem includes us, as we read it, among an elite.

The poem fuses Laforgue, so to speak, with Edwin Arlington Robinson, substituting a southern, genteel context for that of Robinson's "Tilbury Town." As Robinson does in his best poems, Ransom implies a social milieu, its mores, values, and idiom. The lady's relatively easy and protected death seems of a piece with her genteel existence, sheltered from life's rawer, more harrowing moments. The old bits of lace, family kisses, and restorative sips of wine imply benignities but also limitations. And as in Robinson, the speaker belongs to the lady's class and milieu, as we see from what he says and also from the form and diction ("beauty and high degree") of his speech. The concluding cliché—"we bade God rest her soul"—highlights the conventionality and inadequacy of response in this genteel world.

So the interest and complexity of the poem lie chiefly in the attitude of the speaker, the involutions of irony and self-irony. From our perspective, as we try to understand the development of poetic form in the 1920s and 1930s, the significance of Ransom's poem is especially that it makes the reader think. It does not do so by the profundity of its metaphysics, as in the Romantic tradition—Goethe's "Urworte, Orphisch," for example, or Wordsworth's "Intimations of Immortality"; its verbal texture is not dense as in Pound or Eliot; but the reader has to quiz and ponder every detail in order to catch the attitude.

Our next example might be described as the entombment,

amid such solemn splendor, of Modernism; more exactly, it combines Modernism with older traditions. Allen Tate's "Ode to the Confederate Dead," which he composed at the age of twenty-seven in 1926, is a vampire ritual, draining blood from many poets without coming to life itself. Stylistically it assembles an anthology. "Ambitious November with the humors of the year" (line 15) might have come from the later nineteenth century. Other lines are haunted by Yeats:

> you know the rage,
> The cold pool left by the mounting flood,
> Of muted Zeno and Parmenides.

The style of Yeats and Eliot could hardly be more dissimilar, but there is a detached image in the poem that might have been lifted from "Gerontion" or *The Waste Land:*

> the hound bitch
> Toothless and dying, in a musty cellar
> Hears the wind only.

The poems of Pound and Eliot had also juxtaposed different styles, but except in satiric contexts, these were historical styles. In Tate's ode the Modernist styles became no less canonical than the traditional ones that the poem also invokes. This was an inevitable moment in literary history. What seems remarkable is that the moment came so soon.

Struggling to understand and enjoy Modernist poems such as *The Waste Land,* Tate had been compelled to form new methods in reading. As a critic he applied these methods to poems generally, and when he wrote poems, he naturally also concentrated on the same elements of poetic form that he concentrated on when reading, interpreting, and evaluating. In all this Tate was typical of his generation. Explicating was a part of writing, and the conscious, explicating attention focused especially on the manifold connotations and interconnections of images, metaphors, and symbols. Hence, though Tate's notes to his ode were written twelve years after the poem, they reflect the kinds of considerations that motivated him as he composed. At one point, for example, "you" have been looking at an angel carved on a gravestone. Suddenly, "You shift your sea-space blindly /

Heaving, turning like the blind crab." The stare of the angel has
plunged you—such are the violent and pecular psychological
dynamics of the poem—into this metaphoric sea where you behave like a crab. No more crabs appear, but some fifty lines later
"mute speculation . . . like the jaguar leaps/ For his own image
in a jungle pool." (It is not irrelevant to mention that a crab had
figured in Eliot's "Prufrock" and a tiger in "Gerontion.") Just as
in *The Waste Land* the one-eyed merchant is to be associated with
the Phoenician Sailor, as Eliot's notes tell us, and the Sailor with
Ferdinand Prince of Naples, and so on, Tate associates his crab
with his jaguar; "in the entire poem there are only two explicit
symbols for the locked-in ego; the crab is the first and less explicit symbol, a mere hint, a planting of the idea that will become
overt in its second instance—the jaguar towards the end." He
also suggests that we should compare and contrast the jaguar
with Narcissus: "instead of a youth gazing into a pool, a predatory beast stares at a jungle stream, and leaps to devour itself."
Never were irrational leaps of mind performed with more
thoughtful calculation than by the poets we are considering, who
may be said to have analyzed before they leapt. They were, to
repeat, anticipating the analyses they expected their readers
would bring to bear.

Robert Lowell published "The Quaker Graveyard in Nantucket" in 1946 at the age of twenty-nine. This was the hugely
ambitious attempt of a young poet, schooled by Ransom and
Tate, to rival the poem Milton had composed at the same age.
Like "Lycidas," Lowell's long poem is about the death of a
drowned friend. He tries to break out for consolation into the
transcendent, as Milton so grandly does, but his poem is much
less confident and more ambiguous. Its metaphysical ambition
is matched by its formal one. Like "Lycidas," the poem is composed in rhymed, pentameter verse with occasional shorter
lines; unlike Milton, Lowell divides his poem into numbered
strophes, his Roman numerals lending weight and solemnity.
Long vowels resound in the rhymes, and there are strong en-
jambments, alliterations, assonances, functional cacaphonies,
apostrophes—in short, the poem is stuffed with traditional devices. But its primary tradition is that of the New Criticism, and
it realizes in an extreme degree the formal values of this school
as they were developed in practice. For by now the methods of

this criticism had been illustrated in hundreds of published explications; in classrooms throughout the country thousands more were being written, discussed, and graded. According to their ideology, explicators should have focused on all the aspects of a poem that shape its total meaning. But in fact, as we just noticed, they especially emphasized imagery. Hence poets sought to load their imagery with connotations and interwoven associations. In Lowell's third strophe, for example, the drowned cousin has gone down into the ocean realm of Poseidon like Orpheus into Hades:

> All you recovered from Poseidon died
> With you, my cousin, and the harrowed brine
> Is fruitless on the blue beard of the god.

The sea being blue, the god Poseidon becomes Bluebeard of the fairy tale, with the suggestion that whatever knowledge the cousin "recovered" from the depths was horrible, like that of Bluebeard's wife when she looked into her husband's locked room and knew she would be murdered. The ocean is like a field "harrowed"—tormented, farmed, plundered—by the whaling ships, but it is a salt field and remains "fruitless." Christ harrowed hell, descending like Orpheus and bringing back the righteous souls. Unlike the cousin, Christ "recovered" or rescued what the depths held captive. "Harrowed brine" illustrates the artificial idiom you get when you concentrate mainly on packing in connotations.

We move on to 1956. Cleanth Brooks and Robert Penn Warren's *Understanding Poetry* had been telling students how to read for eighteen years. Poets were getting bored with the reiterated message. John Berryman, forty-two, was teaching at the University of Minnesota after ten years in the English Department of Princeton. His subject in "Homage to Mistress Bradstreet" was academic, since only professors and their seminars had perused or maybe even heard of Anne Bradstreet, a pious poet of early New England, dead since 1672, though Berryman said he "fell in love with her." His style is academic too: here is Anne gloating, having just had her baby:

> drencht & powerful, I did it with my body!
> One proud tug greens Heaven. Marvellous,
> unforbidding Majesty.

Swell, imperious bells. I fly.
Mountainous, woman not breaks and will bend:
sways God nearby: anguish comes to an end.
Blossomed Sarah, and I
blossom. Is that thing alive? I hear a famisht howl.

This impassioned interior monologue proceeds in rhyme and stanza. Each ejaculated phrase contrasts in style with adjacent phrases. "I did it with my body!" is intimate, direct, homely, and "sympathetic"; "One proud tug greens heaven," Romantically symbolic or apocalyptic. The spelling of the past participles and the use of the ampersand give seventeenth-century flavorings; "woman not breaks and will bend" might have strayed from "The Wreck of the Deutschland." The biblical allusion in "Blossomed Sarah" seems in character for the Puritan poet, but "Is that thing alive?" sounds too colloquial and tough for any age except our own. The sudden transitions of Anne's thoughts had been familiar since the 1920s, when Modernist poets had explored the uses of extreme discontinuity, often presenting their strange juxtapositions as the stream of someone's consciousness. Berryman the careful workman has remembered to insert the irrational, not only in the transitions but in Anne's projections and transferences of her emotions ("imperious bells"). His phrasing provides the obligatory ambiguities ("sways God nearby"—syntactical and semantic ambiguity), and the images associate with one another (green; blossom) in ways that were then deemed "organic."

Yet in contrast to the ironic poems of Empson and Ransom, Berryman's no longer intends to hold life at a distance. The stylistic tradition does that willy-nilly, even while the poem tries to snuggle as close to life as it can. With its frozen jerkiness the stanza gives an idea of death imitating life. Berryman's attempt in this poem to identify with Bradstreet and his first-person appearance in other parts of the poem indicate that the style we have been following was beginning to lose its appeal.

Since the New Critics did not make their principal impact on young writers until the 1940s and 1950s, the poets here discussed from the earlier generation are Laura Riding, Robert Graves, and the critics themselves—Empson, Ransom, Tate, and Winters. Toward the end of his career I. A. Richards also composed poetry of much distinction in this formal, intellectual style. He is one of the many fine poets omitted for lack of space. Robert Penn Warren was one of the New Critics, of course, and his earlier poetry might be noticed in this chapter. But his poetry usually had novelistic elements that were not characteristic of the New Critical style. Eventually he ceased altogether to work in the neo-Metaphysical mode, and I shall take him up later in a different context. During the 1930s the New Critics were much less influential than Eliot and Auden. The urgency of social and political questions in that decade made the concerns of the New Critics seem mandarin by comparison. But in the 1940s and 1950s, as I said, their premises and tastes were more or less accepted by at least half the young poets in America. Even Allen Ginsberg was at one time "all hung up," he remembers, "on cats like Wyatt, Surrey, and Donne." Even those who completely rejected the influence of the New Critics wrote in response to it if, like Frank O'Hara, they shaped their style deliberately to be unlike this approved mode.

LAURA RIDING

After 1938 Laura Riding (b. 1901) stopped composing poetry, for she concluded that poetry cannot attain the "rightness of word that *is* truth." She did not republish her work for thirty-two years (until *Selected Poems*, 1970). She was born in New York City, and went to Cornell, where she began writing. The Fugitives liked her poetry, and so did Robert Graves, who was exchanging letters with them. She sailed for England in 1925, and she and Graves worked closely together, publishing criticism under their joint names and printing by hand, as the Seizin Press, works by themselves and others. Leaving England in 1929, the two poets lived in a fishing village on Majorca. After the Civil War broke out in Spain, Riding left Majorca and returned after a couple of years to the United States. She married Schuyler Jackson in 1941 and has lived since in Florida. Her authorial name is now Laura (Riding) Jackson.

Riding's *Collected Poems* (1938) begins with an eloquent prose assertion that her poems are written for the right "reasons of poetry." These are not, she notes, the reasons why most people read, for most people are in quest of illusions, exaggerated emotions, and flattering sensations of profundity. She does not state what the "reasons of poetry" are, but in cumulatively suggestive phrases speaks of the uncovering of "reality as a whole," of living "for your very best reasons," of poems as "precisely somewhere in precisely everywhere" and as "incidents in the good existence." The good existence is that of the mind in its quest for completeness of conscious awareness. The end is not knowledge, if by that we mean a portable conclusion. But is is the power of finely discriminating, precisely valuing, seeing things in all their bearings—the intelligence in process.

Her poems have the action of intelligence as their form and their content. Often they are argument; assertions are made, explained, defended, justified, sometimes questioned and countered. In such poems her language may be plain, general, and colloquial. Other poems more resemble the Metaphysical mode (or the version of it that developed in the twenties) and continue a metaphor while exploring its implications: for example, the metaphor of maps in "The Map of Places" and that of jewels in "Auspices of Jewels." Her syntax is generally compressed and elliptical, and she musters an idiosyncratic, resourceful diction ("secretless," "usedness") with many compounds ("lover-round," "day-change," "Self-wonder"). Her perceptions tend to be especially alert to automatic routines of feeling and language. "The final outrage" is a stock phrase; typically correcting it by writing "outrage unfinal" (in "Memories of Mortalities"), Riding comments on both the true state of affairs and the false state of our language, or more exactly, of our ordinary, unthinking use of it. Poems such as "Postponement of Self" and "As Well as Any Other" articulate her rejection of nineteenth-century poetic conventions. Her truth-telling can be aggressively downright, but is often expressed with paradox and irony. Irony is seldom her final position, however, for her mind is more conscientious than it is open, and her predications, though complex, are not tentative. At her best she compresses original insights into forceful, surprising phrases. Among her best poems are "As Well as Any Other," "Postponement of Self," "Hospitality to Words," "All Nothing, Nothing," "The Need to Confide," "Friendship on Visit," and "The Vain Life of Voltaire."

ROBERT GRAVES

Robert Graves (1895–1985) belonged to the generation of poets who started writing in the Edwardian-Georgian days of artful simplicity, singing or colloquial charm, mild, agreeable realism, and fond, pious love of a traditional England, its countryside and ways of life. The schoolboy verse of Graves dwelt "in a romantic vein" (he later said) on "wizards, monsters, ghosts, and outlandish events and scenes," for his father had a library of Celtic folklore and poetry. A teacher sent his poems to Edward Marsh, the Georgian impresario. Marsh gave polite encouragement, but pointed out that Graves's diction was fifty years out of date. So far as inexpert youth permitted, Graves now imitated the Georgian anthologies. Few of these early efforts survive in his *Collected Poems*. Perused in *Over the Brazier* (1916), they astonish; in a youth so sweet and lilting, no one would predict the terse man at fifty and his goddess-ridden passions. Most English poets of Graves's generation fought, as Graves did, in the First World War, and the best of them, Owen and Rosenberg, died in it. The survivors were haunted for years by what they had gone through. But you could not know this from Graves's verse. *Fairies and Fusiliers* (1917) dwelt on moments of rural peace and beauty after battle, happy memories, friendship, and the like, though there were also some war grimness and horror. His work was included in the Georgian anthology for 1916–17, and readers liked it. Marrying, he settled in a rural cottage and raised children, writing amid the diapers. In these immediate postwar years he seemed, like Edmund Blunden or Ivor Gurney, a poet whose development had been arrested by the war. The idyll of his nursery rhymes and ballads, elves and fairies, published in *The Treasure Box* (1919), *Country Sentiment* (1920), and *The Pier Glass* (1921), was incredible in relation to his own experience, not to mention that of the age. In fact, these poems were an effort to escape the shocking images and emotions that hung on in his war-traumatized psyche. Such poems as "The Outlaws," "The Pier Glass," and "The Haunted House" allude to

> . . . lust frightful, past belief,
> Lurking unforgotten,
> Unrestrainable endless grief
> In breasts long rotten.

The use of poetry adumbrated here was to persist throughout Graves's career. He hated and feared his own emotions, or some of them. Moreover, he intuited that the underlying reality—of our emotional nature, existence, world—is terrible. Yet he believed he must confront what he feared. To do so might be therapeutic, might even bring joy, if, as Nietzsche thought, the delight of existence belongs to those who know also its nothingness and horror. And truth was a moral imperative. So in his mature work Graves did not shrink from the shocking and dreadful; yet he did not—dared not—enter immediately into such states of mind. He described and contemplated but did not embody or enact them. He brought them forward in the chains of controlling form. He distracted himself and us from them with conceits. In short, the formal, intellectual, traditional qualities of Graves's poetry, the regularity, elegance, generalization, wit, point, and brevity were defenses against underlying horror. They were means through which he could both express what he knew and felt and also keep it at a distance.

Critics and poets were now regularly assailing the Georgians, and Graves joined the cry, though at first under a pseudonym ("The Marmosite's Miscellany," 1925). How Graves may have felt about *Hugh Selwyn Mauberley* and *The Waste Land* at the time they were published, I cannot say. (His later remarks were colored by the resentment of the neglected.) Their extreme stylistic innovations and close, disagreeable portrait of the modern world were alien to his traditions but not to his feelings, which were veering toward revolt. And he was open to new influences, such as the Metaphysical poets, John Crowe Ransom, and Laura Riding. But he continued for a while to use the blither forms, though with deepening meanings. And he developed also a poetry of ideas, of speculation and generalization on "problems of religion, psychology, and philosophy" (as he put it).

In 1929 Graves and his wife separated and Graves went with Laura Riding to Majorca, where they built the house in which Graves lived for most of the rest of his life. Before leaving England he had collaborated with Riding on *A Survey of Modernist Poetry* (1927) and had written his autobiography, *Good-Bye to All That* (1929). This straightforward, modestly frank and vivid account of school life and war experience proved popular, and its sales contributed to his life on Majorca.

Around 1929 Graves started to write the poems that eventually made him famous, though not all achieved their final form at that time. In "Pure Death" we are told of stark, sudden, overwhelming emotions. The emotions are not particularized—they are just love and terror of death—and the persons subject to them are not individualized. If they exist in any time, or place, or are involved in any circumstances, these are not mentioned. The poem goes on to develop an ingenious conceit: after giving each other everything else they could, the lovers bestowed "pure death" as their crowning gift. That terror of death is the ultimate gift is a fine Gravesian thought. For to feel this "natural terror" is to escape intellectual falsities and to live in presence of reality. But "natural terror" is exactly what the poem will not face, and so it takes refuge in its extended conceit of gift exchange, developing the paradox of the opening lines while diminishing their emotional intensity.

"Sick Love" observes the illness that infects love and dooms it to brevity.

> O Love, be fed with apples while you may,
> And feel the sun and go in royal array,
> A smiling innocent on the heavenly causeway,
>
> Though in what listening horror for the cry
> That soars in outer blackness dismally,
> The dumb blind beast, the paranoiac fury:
>
> Be warm, enjoy the season, lift your head,
> Exquisite in the pulse of tainted blood,
> That shivering glory not to be despised.
>
> Take your delight in momentariness,
> Walk between dark and dark—a shining space
> With the grave's narrowness, though not its peace.

The packed, ambivalent phrasing lays bare the attitude of the speaker, who views love with sympathy, foreboding, and irony. His awareness of love's sickness ends in desire for death. Graves chooses not to speak as one of the lovers, not, in other words, to express their delight and horror, but to speak instead as an encompassing, therefore ironic intelligence, knowing what the lovers feel but also knowing, as they do not, their total situation. The poem is morally sensitive and wounded, pondering and acute.

If Graves began as a Georgian, of what school was he now?—

a question he would have scorned. He was, to recapitulate, lucid, impersonal, grammatical, and logical, regular and careful in form, ironic, and much given to conceits. The emotional states he explored were sensitive and complex. Thus his work somewhat resembled the poetry that developed along with and out of the Metaphysical revival and the criticism of Eliot, Richards, and Empson. But his diction was Romantic (for example, "O Love," "royal array," "horror," "glory," in the poem quoted). If the poetry of the Metaphysical revival was a flowering cactus, Graves was a desert lily.

Between 1925 and the coming of the "White Goddess" in 1945 no strong new impulse entered his work. The conceits of "Ulysses," "Succubus," "Leda," and "Down, Wanton, Down" elaborate the fascination and repulsiveness of sex. They range in attitude from the broad, humorous irony of "Down, Wanton, Down," an address to the phallus, to the shocked self-contempt of "Leda." Given the psychological tensions love activates, it cannot last, Graves believes, and he has no attitude toward this fact. *Carpe diem*, lament, rage, protest, and the like, seem frozen in him, and his many brief stories and far-fetched symbols only tell love's instability over and over.

Graves's attitude can seem splendidly hard, for his rebellions against conventionally poetic emotions, or repression of his own emotions, or control of them through form, intellectuality, and irony can be felt as stoic defiance. Landscape plays no great role in his poetry, but when it presents itself it is likely to be unspoiled, bare, and cruel ("Rocky Acres"); because it has this character, it is welcomed. He celebrates "The Oleaster" because it roots in rock. His symbolisms of servitude in soldiers, prisoners, and galley slaves express his sense and psychological need of a harsh, compelling world. His comfort is pride, the answering energy of resistance or endurance such a world calls forth. In "Certain Mercies" each "new indignity" forced upon the prisoners confers "obscure, proud merit." In "Thief" the speaker condemns himself to the galleys with sadistic vividness of language. Love also is, for Graves, a quasi-external power to which he is subject. The Goddess of his later myth is his richest symbolic expression of the beauty and terror of existence. Since each heightens the other, he wants to accept or even welcome the fear and cruelty for the sake of the intensified life they bring, or possibly for their own sake.

Displaced by the Spanish Civil War, Graves and Riding left Majorca in 1936. Two years later they were in the United States. Riding married and Graves returned to England. By this time he had published his historical novels on the Roman emperor Claudius (*I, Claudius* and *Claudius the God*, 1934) and the Byzantine general *Count Belisarius* (1938), along with other prose items, with all of which he earned his living. In 1948 his *The White Goddess* appeared. This work reconstructs a primitive myth of the Great Mother who was worshipped, Graves argued, throughout the ancient world. The book conflates a great many myths from different traditions in order to present a unified one, and the myth is also a structure of emotions and a vision of life. The Goddess is the beautiful woman, the mother, and the crone who lays out the body of her victim-lover; she is the immortal queen who bears, loves, and kills the hero king. In her triple character she is spring, summer, and winter; the new, full, and waning moon; Hera, Aphrodite, and Hecate; and so forth. The general impulse or meaning behind Graves's cult of the White Goddess is the longing of an Apollonian man for the Dionysian, in other words, of a self-disciplined, morally scrupulous intellectual for self-abandon. He lives in a world of contracts, disinfectants, timetables, and savings banks, abounds in questions, doubts, prudent hesitations, half-measures, and ironies, and is therefore disgusted with himself and seeks ecstasy. He tries through myth to recover the intensity and psychological unity anciently possessed, he imagines, by Celts and Dorians.

Graves's poems seldom require the arcana of the Goddess as glosses. Exceptions come chiefly in poems that tell the myth, or phases of it, in overtly mythological terms. Among these, "To Juan at the Winter Solstice" is magnificent, "Darien" hauntingly beautiful and mysterious, "Return of the Goddess" and "The White Goddess" memorable. When in "To Juan at the Winter Solstice" we read,

> How may the King hold back?
> Royally then he barters life for love,

we are confronted with lore the poem assumes but does not impart. The power of the lines is not in the lore, however, but in the attitude of the speaker. More exactly, the effect lies in the interplay of the speaker's thoughtful contemplation and formal self-possession with the irrational emotion contemplated. Because he views the emotion from without, his approval of it has peculiar weight and solemnity. The lines are cold, deliberate, and splendid, the verbal equivalent of a ritual sacrifice.

Graves's main theme henceforth was love. But of his poems written after 1945, none excel the earlier ones. Readers will linger with pleasure among them, for they are terse, elegant, inventive, and intelligent, but here they need not be noticed distinctly.

Though Graves was writing through the whole Modernist period from the 1910s to the 1950s, he rejected most Modernist styles. Imagism did not impress him. He did not assimilate the perceptions and devices of Joyce, Eliot, or Pound. To Lawrence's preachings and styles he was closed. He was mythopoeic, meditative, and colloquial, like Yeats, but Yeats was not a strong, direct influence on him. From Surrealism he was as remote as it is possible to be. When the younger poets reverberated to Auden, Graves did not. And of course he ignored Postmodern developments. But Graves was an early admirer of Ransom and Cummings, and he contributed in the 1920s to the Metaphysical revival. For these reasons I have discussed him in this chapter.

Eventually Graves was valued precisely for his lifelong independence from Modernism. This was in the 1950s, when the Movement poets in England, reacting against Modernism, commended his taut workmanship, emotional control, lucidity, and realism. They did not sympathize with the White Goddess. And as his growing reputation brought him invitations to lecture and review, the opinions he expressed confirmed his distance from much in Modernist literature, including the New Criticism. His attacks on Yeats, Eliot, and Pound (for example, "These Be Your Gods, O Israel," 1955) doubtless afforded relief to many readers at this time who were themselves struggling against the same idols. Longevity and recognition finally brought Graves many prizes and honors. In later years he wrote about and hoped to serve the Black Goddess of Wisdom.

WILLIAM EMPSON

The first book by William Empson (1906–84) was *Seven Types of Ambiguity* (1930), a work of criticism illustrating that ambiguities in poetry are not necessarily undesirable confusions but may be nodes of intellectual and emotional conflict, expressing divided impulses in the poet. At about the time Empson was writing this book his poems were appearing in magazines. By his mid-twenties he had developed a style that dazzled his contemporaries. Dense, ironic, formal, his poems kept readers at a distance and exercised their wits. In one sense the poems were abstract, for they lacked narrative, scenery, and characters. In another sense they were concrete, for the language of their intellection was metaphor. Each metaphor might suggest several meanings and link with many other metaphors in the poem. Syntax was compact—"strong," as Dryden and Pope would have termed it. Ambiguities and puns abounded and so did paradoxes: "Gods cool in turn, by the sun long outlasted." Though the poetry was not allusive in the way of Eliot or Pound, it was learned in contemporary mathematics and physics, from which it took metaphors: "Space is, like earth, rounded, a padded cell." For literary people these further intensified the impression of dry intellection. Empson's observations were often satiric and, when not satiric, were anti-Romantic and stark:

> Thorns burn to a consistent ash, like man;
> A splendid cleanser for the frying-pan.

In comparison to the work of the high Modernists Empson's naturalism imposed a reduced imaginative scale. The emotion in his "Villanelle" might almost be Yeats's about Maud Gonne except that Empson does not upgrade his love woes into myth, as Yeats did, conflating Maud Gonne with Helen of Troy. And there are no Poundian goddesses or *Waste Land* thunders or *shantihs* in Empson, whose "Supreme God" is to be found in the "ethnological section" of the British Museum. Intricate, ironically poised, sardonic, and disintoxicated, Empson's poems appealed because of their intellectual excitement, complexity, and honest bleakness. Falling upon the thorns of life, Empson had not bled, like Shelley, but had put out thorns himself.

Yet strong emotion was present. If his style was witty and "metaphysical" in some ways, his hurt was Hardy's. He accused God for not existing and man for his mortality. In the round space of the cosmos we are like mites in an apple or beetles in the ground or scorpions penned under glass. (Hardy's gargoyle imagination lies behind such comparisons.) Empson's difficult style had personal motives. It formed the barriers and shunting ways by which a strong personality preserved control over emotion. We may be tempted to justify Empson's style by New Critical considerations, but the state of mind and the psychological struggle embodied in his poems are what fascinates and holds us.

Since I once spent two days trying to read "Bacchus," and this effort was required even after several previous encounters with the poem, I will quote its opening to illustrate Empson's dense, polysemous phrasing:

> The laughing god born of a startling answer
> (Cymbal of clash in the divided glancer
> Forcing from heaven's the force of earth's desire)
> Capped a retort to sublime earth by fire. . . .

The poem continues for another eighty-eight lines in this punning, allusive style.

By the time he turned thirty, Empson had written most of his poems. From 1931 to 1952 he taught English literature, first in Japan (1931–34) and later in China, though he spent some years in England during the war. In the poems he wrote during this period, I do not find any definite development. "Ignorance of Death" may be mentioned for its un-Empsonian technique: it sets down one plain statement about death after another—for example, "Liberal hopefulness / Regards death as a mere border to an improving picture"—and it concludes, "Otherwise I feel very blank upon this topic." Empson returned to England in 1952 and taught at Sheffield University until he retired in 1971. During these forty years he published several volumes of criticism—*Some Versions of Pastoral* (1935), *The Structure of Complex Words* (1951), *Milton's God* (1961), and others, all worth reading, but none of these later books had the ground-breaking importance of his first critical work and of his poems.

JOHN CROWE RANSOM

John Crowe Ransom (1888–1974) went to Vanderbilt University in his native Tennessee and then as a Rhodes Scholar to

Oxford. He returned to Vanderbilt as a teacher in 1914, and two years later "almost blushingly" read his first poem, which he had just written, to Donald Davidson. In 1917–1919 he served in France as an artillery officer. Despite this, his first book, *Poems about God*, appeared in 1919.

With their country and genre scenes, humor, happy senses, and tender sympathies, these poems suggest that he had been reading the Georgian anthologies. The book also includes passages of plain-speaking realism and Hardyesque irony, but such anti-Romantic deflation was as typically Georgian as the agreeableness of style and theme. Robert Graves thought Ransom a Tennessee Frost. His forms and phrasing were direct, obvious, and loose. He never republished these early poems.

Again at Vanderbilt after the war, Ransom helped found and edit the magazine *The Fugitive* (1922–25). Several things converged at this time to change his style radically. Embarrassment with his *Poems about God* motivated a new strictness, and so did the scrutiny that the Fugitives gave each other's poems at their meetings. Editorial reading put him in closer touch with contemporary styles. Pound's *Hugh Selwyn Mauberley* (1920) may have intrigued him. Ransom also read the Metaphysical poets attentively. His breakthrough is said to have come in the winter of 1921–22 with the poem "Necrological." His mature style is present in all its brilliance in *Chills and Fever* (1924) and *Two Gentlemen in Bonds* (1927), and after these two books, he virtually stopped writing verse. He produced a few more poems, but his creative effort henceforth went mainly into essays, and he became one of the most influential critics of the age.

Ransom's prose addressed questions of economics and social organization as well as of aesthetics and literature. With other Fugitives he deplored the new industrial South and argued for a traditional, agrarian society; the self-subsistent farm, he believed, promotes individual independence and responsibility, exercises sensibility, and provides leisure for the "good life." He moved to Kenyon College in Ohio in 1937 and two years later founded the *Kenyon Review*, which he continued to edit until 1959. This was widely regarded as an organ of the New Critics, and Ransom's own critical position was generally that sketched in the first part of this chapter. In his book *The New Criticism* (1941) the movement received its name. Perhaps the most individual point he made as a critic was his distinction between po-

etic "texture" and "structure": "structure" referring to the logical discourse and "texture" the alogical increment carried in
rhythm, sound, diction, and imagery. Critics of Ransom usually
add that his heart was with "texture," for like subsistence farming this was not tethered to scientific reason and efficient progress. But at a time when Symbolist poetics strongly influenced
criticism, Ransom's emphasis on the necessity of "structure" was
unusual.

Ransom's poetry falls within the Romantic tradition. "Janet
Waking" is a redoing of Wordsworth's "We Are Seven." "Of Margaret" alludes to Hopkins' poem. The "Vaunting Oak" seems
massively unassailable and perduring, and the girl in the poem
takes it as "Our love's symbol." Ransom writes of lovers in April,
tirelessly vital children, the ballad hero Captain Carpenter, a "vision" by Sweetwater, Philomela the nightingale, and a good
many people whose lives are governed by some ideal commitment—all typical items in the poetry of the nineteenth century
on its Romantic side. But these are put forward in order to be
criticized, so that within the Romantic tradition Ransom, like
Frost, is anti-Romantic. The Romantic sensibility persisted in
him, in other words, but he was also impelled to correct it. In
the Hardyesque "Vaunting Oak" the girl is "too young" and
"wrapped in a phantasy of good"; her "sorrowing lover" knows
that the oak is already hollow. Captain Carpenter loses his encounters, the vital children die, Philomela's song registers "a
little flat," the vision by Sweetwater is of old age and pain, and
for the sake of their moral, religious, or romantic fidelities the
idealists in "Parting at Dawn," "Necrological," and "Emily Hard-
castle, Spinster," may have sacrificed too much and ended up
with a diminished life. The poems imply mixed feelings about
these idealists. For Ransom's criticism of Romanticism was no
more whole-hearted than his Romanticism. "The Equilibrists"
and perhaps also the "Spectral Lovers," though very much in
love, are kept apart by honor:

> Predicament indeed, which thus discovers
> Honor among thieves, Honor between lovers.
> O such a little word is Honor, they feel!
> But the grey word is between them cold as steel.

Whatever we are to think of them, we cannot—this is typical of
Ransom—think anything simple.

If these were the main points to be made, Ransom might be characterized as a poet of Modernism in its early phase, the phase when poets in transition from the nineteenth century were both invoking and repudiating its conventions. Hardy, Laforgue, Robinson, and Frost were poets of this kind, though in quite different ways, and Ransom has much in common with each of them. But Ransom's irony is extremely pervasive and peculiar. Hardy sympathizes with his victims of life's ironies, and so do Robinson and Frost. Ransom seems not to do so. We have a strong impression of coldness, even of mockery, though there may be a strain of sympathy or tenderness underneath. This defensiveness (if it is that) makes Ransom repellent to some Postmodern readers, and since it is expressed especially in peculiarities of diction and form, it may also make him seem mannered. The "transmogrifying bee" of "Janet Waking" is famous, and "pernoctating" in "Philomela" has a similar effect; combining extreme oddness with extreme exactitude, both words have a pedantry—more exactly, a parody of pedantry—that is felt as mannered wit and creates a wide distance between the speaker and his subject. "Dead Boy" is another example:

> The little cousin is dead, by foul subtraction,
> A green bough from Virginia's aged tree,
> And none of the county kin like the transaction,
> Nor some of the world of outer dark, like me.

Though the tone of this is complex and difficult to define, one's first impression is not. To speak of a child's death as a "subtraction" is peculiar and oblique to the nth degree, and so also is calling it a "transaction." Reinforced by their rhyme, the terms inevitably suggest that the boy's death is not much felt by the speaker. "Foul" therefore seems a cold, half-comic hyperbole, and the "green bough" a cliché, though one that renders the semibiblical speech of this traditional community. But on reflection we note that since the speaker is not one of the kin, he can appropriately view the death from detached perspectives, and whatever sympathy he feels may be the more moving because it emerges through and despite his detachment. But no matter where we finally arrive in our response to this poem, the initial shock is chilling.

In the heyday of the New Criticism, from the 1930s to the

1950s, Ransom's poems appealed by the compactness and rigor of their forms, their impersonality, the perpetual surprise of their diction, and the contrasting feelings and judgments they elicited. Much sensitive comment pinpointed their interplay of sympathy with detachment, seriousness with levity, sorrow and resignation before fate with bitter protest, and admiration and idealism with deflating realism. Sometimes it was claimed that his poems integrated these opposites, thus illustrating the ordered wholeness of impulse that Richards had made the criterion of poetic excellence. Even if it was not integrated, the speaker's state of mind was still valuable, for the ironic tensions of the poem articulated his complex awareness. The poems especially corrected or criticized sentiment, and this still seemed important as a gesture against the nineteenth century. And of course Ransom's earned and growing fame as a critic won still more attention for his poems, and so did the praise of his illustrious students such as Allen Tate, Robert Penn Warren, Cleanth Brooks, Randall Jarrell, and Robert Lowell.

ALLEN TATE

As a freshman at Vanderbilt Allen Tate (1899–1979) dazzled his fellow students and teachers. He was reading Baudelaire, Mallarmé, and *symbolistes* of whom they had only heard. Up to 1922 his poems mixed these sources with such others as Robinson, Dowson, and Pound. But Hart Crane, seeing some of Tate's verse in *The Fugitive*, was reminded of Eliot and said so in a letter to Tate. Between May 1922 and February 1923 Tate read Eliot for the first time, starting with *Poems* (1920) and probably also Eliot's critical essays in *The Sacred Wood* (1920). From this encounter, Tate later said, he matured his style. He now introduced the criticism and poems of Eliot to Ransom and other Fugitives. Advocating Eliot, he identified himself as a Modernist, enjoying in the process the glories of one-upmanship and rebellion. His Tennessee hearers "did not know anything about" this literature, as Ransom later recalled, "and were as likely as not to resist it when they were made to know."

Though a student of Ransom's, Tate was anything but a disciple. He found his teacher "cold, calculating, and highly competitive," and used Eliot as a stick to beat him with. When Ransom did not like *The Waste Land,* Tate wrote him, Ransom says, "with as much agitation as I ever knew him to register." In later years Ransom and Tate were fellow Agrarians, and as critics they referred to each other's essays and shared the same general enemies, but some uneasiness persisted in their friendship. Tate moved to New York City in 1924 with the intention of supporting himself by literary work. His imagination was now naturally carried back to Virginia and Kentucky, where he had grown up, and the South became a major, recurrent theme and symbol in his poetry and criticism. He composed his famous "Ode to the Confederate Dead" in 1926 and wrote biographies of Stonewall Jackson (1928) and Jefferson Davis (1929). He took eager part in the discussions that led up to the Agrarian manifesto *I'll Take My Stand* (1930), and contributed an essay to it. The accumulated mass of his engagement with the antebellum South in family history, biographical writing, social philosophy, polemic, and enormous reading lies behind Tate's brilliant, ambivalent novel, *The Fathers* (1938).

Volumes of his poetry were published in 1928, 1932, and 1936, and from the mid-1920s the *Nation, New Republic, Sewanee Review, Criterion,* and similar magazines printed his critical essays and reviews. But though he was now established as a poet and man of letters, he could not live by his writing. He took up college teaching in 1938, and except for six years from 1942 to 1948, he stuck with it until he retired. During this period he wrote much less poetry. It is interesting, as a comment on the resentments of English departments against New Critics in those days, that he received no tenure offer until he was fifty-two, when the University of Minnesota gave him a position. From this time on he was increasingly invited to read from his poems and to lecture, and the quasi-official recognitions of the literary and academic world piled up in honorary degrees and memberships, awards, prizes, gold medals, and the like. On retiring he returned to Sewanee, Tennessee, where he died in 1979.

By the end of the 1920s Tate's poetry illustrated the emerging style associated with New Critical taste—for example, in "Last Days of Alice" and "The Paradigm." Previously he had responded to diverse models in an eclectic way, and some of these poems written in his twenties—"Mr. Pope," "Death of Little

Boys," "Ode to the Confederate Dead"—were among his finest. His style did not stop developing in the thirties, and if often he produced the type of New Critical poem Robert Lowell described as "symbol-ridden and willfully difficult"—"a symbol hanging on a hatrack"—he could always write in different styles also. Nevertheless, from first to last Tate's poetry was metered and usually also rhymed and stanzaic, with logical syntax, mannered diction, and packed phrasing. It ranged from the difficult to the impenetrable. Perhaps because of his connection with Hart Crane, who greatly influenced him, Tate prized stylistic intensity more than did other New Critical poets. Few of his poems completely lack narrative, dramatic characterization or dialogue, or a personal occasion and speaker, and in some meditative, reminiscent, or monologic poems, such as "The Meaning of Life," "The Oath," or "Aeneas in Washington," these elements are very effective. But generally in his poems such sources of interest hold attention much less than the texture of telescoped images and metaphors. Activating multiple suggestions and interweaving as the poem proceeds, they compel us strenuously to take note and connect. Our reward for so much effort may be the complexity of the many-sided, ambiguous, ambivalent state of mind we achieve. The last two stanzas of "The Paradigm" illustrate this texture:

> For in the air all lovers meet
> After they've hated out their love;
> Love's but the echo of retreat
> Caught by the sunbeam stretched above
>
> Their frozen exile from the earth
> And lost. Each is the other's crime.
> This is their equity in birth—
> Hate is its ignorant paradigm.

Tate's feelings are of the heavy, brooding, intense kind. He lacks Ransom's light touch and charm, and his humor, what little there is, is satiric. Latinate polysyllables resound: "rumour of mortality," "requisitions of a verity." Adjectives are wildly improbable and forced—"mandible world," "punctilious abyss," "verdurous anonymity," spring's "combustible juice"—as they knot together strands of implication in the poem. Transitions of feeling can seem very sudden and unmotivated. And there is a general vehemence of diction and sentiment: "livid wound of love"; "unbaptized" Edmund Wilson, "that sly parody of the devil." In combination with the cerebral demand and the strict form of Tate's poetry, the effect is of a frozen violence.

YVOR WINTERS

In *Primitivism and Decadence* (1937) and later books Yvor Winters (1900–1968) attacked most of the poets he mentioned for the inadequacy of their moral vision. Frost was a "spiritual drifter," Stevens a "hedonist," Pound "a sensibility without a mind," Eliot lost in "acedia." Naturally Winters was much embroiled, the more so since his praise was eccentric. He championed, among others, Charles Churchill, Jones Very, and F. G. Tuckermann. He was deficient in humor, sympathy, irony, sometimes in learning, but never in courage, and if his phrasing of his criticism was too accusatory, his perceptions were acute and his judgments rooted in principles that were systematically thought out.

Winters read contemporary poetry first and went back later to the older works, an order that used to be unusual. In high school he subscribed to *Poetry,* and he also bought copies of Yeats, Pound, and Williams, along with *The Little Review* and *Others.* In college after 1923 he studied literature in Latin, French, and Spanish, and after 1928 he read English and American literature before the modern period. Hence for him, as he began, the modern was the received way to write. Until 1928 his poems were free-verse meditations or, more frequently, Imagistic constructions, drawing on the landscape and folkways of New Mexico, where he was teaching. In this period his poems were typical of the average good work done in the United States in the 1920s. His many poems that imitate William Carlos Williams were among the best. Since later the ideas and values of Winters were bitterly opposite to those of Williams, his fondness for this poet is interesting. Most of our quarrels are with ourselves; in 1928 Winters started writing poems in meters and stanzas, and he adhered to strictness of structure and versification for the rest of his life. Such forms were then coming in, of course, but Winters was not following fashion. Style was a "definition by example." His summings up—formal, economical, controlled, conceptual, generalizing—embodied his ethical ideal as much as they stated it:

> Passion is hard of speech,
> Wisdom exact of reach;
> Poets have studied verse;
> And wit is terse.

Winters' attitude was stoic, though he wrote poems of affection for vegetables, animals, landscape, and California wines. Among the later poets he influenced are J. V. Cunningham (1911–85) and Robert Pinsky (b. 1940), poets of strong intelligence, formal control, and clear statement.

6

THE PERIOD STYLE OF THE 1930s IN ENGLAND

LITERATURE in the 1930s was caught up, with all intellectual life, in the public crises. In this decade of economic dislocation, business collapse, strikes, severe unemployment, and breadlines, liberal democracy appeared ineffective. With the general loss of confidence in it, other modes of government were envisioned, and the prospect of radical social change inspired fervent debate. There was militant political agitation against the existing order, class antagonism intensified, and to many intellectuals a revolution seemed a serious possibility. The revolution might come from the political right, they thought, but they expected it to be Socialist or Communist, and their emotions were generally ambivalent, mingling dread and hope. But in the latter half of the thirties events in Europe caused a sense of doom. The Fascist dictatorships in Germany, Italy, and elsewhere liquidated their liberal, Socialist, and Communist opponents, with whom English writers and intellectuals identified. Germany's march into the Rhineland, Italy's invasion of Ethiopia, and civil war in Spain after 1936 were calamities and portents of greater calamities. Germany and Italy were rearming, and the English and French governments were impotent to prevent this. A second World War was a growing probability. The future looked apocalyptic.

Contemporary history preoccupied the thoughts and emotions of poets as much as it preoccupied other thinking people. The responses of poets to the public events were not different from those of most people, and in voicing these responses, poets could speak to and for a wide audience. These considerations led to changes in poetic style. The esotericism, phrasal density, formal complexity, and avant-garde experiment of high Modernism had less appeal, for they made poetry difficult and thus relegated it to a small number of readers. The persistently concrete presentation in high Modernist style was now viewed as restrictive. Poets wished to address issues in a language appropriate to intellectual discussion, and hence they used discursive or generalizing language. Yet the prestige of high Modernist style was such that departures from it caused misgivings of conscience, and poets feared they could overcome the Modernist isolation of poetry only by diluting the Modernist artistic achievement.

When we think of poetry of the thirties, we have in mind that written by the emergent generation, the poets born between 1904 and 1914, such as W. H. Auden, C. Day-Lewis, Stephen Spender, Louis MacNeice, and William Empson. To those living in the thirties, however, contemporary poetry included older writers. From *The Tower* in 1928 to his death in 1939 Yeats published his greatest lyrics. "*Burnt Norton*," the first of Eliot's *Four Quartets*, appeared in 1935. Edith Sitwell was writing. So were former Imagists such as Richard Aldington and Sir Herbert Read, though neither was still an Imagist. Edwin Muir had started to publish in the 1920s and Robert Graves in the 1910s. C. M. Grieve (1892–1978), who wrote under the pseudonym of Hugh MacDiarmid, had been publishing prolifically since 1923. Since he wrote most of his poems in Scots rather than English, he is not discussed in this history, but he is the most important poet in Scots since Robert Burns. Younger writers such as Basil Bunting, Samuel Beckett, and David Jones had picked up the high Modernist tradition and were carrying it on splendidly; though they were writing in the thirties, Beckett's fame came in the 1950s and Bunting's in the 1960s. Meanwhile in the 1930s Edwardians and Georgians were writing much as they had previously. Masefield brought out seven volumes of poetry in the 1930s, de la Mare nine, and there was also verse from W. H.

Davies, John Drinkwater, Wilfrid Gibson, and Laurence Binyon. Edmund Blunden, Richard Church, and Victoria Sackville-West were somewhat similar to the Georgians in style and spirit, and Siegfried Sassoon had now returned to the Georgian style in which he had begun as a poet. Kipling was still publishing, and so was Arthur Symons. And many younger poets, some of them excellent, continued to write in styles derived directly from the nineteenth century: Gerald Bullett, Peter Quennell, Ruth Pitter, Anne Ridler, Roy Campbell, F. T. Prince, and William Plomer—the last three from South Africa.

Sir John Betjeman (1906–84) and Stevie Smith (1902–71) were already following their highly individual developments. Betjeman, who succeeded C. Day-Lewis as Poet Laureate, wrote as if there had been no Modernist break with nineteenth-century traditions. Much of his verse was light, though as he grew older it deepened. He described, both fondly and satirically, the material and spiritual culture of the upper middle class. In prose writings Betjeman did much to revive appreciation of nineteenth-century architecture, and many of his poems are about the Victorian period, which he knew intimately. Others recollect his own childhood or contemplate the postwar, Socialist transformation of England, a transformation with which he had little sympathy. Many people who ordinarily do not read poetry enjoy Betjeman's, and he is also admired by poets. Florence Margaret Smith, who was nicknamed Stevie, also has a large following, especially in England. Her poems are somewhat embittered, stoic, and tartly humorous. "Not Waving But Drowning" is typical and famous. The poem compares the man it describes—"him"—to a swimmer far out in the ocean; to the people on the shore he appears to be waving. Both Betjeman and Smith were talented poets of limited range, idiosyncratic but also original.

In the mid-1930s Surrealism had a minor vogue. Dylan Thomas and George Barker were not Surrealists, but the Surrealist vogue helped prepare a reception for them. Ruthven Todd, Rex Warner, Bernard Spencer, C. Day-Lewis, Gavin Ewart, and Julian Symons are among the many poets who illustrate the fascination of Auden for their generation. The most formidable of the literary Marxists was Christopher Caudwell (pseudonym of Christopher St. John Sprigg), though his verse was more revolutionary in content than in form. Caudwell died in the Spanish Civil War, and so did Julian Bell, another poet whose traditional art had not yet matured.

Just how diverse the poetry of the 1930s was can be seen in sample years. Among the new books of 1928 were the last of Hardy's and the first of Auden's, and there were also Yeats's *The Tower* and the *Collected Poems* of Lawrence. In 1935 Empson's *Poems* was published, along with Eliot's *Murder in the Cathedral* and "Burnt Norton" and a volume from MacNeice. A year later appeared Auden's *Look, Stranger!,* Thomas' *Twenty-Five Poems,* and *More Poems* from A. E. Housman. It was a decade of opposed tendencies, and the taste and feeling of many a writer and reader were similarly self-divided. We see this with special significance in three impresarios, Michael Roberts, John Lehmann, and Geoffrey Grigson, who collectively did much to obtain an audience for the younger poets and to define the terms in which they were discussed.

It was Michael Roberts (1902–48) who first presented the young poets as a coherent, new development. This happened in his anthology, *New Signatures* (1932). In his preface he argued that Auden, Day-Lewis, Empson, the American Richard Eberhart, and several others shared an effort to overcome artistic isolation and detachment, reject esotericism, "say something to an audience," and "find solidarity with others" ("the essence of the Communist attitude"). *New Signatures* was conceived in a conversation with John Lehmann (b. 1907). As Roberts was describing the percolation of the *Zeitgeist* in the young poets, including Lehmann, the flattered Lehmann thought of presenting them as a *"front,* so that the public, notoriously sluggish in its appreciation of individual poets, should be obliged to sit up and take notice." He persuaded Leonard and Virginia Woolf to publish *New Signatures* from their Hogarth Press.

Lehmann's poems at this time packed Romantic feeling and imagery into firm couplets:

> Through deep-grassed fields I stray with you again,
> Hear wind in elm leaves, rustle of sweet rain;
> Down by the weir in June's hot sun, I see
> Green streams of creeper, where you wait for me;
> The loud clock chimes, and tea-rose evening dies;
> The limes, the spires, are mirrored in your eyes.

During the thirties Lehmann lived for several years in Vienna. There he made friends among the working class and participated in the political effort of the far left. He now wrote poems that were close to propaganda; they documented social wrong and political repression and celebrated the workers and their dawning future. In England a few years later wartime emotions interplayed with those of an unhappy love affair and produced more complex states of mind. His struggle of faith against despair was waged in terms that were simultaneously religious, historical—for an age was ending in the war—and personal between himself and his lover.

> Far in the censored oceans you are lost,
> But lost the world, too, which your longing haunts:
> The blue sky looks across the rubbled inn
> . . . .
> They crack, the giant elms, from rooted shape
> The green cliff-gardens tumble: who shall turn
> From this, love's ravaged landscape, back to praise?

Thus Lehmann's verse still retained the melody and rhythm of the nineteenth century, the elegiac emotions, and the struggle for acceptance, hope, and faith. His images and anecdotes could sometimes be grim, especially for propaganda purposes, but grimness was not his temptation, which was rather toward uplift.

Geoffrey Grigson (1905–85) founded and edited *New Verse* (1933–39), a periodical notable for the poetry it printed and for Grigson's slashing reviews. Though it was not the organ of any particular group, *New Verse* enforced poetic values we associate with the decade—the use of ordinary speech, the report of the outward world, the involvement with politics and society. A fascinated partisan of Eliot while at college, Grigson used Eliot to bait his tutor. Yet the urban setting and "alien quality" of Eliot's poetry did not appeal to him deeply. Auden's poetry was English, and Grigson loved it as he could not love Eliot's. This response was typical of many readers in his generation. In the 1930s Grigson composed poems in Modernist modes, yet, as with Day-Lewis, the influence was only temporary. As time passed, his many editions, anthologies, and volumes of poetry showed him an enthusiastic admirer of poets and artists in the Romantic landscape tradition—Samuel Palmer, John Clare,

George Crabbe, William Barnes, Wordsworth, and Hardy. Thus as editors both Grigson and Lehmann supported styles of poetry that it was not natural for them to write. This perhaps increases their merit, but their sensibility remained self-divided.

I may also illustrate the point by citing the "Sketch of the Author" that Glyn Jones (b. 1905) appended to his *Poems* (1939). Its honest report summarizes several, at least, of the opposed tugs to which poets were subject. Jones began, he says, under the influence of Lawrence; more exactly, he accepted Lawrence's vocabulary and imagery but not his doctrine. Tiring of Lawrence, he next hoped to "achieve a body of workers' poetry." By this he did not mean the "public-school-communist verse which was fashionable at the time" but "poems which the workers themselves could read, understand and appreciate." But the workers did not read his poems. He now (in 1939) seeks only to "communicate with myself, to indulge my love of words and phrases which I had suppressed to a large extent before the scrutiny of my workers." And he states with much firmness that ideas are not what makes a poem valuable. "I have laboured this point so much because I see writers to-day praised for being catholics, or socialists, or contemporary men, or for being killed in Spain, rather than for being poets." Jones's views in 1939 were straws in the wind. The thirties were ending. Poetry was entering a new phase.

THE IMPACT OF AUDEN

Most of the young English poets who started publishing at the end of the 1920s and in the 1930s inhabited more or less the same imaginative world. It was created out of their great modern predecessors—Lawrence, Joyce, Hardy, Yeats, and Eliot— out of Freud and Marx and their followers, and out of the newspapers. By "newspapers" I mean what was news in the 1930s— unemployment, depression, Communism, Fascism, spies, street mobs, dictators, treaties, arms race, wars—and also the fears, hopes, and strivings with which English intellectuals responded to these events. Film and popular fiction, especially the thrillers, were responding to the same events, and poets formed their imaginations and techniques on these arts also.

The major poet of the decade was Auden, to whom I devote
a separate chapter. His poetry gathered more of these sources
together and interwove them more suggestively. He did this,
moreover, when he was young and with astonishing originality.
The delighted surprise of his first readers is now difficult to recapture. His 1930 volume presented a world that was both familiar and strange. The poems drew on literary tradition and
on the images and lore of the present age, and yet they were
unlike any before, as in the following examples:

> "There is a free one," many say, but err.
> He is not that returning conqueror,
> Nor ever the poles' circumnavigator.
>
> But poised between shocking falls, on razor-edge
> Has taught himself this balancing subterfuge
> Of the accosting profile, the erect carriage;

and

> Who stands, the crux left of the watershed,
> On the wet road between the chafing grass
> Below him sees dismantled washing-floors,
> Snatches of tramline running to the wood;

and

> Control of the passes was, he saw, the key
> To this new district, but who would get it?
> He, the trained spy, had walked into the trap.

Charles Madge's egregious lines in "Letter to the Intelligentsia"
are now usually cited with critical *Schadenfreude:*

> But there waited for me in the summer morning
> Auden, fiercely. I read, shuddered and knew.

Yet if we ignore the peculiarities of his metaphors, the response
Madge recalls was widespread among the younger writers.
Vivid, uncanny, fascinating, authoritative, Auden's work gripped
a whole generation. His rhythms, images, and habitual emotions; his comic descents and preachy elevations ("woozy," he
called them); his montage of facts, gestures, or dictions that reveal deep-lying faults in the psyche and in society; his unification
of depth psychology with social analysis, pervade the writing of
the period.

We can observe, for example, the transformation of C. Day-Lewis. He published two books of bucolic, conventional poetry, but meanwhile met Auden in 1925 or 1926, when both were students at Oxford. For the next ten years Auden's stronger personality and style showed itself in Day-Lewis' work. Thus in the first lyric of *The Magnetic Mountain* (1933) Day-Lewis compared joy—"that fleet one"—to a kestrel and asked where to find it:

> No searcher may hope to flush that fleet one
> Not to be found by gun or glass,
> In old habits, last year's hunting-ground,
> Whose beat is wind-wide, whose perch a split second.
>
> But surely will meet him, late or soon,
> Who turns a corner into new territory;
> Spirit mating afresh shall discern him
> On the world's noon-top purely poised.

This poem owes generally as much to Hopkins as to Auden, but only Auden shaped the psycho-moral landscape in which "old habits" are a place and fresh thoughts and feelings a "new territory."

Or there was Gavin Ewart (b. 1916). In his "Political Poem" of 1939, for example, he apostrophized, "O Communists,"

> We believe that you are our enormous nurse
> Helping us not to cry in the dark, not to steal sweets,
> Kindly to many, a saviour of rearrangement.

The lines are saturated with Auden's attitudes and methods: the fusion of depth psychology with politics, or, more exactly, the psychoanalytic explanation of the appeal of Communism as Freudian regression; the detachment from Communism this implies; yet the ambivalence too, for the nurse is also a savior. And the lines pick up Auden's devices of style: the surprising, witty comparison—Communism as nurse; the casual, illustrative particulars—cry in the dark, steal sweets—that set up a complicity with the reader; the pun in "rearrangement" (psychic or social); the concessive qualification that by refusing to claim too much ("kindly" is not "loving," "many" not "all") quickens the lines intellectually.

In a last example, Kenneth Allott (b. 1912) writes:

Against the clock, like the end of a school cricket match,
The human figures in the position of love enjoy
The incandescence which precedes being more lonely than ever.

Against the clock, like a film cross-cut to a climax,
The scholar struggles like a furious ant to add
One more speck to the Himalayas of knowledge.

The metaphors have Auden's generality and wit, and some of them come from spheres he liked to draw on—cricket, film, the monomanias of scholars. The montage of lovers and scholar is also Audenesque; in fact, it appears in his "Lay your sleeping head . . . ," though the scholar is there a hermit. The puns in "figures" and "position" are of Empson's school but also of Auden's, and so are the objectivity, detachment, impersonality, and wide awareness. "Incandescence," for example, might have been a strong term, but the cool, ironic context reduces it to an unemotive, descriptive one, a name for the usual climax that leads to the equally usual postcoital sadness. When the poem was published in his 1943 volume, Allott noted that it was written before September 1939. In the last interval of peace the cricketers, lovers, and scholars were hastening to score, as it were, before war broke out. Most thirties poets would have felt tenderly for the doomed, peacetime pleasures. Some of this enters Allott's poem in later stanzas, but only as one possible response, and the poem is more complicated and honest in its perceptions, though less coherent, than most of the others on this theme. For if there were no war, the scholar would still add only a speck and the sequence of love would still be disappointing and mechanical. Yet at the same time the poem also suggests that awareness of impending war reduces lives and emotions to clockwork.

No other poet, needless to say, sounds just like Auden. And some poets—Dylan Thomas, for example, Empson, Betjeman, and the Surrealists—caught so little from Auden and developed on such different lines that they are more appropriately noticed in other connections and are not discussed in this chapter. In the pages that follow I am thinking chiefly of Allott, Day-Lewis, MacNeice, Charles Madge, Bernard Spencer, Stephan Spender, Randall Swingler, Julian Symons, Ruthven Todd, and Rex Warner, though space permits the separate discussion of only some of these. In varying degrees, to repeat, these poets caught their methods, or some of them, from Auden; at least they did so in the 1930s. What they took from other poets, such as Yeats, was often mediated to them through Auden. And in Auden they found perceptions of the contemporary world, and emotional responses to it, that were their own, though without Auden they would have been less conscious of them and less able to express them in poetry. There were, of course, other factors that also shaped in common the poems of this decade, and I shall come to them presently—the difficulties of coming just after the high Modernist achievement of the 1920s; the ideas and faiths adopted from Freud, Marx, and Lawrence; the inescapable political concerns of that time. But the main single factor creating what we recognize as a period style was the influence of Auden on other poets.

With some of these poets Auden had close personal relationships. And since the young poets naturally wished to think of themselves as a distinct group or movement with characteristics of their own, they wrote critical prose in which they exhibited each other for praise, with Auden as the special, illustrious specimen. Thus in *A Hope for Poetry* (1934) Day-Lewis called Auden the best of the postwar poets, with Spender next, and associated himself, MacNeice, John Lehmann, and a few others with them. In his book *Modern Poetry* (1938) MacNeice also named Auden and Spender as his favorites; they with himself and Day-Lewis were the poets his book most discussed. (In this rather bland work MacNeice's sharpest antagonisms were interestingly directed not against predecessors from whom his generation had to differentiate itself but against contemporaries whose styles and methods departed widely from his own—Thomas, Empson, and the Surrealists.) Noting the admiration of these poets for one another, critics concluded that they were a united band and began to speak of the "Auden Group." Naturally the phrase obscured the major differences among the poets it embraced—chiefly Spender, Day-Lewis, and MacNeice, along with Auden himself.

COMING AFTER THE MODERNISTS

To understand why the poetry of the thirties took the direction it did, we must keep in mind the situation in literary history of these poets born between 1907 and 1917. They were the first generation for whom the development of modern poetry from the 1890s was what it is for us—history, tales of the tribal elders. They felt none of the priestly devotion to art of the *fin de siècle*. Laboriously perfected style was out of date. So was the poet's alienation from society and many another premise of the nineties. They did not share Yeats's Pre-Raphaelite, Aesthetic, and Symbolist convictions that art should not "comment, however wisely," nor "express the socialistic, or humanitarian, or other forces of the time," nor lose itself in opinions and generalizations. Quite the contrary. And if like the Aesthetes and Yeats these poets satirized the bourgeois middle class, it was not for utilitarian values and Philistine tastes but for Marxian belatedness. For these readers of Marx, in other words, the future no longer belonged to the middle class, and they assumed that its members sensed this apprehensively and were riddled with guilt. The young poets had not experienced the moment of Imagist advocacy. Pound's "Use no superfluous word," "Don't be 'viewy,'" "Go in fear of abstractions," were maxims of no force for them. Avant-garde experimentation had now no special cachet; in fact, poets no longer especially aspired to be avant-garde.

Auden, Spender, Day-Lewis, and MacNeice were schoolboys when *The Waste Land* was published in 1922. While they were university undergraduates, in 1928, Yeats's finest single volume, *The Tower*, appeared. They looked back, as they shaped their styles, on an extreme development and an undeniably great achievement in the Modernist mode. In this respect their situation was prototypical for all later poets, yet they were the first to come after, and they were luckier, in a way, than poets since. The high Modernist achievement did not yet seem so hopelessly intimidating in the 1930s as it did twenty years later, when the prestige of Eliot and of Yeats had been raised like twin ziggurats on mounds of critical advocacy and explication. The thirties poets could pretend and almost convince themselves that they had advanced beyond these gifted predecessors, in whom much had always been irrelevant and eccentric and more was now out of date. They had inherited, if you believed them, the poetry of the recent past like family silver and were picking and choosing among the pieces; some might still be serviceable. In reality, as we shall see, the Modernist artistry of the 1920s haunted them.

To this generation the weakest sides of Yeats were his writing about fairies, spooks, and phases of the moon and his hocus-pocus of magical symbols and vision—more generally, his irrationalism. To which might be added his atavistic celebrations of art and style, of personality and aristocracy, and the general irrelevance of his poetry to the unemployed workingman, the Peace Pledge Union, sexual emancipation, the struggle in Spain—the concerns of the responsible intellectual of the 1930s. Yeats was not, as Spender put it, "socially constructive." In fact his Nietzschean or Rocky Face mask of cold rejoicing in history's violence could seem close to Fascism, and so could other Yeatsian manifestations, all hugely offensive to a literary world leaning strongly to the left. Yet even though (or perhaps especially because) Yeats was so easy to criticize and reject, the young poets also admired and learned from him. They caught the rhythms and syntax of his marvelous poetic talk, they adopted his mode of occasional, meditative poem (as in Auden's "Now from my window-sill I watch the night"), and they praised their friends in his way. "These, then, have my allegiance," Day-Lewis enumerated, "the hawk-faced man . . ."; and Spender, remembering Yeats's boast "And I myself created Hanrahan," wrote, "First made I Marston the superb boxer." They delighted in Yeats's strong rhetoric. And they liked his generalizing utterance, for despite his earlier strictures, the later poems of Yeats uttered his moral and intellectual opinions.

With Eliot their relationship was even more complex. Like most of us since, they first read him in secondary school or college, having heard that they were not *au courant* until they did. Since their love of poetry had been formed originally on *The Golden Treasury* or something analogous, Eliot's work at first repelled, baffled, and fascinated them. As gradually they got the hang of it, they were ambivalent. They learned from him, more than from anyone else, to present the modern, urban-industrial world in poetry, but where Eliot had been satirical or appalled, they might express any feeling; the power lines and engines might even be symbols of hope, as in Spender's "The Pylons" and "The Express." "For night express is due," Day-Lewis gushed; "Glory of steam and steel strikes dumb." And although Eliot had exhibited Apeneck Sweeney, the carbuncular lover, the gas works, and the like, he had hardly taken them for granted. The next generation wrote of automobiles, jazz bands, diabetes, and hair oil as familiarly and casually as if they were sunsets and daffodils, and thus took final possession of the modern scene for English poetry.

The thirties poets similarly absorbed yet also rejected Eliot's characterization of the modern mind. Of course it was not Eliot's only, but impressively shared. One could find corroboration of various aspects in Joyce and Lawrence, not to mention Freud and Marx, and even in one's own self-searchings. Yet though the young poets might find themselves quite as bereft of tradition, community, faith, and purpose as the figures in *The Waste Land,* and might feel in themselves the same emotional fragmentation, alienation, guilt, futility, and fear, they denied Eliot's pessimism. What he protrayed was not the ineradicable condition of man, they said, but an expression or result of the social isolation of Modernist art. Or what Eliot rendered was the emotional illness of a social class. Or it was, more vaguely, a mess that could be cleaned up. Eliot was defeatist. He observed in helpless anguish, wringing his hands. And then in 1928 he had declared himself a classicist in literature, a royalist in politics, and an Anglo-Catholic in religion, thus putting himself on the conservative side of seventeenth-century debates. Poetry, these writers believed, should engage more actively and relevantly in the needs of the time. Perhaps it might contribute to social change. But not poetry in Eliot's style.

The trouble was partly, of course, that Eliot's style could not be widely understood. Whoever used it cut himself off from most of his fellow human beings. Yet there was also a second, completely different nexus of motives and considerations. The styles of the Modernists in the 1920s could not be developed further on their own lines. Neither on their own ground could anyone hope to rival the brilliance of these poets. And their artistry had been of the self-critical, painstaking type; striking critical pronouncements of Eliot, Pound, and Yeats had intensified this impression. The Modernists attacked decoration, vagueness, and dilution and urged that scrupulous toil was necessary to avoid such relaxations. Hence in order to exist at all, at least in order to have a distinct identity and *raison d'être*, the next generation was compelled to adopt or discover different styles and values. Inevitably they also reacted against the ideal of perfected workmanship. At least three times in the twentieth century the pendulum has swung from the self-conscious, difficult, and much revised toward the looser and more accessible: in the Edwardian-Georgian reaction against the verse of the *fin de siècle*; in that of American poets in the 1950s and 1960s against the New Criticism and the poetry written according to its premises; and in England in the 1930s. Each time this swing was accompanied and justified by a feeling of reaching out to an audience from isolation and to subject matter and life from form and art. And each time there was a demystifying of poetry. The poetic state of mind was no longer to be conceived as especially privileged—more complex and integrated, or more uplifted toward the beautiful, eternal, and true. And a poem was not, like *The Waste Land* or *The Cantos*, a grand web of myths. A poem was now to be a piece of ordinary consciousness and talk, a poet just a person with a special job. If he made verses imperfectly, with maybe some loquacity, sentimentality, imprecision or cliché, these blots might be badges of humanity. They might even be signs of his refusal to take poetry too seriously, there being so many more important things in the world.

Yet Metaphysical wit was a common note of style in the thirties poets. Their motives for it may again be found in the prestige of Modernism, or more exactly, in the welter of strong emotions—admiration, discipleship, rivalry, intimidation, and fear of competing—that Modernist poetry of the 1920s aroused in them. In fact, that there was a Metaphysical revival especially indicates the force of these emotions. For this brilliant wit was not really appropriate in poets who hoped to address a large, earnest, politically concerned public. It presupposed a sophisticated and thus an elite audience. And writing of the Spanish Civil War, did you really wish to mingle levity with your seriousness? Or did you wish to activate opposed points of view toward the hunger of the unemployed? Or to dance in intricate metaphors about approaching war? Yet Metaphysical wit was an infatuation, and it is easy to see why. Eliot was not himself a source for it. Exactly this, in fact, made it beguiling. Though his criticism had praised Metaphysical wit, his poetry had not much ex-

emplified it. It was an element of the Modernist program that
had not yet been fulfilled. Developing this wit, the young poets
could excel Eliot on his own ground. They adored puns and
conceits.

Moreover, a ready intelligibility meant a loosening of style.
You could so easily seem to yourself dull, slack, and dawdling.
Looking back on the thirties, Spender later recalled that he and
his fellow poets "were aware of having renounced values which
we continued nevertheless to consider aesthetically superior, in
Joyce, Yeats, Eliot, Lawrence, and Virginia Woolf." Hence the
thirties poets were divided among and within themselves. Some
of them—Empson, Thomas, and the Surrealists—could be
quite as formidably compressed and obscure as Eliot, Pound,
and Yeats, though each in different ways. Others, such as Rex
Warner (b. 1905) and Randall Swingler (b. 1909) were perspicuity itself and illustrated its liabilities. Most thirties poets are
found occasionally at one extreme or the other. Except for some
characteristics of rhythm, diction, and the molding of the line,
Auden's broad invective in "Beethameer, Beethameer, bully of
Britain" would hardly seem to be by the same poet as the involuted, introspective "Not, Father, further do prolong / Our necessary defeat," though these poems were written within eight
months of each other.

The dilemma has persisted ever since. However poets have
actually written or whatever they have said in manifestoes, in
their hearts and consciences they have been unable either to accept or to refuse the stylistic legacy of the 1920s. Their situation
has been peculiarly exacerbated also by the accidents of history
and vocabulary in the 1920s that associated particular qualities
of style with the "avant-garde" and "modern" and also bestowed
on these terms a special cachet. Henceforth the more a poet
wished to think himself "modern," the more he had to reckon
with the historical mode thus inevitably brought to mind. But
mainly the Modernist styles have exerted their pressures because
of their brilliance. To reject them has seemed to poets a lowering
of artistic standards, a refusal of technical challenge, a choice
against wit and intelligence. Of course the stylistic legacy of
Modernism includes both particular devices—ellipsis, literary
allusion—and also general values, such as density and complexity of meaning. To avoid the devices is easier; it is the values that

especially fascinate and pull. When poets react against them, they may, like Allen Ginsberg or Frank O'Hara, swing amazingly far in the opposite direction. Yet to accept and continue the complex Modernist styles has also been impossible. I mentioned that to continue them locks the later poet in a rivalry he may feel to be hopeless. But also the poet may find that these styles isolate him in a world that is private or, at best, accessible only to an intellectual elite. "Writing gets shut up," as Auden put it in 1932, "in a circle of clever people writing about themselves for themselves." The artist is closed into an art world that cannot participate in the experiences and feelings of most people. Neither can Modernist art engage itself effectively in social causes. But a poet who writes only for himself and a like-minded few is dangerously vulnerable to a suspicion that his art is nothing more than a cultivated amusement, like crossword puzzles. Or if he persuades himself that his art serves a higher function—psychological integration? truth?—it still assists only a small number of people to these good things. Hence the poet's style troubles his conscience. He may even feel that the isolated person or group cannot achieve psychological wholeness and a sense of purpose, since these must be socially derived and supported. Poets, said MacNeice, "will get their poetry more in order when they have got themselves in order, which in its turn may depend on a re-ordering of society." In other words, a major poetry cannot come from an art in opposition to society or isolated from it. Society itself must be reshaped before poetry can be. And what, meanwhile, is poetry to do, if a great poetry cannot now be written and if the aspiration to create it must divide the poet against himself, pitting his pride as an artist against his conscience as a human being? It must lower its pride and "in tiny measure contribute," urged MacNeice, to the larger cause. Or else poetry might pursue its own technical standards and development and die in its isolation.

So whatever direction poets take, their way is thickly beset with fears and guilts. On the one hand, they feel themselves threatened with self-consciousness, loss of direct emotion, isolation from an audience and from ordinary reality, the futility of the esoteric. Yet perhaps the other way leads inevitably to a bad conscience as a writer and the contempt of one's peers. The self-conflict is even more bitter for the many poets who have or want to have feelings of solidarity with the poor, the victimized, and the oppressed. What can our complicated, elitist art present them? How can it cry aloud in confronting those moral, political, and social issues in which feeling ought not to be complex?

POETRY AS THINKING AND TALKING

The elliptical, discontinuous, persistently concrete style of Eliot in the 1920s precluded many of the acts of mind we ordinarily describe as "thinking"—thinking through, about, over, so. In the style of *The Waste Land* one could not meditate, reason, argue, opine, generalize, judge, or conclude. The absence of such acts of mind contributed to Eliot's inaccessibility. But the issue went much deeper. If "thinking" is a large or essential part of our mental functioning, or an important means of persuasion, or even a vehicle toward truth, a style that makes thinking impossible suffers—this is the least one can say—from a grave limitation. Eliot felt so too; from *Ash-Wednesday* through the *Four Quartets* his verse partially and gradually returned to a more meditative mode. The young poets of the thirties, or some of them, were avid readers of intellectual prose and thinkers of abstract thoughts. Auden had steeped himself in Freud and Jung by the time he was seventeen. Day-Lewis' *Transitional Poem* (1929) had footnotes to Spinoza. MacNeice read philosophy along with classics at Oxford, and his poems often addressed philosophical themes. Having such interests, the thirties poets saw no reason to exclude them from poetry. Reason, logic, and learning played large roles in the work of the Metaphysical poets of the seventeenth century, whom the thirties poets much admired. The political concern of this generation sometimes tumbled them into poetic propaganda. "Conrad," queried Sylvia Townsend Warner,

> Can your cunning foot the swamp
> Where you tread on the dead?—
> Red! Red!

But the same political concern also pushed poets toward styles of thoughtful speech. Poetry reported and editorialized, so to speak; it viewed, argued, and took its stand. Thus, for example, in "Spain 1937" Auden pointed out that "history" now necessitates risk, waste, and guilt.

> To-day the inevitable increase in the chances of death;
> The conscious acceptance of guilt in the fact of murder;
> To-day the expending of powers
> On the flat ephemeral pamphlet and the boring meeting.

For,

> History to the defeated
> May say Alas but cannot help or pardon.

"Spain 1937" is slightly rhetorical, but the general thirties type to which it belongs is best described as intellectual talk. It is also intelligent talk, but "intellectual" more precisely characterizes the speaker. Since readers were also intellectuals, they probably recognized in Auden's lines from "Spain" their own habits of abstract, argumentative consideration, their wrestling with issues (such as necessary murder) that would seem unreal to most people, and their frame of reference within highbrow books and ideas—Marxist thought, for example, behind Auden's "history."

The mode of address could range from the oratorical to the intimate, but for the most part this poetry of intellectual speech was conversational. More exactly, it was a poetic imitation of conversation, more heightened, metaphoric, and formally patterned than ordinary conversation, but more like talk than was common in English poetry. The mental acts performed in this type of poem are generalizing, illustrating, alluding, qualifying, concluding, and the like; the judgments proceed in rational sequence. Such processes of mind, common in other types of poem, as describing, emoting, imagining, envisioning, dramatizing, and symbolizing are much less present in this type, and thus it approximates "normal" (for intellectuals) states of mind as opposed to "poetic" ones. MacNeice's long diary poem "Autumn Journal" is full of examples:

> It is so hard to imagine
> A world where the many would have their chance without
> A fall in the standard of intellectual living
> And nothing left that the highbrow cared about.
> Which fears must be suppressed.

We read this under the convention that it is spontaneous, and only with this convention do we enjoy it. Poetry of this type belongs specifically to poets who formed their styles in the 1930s. It was not found earlier in the modern period, and it has not returned strongly since.

THE ENGLISH TRADITION

In his youth Eliot discovered the French *symbolistes* with an excitement that was almost like a conversion. Pound studied the poetry of ancient Provence, Tuscany, China, and other historical cultures. Moreover, he kept an eye on Modernisms in foreign countries—Futurism, Expressionism, Dada, and the like—and was also much influenced by Modernist painting, sculpture, music, film, and fiction. But Pound and Eliot were Americans living in London. English Modernists—Aldous Huxley, Richard Aldington, the Sitwells, Edgell Rickword, Herbert Read—assimilated the "American-Montparnasse" influence, as Richard Church called it, and they also drew on painting and music. Yet in comparison with that of the United States, the poetry of England in the 1920s seems much less open to foreign literatures and the other arts—in fact, much less Modernist. The reason is that the major volumes in England during the 1920s were not, except for Lawrence, from Modernists but from older poets such as Hardy and Bridges. The younger ones had been killed in the First World War.

By the 1930s all young English poets were aware, through Eliot, of the poetry of France. A diluted Surrealism from abroad was practiced briefly by a few poets. Auden went to Berlin for boys and found Brecht; in later years he identified with Goethe. Rilke was admired. Poets caught much from films and from thrillers. And they had personal relations with foreign writers, painters, and composers. But despite all this, foreign literature made relatively little impact on English poetry in the 1930s. In Auden, Thomas, Empson, MacNeice, Spender, Day-Lewis, and most other poets (including Eliot), English poetry returned for inspiration to its native traditions. Not that these poets, or most of them, could be thought traditional in the sense of "like the past." They were much too colloquial, elliptical, rhythmically irregular and seriously parodic for that. Moreover, they reflected contemporary lore, images, and states of mind, and they were deeply involved, emotionally and intellectually, in the crises of their age. Nevertheless, in contrast to the Modernism of the 1920s, the style of the 1930s derived much less from outside poetry and from abroad. Instead, it synthesized different English traditions or types of poetry. Which traditions? Eliot, of course—Modernism. But also the older poets Eliot had praised in his criticism as he warred against the taste of the nineteenth century. About half the poets of England and America were delighted with the witty, often elegant Metaphysical poetry of the seventeenth century. Yet the Romantic traditions of the nineteenth century also revived in the poetry of the 1930s. Some poets, Auden especially, continued the anti-Romantic polemic of Pound and Eliot, though this did not prevent Romantic elements from looming large in their work. But almost all the poets of this generation paid homage to three premoderns (as they saw them)—Hardy, Hopkins, and Owen—and these three were strong carriers of Romantic convention, which they passed on to their enthusiasts. So was Yeats, who was so much deplored and imitated. Moreover, the brisk, demystifying idea of poetry in the thirties did not foster fundamental and programmatic reconsideration of style. Getting on with the job of writing, poets were vulnerable to whatever conventions were handiest, and these might still be Romantic ones, which some of the thirties poets absorbed and followed without much thinking about it. But mainly the Romantic came back because poets shared so intensely the public and political hopes and fears of the decade. I shall enlarge on this topic later, and here simply note the prevalence at this time of utopian, apocalyptic, and elegiac emotions, which had also been strongly present in the Romantic age and expressed in its poetry.

Many other sources and influences could also be described, from Anglo-Saxon to Laura Riding and Robert Graves, but only four need to be remarked distinctly. Hopkins, Hardy, and Owen have been mentioned; the fourth is Lawrence. He mattered to this generation mainly as a guru, and we shall come back shortly to view him in this role. Specific emulation of his poetry was not common. There was some Lawrentian free verse, and if Lawrence's feelings and vision of things took root in a poet's imagination, so also might the images in which he had expressed them. Hence many images of the sun, Mediterranean landscape, bulls, darkness, and the like in the poetry of the 1930s have a Lawrentian provenance. Though Hopkins was a Victorian, most of his poems had not been published until Bridges' edition of 1918. Ten years later he was being read with such enthusiasm that he was enrolled as an honorary modern. What the thirties poets particularly admired in him was his condensation, sprung rhythm, concrete vividness and particularity ("inscape"), and bold, arresting linguistic means (hyphenated compounds, Anglo-Saxon diction, syntactic inversion, ellipsis, heavy alliteration). "Me, March," wrote Auden, "you do with your movements master and rock / With wing-whirl, whale-wallow, silent budding of cell." "Plover," said Rex Warner, "with under the tail pine-red, dead leafwealth in down displayed."

The presence of Hardy in the poetry of the thirties is usually less obvious. His work drove home the value of real-life subject matter and novelistic interest. The thirties poets shared his elegiac regret for human hopes crushed in the moiling of history. He reinforced general bucolic tenderness, especially in Day-Lewis, and may have contributed to the gray, northern landscape of Auden. Above all, Hardy was a poet of powerful imagination and imperfect execution. One could admire him enormously yet hope to do better, and for this reason, as Auden said, his poetry encouraged and fostered. In his later years Day-Lewis felt so great an affinity or devotion that a number of his poems could hardly be told from Hardy's. Owen was a force for these poets because of his directly emotional poetry of protest. "His unsentimental pity," Day-Lewis said, "his savage and sacred indignation are the best of our inheritance." Sympathizing with the common soldiers, presenting their sufferings realistically, and accusing politicians and generals, Owen taught the thirties poets to voice their own similar feelings in the political context of their time. Owen's feeling of human brotherhood in suffering and death also moved this generation powerfully.

FREUD, MARX, AND LAWRENCE

The enormous impact of Freud, Marx, and Lawrence on the ideas and feelings of the thirties poets would be a subject for a separate book—in fact, three books. The names of Freud and Marx are here used as symbols, "Freud" for Freud himself and also Jung, Adler, and other expounders and theorists of depth psychology, including Lawrence; and "Marx" for himself and his ideological cousins and followers. Particular ideas from these schools appear everywhere in the poetry of the thirties, but Freud and Marx mattered most to these poets because in or from them one could obtain criteria of what may variously be called health, goodness, love, or even salvation. They diagnosed the sickness, they uncovered its hidden causes and workings, and they showed how it might or would be remedied.

In the 1920s much of Eliot's technique had been suggested by psychoanalytic theories of the mind. But the associative, fragmentary, eruptive, symbolic workings of the unconscious were less imitated in the thirties, less, at least, in formal procedure, for the thirties poets returned, as I have said, to grammatical sequence, reasoning, and generalization. Nevertheless, both "Freud" and "Marx" bestowed rich stylistic potentialities. Both lines of thought transformed observed details or seemingly casual images into symbols. The barometer tapper, the wearer of spotless collars, the man who beheads buttercups with his cane are figures of Freudian meaning; caverns and fountains are mother; and so forth. "I cannot believe," Auden said, "that any artist can be good who is not more than a bit of reporting journalist," but the Marxian theory of history, predicting the collapse of the bourgeois system, converted journalistic fact—idle factories, street mobs—into symptoms. The cricket match took on imaginative resonance as a symbol of the dying order, affectionately loved but doomed. Every item associated with the bourgeoisie in its past prosperity and every example of present unrest was full of augury.

Though Freud and Marx were concerned with different spheres of existence, each line of thought led into the other. Depth psychology might explain mass behavior and Marxism individual neurosis; ultimately, the thirties poets might believe, psychoanalysis would transform society or socialism the individual. Certainly it was urgently necessary to reconcile the personal and the social on some ground. To liberate yourself from inhibition, repression, neurosis, to be fully alive, whole, loving, creating—who could dream on this without upwellings of resolve and purpose? The victory would be not for yourself only but for mankind. And yet the slums, the breadlines, the morning newspapers with their ominous headlines, the desperate wrong and threat summoned you forth. You had to commit yourself. Unless, therefore, you could embrace the personal and the social in one thought, and battle in both spheres with one act, your conscience was divided. That Lawrence had addressed both with the same intuitions was part of his fascination.

Metaphor, at least, could link the two realms. Hence in the poetry of this period metaphors from the public and historical may express the intimate and psychic. Strikes, business slumps, dictators, revolutions, diplomatic conferences, and embargoes were witty illustrations of psychological goings-on or of phases of love affairs. Conversely, the tendencies of nations, classes, and history could be characterized in psychoanalytic terms—regression, narcissism, trauma, death-wish—that were partly explanatory, partly metaphorical, but wholly unexpected and apt. Of course the thirties poets created fresh metaphors from other sources also: bureaucracy (memos, progress reports, pink forms, committee meetings); finance ("to sleep on a mattress of easy profits," a life as "intangible as a Stock Exchange rumour"); machinery (brakes, pylons, searchlights); medicine (surgeons, bacilli, cancer); and sports (cricket, mountain climbing, tennis). And the old standbys returned—quests, landscapes, birds, beacons, stars, fires, classical ruins—with much other Romantic convention that had been repudiated and avoided in the twenties.

Moreover, psychoanalysis and Marxism shared, or could be made to share, some basic symbolisms or symbolic orientations. In both, for example, the categories of surface and depth, present and past, were fundamental, and both showed that the present and surface were determined by the past and deep. The Freudian id, infancy, and archaic forms of society, psychological regression and political reaction, could be associated, however illogically. Whoever stood on the border or place of transition was struggling to free himself from neuroses formed in the past and to become a maturely loving adult. History stood also on a watershed, and the necessary psychic crisis of transition could be conflated with the public one, the loving personality with the utopian society of brotherhood. In the borderland one is gripped by the past that must be left behind. One may look back nostalgically to narcissism, cherish one's psychic wound, arm and entrench oneself against revolution. The leaders compel themselves not to look back. Their choice of the future is heroic. It must be made with inadequate data and amid the inevitable ambivalence and self-divisions of the border zone. (The pathos of the leader and the choice was much dwelt on.) The loveless, incurable neurotic and the bourgeois outmoded by history cannot go forward; as they are left behind, they are assailed by dread. The revolution or reordering will be terrible to the regressive, infantile, and capitalist; it will be Lawrentian, Freudian, and Marxist, for the promised land is both utopia and the healed psyche. Spender speaks of "those / Who build a new world in their heart." "Know you seek a new world," says Day-Lewis, "a saviour to establish / Long-lost kinship and restore the blood's fulfilment"—one savior of both society and the psyche. Charles Madge foretells that

> We shall be differently aware, we shall see all things new
> Not as a craze or a surprise, but hard, naked, true.
> And trash heaped up, torn scraps, mud, all shall glow through
>   and through
> When the electric moment passes in, making them new.

Thus the revolution will give us not only leisure, plenty, and brotherhood, but also Whitmanian or Blakean eyes. Meanwhile the secret agent goes before. Living amid the bourgeoisie and disguising himself as one of them, he undermines from within. The writer of middle-class life and leftist sympathies may be one of these spies. In such conflations of "Freud" and "Marx" the thirties poets, especially Auden, possessed the rudiments of a myth.

A guru for this generation, Lawrence also saw and denounced the sickness the poets recognized in themselves and their world. "Perhaps I was the type of cerebral modern writer condemned by Lawrence"—the typical misgivings are Spender's. "A healer in this English land," Auden called Lawrence. As a college student, MacNeice remembered, "My ideology was built up on *Ulysses,* 'The Waste Land,' and the novels of D. H. Lawrence. As the two former are essentially negative works, my positive creed was inevitably Lawrentian." He was looking back from ten years later, and his positive creed was no longer Lawrentian, for the liberal, Socialist, or Communist sympathies of the thirties poets somewhat impeded their discipleship. Neither did they follow Lawrence all the way into the mystical dark where, as he imagined, in sex we commune with deep, salvific powers. Yet they went a little way with Lawrence, for they hoped that by celebrating the sexuality of our being, so to speak, we may achieve wholeness and health. To them Freud seemed to suggest the same thought, and Freud and Lawrence lurk behind many a woolly, urgent formula of salvation in the 1930s. "It is possible," said Spender, "for the individual to save himself by learning to love, and to live." And Auden wrote, "We must love one another or die." Moreover, Lawrence could be mustered as a witness against the social order. As Spender put it in a 1937 review, "the corruption of a society which sets commercial values above human ones is most evident in the sexual relationship. I think Lawrence has gone further in describing the symptoms of a sexually neurotic society than Freud, whose observations are necessarily confined to pathological examples . . . the bourgeoisie has really come secretly to hate and trample on sex." Spender added, "It is not too much to say that Lawrence saw sex as the pivotal point on which would turn a social revolution."

POLITICS AND ROMANTIC CONVENTION

Political events in the 1930s and the strong emotions they generated sent poets back to more Romantic conventions and modes of speech, more Romantic, that is, than was consistent with other attitudes of some of the thirties poets. Though these poets demystified the writing of poetry, talking of it as a job like others and denying that the poetic imagination possessed special insight, they also assumed the prophetic role. We find poems rebuking the sins of the people, or if not of the people exactly, at least of the middle class, and if not sins, at least belatedness. They voiced prophetic warning, foretelling ruin:

> out of the dream-house stumbling
> One night into a strangling air and the flung
> Rags of children and thunder of stone niagaras tumbling,
> You'll know you slept too long.

The words are from Day-Lewis, but might have been almost anyone's. And the poets cried prophetic promise of a savior and a new world. "Light has been let in," exulted Rex Warner prospectively, "The fences are down. No broker is left alive." And in "Freud" and especially "Marx" the thirties poets possessed a lore by which they could prophesy, denouncing the illness and envisioning the New Jerusalem. The images, rife in this poetry, of a longed-for savior reflect the futility, in the contemporary social crises, of the government and, as it seemed, of democratic procedure. The equally current, cognate image of the healer, the all-wise diagnoser and curer, was a projection from the same despair and hope: change must and will come, yet one cannot effect it oneself, not even in oneself. And since amid the huge and impending crises poets were speaking not for their isolated selves, but for so many others also, they felt the more righteous in their urgencies. Utterances that might otherwise have been tentative, tinkling cymbals transformed themselves into sounding brass. Yet again, however, the ambivalence of the thirties poets must be noted. Though they recaptured the prophetic voice, theirs was rarely whole. Much of their prophecy is at the same time a deliberate parody of prophecy; the apocalyptic voice is also buffoonery.

Stout Cortez, Ulysses, Columbus ("Sail on! and on!"), Rabbi Ben Ezra, Merlin, Launcelot, and other heroes and sages of nineteenth-century poetry were discarded in the Modernist revolution. Only Yeats continued to imagine such figures. But the leader-savior (as Comitatus Earl, scoutmaster, Communist boss, cricket captain, and so forth) and the wise healer or scientific Merlin reawakened in thirties poetry some of the old Romantic awe, though the awe was mixed with humor and deflation. So also with the solitary airman and analogous symbols such as the mountain climber and polar explorer. Imperiled, pushing beyond limits, isolated above or past man's towns, cultivated valleys, or loneliest farms, and thus freed of social ties and responsibilities, these symbolic figures expressed in general the need to explore a new world. It was typical of the thirties imagination that these heroes went forth with crampons, ordnance maps, compasses, sled dogs, or whatever; science and technology equipped their venture into the unknown and provided its chance of success. Yet often the poems put in question the heroes they imagined; perhaps their quest was really an evasion or escape, their impelling motive a psychological wound.

Elegy was deep-rooted as an emotional implication in the 1930s sense of crisis. From the fear that Europe was going to be engulfed in war, every present moment of peace—a walk by a river, a concert, a dinner with friends—had its elegiac border. In "Place of Birth" Peter Hewitt (b. 1914) recollected the present moment prospectively, so to speak:

> and tonight's misty trees and mackerel sky
> remembered in the draughty days to come
> tearing at hearts shaken by midnight guns.

Elegiac feeling flowed also toward traditional English or bourgeois ways of life, now sensed to be ending. Even revolutionary utopians were subject to such cross-currents. To speak of an elegiac feeling for a present happiness may seem an abuse of language, since elegy involves a lamentation for the past, now lost and irrecoverable. But the thirties poets placed the present at a distance, seeing it as though it were past and speaking of it commemoratively and wistfully. Or they placed the immediate moment, the private hope or happiness, in the vast context of the world's other goings-on, the panorama of contemporary Europe and history. They caught this from Hardy, but also from their breakfast newspapers, and again and again in their poetry we see the concert, or the cozy pub, or the party on the English lawn in the same moment with some violence in Europe or some festering slum in Birmingham, reminding us of the brooding doom. Furthermore, these young poets, especially Auden, struggled for intellectual objectivity, and this too could strangely foster an elegiac regret for the present. One of their themes was the contrast between subjective wish and objective fact. In the very moment of intense fulfillment and happiness, they knew it would be transient or illusory.

Yet such elegiac tendencies also aroused feelings of guilt. Wistfulness is hardly wrong if it is for feelings of certainty, fidelity, and beauty, not to mention the concerts or lawn parties of a bourgeois world at peace. Yet for these poets the emotion became wrong to the extent that its objects could never or could not appropriately now exist. The wide, changing, present world as it is must be entered and accepted, not only because it is, but because it may offer a fulfillment that is certainly more troubled than the imagined or lost one, yet is also deeper and more significant. "Rest from loving and be living," wrote Day-Lewis, stating the inevitable course of life as a moral imperative. "Find the mortal world enough," Auden concluded his "Lay your sleeping head, my love," invoking for the boy a blessing more in touch with reality and hence more possible than the intensities and illusions of Romantic love. In other love poems of Auden the elegiac feeling could be so blended with acceptance of time and change that it was almost completely lost:

> I, decent with the seasons, move
> Different or with a different love.

And for many poets the revolutionary or anti-Fascist struggle, or the moral necessity of facing up to the war, tinged moments of private happiness with a guilty sense of self-indulgence. Enjoying the moment, they knew also that they ought to renounce it, and so again the poem might include an elegiac feeling of farewell. In Bernard Spencer's "Allotments" the speaker walks happily on a spring day. But behind him in the town are "The sour doorways of the poor" and the radio news reports of "pacts, persecutions, / And imprisonments and deaths," and the speaker, conscious of this, is uneasy in taking his pleasure. Chaucer's "Whan that Aprille . . . ," the burst of springtime joy at the start of the *Canterbury Tales,* was no longer possible because it could no longer be quite innocent. The poet and his lover might be toasting sausages before a fire in Scotland, but in the world's wide concatenation of events—the Hardyesque perception renewed itself with great force in the poets of the thirties—there was off somewhere in Vienna, Madrid, or Warsaw a street riot, an assassination, or a putsch. The poet would have liked to forget it, but could not, for it forebode heavily. In Bernard Spencer's "A Cold Night" the speaker tries to put Europe out of his mind, but it comes flooding back. One would like, he says, not to be always

> Opening one's doors on the pitiful streets
> Of Europe, not always think of winter, winter, like a hammering
>   rhyme
> For then everything is drowned by the rising wind, everything is
>   done against Time.

Geoffrey Grigson's "And Forgetful of Europe" remembers the plants, birds, menus, walks, and guests at a seaside resort. "Europe," in the sense intended, is not mentioned at all; in other words, the poem enacts the forgetting that is its subject. Readers, the poem assumes, will understand what and why the speaker is trying to forget. "Trying," because the more intensely he concentrates on the wagtails and oleanders, the more we are reminded of his motive. Outside the context of the thirties, the poem would be pointless, for "Europe" would have no resonant meaning. But the poem is moving if we know the imagination of the thirties and read within its conventions.

DAY-LEWIS, MACNEICE, AND SPENDER

Of the many poets who shared the period style of the thirties, Auden, Day-Lewis, Spender, and MacNeice were the most distinguished. C. Day-Lewis (1904–72) began as a fondly bucolic poet in *Beechen Vigil* (1925) and *Country Comets* (1928). But at Oxford he met Auden and fell under his influence. He also assimilated the other examples that mattered especially to the young writers of that time and place—Donne, Yeats, Eliot, Hopkins, Lawrence. His *Transitional Poem* (1929), a collection of lyrics arranged to make a sequence, was full of love and metaphysics, more exactly, of both at once; the philosophical love lyric was then a favored genre. Day-Lewis married in 1928. *From Feathers to Iron* (1931) expressed, he said, the suite of his feelings during his wife's pregnancy, but readers saw political meanings in these metaphors. An expectant father might well feel that his days of "Running across the bean-fields in a south wind" were over, along with many another thoughtless joy and pristine passion; he will have to buckle down to work:

> Such and such is our country. There remains to
> Plough up the meadowland, reclaim the marshes.

But the mood seems also postrevolutionary tristesse, expecting a new society as well as a new baby. It illustrates again the fusion, in this generation, of the private and personal with the public and political.

In 1933 Day-Lewis published *The Magnetic Mountain*. He had

not yet joined the Communist party formally, but this was a full-throated cry of social agitation and prophecy in verse. The sequence ranges from deliberate doggerel, satiric invective, and parodic graduation speeches to vague, lyric hails to the wished-for leader and to splendid revolutionary odes:

> You that love England, who have an ear for her music,
> The slow movement of clouds in benediction,
> Clear arias of light thrilling over her uplands
>
> . . . .
> Listen. Can you not hear the entrance of a new theme?
>
> You who go out alone, on tandem or on pillion,
> Down arterial roads riding in April,
> Or sad beside lakes where hill-slopes are reflected . . .

Much in the poem seems to suggest that the savior might be Auden, who is cast in the period role of heroic airman or Hopkins' windhover:

> Look west, Wystan, lone flyer, birdman, my bully boy!
> Plague of locusts, creeping barrage, has left earth bare:
> Suckling and centenarian are up in the air,
> No wing-room for Wystan, no joke for kestrel joy.

One reader of the poem thought that the magnetic mountain, toward which all the express trains are or should be underway, might be Auden.

In 1935 Day-Lewis joined the Communist party. A village householder, with thatch on his roof and romping children in his garden, he distributed leaflets and conducted the "political education" of his Party group. How, then, did he transit from this to the odal commemoration of Winston Churchill ("Who Goes Home?") he published thirty years later, even before he was named Poet Laureate? As he tells the story in his fine autobiography, *The Buried Day* (1960), he was not shaken from Communism by any sudden shock, but realized after about three years that agitation coarsened his art. It might be the right thing to do, but he was the wrong person to do it. And gradually through the years the emotional preoccupations of his personal life took over and his political attachment died, leaving a vacuum into which convention rushed. Hence his verses about the Mother of Parliaments grieving for her dead son.

In the mid-1930s Day-Lewis quit teaching school and lived henceforth as a freelance writer. He commenced his admirable series of detective novels under the pseudonym Nicholas Blake. The more specifically modern influences faded gradually from his verse, and he returned to late Victorian feelings and modes. Where *The Magnetic Mountain* had celebrated the questers and battlers who will save us from psychological inhibition and from capitalism, Day-Lewis now painted more traditional heroics, billboard style, in well-managed narrative poems. "The Nabara" (1938) tells how several little trawlers fought a Fascist cruiser in the Spanish Civil War; the poem is similar to Tennyson's "The Revenge." His metaphors were now from the stock of the nineteenth century. "The Ecstatic" apostrophizes a "soaring" skylark as "a singing star," a "nerve of song." "Poem for an Anniversary" compares young lovers to volcanoes: "A molten rage shook earth from head to toe." At his best Day-Lewis was likely to resemble Hardy, though typically with a touch more of the nineteenth-century elegiac music than Hardy permitted himself:

> Always our time's ghost-guise of impermanence
> Daunts me; whoever I meet,
> Wherever I stand, a shade of parting lengthens
> And laps round my feet.

Day-Lewis' "Birthday Poem for Thomas Hardy" is as warm a tribute as I know to a master in the master's own voice. At about this same time—the later 1930s and the 1940s—Day-Lewis also took childhood memories for his subject, and in the mid-1940s he worked in recollection and analysis over love woes of years before, when his heart had been divided between his wife and another woman. These poems recall Meredith's *Modern Love* but are still more like Hardy's on similar subjects. At his death in 1972, Day-Lewis was buried, according to his wish, in the same churchyard as Hardy.

Louis MacNeice (1907–63), of an Anglo-Irish family, went to schools in England from the age of ten. At Oxford he met Auden and Spender. His work appeared with theirs and with that of Day-Lewis in *Oxford Poetry: 1929,* and henceforth readers associated him with these poets. He taught classics at the University of Birmingham and at Bedford College, University of London, and in 1941 started working for the BBC, where he continued writing and producing for the next twenty years. He also turned out translations (*Agamemnon, Faust*), plays, novels, autobiography, and criticism. He had started writing verse at the age of seven, and he never stopped.

MacNeice's poetry dwelt in the contemporary world with the offhand familiarity of his generation. In the thirties he exhibited more or less the same facts of the age, social, economic, political, psychic, as did his fellow poets: the industrial landscape and the slums; the wealthy—"Old faces frosted with powder and choked in furs"—and the tawdry middle class riddled with fear; the coming smash in war or revolution—

> when the sniggering machine-guns in the hands of the
>   young men
> Are trained on every flat and club and beauty parlour and
>   Father's den.

The future victims—ourselves—avert their eyes from these facts, but their unconfronted guilts and fears translate into vague, clinging dread and retreat from life ("Spring Voices"). MacNeice's justly famous "Bagpipe Music" whirls this confused, aimless society around in its dance. The poem is satire, but of a ticklish kind, for the speaker pretends to share the state of mind he renders—"All we want is a bank balance and a bit of skirt in a taxi"—and no higher values or visions enter into the poem. It ends in futility and ominousness:

> It's no go my honey love, it's no go my poppet;
> Work your hands from day to day, the winds will blow the profit.
> The glass is falling hour by hour, the glass will fall for ever,
> But if you break the bloody glass you won't hold up the weather.

As with Auden and Spender, the genius of MacNeice lay partly in his ambivalence. In a brash sentence of his book *Modern Poetry* (1938) he noted that *The Waste Land* perceived a world in fragments, "but the contemplation of a world of fragments becomes boring and Eliot's successors are more interested in tidying it up." A few poems shared this mood and reached for the feather duster. And to judge from his rhythms, MacNeice was naturally brisk and purposeful. But he lacked hope and faith. Though he exhibited and satirized all that excited his Liberal repugnance,

he had no belief in a better Socialist or Communist world to-
morrow. Sometimes he imagined that a finer society might have
been found at some time or place in the past, maybe in ancient
Greece, but on consideration he doubted that things had been
much different then. He reported a more admirable community
and way of life in "The Hebrides," but typically concluded:

> There is still peace though not for me and not
> Perhaps for long—still peace on the bevel hills
> For those who still can live as their fathers lived
> On those islands.

And though he was inclined to philosophy, and argued with
himself in many a poem about Flux and Permanence, Time and
Eternity, the Many and the One, he only extended his doubts.
So he could not wish to go forward or back; neither Marxism
nor metaphysics nor religion provided a solution for him.

We find him a guilty enjoyer of the moment, an autumnal
lingerer. In the great social questions he often speaks as a member of the group that is doomed, seeing the impending ruin and
feeling that it may be just, and yet holding and tugging in mind,
heart, and belly against the historical tide. He thought life after
the revolution might be less in beauty, excitement, artistic
achievement, and "grilled steak," or even if better, maybe better
in a way that would not suit him. "An Eclogue for Christmas"
speaks of that future as a time when "faces are all dials and
cannot smile or frown." Ultimate metaphysical reality was for
him similarly alien and threatening, and he tended to speak of
it and of the historical future in the same metaphors. Both are
like the ocean around our island, around our cozy Now, and the
"tripper" in "Upon This Beach" is advised to turn his back on
the falling and exploding "wall of the sea," to head inland, "And
boarding bus be jolly."

MacNeice also composed poems of the personal life—recollections of childhood, self-analyses, love lyrics, journal poems—
and like the other poets of his generation he tended to conflate
the private and public spheres, referring to both at the same
time. "Riding in cars / On tilting roads," we forget past and future and live only in this reckless moment, "we" being lovers and
also the whole social and political order. His haunting "The Sun-

light on the Garden" draws its complex resonance from this conjunction. Time is passing; an end is coming; the autumnal or
late afternoon setting suggests that the subject is old, age and
natural death; the quotation from *Antony and Cleopatra* adds that
the end is also of a love affair and an empire. A reader versed
in the poetry of the thirties might assume that the love affair is
approaching its end because the crisis in the public, historical
order is advancing and will overwhelm private lives.

> The sunlight on the garden
> Hardens and grows cold,
> We cannot cage the minute
> Within its nets of gold,
> When all is told
> We cannot beg for pardon.
>
> Our freedom as free lances
> Advances towards its end;
> The earth compels, upon it
> Sonnets and birds descend;
> And soon, my friend,
> We shall have no time for dances.
>
> The sky was good for flying
> Defying the church bells
> And every evil iron
> Siren and what it tells:
> The earth compels,
> We are dying, Egypt, dying
>
> And not expecting pardon,
> Hardened in heart anew,
> But glad to have sat under
> Thunder and rain with you,
> And grateful to
> For sunlight on the garden.

Though the wish is to hold or prolong the moment, the recognition is that we cannot. But the form of the poem enacts the
impossible wish: with echoing rhymes (garden / Hardens; minute / Within its); with the rhyming of the first and last lines in
each stanza; with the repetition of the opening line of the poem
in the final one. That "When all is told" (made known, reckoned,

with a pun on "tolled") we cannot "beg for pardon" implies that we are guilty. "Free lances" can fight on whichever side they choose, write what they will, but the coming world will not permit of this. "Flying" in this context images free individualistic soaring, reckless and socially irresponsible, like Antony and Cleopatra's defying of the signals of alarm. In connection with flying, the phrase "the earth compels," with its gravitational suggestions, makes us think, among many other things, of a crash. "Hardened" in the final stanza refers no longer to the sunlight but to ourselves, tempered to undergo what we must. "Anew" suggests that we have been "hardened in heart" before, and hence that the nostalgia and regret of the poem may express a moment of backsliding self-indulgence. If so, the poem ends in anything but renewed readiness for the future, for the final lines turn fondly again toward the past and the present.

In this poem MacNeice employed his facility and ingenuity to make music, but more usually he percolated in puns ("pigeons banking on the wind"), surprising comparisons ("light delicate as the chink of coins"; "he would . . . fly / In search of a future like a sycamore seed"), satiric allusions ("Give us this day our daily news"), and reversed clichés. He proliferated inventive conceptions of poems, and his construction was always purposeful—"good carpentry," as Auden put it—but as the other side of his clarity, his phrasing could be loose, and his vigor manifested itself at times in a coarsely swinging rhythm. (In his youth MacNeice had greatly admired Alfred Noyes, though he forgot this when in *Modern Poetry* he gave a three-chapter history of his personal tastes.)

In the 1940s and 1950s MacNeice wrote often in the then-favored genre of the essay-poem. Derived partly from the contemporary example of Auden, these were longish, colloquial, perspicuous, mildly witty, and pleasant utterances. "Mahabalipuram," a descriptive travel piece, is an example. He also wrote dramatic monologues and, as his longest effort, "Autumn Sequel" (1953), a poem in twenty-six cantos that corresponds to his "Autumn Journal" (1938), the famous, slapdash record of his feelings in that season of personal troubles and of Munich. His poetry centered less now in the public realm, and as the years passed, the feelings voiced in his poems tended toward ennui and depression. "Charon" is typical. In this fantasy the apocalyptic end is just wearisome, and the old ferryman to death is a rude official.

Stephen Spender (b. 1909) was living in Germany through the collapse of democracy and the start of the Nazi terror. He was in Spain during the Civil War, and he fought fires in London during the Blitz. He joined the Communist party in 1937, later renounced it, and was energetically anti-Communist in the 1950s. He has described these experiences and emotions in important works of autobiography and political argument—important because they help us to understand feeling and opinion in the years he describes—including *Forward from Liberalism,* (1937) and the autobiographical *World Within World* (1951). He has also written fiction and drama. As a critic he helped to formulate the literary ideals of his generation in *The Destructive Element* (1935). He was co-editor of *Horizon* (1939–41) and of *Encounter* (1953–67). He has traveled widely, lectured, taught at universities in England and the United States, participated in conferences, and corresponded, dined, drunk, or visited with a great many of the leading writers of the last fifty years. In short, he is a veteran whose perceptions, advice, and reviews have special authority.

Spender has not published much poetry since his *Collected Poems* (1955), and in that volume more than half the pages, including nearly all the especially significant ones, come from the 1930s. They express conflicting emotions and opposed ideals, typical of that generation torn between the pursuit of personal, emotional liberation and fulfillment and the menace of politics and history. "In 1929" presents three naked friends: "the new, bronzed German, / The communist clerk, and myself, being English." Twelve years earlier he and the German would have killed each other in the war; in the revolution ten years from now the Communist will execute them both. Thus the personal life is vulnerable to history, but now for this moment the friends feel their common humanity, which lies precisely in this vulnerability. History has made their "love" briefly possible, and the "love" grounds itself in their shared awareness of life's randomness and the doomed separation of death.

> Lives risen a movement, joined or separate,
> Fall heavily, then are always separate,

>Stratum unreckoned by geologists,
>Sod lifted, turned, slapped back again with spade.

This poem has much of Wilfred Owen in it, not least in that it spreads the meaning of the love it proclaims from sexuality to universal brotherhood. But in another poem, "The Shadow of War," the awareness of coming war stops emotion. "I think continually of those who were truly great" applies such terms as "great," "ambition," and "honor" to persons who delight in the senses and the "blood." But "Not palaces, an era's crown" commands the senses to "leave your gardens, your singing feasts" and enlist in the revolution. Spender was here telling himself what sort of poetry he ought to write, but his vivid love for all he must not now permit himself confirms his ambivalence:

>Eye, gazelle, delicate wanderer,
>Drinker of horizon's fluid line;
>Ear that suspends on a chord
>The spirit drinking timelessness;
>Touch, love, all senses;
>Leave your gardens, your singing feasts.

Though Spender can be fine, he can also be vague and sentimental. His imagery and diction draw amply on Romantic kitsch and cliché; stars, seas, mountains, winds, eyes, fires, and suns glitter on his pages like sugar candy. Such phrases as "terrible river of grief," "war on the sun," "the untamed horses of the blood," "touched with fire," "flowering of the spirit," and so forth are quite as frequent in his best poems as in his lesser ones. His emotions are sometimes rhetorical; in other words, they rely for their impact on the ready agreement they assume or coerce in the reader. "Not Palaces," a splendid poem, ends declaring that "our programme" ("our" is not editorial but refers to some collective group or party) is "Death to the killers, bringing light to life." A program of killing killers may disturb the moral ideas of some readers, but "bringing light to life," whatever it may mean, overwhelms protest, for everyone must be on the side of light and life. Spender's sentimental emotion often allies itself with revolutionary accusation or utopianism. "An Elementary School Classroom in a Slum" concludes with a fervent prayer (though not, of course, to God) to make the "world" of the slum children

Run azure on gold sands, and let their tongues
Run naked into books, the white and green leaves open
History theirs whose language is the sun.

Such words do the heart good even if they do not satisfy the mind.

7

W. H. AUDEN

I FIRST read Auden as a college student around 1950 and
with impressions that must in part have matched those of
readers in the late twenties and thirties, when he started
publishing. It struck me as the first poetry I had read that simply
took the modern world for granted, as though it were entirely
natural for poetry to speak of golf balls, gasworks, stockbrokers,
bureaucratized work, and the like. Moreover, I seemed to find
in Auden a kind of sophistication that was beguilingly intellectual and contemporary. He was the familiar highbrow who had
digested Marx, Freud, Fraser, Kierkegaard, and so on and alluded to names, doctrines, and works in several languages. At
that time I was also taken with the prose of Matthew Arnold,
and I see now that Auden and Arnold have much in common:
the pose of almost jaunty self-confidence in diagnosis and prescription, the agile one-upmanship, the dilettante and ironic
manner combined with moral concern and quest. Above all I
was charmed in Auden by what seemed the ultimate sophistication, which was not disillusion but instead minimal expectations. More exactly, it was the combination of unillusioned insight, anti-Romantic and scientifically objective, with the ability
to believe in and feel, however mutedly, traditional positives.
Lines such as

> Lay your sleeping head, my love,
> Human on my faithless arm
>
> . . . .
>
> Mortal, guilty, but to me
> The entirely beautiful,

seemed a fascinating poetry of deflated affirmation, in which the lover expects little of himself or of human nature and sees through romantic love, and yet also sees that it has a kind of reality and value. And so far as literary history is concerned, it was clear that Auden, with his tolerant imperfection of phrasing and his colloquial tones, had extended the range and hence the potential relevance of poetry, making it possible—to the extent that his poetry was talk—to talk about anything.

Wystan Hugh Auden was born in 1907 in York, the third son of a distinguished physician of wide scientific interests. Encouraged by the atmosphere of his home, Auden planned a scientific career. At St. Edmund's School he made a hobby of geology and metallurgy, intending to become a mining engineer. Then at Gresham's School in Norfolk he specialized in biology and read deeply in psychoanalytic writings. He later described himself during his school years, rather too harshly, as "mentally precocious, physically backward . . . untidy and grubby . . . dishonest, sentimental, with no community sense whatever, in fact a typical little highbrow and difficult child."

Auden then went on to Christ Church, Oxford. Already at school he had written some poetry. Later he would movingly describe the impact on him of the poetry of Hardy; Edward Thomas and Robert Frost were also favorites. Ebullient, brilliant, and with a gift for comedy, he won the admiration of fellow students; and if he studied literature with diagnostic, even quasi-clinical curiosity, he did so also with an increasingly broad, imaginatively receptive awareness. This openness and variety of interest were to prove self-corrective and formative as he progressively shed the stock responses of the precocious, avantgarde youth—indeed saw through them with the earned insight of direct experience. Meanwhile, at nineteen, he discovered the poetry of Eliot and at once recognized its revolutionary potentialities. He edited *Oxford Poetry, 1926,* and *Oxford Poetry, 1927,* which included some of his own poems, and brought out his own first volume, *Poems,* in 1928. Other influences besides Eliot included Anglo-Saxon verse, Gerard Manley Hopkins, Emily Dickinson, and Edward Arlington Robinson.

Offered a year abroad after Oxford, Auden went to Germany (1928–29), where his life-long interest in German literature began. He then spent five years as a teacher at Larchfield Academy, Scotland, and the Downs School, near Malvern, publishing *Paid on Both Sides: a Charade* (1930); *Poems* (1930); *The Orators* (1932); a play, *The Dance of Death* (1933), written for the Group Theatre; and another play, *The Dog Beneath the Skin* (1935). In the next few years he took trips to Iceland, Spain, and China, meanwhile publishing, besides several critical essays and reviews, two plays, *The Ascent of F6* (1936) and *On the Frontier* (1938), both written with Christopher Isherwood; *Look Stranger* (1936), which was published in the United States as *On This Island* (1937); and *Letters from Iceland* (1937), written with Louis MacNeice. He also edited the *Oxford Book of Light Verse* (1938).

Early in 1939 Auden left England for the United States (he became a citizen in 1946). He made his living by teaching in schools and colleges. Works during these years included *Journey to a War* (1939), with Isherwood; a choral work, *Paul Bunyan* (1941), with Benjamin Britten; *The Double Man* (1941), published in England the same year as *New Year Letter; For the Time Being* (1944); *Collected Shorter Poems, 1930–1944* (1950); a book of essays, *The Enchaféd Flood* (1950); *Nones* (1951); and *The Shield of Achilles* (1955). His continuing interest in music is illustrated by writings on opera and his collaboration with Stravinsky on *The Rake's Progress* (1951), for which he wrote the libretto with his friend Chester Kallman. Meanwhile his reviews, critical articles, and introductory essays ranged from Greek literature and Icelandic sagas to modern poetry and fiction, folklore, children's literature, psychology, religious writing, history, biography, light verse, and music. He was awarded the Bollingen (1954) and Feltrinelli (1957) Prizes. From 1956 to 1961 he served as professor of poetry at Oxford, and in 1957 he began spending summers in Austria. Later works included, besides his usual prolific output of reviews, critical essays, and introductions to selections he had edited, *Homage to Clio* (1960); the libretto (with Kallman) for an opera by Hans Henze, *Elegy for Young Lovers* (1961); an English version (with Kallman) of *Don Giovanni* (1961); *The Dyers Hand and Other Essays* (1962); *About the House* (1965); a libretto (with Kallman) for Henze's *The Bassarids* (1966); *Collected Longer Poems* (1968); *City Without Walls* (1969); and *Epistle to a Godson* (1972). Auden died suddenly in Vienna in 1973.

AUDEN IN THE 1930s

The hegemony of Eliot in avant-garde circles had been quickly established with the publication of *The Waste Land* in 1922, and perhaps nothing since has equalled the impact that poem had on young readers at the time. But since any style specializes to particular effects and precludes others, to cry a writer up at once stimulates poets, critics, and readers to watch for an alternative or successor. As Auden's publications appeared in rapid succession, it seemed to many that this brilliant young poet, who was twenty-three in 1930, was the next step beyond Eliot. Here was an apprentice who had assimilated the skills and principles of the master, yet was using them in a different way and in combination with other influences (for example, Hopkins, Owen, Yeats, Anglo-Saxon poetry) and with resources of his own. The general trend of his writing, regarded as a reaction against Eliot, seemed to be toward accessibility (though it was still "difficult" poetry), a more conversational tone, and a freer use of discursive or generalizing language.

In the thirties, however, critics and readers especially noticed the leftist political commitment that seemed to run through his writing. Their view of Auden was too simple, but it was inevitable at a time when an approach to literature and criticism (often Marxist) stressing social orientations and implications was widely influential. The left intelligentsia, who most thoroughly adopted this approach, had abandoned Eliot when in 1927 he had, from their point of view, revealed himself a "reactionary," and they were eager to welcome a new poet on their own side. Moreover, the notion or critical fabrication of a so-called Auden Group, a coterie of like minded young poets centered around Auden, meant that his poetry was read as though it were by other poets in the Group, such as Day-Lewis or Spender, who were politically more committed than Auden was.

But political commitment, or at least political concern, is vividly present in Auden's poetry. If "concern" seems the better word, it is because Auden's own attitudes at this time were rarely undivided. He explored with allusive power the sick atmosphere of the age: the industrial decay reflected in images of "silted harbor" and "derelict works"; the contrast of the jobless and brutalized poor with the pleasure-seeking rich "constellated at reserved tables," "Supplied with feelings by an efficient band," guilt-ridden, and subject to "immeasurable neurotic dread" and death-wish; the obscure, vicious struggle between secret agent and secret police; the brooding threat of international distrust:

> In the nightmare of the dark
> All the dogs of Europe bark,
> And the living nations wait,
> Each sequestered in its hate.

And he proclaimed the urgent need for renovation, promising a 'tomorrow" that would bring after the struggle,

> the poets exploding like bombs
> The walks by the lake, the winter of perfect communion;
> To-morrow the bicycle races
> Through the suburbs on summer evenings.

Yet the utopian note was rarely sounded with much conviction, and his state of mind was much too changing and uncertain to be reliably partisan. Feelings of guilt, battle, and doom were frequent in his poetry, but who is guilty and doomed was a question. The guilty ones might be the bourgeoisie as a class, England, Western society, or all mankind. A battle was coming, but who the enemy was, or how "they" differed from "us," or indeed who "we" were, remained clouded. Nevertheless, there was the anxious thought that one ought to be joining the fight; a characteristic poem of 1932 was entitled "Which Side Am I Supposed to Be On." Half-parody, unsure and shifting in tone and attitude, the poem is a speech to troops before battle. But one does not know what to make of the speaker, or what his "side" stands for, or which "side" to prefer, or whether in fact each side is guilty, each having vitiated the other.

Still another source of complexity and sometimes confusion is that Auden swings between sociological and psychological modes of analysis, and that, exactly reversing usual leftist doctrine, he is likely to think that psychological ills are primary, political and social wrongs being merely derived from them. The process of diagnosis and healing, with which he was always so much concerned, must thus start not with social institutions but with the human heart. Some of his poems are chiefly psychological analyses or exempla, such as the ballad of Miss Edith Gee, and in many others the point of view is clearly, often reductively that of psychoanalytic lore. He makes a deliberate and knowing use of dream-like imagery:

> Though in the night
> Pursued by eaters
> They clutch at gaiters
> That straddle and deny
> Escape that way.

And in a great many poems he mingles psychological and sociological references in a way that especially characterizes him and can be both illuminating and hard to follow, involving as it does a long mental leap. The last line of "Petition" is one instance, where he prays for "New styles of architecture, a change of heart"; but a more typical, because more obscure, example is the reference to the "father" (here perhaps the conscience or superego) in the poem beginning, "Now from my window-sill I watch the night":

> But deaf to prophecy or China's drum
> The blood moves strangely in its moving home,
> Diverges, loops to travel further
> Than the long still shadow of the father,
> Though to the valley of regret it come.

In a sense, however, Auden's analysis is neither sociological nor psychological, nor simply a mixture of both, for from the start he was primarily a moralist. His application of sociological and psychoanalytic lore goes with a semiscientific or technical vocabulary but is without genuine scientific detachment. The chief importance of these modes of thought for him is that they provide criteria of the "good." (The "clinically detached" Auden is, at least on the evidence of his poetry, a myth.) The movement of his mind as he reflects upon the phenomenon of Hitler is typical. Hitler may be explained sociologically through German cultural history, or psychoanalytically through Jungian concepts

(Hitler lived briefly in Linz as a child), but Auden sets both aside in favor of copybook morality:

> Accurate scholarship can
> Unearth the whole offence
> From Luther until now
> That has driven a culture mad,
> Find what occurred at Linz,
> What huge imago made
> A psychopathic god:
> I and the public know
> What all schoolchildren learn,
> Those to whom evil is done
> Do evil in return.

This characteristic mixture of moral concern with sociology and psychoanalysis comes especially to focus in the theme of love. The idea of "love" fascinates Auden, and the question is whether or in what sense "love" is possible and, if possible, a good thing. Romantic love is not, he feels; however tender it may be, it is an illusion:

> What right have I to swear
> Even at one A.M.
> To love you till I die?

And in the ebullient ballad that begins "As I walked out one evening," he parodies such vows:

> I'll love you till the ocean
>   Is folded and hung up to dry
> And the seven stars go squawking
>   Like geese about the sky.

Moreover, romantic love is, he suspects, narcissistic, projective. And even if love is something less illuded and egoistic, it is still guilty, for it is or tends to be socially irresponsible: we

> From gardens where we feel secure
> Look up, and with a sigh endure
>   The tyrannies of love:
>
> And, gentle, do not care to know,
> Where Poland draws her Eastern bow,
>   What violence is done;

> Nor ask what doubtful act allows
> Our freedom in this English house,
> Our picnics in the sun.

And even if it were not irresponsible, love—or a love affair—is doomed, for its context is a society rushing toward catastrophe. And perhaps just as well, Auden feels, for "love" must become a wider social bond or brotherhood: "You shall love your crooked neighbour / With your crooked heart."

Auden's style in the thirties was a considerable creative achievement. He approached poetry with abilities and assumptions that must have made the writing of it easier for him than for most modern poets, and these may help account for his large productivity. For one thing, he had a mockingbird's ability to pick up other styles. He could sound like Yeats, Anglo-Saxon verse, Henry James, Byron, Restoration court lyrics, Rilke, or Emily Dickinson, among others, and he wrote effective ballads. A particular style was a problem to be mastered, and once mastered, a permanent part of his repertoire. He had a very skilled ear and a strong interest in versification, and throughout the thirties, as later, he was reaching out to experiment with new, sometimes quite intricate forms. As Isherwood says,

> You could say to him: "Please write me a double ballade on the virtues of a certain brand of toothpaste, which also contains at least ten anagrams on the names of well-known politicians, and of which the refrain is as follows . . ." Within twenty-four hours, your ballade would be ready—and it would be good.

In many of Auden's poems the formal challenge must have been the chief conscious motive for writing. He had much pleasure in the lighter sorts of poetry. He wrote songs, such as the lovely "Look, Stranger, on this island now," or "May with its light behaving." Many poems were comic verse, such as the "Letter to Lord Byron," and many passages in the plays, especially in *The Dog Beneath the Skin*, were music-hall entertainment or slaphappy doggerel. This experimental, blithe, problem-solving, versifying, craftsman's approach to poetry would naturally have tended to free him from the psychological inhibitions of poets frozen in awe before their own ambition or self-imposed responsibility. Of all modern poets Auden may be said to have

most taken to heart Goethe's (or his stage manager's) advice in
the "Prelude in the Theater" of *Faust:*

> Was hilft es viel von Stimmung reden?
> Dem Zaudernden erscheint sie nie.
> Gebt Ihr Euch einmal für Poeten,
> So kommandiert die Poesie.

("What good is it to talk a lot of mood? If you hesitate, it won't
come. If you claim to be a poet, command poetry.") Moreover,
much as with Wallace Stevens, Auden's impersonal and generalizing habit of mind undoubtedly meant that he was less likely
than many writers to be at a loss for a subject; anything could
lead to a generalization, or rather set off the collision and rico-
chet of general points of view in which so much of his poetry
consists.

In the thirties he exploited an idiom that made for velocity,
compression, ambiguity, wit, and concrete impact. Among the
elements of this were, in syntax, ellipsis (especially of articles,
demonstrative pronouns, conjunctions, and prepositions), peculiar and ungrammatical constructions, and inversions; in diction, archaic words, technical words, personified abstractions,
periphrasis, puns, and a characteristic, un-English use of the
definite article, either for emphasis or for an air of detachment,
generalization, and knowingness:

> To lie flat on the back with the knees flexed
> And sunshine on the soft receptive belly,
> Or face down, the insolent spine relaxed.

The wit was very much a matter of the incongruous or unexpected—for example, on music:

> Only your notes are pure contraption,
> Only your song is an absolute gift.

As for concrete impact, his discursive and generalizing methods
made it unusual for him to describe objects, scenes, or actions at
length. But he used allegorical metaphors, so to speak: extended
metaphors that give the suggestion of a "plot," such as the quest
or the detective novel. Or he made use of his skilled reporter's
or notetaker's eye for the significant detail. He could agglom-

erate such details *en masse* to serve an argument, or could even argue by means of them; as in film technique, he replaced generalization with concrete instances. He often presented the concrete instance through synecdoche, writing with an extreme compression in which the general situation is evoked through concrete fact and the fact itself through only one of its elements. If all this resulted in poems that often seemed inorganic and contrived, the contrivance and improvisation were quite brilliant.

To illustrate this style briefly is impossible, simply because it is too variously resourceful and changing. But two passages may be cited to show at least some of the possibilities. The first is a chorus from *Paid on Both Sides* (1930), in which one notices the ellipsis, the influence of Anglo-Saxon (and also of Hopkins) in diction and versification, the allusive concreteness and synecdoche (for example, the phrase "the legs sucked under" evoking a drowning), the speed, and the generalizing habit of mind. Like some other of Auden's best passages (notably the elegy on Yeats), the poem is a modernization of a familiar convention (in this case the Greek tragic chorus) and gains its effect through the combination of nimble intellection with direct emotion:

> Can speak of trouble, pressure on men
> Born all the time, brought forward into light
> For warm dark moan.
> Though heart fears all heart cries for, rebuffs with mortal beat
> Skyfall, the legs sucked under, adder's bite.
> That prize held out of reach
> Guides the unwilling tread,
> The asking breath,
> Till on attended bed
> Or in untracked dishonour comes to each
> His natural death.

The second passage, the conclusion to "Consider this and in our time," illustrates among other things the extent to which Auden's style, accommodating diverse points of view through ambiguity (the word "ruined") or rapid shift, was the expression of uncertainty and self-conflict. Here the doom predicted is that of the bourgeoisie riddled with selfishness and irresponsibly seeking private happiness. Auden cannot, however, contemplate this with a simple emotion—for example, the fear of the rentier or the righteous joy of the revolutionary—and so in this prophecy of doom there is a mixture of threat, fellow-feeling, derision, condemnation, understanding, and malice. He combines the tone of a biblical prophet warning the people with that of a bright schoolboy gibing, and yet also feels elegiac or at least tender at the inevitability of human defeat.

> Seekers after happiness, all who follow
> The convolutions of your simple wish,
> It is later than you think; nearer that day
> Far other than that distant afternoon
> Amid rustle of frocks and stamping feet
> They gave the prizes to the ruined boys.
> You cannot be away, then, no
> Not though you pack to leave within an hour,
> Escaping humming down arterial roads.

Auden's work of the thirties makes a striking impression. Especially in view of the original contribution he was making, the mere amount of publication is remarkable: nine volumes in ten years. The charges that were later so often leveled against him —carelessness, mannerism, obscurity, cliquishness, muddled thinking, frivolity, glibness, lack of integration, and a habit of amputating his own past, so that, the argument goes, he achieved virtuosity in different roles or styles rather than cumulative growth—up to 1940 seem either less warranted or less important. He created styles that were completely his own and, in doing so, widened the possibilities of poetry for other writers. His penchant for comic entertainment and for song, his ability to write at times with open perspicuity, his informality and imperfection were healthy at the time. He was wholly a poet of the contemporary situation, not only by topical allusion and reportage but also because he explored and expressed the feelings of vague guilt, anxiety, isolation, and fear that so many shared. He was never without something to say. However pessimistic the poems might be, the general spirit of his poetry was adventurous, experimental, buoyant, full of intellectual gusto. He was the most significant new voice of the thirties, and because he was so young he seemed boundlessly promising. Yet Auden's poetry changed in ways that disappointed most of his readers.

LONG POEMS OF THE 1940s

The general direction of Auden's development throughout the thirties was toward a clarification of attitude and a more accessible style. These tendencies reached something of a climax in four long poems published in the 1940s: "New Year Letter" (1941), "The Sea and the Mirror" (1944), "For the Time Being" (1944), and *The Age of Anxiety* (1947). The "New Year Letter" is a didactic, argumentative poem in tetrameter couplets. It roams through politics, aesthetics, ethics, and religion, with many learned allusions but with a witty touch. It is not all argument, for it includes personal recollections and tributes to friends and poetic masters (Blake, Rimbaud, Dryden, Catullus, Baudelaire, Rilke, and others) and allusive sketches of the contemporary world drifting toward war.

"The Sea and the Mirror" is described in a subtitle as "A Commentary on Shakespeare's *The Tempest*." It presents the characters of *The Tempest* on the boat sailing from Prospero's island to Milan. Each speaks in a different verse form, some quite complex (villanelle, sestina, sapphic, terza rima, elegiac), so that the work is among other things a display of technique. The last half is a prose speech of Caliban, who has been left behind on the island, the lump of shocking reality Prospero's art could not transform. With a typical Audenesque irony Caliban addresses the audience in a style that alludes to the intricate, artificial style of Henry James in his later period. "The Sea and the Mirror" cannot be summed up, but it is at least not false to say that the theme is the relation of art and the imagination (the mirror) to reality (the sea). At the end of his speech Caliban turns to the general dilemma of the artist in relation to divine and ultimate truth. The artist cannot mirror both the divine and the human estrangement from it. The more faithfully he represents the human condition, the further he is from indicating the divine from which it departs. And the more his mirror of their plight satisfies the aesthetic needs of his audience, the less it moves the will to action, the necessary religious action of contrition and surrender. Life itself, Caliban concludes, is a stage performance, an acting of roles in which we display "our personalities and our looks," but the performance is always bungled, and so, when at the end the embarrassed actors stand on stage with no applause, realizing that even the "huge stuffed bird of happiness" has fooled no one, they see themselves as they are: "swaying out on the ultimate wind whipped cornice that overhangs the unabiding void." And they hear for the first time not the words of their performance but the "real Word which is our only *raison d'être.*"

"For the Time Being" was written as a Christmas oratorio and, in an abridgment, was later set to music and performed. It is a retelling in oratorio form of the Nativity story. As in "The Sea and the Mirror," different speakers adopt different meters. The philosophical theme, which may be characterized as the historical and religious meaning of the Incarnation, is put forward especially in a long prose discourse by Simeon. To this story and theme the poem brings a point of view strongly influenced by Kierkegaard. Thus the opening section shows the despair of the ancient world previous to the coming of Christ, and the speech of Simeon reiterates that total despair must be suffered before the Incarnation can occur.

The Age of Anxiety, subtitled "a Baroque Eclogue," presents four characters typical of the lonely crowd of the modern world. They meet in a bar, talk, and the drunken evening ends in the apartment of one of them, Rosetta. After more talk, the older persons leave and the young Emble disappoints Rosetta by passing out. Using the alliterative stressed line of Langland's *Piers Plowman,* the poem explores the spiritual disease of these characters and the society they represent, purposeless, anxiety-ridden, haunted by memories or fantasies of innocence and what Auden would call the Good Place, on a quest of which they are only vaguely aware.

By 1940, then, Auden had committed himself to Christianity, becoming a member of the Anglican communion. His poems of the early 1940s embody this point of view, in which much of the former tension and self-conflict of his poetry has been left behind. In these poems he was trying to find an effective form for an extended poetic statement, a problem with which almost every modern poet has struggled. In the "New Year Letter" Auden's solution was a traditional one, the discursive poem in a didactic or meditative vein. "The Sea and the Mirror" and "For the Time Being" had the advantage that, though they are not themselves narratives, they are at least commentaries on known

stories. Moreover, different speakers permit different points of
view, so that to the play of ideas a more human and dramatic
interest is added. This tendency was carried further in *The Age
of Anxiety*, which has characters interacting and a plot of sorts,
though it still has considerably less narrative and dramatic (as
well as essayistic) interest than, say, Samuel Johnson's *Rasselas*.
The formal problem in these poems was further complicated by
the habitual split in Auden's thinking between "poetry" and
"truth," and by his tendency to think of poetry as entertainment
or "play." This meant that the Nativity story, for example, must
be felt with reverence, interpreted with theological or philosophical depth, and yet somehow be made amusing. In all these
poems discourse must be enlivened by wit, technical stunts,
comic songs, or whatever. The trouble is that the light touch, at
least Auden's, seems not suited to the subject matter. A dry passage can be relieved by a chuckling comparison, for example of
our lives to attractive wives:

> We cannot, then, will Heaven where
> Is perfect freedom; our wills there
> Must lose the will to operate.
> But will is free not to negate
> Itself in Hell; we're free to will
> Ourselves up Purgatory still,
> Consenting parties to our lives,
> To love them like attractive wives
> Whom we adore but do not trust.

But in the long run the cost is too great. Auden's own sincerity
or seriousness is not in question. The point is only that his methods inhibit a deeper emotional response, which is another way
of saying that the subject matter is not fully grasped in the
poems. Recollection of Eliot's *Four Quartets* is inevitable, and one
is reminded of the value of Wordsworth's remark that poetry is
"truth carried alive into the heart by passion."

POETRY AS CONVERSATION

Before turning directly to the later volumes of lyrics, I should
say something about one of the most striking features of Auden's

style from almost the start of his career, namely his use of the conversational. It developed early as one possible mode of his poetry, increasingly took over, and, except in dramatic or quasi-dramatic works, found its most extended employment in the "New Year Letter." The attractions of this style to Auden are obvious. By lessening the distance between "poetry" and ordinary speech, it widens the range of possible subject matters. It permits a characterization of the speaker through his style of expression, and thus gives play to Auden's mimetic talent, as for example in the words of a worried bureaucrat who had

> Issued all the orders expedient
> In this kind of case:
> Most, as was expected, were obedient,
> Though there were murmurs, of course.

Or when, as was more frequently and increasingly true, the speaker was Auden himself, it made his own personality (or the version of it put forward by his poetry) a source of interest. Not that Auden was a self-expressive writer; on the contrary, he was relatively impersonal, taking his subject matter from without and treating it in a generalizing way. But a speaking voice brings us into contact with a speaker. Finally, since a conversational stance, like any other, controls the expectations of readers, it provided Auden with a means by which he could convert his limitations into advantages, something every writer must do. From a poetry that is talk one cannot expect prophetically sustained emotion, or perfected phrasing, or tight integration. The mode excuses impatience, imprecision, doubtful taste, long-windedness. As Auden put it,

> I relapse into my crimes,
> Time and again have slubbered through
> With slip and slapdash what I do.

But "slip and slapdash" cannot be felt as crimes when the style is anyway so pleasantly gabby. They even play a positive role in reminding us that we are, after all, not in the church of poetry but at the kitchen table, enjoying the conversation of this amply ideaed, unpredictable, engaging speaker.

Though they shade into one another, Auden had in fact several conversational styles adapted from different sources. One continuing influence was Yeats, on whom many an occasional, meditative poem in the *Collected Shorter Poems* is modeled. This note was struck already in Auden's first volume (1928), for example in "From the very first coming down":

> to-day
> I, crouching behind a sheep-pen, heard
> Travel across a sudden bird,
> Cry out against the storm, and found
> The year's arc a completed round.

But Yeatsian talk is incredibly exacting, since every seemingly casual word is right and the flow is marvelously energetic, limpid, and sustained. Neither could Auden be quite at ease with the nobility of this speech, and he found other, probably more congenial models in such different figures as Byron, Frost, and Marianne Moore. Byron in *Don Juan,* Auden remarked, is "the master of the airy manner," and his "Letter to Lord Byron" (1937) catches this perfectly:

> Art, if it doesn't start there, at least ends,
>   Whether aesthetics like the thought or not,
> In an attempt to entertain our friends;
> And our first problem is to realise what
> Peculiar friends the modern artist's got.

Auden's usual conversational style, however, is less directly borrowed and more difficult to characterize. From the beginning of his career it was a flat, open, unemotional, prosaic talk, though this could easily gather into eloquence or lower itself for a joke. In his later verse he excelled at the completely casual observation—

> And it is curious how often in steep places
>   You meet someone short who frowns,
> A type you catch beheading daisies with a stick;

the aphorism—

> Thousands have lived without love, not one without water;

and personal chat—

> I should like to become, if possible,
> a minor atlantic Goethe,

> with his passion for weather and stones but without his silliness
> re the Cross: at times a bore, but. . . .

A poem that well illustrates his conversational technique is the familiar "Musée des Beaux Arts." Taking the concluding lines, we may notice again the prose word order, the colloquial phrasing ("must have seen something amazing," "had somewhere to get to"), the deliberate use of almost empty phrases ("for instance," "quite leisurely") to produce uncompressed and dawdling lines, and the skillfully exploited versification. The lines can be scanned, but the prosody is quite irregular (stress meter with a varying number of stresses per line, though they are usually six), so that the norm hardly establishes itself to the ear. At moments Auden allows prose rhythms to take over almost completely: "But for him it was not an important failure"; "Had somewhere to get to and sailed calmly on." The rhymes are arranged in no pattern and are not emphasized. The integrity of the line is broken by run-ons, strong caesuras, and caesuras in unusually late or early positions in the line. This is, in other words, a poetry that preserves meter and rhyme—it is not free verse—and yet in reading it, especially in hearing it read, the sense of metrical form recedes and the prose meaning takes over:

> In Brueghel's *Icarus*, for instance: how everything turns away
> Quite leisurely from the disater; the ploughman may
> Have heard the splash, the forsaken cry,
> But for him it was not an important failure; the sun shone
> As it had to on the white legs disappearing into the green
> Water; and the expensive delicate ship that must have seen
> Something amazing, a boy falling out of the sky,
> Had somewhere to get to and sailed calmly on.

THE LATER AUDEN

Auden's work after the late 1940s included a great many essays and reviews, opera libretti, and six volumes of poems. Only the poems concern us. In some respects they continue tendencies already dwelt on: they are colloquial, meditative, and generalizing in manner; they pursue technical problems, the most important new development being syllabic verse; the light touch is almost omnipresent. Yet when compared with Auden's poetry of the early thirties, the style has changed completely. The velocity and compression, the sudden shifts of tone or direction, the ambiguity, ellipsis, and wrenched grammar, the brilliance and the difficulty have vanished and been replaced by a way of speaking that is loose, leisurely, fully articulated, and perspicuous. It is a style without depths, so to speak. Everything that is to be understood is said. The poet who wrote "Consider this and in our time" or "Which Side Am I Supposed to Be On" now writes like this "In Praise of Limestone":

> If it form the one landscape that we, the inconstant ones,
>   Are consistently homesick for, this is chiefly
> Because it dissolves in water. Mark these rounded slopes
>   With their surface fragrance of thyme and, beneath,
> A secret system of caves and conduits; hear the springs
>   That spurt out everywhere with a chuckle,
> Each filling a private pool for its fish.

Or like this in "Whitsunday in Kirchstetten":

> *Komm Schöpfer Geist* I bellow as Herr Beer
>   picks up our slim offerings and Pfarrer Lustkandl
>   quietly gets on with the Sacrifice
> as Rome does it: outside car-worshippers enact
>   the ritual exodus from Vienna
>   their successful cult demands.

Who—this perhaps was the first impression of most readers—would have thought Auden could be dull?

But in fact this work is not dull. It is just that as one goes from the early to the later poetry, radical readjustments of expectations and reading habits must be made, and in particular one must read more rapidly. These poems are written for cultivated people to enjoy without much effort. Approached that way, they are continually amusing and interesting. They show no loss of mastery. In fact, in control over the style and in appropriateness of style to content, the mastery is greater than ever before. But the style is much less ambitious. It is also less impersonal. The point is not simply that the persona, the graceful and charming voice, counts for more in the total effect. Increasingly, Auden refers more openly to himself. To some extent, his style has simply moved with the times, he adopting in his own way the suburban blandness of much poetry in the fifties and the confessional mode of the sixties. But the change in style was accompanied by a refocusing of attitudes.

At first impression it might seem that the political concern of the thirties has vanished. The poet who now jocularly identifies himself as an Arcadian rather than a Utopian, or who calls neither for a change of society nor for a change of heart, but for a defense of the modes and declensions of grammar—"Guard, Civility, with guns / Your modes and your declensions"—is by the standards of the thirties trivial, if not something worse. Yet in another sense political feelings are more than ever present in his poetry, which catches a mood of the fifties and sixties just as much as earlier it did that of the thirties. One may begin by noting the sense of personal helplessness. As long ago as 1939, faced with the political realities of those days, Auden had asserted that "poetry makes nothing happen." More exactly, poetry can redirect the way we feel about events, but not the events themselves. He would now add, it seems, that nothing, in the sense of betterment, ever happens anyway. The ills and crimes of the world go on just the same from age to age, and though there are many revolutions, there is no reform. For a poet this means, among other things, that different ages can coalesce in imagination, and this technique, which Auden had always exploited, becomes more central now. "The Shield of Achilles," for example, pictures simultaneously the Homeric, Imperial Roman, and contemporary worlds, all equally brutal. The poet looks on these and similar scenes with an emotional detachment and a wide, impartial gaze (and these are also not new in his work), noticing in one view the diverse goings-on of human life and the unchanging natural environment:

> That is the way things happen; for ever and ever
> Plum-blossom falls on the dead, the roar of the waterfall covers
> The cries of the whipped and the sighs of the lovers.

As an individual he is utterly vulnerable before the violence of history, but he now accepts this with humorous resignation: he may be blown to nothing "at the nod/ of some jittery commander," or his "bailiwick" may be invaded in a "conventional" war:

> I shall of course
> assume the submissive posture:
> but men are not wolves and it probably
> won't help.

What is missing is the feeling that he or "we" ought to be doing something about it, ought at least to be taking sides. There is, in fact, no side to take. The poetry is the record of a civilized intelligence that finds itself in a crass, overwhelming, and nonsensical society. A recurrent symbol is the Roman empire in a late period, with its poets and cultivated minds trying as best they could to keep up civilized tradition, scattered and "ironic points of light" amid the dark, as Auden had put it in 1939. Amid windy Caesars, neanderthal generals, bored and overworked civil servants, press agents, ideologues, and barbarians, what can such a person do? He can *cultiver son jardin,* which means, for Auden, first of all the *jardin* of the English language and of literary tradition. The more difficult the form, the more fantastic and *recherché* the vocabulary, the more the poet is asserting, with a kind of heroic foppery, his values of civilized wit and sanity. When the "gutteral tribes" crossed the Great River, the Epigoni did not break out into "sonorous clap-trap about death" but rather into "preposterous mechanical tricks" of style—"Epanaleptics, rhopalics, anacyclic acrostics":

> To their lasting honour, the stuff they wrote
> Can safely be spanked in a scholar's foot-note,
> Called shallow by a mechanised generation to whom
> Haphazard oracular grunts are profound wisdom.

And the more that direct, "affirmative speech" is captured and perverted by generalissimos and journalists, the more the poet must speak in a minor voice, the "civil style" that is wry, sottovoce, ironic, and monochrome. Auden uses this style to puncture the "Makers of History":

> these mere commanders,
> Like boys in pimple-time, like girls at awkward ages,
> What did they do but wish.

And he takes much pleasure in the reflection that the name of Tamburlaine, which was once

> A synonym in a whole armful
> Of languages for what is harmful,

now survives only in the minor intellectual pleasures of a cultivated few:

> Eg, as a crossword anagram:
> 11 Down—A NUBILE TRAM.

Along with this interest in deflating the pompous, pretentious, and falsely imposing goes a quiet appreciativeness of the minor decencies of cultivated living, a tendency that reaches its climax in the series of poems called "Thanksgiving for a Habitat" in *About the House.* He praises the bath where he can "present a Lieder Abend / to a captive audience of his toes"; and he is grateful for a well-cooked dinner:

> surely those in whose creed
> God is edible may call a fine
> omelette a Christian deed.

There should be not more than six persons at a table (with allusions to the Last Supper and to King Arthur's Round Table):

> six lenient semble sieges,
> none of them perilous,
>
> is now a Perfect
> Social Number;

and "After dinner, music or gossip." It is not surprising that the volume contains many *haiku* and also asserts that

> Even a limerick
> ought to be something a man of
> honor, awaiting death from cancer or a firing squad,
> could read without contempt.

I have been trying to give the impression of a retreat, for perfectly understandable reasons, into the minor and unpretentious in subject matter and style. This poetry disarms criticism or else puts it on the defensive, helpless before charm and unwilling to seem to prefer "haphazard oracular grunts." And yet there remains the fatal fact that, though it is intelligent, amusing, graceful, and gracious, this work is not very exciting. To the extent that Auden's poetry survives, it will be the poetry of the thirties, with much of the later verse noticed primarily "in a scholar's foot-note."

8

THE ENGLISH ROMANTIC REVIVAL,
1934–1945

E
VEN during its hegemony, Modernist style seldom possessed the undivided allegiance of the heart. However much they were excited by it, most poets could not wholly accept it. The reasons were partly, as I have stressed, that this style imposed serious limitations on both the powers and the potential readership of poetry. Using the methods of *The Waste Land* or of Yeats's densely symbolic poems, one could not discourse, converse, or even think logically, and one could not hope for a large audience. Moreover, the achievements of Modernism in the 1920s were too brilliant to be excelled in their own mode. To make an impression one had to write differently. For these reasons English poets in the thirties had already begun to modify and retreat from the high Modernist style, and this development continued in the 1940s.

The deepest, most pervasive reason for the widespread uneasiness with Modernism, however, was that it cut poetry off from the Romantic traditions of the nineteenth century. These were deeply loved. Shelley, Keats, Wordsworth, Tennyson, and Hardy (and Whitman in the case of American poets) had been cherished in adolescence. They had formed your idea of poetry when you first started to write. They still afforded a warmer emotional release than was available in Modernist or Metaphysical poetry, and most poets wanted this. Modernist critical demolitions might shake belief in the Romantic mode, but nothing could shake affection for it. After the hiatus created by high Modernism, the history of modern poetry is in part the story of a reconnecting to Romantic roots. At first this impulse was half-suppressed and embarrassed, but by the 1940s in England it had become rebellious, and it became similarly open in the United States during the 1950s.

The interplay in twentieth-century poetry of the Modernist mode with Romantic tradition is a subject for many books. Scholars have plausibly argued that Modernism develops out of Victorian poetry as an extension of it. Others have traced the premises of Modernist poetics to the Romantic period. It is easy to show that many modern poets from Eliot to the present are Romantic in some ways. In Wallace Stevens one can cite the play of his mind upon the central Romantic concept of the "imagination." Stevens, Robert Penn Warren, Theodore Roethke, and a great many other modern poets took up the Wordsworthian, Emersonian theme of the solitary mind seeking relation with the cosmos. Romantic convention represents the cosmos in nature or landscape, and both the meditation on landscape in A. W. Ammons and the parody of this stock situation in John Ashbery extend the Romantic poetic tradition. James Wright, Robert Bly, Gary Snyder, and W. S. Merwin are Romantic primitivists, as we shall see in Chapter 23, and even Charles Olson, though a follower of Pound and Williams, sounds more like Thoreau in many of the Maximus poems; the countryside about Gloucester, Massachusetts, is Olson's Walden. Allen Ginsberg caught his visions and mysticism more from Blake and Whitman than from William Burroughs and Jack Kerouac, and Robert Duncan has committed himself to Romantic emotional spontaneity and Romantic hermeticism.

A "Neo-Romantic" style developed in England during the 1930s and was briefly ascendant during the 1940s. Dylan Thomas was its major poet. "Romantic" was the word used at the time, and implied that the Neo-Romantics were challenging the high Modernism of the 1920s and the discursive, intellectual styles of the 1930s. Thomas was typical in this respect. He had the mystical intuitions, emotional intensity, personal utterance, and natural imagery of a poet in the Romantic tradition. But in the same poems he was also a poet of Metaphysical wit and Symbolist technique. Other poets of the Romantic revival similarly absorbed Modernist influences while also rebelling against them. Vernon Watkins was a disciple of Yeats. George Barker sounded at times like Auden. If we accepted Roland Barthes' description of Modernist poetry as an "explosion" of autonomous words, the paradigmatic English Modernist would be David Gascoyne in his youthful Surrealist phase. In short, the interrelations between Neo-Romantic style and other tendencies of the age defy brief or simple description. No minor part of the problem is that Neo-Romantic styles varied from poet to poet as much as Modernist styles did.

Yet the poets now to be discussed conceived that their work opposed that of the dominant groups. By 1940 they considered themselves the wave of the future. When Sidney Keyes, then twenty years old, introduced *Eight Oxford Poets* (1942), a collection of poems by himself and some friends, he explained that "we have, on the whole, little sympathy with the Audenian school of poetry." We are all, he said, "*Romantic* writers," though he modestly added, "by that I mean little more than that our greatest fault is a tendency to floridity." Early in the 1940s the poets of the so-called New Apocalypse, to cite one more instance, captured attention by asserting that their "Romantic" generation was succeeding Auden, Spender, and MacNeice. The vogue of Dylan Thomas, the spread of "Romantic" self-identifications, and the "florid" writing these encouraged in turn evoked in reaction the poets who in the 1950s made up the anti-Romantic "Movement." Whatever the ambiguities of the term "Romantic," in other words, English poets were divided between those who subscribed to it and those who thought it a stigma. The former group are discussed in this chapter, and we shall find, after all, that the term applies.

To see why it could apply, we may point to some of the obvious contrasts between Dylan Thomas, on the one hand, and Auden and Empson, on the other, since Auden and Empson were the leading poets in the main new tendencies of the 1930s. What differentiates Thomas from Auden and Empson describes, in the ensemble, a poetry based on essential Romantic values—the self and nature as opposed to society, emotional intensity, sacred awe—and at this level of generalization Thomas represents most of the other poets this chapter considers. Taught by Eliot, the "Audenian school"—Pylon Poets, they were sometimes called—dwelt on the industrial waste land. For those who were Communists or Socialists, polluting factories and slums imaged the capitalist economy. As Socialists they might imagine more hopeful industrial views in the future. In writing of the present they focused on revolutions, counterrevolutions, secret police, dictators, and the growing probability of total war. Neither the industrial images nor the political themes appear in Thomas, whose subject was Wordsworth's, the human psyche finding the divine in nature. His imagination dwelt among myths and archetypes—light, dark, ocean, blood, seed, grain, harvest—as though he were perusing Frazer, Jung, and Lawrence rather than the newspapers. Empson and Auden discoursed, argued, or sometimes merely chatted, but Thomas prophesied. They were rational and intellectual. Thomas recaptured the emotions of childhood, or entered in imagination into primitive forms of life, or identified with bodily and sexual urges. The sense of the sacred, which Empson debunked and Auden was reticent about in the 1930s, emanated strongly from Thomas' poetry. His rhetoric conveyed, though with desperate ambiguity, an affirmative, mystical insight. As compared with Auden and Empson, his language was more melodious, sensuous, and irrational, with vaguer meanings.

Among Romantic poets in the 1930s there were significant generational and period differences. Ruth Pitter, Roy Campbell, and William Plomer were born around the turn of the century. These older poets did not revive Romantic styles but continued them, for when they were growing up the Romantic tradition had not yet been broken by the Modernists. Ruth Pitter resembled Alice Meynell and other late Victorian poets of devoutly Christian faith who returned to the English poets of the early seventeenth century. Campbell's bold rhetoric and rollicking satire were Byronic, but his best work derived from French poets of the nineteenth century, such as Baudelaire and Rimbaud.

Poets born between 1908 and 1916 represent an altogether different phase, for these poets—Kathleen Raine, Vernon Watkins, Anne Ridler, George Barker, Dylan Thomas, and David Gascoyne—encountered the high Modernist poetry of the 1920s during their adolescence. When they began to write, the literary milieu was not, on the whole, sympathetic to Romantic values; to the extent that they pursued such values, they opposed contemporary tendencies. But their reaction nourished itself, as I have noted, on modern as well as Romantic sources. If they read devotedly in Blake, Wordsworth, Hölderlin, Baudelaire, and Whitman, they were also disciples of Yeats, Rilke, and Lawrence. With the Second World War the poetry of the Romantic revival again changed. One sees this in Thomas, Gascoyne, and Barker as well as in younger poets—John Heath-Stubbs, Keith Douglas, and Sidney Keyes—who had been born between 1918 and 1922 and were just beginning to publish. Poets of other schools, such as Auden, underwent a similar transition during the war years, and the same general alteration of taste and feeling accounts for the suddenly more favorable reception of Kathleen Raine and Lawrence Durrell, who had earlier been publishing without much recognition. That Vernon Watkins brought out his first book in 1941 had nothing to do with the war—he did it because his friend Dylan Thomas encouraged him—but he found an audience he would not have had a few years before. The mood of the late thirties and early war years was complex, as we shall see, but in brief the war evoked a more somber, compassionate, and religious state of mind. But though the war was the main cause of the change in poetic style and emotion, literary influences were also important, as they always are for poets. The most significant of these was Eliot's *Four Quartets*, which, though begun several years before the war, expressed feelings that were widely shared in 1940 and 1941.

THE BEGINNINGS OF THE ROMANTIC REVIVAL: DYLAN THOMAS, DAVID GASCOYNE, AND GEORGE BARKER

For readers in the 1930s the Romantic Revival originated independently with two young writers of genius, Dylan Thomas and David Gascoyne. They emerged at roughly the same time: Thomas in 1934 with his first collection, *18 Poems*, and Gascoyne in 1936 with his Surrealist volume, *Man's Life Is This Meat*.

Dylan Thomas (1914–53) grew up in Wales. Neurotically self-absorbed, he exploited, like Hart Crane, his fragile health in childhood and youth to resist the demands of the outer world. Amid his rich, inward preoccupations, parental hopes and school (as, later, jobs, contracts, politics, and the like) could hardly make themselves heard. Yet in his own sphere of words and poetry he labored with ardor and self-discipline. He was fascinated with words, with their sensory qualities, meanings, and connotations. *Finnegans Wake*, he later said, is the greatest work of our time, and though there is no evidence that he had read much of the book, he imitated the hynotic incantation and associative density of Joyce's language. Hopkins' poems were "obscure" to him, but Thomas loved them for the lavish, patterned use of sound he caught from them. Hopkins' sprung rhythm extended his own rhythmic resources. The vivid imagery of nature in both Hopkins and Lawrence, whose collected poems Thomas read from cover to cover, impressed him greatly; both poets presented a nature charged with sacred being, and Lawrence especially provided Thomas with his vocabulary of archetypal images. He read Eliot and Auden, and though he rebelled against them, they also influenced his style, and he was led by Eliot's critical essays to read in Herbert Grierson's anthology of English poetry of the seventeenth century. He admired the complex metaphors and puns, and was moved also by Donne's pervasive sense of mortality. He was amazingly precocious. "And death shall have no dominion" was composed when he was eighteen, though some revisions were made three years later. Six months afterward he wrote "The force that through the green fuse drives the flower." In the next month came "Light breaks where no sun shines." Published in March 1934 in the *Listener*, this poem caused a stir in literary London, and the young Thomas received letters from Eliot, Spender, and Geoffrey Grigson, the editor of *New Verse*. By the time he was twenty-one, he had completed approximately half of his final *Collected Poems* (1952).

Henceforth his biography is sad reading. He drank excessively. Money was scarce, for he had no regular job, and what he obtained through short stories, reviewing, film scripts, poetry readings, and sponging slipped through his fingers. He had spectacular quarrels with his wife. His talent was deserting him;

at least, he found it increasingly difficult to compose, and months would pass with nothing to show for them. He died in New York of overdrinking at the age of thirty-nine. Reading poems over the BBC, Thomas had attracted a relatively wide audience in England. On his three American tours in 1950, 1952, and 1953 thousands of persons heard him read. His voice was bardic, and the effect of his own poetry, as he read it, was overwhelming. Moreover, his indecorous, drunken behavior satisfied adolescent ideals of rebellious genius. For superficial observers it also substantiated the pose of a randy, life-hungry, and life-affirming man that his creative work projected. He became a legend. And although his style had usually been difficult, he had written during and after the Second World War a number of accessible poems that appear in almost every anthology: "A Refusal to Mourn the Death, by Fire, of a Child in London," "Do Not Go Gentle into That Good Night," "Poem in October," and "Fern Hill." His radio play, *Under Milk Wood*, was also popular when it was posthumously published in 1954.

Because Thomas' style challenged the dominant tendencies of the 1930s, it appealed all the more. Not that readers were tired of Eliot, Auden, Empson, and Ransom. But while you rejoiced in the brilliant velleity, intellectual discourse, and sparkling, bitter, or Mandarin wit of these poets, you might still find yourself wistful for strong, direct emotion. No poet in the 1930s and 1940s, not even Spender, released emotion—moreover, affirmative emotion—in greater force and volume than Thomas. Technically the means to this included sweeping, unqualified assertion, traditionally rhetorical syntax with much repetition and apposition, lavish alliteration and assonance for emphasis, immensely energetic diction and rhythm, semantic vagueness, and a bardic or vatic pose. "And death shall have no dominion"; "The force that through the green fuse drives the flower/ Drives my green age"; "Light breaks where no sun shines." Such assertions may not completely satisfy the intellect as it sifts the texts to discover their exact meaning. But they are glorious. Beginning the poem with "And" strikes the keynote of ongoingness; the syntax enacts the quality the poem attributes to life. "Death" (the vague, emotionally loaded personification) "shall" (prophetic promise) "have no dominion," the emphasis enhanced by alliteration (*d*eath-*d*ominion) and assonance (n*o* d*o*minion). The interplay of Anglo-Saxon with Latin roots (death-dominion) is a traditional device of English eloquence. The line is biblical. "The force that through the green fuse drives the flower" telescopes metaphors. The green fuse or plant stem terminates in an explosion or flower (with a pun on fire). But "drives" implies resistance. On the gunnery or dynamite metaphor Thomas has mounted one of forcing a flower through a narrow tube, with other connotations also. His "green age" is analogous to the flower. That Thomas' metaphors have such complexities is a consideration to which I shall return. For the moment my point is the immense energy of the diction. It pictures a world of driving forces, resistances, and explosions. To its first readers "Light breaks where no sun shines" seemed magnificently spooky and cosmic. Thomas satisfied hungers for emotional force, boldness, and grandeur that are always present in readers of poetry, hungers that the dominant, intellectual modes of the 1930s did not much address.

Yet Thomas' poetry was also very much of its time. The literary world would hardly otherwise have proved receptive. The density of his poetic texture—more exactly, the ways in which it is dense—reflects the post-Eliot moment when Symbolism was amalgamated with the Metaphysical style of the seventeenth century. "Altarwise by owl-light," the first phrase of a sonnet sequence, illustrates Thomas' Symbolist verbal rites. The phrase is practically a poem itself, with densely interlaced sounds (alowl; by-wise-light) and connotations (owl-wise). A phrase from the "Author's Prologue" to Thomas' *Collected Poems*—"the moonshine/ Drinking Noah of the bay"—exemplifies his use of Metaphysical wit. The poet, Thomas, is Noah; his poems are his ark. In medieval drama Noah was traditionally drunk, as Thomas was much of the time, and the complex pun in "moonshine" refers to the homemade Appalachian liquor, the moonlight shining on the water, and the fantasies that moonshine (in both previous senses) produces.

Free verse was not much written in Thomas' time. Neither did poets then experiment with either Symbolist lapsed grammar or "Projective" grammatical transformations. In these respects Thomas followed the decorum of the period. His prosody was usually regular and traditional, like that of Auden and the Neo-Metaphysical or New Critical poets. With a few exceptions his syntax was correctly grammatical, though the grammar was often extremely complicated and elliptical. This suggested to readers of the time that his dense, concrete phrasing was rationally articulated and ought to be intelligible. Yet his earlier poems seemed impossible to understand in detail. Most readers caught the emotion and attitude, at least vaguely, but not much more. His predications seemed alogical and connectionless. The reader could not tell what, if any, actions or circumstances his poems referred to. Suggestions wafted like feathers from a torn pillow. In the poems Thomas wrote during and after the war, however, much of the difficulty vanished. "Poem in October," for example, tells the plain circumstances of a walk out of town on his birthday. The phrasing is accessible on first reading. The sensory, vivid imagery paints the Romantically pleasant landscape of nature; it is descriptive as well as connotative and symbolic. The nostalgia for childhood communicates itself easily, the life-affirming mood is sympathetic, and inevitably this dewy, teary, reverential poem became popular.

Thomas' poetry returns to the same large themes over and over. He asserts a Blakean-Wordsworthian-Whitmanian intuition of the unity and holiness of all existence. He wants to celebrate the life-process totally. But individuation, time, and death are involved in the process, and force him into ambivalence and paradox. If death is a return to the whole, it is a positive. If it is extinction, it is dreadful. Hence,

> Do not go gentle into that good night,
> Old age should burn and rave at close of day;
> Rage, rage against the dying of the light.

If "good night" is the phrase said at parting for sleep, the metaphor deprives death of terror. But "*that* good night" is final; hence the urgent imperative, "Do not go . . ." But "that *good* night" asserts that night is desirable, presumably as a return to the all. Thomas delighted to dwell on childhood because children have, he believed, no consciousness of being separate from the world. Or reaching further back before the tragic fall into individuation and separateness, he tried to reenter in imagination the being of an embryo, or even of the first germinal life before the embryo is formed. Taking death as an aspect of the ongoing process of life, he denied its ultimate reality. We return, he said, with the daisies. But neither mysticism nor rhetoric could overcome his mindfulness that, though life will go on, "we" will not be part of it. The famous lines just quoted reveal the fear of death that motivates Thomas' imaginary flights from individuation. "The dying of the light" does not suggest merely "close of day"; it is the end of the world. Literally speaking, of course, not the light but Thomas' father is dying; the light will return the next morning. But from the point of view of the individual person, the world ends with his death. "The dying of the light" expresses the solipsism Thomas wanted to deny but could not. Out of such tensions came the perhaps muddled, perhaps mystical lines and poems that sound like magnificent affirmation, though as we ponder them, we cannot say exactly what is affirmed.

Like Thomas, David Gascoyne (b. 1916) was amazingly precocious. The Surrealist poetry he published at the age of twenty was not the only manifestation of this school in England during the 1930s, but it was certainly the best English verse in this style. And though Thomas hotly denied that he was a Surrealist, many readers associated him with Gascoyne. In Thomas one reads, for example, "A million minds gave suck to such a bud / As forks my eye"; and in Gascoyne,

> The face of the precipice is black with lovers;
> The sun above them is a bag of nails; the spring's
> First rivers hide among their hair.

Thomas' lines were conceived as a web of Symbolist implications, while Gascoyne pursued Surrealist liberation of the unconscious. But we may easily forgive those readers for whom Gascoyne's *Short Survey of Surrealism* (1935) seemed to explain both poets. In Gascoyne's spiritual quest, however, Surrealism was only a brief episode.

By the age of sixteen Gascoyne had published a book of poems and completed a novel. He moved to Paris and lived there much of the time until the war, subsisting precariously on advances from publishers. His diaries from this period have been published, and give a fascinating picture of the expatriate, intellectual-artistic milieu in Paris in the late 1930s. He was acquainted with French poets, but most of his friends were painters, writers, and philosophers from England, Denmark, Russia, and the

United States. Their thoughts revolved about Existentialism, Freud, Surrealism, and Communism. Gascoyne's diaries also engage us intimately in the moving struggle of a young writer to develop his talent. He steeped himself in Rimbaud, Hölderlin, Dostoevsky, and other writers congenial to his Romantic, pessimistic *Weltanschauung.* He read contemporary poets, forming judgments of precocious independence and insight. He explored ideas in night-long conversations. Music and painting moved him deeply. He isolated himself for weeks at a time to write, or try to do so. He was intense, sincere, striving, and idealistic, as well as sensitive and imaginative; and yet, reading his journal, one fears for his sake the too continual and self-castigating introspection. Yet while he made little progress with novels and poems, he was finding his vision of truth.

The son of a middle-class family, Gascoyne violently rejected the "English death" (a phrase he borrowed from Lawrence Durrell) in which he had been reared. By this he meant what D. H. Lawrence would have meant: the inhibitions, social pretensions, economic order, and unexamined, second-hand ideas by which middle-class existence sheltered itself from genuine personal relationships, "life," and "reality." The menace of Hitler and total war further intensified his protest and revolt. But he had internalized the "death" he hated, and his struggle to overcome it pitted him not only against bourgeois society but against himself. His poetry and journals are full of images of constriction and release—of frozen glaciers and melting, walls and windows, blindness and seeing, prison and freedom, dismemberment and wholeness, guilt and innocence, statues and live human beings, flesh and spirit, grave and resurrection—but the constriction is experienced, the release only prospective or hypothetical. In many of his poems the prisoner is not freed but dies within his cell.

These rebellions and hopes predisposed Gascoyne to Surrealism and echoed through his Surrealist manifestoes and poems. After his brief allegiance to Surrealism, he brought out *Hölderlin's Madness* (1938), a collection of loose translations from Hölderlin with some original poems in his vein. *Poems 1937–42* (1943) contained work of extraordinary imaginative and emotional intensity, including a sequence ("Miserere") in which Gascoyne's pessimistic vision expressed itself through Christian symbolism.

In *A Vagrant and Other Poems* (1951) he deliberately loosened his style. Periods of psychological depression and breakdown lessened his productivity.

Much of his poetry after 1938 is couched in theological terms and spoken in despair. He pictures the world as a night, dark pit, empty void, hell, and the like, a place of meaninglessness, guilt, rage, and torment, from which there is no escape. Instead of love, the heart is "foaming with helpless fury." At any moment, he writes in "Inferno," the "scarlet and black flag" of "anger and despondency" may lead us on to behold the "Void that undermines the world . . . Bottomless depths of roaring emptiness." In "De Profundis" he questions

> what shamefaced cry
> Half choked in the dry throat, as though a stone
> Were our confounded tongue, can ever rise

out of these depths. But fidelity to the truth, though in despair, is, he feels, a moral imperative. "Artist" affirms that so long as the artist continues to perceive and record the evil or nothingness, keeping his wound open, he may hold the demonic host at bay. And because a life in despair grounds itself in knowledge of man's authentic condition, it attains an intensity of being unknown in the comfortable "death" of the middle class. Gascoyne even suggests a paradoxical hope through fidelity in hopelessness. He writes in "Sanctus" that if he accepts that his "blind eyes" can see only night, "then they may see at last; / And all they see their vision sanctifies." All such promises, or rather guesses, in Gascoyne's poetry are necessarily vague and ambiguous, for he cannot say what lies beyond despair, or even that anything does. He writes as one in a windowless dungeon, knowing only the dark and the wall, yet surmising that there may be something outside. (Many of these poems were composed between 1939 and 1943 and express Gascoyne's feeling about the war as well as about the human condition in general.) And he has no means of breaking through the wall except to accept it. This paradox underlies "Tenebrae" and similar poems in which he appeals not for release but for a deeper descent with Christ into hell.

> "*It is finished.*" The last nail
> Has consummated the inhuman pattern, and the veil

Is torn. God's wounds are numbered.
All is now withdrawn: void yawns
The rock-hewn tomb. There is no more
Regeneration in the stricken sun,
The hope of faith no more,
No height no depth no sign
And no more history.

Thus may it be: and worse.
And may we know Thy perfect darkness.
And may we into Hell descend with Thee.

From these quotations it will be obvious that Gascoyne does not sing, enchant, or reassure. He appalls. And he is an imperfect craftsman; his poems tend to lack construction and his rhythms and phrasing can lapse into honest prose. But the sincerity, intelligence, powerful imagination, and emotional shock of his work make him a poet to be reckoned with. Some of his lines are unforgettable, as when he writes in "Winter Garden" that within his blocked self "A savage sun consumes its hidden day."

In 1937 George Barker (b. 1913) startled readers with *Calamiterror*. In ten obscure books the poem recorded a vision of truth and a quest for purpose in living. Its language was irrational, musical, and densely associative. Symbols crowded and recurred, and they were the deep, pregnant, ready-made symbols of the "archetypal" style:

The green dream hung in the male tree bled when I burst
And burning boy out of the apple I fell.

Literary adolescents such as Anthony Thwaite and Robert Duncan read *Calamiterror* with delight. Because of this poem Barker was associated with Dylan Thomas.

Calamiterror was not the first of his publications, for, like Thomas and Gascoyne, Barker was a gifted writer while still very young. Volumes of his poetry had appeared in 1933 and 1935, the second having been chosen by T. S. Eliot for publication by Faber and Faber. Yeats had included two of Barker's lyrics in the 1935 *Oxford Book of Modern Verse*. Barker's early poems showed him absorbing Joyce, Eliot, Yeats, Blake, Auden, Spender, and Hopkins, a typical reading list for the time. After *Calamiterror* he did not continue with this style. Now twenty-five years old, he retired from ultimate dragon fights and confronted the history of his time. His poems indicted the social and international orders. Their contemporary reference and looser, plainer idiom made them more accessible than *Calamiterror*. But they were still visionary, archetypal, and subjective. Barker did not, in other words, describe the outward scene but expressed it in imaginative symbols, thus transposing the real world into a visionary one. And he projected his own metaphysical preoccupations— his controversy with the hidden God, or, as it sometimes seems, his effort to accept a Manichaean universe—into contemporary history. His sonnet "To Any Member of My Generation," for example, voiced a sense of things shared by many poets of the 1930s as the Second World War began:

> Whenever we kissed we cocked the future's rifles
> And from our wild-oat words, like dragon's teeth,
> Death underfoot now arises; when we were gay
> Dancing together in what we hoped was life,
> Who was it in our arms but the whores of death
> Whom we have found in our beds today, today?

But feelings of disillusion, failure, guilt, and evil did not arise in Barker as a reaction to political events, or if they did, it was because such feelings were inveterate in him and saturated all his reactions.

Sex had been, Barker tells us, a personal and literary preoccupation of his since the age of nine. In the 1940s sexuality and love became his major theme, or rather, his poetic arena, in which he confronted his appalled sense of evil. There are some joyous poems, but the ambivalence, suffering, and disgust of love were his usual burden. "Four Cycles of Love Poems" should especially be mentioned. In the first part of the satiric *True Confessions of George Barker* (1950; with Part II added, 1964) his reductive vision reached its *ne plus ultra*. The poem spoke with mockery and contempt of himself from childhood on, of reason, poetry, religion, and ideas generally, and most especially of love, marriage, sex, and the body with its glandular squeezings and defecation odors.

> The married lovers, cock and snake,
> Lie on a Mount of Venus. Traitor
> Each to each, fake kissing fake,
> So punished by a betrayed creator.

The *True Confessions* maintains a pose of jovial frankness and hard indifference. Every reader, the poem assumes, knows that its insights are true. But the ribald, blasphemous poem was attacked, fussed about in the House of Lords, and omitted from Barker's 1957 *Collected Poems* "at the publisher's request," the publisher being Faber and Faber. And since sex is sacred to many modern readers, Barker's reductive and tormented analyses are still often dismissed with the sort of epithet—"immature," "unbalanced," "pathological," "obsessive"—by which we whisk out of sight what we do not wish to consider.

What weakens Barker is not his vision but his imperfect craftsmanship. Slapdash is appropriate in the *True Confessions; le mot* that is ostentatiously not *juste* belongs to the satiric, jaunty aggression. But a similar making-do disappoints in other poems. Barker has an unfortunate penchant for jingles (the lover will "sleep and keep by me") and bad puns ("These errors loved no less than the saint loves arrows"). And the deliberately loose, talky poems written since the 1960s are less interesting than his earlier ones without being less uneven. Nevertheless, he always communicates his emotion and fuses it with intelligent thought. Among his typical, better lyrics are the earlier of the two entitled "Kew Gardens" ("Two who were walking together . . ."), "On the Approaching Birth of a Child to Friends," "Epithalamium for Two Friends," and "Channel Crossing."

The first period of W. S. Graham (b. 1918) culminated in *The Nightfishing* (1955), a poem that has wonderful descriptions of the herring fishery off Scotland. At this time Graham was strongly influenced by Dylan Thomas. From 1955 to 1970 he published nothing, and in *Malcolm Mooney's Land* (1970) and subsequent volumes, the lush, obscure rhetoric of his first period was gone, and in its place was a poetry of spare, simple statement, intense with thought. Many of his later poems take for their theme the inadequacy of language as incarnation or communication.

Meanwhile in the 1930s, while Thomas, Gascoyne, and Barker were creating new Romantic styles, Roy Campbell (1901–57) was continuing more traditional ones. With Campbell I may also mention the Canadian poet E. J. Pratt (1883–1964). Had I strictly observed chronology, I would have begun this chapter with them rather than with Thomas, since they were the oldest and earliest published (Pratt for the first time in 1923, Campbell in 1924) of the poets discussed here. But the work of Pratt and Campbell had little influence, except that William Plomer and F. T. Prince, who like Campbell were from South Africa, caught Campbell's exotic and colorful imagery of African beasts and landscape.

Edwin John Pratt was born in a Newfoundland fishing village, the son of a minister. He attended Victoria College, University of Toronto, and then, as a graduate student, specialized in theology and psychology. After much hesitation he decided not to become a clergyman, and made his career teaching English literature at Victoria College. *Newfoundland Lyrics* (1923) presented the landscape and people of his native region. These were vivid poems, but from them no one could have predicted the verve and individuality of Pratt's next phase, when he wrote long, narrative poems in octosyllabic couplets. *The Witches' Brew* (1925) was a fantasia on alcohol. "The Cachalot" (in *Titans*, 1926), Pratt's finest single poem, described a sperm whale, its fight with a giant squid, and its final combat with a whaling ship. Pratt's sympathy with the hugely powerful whale and his battle-joy combined in this original poem with a comic perspective. For the rest of his life Pratt continued to publish both lyrics and narrative poems, but the latter especially established his popularity. The extent to which his poetry draws on Canadian history and landscape has been important to readers and other writers in that country. Among his better-known lyrics are "The Highway" and "Come Away, Death." As a stylist Pratt rejected the various Modernist developments of his time; they moved, as he said, "away from clarity of expression into obscurity, which I think is a bad drift."

Roy Campbell grew up in South Africa and went at the age of seventeen to England. He spent a year at Oxford, mingling with other writers and reading voraciously in English and French poetry. His *The Flaming Terrapin* (1924), a long poem, was favorably reviewed. The plot and symbolism of this work are incoherent, but its descriptive patches have a wild verve:

> Down unimagined Congoes proudly riding,
> Buoyed on whose flow through many a grey lagoon,
> The husks of sleepy crocodiles went sliding
> Like piles of floating lumber in the moon;

. . . .
And gleaming serpents, shot with gold and pearl,
Poured out . . .

He moved in 1928 with his wife and children to southern France. Here he composed a satire on the English literary world, *The Georgiad* (1931), a forty-page mock-epic in heroic couplets. With slight exceptions the poem does not attack the major writers of the time, such as Joyce, Eliot, Forster, Yeats, and Woolf, but ridicules small fry such as Humbert Wolfe, J. C. Squire, and Victoria Sackville-West, who are presented as characteristic of the Georgian-Bloomsbury milieu. In Campbell's portrait the modern literatus is intellectual, effeminate, leftist, and cliquish; he or she wears glasses, chatters affectedly ("drawling out long O's / Along its draughty, supercilious nose"), and bores.

In the early 1930s Campbell published the lyrics that keep his name alive, poems such as "The Zebras," the first of the two entitled "The Olive Tree," "Horses on the Camargue," and "Toledo." Though hardly subtle, and not even fresh in language or feeling—in fact, they are full of Byronic pose, rhetoric, and cliché—they are appropriate and expressive; their unrestrained emotion, headlong movement, and vivid, energetic phrasing enact the values of strength, untamed courage, defiance, and independence to which Campbell was committed. And the images that embody these ideals are sometimes fine: the horses of the Camarge "With white tails smoking free"; the tough, twisted olive tree; the zebra stallion, "Engine of beauty volted with delight."

A convert to Roman Catholicism, Campbell moved to Spain in 1933, where he supported the Nationalist cause. He returned to England in 1939 and fought as an NCO in the British army during the Second World War. He lived in England thereafter, working for the BBC and writing autobiographical narratives of his adventures. They had been numerous and lost nothing of their violence in his telling.

EDWIN MUIR

Edwin Muir (1887–1959) lived on farms in the Orkney Islands until he was fourteen. In his fine *An Autobiography* (revised 1954) he remembered his childhood with fond love for the traditional, unchanging ways of life. He suffered the intense terrors and guilts of a strongly imaginative child, and he also beheld wonders. "Horses," for example:

> Their conquering hooves which trod the stubble down
> Were ritual that turned the field to brown,
> And their great hulks were seraphim of gold,
> Or mute ecstatic monsters on the mould.

In later years he was sure that all children see things this way. A child, he added, has not yet fallen into time; with the permanence and security it feels, the naturalness things have for it and the harmony they make, a child's world is paradisal—an Eden. As Muir remembered his childhood in *An Autobiography:*

> That world was a perfectly solid world, for the days did not undermine it but merely rounded it, or rather repeated it, as if there were only one day endlessly rising and setting. Our first childhood is the only time in our lives when we exist within immortality, and perhaps all our ideas of immortality are influenced by it. . . . there is a completer harmony of all things with each other than [we] will ever know again.

But the exactions of landlords and his father's ill health brought this Orkney idyl to an end. The family moved to Glasgow. Walking through the slums to his job as an office boy, Muir was appalled by "the crumbling houses, the twisted faces, the obscene words casually heard in passing, the ancient, haunting stench of pollution and decay, the arrogant women, the mean men, the terrible children." Even the country fields, when he escaped to them, "seemed blasted by disease." Later he worked in a factory where bones were rendered: "The bones were yellow and greasy, with little rags of decomposed flesh clinging to them. Raw, they had a strong, sour, penetrating smell. But it was nothing to the stench they gave off when they were shovelled along with the maggots into the furnace." A feeling of shame, he said, "slowly settled within me." The odor from the bones was "so insinuating that I came to believe that I smelt of them." His father, mother, and two brothers died shortly after the move to Glasgow.

Evenings, Sundays, during illnesses, and on vacations Muir read. Converted to Socialism, he embraced its utopian promise and devoured Shaw, Ibsen, Whitman, and Heine. Inconsistently, he read Nietzsche with equal faith. He started writing, submitting prose to Orage's *The New Age*. In 1919, still a clerk in Glasgow, he married, and later that year he moved to London and underwent psychoanalysis. He started to write poetry in 1921 while he and his wife were living on the Continent.

I had no training; I was too old to submit myself to contemporary influences; and I had acquired in Scotland a deference toward ideas which made my entrance into poetry difficult. Though my imagination had begun to work I had no technique by which I could give expression to it. . . . I must have been influenced by something, since we all are, but when I try to find out what it was that influenced me, I can only think of the years of childhood which I spent on my father's farm . . . these years had come alive, after being forgotten for so long.

From this time forth he supported himself by translating with his wife from German into English, by occasional teaching, and by writing articles and reviews. His six volumes of poetry are his lasting achievement.

Muir's poems center on archetypal images. He finds these images in dreams, classical myth, the opening chapters of the Old Testament from the garden of Eden through the stories of Abraham, Isaac, and Jacob, and the life of Christ. For Muir an archetype was also given in recollection of his own childhood. The primitive, rural community of the Orkney Islands had given him, as he felt, a vision of what human life essentially is and should be, man "standing on earth, looking at heaven." As he writes in "Labyrinth,"

> For once in a dream or trance I saw the gods
> Each sitting on the top of his mountain-isle,
> While down below the little ships sailed by,
> Toy multitudes swarmed in the harbours, shepherds drove
> Their tiny flocks to the pastures, marriage feasts
> Went on below, small birthdays and holidays,
> Ploughing and harvesting and life and death,
> And all permissible, all acceptable,
> Clear and secure as in a limpid dream.

Events may depart from the archetype, or our perception of it may be obscured, but the archetype eventually reasserts itself.

Gradually and with increasing clarity toward the end of his career, Muir elaborated also the notion of a single pattern that appears both in the story of mankind as a whole and in the lives of individuals. He called this the "Fable." It is essentially a mythological interpretation of his own experience in the light of the early chapters of the Bible and the Christian doctrine of the Fall. His childhood on the Orkney Islands is or corresponds to the Garden of Eden ("Variations on a Time Theme," III):

> A child in Adam's field I dreamed away
> My one eternity and hourless day.

He dwells on the simplicity and beauty of this lost paradise, the feeling of harmony with the animals and the natural environment, and, above all, the sense of timelessness ("The Myth"):

> My childhood all a myth
> Enacted in a distant isle;
> Time with his hourglass and his scythe
> Stood dreaming on the dial.

The sudden move of his family to the utterly different, grimly industrial Glasgow, with the suffering that attended it, is the Fall from Eden, after which, so goes the myth, come years of wandering in the desert. The Fall is not, as in Christian doctrine, a fall into sin. It is rather a fall into time, and the realm of time is characterized by grief, pain, dread, and meaninglessness. In the desert of time we still remember or imagine Eden and we are on a quest for it, seeking Eden's gate. The final part of the pattern is the return to paradise. The fable is the most comprehensive of Muir's archetypes, but, to repeat, he discovered it only gradually. His poems are subtle, diverse, and exploratory in their meditations; it would be a mistake to treat the Fable as a "key" to all Muir's poetry. But its essential elements—the feelings of loss or separation, of waiting and questing in suffering, and of final restoration—appear in a great many of his poems—those, for example, on Moses, Prometheus, Penelope and the return of Odysseus.

The archetypes confer meaning on our experience. They are universal and timeless. And they are the objects or contents of everybody's imagination. As the imagination beholds them, we escape from time, a possibility Muir glories in ("The Stationary Journey"):

> To the mind's eternity I turn,
>   With leaf, fruit, blossom on the spray,
> See the dead world grow green within
>   Imagination's one long day.
>
> There while outstretched upon the Tree
>   Christ looks across Jerusalem's towers,
> Adam and Eve unfallen yet
>   Sleep side by side within their bowers.

From Eden, in other words, through the crucifixion to the New Jerusalem the myth describes a temporal sequence; but to the imagination each of the archetypes or eternal forms (as Blake called them) that enter into the myth is present simultaneously with the others. In fancier language we might say that every moment of imaginative energy is apocalyptic: time is annihilated and all that ever was may rise again in new and eternal life ("Into Thirty Centuries Born"):

> Ilium burns before our eyes
> For thirty centuries never put out,
> And we walk the streets of Troy
> And breathe in the air its fabulous name.
> The king, the courtier and the rout
> Shall never perish in that flame.

That these passages flow with such energy back in time is typical of Muir. His deepest emotional longing was for restoration or return. Timelessness meant to him the world of his childhood.

Beyond the conceptions I have mentioned Muir was not really willing to go, yet with them he was not quite willing to stop. When it came to that which finally (to quote Wordsworth) "is, and hath the name of God," Muir would speak only in the most noncommittal way, yet he would speak. And so he adopted Hölderlin's symbolism of the Olympian gods ("they"), perhaps because no one could mistake this for a church affiliation. Or he spoke, with Prospero, of our lives and world as a dream, and with Shelley of a dream within this dream, and putting whatever he was contemplating still further off, said that within this deeper dream we come upon an "unending thought/ Which has elsewhere its end." Or he spoke of a "place of peace, content to be," or a "love" that "gathers" all strife. In "In Love for Long" he writes:

> I've been in love for long
> With what I cannot tell
>
> . . . .
>
> It is not any thing,
> And yet all being is;
> Being, being, being,
> Its burden and its bliss.
> How can I ever prove
> What it is I love?

Muir's poems, then, present an imaginative image—the dream, memory, or myth. For readers who accept the Romantic premise that poetry is imagination, imagination poetry, and ask for nothing more, Muir is powerfully compelling. But his poems are also meditative, and in this mode he appeals to another type of reader, who loves him for moral qualities, for integrity, wisdom, and goodness. Not to sympathize with his feelings would be fiend-like, for amid his psychic wounds he is patient, loving, and hopeful. His longing for a simpler, more rooted way of life is attractive, if nostalgic, and so is his serious respect for his own life and for all lives as story and Fable. And something about Muir makes readers construe everything he does for the best. When his diction is naive, we take it as sincere. When his rhythms stumble, we are pleased that we are in touch with authentic, first-hand thinking. When Muir is too leisurely, what impresses us is his calm confidence in his vision. Our impression of his wisdom arises partly from his perspectives. Whoever sees things within so wide or long a field of vision must be a sage. And Muir is always thinking and, at his best, his thoughts and perspectives are startlingly his own.

No poem better illustrates this than the famous "The Horses" from *One Foot in Eden* (1956):

> Barely a twelvemonth after
> The seven days war that put the world to sleep,
> Late in the evening the strange horses came.
> By then we had made our covenant with silence,
> But in the first few days it was so still
> We listened to our breathing and were afraid.
> On the second day
> The radios failed; we turned the knobs; no answer.
> On the third day a warship passed us, heading north,

> Dead bodies piled on the deck. On the sixth day
> A plane plunged over us into the sea. Thereafter
> Nothing

The calm, declarative sentences are typical of Muir, and so is the logical and orderly progression. He creates suspense as he ticks off the seven days. Details are selected effectively, such as the mysterious airplane plunging into the sea. He obtains resonance by allusions to myth: the destruction of the world by man takes six days, just as God took six days to make it; the covenant with silence recalls God's covenant with Noah; the warship is the archetypal ship of death or Flying Dutchman. All this seems to me skillful but within the range of maybe two hundred modern poets. The genius of Muir's poem lies in the opening lines. They put nuclear war as the subject into a subordinate clause. They are spoken from a time after the war, and they say not only that there was an "after" but that what happened afterward was more important than the war. The calm strength of Muir's amazing faith is moving in itself, but all the more so in the context of innumerable poems on nuclear war written in the 1950s and 1960s, virtually all of them envisaging doomsday and most of them in a rhetoric of frenzy. Such poems might in fact be wiser than Muir's, but as literature they are more conventional and less imaginative. Muir is again envisioning a return to the world of his childhood, and the rest of this beautifully thought out poem describes it.

"One Foot in Eden," the title poem of this late volume, is unusual and the more moving because in it Muir checks his nostalgia with a deeper consideration. Though not formally a Christian, he was now sympathetic to Christian teachings, and this poem develops a thought analogous to the Christian doctrine of the fortunate Fall. Precisely because it is clouded with pain and fear, he says, the world of time bears

> flowers in Eden never known.
> Blossoms of grief and charity
> Bloom in these darkened fields alone.
> What had Eden ever to say
> Of hope and faith and pity and love
> Until was buried all its day
> And memory found its treasure trove?

> Strange blessings never in Paradise
> Fall from these beclouded skies.

The poem is Muir's acceptance and even blessing, after so many years, of Glasgow.

THE WAR YEARS

The poets we especially associate with the years 1939–45 are those who first began to publish then or who, having published earlier, first won recognition. The most important of them are Kathleen Raine, Vernon Watkins, Lawrence Durrell, Bernard Spencer, Ann Ridler, Norman Nicholson, Alun Lewis, Roy Fuller, W. S. Graham, F. T. Prince, John Heath-Stubbs, Keith Douglas, and Sidney Keyes.

Sidney Keyes, Alun Lewis, and Keith Douglas are usually noticed as a separate group, the reason being the eagerness of readers for "War Poets" comparable to those of the First World War. That Keyes, Lewis, and Douglas served as soldiers, wrote sometimes of their military experience, and died in the war makes them available for this role. There were other poets, such as Roy Fuller, who also fought in the war and described their experience in poetry, but since they survived and wrote in later years on other subjects, they are not usually noticed in this connection. Even when Keyes, Lewis, Douglas, and Fuller were in the army or navy, their poetry addressed many things besides military life and combat. Moreover, in contrast to the poets of the First World War, experience of soldiering and battle did not greatly modify the imaginative responses and emotions of these poets. For the Second World War was entered with an altogether different state of mind from the First. Since there was not the patriotic idealism and optimism of 1914, there was less of the savage grief, revulsion, and satire that came in 1917, and without these emotions as motives, there was less cause to focus on battle as a subject matter. I have raised the topic of war poetry in order to dismiss it. The poets who served in the war expressed much the same complicated and profound state of mind as those who lived through it as civilians.

By 1939 the liberal or leftist optimism of the early and mid-1930s had been swept away. The triumph of Franco in Spain had been a bitter and ominous disappointment. Events during the Spanish Civil War—especially the atrocities committed by the workers as well as the Fascists and the ruthless internecine struggle for power among the various Anarchist, Socialist, and Communist groups—had disillusioned many English idealists, whom life in England had not prepared for the realities of an actual revolution. The alliance between Communist Russia and Nazi Germany was a shock, and the descent of Europe into total war seemed a final defeat to those who had hoped for the progressive or revolutionary creation of a better world.

No few terms or generalizations can adequately convey the state of mind that ensued, but feelings of guilt, helplessness, and defeat revived pessimistic interpretations of human nature and of history. Many persons felt a heightened religious need. Expressions of religious quest or faith, which earlier would have seemed atavistic to most intellectuals, could now be read with sympathy. Poets such as Ann Ridler and Norman Nicholson expressed a traditionally Anglican faith; they were much influenced by Eliot. Other poets, such as Kathleen Raine and Vernon Watkins, were imaginative, archetypal, or mystical. Their sense of the sacred had no necessary connection with Christian belief. It was during the early war years, as I noted, that David Gascoyne voiced emotions of religious despair, using biblical and Christian symbolism.

At least in its ideology, the short-lived "New Apocalypse" was also representative of these years. This movement presented itself in a 1941 anthology, *The White Horseman: Prose and Verse of the New Apocalypse*, edited by J. P. Hendry and Henry Treece. The anthology included poems by the editors and by Nicholas Moore, Alex Comfort, and Vernon Watkins, along with criticism and fiction, and was followed by similar anthologies. Essays by G. S. Fraser, Treece, and Hendry explained that the poetry of Auden, Spender, MacNeice, and their followers had been dominated by politics and "mechanism." These poets had idealized the subordination of the individual to a social imperative. But, said Treece, the "salvation of the individual man is via the individual man himself . . . and not by way of the Commonwealth, the State, or the International Collective." The poetry of the

New Apocalypse would explore personal and subjective experience, and would not do so with rosy spectacles. For the thirties poets had not adequately seen the "dark, fundamental impulses and subconscious motives" of human nature or the "explosively chaotic nature of life." Treece was favorably singled out by other essayists for the terror and horror in his poetry, while Treece himself urged acceptance of the irrational as necessary to wholeness of being. All the Apocalyptics, but especially Hendry, stressed the importance of myth as the basis of individual and societal life.

Tracing the history of their own movement, these writers explained that they derived from Freud, Jung, Lawrence, Surrealism, and, on the political side, from the anarchism of Herbert Read. They had "codified their aims," Treece said, "two or three years before Munich," yet Munich and the fall of France were also influences. These were, Treece aphorized, "aesthetic no less than political events." The link between the defeat of France and the New Apocalypse lay in the feeling that Hitler's *Blitzkrieg* had destroyed liberal rationalism and optimism as well as the French armies, and that a more pessimistic awareness centering on horror and the irrational was now necessary. Of course this conviction reflected not just the events in France but also the foreboding of worse still to come as the war continued. The stories and poems of New Apocalyptic authors were, however, less interesting than their essays, and by the end of the 1940s the movement had expired.

Though "history" was a major theme of poetry in the 1930s, poets then had in mind, when they used the term, not so much the past as the looming crises of the present. At any moment these might sweep away the loves and hopes of personal life, which therefore were attended with a constant feeling of their vulnerability and transience. We might suppose that this complex of feelings would have been even more strongly present during the war, and indeed it was, but it combined with a different perception of history. Poets thought now of the long past and the innumerable fellow human beings who had lived out their suffering and trapped lives, and as the imagination dwelt on this, a grave awe and compassion were felt, as in many of the poems of Sidney Keyes. A similar sense of history is often present, at least as an undertone, in the sensitive impressions of place—Cairo, Greek islands, India—found in Alun Lewis, Bernard Spencer, Lawrence Durrell, and Keith Douglas. One thinks also of F. T. Prince's well-known "Soldiers Bathing." The major expression of this response to history is Eliot's *Four Quartets* and especially the last of these, "Little Gidding," which was published in 1942.

Poetry was now stylistically far from anything that could be called avant-garde. We saw this in the *Four Quartets*, which amalgamated older, more familiar styles of English poetic utterance with Symbolism. And we noticed a similar modification toward accessible language in Thomas, Barker, and Gascoyne during and after the war. These developments reflected a general emotion of the early war years, for the war united the English people emotionally as well as socially and caused them to identify more consciously with their own national past. In earlier or later periods the styles of Heath-Stubbs, Prince, and even Keyes might have seemed not merely traditional but even academic, yet precisely in this quality they expressed an emotional need of the time.

So far as the religious emotions of the war years associated themselves with Anglican tradition, the *Four Quartets* was incomparably the major poetic utterance. Norman Nicholson (b. 1914) and Anne Ridler (b. 1912) were minor Christian poets. Ridler's simple, meditative lyrics were somewhat influenced by the Anglican verse of the seventeenth century. Though her topics and styles were more contemporary, her work recalled that of Ruth Pitter. The poetry of Nicholson expressed his lifetime residence in western Cumberland, his devotion to it and the adjoining Lake Country, and his effort to find in it a microcosm of human life and experience. Reading T. S. Eliot encouraged Nicholson to seek through Christian belief a profounder meaning to life, and at the age of twenty-six he was reconverted to the Anglican Church, an event he regarded as the turning point of his life. The interplay of his religious interests with his regional subject matter gave his verse dramas and poems, which he started to publish in 1944, their special character.

In contrast to Nicholson and Ridler—or to Eliot—Kathleen Raine (b. 1908) and Vernon Watkins (1909–67) continued the Romantic mode of Blake and Yeats that seeks religious truth through the imagination. Watkins worked as a clerk in Lloyd's

Bank near his home in a small, seacoast town in Wales. At night he wrote poems. And he rewrote constantly. Some poems went through five hundred drafts; the average, fifty. He submitted nothing for publication until he was thirty-one, and then only because he was urged by Dylan Thomas, whom he loved for his poetry.

Though he admired many other poets, Watkins especially gloried in Yeats and identified with him. Not the early "Celtic" Yeats, as one might have expected, so much as Yeats after his major transition of style in the early years of the twentieth century. For Watkins felt that Yeats had gone through an emotional trauma analogous to his own (which is described below), and had shaped the harder, more vigorous style of his later years as a result of it. Identifying with Yeats, Watkins adopted his rhythms, forms, and diction, and, to some extent, his symbols. I am of two minds about this discipleship. On the one hand, Yeats gave Watkins his concrete, forceful diction and density through aphorism and paradox. On the other hand, Watkins is not Yeats, and as with Roethke, to sound like Yeats without equaling him is anticlimactic. But this point should not be overstressed. The Yeatsian poems are fine in themselves, and many of Watkins' good poems have little of Yeats in them.

"At the age of twenty-one," Watkins later recalled, "the poems and letters of Keats, and the poetry of Shelley, Milton and Blake so governed me that the everyday world hardly existed for me except as a touchstone for protest and indignation." In fact, he was losing his sanity. He had entered Cambridge University, found the atmosphere inimical to the Romantic poetry he loved and wrote, and left after two years. But then, instead of living the free, aspiring life of a young Milton as rural *Penseroso*, Watkins was forced to take a job in a bank. With his dreamy, heroic ideals defeated, he felt disgusted, guilty, and lost. He sank into depression, which deepened over a couple of years into acute schizophrenia. Placed in an asylum for the insane, he kept his fellow patients from sleeping by reciting Blake throughout the night. He recovered, but henceforth his life and work suggest the rigidity of the traumatized. He returned to the bank, but refused promotion and continued all his life as a clerk. And he identified still more fiercely with the traditional mode of poetry that he associated with his ideal of life. He associated it also with

his schooldays, during which he had been able to adhere more
closely to his ideal. He could not possibly have sympathized with
the period style of the thirties, rooted as it seemed to him in the
newspapers. His theme was the nothingness of time in relation
to eternity. He wrote his poetry not merely to escape from everyday reality but to deny it.

His themes are death, poetry, eternity. He contrasts the brief
life of man with perduring nature and feels consoled. Though
mysterious and fearful, death comes as a cleansing and a release.
A poet is a watcher of eternity, like a motionless heron eyeing
the light in the water ("The Heron"). Watkins' best symbols derive from the landscape of Wales, where he lived. The endlessly
restless sea is the world of time; the light of eternity reflects from
it. From the rocky cliff he gazes out into the sea and the light.
The cliff is a symbol of his life, conceived both as the point from
which he looks and as unchanging. It defies the flux of the sea—
a strange feeling about one's life but typical of Watkins. His past
lies buried and inaccessible within the rock. Summarizing thus,
I may seem to suggest that Watkins' poetry is merely Romantic
cliché, but this is far from the case. The Romantic themes and
symbols express a complex, individual vision. "The Dead Shag,"
a marvelous poem, contrasts the vitality of the living seabird with
its dead, mummified body sunk in a pool. In the paradoxical
concluding lines—

> I have lost the light of day
> If once I have lost that dark

—the "dark" is death, or the abiding sense of it, but the lines
have their full weight only if we understand that the living bird
symbolizes the poet's own life before his breakdown; his "light"
comes from the memory of that trauma.

A believing student of occult lore, Kathleen Raine startles her
readers with uncanny speculations. Remembering a place where
she once lived, for example, she asks whether she was ever actually there, "Or had we, thinking we were on bodily ground,
walked in the eternal mind?" When she does not question, she
affirms. "The Journey," for example, tells that she has been born
and died many times (as animals) and still must do so many
more:

I was the trout that haunts the pool,
The shadowy presence of the stream.
Of many many lives I leave
The scattered bone and broken wing.

Raine's mind has no tendency to exceptions, modulations, and qualifications, and, indeed, they would be inappropriate to her prophetic style of utterance. But as a prophetess, she is anything but sibylline. Her poems are clear, neatly patterned, and definite in form, however mysterious and Delphic in their suggestions. "Triad" may illustrate:

To those who speak to the many deaf ears attend.
To those who speak to one,
In poet's song and voice of bird,
Many listen; but the voice that speaks to none
By all is heard:
Sound of the wind, music of the stars, prophetic word.

Raine voices her insights in symbols drawn from nature. Her natural images are clear and unparticularized. Her adjectives are predictable within Romantic convention: "great" ash tree, "roofless house," "inarticulate cry," "holy water," "gray stone," "lonely rowan," "dark pool," "bright mountains," "bitter berries red," and "water cold and clear" all are phrases from "The Wilderness," a poem of fifteen lines. Obviously Yeats and the poetry of the Celtic revival lie behind this diction. Such phrases are "clichés" only in the sense that "lucent stream" or "smiling plain" are clichés in the poetry of Alexander Pope; the tradition behind them gives them a resonance that does not belong to the merely clichéd. Raine excels in imagining or remembering natural paradises, which she fills with bright, glittering light, birds, water, flowers, and blossoming trees. She sees the world in archetypes—Eden, the Fall, Hell, the Resurrection—and she proclaims or symbolizes emotions or archetypal situations rather than enacting them.

Lawrence Durrell and Bernard Spencer were associated in bringing out the quarterly *Personal Landscape* in Cairo during the war. In many qualities of style and imagination they recall the period style of the 1930s. The poems of Durrell (b. 1912) recreate the same world as his novels and travel books—the Mediterranean littoral, its towns, islands, landscapes, and types of people—and relish its sensory color. He seems more an observer of life than a participant in it, and the wisdom of his poems lies in this detached, appreciative, compassionate, tolerant point of view. The sense of a long, complex past usually looms large in his impressions of place, and intrudes a somber theme amid the picturesque, sensory appeal. Durrell also writes poems about artists and writers, and he composes songs, comic or satiric pieces, and Audenesque essayistic lyrics.

Spencer (1909–63) is the more considerable poet. He spent most of his adult life in countries about the Mediterranean. His poems present objects, sights, occasions, or memories with sensory vividness, and suggest that the life of the senses is good in and of itself. As he asserts this Spencer, like many poets of his generation, catches much from D. H. Lawrence, and especially his primitivism. Hence he celebrates natural, simple, and universal objects of sensation, as opposed, for example, to the exotic and artificial—the jewels, brocades, perfumes, and the like of the *fin de siècle*—and his attitudes are not merely hedonistic but also vaguely religious. "The dark bread/ The island wine and the sweet dishes," and "Touch of skin, touch of hair" are almost numinous. Spencer dwells on possibilities of simple, natural happiness tragically wasted by history, that is, by poverty, war, and by our duty to oppose such evils. In "Salonica June 1940" he observes

> The dancing, the bathing, the order of the market, and as day
> Cools into night, boys playing in the square;
> Island boats and lemon-peel tang and the timeless café crowd,
> And the outcry of dice on wood.

He "would shut the whole if I could out of harm's way," but nowhere now

> exists a word or a lock which gunfire may not break,
> Or a love whose range it may not take.

The work of Alun Lewis (1915–44), in poems suggested by what he saw as a soldier in India ("The Mahratta Ghats," "Karanje Village"), may be compared with the similar sketches by Spencer and Durrell. But Lewis' attitude is different. Where Durrell and Spencer admired the Mediterranean ways of life and mores, at least as a release from what Durrell called the "English death," Lewis had no such quarrel to pick, and his reflective, emotional nature was shocked by the age-old, hopeless poverty he witnessed in Egypt. The same combination of compassionate feeling with realistic description appears in his poems on army life, such as "After Dunkirk" and "A Troopship in the Tropics." His army poems record the experience and seek the point of view of the ordinary soldier, describing the inevitable monotony he endures ("All Day It Has Rained") and the toughness he displays ("Infantry"). Lewis' direct emotion, thoughtful concern, sensitivity, and power of vivid, intimate communication made him a poet of major promise. He died of an accident in Burma before his thirtieth birthday.

John Heath-Stubbs, Sidney Keyes, and Keith Douglas were the youngest poets of the Romantic revival to emerge during the war years. Had Keyes survived the war, neo-Romantic poetry might have enjoyed a higher reputation in the 1950s, while Douglas, had he lived, would probably not be discussed with the neo-Romantic movement at all. Heath-Stubbs and Keyes knew each other at Oxford, and Heath-Stubbs, who was slightly older, somewhat influenced his friend. Heath-Stubbs (b. 1918) became less Romantic and more simply academic after 1950. The difference appeared in his diction, which went from "dove-winged chords" and "roses that are red with pain" to more colorless though equally conventional phrases such as "vault of the stars." "Disdain, my verse, the language of the age," he exhorted in the first poem of *The Triumph of the Muse* (1958), and his verse has generally followed this injunction. His subjects are derived from Greek and Roman literature, classical myth, Christian legend, and the like, as in "Tibullus Gone to War," "Horace to Lydia," "Saint Cecelia," "An Heroic Epistle from William Congreve to Anne Bracegirdle, circa 1729," and "Tiberius on Capri." Within Romantic tradition his poetry resembles that of the generation of Dowson and Lionel Johnson, not of Wordsworth or Shelley. In many of his later poems he tries to escape from the ornate and mildly archaic, but is able to become colloquial only when he writes in a quasi-jocose vein.

Sidney Keyes (1922–43) was killed in Tunisia just before he reached the age of twenty-one. He wrote over a hundred poems during his short life as well as two plays and some short stories.

After he joined the army he put together a small volume of verse, *The Iron Laurel* (1942), and assembled poems for a second, *The Cruel Solstice*, published posthumously (1944). Other poems, many of which had appeared in magazines, were added to form his *Collected Poems* (1945). Such an early death naturally moved readers, and ensured a sensitive response. The poets Keyes most admired were the major English Romantics and, in the twentieth century, Hardy, Housman, Rilke, Yeats, and Eliot. A union of bleakness with tenderness, reminiscent of Hardy, characterizes several of his poems (such as "Seascape"); but, as in "The Wilderness," one of his best poems, there is determination to find meaning through loving communication. The love must, however, fully confront evil and death without retreating to some imagined oasis. A generalized religious mood, with no specific theological commitment, pervades many of his poems. Extending it are symbols and imagery that draw upon primitive religion and myths. Keyes is by no means a "war poet." Though the war was inevitably in his mind as he wrote of "pain" (a recurring word) and death, he seems to have tried to keep it at a distance as a specific subject. Exceptions are poems such as "Moonlight Night on the Port," an elegy for soldiers and sailors who went down in their ships, "An Early Death," about mothers of sons lost in battle, and especially "The Foreign Gate." In imagination and rhythm he more resembles Rilke, whom he greatly admired, than he does any English poet, as when in "The Foreign Gate" he speaks of the departed lovers:

> Their images remaining in the lake
> Like written words, the grateful air retaining
> Their impress, like a dancer's or a bird's.

Keith Douglas (1920–44), who was killed in the invasion of Normandy, disdained literary fashion in favor of a direct and independent realism, and, in language, sought a spareness in which, as he said, "every word must work for its keep." Rhythm must "enable the poems to be read as significant speech." These aims were not the product of his experience during the war. They were present from the start. Most of his extant poems, written from the age of fourteen through his first year at Oxford, are, for someone so young, surprisingly spare and firm. Especially effective, within their limits, are "Encounter with

God" and "Forgotten the Red Leaves." But though the impact of the war did not create his resolve to strip away the "decorative," it certainly confirmed and strengthened it. If this stripping away worked against lyricism, it would be for the sake of something truer to the circumstances of the time. "I see no reason to be either musical or sonorous about things at present." Battles in the North African desert and other experiences in the Near East (recorded in his war journal, *Alamein to Zem-Zem*, published in 1946) provided Douglas with new subject matter, which appears in stark impressions of the land ("Syria I and II," "Enfidaville," "Landscape with Figures"), images of a corrupt society ("Cairo Jag," "Egypt," "Egyptian Sentry, Corniche, Alexandria"), and an omnipresent sense of death ("How to Kill," "Dead Men," "Gallantry"). Like so many poets whom we associate with the war, he was not—nor did he regard himself as—a "war poet": "I never tried to write about war (that is battles and things)." Yet it is impossible to imagine his poetry being what it was, by the time he died, without the influence of the war, which hurried him to maturity and strengthened his perceptions. Some lines from "Bête Noire," his best (though never finished) poem, may illustrate his style:

> This is my particular monster; I know him;
> he walks about inside me: I'm his house
> and his landlord. He's my evacuee
> taking a respite from hell in me
> he decorates his room of course
> to remind him of home. He often talks of going.

In Douglas the Romantic impulse of his generation was less present, and his work points to a harder strain in English poetry of the 1950s and 1960s.

PART TWO

THE RESURGENCE OF POUND, WILLIAMS, AND STEVENS

9

REAPPRAISING THE MODERNISTS

I N 1925 most readers thought the great living poets of the
English language were Hardy, Bridges, and Yeats. Looking
back on that same date from twenty years later, they saw a
different topography. Yeats and Eliot had been the major poets
of the 1920s, in fact, of the twentieth century. But in 1945 the
reputation of Yeats, though enormous, was less than Eliot's. Besides Eliot, the most significant living poets seemed to be Frost,
Auden, and Pound, though Pound was esteemed for his early
work much more than for the *Cantos*. Other living poets who
would have been mentioned on most short lists in 1945 were, in
England, Graves, Thomas, Spender, and Day-Lewis, and in the
United States, Cummings, Stevens, Ransom, Tate, Moore, and
Williams.

What is striking about these former estimations is how far they
lifted Eliot above Pound, Stevens, and Williams. Pound seemed,
as I said, almost a back number, an important figure of the
1910s. The *Cantos*, his only poetic effort since *Hugh Selwyn Mauberley* (1920), seemed a progressively worse failure. After some
stunning passages the poem had ended in the long, dreary eccentricity of the Chinese and American Cantos published in
1940. Pound was no longer an influence. At least the young
poets of whom one heard in the 1930s—Auden, Thomas,

Spender, Day-Lewis, MacNeice, Empson, Delmore Schwartz, Robert Penn Warren, Stanley Kunitz—had not formed their styles on him. And in 1945 Pound was in jail, having been arrested for treason. Of itself this crime would not have injured his literary standing, but his pro-Fascist and anti-Semitic polemic damaged his reputation deeply.

Wallace Stevens in 1945 was still seen as the poet of his 1923 volume, *Harmonium*. As the consensus then went, this was brilliant, somewhat precious, and isolated. No traditions of American poetry led into it, no important developments stemmed from it. Because of his elegance and wit, Stevens was admired by younger poets in the new Critical mode, and one heard a tone of Stevens sometimes in, for example, Richard Wilbur or James Merrill. Since 1930 he had been writing again, ending the six-year silence that followed *Harmonium*, but his more recent poems had not been widely assimilated by 1945, and he had not yet published several of the late, long poems—"Credences of Summer," "The Auroras of Autumn," "An Ordinary Evening in New Haven"—that are among his masterpieces.

The case of William Carlos Williams was lamentably simpler: he had never enjoyed much recognition. He was known to other poets in the United States. He and his work gave pleasure. But in a critical milieu dominated in the 1940s by the traditionalism, formalism, and intellectualism of Eliot, the New Critics, and Auden, Williams seemed likable but light. No one could have predicted that within ten years he would be the most influential of all the pristine moderns on young poets in the United States.

The chapters that follow tell the moving story of the later careers of Pound, Williams, and Stevens, of their growing reputations, and of their great impact in the 1950s and 1960s. Pound and Williams were very dissimilar, but, for the most part, if in the 1950s a reader admired one, he probably also admired the other, and if a poet built his style on their basis, he conflated elements from each. Stevens' was an altogether different kind of poetry, and it attracted a different group of followers.

The first major events in the postwar ascension of Pound and Williams were their own publications. In 1948 came Pound's *Pisan Cantos*. To my mind the *Pisan Cantos* and the *Four Quartets* are the greatest long works in modern poetry. Few readers could share this opinion in 1948, for without the glosses now available, the text of the *Pisan Cantos* was very obscure, but the poem had a moving humanity beyond anything else Pound had ever written. The *Pisan Cantos* received the Bollingen Prize in 1949, and the controversy this aroused, pitting believers in the poem against deplorers of Pound's political record and opinions, heightened general awareness of him. The *Pisan Cantos* were followed by further Cantos and other publications and republications, but remained the decisive new work from Pound. In the career of Williams a similar influence stemmed from *Paterson*, of which the first book appeared in 1946. A poem in the Modernist tradition of *The Waste Land, The Bridge,* and the *Cantos, Paterson's* formal procedures and moral vision—because they were also pure Williams—made a new start within that tradition. *Paterson,* in other words, was rooted in the Modernism of the 1920s but led into such works of the 1950s as Allen Ginsberg's *Howl* and Charles Olson's *The Maximus Poems.*

To young poets the styles of *Paterson* and the *Pisan Cantos* presented clear alternatives to the dominant, New Critical mode. The free verse of Pound and Williams challenged the prevalence of traditional meters and stanzas. Pound's stream-of-consciousness and ideogrammic presentation could be read—or misread—as spontaneous, open, and agrammatical. The speaker was Pound ("old Ez," he calls himself), not a New Critical "persona," and his elegiac memories and present sufferings in a concentration camp seemed unconcealed autobiography. His tones and emotions—weeping, defiance, fear, scorn, religious reverence, sagelike serenity, prophetic wisdom—went far outside and beyond the urbane irony by which poets in the New Critical and Audenesque schools kept life at a distance. In *Paterson* Williams continued to root himself, like his chicory flower, in the ordinary American locality and speech. Moreover, his poem plainly asserted and exemplified his rejection of New Critical closure, for it was always beginning anew.

Style embodies a moral vision, and Pound's was congenial in some respects (if hateful in others) to many in the younger generation. Williams' was still more so. I shall sketch the congeniality later on, but may here quickly note that the *Cantos* voice a reverence for the "green world" of nature. At moments they are mystical. But their religious emotion is personal, eclectic, syncretic, not structured by Christianity. The *Cantos* seek to recover the primitive sense of a divine world. One sees the attraction to Ginsberg, Olson, and Robert Duncan. And almost everything about Williams was appealing. He was against the academics, against preciousness, against Eliot, against anything already done; he was receptive to the untried, to anybody's experiment. Democratic, honest, warm, sexual, he and his poetry did not, like Eliot, hold a poet to an impossibly high standard of performance. In fact, he bestowed worth upon one's self and speech just as they were.

Finally, Pound and Williams were of the high Modernist generation. They carried the prestige of the 1920s and could hand it on, as the ancient fathers of Israel passed the tribal blessing to their sons. They were in the United States. You could visit them. They were interested in your work. You could write them, enclosing poems, and Williams, at least, sent enthusiastic replies. That Pound and Williams were somewhat neglected made them all the more appealing. To follow them conferred in 1950 an anti-establishment identity. It also gave you poets to fight for.

Pound and Williams alerted their young visitors and correspondents to a number of old friends, associates, or disciples who were working in obscurity and neglect. These were chiefly Basil Bunting, Louis Zukofsky, and the others briefly linked with Williams in the "Objectivist" movement of the 1930s—Charles Reznikoff, Carl Rakosi, and George Oppen. As the young poets gained standing, the writings of these older ones were reissued and favorably reviewed; in short, they were discovered for the first time. The sense of an audience now caused these older poets to resume writing—for some of them had stopped—or to write more abundantly, and much fine work, such as Bunting's *Briggflatts*, would not have been produced without this belated recognition.

Of Williams and the Objectivists David Jones had, probably, never heard. According to his own statement, he owed very little to Pound. Though Jones's writing was not widely known in the 1940s, it already had a small, elite following. I discuss him in the same chapter with Bunting and Zukofsky because his growing reputation is part of the same transition of taste that also brought them forward. The present fame of his great works, *In Parenthesis* and *Anathemata,* owes much to the labors of friends who believed in him, much to mere time, but much also to heightened enthusiasm in the 1950s for long poems in the high Modernist mode.

Finally, I should acknowledge the impact of graduate students in English and their professors. The seminars on modern literature and the Ph.D. theses followed (with a time lag) the changing values in poetry, but they were also propelled by independent mechanisms that helped bring on the transition of the 1950s. Partly, English departments did this negatively by including New Critical explicators on the faculty. Thus the methods and taste of the New Criticism, which had once seemed subversive, became "academic" and could arouse rebellion. Tenured poets, creative writing programs, and courses in contemporary literature were also increasing in English departments during the 1950s. Along with the expanding postwar empires in American Civilization and American Literature, they heightened hopeful attention to present-day poetry. Perhaps the most important mechanism was the simplest: new subjects were needed for Ph.D. theses. Of the modern poets, Yeats and Eliot were the first to become respectable subjects for the professoriat. (When Eliot visited Harvard, he used to spend time in the archives, chuckling to himself as he read the theses written about him.) But Pound was highly visible in the literary history of the 1910s; moreover, if the *Cantos* were worth reading at all, research productive of glosses was a necessary contribution. And Pound led on to Williams. These remarks pertain especially to the United States, but similar developments followed in Great Britain a little later.

The young poets who admired and built on them are not discussed in the next chapters on Pound, Williams, Stevens, and minor authors of long Modernist poems. But since by the 1950s Allen Ginsberg, Charles Olson, Frank O'Hara, Robert Creeley, Denise Levertov, Robert Duncan, and many others—Robert Lowell in his *Life Studies* (1959), John Berryman in his *Dream Songs* from 1964 on, Randall Jarrell in his poems of the 1960s— were responding to Pound, or Williams, or both, and transforming the context in which they were read, the younger poets and the transition in taste they express are very much a part of the story of Pound and Williams and should be kept in mind throughout the following pages. A plain line of succession extends from the high Modernism of the 1920s to the new poetry of the 1950s and 1960s.

The manifestations of this succession are extremely numerous, diverse, and complicated, as we shall gradually see, but even the quickest overview of one genre, the Modernist long poem, illustrates that the succession occurs. The history of this genre begins with *The Waste Land* (1922) and the first sixteen *Cantos* (1925), for these works gave other poets new conceptions of form and subject for a major poem. In *The Bridge* (1930) Hart Crane took his discontinuous, leitmotific methods and urban materials from Eliot while challenging Eliot's pessimistic vision. The *Four Quartets* (1936–42) represent the next major step in the development of the genre. They fused the Modernist type of long poem with older styles, such as the descriptive-meditative poem of the Augustan age and the seventeenth-century lyric. Pound's *Pisan Cantos* were a response to the *Four Quartets,* for Eliot's poem helped to instigate the exploration of personal memory in the *Pisan Cantos,* the references to English history and tradition, and the religious themes. Williams' *Paterson* would not have been written without the earlier poems of Eliot, Pound, and Crane on which it builds, but it makes a formal innovation by abandoning the ideal of a finished, perfected, and coherent work. A similar theory of "open" form underlies Olson's Maximus Poems (1953–68), and Olson also took from Williams the idea of concentrating for his subject matter on the "local" place. *The Maximus Poems* alludes in its opening pages to the *Four Quartets* and *The Bridge,* but generally Olson's form and vision derive more from the *Cantos* than from any other poem. Meanwhile, Zukofsky's *"A"* started in the late 1920s in the style of the *Cantos* and followed this changing model in the 1930s. Among the many other works that also extended the genre in various directions were MacLeish's *The Hamlet of Archibald MacLeish* (1928), Edith Sitwell's *Gold Coast Customs* (1929), Langston Hughes's *Montage of a Dream Deferred* (1951), David Jones's *Anathemata* (1955) and Galway Kinnell's "The Avenue Bearing the Initial of Christ into the New World" (1960). The use of regional landscape and history aligns Basil Bunting's *Briggflatts* (1966) with the Maximus Poems and with the Welsh "deposits" in *Anathemata,* and Geoffrey Hill's *Mercian Hymns* (1971) owes, in turn, something to Bunting's landscape and vision. The *Mercian Hymns* is an allusive, discontinuous, leitmotific poem of juxtaposed vignettes and interwoven themes in the generic tradition I have been tracing. Robert Duncan's *Passages* is still close enough to the *Cantos* to be included in this tradition also, but by this time the genre has evolved far from its beginnings and the descent is less apparent. Of course many long modern poems—for example by Stevens, Auden, and Merrill—derive from other sources and belong to different genres, for modern poetry, as this book exists to testify, is enormously varied, and no one or few lines of development can sum it up or display its excellence.

10

EZRA POUND: THE *CANTOS*

THE early career of Pound, his great influence on other poets from 1912 to 1922, and the steps by which he modernized his style were discussed in the first volume of this history; I here concentrate on his later life and especially on his *Cantos*. Pound was born in 1885 in Idaho and grew up in suburban Philadelphia. In college he concentrated especially in Romance languages and literatures; his interest in Dante, Guido Cavalcanti, and the troubadour poets of Provence was to be lifelong. In 1908 he emigrated to Venice and then, in the same year, to London, where he married in 1914. He plunged into London poetry circles, attending Yeats's Monday evenings at home, Ernest Rhys's evenings, T. E. Hulme's evenings, and the meetings of the Poets' Club. Between 1908 and 1911 he published four volumes of verse. At first he was enthusiastic about contemporary English poetry, but gradually he saw in it vices of vagueness, sentimentality, literary diction, and looseness. He learned to value a hard, precise, objective presentation of fact in a language that departed "in no way from speech save by a heightened intensity." In 1912 and 1913 he propagated these and other values as Imagism. The provocative, explicit directions "how to write" that he published at this time have had an impact on poetry in

America ever since. *Cathay* (1915) and *Lustra* (1916) show Pound in his Imagist or first Modernist phase.

In September 1914 he met T. S. Eliot. By now he was corresponding with Joyce and reading his work. Through Wyndham Lewis he encountered Modernist painters and sculptors, and he joined with them to launch another movement in the arts—Vorticism. He felt that he and his friends were harbingers of a new sensibility, a new civilization. He created more radically Modernist styles in *Homage to Sextus Propertius* (1919), *Hugh Selwyn Mauberley* (1920), and his early *Cantos*.

The war years brought a terrible disillusion. Like most sensitive people, he was appalled at the slaughter abroad and the jingoism at home. His selfless efforts to get Modernist literature accepted ran into resistance of the crassest kinds. Now thirty-five, Pound was fed up, he said, with England—its cultural life, politics, religion, economic system. Though all Western societies seemed to him venal, stupid, and brutal, intellects seemed clearer, the arts livelier in Paris. He lost his chief economic attachment to London when the *Athenaeum* fired him from his job as drama critic. Maybe he sensed that he was being surpassed as an artist by Joyce and as an influence by Eliot. He doubted his own poetry. He had begun the *Cantos* in huge ambition and hope. They would be the grand poem of the age, comparable in scope and importance to the *Odyssey* or the *Divine Comedy*. But now, briefly, his confidence failed.

In 1921 he moved to Paris. The *Little Review* that year printed a calendar he had made, a zany expression of his resolve, as he approached middle age, to shake off his past and begin again. The Christian Era had just ended, his calendar revealed, and a new age had commenced, to be known as the Pound Era. He tended to identify with founders of civilizations and cultures, and he was now also flirting with Dada. (His brief interest in Dada illustrates again how much he was fed up and in search of novelty, for Pound's idea of poetry was really about as close to Dada as Dante's would have been.) He formed a liaison—it was to be lifelong—with Olga Rudge, a violinist and later a musicologist, and a daughter, Mary, was born. About this time he also had a son, Omar (named for Omar Khayyam), by his wife. *A Draft of XVI Cantos* was published in 1925. The title reflected his doubts; it protectively implied that these Cantos were unfinished, merely provisional. He made friends with several younger writers, notably Cummings and Hemingway. His fascination with history had not at first led him to study the American past, but by 1922 he was going through the writings of Thomas Jefferson, using a set Eliot had given him. One of his important literary works came in 1921, when Eliot laid before him the manuscript of *The Waste Land*. It was "damn good," Pound said, but he blue-penciled through it, slashing boldly, and the poem was published much as it had left his hands. He continued his magazine campaign for Eliot and Joyce, and he wooed correspondents for money to liberate Eliot from the bank where he was working and to publish *Ulysses*. He now also pushed the ideas and writings on economics of C. H. Douglas, whom he had met in 1918, as much as he pushed Eliot and Joyce.

In 1924 Pound settled in Rapallo, Italy, where he was to live for the next twenty years. His rooftop apartment looked over the sea. He swam, played tennis, and read detective stories, but mostly he worked. He translated Confucius. He read further in early American history. He published articles on literature, music, government, and economics. Partly to his championship we owe the rediscovery of Vivaldi's music, though the research of Miss Rudge was more important in the long run. Beginning in 1933 he organized annually a series of concerts in Rapallo. He wished to show how much one person's effort can enhance civilization in his locality. He kept up a wide correspondence. The contemporary writers he now praised were chiefly Williams, Zukofsky, Basil Bunting, Cummings, Hemingway, Marianne Moore, and Eliot. He wrote the *ABC of Economics* (1933). In 1933 he met Mussolini, who observed to Pound's great pleasure that the *Cantos* were amusing. The "Boss," as Pound called him, seemed also to share Pound's economic theories.

In London before the First World War Pound had devoted himself almost exclusively to poetry and the other arts. His thoughts, talk, friendships, doings, and aspirations all centered on them. Some twenty years later, in the 1930s, he was more preoccupied with economics and the social order than with art and literature. How to write concerned him far less than how to govern. Where formerly he had advised and aided Eliot and

Joyce, he now tried to advise senators and congressmen, Roosevelt and Stalin.

Devoted to his ideal of the good society, Pound thought he saw it materializing in Fascist Italy. His sympathy with Fascism, like his anti-Semitism, will always be deeply damaging to his fame. Since the Italian news media were controlled by the government, Pound could not know all that was going on in Italy, especially during the war when newspapers from England and America did not arrive. He dismissed much that he did hear as propaganda. His ideal of a good society incorporated a religious dimension, a conviction that communal life should reflect a reverence for nature and the "gods." The contrast with modern capitalism or socialism was clear, and Pound confused his own piety with its perversion in Fascist cultural propaganda. In short, when we take into account his loathing of the economic system in England and the United States, his conviction that Mussolini was adopting economic remedies Pound had long battled for, his sympathy with paternalistic governments (Founding Fathers in America, emperors in China), his admiration for heroically energetic leaders who get work done ("Tching Tang opened the copper mine"; Mussolini "drained off the muck . . . from the marshes . . . grain from the marshes"), and his religious attitudes, we can begin to see how it happened. What is more, in Italy Pound witnessed the enthusiasm of Fascism and was subjected to its propaganda. And he tended, more than most of us, to project his subjective life upon the outer world. Nevertheless, his sympathy with Fascism highlights, at the very least, a certain crudeness, hardness, and violence of temperament.

As Europe drifted toward the Second World War, Pound felt a terrible urgency. Would he take time to do an article on Joyce? No, for "There is too much future, and nobody but me and Muss and half a dozen others to attend to it." In *Jefferson and/or Mussolini* (1935) he tried to show the "fundamental likeness" between these two heroes, and to explain Italy to the United States. With the same purpose he kept writing letters to American magazines and to friends, senators and congressmen. Only if Americans were ignorant or bamboozled could they enter a war against Italy. He sailed in 1939 for the United States. He had hoped to talk with Roosevelt, but managed to see only a few legislators. An honorary degree from his undergraduate college, Hamilton, was not much consolation before he returned to Italy. It was now June.

When the war broke out, Pound stayed in Italy, continuing his usual activities. Bankers' greed for profits was the root cause of the war, he thought—at least on the Allied side. In letters and other writings he strove to prevent the United States from entering against Italy. But Pound felt that his own ideas on economics and government were far more important to the future of the world than the war could be, whoever won. In January 1941, after two years of trying to obtain permission, he began broadcasting his thoughts over the Rome radio. When Pearl Harbor was bombed, he paused seven weeks, pondering whether to return to America and perhaps attempting to do so. But with the United States now at war with Italy, he resumed his broadcasts.

On the air Pound talked about Social Credit, Confucius, usury, Noh drama, modern poetry—in short, his usual topics. He skipped unpredictably from topic to topic: he used an assortment of English and American dialects; he read occasionally from his *Cantos*. Hardly anyone was listening, needless to say, but Italian and American officials were. Hearing such passages as this one from Canto 46 (here as transcribed by official American listeners)—

And if you'll say that this day teaches a lesson, all that the Reverent Elliot (Haston) more natural language, you who think you'll get through hell in a hurry, huh, ah . . .

—the Italians naturally suspected he was transmitting in code. Doubtless the U.S. Department of Justice was equally puzzled, but some statements were lucid: "For the United States to be making war on Italy and on Europe is just plain nonsense . . . Roosevelt is more than any other one man responsible"; "You are not going to win this war," he told America; "You have never had a chance in this war." In 1943 he was indicted in the United States for treason.

At the end of the war he was seized by partisans and then arrested. He was taken to the Disciplinary Training Center at Pisa—a concentration camp to which the U.S. Army sent for "training" its worst criminals—and confined in a wire cage. He slept at first on blankets laid on the concrete floor and later under a pup tent. He was exposed to rain, sun, and dust. No one was permitted to speak to him. After three weeks he broke down, and the doctors, fearing for his life, transferred him to the medical compound, where a tent was set up for him. Under these conditions he gradually resumed, so far as he could, the routine that embodied his ideal of how to live. He composed verse, translated Confucius, and, for exercise, walked and played imaginary tennis with a lath and stones. Late at night he was allowed to use a typewriter in the dispensary. Here between September and November in 1945, amid the wreck of all personal and political hopes, he composed his "testament" and vision of paradise, the *Pisan Cantos*.

From the prison camp in Pisa he was brought in 1945 to Washington for trial. Four examining psychiatrists found him unable to comprehend the seriousness of the charges against him or to aid in his own defense. He was, they told the court, distractible, illogical, grandiose, delusional, and paranoid. He was confident he could rehabilitate the world through Confucian government and Douglasite economics, which he could not explain coherently; he thought himself persecuted by bureaucrats; he had not been taken prisoner, he said, but "gave himself up" to meet President Truman, who needed his information on Japan and Italy. At this time and within the psychiatrists' frame of reference Pound was insane. That the *Pisan Cantos* contributed slightly to their conclusion is unfortunate but understandable.

In view of the psychiatrists' testimony it was legally impossible to try him. He was sent to the government's asylum in Washington. Living in the insane asylum, he did not collapse in self-pity. He had "enormous work to be done."

He studied Confucius. He battled for monetary reform. In 1949 the *Pisan Cantos* won the Bollingen Prize for poetry. He wrote more Cantos, and translated Sophocles' *Women of Trachis*. A selection of his letters was brought out in 1950. In 1954 he published a volume of translations from ancient Chinese poems. *The Classic Anthology Defined by Confucius* is uneven and contains no poem of the first order, but makes, with its variety of lyric styles, a fascinating and delightful book. His work was being broadcast over the BBC, his writings being reprinted, his reputation spreading, and various efforts were under way to have

him released from St. Elizabeth's asylum. Finally in 1958 the
Department of Justice made no objection and the indictment
was dismissed. Among the writers who worked for this were
Eliot, Hemingway, MacLeish, and Frost.

Out at last, Pound visited his boyhood home near Philadelphia, stayed with friends, and sailed after two months for Italy.
He took up quarters with his daughter and her husband in their
castle in the Italian Tirol. Now seventy-two, he was, as ever, full
of projects—a marble temple to be built nearby on a mountain
summit, sugar maples to be planted in Italy, five hundred grape-
vines to be set out in the castle vineyard to provide the white
wine he preferred. In 1955 *Section: Rock-Drill* (Cantos 85–95)
and in 1959 *Thrones* (Cantos 96-109) had been published. Despite fine passages, these Cantos did not equal the great testament he had written as he awaited execution in the Pisan prison
camp. Struck by illness, he recovered, but felt himself old. In
1965 he attended the memorial service for T. S. Eliot in West-
minster Abbey. He visited Paris again and the United States. He
had left it sixty years before with a swelled head, he said, and
returned with swelled feet. Mostly he lived in Venice with Olga
Rudge. As energy ebbed in these last years he doubted the value
of his life's work. Often he was depressed, silent, rueful. He died
in 1972 in Venice and was buried there.

After 1920 Pound composed almost no poetry, except translations, that was not part of the *Cantos*. The other important
poems he published earlier—in his four books between 1908
and 1911 and in *Cathay* (1915), *Lustra* (1916), "Homage to Sextus
Propertius" (in *Quia Pauper Amavi*, 1919) and *Hugh Selwyn Mauberley* (1920)—were noticed in the first volume of this history, and
in this one I discuss the *Cantos* only. The poem is about twenty-
three thousand lines long. It extends in time from the modern
word back through history to the ancient and primitive. In space
it ranges through America, London, Gibraltar, Italy, Greece,
China, Africa, Russia, and Japan. Its tone of voice varies from

> Hey Snag wots in the bibl'?
> Wot are the books ov the bible?
> Name 'em, don't bullshit ME;

to

       Kuanon, this stone bringeth sleep;

to

And then went down to the ship,
Set keel to breakers, forth on the godly sea, and
We set up mast and sail on that swart ship;

to

      woe to them that conquer with armies
      and whose only right is their power

—tones that we may call low colloquial, lyric, epic, and prophetic—and it includes a huge variety of other tones. Its mass
contains, among other things, laws of ancient China, quotes
from Jefferson and John Adams, extracts from account books
of medieval Venice, vignettes of Edwardian London, ideograms that the Chinese emperor Tching Tang wrote on his
bathtub—

      Day by day make it new
  cut underbrush,
  pile the logs
  keep it growing

—Douglasite explanations of cost and purchasing power, instructions of Sigismundo Malatesta to his architect, descriptions
of hemorrhoids, and moments of mystical vision. It is humorous, grand, startlingly beautiful in places, relentlessly boring in
others, nobly intended, and sometimes morally repulsive. Lay-
ing different historical times and places "ply over ply," it tries to
show the recurring basis of just societies—the few to be found—
and creative civilizations. It asks what sustains the human spirit
amid the confusion and fear of existence.

COMPONENTS OF THE TEXTURE

Whether or not the *Cantos* have an overall structure is a vexed
question. There is also the question whether or how much it

matters. On one occasion (in "Dr. Williams' Position") Pound suggested that "Major form is not a non-literary component. But it can do us no harm to stop an hour or so and consider the number of very important chunks of world-literature in which form, major form, is remarkable mainly for absence," and he mentioned, among others, the *Iliad,* the *Prometheus* of Aeschylus, Montaigne, and Rabelais. "The component of these works and *the* indispensable component is texture." As Coleridge once explained it, a poem must provide "a distant gratification from each component *part.*" The "reader should be carried forward, not merely or chiefly by the mechanical impulse of curiosity, or by a restless desire to arrive at the final solution; but by the pleasurable activity of the mind excited by the attractions of the journey itself."

For many persons reading the *Cantos* is not pleasurable, since the texture seems hopelessly difficult. For example, the opening lines of the *Pisan Cantos:*

The enormous tragedy of the dream in the peasant's bent shoulders
Manes! Manes was tanned and stuffed,
Thus Ben and la Clara *a Milano*
          by the heels at Milano
That maggots shd / eat the dead bullock
DIGONOS, Δίγονος, but the twice crucified
                    where in history will you find it?
yet say this to the Possum: a bang, not a whimper,
     with a bang not with a whimper,
To build the city of Dioce whose terraces are the color of stars.
The suave eyes, quiet, not scornful,
                    rain also is of the process.
What you depart from is not the way
and olive tree blown white in the wind
washed in the Kiang and Han
what whiteness will you add to this whiteness,
                    what candor?

The main elements of this texture are concrete and fragmentary presentation, allusion, ellipsis, discontinuity, and juxtaposition. The "peasant's bent shoulders" may refer among other things to Benito Mussolini ("Ben" in Pound's brash way of talking). "Manes" (or Mani), founder of the Manichaean religion, was crucified, his body flayed, and his hide, the poem says, tanned and stuffed. "Thus" or analogously with Mussolini and his mistress, whose dead bodies were hung up by the heels at Milan. In the context of the *Pisan Cantos* the reference to Mussolini's downfall begins to suggest what the "dream" was and why it was tragic. "Shd" might indicate a rhythmical effect—we do not accent or pause on "should" in this line—but more probably reflects merely Pound's impatience in typing this passage. The image of massive strength in the bullock connects with the peasant and with Mussolini. DIGONOS in Roman and then in Greek letters evokes the god Dionysus. Bringer of a new religion and a new culture, Dionysus makes a subject rhyme with Manes and Mussolini. Like them he was violently killed—torn to pieces. The form of his name here alludes to the myth that he was born twice. The "twice crucified" may be Mussolini, whose body was first trampled and hacked by the mob and then strung up. Perhaps we should also think of Pound: he was stood by the partisans against the wall to be shot, and then brought to the prison camp, where he expected to be hanged. Certainly Pound identified himself with the founders and prophets he alludes to.

"Crucified" is one of the several details in these lines that bring Christ to mind; but we notice that while Pound names Mani, Mussolini, and Dionysus, he does not name Christ although the context seems inevitably to summon the thought of Christ ("crucified," "way," "olive"). It is a typical moment in his lifelong quest to replace Christianity with a truer and finer vision and a better basis of social order.

"Possum" is of course T. S. Eliot, author of *Old Possum's Book of Practical Cats,* and Possum's *The Hollow Men* had ended with the famous lines:

> This is the way the world ends
> This is the way the world ends
> This is the way the world ends
> Not with a bang but a whimper.

The allusion tells us that in this moment and for this speaker the world is ending.

Thus the lines establish a coherence, a meaning, and a dramatic development of emotion; but my subject here is not this creative achievement—I do not aim to "read" these lines—so much as the methods Pound employed. Obviously the presentation is concrete throughout. We are given images, metaphors, examples—the "peasant's bent shoulders," the "dead bullock," Mussolini hung up by the heels. The strength and truth of language lay for Pound in its power of concretion. It is one thing to say "prison" or "concentration camp." But to show the barbed-wire fence and guard towers, as Pound does in the *Pisan Cantos*, speaks "prison" to the imagination. The pictureless general term lies inert on the page; the images, activating imagination, compel us to undergo something of the experience. Conferring felt knowledge, the images penetrate, hold in memory, form feeling. They have the suggestiveness and complexity of reality. No wonder Pound distrusted thought that lost touch with the concrete. For Pound it was a question of sincerity, of knowing and feeling that of which you speak. We can know, to repeat, particulars, not generalizations. We may, for example, have encountered a person who is on the whole virtuous; "the good man" is a meaningless abstraction. Thus if we wish to speak sincerely we will not say, "the good man is modest, loyal, true, and brave," defining an abstraction by more abstractions. Pound will say "Confucius," or, maybe, "John Adams." (He is still more likely to say "Confucius/John Adams," but this is a different, more sophisticated technique—the "ideogram"—to which we shall come.) He will show their acts, quote their words.

These concrete presentations are almost always fragmentary. Fragmentation in *The Waste Land* is mimetic: the technique expresses the modern "mind," our incoherent experience or world, which Eliot renders in satire and despair. But Pound thought that in all times life has always presented fragments to the mind. This is the natural case. The world is coherent—this was Pound's faith—but our data are always incomplete. The event is a complex whole, but only aspects, snatches, bits come to our cognizance. As when historians reconstruct the past from surviving documents, or scientists Sinanthropus from his bones, or archaeologists the ancient city from their digs, we must intuit the living reality from the snippets we can know of it. Some details are especially telling or "luminous," and afford "sudden insight into circumjacent conditions, into their causes, their effects, into sequence, and law." Naturally Pound tried to give such details in his poem. Since life presents fragments, it is not surprising that our minds are inherently disposed to work with them. "All knowledge is built up from a rain of factual atoms . . . Real knowledge goes into natural man in titbits. A scrap here, a scrap there; always pertinent, linked to safety, or nutrition or pleasure. Human curiosity survives and is catered for, by the twopenny weeklies, 24 lines on chromosomes, six lines on a three-headed calf." And as life does not comment on the concrete fragments it provides us, neither do the *Cantos*. If most important poems may be called a reading of life, the *Cantos* aim also to be a course of education in how to read life's page. As we go through the poem we are learning by concrete experience—this was Pound's hope, at any rate—how much and how we can know people, events, civilizations, historical transitions. The rule of procedure is synecdoche. The fragments evoke the whole context from which they come. They may be very brief or extended. Three words, "Adamo me fecit," carved in the stone of a church bring to mind the ethos of medieval craftsmanship as opposed to modern factory production. At an opposite extreme John Adams is evoked (if Adams is the ultimate object and if "evoked" is the right word) in eighty pages (Cantos 62–71) of selections from his works. Though Pound's fragments are perfectly definite, their implications are endless and often contradictory.

Allusion is an aspect of Pound's concrete presentation. Instead of generalizing about crucified founders of cultures, he writes Manes, Mussolini, Dionysus. Thus he obtains the depth and complexity of the concrete, for whatever we know about these figures may enrich our response. So also with allusions to places, works of literature (usually brief quotations), history, philosophies, and religions; the allusion brings its context into the poem's context, setting up a system of interrelations. All this is familiar in Modernist literature.

Presenting concrete fragments, Pound boldly elides, ignoring conventions of grammar and giving only the words necessary to his effect. "The enormous tragedy of the dream in the peasant's bent shoulders" is a line but not a sentence, the verb being elided. "Thus Ben and la Clara *a Milano*" tells us who and where but not what: we have to supply the predication for ourselves. A more perspicuous and wordy writer might have said, "My ideal is to build the city of Dioce . . ." Eliding, Pound secures speed and compression; his fragmentary or unfinished units of grammar work suggestively, summoning the reader's imagination to complete them. When the verbs are elided or are present only in participial forms, as often happens, Pound's lines give the effect of fact after fact laid down with finality. But the omitted verbs may be implied, charging his images with energy and potential action.

His transitions are discontinuous. To some degree they are always disruptive and disorienting also. When we read,

> olive tree blown white in the wind
> washed in the Kiang and Han,

we do not imagine an olive tree washed in the sacred rivers of China. Whatever the interrelations between these lines, the second does not proceed in an ongoing unit of grammar from the first. It is not as with Keats's wine in the "Ode to a Nightingale,"

> Tasting of Flora and the country green,
> Dance, and Provençal song, and sunburnt mirth,

where the images of the second line refer back to the first line, extending and completing it. The units Pound works with may be images, single lines, groups of lines ("ideograms"), continuous passages, whole Cantos, or clusters of Cantos. Larger ones are built by assembling many smaller. Juxtaposed, they make a system of relations. But each remains a discrete piece.

When two things are given together, the mind naturally strives to connect them. We respond to Pound's discontinuities with an initial surprise and shock, and this gives way to heightened mental activity as we explore possible interrelationships among the separate units. The process may end in illumination as we discover implications in the juxtaposition. To speak of this mode of composition as construction oversimplifies, but emphasizes the contrast with the Romantic convention of spontaneous flow, of the poem conceived as an organically evolving process.

Different styles may be juxtaposed. Not merely literary styles from Homer to Henry James to newspapers, but spoken styles, the way diverse people express themselves—a contemporary swindler named Baldy Bacon, or Confucius, or Malatesta. For a style is associated with and implicitly expresses values. It registers a state of mind. The guard's words in the prison camp—

"wd." said the guard "*take* everyone of them g.d.m.f. generals
c.s. all of 'em fascists"

—reveal that the "paraclete" of precision does not dwell in his
soul. On the same page we can read about the music of the good
emperor Shun, "the sharp song with sun under its radiance." A
fragment of "Shun's music" as well as a characterization, the line
highlights by contrast the guard's confusion and rage. With its
civilized theme, its shapely, definite rhythm, and its density with
clarity of utterance, the emperor's music shows the guard's mind
for a pigsty.

Since any distinctly recognizable style—of a particular writer,
a period, a social type or class—brings with it a system of associations, a writer can use a bit of that style as an allusion, even
as a symbol. Moreover, every style (that is in any degree admirable) has particular capabilities and limitations. It can convey
some states of sensibility and feeling, but not others. You cannot
say in biblical style what you can in the voice of Henry James, or
vice versa. At least in theory, then, a writer might adopt whatever
style can best express his state of feeling, and if this state changes
suddenly and radically, so will his style. It may change to a different language, since we should not think merely of English
styles, but of the much wider vocabulary of styles possible to a
writer who knows foreign languages and literatures as well. And
of course if a writer speaks in some historical or otherwise familiar style, the allusive or symbolic values of this style will contribute along with its intrinsic capabilities. We may, for example,
be puzzled that the *Pisan Cantos* end in doggerel—

> If the hoar frost grip thy tent
> Thou wilt give thanks when night is spent

—until we recognize that in meter, diction, and sentiment the
lines both use and allude to a style of folk poetry in the oral
tradition. "Pound's" experience in prison camp has united him
with mankind's experience through the centuries.

However various the styles it includes, a work of art has a stylistic unity also. It is "in," as we say, a style. And usually it does
not criticize its own style. But in a work of art such as the *Cantos*,
which deploys many radically different styles in rapid juxtaposition, each style is implicitly criticized by the other styles that
are also present. Because we are made to be conscious of them,

the specific values and expressive capabilities of any particular style are thus enhanced and liberated. But there may be a cost. The means of expression may become the subject equally with the thing expressed. We may not identify with the emotion as we compare the styles and admire the virtuosity.

IDEOGRAMS

Concrete presentation, ellipsis, allusion, fragmentation, discontinuity, and juxtaposition were fundamental to the *Cantos* from their start. But gradually Pound began to speak of his procedure as the presentation of "ideograms" or the "ideogramic method." Just before the First World War he had come into possession of Ernest Fenollosa's manuscript "Essay on the Chinese Written Character." In Chinese script, Fenollosa explained, some of the characters are "simple, original pictures"; others compound two or more pictures. The ideogram for "messmate" shows a man and a fire. And at every reading. No matter how often we encounter the ideogram, Fenollosa argued, we never respond to it merely as a conventionalized sign. We always perceive it as a complex of images, and our minds work actively from the images toward the meanings they embody. Teaching himself the Chinese script, Pound tried to do just this. Thus the ideogram that combines pictures of the sun and the moon articulated much more than the abstraction "bright." It presented two bright objects, the sun and the moon, and as we think what is meant by putting the sun and moon together, we realize that this ideogram speaks of "the total light process, the radiation, reception, and reflection of light; hence, the intelligence. Bright, brightness, shining."

Precisely when Pound began writing what he considered ideograms is hard to say. (Ronald Bush notices that Pound's characteristic uses of the term began in 1927.) For Pound had been composing by the agrammatical juxtaposition of fragments since 1917 at least. And how would ideograms differ? The question raises a more general one: What conventions did Pound invoke to explain and legitimate his discontinuities, both to himself and for his readers? When he started the *Cantos*, he conceived that the reader would assist in the theater of somebody's mind—for simplicity we may call this person "Pound." The content and flow of the poem would be what "Pound" sees, tells, thinks, remembers, and associates. This was in the Ur-Cantos of 1917. This convention was never wholly abandoned. But though it persisted, the convention had ceased to govern firmly before any Cantos had reached the form in which we now read them. For it was "subjective"; Pound sought a more "objective" presentation. One possibility was the repetition of radicals in a design (something learned from Wyndham Lewis). He borrowed hints from Cubist collage and from music. Each conception of his procedure somewhat influenced his actual way of writing, but also rationalized methods that had been formed (and gradually transformed) under quite different pressures and considerations. None of these conceptions provides a convention throughout the poem. We have to keep them in mind, but they do not completely interpret what we find.

The "ideogram" was another theory of "objective" presentation. Pound explained and espoused it more persistently than the others, and the *Cantos* are often said to be "ideogramic" from start to finish. The ideogram, to repeat, is visual and spatial. In theory it is as far as possible from interior monologue. With the convention of interior monologue, we take the fragments as occurring one after the other, enacting the movement of consciousness. With the ideogram we take the component images as interacting simultaneously to present a complex of meaning. The interior monologue reflects or, more exactly, *is* somebody's subjectivity. The ideogram is objective in the same sense as is a character in Chinese script. In fact, both conventions—of the interior flow of consciousness and of ideogramic objectivity—can operate at the same time in the *Cantos*. Since the one convention was present at the start and the other came gradually later, the fact that both may be observed in the same passage illustrates that ideogramic writing did not involve a radical change from earlier procedures.

Thus far I have been speaking of Pound's "ideogramic method" as a way of presentation. But Pound also advocated and practiced it as a way of thinking. "I am not putting these sentences into monolinear syllogistic arrangement," he explained in *Jefferson and/or Mussolini,* "and I have no intention of using that old form of treachery to fool the reader, my reader, into thinking I have proved anything, or that having read a paragraph of my writing he knows something that he can only *know* by examining a dozen or two dozen facts and by putting them all together." Pound regarded the *Cantos* as a vast process of ideogramic thinking. When he tried to convert George Santayana to this mode of mental procedure, Santayana asked how we know which "facts" or "components" should be heaped up. "A *latent* classification," he said, "or a *latent* genetic connection would seem to be required, if utter miscallaneousness is to be avoided." Ideogramic method claims to eliminate "abstraction," but an unacknowledged (hence nebulous and uncriticized) abstraction stands at the first step, determining which cases are relevant.

INCREMENTAL REPETITION

As we read the *Cantos*, one passage refers us back or forward to another, usually to several others. The connection comes often by allusion to the same memory, historical episode, myth, quotation, landscape, and so forth. It is sometimes as though the circumstance, or the presentation of it, had been shattered into separate fragments, and a fragment were given here, a fragment there. Readers must reassemble the fragments as they read, thus bringing different moments of the poem together. Of course, the actual process and effect is far more diverse and complex than I can suggest. A fragment may enter into different wholes. Events are reinterpreted by the changing contexts in which they reappear. And there are the less describable but no less important incremental effects created through cross-cultural "rhyming" of myths (for example, the Chinese goddess Kwanon with the Greek Artemis), or of myth with history (Helen of Troy with Eleanor of Aquitaine), or of legendary, historical, or literary figures or events with contemporary ones (Malatesta with Baldy Bacon). There is the repetition of images (saffron) and themes (the underworld descent, linking Odysseus with an infant wasp). And there are such unclassifiable associations as the croissant for breakfast with Artemis, the crescent moon. All this presupposes, for its full working, that we have the entire poem intimately in mind before reading any part of it. Few readers do, but every reader experiences that the more one reads the *Cantos,* the more meaningful and moving any passage is likely to become.

MAJOR FORM

When Pound started the *Cantos,* he had methods but not a structure. He had only general notions of what "sort of design and architecture" his poem might acquire. Never mind, he would write on anyway. He would heap up "components," hoping they would eventually cohere. He would make a radical and literal experiment in organic form: the Cantos would develop out of their own dynamics and out of the vicissitudes of his life. He intended a relation to the *Odyssey* and the *Divine Comedy.* Within the first sixteen Cantos he alluded to Homer and Dante in ways that force us to look in his poem for plots parallel to theirs. Occasionally thenceforth, both within the poem and in remarks about it, he indicated that the parallels were still in his mind. And both epics help interpret the course and meaning of the *Cantos.* But no reader has been able to use the *Odyssey* or the *Divine Comedy* as a map. Neither have readers found any other plot or comprehensive design—none, at least, on which they agree. Complaints began early, throwing Pound on the defensive. On most occasions he urged his readers, "as to the *form* of *The Cantos . . . wait* til it's there. I mean wait till I get 'em written and then if it don't show, I will start exegesis." But the *Cantos* were never finished.

Overstating to make the point, we could say that the *Odyssey* has a plot because Odysseus has an aim. Were he not trying to get home, his adventures would be unconnected episodes. Only his volition makes his pleasures with Circe a threat and Ithaca a denouement. But suppose Odysseus willed the purpose of his voyage only gradually in the midst of it. In this case the early episodes of the *Odyssey* would be random, disconnected, and without significance (except that Odysseus survives) when they occur, but would acquire a structural function and a meaning retrospectively as his purpose formed and clarified. In *The Divine Comedy,* in contrast, the world has a structure of its own, independent of any human will. There is only one valid perspective, and every experience is placed within it. But this order and meaning are not fully possessed by the protagonist from the start. They are unfolded gradually through the encounters of his journey. And suppose Dante recognized that he was in hell only after he had caught a vision of paradise. In these respects Pound intended that the *Cantos* would blend their two great prototypes. He was Odysseus, but he was voyaging in order to choose the purpose of his voyage. He was Dante in the dark wood, and he hoped that if he went through the chaos of experience and history, he would gradually see that it had a structure. In other words, Pound was in search of an order of values, and he was also exceptionally mindful of the difficulties of the search. Values are exhibited and must be judged in the concrete. But how much can we know about persons or events, not to mention such more nebulous entities as states of mind and civilizations? To the extent that we have information, how reliable is it? And then there are the truisms Pound tried to keep vividly in mind: any event is complex, its components multiple and their interrelations often contradictory; moreover, the event changes as we see it in different contexts and perspectives.

Nevertheless, if Pound did not possess a coherent vision of things, and so could not articulate one in his poem from the start, he had a faith. He thought that if he looked hard at a great many different persons, events, civilizations, and states of mind, and set each in numerous diverse contexts or perspectives, juxtaposing and so implicitly comparing each with others, gradually an order would emerge. It would be not an order he had imposed but an order inherent in things, which his method had compelled them to reveal. The classifications of biology into genera and species provided a metaphor. These groupings exist objectively in the materials, but are not known until the materials are collected, observed, and compared. His poem would enact the observing and comparing. At every point it would remain honest to the concrete complexity of things, the shifting perspectives from which they can be viewed, and the plurality and contradiction of values in the world. If eventually an order of values revealed itself, it would also interpret the earlier portions of the poem.

But though Pound believed that values were to be discovered and tested empirically, of course he began the poem with moral and even with religious convictions. They were expressed from the start. They change somewhat in the course of the poem, but because of all Pound's experience, not merely because of the examination performed by the poem.

Should we then say that the *Cantos* lack a major form? Obviously they have no "plot" in the ordinary sense, and, except in episodes, generate no narrative interest. There is often a central sensibility, but except in the *Pisan Cantos* that sensibility is too little characterized to hold the poem together. There is much argument, but no logical progression to the whole. There is an order of values, but it does not give structure to the poem. In short, much that in other long poems sustains interest and relates episodes to one another and to the whole is absent from the *Cantos*.

Yet our experience as readers must be the test, and as I go through it, the poem does not seem, on the whole, to lack coherence and development. The sense of coherence is produced mainly by the incremental repetition. And though we are not at every moment aware of it, a "hierarchy of values" is establishing itself. As things and persons recur in different contexts, our judgment of them varies with the context. This holds true throughout the poem. There is never a final view. But amid the multiplicity of different experiences and perspectives, ideals are being ordered in relation to each other. Consider the condottiere Sigismundo Malatesta, whom we encounter in Cantos 8 to 11. He is phenomenally busy, a man of many projects who gets work done, and Pound identifies with him. Also, he embodies the Renaissance "mind" in one of its early expressions. Pound's characterization of him assembles "a great number of . . . violently contrasted facts," as Pound thought historical interpretation must do "if it is to be valid." Malatesta is individualistic, mercenary, violent, treacherous, brave, generous, vital, productive, and a patron and student of the arts and philosophy. And if amid these contrasts we ask what judgment we are to form of Malatesta, the Cantos about him do not tell us. We look at their context in the poem, but the immediate context opens contrasting perspectives. Compared to Baldy Bacon (Canto 12), a modern soldier of fortune interested only in money, Malatesta is admirable. So far as vitality and purpose are better than their opposites, he is also a positive figure when compared with the

living dead of Canto 7. But Confucius in Canto 13 measures him
by a different scale.

> Kung walked
> > by the dynastic temple,

the Canto begins, and the rhythm has a serenity lacking in the
Malatesta Cantos. As more Cantos accumulate, we see Thomas
Jefferson, a ruler no less busy, vital, and many-sided than Malatesta, but less violent and more thoughtful. Pursuing useful
inventions, improvements, trade, the regulation of the economy,
he represents the "mind" of the Enlightenment, and we would
rather be governed by Jefferson than by Malatesta. And in Canto
53 there is the Emperor Yao, "like sun and rain" to his people.
And by the time we come to the *Pisan Cantos* and read, "To study
with the white wings of time passing," and "in the light of light
is the *virtù*," and "have I perchance a debt to a man named
Clower," we are far in spiritual geography from Malatesta. We
may look back on him as one of those "lost / Violent souls" of
whom Eliot speaks in *The Hollow Men*.

THE *PISAN CANTOS*

The *Pisan Cantos* have a human interest beyond anything
Pound had written hitherto. For "Pound" is the central character. We see his immediate circumstances in the concentration
camp, with all their drama and pathos:

> The moon has a swollen cheek
> and when the morning sun lit up the shelves and battalions
> of the West, cloud over cloud
> > Old Ez folded his blankets
> Neither Eos nor Hesperus has suffered wrong at my hands.

His memories come back: the young sculptor, Gaudier-Brzeska,
eyeing "the telluric mass of Miss Lowell"; "the noise in the chimney" that winter when he shared a cottage in Sussex with Yeats—

> as it were the wind in the chimney
> > but was in reality Uncle William
> downstairs composing.

He remembers the trees in Paris, seen from under the frame of
a bridge arch:

> as it might be L'Ile St Louis for serenity, under Abélard's bridges
> for those trees are Elysium
> > for serenity
> > > under Abélard's bridges.

And he remembers a time of despair in Venice in 1907, when
he almost threw the manuscript of his first volume into the canal: "by the soap-smooth stone posts where San Vio / meets with
il Canal Grande . . . shd/ I chuck the lot into the tide-water?"
That moment comes to mind because his despair now reminds
him of then, but he was "free then, therein the difference." Occasionally he judges his own character and life—

> Les larmes que j'ai crées m'inondent
> Tard, très tard je t'ai connue, la Tristesse,
> I have been hard as youth sixty years.

and he sifts his past and present for values that sustain. "Mi-
hine eyes hev," he quotes the "Battle Hymn of the Republic,"
heard on the radio, and reflects,

> > > well yes they *have*
> > seen a good deal of it
> > > there is a good deal to be seen
> > fairly tough and unblastable.

The "glory" is always there, like the "green world" of vital nature, or like the crystal air.

Because he was writing with a personal and autobiographical
dimension, Pound emphasized elements of style that would put
even his most intensely personal feelings at a distance. Unlike
many poets since who also worked with personal materials, he
was not striving to enhance our impressions of intimacy and sincerity by diminishing our impression of artistry. On the contrary,
his thoughts, memories, and immediate sufferings were to be
placed in a context and handled in a way that would give them
the hardness and objectivity of art. Irony is omnipresent, almost,
and in inexhaustibly various forms. Pound mythologizes his experience. In one breathtaking transformation the four guard
towers at the corners of the concentration camp become four
giants, and the camp itself the legendary city of Wagadu, an

African folktale version of the ideal city of Pound's dream, "now in the mind indestructible." At many points in the poem Pound uses words, phrases, and lines in foreign languages. At times these are literary or other allusions, but often they are not. Pound had no one reason or justification for this technique, no motive or intention that explains all instances. Each bit of foreign speech must be studied in its context, and usually its appropriateness or enhanced effectiveness will be clear. (That such phrases arrest attention and cause us to reflect on them would of course be one reason for them.) Often in the *Pisan Cantos* Pound seems to have adopted the foreign phrasing as a means to emotional reticence or control. In Canto 76 Pound in his isolation speaks to the swallow, asking it to carry a message to the woman he loves:

> O white-chested martin, God damn it,
> as no one else will carry a message,
> say to La Cara: amo.

And in Canto 83, remembering Venice, he asks himself "Will I ever see the Giudecca?"

> or the boats moored off le Zattere
> or the north Quai of the Sensaria   DAKRUON   ΔΑΚΡΥΩΝ

the Greek spelling "weeping."

Each quotation in the *Pisan Cantos* works in particular ways in its own context, but generally they remind us that the poem is not to be read as the natural voice of "Pound." More exactly, they have this alienating effect, but we continually reinstate our sense of intimate connection with the speaker. As an external or objective element of "poetic tradition" in the style, quotation generalizes the utterance of "Pound," makes it less personal and more authoritative. But at the same time it serves as a means to Pound's self-expression, for it further defines his emotion through the associations it evokes.

Up to the *Pisan Cantos* Pound had either composed in the mode of impersonal construction by juxtaposition, which gradually he came to call the "ideogramic method," or alternatively he had created a persona as speaker or central consciousness. A passage could be read by both conventions at the same time. The great advantage of impersonal construction was the freedom it afforded in the materials and styles that could be combined. When, for example, the persona is John Adams, the materials must be limited to those which could conceivably have existed within Adams' field of consciousness. And the diction, syntax, imagery, and rhythm—in short, the voice—must similarly restrict its range. (Though Adams' own sentences and phrases became remarkably condensed and elliptical in Pound's extracts.) Thus Adams can utter "Indian pudding and pork greens on the table," but imprisoned in Adams, Pound cannot combine this with Ling Kong's menu—"this prince liked eating bears' paws"—as was possible in an ideogram.

But a persona holds the poem together. Each detail refers to the central figure and characterizes him. In Canto 71, for example, Adams' thoughts move in four lines from Chief Little Turtle's horror of rum to Adams' own of the banking system. The aversions have an ideogramic connection, but if a reader did not follow this thread, each of the items separately and the leap from one to the other would still contribute to the portrait of Adams. Impersonal construction, on the other hand, can seem incoherent. When the thread is lost, the juxtapositions seem a jumble, and we have no way of relating to the poem.

Creating himself as the associating, self-expressing consciousness in the *Pisan Cantos,* Pound did not tie himself to any particular range of materials or style of expression. He illuminated by explosive juxtapositions, as in impersonal construction, but these now also registered complexities and rapid transformations of feeling in a person with whom we identify. That the thoughts and images are fragmentary, elliptical, and dissociated simply contributes in this case to the dramatic characterization. As in Eliot's *The Waste Land,* discontinuity presents a mind *in extremis.*

The *Pisan Cantos,* in other words, must be read both as ideogram and as interior monologue. Yet since this could also be said of some earlier Cantos, the *Pisan Cantos* are so much different not simply because they unite the two modes, but because in them the ideograms have an imaginative splendor, the characterization of the persona an emotional appeal beyond anything Pound elsewhere achieved. For example,

I don't know how humanity stands it
with a painted paradise at the end of it
without a painted paradise at the end of it
the dwarf morning-glory twines round the grass blade
magna NUX animae with Barabbas and 2 thieves beside me.

In the "death cells" awaiting execution, Pound thinks of man's illusory hope for an afterlife, the "paradise" so frequently "painted" for our consolation. Because it is artificial, we cannot bear it. Yet without it we cannot bear to confront death. His attention fixes on the dwarf morning-glory and then on the great night of the soul. In this moment of agony he identifies himself with Christ on the cross. The passage enacts a plunge of the mind facing death into despair and self-pity.

Yet when we view this passage as an ideogram, the morning-glory changes its value. It is not just a brief eddy in a stream of consciousness, but a stable and lasting component of a complex of meaning. The passage reflects on Christianity, and since "Possum" is mentioned two lines before, probably T. S. Eliot's Christianity was hovering before Pound. Possum had dwelt in his *Four Quartets* on the concept of the great night of the soul. Pound was always concerned to set Eliot right. In the interrelations of the ideogram the morning-glory exhibits the paradise that is not "painted," the real, always present, vital nature, as much in this one small, frail thing as anywhere. "Morning" and "glory" flood the line with light, contrasting with the NUX. The interrelations of the flower held on the grass blade with Christ on the cross defy description.

PARADISO

The old reverence before sacred nature is gone in the modern world. This fact connects, Pound believed, with the artistically unproductive, deeply unnatural character of modern life, and the *Cantos* facilitate comparison by placing their images or evocations of the ideal next to other images of venal art, sterile luxury, inert sloth, ruthless greed and swindles. All this is hell, and Cantos 14–16 express it as scenes in Dante's *Inferno*. But it is not just a spiritual state, it is the result of an economic system, and the relation between these two orders of reality is not always clear in the *Cantos*. For on the one hand, the evil lies in the human will. The *Cantos* are the most intense indictment yet made, in the poetry of our century, of greed blighting human affection, coarsening intellect, depraving art, perverting government, kindling wars. But on the other hand, the evil lies in certain malfunctionings of the economic machine, and, in Pound's opinion, only a little expert tinkering is needed to adjust it and keep it working infallibly, a cornucopia steadily distributing.

Just before he was imprisoned in the Pisan concentration camp, Pound had started to prepare himself for writing the final part of his *Cantos*. He was going to write his *Paradiso*. The relation between his ideals of paradise and of communal order is tricky. Pound intensely hoped that the just state would someday become a reality. Passages in the *Cantos* that imagine this might be said to portray an earthly and possible paradise. Still, his *Paradiso* could not be merely a description of a future social order. For paradise must be now or nowhere. There is no afterlife, no future heaven. A future golden age of history was, in Pound's view, no glorious promise for those who would never see it. Our one existence is now, in this moment, for example, of dawn that Canto 47 pictures:

> And the small stars now fall from the olive branch,
> Forked shadow falls dark on the terrace
> More black than the floating martin
>   that has no care for your presence,
> His wing-print is black on the roof tiles
> And the print is gone with his cry.
> So light is thy weight on Tellus
> Thy notch no deeper indented.

If there is any "paradise," or hope of it, for us now, it must be individual and mystical, the soul's vision of the divine or union with it. Pound believed, in his own way, in this. He had partly beheld the vision, or thought he had.

When asked his religion, Pound used to call himself a "pagan." I hesitate to attach a less interesting label, but his religion was a mode of pantheism. It was of course an intuition, not a logically consistent or theologized creed. He believed that man is a part of nature and that nature in its inmost being is divine. "'Consciousness of the unity with nature,'" Pound had written as far back as 1931, "is at the root of any mystery." He found this intuition of "unity with nature" expressed in the paganism of Confucian China and of the ancient Mediterranean world. He "believed" in the gods—gods, for belief in one God tends to divert the mind from this world to some other, purely imaginary one. And it seemed to Pound that monotheism has regularly been associated with religious and moral tyranny. "The glory of the polytheistic anschauung is that it never asserted a single and obligatory path for everyone." Another of its glories was that it did not "disdain" but instead "celebrated and exalted" the erotic. Pound felt that nature incarnates in the sexual as in every other of its manifestations a divine mystery. Hence when the *Cantos* present Dionysus, Demeter, Persephone, Aphrodite, Adonis, and the like, Pound is expressing both his nostalgia for an age or culture that sensed and revered the divine in nature and also his own reverence for all that these mythical figures invoked. Above all, he is saying that the gods are still present:

> Gods float in the azure air,
> Bright gods and Tuscan, back before dew was shed.
> Light: and the first light, before ever dew was fallen.
> Panisks, and from the oak, dryas,
> And from the apple, mælid,
> Through all the wood, and the leaves are full of voices,
> A-whisper.

And there is light. It was Dante's symbol of the divine, and Cavalcanti's; it went back to Plato, neo-Platonic philosophers, mystics, Schoolmen, Provençal poets, and Confucius—in Pound's version of Confucius. Light descends from heaven:

> Thus the light rains, thus pours, *e lo soleills plovil*
> The liquid and rushing crystal,

as Pound or his musing protagonist had summed up as long ago as 1919 in Canto 4, the phrase in Provençal ("and the sun rains") taken from Arnaut Daniel. Light is everywhere. "Overstanding the earth," light "fills the nine fields to heaven." It is a symbol of the intellect in its perfection. Studying the Chinese ideogram "hsien" ("to manifest," "to be illustrious"), as Hugh Kenner has explained, Pound thought he saw in it the signs for sun and silk, and imagined the sun's ray or beam as a strand of silk:

> Light tensile immaculata
>   the sun's cord unspotted

(saying it in scholastic Latinity and in Chinese ideogram to invoke two different civilizations). Stretching between heaven and earth, hitting the mark, in other words, tense, precise, focused, clear, radiant, this sun silk or light or intelligence is the "paraclete that was present" in the good Chinese emperors. Drawing on neo-Platonic and medieval philosophers, Pound could say that the intellectual being or light of the divine dwells not just in the mind of man but in all things as their inmost principle or essence. In his brash, familiar way he cites Scotus Eriugena, a ninth-century philosopher from Ireland:

> "sunt lumina" said the Oirishman to King Carolus,
>   "OMNIA,
> all things that are are lights."

And Pound identified this indwelling light with the "inborn nature" of which Confucius (in Pound's translation) speaks: "What heaven has disposed and sealed is called the inborn nature. The realization of this nature is called the process."

Light shining from everything, a moving energy within, without, over, on. You cannot help seeing it, as well as by means of it. At least, that is what the symbolism seems to imply, but hardly anyone using the symbolism has wished to suggest that we knowingly and feelingly behold the divine in every moment of our earthly lives. Neither did Pound. He thought, instead, of a light that is always there, but, somehow, not always seen. So also with his other main symbolism. "God floats in the azure air."

> And we have heard the fauns chiding Proteus
>   in the smell of hay under the olive-trees,
> And the frogs singing against the fauns
>   in the half light.
> And . . .

The last line ("And . . .") reminds us that in the unresting flow of temporal experience these moments are followed by other, quite different ones. The crescent moon is Artemis, but the moon comes and goes. The leaves of olive trees ripple in the wind, their white undersides glittering as they catch the light, and Athena is there, Homer's "gleaming eyed" goddess. But suddenly the eyes are not there again, and "olivi" image

> That which gleams and then does not gleam
> as the leaf turns in the air.

Canto 81 implies that the eyes of the goddess are present in nature as

> sky's clear
> night's sea
> green of the mountain pool,

and adds that once, at least, "Pound" beheld the eyes directly, though even this moment was not one of full communion or knowing.

If the divine light is not beheld, the cause lies in the human psyche, which may not be prepared to receive it. Drawing mainly on his interpretation of Confucius, Pound urges that we must become like light to see it.

> The wind is part of the process
> The rain is part of the process,

and the end of the process or way is the inborn light, manifested as rectitude, candor, clarity. To the person who has gone or undergone the way of purification, the divine is present in the world. Nowhere do the *Cantos* put this more beautifully than in the penultimate Canto 83 of the Pisan suite, where the world appears as water, and light, and light on water.

The Cantos Pound wrote after Pisa are impersonal in presentation. "Pound" is not in them as a central figure except sporadically; the human and dramatic interest of the *Pisan Cantos* is gone. The presentation is more continuously elliptical and fragmentary than it was before the *Pisan Cantos,* and since we cannot now also understand it as somebody's interior monologue, we confront only ideograms. Chinese written characters make frequent components of the text. The subjects recapitulate previous ones. Usury is exposed, right principles of economics and government are inculcated. Cantos 90 and 91 again beautifully enact the ascent to paradise.

How good are the *Cantos* as a whole? Or since evaluation is always personal, how much do I admire and enjoy them? Huge indictments can be brought against them. Pound's Fascist sympathies are and will remain troubling for as long as mankind remembers what Fascism was. His anti-Semitism is obvious and repulsive. Though there is much to be said for ideograms as a method of presentation, ideogramic thinking, as the poem exemplifies it, is undisciplined and self-indulgent. In many places there is a ludicrous disproportion between the importance of the ideas, in Pound's view, and his unclear, distracting articulation of them. We cannot argue that such intellectual and moral offenses are irrelevant to the poem, for they pervade the poem, influencing subject matter, intention, and form. And in long stretches the *Cantos* are boring.

Nevertheless I admire the *Cantos,* and not only for the lyric passages everyone responds to. Pound's sense of the importance of texture justifies itself, for, however maddeningly difficult the texture of the *Cantos* may be, it rewards by brilliant effects that could be obtained in no other way. And it stays fresh. Passages can be read over and over with pleasure, for they summon creativity and always disclose new interrelations and possibilities of meaning.

The poem is vigorous, bold, and packed with personality and diverse life. Though it differs enormously from *Don Juan,* in some essential virtues it has more in common with Byron's masterpiece than any other long poem of the twentieth century. The sweep of the poem in time and geographical space brings into it an extraordinary diversity of settings, manners, and ways of speaking. Throughout there is a sympathy with human nature, a cocking of an interested eye on the habits, oddities, ingenuities, virtues, costumes, speech—in short, on the characters and doings—of people. Even the villains are observed, often, with an ironic, humorous appreciation of their bustle, effrontery, and hoggishness. Always fascinated by technique, Pound could not help taking a certain pleasure in the ingenuity of their wangles.

In compressed imagination the poem is, at moments, more brilliant and moving than any other poem of the twentieth century. Pound's sensitivity to what in Byron's time (perhaps we should here think rather of Shelley) would have been called "beauty" and his power of rendering it exceed that of any other modern poet. In Canto IV, for example,

> Smoke hangs on the stream,
> The peach-trees shed bright leaves in the water,
> Sound drifts in the evening haze . . .

In Canto 49, again evoking an evening river in China, Pound gives images of the "Sharp long spikes of the cinnamon," the "cold tune" of the water "amid reeds," and the boat that

> fades in silver; slowly;
> Sun blaze alone on the river.

Always attention is carried out and away from the self. An other is there, offering release. Especially in the *Pisan Cantos* this sense of an other is expressed in nature—ultimately it is more than nature—and nature is always present even to the prisoner in his "cage": "Came Eurus"—the southeast wind—"as comforter"; "Be welcome, O cricket my grillo, but you must not sing after taps";

> and there was a smell of mint under the tent flaps
> especially after the rain
>   and a white ox on the road toward Pisa.

Pound's habitual going out from himself finally expresses a religious faith. Late in the *Cantos* Pound speaks of himself in old age as "A blown husk that is finished." To this moving image he adds what will not be found in most other twentieth-century writers: "but the light sings eternal":

> A blown husk that is finished
>   but the light sings eternal
> a pale flare over marshes
>   where the salt hay whispers to tide's change.

The Rock-Drill section of the *Cantos* states as a doctrine that the essence of the soul is

> Not love but that love flows from it
> ex animo
> & cannot ergo delight in itself.

Forty years earlier Pound's Imagist doctrine had repudiated self-expression and stressed the imperative of "presenting an image." The same underlying attitude has now developed into a moral and religious conviction. The final line of this passage falls

into Latin capitals for weight and emphasis as in an inscription:
UBI AMOR IBI OCULUS EST. Occasionally toward the end of his life Pound tried to judge his work as a whole. In these profound moments he speaks for mankind: A "man seeking good, / doing evil"; "Many errors, / a little rightness"; "a little light / In great darkness . . . a tangle of works unfinished . . . I cannot make it cohere." Yet in that typical transition which is his deepest truth he again goes out from his own being to the other. "Even if my notes do not cohere," it—the world—"coheres all right":

> Do not move
> Let the wind speak
> that is paradise.

11

THE IMPACT OF WILLIAM CARLOS WILLIAMS

WILLIAM Carlos Williams was born in 1883. He went to medical school at the University of Pennsylvania and practiced all his life as an obstetrician and pediatrician. Except for literature, he led an ordinary life—marriage, long days doctoring, extramarital affairs, two sons, a shady suburban home, a cat, roses, and rhododendrons.

He remained where he had been born, in Rutherford, in his time a moderately pleasant, suburban town. Around it stretched the drab, doleful landscape of northern, industrial New Jersey. Here by the filthy Passaic Williams found not the waste land but spring. In weeds, melon flowers at the garbage dump, "Hot Jock" in red paint on a fence, his patients—"Doc,"

> I got
> a woman outside I want to marry, will
> you give her a blood test?

—he celebrated the tough, always renewing vitality of the world, and in a way that put him, he thought, at opposite poles from Eliot. As Marianne Moore once remarked, Williams' imagination was like the boll weevil he noticed in Carl Sandburg's song. In successive verses the cotton pickers threaten to put the weevil in sand, in hot ashes, in the river, and the weevil always replies, "That'll be ma HOME! That'll be ma HOOME!"

Williams began writing at Horace Mann High School, and, ever prolific, by graduation he had heaped up twenty-three notebooks full of "Whitmanesque thoughts." Having decided to become both a writer and a doctor, he pored over Keats's *Endymion* in medical school and composed a long poem in Keats's style. At the University of Pennsylvania he made friends with Pound, Hilda Doolittle, and the painter Charles Demuth. His first book, *Poems* (1909), was published at his own expense in Rutherford. Acknowledging his copy, Pound told Williams that he was "out of touch"—not up to the standards of London, the literary center. Williams' career could be interpreted as a long, stubborn protest against this judgment—against Pound, London, and even, with ambivalences, against standards.

But this was later. Meanwhile he imitated Pound and hoped for London's approval. *The Tempers* (1913) was published in London, Pound having pursuaded Elkin Matthews to bring it out. These poems were influenced, Williams later said, "by my meeting with Pound, but even more by *Palgrave's Golden Treasury*." The impact of Pound showed itself in Renaissance and Browningesque lyrics, but soon Williams was impressed by the March 1913 issue of *Poetry*, which contained Pound's famous brief statement of the principles of Imagism. At about this time Williams struck up friendships with other young writers and painters, and started publishing in little magazines. In 1915 he acquired some measure of editorial control over one of these, *Others*. He now felt himself to be a member of the avant garde. To him this implied that his attitudes, sympathies, way of life, and form of poetry were and ought to be unbourgeois and anti-establishment. It was an exhilarating new pose, though only a pose. Paying his debts, seeing his patients, fathering his family, Williams remained safely within the bourgeois fold.

The literary and artistic milieu in and around New York differed considerably from that of Pound or Eliot in London. The First World War was far away and had little impact on New York imaginations. The uses of past literatures in Pound and Eliot did not appeal. Neither was Greece, China, or Provence the scene of this poetry, which was completely contemporary. In Alfred

Kreymborg, Donald Evans, Marianne Moore, Mina Loy, and Wallace Stevens, New York writing was humorous, whimsical, sometimes dandified, and innovative in form. Most of these poets had heard of the French *symbolistes,* and some, such as Mina Loy, knew them well. But *symbolisme* and other French literature seemed less exciting than the painters and paintings just come to New York from Paris. The Armory Show of 1913 exhibited works by, among others, Renoir, Matisse, Picasso, Cézanne, Braque, Gauguin, and Picabia. Duchamp, Picabia, and Albert Gleizes were in New York during these years. Walter Conrad Arensberg already had a collection of Cubist paintings on his apartment walls. Painter friends of Williams, such as Charles Demuth, adapted Cubism in their own work and helped Williams understand and appreciate it. Arguments, anecdotes, manifestoes, attacks, patrons, parties, and disciples sprang up. "We'd have arguments over cubism which would fill an afternoon," Williams later recalled. "Impressionism, dadaism, surrealism applied to both painting and the poem." All this gave Williams a *point d'appui* for his thinking about poetry, a collection of ideas from outside the traditions of English and American literature. Also it intensified his dispositions to astonish the bourgeois, including the bourgeois in himself, and to welcome almost anything if only it was new. As Williams summed it up, the French paintings and painters "created an atmosphere of release, color release, release from stereotyped forms, trite subjects. There was a lot of humor in French painting, and a kind of loose carelessness."

Amid these excitements Williams' lyrics took an immense stride from the still traditional *The Tempers* to *Al Que Quiere!* in 1917. By 1923, when he published *Spring and All,* he had further developed his vision and technical methods. Meanwhile, *Kora in Hell* (1920) experimented in spontaneous improvisation; Williams hoped thereby to escape the limitations of the too-conscious mind. "For a year [1917–18] I used to come home and no matter how late it was before I went to bed I would write *something.*" Of the 365 pieces of writing thus produced, 84 were eventually kept, arranged, and accompanied by "interpretations."

In the Prologue (1918) to *Kora* Williams began his lifelong quarrel with Eliot and Pound. He objected to their preoccupation, as he saw it, with the literature of the past and of Europe. Their work is "conformist," "rehash," academic. Paris must be surprised "to find parodies of the middle ages, Dante and *langue d'oc* foisted upon it as the best in United States poetry." Their influence would obstruct the creation or at least the acceptance of a vital new art. In the pages of *Contact* (1920–23), a short-lived magazine he started with Robert McAlmon, Williams went on theorizing and manifestoing. More of this moiling prose was interspersed among the lyrics of *Spring and All,* and still more constituted *The Great American Novel* (1923). This book gave the thoughts of someone who is trying to start a novel but is unable to accept the conventions of the form. It was a slightly Dadaist critique of fictional art by the criterion of reality. Despite or because of this formal impasse, Williams wrote mainly novels and short stories for the next fifteen years. *In the American Grain* (1925) was not a novel but portrayed worthies and unworthies of American history: Eric the Red, Daniel Boone, Montezuma, Cotton Mather, and so forth. Williams aimed to discover the psychological, imaginative, and moral character of Americans. But in his *Studies in Classic American Literature* (1923), D. H. Lawrence had already carried out the same exploration. Though Williams' book was not "rehash," his point of view was not new to readers of Lawrence.

He traveled in Europe in 1924 and 1927, renewing contacts in literary circles there. In the late 1920s and early 1930s he involved himself in Objectivism, a minor movement I shall describe in Chapter 13 in connection with Louis Zukofsky. Amid the political strife of the 1930s Williams was just a busy doctor who sympathized with the poor, as may be seen in the short stories of *The Knife of the Times and Other Stories* (1932) and *Life along the Passaic River* (1938). But the *Partisan Review* labeled him a "bourgeois decadent," an attack matched from the far right in the 1950s, when an obscure McCarthyite raised a minor persecution by calling Williams "the very voice of Communism." In 1938 he started serious work on his long poem, *Paterson.*

Williams' reputation had spread very slowly, a fact that greatly distressed him. He had favorable reviews in the 1920s from friends and acquaintances around New York—Marianne Moore, Kenneth Burke, Gorham Munson, and Paul Rosenfeld—and by the end of the 1920s these reviewers had established what is still, mutatis mutandis, the usual critical portrait. But outside this circle hardly anyone, it seemed, was paying attention. The *Dial* Award in 1926 and the *Poetry* prize in 1931 were not much consolation, especially when compared with the éclat of *The Waste Land*, which, Williams later said, "wiped out our world as if an atom-bomb had been dropped on it." "My contemporaries flocked to Eliot."

But in the 1950s and 1960s young poets flocked to Williams. His poetry was unchallengeably Modernist—in fact, he said, it was the vanguard—yet offered an alternative to Eliot, Tate, Ransom, and others who now seemed academic. It was supported with theorizings, a program. Its style was not intimidating. Williams' feelings and values were sympathetic and he himself was encouraging. He belonged to the now almost mythical generation of Joyce, Pound, Eliot, yet he praised the poetry his young admirers sent him to read. When, for example, he included part of Charles Olson's essay on "Projective Verse" in his *Autobiography* (1951), Olson gratefully exploded: "My god, BILL, OF COURSE, god, how wonderful . . . crazy good, crazy wonderful, crazy manna." The young poets—Ginsberg, Olson, Creeley, Levertov—naturally reinterpreted Williams by their own lights, but they acknowledged his importance.

Even the disciples of Eliot and the New Criticism were building bridges toward him. Williams had classified Randall Jarrell among these picky and snippy ones, but in 1946 Jarrell reviewed Book I of *Paterson* favorably. Williams was delighted, and in 1949 Jarrell edited his *Selected Poems*. (But Jarrell cooled toward *Paterson*, and Williams toward him.) Though trained in the enemy camp, Robert Lowell also liked *Paterson* I, and later told Williams, "I have crossed the river into your world." Between 1946 and his death in 1963 Williams received five honorary degrees and seven prizes or awards for his poetry. In the 1950s graduate students and professors of English began to explain his poems and arrange his theorizings into coherence. Having damned "academics" all his life, Williams was now delighted by their analyses and deeply grateful.

But when the house is ready, death comes. Williams was hit by a heart attack in 1948, followed within the next years by a series of strokes. He resigned his medical practice, lost the use of his right arm, was often depressed. But he bravely taught himself to type with his left hand and went on writing until his death in 1963.

THE WILLIAMS LYRIC

By 1917, when he published *Al Que Quiere!*, Williams sympathized eagerly with the Modernist revolution. But this was still Modernism in its first phase, the phase of Sandburg and Amy Lowell, of Pound's *Cathay* (1915) and *Lustra* (1916), of the *Spoon River Anthology* and the Imagists—which, in the first volume of this history, I have called popular Modernism in order to distinguish it from the high Modernism of the 1920s. Repudiating the poetically Genteel and the Victorian, Modernists of this phase eliminated "Thous!" and "Ahs!," allusions to classical myth, capital letters at the start of lines, meter, rhyme, and stanzas, beautiful objects, glamour, romance, uplifting thoughts, idealism, philosophy and philosophic pathos, and strong, urgent emotion. Though they sometimes exhibited ancient Greece or China for exemplary purposes, mostly they dwelt in the contemporary world, which they delineated in simple, colloquial words and sharp-edged clarity.

Still in its infancy, the Modernist movement appeared to be relatively homogeneous. What separated Pound, Eliot, Amy Lowell, Sandburg, Bodenheim, Kreymborg, and Williams mattered less than the vast gulf between these rebels and the Genteel establishment. But in England there was another Modernism. So far as I know, F. R. Leavis is the only critic who has mentioned likenesses between Williams and the English Georgians. Since the Georgians still rhymed, metered, and capitalized at the start of lines, and Williams did not, his poems had a more modernized look and sound. But if the pleasures of Georgian poetry include especially an easy, natural speech, a close, appreciative rendering of suburban and rural existence, charm of personality—the tender, sympathetic, yet humorous speaker—and an outward unpretentiousness with inner subtlety, these characteristics may also be claimed for *Al Que Quiere!* Unlike Rupert Brooke, Williams would not have described himself in so many words as a "great lover" of "White plates and cups . . . the strong crust / Of friendly bread," but he enacted this role:

> In brilliant gas light
> I turn the kitchen spigot
> and watch the water plash
> into the clean white sink.
> On the grooved drain-board
> to one side is
> a glass filled with parsley—
> crisped green.

In *Sour Grapes* (1921), Williams' next collection, the talky "I" was less present. The engaging doctor telling his feelings and responses was replaced by relatively impersonal descriptions which were actually extended metaphors ("Spring Storms," "To Waken an Old Lady") or by packed images of two or three lines as in Pound's *Lustra* (1916). With Williams the speaker, Rutherford the place also disappeared, and the images of flowers and landscape lacked local provenience. Poems without a first-person speaker made their effect by the interactions among their images; in retrospect they showed a transition toward *Spring and All* (1923).

In this famous volume Williams entered the high Modernist phase of poetry. A myth of spring's coming is implied in many of the poems, and tends to link the separate lyrics. The formal principle is less that of Romantic, continuous transition, articulating somebody's evolving thoughts and emotions, and more that of Modernist composition by juxtaposition. The images may be fragmentary and the connection of one to another elliptical or broken. Williams experimented with collage ("Young Love," "Rapid Transit"), with free association ("At the Faucet of June") and with surrealism ("The Agonized Spires"). Some poems juxtaposed different voices in dialogue. The famous or notorious "The Red Wheelbarrow" suspended a few images in no context, like a mobile sculpture. "The Rose" illustrated a Cubist way of seeing:

> The rose is obsolete
> but each petal ends in
> an edge, the double facet
> cementing the grooved
> columns of air.

Between *Spring and All* and the late 1930s, when he started working on *Paterson,* Williams devoted most of what little time

he had for writing to prose fiction. In his poems the Rutherford
doctor talked as in *Al Que Quiere!* ("This Is Just to Say"); or descriptions implied metaphors; dramatic monologues portrayed
character ("Invocation and Conclusion"); selections of images
conveyed impressions ("Nantucket"); syntactical and grammatical tricks ("The Lily") went along with a general freedom from
grammar; short lines ended in "the," "of," and the like. In summary, the variety was great but the elements of it were familiar
from previous volumes. Occasionally there was mastery.

Williams prided himself that the diction and syntax of his poetry was based on the spoken language—Rutherford's talk.
Sometimes the talk characterizes the speaker dramatically, and
sometimes its virtue is just that it doesn't get in the way. The
clear, easy, familiar medium transmits the object without calling
attention to itself. To Williams the more idiosyncratic conversational mode of Robert Frost, with its allusion to Yankee dialect,
must have seemed mannered, a kind of clutter. Dramatic characterization, in contrast, was obviously intended to be noticed,
and Williams was skilled in bringing a person vividly before us:

> Her milk don't seem to..
> She's always hungry but..
> She seems to *gain* all right,
> I don't know.

Even when the speakers are versions of Williams, their voices
may differ widely. "To a Solitary Disciple"—

> Rather notice, mon cher,
> that the moon is
> tilted . . .

—strikes an opposite pose from the warm, abashed "January
Morning":

> But—
> Well, you know how
> the young girls run giggling
> on Park Avenue after dark
> when they ought to be home in bed?
> Well,
> that's the way it is with me somehow.

Ways of speaking characterize not just a speaker but also a social
and cultural context. "The pure products of America," begins

"To Elsie," and the line, as has often been remarked, fetches some of its irony from its vague echo of advertising or Chamber-of-Commerce boosterism. "Go crazy" is the surprising next line, returning us to blunt, everyday speech and to reality. "Somehow," the poem winds toward its conclusion, "it seems to destroy us." The colloquial signal of puzzled rumination—"Somehow"—is too comfortable to be urgent. "It" in this context is just America. So "somehow" points out something—to speak the same language—wrong with us. It is a small, additional point in the general indictment.

In the latter part of the eighteenth century one of the modern or contemporary kinds of poetry, represented by Cowper's *Task* or Coleridge's "conversation poems," was domestic, sincere, appreciative, and formally relaxed or "natural." Part of its complex appeal depended on its moment in literary history, for these poems "Affecting Not to Be Poetry" (as Coleridge put it) came as a reaction and relief after the formally tight, brilliant, often satiric work of Dryden and Pope. To a literary historian Williams' achievement and appeal seem somewhat analogous. Unlike Cowper or Coleridge, he developed his alternative mode at the same time as Eliot—his Dryden and Pope—but, as I mentioned, he was not widely recognized until the next generation itself reacted against his rival. His work raises critical issues similar to those raised by Cowper's. His naturalness and ease involved a lowered pressure or intensity, and for his followers he made poetry easier to write. Once the corset of Eliot's example and hegemony had been thrown off, it was easier to do handsprings, but it was also easier to loll and sprawl. But these central issues need concrete illustration. A "Pastoral" from *Al Que Quiere!* will bring them to a focus.

> When I was younger
> it was plain to me
> I must make something of myself.
> Older now
> I walk back streets
> admiring the houses
> of the very poor:
> roof out of line with sides
> the yards cluttered
> with old chicken wire, ashes,

>furniture gone wrong;
>the fences and outhouses
>built of barrel-staves
>and parts of boxes, all,
>if I am fortunate,
>smeared a bluish green
>that properly weathered
>pleases me best
>of all colors.
>　　　No one
>will believe this
>of vast import to the nation.

Though it seems spontaneous and simple, the poem activates reflection—for example, in the interplay between ideas of making something of oneself and admiring the houses of the very poor. (The contrast is not just the obvious one between the middle-class rat race and the aesthetic, drop-out, take-things-as-they-come mood, for the values associated with the lives of the poor are complex.) The connoisseur's pleasure in bluish green (if "properly weathered") is blithe and eccentric, but expresses his way of taking life, his appreciative responsiveness, his readiness to make the most of whatever slight thing he may happen upon. The unpretentious idiom is that of talk. The lines break at natural pauses in speaking. They exhibit the ordinary by putting a frame around it. So does the poem as a whole.

Fresh, clean-edged presentation, swift, with humor and a marvelous lightness: so long as we are under Williams' spell, other poets seem cluttered and artificial. Milton's opening line in "Lycidas"—"Yet once more, O ye laurels, and once more"— is inconceivably fine in its context, and so, in *The Waste Land,* is:

>Under the brown fog of a winter dawn,
>A crowd flowed over London Bridge, so many,
>I had not thought death had undone so many.

Yet after we have lived for a while with Williams, we may find even such famous verses slow, contrived, too elevated, and perhaps even empty. Had Williams rewritten "Lycidas," he would not have begun, "Here we go again," but the phrase is closer to his poetic world and may suggest something of its pleasantness.

Of course his effects depend on the tradition they reject. His uncompressed, short lines seem peculiarly weightless and rapid because they offer in a line a lesser nexus of stimuli than our normal experience with verse has prepared us to expect. But since traditional poetry has trained us to bring a more active and concentrated attention to verse than we would to the same words in prose, we make the most we can out of whatever a Williams line presents. Attention creates vividness. Meanwhile the momentum is all the greater because these short lines tend also to be enjambed—sometimes violently so, for the lines may have very weak terminations ("of," "as"). And the accelerated momentum heightens attention all the more because it intensifies the counterpoint of the rhythm of the individual line against the rhythm of the syntax. These techniques were developed more radically over the twenty years after *Al Que Quiere!,* as in "The Flowers Alone" (1935):

> Now!
> > the cherry trees
> white in all back
> yards—
>
> > And bare as
> they are, the coral
> peach trees melting
> the harsh air—
> > > excellence
> priceless beyond
> all later
>
> > fruit!

My argument, to repeat, is that the lightness, speed, and vividness of the Williams lyric in the 1920s and 1930s are permitted in part by the fact that his lines, individually considered, perform less than a poetic line ordinarily does. I say this in Williams' praise, for he saw and seized an opportunity that had not before been exploited, at least not systematically. Later poets adopted and developed the new type of poetry Williams created. But when the Williams line is the norm rather than the exception, the pleasurable effects I have described are much less felt.

In works such as "Pastoral" the underlying concept of poetry has much in common with Marcel Duchamp's "ready-mades." With this in mind, I may phrase my point another way. "One day," Williams recollected, "Duchamp decided that his composition for that day would be the first thing that struck his eye in the first hardware store he should enter. It turned out to be a pickax which he bought and set up in his studio." On another occasion Duchamp submitted a porcelain urinal for an art exhibition, calling it "Fountain." Williams' *Autobiography* does not rehearse the controversy this provoked, but it impressed him at the time. That Duchamp had not made the fountain with his own hands, his friends explained, "has no importance. He CHOSE it. He took an ordinary article of life, placed it so that its useful significance disappeared under the new title and point of view—created a new thought for that object." So also with Williams placing the ordinary under the title "Pastoral." To exhibit a urinal makes a statement about the nature of art. But the significance is in the gesture, in exhibiting the pickax or the urinal as art. Once we accept the gesture without protest and consider these useful objects as art, the question arises, how good are these works of art? Do we now, sixty years later, take much interest in Duchamp's "Fountain"? Or in Williams' talky, minimal lines?

Whatever we think of him as an artist, we like Williams as a person—the "I" we meet in the poems. Characterizing him, we may begin with his feelings about spring, for spring and winter make virtually all his seasons. "Whan that Aprille with his shoures sote," Chaucer starts his *Canterbury Tales,* and heaps up the conventional images that were carried down through English and American poetry: the sweet showers of spring, the gentle west wind, the tender new shoots, the small birds singing. "The birds thus sing a joyous song . . . the young lambs bound," wrote Wordsworth in May. Of course this is the English spring, hateful to Williams when it appeared in American poetry, as it often did. But Whitman had noticed the lilacs "With many a pointed blossom rising delicate" in spring, and a "shy and hidden bird is warbling a song." Williams had a gift for seeing as if for the first time, and in his "Spring and All" the traditional associations do not exist. His spring is not in the least sweet, delicate, joyous, or shy, but tough, tenacious, dynamic, and unstoppable; the rooted bushes "grip down and begin to awaken."

How is spring in other poems?

> Maple, I see you have
> a squirrel in your crotch—
>
> And you have a woodpecker
> in your hole, Sycamore.

Another tree has

> knocking knees, buds
> bursting from each pore
> even the trunk's self
> putting out leafheads—
>
> Loose desire!

Thus Williams fetches his readers with humor, vitality, fresh imagination, and sympathy.

But though "Williams" is sunny and likable, the world he describes usually is not. Birth and old age, the spring season of startings up and the winter of endings can seem strangely similar in his cold, bare landscapes. Life just manages to hang on in winter; in spring it pushes up or out into a climate that does not warm or flatter it forth. In both seasons the world is adverse and the living thing needs all its toughness. Surviving is what Williams admires, but he does not mean just continuing to exist. He also means integrity, the thing being itself despite or against its environment, including the environment of social conventions. He sympathizes with resisting integrity that does not conform. Images of this virtue are everywhere in his poetry: in the defiance of the impoverished woman who says,

> Try to help me
> if you want trouble
> or leave me alone—
> that ends trouble;

in the chicory "out of the scorched ground"; and in "El Hombre,"

> It's a strange courage
> you give me ancient star:
>
> Shine alone in the sunrise
> toward which you lend no part!

What Williams admired, if we look closely, was not just surviving as oneself, but making something—enough—out of very little. For since the world is unnourishing, wintry, very little is all there is to work with. But our imagination creates spring. The greatest and most necessary toughness, in other words, is that of the imagination. Williams and Stevens took this theme from poets of the Romantic period, who had also affirmed the power of the imagination to go out in "greeting," as Keats put it, to the world and to find or make it a place of fulfillment and happiness. Williams demonstrated or enacted the imaginative process in a different way from Stevens. He presented his world with vivid and graphic concreteness, and he displayed himself in the role of someone going out to it with creative, exemplary response. Hence his poetry is realistic, dramatic, and intimate in senses that are not true of Stevens'.

For Williams our creative response or greeting is more exactly a finding, a making vivid what is actually there. If it is winter, our greeting does not change its character, but realizes its sufficiency for us. For the other pole of Stevens' musing—that the imagination creates what did not exist before, and that this also may be real—Williams had no affinity. In *Kora in Hell* a few sentences on chicory beautifully express the interaction, as he construes it, between the world and the mind. Chicory is a wild, long-limbed, almost leafless plant with a blue flower. "A poet witnessing the chicory flower and realizing its virtues of form and color so constructs his praise of it as to borrow no particle from right or left. He gives his poem over to the flower and its plant themselves." But the flower and plant "benefit by those cooling winds of the imagination which thus returned upon them will refresh them at their task of saving the world."

If we think of the world he sees, rather than of his creative response to it, Williams seems pessimistic. If we emphasize his imaginative ebullience, he is an optimist. In a sense the optimism is greater as the world is grimmer. This, I should say, is Williams' essential theme—the possibility of making much out of little.

He pictured the urban scene vividly and authentically: "the oil-streaked highway";

> the old man
> in a sweater and soft black
> hat who sweeps the sidewalk;

the billboard that pictures "two / gigantic highschool boys / ten feet tall" and adds that "¼ of their energy comes from bread"; and the advertisement in neon lights (which Williams renders in concrete poetry),

```
        * * *
        * S *
        * O *
        * D *
        * A *
        * * *
```

He sympathized with every impulse and type of person in rebellion against, or escaping from, or never touched by middle-class conventionalities, though he himself was riddled with them. He had a special understanding and compassion for the poor, old, and derelict. Yet Williams' compassion is a complex recognition that includes identification—he feels himself to be like them—aesthetic interest, and even admiration. A poor old woman eating plums is both pathetic and exemplary.

> They taste good to her
> They taste good
> to her. They taste
> good to her.
>
> . . . .
>
> Comforted
> a solace of ripe plums
> seeming to fill the air
> They taste good to her.

The intensity of her satisfaction expresses her poverty. But also her gusto is happiness and is a lesson in living.

Like so many of Williams' poems, this is also a writing lesson. It repeats an ordinary, colloquial sentence three times. Though the words and their order do not change, the line-breaks in different places slightly change the meaning. With each repetition there is an increment of emphasis and significance, the stanza thus rendering the continuing and deepening pleasure. The verbal resources and techniques could hardly be more minimal, but they create a fairly rich, evolving complex of stimuli. Just as it is a lesson in writing, the poem is—also typically—a lesson in seeing: the poet making much out of a completely familiar sight.

When the intricate sensitivity of his reaction—his superior "emotional equipment," as Pound put it—was fully engaged, Williams achieved a remarkably balanced, objective vision. In his best poems—"An Early Martyr," "The Yachts," "Spring and All," "To Elsie," "Burning the Christmas Greens"—the finest thing is the delicacy and complexity of his awareness. The poems embody this in ambiguities within and tensions between their images and gestures. "Winter" offers a brief example:

> Now the snow
> lies on the ground
> and more snow
> is descending upon it—
> Patches of red dirt
> hold together
> the old
> snow patches
>
> This is winter—
> rosettes of
> leather-green leaves
> by the old fence
> and bare trees
> marking the sky—
>
> This is winter
> winter, winter
> leather-green leaves
> spearshaped
> in the falling snow.

Winter may here express a state of mind, or time of life, or even the general adversity of the world, but the poem remains objectively focused on what is seen. Yet the intensity of recognition at the end ("This is winter / winter, winter") suggests that something more than the season is being talked about; otherwise the emotion would seem too great for the subject. If we ask what is realized about winter, we find harshness, bleakness, lifelessness or life just hanging on, and more snow coming. The central image is of leaves:

> rosettes of
> leather-green leaves
>
> . . . .

> leather-green leaves
> spearshaped
> in the falling snow.

The suggestions are of endurance and hostility ("spearshaped"). But the green leaves are at least surviving. There is a certain promise, not exactly cheery, that the plant will withstand and outlast winter. And—typical Williams touch!—the leaves make "rosettes." The word contains the flower: a rose, of sorts. Even in the winter the plant blooms in a way. It is like the broken bottle that shines in the cinders, or the dandelion at the sewage treatment site, or the chicory lifting its flowers from "the scorched ground," or all the people in Rutherford and Paterson, including the poet speaker, whose undefeated vitality and integrity are a kind of beauty. The exclamations of the speaker at the end celebrate a tough, minimal flowering.

THE THEORY OF THE POEM

Though imperfectly qualified for theorizing—his worst bedevilment, he once wrote Pound, was "confusion of thought"—Williams kept it up in little magazines, books, letters, and diaries all his life, scribbling away hastily but with passionate concern. Poetry—how to do it and to what end—is also a subject of many of his poems. His poetry agrees with his ideas, but not completely, for his practice was more old-fashioned than his program. Except for his views on meter, his main emphases did not change after the 1920s. Neither was his career of influence in the world gradual. Instead, as I said, when the young poets in the 1950s and 1960s looked around for an alternative to Eliot and the New Critics, there was Bill Williams with his argument, an argument backed by his poetry, his credentials as a veteran poet, and his warm personal presence.

Poetry, he said, must always make "a fresh beginning." Otherwise it dies. Like life itself, he had told Harriet Monroe, poetry must be "at any moment subversive of life as it was the moment before . . . Verse to be alive must have infused into it . . . some tincture of disestablishment." In 1947 he was still of the same mind. Eliot, Pound, Auden, St.-John Perse are "dead"—"not a breath of anything new"—but the work of some Italian poets he was reading "really breathes the air of the present-day world as if it wanted to be alive." A poet does not become contemporary by mentioning automobiles or jazz bands in poems that are otherwise traditional. He must restructure "the poem" (Williams' word for poetry) if he wants to express the present sensibility. He might begin by reshaping the poetic line. Since the poetry of the past was formed by a different sensibility, it cannot be a model. Europe's "enemy is the past. Our enemy is Europe, a thing unrelated to us in any way." It was because of such attitudes that Pound thought Williams a Futurist.

Live poetry will necessarily be unfinished, imperfect. The generation of the nineties had taught that poetry is not immediate impulse but deliberate art. Frost and many of his contemporaries artfully shaped poems that sounded like spontaneous talk. D. H. Lawrence defined a poetry of "the immediate present": "there must be mutation, swifter than iridescence, haste, not rest, come-and-go, not fixity, inconclusiveness, immediacy, the quality of life itself, without denouement or close." Differing in kind from traditional poetry, a poem of the immediate present, as Lawrence conceived it, might still be unbetterable in its own way. Believing with Lawrence that a poem should be of the present, Williams also believed, with Pound and Eliot, that a poetic form can be fully developed and perfected only gradually through experiment. But since the present is always "at that very moment moving on," by the time a form has been perfected, it will express a sensibility that is past. Any form that is in touch with the new moment will be "defective and ineffectual." "The new . . . cannot be correct. It hasn't time." "Nothing but a gnat is born the week following its conception." Hence a "really first-rate modern movement" must have "gross imperfections." Conversely—triumphant paradox!—whatever is brilliantly finished must be passé. The next step of the argument could easily follow: "Write carelessly," says a voice in *Paterson,* "so that nothing that is not green will survive."

He wanted to present "the truth of the object," and could have said with Wallace Stevens in his stronger rhetoric,

> Let's see the very thing and nothing else.
> Let's see it with the hottest fire of sight,
> Burn everything not part of it to ash.

Any new, any authentic poetry could begin only in contact with the thing. And maybe it would end there: "poetry should strive for nothing else," he said, and added, virtually quoting T. E. Hulme, "this vividness alone, *per se*, for itself . . . makes the poem." The object was the outward world known by the senses— bedraggled poplars, a man sweeping the street, birds piping. "Why do you write," Williams asked himself, and replied, "To have nothing in my head." No thoughts, that is, no ideas, considerations, opinions. Nothing but the object. It came "as joy, as release."

But how to achieve contact "with an immediate objective world of actual experience"? Maybe it seems contact cannot fail. We are in the world; our senses register it. But like all arguers of this tendency, Williams means that we live too much in our minds, not our bodies, in concepts, memories, worries, hopes, desires, not in the fullness of the moment. The thing offers itself, now and always, in all the particularities of its being, but we are too busy, abstracted, repentant, or dreamy, too beset by our own internal uproar or too stereotyped and conventional in our responses. So we do not take it in. It is an old theme. Maybe any perception we can have of anything must inevitably be a stereotyped one, so great is the pressure of culture on us, of "the tradition."

To see the thing, breaking through all this, and to present it in poetry are almost the same. Certainly the technique can be described in the same terms. Negatively, you do not cogitate the thing or ask questions about it. You approach without presuppositions and draw no conclusions. You don't compare it, or make it into a symbol, or associate it with anything, for associations lead the mind away from it. In fact you dissociate the thing. You isolate it, put white space about it, make it stand out by framing it. You juxtapose it with objects that no one would expect to find near it. Williams learned from Duchamp that "a stained-glass window that had fallen out and lay more or less together on the ground was of far greater interest than the thing conventionally composed *in situ*." Encrusted connotations must be stripped away. Hence the value of the nongrammatical, nonlogical style of the Surrealists or of the "destructive" moments in Poe, who sometimes "used words so playfully his sentences seemed to fly away from sense." Forced thus to look attentively at single words, we recapture their "elemental qualities," find them "clean" again.

Beyond such few practical pointers, Williams could only wait for moments of heightened being, when the longed-for contact would come. Everything depends on the psychic state in which a poet writes. He must be all immediately there, unlocked, focused, and flowing. As Williams put it, we must "perfect the ability to record at the moment when the consciousness is enlarged by the sympathies and the unity of understanding which the imagination gives." This view of the matter was present as a strong element in the poetic theory of the Romantics. Lawrence and Williams caught it especially from Whitman and transmitted it to the Beat poets. It overcame the distinction between writing and living—so sharply drawn and fateful for the *fin de siècle* generation—by asserting that they are the same thing.

Since writing is living, and since you "cannot live after a prearranged pattern, it is all simply dead," you cannot know where your poem may be going as you compose it. At any point it should be open, its next gesture undetermined, its direction unpredictable. A poet's greatest single gift is motion, a rapid, energetic, changing onwardness of mind. A motion, Williams says, like a tree, for his trees are not "great rooted" Yeatsian ones, interwoven and perduring, but images of dynamic thrust with branchings and windy tosses:

> the tree moving diversely
> in all parts;

the young sycamore that rises

> into the air with
> one undulant
> thrust half its height—
> and then

> dividing and waning
> sending out
> young branches on
> all sides.

We have been taught to suppose, Williams says, that either the mind moves "in a logical sequence to a definite end which is its goal," or else the mind "will embrace movement without goal other than movement itself for an end and hail 'transition' only as supreme." But neither alternative describes the motion of intelligence at its "optimum." Such motion is not preconceived or logical, but neither is it aimless or happy-go-lucky. It has an inner direction, but is alert at every moment to alternatives, contrary impulses, and new departures that are possible. Ideally speaking, each word in a poem will be a node, defining a direction but charged also with counter-tensions and fresh suggestions.

Hence though Williams talked as if contact with exterior objects were the aim, he also harbored a subtler idea of mimesis as union with life's ongoing, dynamic creativity. This thought had come to the fore in the Romantic age, especially in Germany. Doubtless Williams caught it from the theorizings of modern art movements, for the premise was current in them. A work of art, they explained, should not represent what already exists, but should bring a new object into the world. Williams said that "The Red Wheelbarrow" illustrates how "Poetry has to do with . . . the perfection of new forms as additions to nature." But though they are "additions," the new forms will be just as "natural" or "real" as the chicory flower. As Coleridge had put it, if "the artist copies the mere nature, the *natura naturata*" or objects in nature, "what idle rivalry!" The artist must imitate the productive process of nature, not what nature has already brought forth but the bringing forth, "the *natura naturans*," as Coleridge calls it—nature naturing. "The work of the imagination is not 'like' anything," Williams explained in *Spring and All*, but it is "transfused with the same forces which transfuse the earth."

In the 1910s Pound had judged most American poets "provincial." Some of them had returned the insult, attacking Pound and Eliot as "cosmopolitan." Williams urged that poetry must be rooted in the "local." What he meant by this is not easy to say. Though their subjects were hardly local, he did not, for example, wish to criticize Shakespeare for writing *Antony and Cleopatra* or Dante the *Divine Comedy*. His most considered meaning was that art begins in sensation and the sensory response must be your own. If we think how at the end of the nineteenth century Genteel writing borrowed its sensibility from earlier, English work, we can sympathize with Williams' point. Additionally, when Williams said a writer must "become awake to his own locality," must "know his own world," he was asserting his moral doctrine: if you live in Rutherford—or Omaha, or Albuquerque—your imagination should inhabit it also, should make something out of it by creative response, so that your experience becomes full and vivid. The cathedrals, castles, museum hoards, and whatnot that one can enjoy in the "old world" are no advantage. A sensibility formed in Rutherford will be no less valid for art.

In fact, it will be more so. If Williams' argument were only for the "local phase of the game of writing," it would apply to any locality, for it would point out that all localities are equal. If there is no reason for an American to hie himself to Europe, there is equally no reason for a Frenchman to move to Des Moines. What Williams really had in mind was something else. It went back to his first premise. "Nothing is good save the new." Rutherford—America—was new. His argument was that sensibility is formed by "contact with experience"; experience in the American environment is a new thing in the world; therefore, Rutherford forms a new sensibility and it, not London, is the place to create a new poetry. Pound had forgotten that poetry depends on sensation, not sophistication; he "left the States under the assumption that it was mind that fertilizes mind," headed for London and "straight for literary sterility." He and Eliot had been "too quick to find a culture (the English continental) ready made for their assertions. They ran from something else, something cruder but, at the same time, newer, more dangerous but heavy with rewards for the sensibility that could reap them. They couldn't. Or didn't." The cachet of newness had come to Williams as an artistic value mainly from the avant-garde of Europe. Bestowing it on America, Williams hoped to outstrip Eliot and Pound by staying at home.

Obviously Williams' theories were shaped self-defensively under pressure from the prestige of Pound and Eliot. He had to stand for an alternative or be eclipsed. For if a poet must be aware of the "mind of Europe" and of the "order"—to continue Eliot's phrasing—that subsists within the "whole of the literature of Europe from Homer," how could a busy doctor in Rutherford hope to compete? Hence Williams dwelt on the distinction of his kind of poetry from Pound's and Eliot's and also, rather more than was generous, on their shortcomings. His wounds and rage were understandably exacerbated by Pound's tone of patronage. The tone was appropriate—for many years Williams was able to publish only in outlets Pound influenced—but that did not lessen resentment. Eliot, meanwhile, seemed totally unaware of Williams' existence, and Williams naturally assumed his silence was a deliberate insult.

Of course he did not view Pound and Eliot the same way. With Pound, his old college friend and sometime encourager, he kept up cordial relations. But the academic, deracinated, repressive, perfectionist, successful Eliot became his bogey. What Williams allowed himself to say about Eliot in public was nothing to his comments in private. In a letter of 1944, for example, "I don't know what it is . . . about Eliot that is so slimy. It is the affectation of authority, an offensive leaking from above so that the water is polluted whenever he appears in print." During the Blitz over London Williams came forth with a poem, never republished, that appeared to celebrate the bombing because it would cleanse England of all that Eliot represented.

It requires no odious suspicion of human nature to understand that Eliot and Pound offended Williams partly because his poetry derived from theirs to a far greater extent than he wanted to acknowledge. Not just from Pound's Imagism. I noted that Williams would hardly have conceived *Paterson*, his main poetic work in later years, without the *Cantos* and *The Waste Land* as precedents; moreover, the rhythm, perhaps also the meditative phrasing, of his late poems occasionally owe something to the *Four Quartets*. The other, even greater crime of Eliot and Pound was that they held the central position Williams wanted to hold. Young poets, as yet unknown or unestablished, could always count on Williams for warm praise and encouragement. It was lovely, but it was also political; he was trying to enlist them. To established poets of his own generation he was less receptive. He could usually be relied on for favorable reviews of old friends. Where praise was plainly due, he honorably struggled to give it, even to Eliot. But the effort usually collapsed, and his typical comments are querulous. "Dear fat Stevens, thawing out so beautifully at forty!" That was in 1918 in *Kora in Hell*. Or, for another example, there is the 1932 letter in which he goes through living American poets—Robinson, Stevens, Winters, Jeffers, Frost—and finds that none will do. He also implies that he himself won't do, thus raising himself to equality with the others. As for Eliot and Pound, he concludes elsewhere, "I dunno, I dunno—. If they are great then I'm just a pig."

The language of poetry, Williams said, should be based on ordinary and local speech. The idiom of American poetry has hitherto been a conventional one, a "poetic diction," formed out of the "unrelated traditions" of England. But in their own idiomatic talk, if only they dare exploit it, poets have the basis for an aesthetic medium that will unseal their own sensibility. And American talk, differing radically from English, is especially a medium with possibilities not yet explored. "The inner spirit of the new language is original. Its difference from standard English is not merely a difference in vocabulary . . . it is above all a difference in pronunciation, in intonation, in conjugation, in metaphor and idiom." In fact, a poet who draws on contemporary speech will always have a medium that is unexplored because the spoken language is always changing. Rutherford's speech today has "jumps, swiftnesses, colors, movements" that were not present twenty years before. Williams did not necessarily intend that poets should reproduce contemporary speech. His argument was again influenced by the anti-illusionist strain in modern art. Modern painters or composers develop aesthetic possibilities suggested by the visual forms or sounds of contemporary life. They do not render contemporary life in a naturalistic way. So also the poet should develop the "new means" and "expanded possibilities in literary expression" that are latent in the speech habits of his time.

On the subject of prosody Williams began to change his mind in the 1920s. Until then he had practiced and believed in free verse; his prosody had carried his own stylistic signature and developed from volume to volume, but he had not talked much about it. In the 1920s, however, he began to feel that poets were not going to "discover beyond" Eliot and Pound by "slopping about in vers libre." He was joining a trend, for a reaction against free verse was general at this time. Trying to conceive a new prosody, he urged that there must be a "measure" (a term he first used in 1928), "some sort of discipline *to free* from the vagaries of mere chance." The measure must be "new" and "intrinsic" to actual American speech. "Speech is the fountain of the line," and "it is in the newness of a live speech that the new

line exists." And the new line must express our modern civilization, just "as the Homeric line included Greece . . . and the
Shakespearian line England." But what is the modern reality?
And what measure does it determine? Williams did not know,
but was willing to grope. The new line would have "internal tension" and be "pliable" to register "the intricacies of the new
thought." Its foot would be capable of more modifications than
the old, rigid foot and would contain more. Pound's line in the
Cantos is "something *like* what we shall achieve," but its inspiration is medieval, not modern; it will have to be "realized in living,
breathing stuff." The main thing to hold on to is that "Speech
for poetry is nothing but time—I mean time in the musical
sense"; and our search must be for "a new time that catches
thought as it lags and swings it up into the attention." Williams
had got this far by the end of 1932.

His breakthrough, as he saw it, occured in the 1940s. He located it in the lines in *Paterson* II (published in 1948) that begin,

> The descent beckons
>   as the ascent beckoned
>   Memory is a kind
> of accomplishment
>   a sort of renewal
>   even
> an initiation, since the spaces it opens are new places
>   inhabited by hordes
>   heretofore unrealized . . .

This passage, he later said, "brought all my thinking about free
verse to a head." "It took me several years to get the concept
clear," but gradually he saw that "in our new relativistic world"
the poetic foot would also have to be relative or "variable." But
since the "variable foot" is a paradox, a self-contradiction, Williams never got the concept clear, though he revolved it perpet-
ually thenceforth. In practice the "variable foot" was the "measure" he had discovered in *Paterson* II, and he wrote in it
(naturally with many variations) during the last ten years of his
life. But if we ask how this measure is to be interpreted, Williams
offers little help, for his many remarks were maddeningly general, inapplicable, or inconsistent. He has a "triadic" or three-
part unit. Each part may be considered a foot, a single "beat,"
but evidently the "measure" does not lie in any regularity based

on quantity, stress, number of syllables, or duration. Neither do the parts of this triad necessarily coincide with units of natural breathing or of syntax, though they tend toward this. If we accepted Williams' idea of a prosody consonant with Einstein's theory of relativity, we might say that the "measure" is constantly changing, each foot determining a new measure. But in prosody I remain stuck at Copernicus, and a variable or relative measure seems none at all. Three parts in each unit is the only regularity in this prosody, and since this would never be heard, it is a regularity only for the eye. Nevertheless, it is a regular pattern; Williams was no longer composing vers libre as this had ordinarily been conceived in the 1920s.

PATERSON AND THE LAST POEMS

Paterson is Williams' long poem, his challenge to the *Cantos* in five books, 178 pages. He published it book by book from 1946 to 1958. The *Cantos* roam the history of the world, but *Paterson* roots itself locally, dwelling on a New Jersey city with its diverse life. Williams wanted, he explained in his *Autobiography,* "to find an image large enough to embody the whole knowable world about me."

At least since the early nineteenth century, "poetry" has meant primarily the lyric, the short utterance in verse. Not in dictionary definitions, but in the far more important realm of half-conscious expectation. But the idea of a major poem continues to presuppose length. As Williams put it, "isolated observations and experience" in short poems need "pulling together to gain 'profundity.'" He puts "profundity" in quotes to apologize, with aggressive defensiveness, for so Victorian a value, and one so contrary to his pose. But his thought was typical of modern poets. He had written short poems for forty years, but from early on he had been restless under their restrictions.

Paterson the city is also, in Williams' poem, a giant figure, a poet and doctor, whose thoughts or dreams are the images and vignettes presented. These render the landscape around Paterson, fragments of conversation, snapshot characterizations of persons, love affairs, religious sensibilities, and American life histories. All this comes in discontinuous, concrete, juxtaposed

fragments and, as in *The Waste Land* or the *Cantos*, different attitudes, tones of voice, and styles play suddenly against one another. There is social protest and criticism of the culture or civilization of the United States. So many of Paterson's people are
like flowers the bee missed; they are divorced from their own
bodies, from their lives, and from the power to express themselves adequately. The poem evokes the historical past of the city
along with its present; the past is brought to bear chiefly by the
collage of prose passages, bits from old newspapers that Williams extracted from local histories. (Among its literally "real"
materials the poem also includes extracts from letters that had
been written to Williams.) Images and symbols recur incremen-
tally (the river, the waterfall, marriage and divorce). Myth is created; the giant Paterson, for example, reclines against the feminine figure of the landscape. The poem is not continually
concrete, for it includes reflective passages and lyrics in many
styles.

The great difficulty in the Modernist long poem is to shape a
coherent and developing structure. I discussed this problem in
connection with Pound's *Cantos*, where discontinuous juxtaposition of fragments, allusion, and evocation of myths assemble
an extraordinary number of diverse materials, and Pound
hoped and struggled to order them into a "major form," a comprehensive yet organized whole. Williams cared much less about
creating an ordered total form. He did not believe that experi
ence is mere chaos and flux, meaningless or of no knowable
meaning, so that any order would be a falsification, but he set
other values—contact with experience, openness, flexibility,
continuously fresh creativity—before those which might make
for structure and coherence.

Like all Modernist long poems *Paterson* makes its own form a
part of its subject. Explaining and justifying its procedures, it
deploys metaphors of formlessness, jumble. Life, Paterson's
thoughts, and the poem itself are like the flowing Passaic, rolling
things up and along miscellaneously—

> the drunk the sober; the illustrious
> the gross.

Always immediate, new, changing, ongoing, Paterson's thoughts

> interlace, repel and cut under,
> rise rock-thwarted and turn aside
>
> . . . .
>
> Retake later the advance and
> are replaced by succeeding hordes.

As the waterfall crashes down, the "tumult" and "spray" fill "the void." Nothing more could or should be desired. The amnesiac "roar of the present" is "of necessity, my sole concern." The metaphors, in short, suggest diversity, multiplicity, one thing replacing another in no meaningful order. Even memory is discovered, paradoxically, to be a "sort of renewal" that opens "new places." In Williams' extreme Romantic celebration of open possibilities and spontaneous creativity, the form must begin anew in every moment. Otherwise it would be dead.

It can be argued that the poem belies its own programmatic formlessness. Themes recur and interrelate, and the longer we read and study *Paterson,* the more we find it coherent. Of course. But maybe, even so, not very coherent, relatively speaking. Our judgment or response will depend especially on the expectations we bring to bear. If we come to *The Waste Land* from earlier poems, as its first readers did, it seems disjunctive, but it is integrated in comparison to *Paterson.* The important point is that the less a work of art has or seems to have a coherent structure, the more emphasis falls on its texture, in other words, on the workmanship and imagination in each successive detail. For as I remarked in connection with the *Cantos,* something must motivate us to continue reading, and if it is not an emerging sense of a whole, meaningful experience, it can only be the delight we have from moment to moment. In this aspect *Paterson* fails in a way that matters seriously. From page to page there is much dull or even bad writing. Whoever disagrees will not be convinced by brief demonstrations; examples I cited could always be ingeniously defended or called exceptions. And there is no pleasure in citing a botch. Readers of the poem who consult their own feelings as they read, rather than the arguments of specialist defenders, will probably find that if they go on to the end, the cause is conscience rather than interest or pleasure.

In the short poems of his last fifteen years Williams' style changed, becoming much more continuous, relaxed, and per-

spicuous. Transitions are leisurely. Diction and syntax are as natural and ordinary as ever, but merely so. There are fewer of the
experimental "jumps, swiftnesses, colors, movements" caught,
supposedly, from contemporary Rutherford speech. The poetry
goes like the following passage from "To Daphne and Virginia":

> Staying here in the country
> > on an old farm
> > > we eat our breakfasts
> on a balcony under an elm.
> > The shrubs below us
> > > are neglected.

Poetic tradition had been his "enemy"; now he sometimes invoked it. "Asphodel, That Greeny Flower," begins with the epic
propositio:

> Of asphodel, that greeny flower,
> > like a buttercup
> > > upon its branching stem—
> save that it's green and wooden—
> > I come, my sweet,
> > > to sing to you.

The domestic intimacy of this also typifies Williams' new manner; this long poem retains some of the incremental symbolism
and mythical allusion of *Paterson,* but it is addressed to his wife
and filled with reminiscences of their marriage. "No ideas but in
things" had once been his slogan. He now generalized:

> What power has love but forgiveness?
> > In other words
> > > by its intervention
> what has been done
> > can be undone.
> > > What good is it otherwise?

We might call this "abstract," but the speaker is strongly characterized and so is the dramatic moment: he is about to plead
for forgiveness.

Not just Williams' style but his whole conception of poetry was
shifting. He had once composed in the convention that a poem
is a made thing, impersonal and objective with respect to its author. But traditionally Romantic conventions had always shaped

his work also, and now they emerged more strongly. Quite as much as Keats's "Ode to a Nightingale," his poems might now embody the poet's intimate thoughts and feelings as they flow and develop in a brief moment of time. As their careers drew toward a close, almost all the Modernist poets of his generation modified their revolutionary techniques and returned partly toward the elegiac poetry of the nineteenth century. So also with Williams:

> So we come to watch time's flight
> as we might watch
> summer lightning
> or fireflies, secure,
> by grace of the imagination,
> safe in its care.

12

THE LATER POETRY OF WALLACE STEVENS

ORN in 1879 in Reading, Pennsylvania, Stevens grew up in comfortable, middle-class circumstances. Everyone in the family spent his time, he later said, reading in a separate room. At Harvard he was president of the college literary magazine, the *Advocate*. He wanted to become a writer, but, like Crispin in "The Comedian as the Letter C," he also wanted "A Nice Shady Home." After a brief try at journalism in New York City he became a lawyer. He married Elsie Kachel of Reading in 1909 and had one daughter, Holly. In 1916 Stevens joined an insurance firm, the Hartford Accident and Indemnity Company, and moved to Hartford, Connecticut, where he lived until his death in 1955.

His first volume, *Harmonium* (1923), suggests that he had been reading the English Romantics and French *symbolistes*, the late Victorian Aesthetes and Dandies, the Impressionists and Imagists, but, like most lovers of poetry, he read all kinds and enjoyed most that he read. Around 1907 he even felt a brief but strong enthusiasm for the "vagabondia" verses of Bliss Carman and Richard Hovey. He was not a fast developer, and was still capable in his late twenties of writing hopelessly conventional poems. "Quick, Time, go by—and let me to an end. / To-morrow, oh to-morrow," begins one genteel sonnet. Several of his early poems were composed for his "Little June Books," manuscript collections of his verse that he presented to Elsie Kachel on her birthday in 1908 and 1909. In later years she did not read his writings. Everything in the world, as Goethe said, can be endured except a succession of fine days. Once he had married and become a lawyer, Stevens' methodically capable, secure, well-fed, affluent, detached, orderly existence left him glum. He found his days at the office satisfying, on the whole, but his satisfaction seems to have been in the routine. The office did not fill him with zest. Of course it is hard to find zest in a career you did not really want. What someone else might have made out of Stevens' professional days I do not know, but Stevens had already invested his hopes for glamour and purpose in an earlier, quite different plan of life, for he had intended to proceed from college to romantic *Wanderjahre* and a writer's life in the cultural center. He continued in later years to feel the pull of this prudently renounced dream. "You have so thoroughly lived the life that I should have been glad to live," he wrote to the wealthy Henry Church, who had made his home in Paris, read many books, and edited a little magazine. But Stevens had not wholly surrendered his plan; he pursued it so far as evening leisure, provincial Hartford, and the limitations of his purse allowed. His evening and weekend avocations—serious literature, Parisian paintings and bookbindings, wine and cheese from France, little magazines, poetry—were tokens and samplings, keeping him in touch with a way of life that remained his ideal.

The deeper truth, however, is that Stevens, at least by the time he reached middle age, felt that his professional routine and his imaginative escapes from it were interdependent; one would have been less desirable without the other. He would not have wanted these separate spheres of his life to unite, supposing that had been possible. (Stevens differs strikingly from William Carlos Williams or T. S. Eliot in that his professional work seems not to have entered into his poetry.) What he valued was the going back and forth from one to the other, so that each pleased and refreshed in its turn. In one of his letters Stevens mentions "the energizing that comes from mere interplay, interaction. . . . Cross-reflections, modifications, counter-balances, complements, giving and taking are illimitable. They make things interdependent, and their inter-dependence sustains them and gives them pleasure. While it may be the cause of other things, I am thinking of it as a source of pleasure, and therefore I repeat that there is an exquisite pleasure and harmony in these interrelations, circuits." His going from office day to evening avocations was a "circuit." It connects with the central, continuing topic of his poetry, which revolved incessantly in meditation from "things as they are" to "things imagined" and back again.

His verse had appeared in little magazines since 1914, and a few friends and editors valued his talents, but to the larger literary world he was unknown. Brilliant books of Modernist poetry by Pound, Eliot, Marianne Moore, Williams, and D. H. Lawrence had appeared between 1918 and 1923. Thus when Stevens brought out *Harmonium* at the age of forty-four, it may have been lost in the dazzle. Certainly it stirred little interest. For the next few years Stevens wrote almost nothing. *Harmonium* seemed an end rather than a beginning.

HARMONIUM

Though I discussed this now famous book in the first volume, I briefly notice it again in order to highlight the enormous change in Stevens' work as he grew older. Among the brilliant poems included in *Harmonium* were "The Snow Man," "The Emperor of Ice Cream," "Peter Quince at the Clavier," "Sunday Morning," "Anecdote of the Jar," "Domination of Black," and "Thirteen Ways of Looking at a Blackbird." Longer poems, such as "The Comedian as the Letter C" and "Le Monocle de Mon Oncle" also contained stunning passages. Many less significant poems were attractive and fascinating, for example, "Earthly Anecdote," "Anecdote of the Prince of Peacocks," and "Tea at the Palaz of Hoon." Some poems were hardly more than exercises, yet were flawless performances, such as "The Load of Sugar-Cane" and "Disillusionment of Ten O'Clock." Naturally among 125 pages of verse there was occasional dullness, but on the whole the poems were fresh, exuberantly decorated, inventive, and intriguing. And though one or another poem might faintly recall Mallarmé, Laforgue, Valéry, Alfred Kreymborg,

Williams, or Donald Evans, the book had its own voice throughout, idiosyncratic and unmistakable.

Harmonium created a comic world of artificial simplicity, high
spirits, humorous exaggeration, parody, Dandy sophistication,
affectation, archness, burlesque, and fairytale fantasy. Wit and
irony were omnipresent. Images or props were cheery—stupid
giants, angels on muleback, the Palaz of Hoon, watermelon pa-
vilions, portly Azcan and his hoos, floral decorations for bananas. Nonsense syllables and happy bangings were heard, as in
"Ploughing on Sunday":

> Tum-ti-tum,
> Ti-tum-tum-tum!
> The turkey-cock's tail
> Spreads to the sun.

The comedy of *Harmonium* was showmanship, however. "Whatever life may be . . . *here we are* and *il faut être aimable*," as Stevens
had put it in a 1908 letter. Behind the show his mood was much
less blithe or complaisant than hurt, bitter, cold, and desparing.

His style had a deliberately affected and fantastic obliquity.
"Invective against Swans" is about the coming on of "winter" and
presumably had its basis in the personal feelings of the middle-
aged poet. In elaborately pompous address ("The soul, O gan-
ders . . .") it explains that as autumn begins the soul rejects
parks, moonlight, sex, and swans, and seeks a reality beyond.
Despite the zany title, the poem contains no invective, though it
strikes an attitude of superior condescension and mockery. "The
Plot against the Giant" can be read as a metaphor of Stevens'
own plan of life. Refined objects and pleasures, personified as
three girls, counteract the impoverished, boorish giant of quotidian reality. The poem is arch, tittery, and adroit; for example,
the third girl will whisper

> Heavenly labials in a world of gutterals.
> It will undo him.

A mood of "Depression before Spring" is expressed in a disjunctive sequence of images: the disenchanted comparison of
"The hair of my blonde" to "the spittle of cows / Threading the
wind" is plain enough, however disagreeable. But the next
image,

> ki-ki-ri-ki
> Brings no rou-cou,
> No rou-cou-cou

(the cock speaks German, the dove, French), has Stevens' far-fetched fantasticality, and the final image in the sequence exhibits a familiar item from his stock:

> But no queen comes
> In slipper green.

The reasons for Stevens' obliquity were partly temperamental and partly historical. He was a reserved man for whom intimate and direct emotional expression was not natural, though some of his early poems are in this vein. By 1913 the convention of sincere, personal utterance had lost its grip on the avant-garde centered in New York City. A poem was an image, a metaphor, an impersonal construction. For Stevens it was an escape into fantasy that lifted the pressure of reality, while also highlighting reality in some aspect. To present a boorish giant rather than, in an Eliot image, the "smell of steaks in passageways," sets the quotidian at a distance. The coarseness and ennui of actual life are "transformed," "metamorphosed," "placed in the imagination" —the terms are Stevens' usual ones—where, as a boorish giant, they can be contemplated with happy interest. To the end of his life his obliquities served this fundamental need to remove, to abstract, to transform, and thus to create a no longer depressing, a pleasurable "mundo" of his own.

Stevens was unlike any other American poet in the combination of qualities shaping the poems of *Harmonium*—irony, deliberate affectation, humorous fantasticality, obliquity, lightness, brilliance, and cool, impersonal performance as of a show arranged or a Pierrot's clowning. His work seemed exotic, Parisian, and thus for some readers acquired an extra cachet. But that his manner kept his matter at an enormous distance also troubled readers from the start. Moreover, his matter did not include human beings. To relishers of character and action his poems seemed glassy glitters of a kaleidoscope. Dexterity of style and dizzle-dazzle of wit—but what of life? what of the heart?

The poems in *Harmonium* had been written over the previous nine years and there was much variety. "Sunday Morning" was a richly imaged, meditative poem of a traditional Romantic kind.

Passages of a Keatsian concrete density, toned toward comedy, could be found in "Le Monocle de Mon Oncle":

> Our bloom is gone. We are the fruit thereof.
> Two golden gourds distended on our vines,
> Into the autumn weather, splashed with frost,
> Distorted by hale fatness, turned grotesque.
> We hang like warty squashes, streaked and rayed,
> The laughing sky will see the two of us
> Washed into rinds by rotting winter rains.

"To the One of Fictive Music" and a few other poems were voluble, rhetorical, and abstract in ways that most modern poets repudiated. At times Stevens mentioned the need to speak with sinewy directness, gripping

> more closely the essential prose
> As being, in a world so falsified,
> The one integrity for him, the one
> Discovery still possible to make.

He could write with aphoristic brevity, and he could shape in few words a concrete, sharply focused image. The free-verse, haiku-like austerities of "Thirteen Ways of Looking at a Blackbird," first published in 1917, exemplified brilliantly one stylistic ideal of the avant-garde at that time.

Goethe, to cite him again, would not express or not publish some of his particularly disagreeable insights, for why trouble good and useful citizens with useless truths? Despite the obliquity of his style, Stevens conveyed his somber vision of things. "The Emperor of Ice-Cream" says that ice cream, or the tawdry, concupiscent pleasures it represents, is the only pleasure that is real. "The Snow Man" is "nothing himself" and beholds "Nothing that is not there and the nothing that is." "Frogs Eat Butterflies. Snakes Eat Frogs. Hogs Eat Snakes. Men Eat Hogs," as the title of another poem sums up. In "The Comedian as the Letter C" Stevens' protagonist and alter ego, Crispin, achieves middle-class comforts and gradually gives up his grand ambitions as a poet. His failure, as Stevens presents it with his typically depressed honesty, is not tragic or even pathetic. Neither is it ironic. It is simply of no interest or importance whatsoever. Any significance it might have had dissolves in Gerontian-like questioning:

> What is one man among so many men?
> What are so many men in such a world?
> Can one man think one thing and think it long?
> Can one man be one thing and be it long?

Such middle-aged awareness made Stevens formidable and impressive, but, still more impressively, his sense of things was also complex and qualified. Even the most unpleasant truths, such as those of "The Snow Man" and "The Emperor of Ice-Cream," were represented as true only within a particular context or from a particular perspective. Stevens was never sentimental, but neither was he tough-minded in a simplistic or reductive way. "Crow is realist," as he once said. "But, then, / Oriole, also, may be realist." His finest poems preserve a remarkable balance between opposed truths. "The Death of a Soldier," for example, considers both the disturbances and also the lack of disturbance a death makes:

> Death is absolute and without memorial,
> As in a season of autumn,
> When the wind stops,
>
> When the wind stops and, over the heavens,
> The clouds go, nevertheless,
> In their direction.

The attitude here is objective, poised, and final in a way that might be called classical.

Harmonium was published in a second edition in 1931 with fourteen new poems, of which the most notable was "Sea Surface Full of Clouds." Four years later Stevens had composed enough lyrics to make a second book, *Ideas of Order* (1935). His gaudiness had diminished somewhat, and his "Gubbinal" mood of slight depression was more visible and frequent. "Anglais Mort à Florence" took stock of the dwindling into middle age— "A little less returned for him each spring"—more directly and bitterly than "Le Monocle de Mon Oncle," and it lacked the comic brio of the earlier poem. The imagery of the Deep South and the tropics had largely gone, as "Farewell to Florida" announced, and his landscape and climate were now of the North, usually in a season extending from late autumn to early spring. His convictions had not changed in the years since *Harmonium*, but he now dealt more persistently and more directly with the loss of religious belief and the consequences of that loss. Evening is "without angels"; we are "empty spirit / In vacant space"; "vacancy glitters round us everywhere." Traditional moral values of the copybook are no longer puissant or even appropriate, like "Lions in Sweden." Stevens confronted this state of affairs without anguish, however. He was not excitable, and perhaps the collapse of values and beliefs meant that more authentic ones would be devised. His "Sad Strains of a Gay Waltz" begins with the same perception as Yeats's "The Second Coming." "Too many waltzes have ended," as Stevens puts it, and order—social, imaginative, intellectual, religious—has broken down. There are "sudden mobs of men," "voices crying without knowing for what." But the poem typically lacks Yeats's dramatic immediacy and intense emotion. The "epic of disbelief / Blares oftener and soon, will soon be constant," but in due course the world will be put back together again in a new form. Similarly with the loss of the old, imposing morals. If these "lions" must now be sent back, there are still others alive in the "vegetation." Meanwhile, until the new music has been created, we must learn to live rejoicing in the vacancy, in the "winter" of reality, to cite another favorite metaphor. This question—how we can both confront reality and rejoice—was the urgent object of Stevens' imaginative speculation throughout his life. The answers proposed in *Ideas of Order* are the same as in all his other volumes, but except in "The Idea of Order at Key West," his tone of voice was less assured than it could sometimes later become.

Ideas of Order originally opened with a complaint, in "Sailing after Lunch," that the "old boat" of his imagination will hardly "get under way." What holds it back, the poem says, is doubt whether his "romantic" kind of poetry is appropriate. In fact, Stevens felt himself on the defensive in the 1930s. Since social and political questions dominated intellectual life, literature was often judged by its commitment or, at least, its relevance to such issues, and from "the point of view of social revolution," as Stevens said, *Ideas of Order* was "a book of the most otiose prettiness; and . . . probably quite inadequate from any social point of view." He was commenting on Geoffrey Grigson's notice of his work under the caption, "A Stuffed Goldfinch." He took other hard knocks too, and he made an effort to write about social problems in his own manner.

Owl's Clover (1936), a sequence of longish poems, began by contrasting a statue of marble horses in the park and a destitute woman there. The statues embody the noble elevation of art, at least of much art in the past, and the poverty-stricken woman with her "bitter mind" exemplifies a side of truth not much noticed in such art. The contrast should activate meditation on the proper social responsibility or irresponsibility of art, but as the sequence proceeds it loses specific focus. Argumentative, elaborate, and vague, *Owl's Clover* was otiose without being pretty, and Stevens never republished it after 1937. In his next major poem he retrenched to his own theme.

The Man with the Blue Guitar (1937) presents "reality," the "imagination," and their interrelations from different and changing points of view. Stevens thought it boring at times, but a better book than *Ideas of Order*. The thirty-three poems of this sequence are barer and more direct than Stevens' verse had been hitherto, with, sometimes, short sentences and a driving energy in the syntax. Among all Stevens' volumes this makes his nearest approach to an undecorated, severely "functional" expression. In 1942 he published another collection of lyrics, *Parts of a World*. It contained memorable poems, such as "A Rabbit as King of the Ghosts," but readers of these last two volumes might have concluded that Stevens, now in his sixties, had made his contribution. Most readers felt, in fact, that no volume since had equaled the brilliant *Harmonium*. After *Ideas of Order,* they agreed, there were not even individual poems to be compared with the finest of the earlier ones—an opinion Stevens sometimes shared.

In fact, a remarkable, ten-year period of poetic energy and renewal had already begun. *Notes toward a Supreme Fiction* appeared in 1942 and was included with "Esthétique du Mal," "Credences of Summer," and other poems in *Transport to Summer* (1947). This was followed by *The Auroras of Autumn* in 1950 and by the splendid group of poems included in "The Rock" section of the *Collected Poems* of 1954. Approximately half of all Stevens' verse was written in this final decade. There is no evidence that Stevens ever composed by painful, perfectionist squeezes, and so much verse could not have been produced except by a mind that was quick, practiced, ingenious, resolved to proceed, and ready to be pleased with its own doings. The results are sometimes a little bland and sketchy. Especially in his longer poems there are always passages that Stevens might have revised more anxiously. Yet in the significance of its central concerns, in its pervading intelligence, fecundity of illustration, original imagination, and unmistakable individuality, it was a major poetry; gradually by the late 1940s Stevens was seen to be among the four or five greatest American poets.

"WINTER DEVISING SUMMER IN ITS BREAST"

Stevens in his sixties was large, heavy, blue eyed, healthy. He went to bed and got up early, and liked "to read a little philosophy after breakfast, before starting downtown." As he walked to the office, he composed his poems, jotting "notes" as he went, since, "otherwise, by the time I got to the end of the poem I should have forgotten the beginning." The notes would then be "arranged" and the "thing" written out, typed, and revised.

He led a stangely isolated existence. In New York before his marriage he had made few friends. After his day's work he had usually returned alone to his apartment and read. On weekends he had taken walks of up to forty miles, noticing and later recording in his journal or in letters to his future wife the look of countryside and weather. The same way of life continued, more or less, after his marriage, except that he gradually walked less. His letters make little mention of sociability in Hartford. Except for his wife, his daughter, and three or four other persons, the relationships that meant most to him were with people he had never met, but with whom he had fallen into an exchange of letters. His pleasures had little to do with other people, a fact which sometimes caused slight compunctions of conscience. "I detest 'company' and do not fear any protest of selfishness in saying so." "Life is an affair of people not of places. But for me life is an affair of places and that is the trouble." "Most people are a great nuisance."

> It needed the heavy nights of drenching weather
> To make him return to people, to find among them
> Whatever it was that he found in their absence,
> A pleasure, an indulgence, an infatuation.

Boredom, he said, is "practically unknown to me. Perhaps I have been bored at Church, or at the Theatre, or by a book, but certainly, I have never been bored in any general sense." In fact, he put much time, thoughtful planning, and willpower into not being bored. He was determined that if life and the world could not be understood, they could at least be enjoyed. He read a great deal, though less as he grew older, when often he just sat around thinking. He thought himself a lover of nature, though actually he seems to have noticed mainly flowers and the weather. He had a large collection of records. He liked handsomely printed and bound books. A dealer in Paris supplied his requests for editions and bindings from that city and occasionally also forwarded cheeses. If you buy cheeses from France, you are living in France, Stevens said. He also said he enjoyed "nothing more than seeing new places," but he traveled little. He was frequently in Florida on trips that were partly business, but except for a couple of stops in Havana he never left the United States, and mostly he stayed in Hartford. He loved to "rush out of the office on Saturday morning, reach New York in time for lunch, have a really fastidious lunch and then spend a few hours looking for books," fancy fruits and cakes, and the like. This was his ordinary refreshment through change of place. After these outings in New York he also relished more vividly the order and coolness of his Hartford home.

But though he did not himself travel, he feasted on postcards from friends abroad. He had a correspondent in Ceylon and another in Cuba, and delighted in the glimpses their letters gave of ways of life in other, non-Hartfordian scenes. The correspondent in Ceylon and Harriet Monroe's sister in China were pressed into service to send little characteristic things—fans, carved Buddhas, a jade screen, unusual teas, black crystal lions—that stimulated his imagination. He could evoke novel impressions just as well from a letter from Cuba as from Cuba itself. If I understand him rightly, the letter was even more satisfying in some ways. Munich—to change the scene—is large, bustling, diverse, and sometimes disagreeable. Postcards from Munich are not. You can study postcards to the least details. You can depart from them in reverie. You may feel finally that you have exhausted all the stimulus they can give. Stevens enjoyed concentrating his mind. He liked to pursue his subject to the end, though he rarely did. He was aware of the complexity, the many-sided and fluctuating character of things, and he felt a counter-need to fix them in contemplation and master them. Small bits or tokens of experience, isolated from the large, weltering mass, could be thoroughly explored and appreciated. Paintings, for example. Stevens had strong visual and aesthetic responses. But his delight in paintings was probably also that each presented a manageably limited, fresh world. He could hang them up and contemplate them, or any detail in them, for as long as he liked. But again, as with his enjoyment of "new places," there was a fundamental vicariousness. He pored over catalogues and wrote anxious letters discussing possible buys, but he did not choose his paintings himself or see them before he had bought them. His Parisian book dealer and, later, the dealer's daughter were employed to purchase his paintings for him, exercising their own taste and judgment. When the paintings arrived, he found much refreshment living with and in them. Eventually he would tire a bit and feel the need of another painting.

He enjoyed sitting in his garden of a summer's day with cheese and chilled wine. He felt sensuous, wicked, and defiant when he ate an apple with a mound of mayonnaise as big as the apple, the mayonnaise having been purchased from someone in upper New York state who made sauces. He had woodapple jelly and Ceylonese tea for breakfast. "One likes to look at fruit as well as to eat it," and "When I go into a fruit store nowadays and find there nothing but the fruits du jour: apples, pears, oranges, I feel like throwing them at the Greek. I expect . . . sapodillas and South Shore bananas and pineapples a foot high with spines fit to stick in the helmet of a wild chieftain."

He might be called a hedonist, but a hedonist on principle and with nothing gross in his pleasures. They were imaginative. When he contemplated his paintings, he entered and dwelt in the imagined France that he made out of the painter's France. His attention to *objets d'art* and to the sensations, impressions, and imaginative moods they set off in him shows a *fin de siècle* side to his sensibility. But it was not the fine carving of his jade screen or his wooden god that delighted him so much as it was the imaginative release they stimulated. Ceylonese tea for breakfast activated reverie and fantasy as well as digestion. Sipping wine and nibbling cheese amid roses or chrysanthemums, he enjoyed the mental image or idea of himself engaged in such civilized pleasure, and when he ate a mound of mayonnaise with his apple, he saw himself in another, equally enjoyable light, as Wallace Stevens the plump relisher of the earth's fatness, amoral, reckless, and happy.

"THE THEORY OF POETRY IS THE THEORY OF LIFE"

"Felicidad," Stevens once said, is "after all . . . the great subject," and all his poems deal with it. The question, as I said, was how can we see and feel our situation as it really is and nevertheless be happy. That we must face up to "things as they are" was Stevens' first imperative. He almost never budged from it; in moments of difficult decision in his personal life he asked himself what "reality" dictated and took, however sadly, that path. But his allegiance to "reality" was a moral instinct, an expression of temperament. Like most of us, he had only vague and inconsistent notions of what he meant by "reality." Admiring critics have tried to make him precise and consistent, but they violate his own sense of his situation. He felt himself teased and preoccupied by quasi-philosophical questions—"a constant source of trouble to me"—that he could not resolve. Settling them for him, critics substitute abstractions for the human drama of his effort. His poems express rival premises and opposed emotional needs, going back and forth or hesitating between. Whether or not he deeply wanted to reconcile them I do not know. If he did, he was of too many minds and too honest to succeed.

From one point of view reality was the facts—winters, roses, machine guns, oceans, hunger, clouds, aging, death. In other words, things and conditions existed objectively, could be known, and had consequences. Did the sum total of the facts make, in most cases, for more pleasure than pain? For "felicidad"? Can human beings hope to find "the honey of common summer" enough? Stevens dearly wanted to say so. But obviously he could not forget all the "mal" of existence—the limitation, pain, moral evil, death. Life was not summer, reality not framed for our happiness:

> From this the poem springs: that we live in a place
> That is not our own and, much more, not ourselves
> And hard it is in spite of blazoned days.

And if the facts are wintry, exigent, and hard to bear, what then? Do they necessarily depress our spirits and inhibit imagination? Or can they, on the contrary, summon our imagination ("from this the poem springs") to press back against them, altering them and so making an affluence amid our essential poverty? Perhaps they waken a heroic joy precisely because they are adverse. If we rejoice, should we rejoice in our moral strength to confront reality or in our creative power to change it?

But can imagination transform reality? Yes, says Stevens—or maybe. Or up to a point. We lack space to pursue his elaborate and changing analysis of the imagination's acts and powers, but some main heads may be noted. We focus on things, Stevens says, making them more vivid and present to us by the attention we give them. "Description is revelation." We relate different objects or sensations, spontaneously ordering whatever the world brings. We modify what we perceive by adding something, maybe creating a freshness thereby:

> The way some first thing coming into Northern trees
> Adds to them the whole vocabulary of the South,
> The way the earliest single light of the evening sky, in spring,
> Creates a fresh universe out of nothingness by adding itself.

We project ourselves into things—"Her green mind made the world around her green"—and so dwell in a world to which we feel ourselves related. We make metaphors, thus contemplating facts in metaphorical versions. The facts persist amid such doings of the imagination. We have not closed our eyes to them. Neither, admittedly, have we literally transformed them. But we have changed our perception of them. Thus, maybe, we have made the facts vivid, meaningful, pleasureable despite their "mal."

But, on the other hand, do we actually know the facts at all? Certainly not if by "facts" we mean things as they objectively are. Our senses take in only those aspects to which they are attuned. What they collect they represent in accordance with their own inherent form and working. Sensation is a process of translation, selective and free, of an original that can never be known. Stevens calls what the senses report "the eye's plain version," the "plain sense of things." Almost invariably in the process of perception we further modify "the eye's plain version" in accordance with our fears and hopes, our understanding and past experience—a banging door may be terrible to a shell-shocked hearer. This automatic and instinctive rendering of unknowable stimuli into sensations, and of sensations into charged perceptions, is not what we usually mean by imagination, but involves many of the same processes. In the least imaginative representation that is possible to us we have "the eye's plain version." At the opposite extreme we have fantasies. In either case the mind contemplates what it has itself produced. Have we, then, imagined the facts, the bitter and exigent circumstances we thought we confronted? Perhaps not entirely. What we imagine may be (as Santayana taught) our subjective version of what really is. And yet even the "absence of imagination" has "itself to be imagined"—the pond "without reflections," the "water like dirty glass, exposing silence." And since what Stevens wrote of the girl singing on the shore in Key West is true for all of us—

> there never was a world for her
> Except the one she sang and, singing, made

—why shouldn't we call this "world" reality? In this redefinition reality becomes

> a thing seen by the mind,
> Not that which is but that which is apprehended.

But though Stevens entertained this redefinition often enough, he was seldom willing to accept it. His fidelity was still to an objective reality, even if it was unknowable. We cannot cease striving to conceive it, and we come closest to the truth—at least we most guard ourselves against illusion—to the extent that we refuse to indulge our exuberant creativity. If we speak of reality in metaphors of emptiness, bareness, blankness, grayness, silence, and the like, such metaphors, though themselves illusory, will at least purge our minds of the notion that reality is accessible to us. Especially they will not suggest that reality has any relation to human emotions, moral instincts and meanings—no more than rock or empty air.

If we ask "How to Live? What to Do?" the answer can only

be—imagine! Proceeding toward reality, the imagination strips away imaginations: the angels are taken down and the backdrop of rosy dawn repainted to featureless gray. This is still an imagined backdrop, but hardly a wishful or self-indulgent one. Or starting from the featureless gray and working in the other direction, the imagination creates a humanized and delightful "mundo" where it is at home—our transformation of the world. In the one case we heroically strive for truth; in the other, facing nothingness, we heroically assert our own creativity. In both cases the imagination is roused, active, intensely engaged. And that is what matters. The world of the unimagining is dull and incoherent. More exactly, since any world is an imagined one, whoever does not exert imagination is invaded by the common imagination, and in our time, at least, the common imagination is remarkably unorganized, inert, unconscious, sordid, and clichéd. In contrast, the person of strenuous imagination lives in a world that is not real, of course, but is fresh, ordered, meaningful, and essentially happy. The difference imagining makes is between vivid life and living death. Poetry is imagining. Hence it is "the heroic effort to live expressed / As victory."

The imagination also creates total myths or "supreme fictions." Having lost the faith of his youth, Stevens was both bitter and nostalgic. He wanted to kick at the Archbishop of Canterbury, as he once put it, for propagating an illusion, and he mocked Christian faith aggressively. But he also wrote movingly about the dimensions and shock of the loss of faith:

> How cold the vacancy
> When the phantoms are gone and the shaken realist
> First sees reality.

In short, a total myth is necessary, but if it would be crude to dismiss such myths as mere illusions, it would be something worse to think them true. Stevens concluded, at times, that we must believe in a fiction while knowing that it is a fiction:

> The prologues are over. It is a question, now,
> Of final belief. So, say that final belief
> Must be in a fiction. It is time to choose.

The position is ironic, desperate, and maybe profound.

But our leap of faith could not nowadays land us amid the

saints and angels or the Olympian gods. A supreme fiction must be "credible." If only for this reason, supreme fictions must change from age to age, the no longer credible being discarded and the new created. A "second giant" must kill "the first—A recent imagining of reality."

These ideas had been developed and brilliantly explored long before Stevens adopted them. They were central to the great literature of the Romantic age—Coleridge, Emerson, Shelley, Keats, Wordsworth—and they had been partially restated in more modern forms by philosophers such as Bergson and Santayana. The more pessimistic aspects of them in Stevens had, naturally, the more modern sources; the paradox of believing in a fiction, for example, was presumably suggested by reading Nietzsche. That the ideas were generally typical of a less "recent imagining of reality" does not limit their significance. And Stevens' attempt to resurrect the Romantic imagination as a live option, a possible *magister vitae*, has much human interest also, the age lending it so little credibility. But since interpreters of Stevens sometimes give the opposite impression, it may be useful to say plainly that Stevens was not a powerful contributor in the realm of ideas, as he himself well understood. His prose pieces collected in *The Necessary Angel* are helpful if we are interested in Stevens, but as *Essays on Reality and the Imagination,* as the subtitle puts it, they are vague and muddled.

Poets differ from the rest of us, Stevens says, because their imaginations are stronger and more active. Through their writings, however, readers also are lifted into the concentrated and radiant atmosphere of the poetic imagination. The great Romantics before Stevens, having also identified poetry with the imagination, had equally rested their justification of poetry on an analysis of this "glorious faculty"—thus Wordsworth—"its acts / And its possessions." But the enormous difference was that the earlier Romantics held, though with many doubts, that the imagination could embody knowledge, whether of immediate, particular things or of ultimate truth. A hundred years later Stevens could seldom credit this. The purpose or end was imagining, the activity itself, not whatever might be imagined. Imagining is happiness, and happiness justifies itself. Having composed a poem, or read one, we can only go on to another. So long as we are imagining, life is heightened, and the only thing to do is to keep on heightening life from moment to moment until it ends.

THE MYTH OF A SUFFICING NATURALISM

In contrast to Blake or Yeats, Stevens made no attempt to create a supreme fiction himself. His "Notes toward a Supreme Fiction" pretend merely to suggest some necessary characteristics of any supreme fiction. Yet from the start to the end of his career, his poems speculate in desperate hope that "the health of the world might be enough," that "the honey of common summer / Might be enough." In such passages he thinks of reality as things as we see, hear, touch, taste, and smell them; our imaginative response is merely a focusing of attention through which the "visible" is "announced" but not otherwise changed. "We observe," says Stevens, "and observing is completing and we are content."

Stevens hopes with Nietzsche, in other words, that if we surrender our illusion of a Father in heaven—of a supernatural ground and purpose to our existence—and turn to this world as all we have, maybe this world will take on a fullness, richness, and vividness so intense as to suffice. The earth will be

> a jostling festival
> Of seeds grown fat, too juicily opulent,
> Expanding in the gold's maternal warmth.

We will be merely and wholly physical and natural beings, for whom

> Day is desire and night is sleep.
> There are no shadows anywhere.

And so we will be free to rejoice in "this present ground." This "thesis" is "scrivened in delight"; its "reverberating psalm" or "right chorale" must take the place of the no longer credible hymns of the Church. "What more is there to love than I have loved?" Stevens asks. If the answer is, "nothing," the glory once bestowed on heaven returns to earth:

> And if there be nothing more, O bright, O bright,
> The chick, the chidder-barn and grassy chives.

The myth of a sufficing naturalism may make life possible. Certainly to desire to be anything else except a "race / Completely physical in a physical world" would be to desire the incredible, the impossible. It would be a desire "too difficult to tell from despair."

THE MAJOR POETRY OF THE FINAL PHASE

In his confident and astonishingly productive last phase, beginning in the early 1940s and ending with his death in 1955, Stevens' style differed widely from that of *Harmonium*. The doctrines of the Imagists, which had modified many of the poems in *Harmonium*, were now violated wholesale. Instead of using no word "that did not contribute to the presentation," as Pound had urged in his 1913 statement in *Poetry*, Stevens was voluble and diffuse. He now seldom followed the Imagist principle of composition in "sequence of the musical phrase," but wrote in meters, especially iambic pentameter. He did not take the Poundian advice to "Go in fear of abstractions"; he abounded in them. The high spirits of *Harmonium*, the ironic wit and corruscations of sound were still present but generally much toned down. As he put it in "An Ordinary Evening in New Haven,"

> The color is almost the color of comedy,
> Not quite. It comes to the point and at the point,
> It fails. The strength at the center is serious.

In fact, much of his later poetry was without pose of any kind, unless straightforward reflective utterance was itself a pose.

To read the poems of his last phase is to enter a coherent world, continually changing yet always characteristic. That there is a central topic or preoccupation helps create this sense of coherence, but mainly it depends, I think, on the imagery. Stevens never organized his vocabulary of images as Yeats did in *A Vision*. Probably he never exploited the association, cross-reference, and incremental return of images as consciously as Eliot did in the *Four Quartets*. But he thought in images; the same or similar images tend to recur from poem to poem; to each poem they bring implications already gathered in other poems; and thus they enhance imaginative resonance or connotation. Fully to explore this vocabulary of images would take another book, the more so since each image is richly evocative and changing in its suggestions. The sun and summer are generally associated with natural and physical reality; they may be fierce, fecund, tropical, and Stevens' many images of the Deep South and Florida are part of this large cluster of associations. From the point of view of winter, summer is an illusion, and as autumn blows "the silence of summer away," the true reality emerges:

> It is a coming on and a coming forth.
> The pines that were fans and fragrances emerge,
> Staked solidly in a gusty grappling with rocks.
>
> The glass of the air becomes an element—
> It was something imagined that has been washed away.
> A clearness has returned. It stands restored.

Since "summer" and "winter" were interdependent opposites, the imaginative "circuit" or going round from one to the other, including and experiencing both points of view, would have seemed truer and more satisfying to Stevens than any choice between them. But had he been forced to choose, my opinion is that he believed more deeply in the reality of winter and probably loved it more.

While the imagination of daylight holds fast to "the plain sense of things," moonlight transforms, weaving the gorgeous gowns of illusion by which we cover our nakedness, make an affluence amidst our poverty. For the imagination of moonlight reality is made of words and thus is endlessly transformable:

> It is a world of words to the end of it,
> In which nothing solid is its solid self.

Metaphor is moonlight, and the imagination of moonlight especially suggests unreality. Hence Stevens' many gestures against the moon: "It is fatal in the moon and empty there." In such moods he also rejects the transformations of metaphor as evasions. They are a "beau language" that fobs off "The precisions of fate." The imagination that seeks "Nothing beyond reality" needs a language

> untouched
> By trope or deviation, straight to the word,
> Straight to the transfixing object.

Among his habitual images, to be fat means, among other things, that you fill the space of the world, leaving no room for anything that is not you. More exactly, you are projecting yourself into the world, which thus reflects you, and you feel at home in it. Stevens usually presents this "fatness" with irony because it is manic. Those who feel the vast indifference of the cosmos are thin, pressed into little space by the alien world they dwell in. Straight lines and figures suggest rational thinking. Statues, especially bronze ones, suggest points of view that cannot change. They become "rubbish in the end."

Major symbolic images may come from the realm of fairytale and romance: "A giant, on the horizon, glistening"; "The pensive giant prone in violet space." Stevens does not retell the ancient myths, and, with very few exceptions, his poems are not based on them. But he saw or imagined things as they exist for the myth-making imagination: the sun is a "brave man," the night a "noble figure . . . Moving among the sleepers . . . the archaic queen."

If his imagery is one main source of Stevens' power, the other, complementing this concrete, imaginative tendency, lies in the active play of his intellect. His paradoxical generalizations surprise: "It is an illusion that we were ever alive." Phrases demand analysis. By definition a hypothesis is not fixed and solid. A "crystal hypothesis," however, must be clear, solid, and radiant, hardly a hypothesis at all. Such wit is omnipresent. Already in *Harmonium* Stevens' poems had a quasi-philosophical dimension. One poem asks whether a plum survives "its poems." Does it persist in "its own form," or does it exist only in and as the "poems" or images we entertain of it, each shaped and colored by the obliquities of a momentary and personal contact? Whether or not his utterances have any value as philosophy, the quasi-philosophical aspect of his poetry undeniably impresses readers with feelings of its seriousness and dignity.

In the latter part of his career Stevens became a major poet in the meditative mode. In the religiously meditative verse of the seventeenth century, in much of the so-called descriptive-meditative writing of the eighteenth century, and in such later examples as Wordsworth's "Tintern Abbey" and portions of Eliot's *Four Quartets*, meditative poetry enacts a strenuous effort of thinking leading toward realization. The main formal prin-

ciple of such poems is the rendering or imitation of the natural
movement of the mind "in the act," as Stevens put it, "of finding
/ What will suffice." In Stevens as in Wordsworth or Coleridge
the motion of the mind in meditation is presented as a continual
transition or "manifold continuation," an "endlessly elaborating"
and "deluging onwardness."

At one extreme Stevens' meditations may be dense with images, rapid and surprising in transitions, and continuously witty,
thus providing a distinct node of interest at every moment. This
stanza in "Esthétique du Mal," for example:

> Life is a bitter aspic. We are not
> At the center of a diamond. At dawn,
> The paratroopers fall and as they fall
> They mow the lawn. A vessel sinks in waves
> Of people, as big bell-billows from its bell
> Bell-bellow in the village steeple. Violets,
> Great tufts, spring up from buried houses
> Of poor, dishonest people, for whom the steeple,
> Long since, rang out farewell, farewell, farewell.

The allusion in "aspic" to Cleopatra's death, the swift contrast of
jellylike aspic with the similarly transparent but invulnerable
diamond, the unexpected transition to paratroopers, the odd
comparison of the trailing parachutes to the grass-catchers of
lawnmowers, the quick presentation of another image of death
in the sinking vessel, the shock (emphasized by the line break)
of "waves / Of people," the movement by rapid association from
the ship's bell to the steeple bell, and from waves of drowning
people to the more traditionally elegiac scene of a village so old
that in it violets spring where houses once stood, the rude check-
ing and violation of elegiac sentiment as Stevens (typically) keeps
in mind that the dead were dishonest, like all of us, and the final
repetition of "farewell," insisting with a bell-like sound and an
indefinable feeling of sorrowful yet almost angrily mocking dis-
missal that the dead do not rise again—in short, the phrasing
continually arrests attention and routs the giant of ennui.

At an opposite extreme of his style, however, Stevens holds
attention no less effectively despite a texture in which no word
or phrase can attract special notice. In such cases the effect depends on tensions generated by the movement of thought and
feeling, that is, by the syntax. A well-known passage in "Notes

toward a Supreme Fiction" builds by suspended constructions
and by repetitions expressing urgency:

> But to impose is not
> To discover. To discover an order as of
> A season, to discover summer and know it,
>
> To discover winter and know it well, to find,
> Not to impose, not to have reasoned at all,
> Out of nothing to have come on major weather,
>
> It is possible, possible, possible. It must
> Be possible . . .

Because these passages represent opposite stylistic poles, they
are not quite typical of Stevens. Usually his writing combines
elements of both styles in a texture and movement to which
everything we have noticed contributes—his vocabulary of images, surprising juxtapositions, humorous fantasies, wit, generalizing diction, play of ideas, "philosophical" largeness, and
strong, varying flow of syntax. "The Plain Sense of Things" may
be quoted as an example:

> After the leaves have fallen, we return
> To a plain sense of things. It is as if
> We had come to an end of the imagination,
> Inanimate in an inert savoir.
>
> It is difficult even to choose the adjective
> For this blank cold, this sadness without cause.
> The great structure has become a minor house.
> No turban walks across the lessened floors.
>
> The greenhouse never so badly needed paint.
> The chimney is fifty years old and slants to one side.
> A fantastic effort has failed, a repetition
> In a repetitiousness of men and flies.
>
> Yet the absence of the imagination had
> Itself to be imagined. The great pond,
> The plain sense of it, without reflections, leaves,
> Mud, water like dirty glass, expressing silence
>
> Of a sort, silence of a rat come out to see,
> The great pond and its waste of the lilies, all this
> Had to be imagined as an inevitable knowledge,
> Required, as a necessity requires.

Few readers would call this a "great" poem, for it lacks the magic of phrase, the intensity and drama of emotion, the depth of connotation and profundity of symbolism that are now associated with this adjective. But if it is not "great" it is good in the extreme. It presents a sustained, lucid, equable, tough, ongoing, tenaciously working activity of mind, touched with imagination and pleasurably surprising at every point.

In all Stevens' meditation there is no finality. I quoted a moment of climax—"It is possible, possible, possible"—in "Notes toward a Supreme Fiction," but, typically, the climax was not the end. The line continued—"It must / Be possible"—and the slight variation sadly qualified and began to withdraw from the triumphant assertion. And so it goes in Stevens. Whatever is affirmed is at once questioned. Eventually the unresting flow of thought and feeling may lead to an opposite affirmation, which also becomes, in turn, a starting point for further meditation. His sentences can be long and shapeless, and, as Helen Vendler has pointed out, we almost irresistibly forget how often the accumulating clauses stand under some introductory sign ("One might," "If," "It must be") that makes them hypothetical, contingent, or merely hopeful. That there can be no "last deduction" or "grand pronunciamento" Stevens understood very well. It was implied in what he meant by meditation, of which the formal essence was ongoingness. It was intrinsic to the restless, questioning, and skeptical habit of his mind. And he wished that meditation should be "never ending" because it was pleasurable.

13

OTHER MODERNIST POETS

WHEN after the Second World War many young poets in the United States adopted Pound and Williams as their masters, they praised their styles and repeated their literary opinions. This enthusiasm inspired similar responses in university students and teachers of English, though for a long time academic admirers of Pound were on the defensive and therefore militant. In England during the same period some poets, such as Charles Tomlinson and Donald Davie, believed that American influences would be healthy, and were therefore receptive to them. This new, sometimes belligerent sympathy with Pound and Williams led to a heightened appreciation or even to a discovery of poets who had been writing all along as their disciples or, at least, had composed in analogous modes. The most important of these newly recognized poets were Basil Bunting, David Ignatow, Louis Zukofsky, and three others—Charles Reznikoff, Carl Rakosi, and George Oppen— who had been associated with Zukofsky in the "Objectivism" of the 1930s.

They had been working for thirty years in obscurity. Though they were contemporaries of E. E. Cummings, Hart Crane, and Allen Tate, much of their poetry had not even been published; what had appeared, had perished. In the 1950s and 1960s they found for the first time publishers and critical attention. This reception released their creativity, and they wrote more or better than they had for years before.

The story of Louis Zukofsky is typical. In 1932 he edited an "Objectivist" issue of *Poetry* magazine, and in 1938 Pound dedicated his *Guide to Kulchur* to Zukofsky and Bunting. Otherwise, Zukofsky's name was scarcely known. But in the 1950s and 1960s poets such as Charles Olson, Robert Duncan, and Robert Creeley sought out Pound and Williams, and these older poets alerted them to Zukofsky's existence. They visited him, they read his poems, they sent theirs to him, they got him published, and Creeley wrote an admiring Introduction for "A" 1–12 (1967), a first installment of the long poem Zukofsky finished in 1974. His *Collected Short Poems* were published in two volumes in 1965 and 1966, and in 1978 the complete "A" came out in a handsome, one-volume edition of eight hundred pages.

I also discuss the poetry of David Jones in this chapter, although he was not an associate or follower of Pound and probably had never read Williams. Moreover, the world had not been blind to Jones. With his first book, *In Parenthesis* (1937), his genius had been perceived by readers whose opinions were worth having, such as T. S. Eliot, and when Auden hailed Jones's *Anathemata* (1952) as "very probably the finest long poem written in English in this century," the opinion seemed at least possible. I notice him here because the growing appreciation of his poetry in the 1950s and 1960s was part of the complex event I am tracing, the postwar resurgence of the high Modernist mode.

DAVID JONES

What David Jones (1895–1974) observed and underwent as a soldier in the trenches during the First World War was traumatically imprinted on him. He drew on it for *In Parenthesis* (1937), and to the end of his career soldier life was a recurrent subject of his art. He suffered from frequent migraines and other health problems that were drags on his productivity, including a nervous breakdown, and these probably had their main causes in the war, though one close friend attributed them rather to the intensity of Jones's creative effort. In 1919 he returned from the

trenches to enter art school, and three years later he was associated with the community of Roman Catholic artist-craftsmen
centered about Eric Gill in Wales. He gradually acquired a minor
reputation, especially for watercolor. In 1921 he was received as
a convert into the Roman Catholic Church, and his thoughts and
works henceforth were steeped in Church lore, ritual, and tradition.

Welsh "deposits," as he would have called them, were also important in his work, for he identified with his Welsh background.
He studied the early literature of Wales and the history of Celtic
and Roman-Celtic Britain, and pored over the Arthurian legends and their explainers. He tried to learn the language, and
words in Welsh dot his texts. He was fascinated by anthropological interpretations of Arthurian and other myths, such as Jessie
Weston's and Sir James Frazer's, for these opened vistas into the
prehistoric mind and world.

For reasons of health and temperament Jones led a somewhat
ascetic, withdrawn life. He never married or had a domestic establishment of his own, but stayed with his parents, or with
friends, or in rented rooms. *In Parenthesis* and *Anathemata* were
followed, at least in order of publication, by various shorter
pieces, though some of them were partly composed in the same
years as *Anathemata*. They were brought together in *The Sleeping
Lord and Other Fragments* (1974). His essays on literature and art,
collected in *Epoch and Artist* (1959) and *The Dying Gaul* (1978),
illuminate his work.

In Parenthesis is certainly the greatest literary text that deals
with the First World War. But it is a "war book" only if the *Iliad*
belongs in this classification. It presents roll calls, inspections,
fatigue duties, patrols, wounds, deaths, and corpses, but from a
universal perspective. In it the battle of the Somme is conflated
with that of Agincourt, and also with an obscure, doomed raid
by three hundred Welsh in the sixth century, not to mention
other battles in many times and places. Its subject is the First
World War and also war and soldiering perennially, and war and
soldiering are themselves only symbols through which a wider,
more comprehensive view of human existence comes to a focus.
Of the *Anathemata* I am less sure, but the least one can say is that
it has imaginative brilliance.

Both works are commemorative, and see the past in the present, the present in the past, reenactments and prefigurings. In a generation that had read *The Golden Bough* and observed the modernity of the Lascaux cave paintings, it was natural to assume that time, even thousands of years, does not change man's nature and situation essentially. Neanderthal scratchings on burial stones are of the same essence with ritual prayers in the Mass for the faithful departed, and we shall see that a stunning passage in *Anathemata* brings them together. Joyce, Yeats, Pound, and Eliot made similar "rhymes," as Pound called them, linking events across epochs and cultures. But Pound and Eliot dwelt on contrasts as well as resemblances; their juxtaposition sometimes assayed the comparative quality and worth of different historical ages. In the more directly pious, passive, and hopeful work of Jones the imaginative effort was to "uncover the mystery," to see in the foregrounded event all the others it repeats or anticipates and thus symbolizes.

Jones was a lover of ritual. He revered the *disciplina*, as he called them, the forms and the procedures that are proper and traditional in every line of effort—surveying, shipbuilding, stone carving, warfare, worship. Military practices and routines—the aloofness of officers, the hectoring of sergeants, the fallings in, roll calls, inspections—are age-old because they are appropriate to the end in view. So also there is a good reason why the ship's helmsman must always repeat aloud and with the same emphasis a cry from the crow's nest, such as "Lánd afóre the béam to stárb'd." But while such forms are traditionally prescribed because they are efficacious, Jones felt a further propriety in them. They were a ceremonial link with the past. They had a virtue of fidelity to it.

For a writer thus devoted to commemorating and handing on the past, self-expression could not be an important value. Art is, as Jones put it, a "showing forth of our inheritance," a "kind of *anamnesis* of . . . an effective recalling of, something loved." The self is never his subject, and he never uses the first-person, lyric convention that "I" am speaking. *In Parenthesis* draws on sensations, feelings, and experiences Jones had known personally, but they are attached to a fictive character named John Ball and used objectively as materials in a literary construction. Jones's training as a craftsman also contributed to his impersonality as a writer. He regarded his writings as things to be made, and the processes of such making are assembling the motifs and shaping a whole or "complex" out of them.

In Parenthesis follows a small army unit from its embarkation for France to the battle of the Somme. The troops disembark, move from the rear areas toward the front, come eventually within the range of shells, enter the wilderness of trenches, and find after much confusion their own assigned strip. Part 4 presents the routine of trench life through one day. Pulled out of the line for recuperation, the company is then marched as reinforcements toward the battle of the Somme. The final pages describe their assault, in which most of them are killed. This summary may perhaps convey the outline and the distribution of plot emphases: how little is actually fighting, how much is initiation. In fact, the poem activates what might be called an initiation archetype of gradually learning the ways and rituals of an alien, waste world, of penetrating steadily deeper and becoming accustomed. In one sense the catastrophe of the battle at the end is foreknown; from the start of the poem a web of allusion creates a sense of doomed fatality. The title, for example, of the first page, "The Many Men So Beautiful," is from Coleridge's *Rime of the Ancient Mariner,* though Jones does not print the line that follows in the poem, "And they all dead did lie." This atmosphere of tragic fate envelops the soldiers as a dark background, setting off their ordinary human qualities—their kindness, faithfulness, humor, and pride—and investing them with pathos.

But in another sense the reader does not foresee the catastrophe. For our perspective as we read is that of the common soldiers, and they usually do not know where they are or what the purpose of their marches may be. Other areas of the front are to them like far-off continents from which rumors come. They have no sense of the whole. Hence what happens seems aimless. The book does not press this as an indictment of the war but as the inevitable experience of soldiers. They go through the war as through a demonic wonderland in which they are Alices, quite unable to know what may come next. And until the battle in the final pages it seems, moreover, that nothing much is happening. The packed style and slow tempo of the narrative contribute also to this impression. Jones conveys a great many sensations and thoughts in a very few words, so that, in this sense, a great deal happens on a page. But most of the events are routine ones, and they are rendered at length and in very close detail, so that, in another sense, the "plot" hardly moves forward. In the first three pages, for example, the company merely falls in and starts marching off. Thus while the narrative fascinates, appalls, lifts the imagination and pulls at the heart, it also bores relentlessly, with a boredom that is altogether necessary, appropriate, and expressive.

To illustrate the perspective that *In Parenthesis* shares with the *Iliad*, we may take the sketch of Mr. Jenkins, the young lieutenant in charge. We come to know him through a few brief passages interspersed throughout the book. He has, we are told on the second page, a "flax head," and looks like a squire in a Uccello painting. He is twenty years old. When the troops were training in England, he would, if no major was looking, let them loaf a bit by the stream, himself gazing "for long at a time without moving" into the water. He is aloof from his men, as he is from the discipline of war, but he is a conscientious shepherd, concerned that the soldiers should get some sleep, that "no one falls out, see them all up." Yet the troops, seeing he is young and new to his job, think, "how should his inexperience not be a broken reed for us—and fetch up in Jerry's bosom." On his twenty-first birthday he gets "a parcel from Fortnum and Mason," but he grieves "for his friend, Talbot Rhys," and feels "an indifference to the spring offensive." Still, on a fine day in the rear areas he "would strike at midge-flies with his cane, and forget a bit about Talbot Rhys." And so, because these references to Mr. Jenkins have made him vivid to us as a typical young officer, his sudden death in the battle comes as a shock. There is something deeply suggestive and moving about the way the shot boy gropes with ebbing strength to unbuckle his shrapnel helmet ("iron saucer"), which has fallen forward over his face, masking and blinding him from the light and air:

> He sinks on one knee
> and now on the other,
> his upper body tilts in rigid inclination
> this way and back;
> weighted lanyard runs out to full tether,
> > swings like a pendulum
> > and the clock run down.

> Lurched over, jerked iron saucer over tilted brow,
> clampt unkindly over lip and chin
> nor no ventaille to this darkening
>   and masked face lifts to grope the air
> and so disconsolate;
> enfeebled fingering at a paltry strap—
> buckle holds,
> holds him blind against the morning.
>   Then stretch still where weeds pattern the chalk
> predella—where it rises to his wire—and Sergeant T. Quilter takes over.

External, impersonal, and precise, the passage focuses on a sequence of bodily motions and thus prolongs the narration while keeping it tethered to observed fact. The narrator feels a decent sympathy and pathos, and the grotesque image of the masked face lifting to grope the air is poignant, but the clear, exact rendering and mechanical metaphors keep an emotional distance; in fact, they chill the episode to a surprising degree and thus lodge it all the more in our memory.

"The more imaginative a writer," Jones once observed, the more we probe the text "for possible significances, allusions, clues, in every line and every word." The dense, packed texture of the writing in *In Parenthesis* is typically Modernist. The presentation is undeviatingly particular and concrete. Historical and literary allusions weave through the generally realistic vignettes. The diction ranges from the colloquial to the heroic and biblical. The range of juxtaposed feelings is also very wide—the cynical humor of the soldiers, disgust, fear, ironic protest, and elegiac sadness at the waste of war—and the diverse emotions interplay complexly.

Jones had read little Modernist literature by the time he began *In Parenthesis,* but he knew *The Waste Land* and a bit of Pound. He had not yet dipped into Joyce, but had acquired some information about Joyce's work and heard a portion of *Finnegans Wake* read aloud. That his own writing was similarly high Modernist in form was to be attributed, Jones later said, less to influences than to the "civilizational situation." The works of writers who "have somewhat the same attitude toward or reaction against or apperception of the time and site to which they belong" will show "an affinity" in form and content. It may look like direct borrowing when in fact it is "a similar response to an identical 'situation' on the part of persons of similar perception." Jones also explained that when he began *In Parenthesis* he tried to transfer to literature techniques he had first learned in painting. The conjunction of what little he knew of Modernist writings— genius does not require many hints—with his professional knowledge of contemporary painting may sufficiently account for his Modernist style.

In Parenthesis might be classified as either prose or poetry, depending on definitions of them. Jones called it a "writing," leaving the question open. Much of it is prose by any definition. But many passages are arranged as free verse. In army routine Jones typically saw aesthetic form and ritual, and so his narrator tends to fall into syntactical and rhythmic patterns akin to antiphonal response. In one passage, for example, the soldiers are ordered to stand-to at dawn (an hour when attack might be expected; the stand-to was a twice-daily ritual at dawn and twilight in the trenches). The crack of repeated commands composes a text that is completely realistic yet highly formalized; the reference to *Macbeth* brings to mind other armies in the past, hearing similar commands as they peered into the distance. They are watching the currents of fog on the woods opposite, as soldiers have always done, wondering whether enemy troops are moving toward them:

> To their eyes seeming a wood moving,
> > a moving grove advisioned.
> > Stand-to.
> > Stand-to.
> > Stand-to-arms.

> > Out there,
> > get out there
> > get into that fire trench.
> > Pass it along to Stand-to.

Much of Jones's verse might be thought experimental. We find collages of the thoughts of different soldiers, recitals of titles and epithets, and conversations formalized through repetition. There are inserted set pieces of poetry, such as that on the rats heard in the silence at the end of Part 3 and the long speech of the Welsh soldier in Part 4. A shorter example is the poem on the sentry in Part 3 ("them" refers to the enemy; the long-barrows are the ancient Celtic tombs, in which the warriors were buried with their weapons):

> foremost toward them
> and outmost of us, and
> brother-keeper, and ward-watcher;
> his mess-mates sleeping like long-barrow sleepers, their
> dark arms at reach.
> Spell-sleepers, thrown about anyhow under the night.

Most of the last part, presenting the assault and battle, is in verse. In one passage, as an example of the whole, the attacking soldiers drop down for safety as a shell bursts nearby, its blast followed by a deluge of mud. Private Weavel is killed, and the others move forward again, feeling as though they were already dead and floating above the earth, like the saved borne upward on clouds in the old paintings. The underlying metaphor is of the Day of Judgment, but the image of the saints assumed into heaven here expresses the soldiers' state of psychological shock and detachment. The irony of the psalm in conjunction with Weavel's death is especially complex:

> You drop apprehensively—the sun gone out,
> strange airs smite your body
> and muck rains straight from heaven
> and everlasting doors lift up for 'o2 Weavel.
>   You cant see anything but sheen on drifting particles and
> you move forward in your private bright cloud like
> one assumed
> who is borne up by an exterior volition.

The Anathemata is a poem of two hundred pages in eight parts. Unlike *In Parenthesis*, it has no continuing narrative or "plot." In his Preface Jones called it a "heap," quoting the medieval Welsh writer Nennius—"I have made a heap of all that I could find"— and he also compared it to "meanderings," "fragments," "free associations," and "a longish conversation between two friends, where one thing leads to another." These terms, in their slightly ironic modesty, do not convey Jones's whole opinion about the governing form—or lack of it—of his poem. But they address the question more accurately than most of the suggestions and metaphors other critics have offered. *Anathemata* is not, for example, a history of the world, though a lot of history is allusively included. To think of it as meditations and associations coming to mind in church during the Mass provides little help in reading. For though Jones had this idea himself, at least when he wrote the Preface, we have no continuing consciousness of a Mass being celebrated, and the form of the Mass does not interplay with or organize the form of the poem. To fancy that the construction of the poem resembles the design of a Celtic cross, or the ground plan of an ancient Celtic fort, or the narrative method of a medieval Welsh poem is merely to restate the problem—elaborate interweaving without architecture or central focus. *Anathemata* can be compared only with the greatest Modernist long poems, but making this comparison, I acknowledge that I do not read it as eagerly as *The Waste Land, The Cantos* or *The Bridge*. Nevertheless, *Anathemata* is a work of brilliant imaginativeness, scope, and grandeur.

If we sense, as we read *Anathemata*, that the whole coheres and develops, the main cause of this impression is the incremental recurrence of themes and images. A passage picks up, echoes, and adds to previous ones in widely diverse contexts, and thus the poem becomes a complex of cross-references. The web of associations binds every part with the whole; the background of the whole gives the part resonance. Since we collect the recurrences and interassociations only gradually as we read, *Anathemata* seems a more unified poem on page two hundred than on page twenty and on the twentieth reading than on the first. How coherent we find it to be depends, at least in part, on how well we know it.

To illustrate the texture of Jones's style I may quote a passage from the first part. At this point Jones is arguing that the specific note by which we recognize the human is "artefacture." Or since wrens make nests and beavers dams, the properly distinguishing note of man is that he makes things gratuitously as signs, as "anathemata." Hence when on Neanderthal tombs we see "uteral marks" scratched on the covering stone, we know the maker was human, and the prayer in the Mass of All Soul's Day "For all WHOSE WORKS FOLLOW THEM" is also for the Stone Age craftsman.

> For all WHOSE WORKS FOLLOW THEM
>   among any of these or them
> *dona eis requiem.*
>   (He would lose, not any one
>   from among them.
> Of all those given him
>   he would lose none.)
>
>   By the uteral marks
> that make the covering stone an artefact.
>   By the penile ivory
> and by the viatic meats.
>   *Dona ei requiem.*

Biblical and liturgical fragments are juxtaposed with fragments referring to objects found in Stone Age burial sites. The general theme is, to repeat, that these works of art and religious symbols show that their makers were human and hence among those Christ would not lose. Their "uteral marks" and our *dona ei requiem* are equally prayers for the dead. The "covering stone" lies over the dead caveman, but since Christ's words ("Of those whom thou gavest me," Christ said in the garden, "I lost not one") were spoken just before his arrest and crucifixion, the phrase may also bring to mind the stone against the door of Christ's rock-hewn tomb. Christ in his resurrection was also a caveman.

This passage is solemn and liturgical, but much of *Anathemata* is not. "Nudge Clio / she's apt to be musing," says the narrator, finding a bit of history dubious as reported. The pun is typical. Other voices interrupt the narrator and sometimes take over for extended passages. There is, for example, the prose monologue of Ilia, mother by Mars of Romulus and Remus. In language one might not expect of a vestal princess she remembers how the god made love (she calls him a "Georgie," farmer, with social contempt; Mars was connected with agriculture before he beat his ploughshare into a sword):

nor had he gratitude to unlace the mired greaves of surly iron—the squat Georgie!

B'the clod smell on him *that's* what he *was* . . . by the manners of him. Yet—Verticordia [Venus], prevent us continually! . . . his glory filled the whole place where we were together.

Almost the whole of Part 5 is a monologue, often similar in tone to the passage just quoted, by one of London's daughters. Other passages are in archaic forms of verse such as the catalogue, the boast, and the list of appellations: "Bough-bearer, harrower / torrent-drinker, *restitutor.*" There is much vivid descriptive writing: a bay, for example, as the ship enters, with the white waves rolling shoreward ("grinders" because they have been dangerous teeth and churning millwheels to the ship) and a shaft of sunlight hitting the harbor mole:

> A sky-shaft brights the whited mole
> wind-hauled the grinders
> white the darked bay's wide bowl.

But mainly the imaginative power of the poem comes from the allusions and incremental repetitions, both enormously expanding the foregrounded event by opening a long vista behind it. Through allusion the vista is of historical parallels and mythical dimensions; through repetition it is of previous contexts and images in the poem. To illustrate the incremental repetition I may point to the many ships and voyages. In Part 2 an ancient ship rounds Cape Sunium in Greece, and another from the Mediterranean reaches Cornwall. Part 3 presents an Anglo-Saxon ship approaching England, and elsewhere the poem briefly mentions or describes many other voyages. Part 4 is mostly the monologue of a shipwright and Part 6 a meditation on the keel, ram, and mast (the "stauros" or cross) of an ancient ship. The different episodes present similar situations, emotions, and characters—peril, vigil in the crow's nest, supplication to the divine, the battered captain who finally makes his port—and the text does not keep these voyages perfectly distinct from one another. The voyages are not allegorical, but in their recurrent elements the meditating imagination finds widening significance. The church, for example, is constructed like a ship (nave, Latin *navis*) and was, as an institution, traditionally compared to a ship on which mankind is embarked. (The keel or "central *arbor* . . . on which our salvation sways" is the cross.) Through the Good Friday vigil at the mast Christ "berthed" (with puns) the ship. The Mass reenacts this voyage; the solitary cantor may be compared to the ship's boy peering for landfall from the crow's nest. The poem, *Anathemata*, is a voyage and also a ship carrying "deposits" of the past. And, of course, the ships in this poem are among those artefactures and symbols to which the poem refers in its title, those things donated, votive, dedicated, made separate and "laid up from other things," signs "of something other," "set up, lifted up, or in whatever manner made over to the gods."

In connection with *Anathemata* I may mention Ronald Duncan's (b. 1914) unfinished poem, *Man* (Part 1, 1970; Part 2, 1971). The poems are not comparable in quality or similar in philosophy, but are the two most ambitious recent attempts I know to express scientific lore in poetry. Where the first part of *Anathemata* presents the geological history of the earth and the evolution of man, Duncan's poem narrates and reflects upon the history of the universe from primordial subatomic particles to the Pleistocene era at the end of Part 2. Six years of reading went into it. Its theme is the evolution of consciousness. "Without an awareness of science," Duncan says, "the contemporary sensibility is fractured and its literature will become a cul-de-sac . . . if serious still trivial, obscure without depth, basically frivolous even when expressing despair."

Ninety percent of poetry, Duncan added in his Introduction to *Man,* "is no more than a mating call." He was repudiating his own poetry, for prior to *Man* his best work, aside from verse dramas, came in *The Solitudes* (1960), a volume consisting mainly of lyric sorrows and avowals in the course of a love affair. The affair ended unhappily and the loved woman later committed suicide. *Man* was written in an attempt to suppress pain and guilt. The impersonality, objectivity, and intellectual demands of science were instruments to this end. This motive, to which the poem keeps adverting, perhaps converts *Man* also into "amatory doodling," though of an unusually strenuous kind. At any rate it lends human interest. And it also provides a moving personal background to the poem's continuing meditation on cosmic evolution. Suffering is intrinsic to consciousness. Among the starfish and sponges of the Proterozoic ocean "pain was brief" and remorse was "happily unborn." But though consciousness is a tragic endowment, man is somberly grateful for it, as Duncan is also for the love he experienced.

In rhythm and phrasing *Man* is not nearly so impressive as in its conception, but it is formally inventive. A friend and in some respects a follower of Eliot and Pound, Duncan caught from Pound's *Cantos* the freedom and bravura of his methods. He writes the purple passages traditional in cosmological poems, such as dizzying contemplations of cosmic vastness, of the energy of the sun, and of alien forms of life in past ages, and he also uses mathematical formulas. The mathematical formulas are visually impressive and semantically impenetrable—at least to most readers; in these respects they resemble the Chinese phrases in Pound's *Cantos*. To sum up, I hope that *Man* will be read, for though it is seriously flawed, it interestingly suggests how fine a poem might be made out of scientific cosmology.

BASIL BUNTING

Basil Bunting (b. 1900) grew up in the north of England, went to a Quaker school, and was a conscientious objector during the First World War, spending some time in prison. He helped Ford Madox Ford edit the *Transatlantic Review* in the 1920s and was closely associated with Pound. He worked as a sailor, journalist, music critic, film extra, army interpreter, and college teacher, living in Paris (1923), Italy (1929–33), the Canary Islands (1933–36), Iran (1943–51), the United States, and England.

Though much influenced by Pound, Bunting learned his art from many other sources also, including the Latin classics. He was associated with Zukofsky in Objectivism and included in the *"Objectivists" Anthology*. Wordsworth, he later said, had held him all his life. His poems of the 1920s, at the start of his career, present the seeming paradox, not uncommon in either the Modernist or the classical tradition, of a strongly individual, emotionally intense, and rebellious personality expressing itself with objective, painstaking craftsmanship and self-discipline.

His style in the 1920s was direct, rather generalizing, and slightly declamatory, with vivid images, Latinate and vigorous diction, and studied rhythm and sound. In the 1930s and 1940s his work slightly recalled that of Pound in *Lustra* and *Cathay*. Bunting also translated Persian poetry, especially Firdousi. Satiric verses mocked the economic system. Bunting's lines "On the

Fly-leaf of Pound's Cantos" may be quoted for their typically harsh strength:

There are the Alps. What is there to say about them?
They don't make sense. Fatal glaciers, crags cranks climb,
jumbled boulder and weed, pasture and boulder, scree,
et l'on entend, maybe, *le refrain joyeux et leger.*
Who knows what the ice will have scraped on the rock it is smoothing?

There they are, you will have to go a long way round
if you want to avoid them.
It takes some getting used to. There are the Alps,
fools! Sit down and wait for them to crumble!

The Spoils is a poem of about 370 lines in three parts. Composed in 1951, it draws on Bunting's impressions and experiences during the Second World War and, later, in Iran. It cuts without transition from one brief vignette to another, and, as in most long Modernist poems since *The Waste Land,* the discontinuous method permits panoramic effects. In a couple of hundred lines we traverse Iran's landscapes, ways of life, historical past, culture, and art. Different styles and moods are juxtaposed. The language is conversational and ranges from sclerotic expostulation—"absolute idiots"—to straightforward reflection—

> sea-gardens
> between Lofoten and Spitzbergen,
> as good a grave as any, earth or water.
> What else do we live for and take part,
> We who would share the spoils?

But the dominant style might be called Imagist (or Objectivist): short, rhythmic lines, compressed syntax, and one image after another. Thus along the Tigris river are

> Naked boys among water-buffaloes,
> daughters without smile
> treading clothes by the verge,
> harsh smouldering dung:
> a woman taking bread from her oven
> spreads dates, an onion, cheese.

Strong, direct, uncivil, Bunting's style accords with his vision of things, as this is imaged in Iranian life and in war memories.

The world of his poem is stark, predatory, and impoverished, but with moments of sensuous or aesthetic pleasure. Peril and violence are omnipresent. Yet the merchant hoarders who live in fear and for money were "better dead." The "spoils," as the epigraph in Arabic says, "are for God," but are won by living at risk.

After *The Spoils* Bunting, completely forgotten as a poet, seems to have stopped writing. He was then working in the north of England on a newspaper. When in the 1960s poetry readings were started in his locality, Bunting proved to be a stunning performer, and the sense of an audience at these readings led him to resume composition. *Briggflatts*, his masterpiece, was completed in 1965 and published a year later.

Briggflatts has about seven hundred lines, condensed from fifteen thousand in earlier drafts. Subtitled "An Autobiography," it draws in some passages on personal memories. The allusions in it to the landscape, ways of life, and historical past of Northumbria enhance the appeal of the poem for English readers. In the course of life that is vaguely sketched the poem finds a pattern, one that is analogous in some ways to Muir's "fable." The pattern is of separation—from a lover and from a native, rural place—and final, though ambiguous, return. A youthful love affair was broken off ("murdered," the poem says) and the poet went out into life "self-hating." The poem alludes to years of wandering thereafter. Amid all his experience the "unconvinced deserter" feels that "something is lost." Neither can the "self-maimed" poet write well or much. He is like a "reproached / uneasy mason" or stone-cutter who is "Shaping evasive / ornaments" and "littering his yard / with flawed fragments." The cycle of life (and of the poem) runs from dawn to night, from spring to winter, and as the poem concludes, the speaker watches the winter stars rise one by one. The light from a star now at its zenith was sent out from that star fifty years ago, at the moment of youthful love. Now that the "sheets are gathered and bound," and all is over, the speaker welcomes the night as death and as the return of love, now to be "uninterrupted."

> Finger tips touched and were still
> fifty years ago.
> Sirius is too young to remember.

Sirius glows in the wind. Sparks on ripples
mark his line, lures for spent fish.

Fifty years a letter unanswered;
a visit postponed for fifty years.

She has been with me fifty years.

Starlight quivers. I had day enough.
For love uninterrupted night.

In many respects, then, *Briggflatts* exerts a strongly Romantic appeal. Its Northumbrian setting offers local color, it has sympathetic images of nature and young love, its tone is frequently elegiac, its story is of a quest, its verse is musical, and it enlarges its significance into the mythical. The mythical element is present not only in the poem as a whole, with its cyclic governing symbol of a turn or return from spring to winter, from day to night, but also in individual passages. A girl washes her lover with rainwater from a barrel, for example, and though the episode is described realistically, his body is identified with the land in the spring rain.

The poem is in the formal tradition of *The Waste Land*. As in *The Waste Land* and *Four Quartets*, the five movements of *Briggflatts* differ from one another in subject matter and style, yet symbolic images—the bull, the slowworm, the mason recur across these discontinuities. The associations gathering and interweaving around these images interrelate the separate parts of the poem. But *Briggflatts* differs from *The Waste Land* by including personal recollections within its symbolist impersonality. Moreover, the syntax of Bunting's utterance is, though condensed, not fragmentary or distorted. Such modifications of Modernist-Symbolist form were frequent in Modernist poetry after Eliot's "Burnt Norton" (1935).

When he discusses his own poetry, Bunting almost always dwells on formal aspects. "Interpretations" are endless, he says, and adds that some of his symbols are obscure even to him. *Briggflatts,* he told some interviewers, originated as an abstract diagram, an arrangement of climaxes in a poem of five parts. He had this in mind before he had subjects or materials. He was also thinking of "the *B minor fugato* of Scarlatti" at the "same time as the diagram." He shared with Zukofsky the conception of poems as musical forms, and classified all his long poems, including *Briggflatts*, as "sonatas."

DAVID IGNATOW

David Ignatow (b. 1914) grew up in Brooklyn, the son of a small businessman. Whitman was imprinted on him in adolescence, but so was his father's bindery, and the gap between them was vast. In daily life on the job he observed no democracy, brotherhood, freedom of the spirit, or divinity in man. Instead, there was pressure, worry, bickering, threat, and resentment in the unceasing struggle to meet work schedules. Had Ignatow's imagination soared less in Whitman's vistas, he might have been less shocked. As it was, he could believe in Whitman's direct methods and realism but hardly in his "transcendental evaluation." T. S. Eliot appealed to Ignatow in his disillusionment, but Ignatow was still a follower of Whitman, though denying him, and could not sympathize with Eliot's style. He read William Carlos Williams and at first thought him literal and prosy, but as he read more, he admired. With Williams as his model, he could, he felt, depict the urban world he knew with direct honesty. Each poem could focus on a piece of it. As Ignatow read the lesson, a poet in Williams' school was not required to have an attitude toward his subject or to be imaginative about it. He would not be tempted, for the sake of "poetic" effect, to satirize, sentimentalize, philosophize, or mythologize, and could thus avoid the various false romanticisms of Eliot, Sandburg, Pound and Crane. To present the thing itself was enough, was poetry. And the language of poetry, as Ignatow gathered from Williams, was natural talk. Thus Williams enabled Ignatow to write.

Like Williams himself, Ignatow at first had few readers. But when Williams began to be a strong influence on younger poets, Ignatow was read with more appreciation. Having a place in the literary world, he was able to sell the family business and begin a new career as a college teacher. Meanwhile, his poetic style had been assimilating Symbolist and New Critical methods. His work was touched by Surrealism in the 1960s, and at the same time he published his notebooks and started writing prose poems. But throughout his career the power of his poetry depended on its unshrinking truth to his harsh experience of life. Sometimes his pessimism is so baldly stated and extreme that it surprises and seems almost witty. A poem on the suicide of Berryman makes the suggestion that Berryman might have lived on as Ignatow does, "half a suicide." The poem he is proudest of is "Rescue the Dead," a poem that debates whether it is better to love or not to:

> Finally, to forgo love is to kiss a leaf,
> is to let rain fall nakedly upon your head,
> is to respect fire,
> is to study man's eyes and his gestures
> as he talks,
> is to set bread upon the table
> and a knife discreetly by,
> is to pass through crowds
> like a crowd of oneself.
> Not to love is to live.
>
> To love is to be led away
> into a forest where the secret grave
> is dug, singing, praising darkness
> under the trees.
>
> To live is to sign your name,
> is to ignore the dead,
> is to carry a wallet
> and shake hands.
>
> To love is to be a fish.
> My boat wallows in the sea.
> You who are free,
> rescue the dead.

LOUIS ZUKOFSKY AND THE OBJECTIVISTS

Louis Zukofsky (1904–78) spoke Yiddish as a child and learned English as a foreign language. Resolved to be a writer, he studied literature at Columbia. He taught English at Brooklyn Polytechnic Institute, but his life was elsewhere—in reading philosophy, in music and poetry, and in the small family of his wife, Celia, and their son. He had the normal resentments of the neglected artist, but was a generous man, and he was touchingly loyal to Pound, whom he much admired, amid Pound's troubles. He was thin, bony, intellectual. In his later years he was fabulously hypochondriacal. He would say to his doctor, "I have, I'm not quite sure, but it may be just the beginning of TB. I coughed last night." His works were sometimes eccentric. *Bottom: On Shakespeare* (1963), on which he spent years, explored Shakespearean epistemology in many pages of baffling commentary. (The second volume is Celia Zukofsky's music for Shakespeare's *Pericles*.) His *Autobiography* (1970) consists of eighteen short lyrics, interspersed occasionally with bits of prose and set to music by his wife. He translated Cavalcanti's canzone *Dona mi prega* into Brooklyn dialect ("A foin lass bodders me I gotta tell her").

Some of the formal complications he imposed on himself would never have been noticed had he not pointed them out. (A few have been detected only through his manuscript notes, now stored at the University of Texas.) In the first half of *"A"* 9, a canzone, the mathematical formula for a conic section governs the distribution of n and r sounds, and the words and phrases of the poem are culled from two books by Marx. The opening stanzas of *"A"* 19 take most of their words and phrases from Mallarmé; in a later section the verses are extracts from the rules for the Paganini Prize.

Ingenuity can, of course, suggest explanations. As a hard, arbitrary rule the conic-section formula resembles the intricate canzone rhymes (which Zukofsky preserves), and the difficult exactness of the form may imply, though for no good reason, a corresponding quality of thought. The words of Marx and Mallarmé, if we know them for such, bring to mind an associated train of ideas about these writers. To quote the brochure of the Paganini Prize Committee tells the story of the competition, in which Zukofsky's son took part. But such expressive considerations were not the main reasons. Neither do they explain the effect of Zukofsky's esoteric procedures on readers. Just why Zukofsky needed to make writing so much more laborious for himself than it might have been, or why, to put it another way, he diverted the difficulties of writing from the expressive to the objectively formal sphere, or why, to put it a third way, he hid within his poems what only he could be expected to know was there, is a question for a psychiatrist. But as with Joyce, Mallarmé, Nabokov, and many another elaborator of similarly private rules, including the troubadours, when we know such ways of working might have been involved, we approach the work in a more than usually vigilant, ingenious, or paranoiac state of mind. Where we would ordinarily think a passage flat or obscure, we suspend judgment. There must, we suppose, have been an intention, a theory, however misguided, behind it, and if we knew the intention we might think better of the passage. Or there must be a meaning we have missed. In the presence of the enormously painstaking and esoteric, we cannot easily suspect ordinary dull writing.

Before turning to Zukofsky's poetry, however, I must briefly notice the "Objectivist" movement, which was really not a movement. There was an Objectivist press, an *"Objectivists" Anthology* (1932), an Objectivist number of *Poetry* magazine, and a band of Objectivists, including George Oppen, Carl Rakosi, and Charles Reznikoff along with Zukofsky, but, nevertheless, Objectivism was fugitive, vaguely defined, and had no influence. In the careers of the poets involved it was only an episode, and they later wrote in other styles. For this reason they are more appropriately discussed individually than as members of a group. The reason for mentioning Objectivism here is mainly that the supposed movement is often referred to and readers may be curious. And the term is sometimes misunderstood. Whatever the Objectivists advocated, it was not, in any simple sense, a concrete representation of objects. Zukofsky later said that the Objectivists had no program. As he told the story, Harriet Monroe, bombarded by Pound, asked Zukofsky to edit *Poetry* magazine for February 1931. "You must have a movement," she said. "No," Zukofsky replied, "some of us are writing to say things simply so that they will affect us as new again." "Well, give it a name."

Zukofsky wrote an essay for *Poetry*, "Sincerity and Objectification." Unlike many poets before and since, he did not associate "sincerity" with simple honesty, confessional intimacy, emotion rather than thinking, or with a process of mind developing in a free, unplanned way. Instead, like Pound, he found sincerity in the perfecting of melody and form (and therefore of the image and thought which are formed) in the least detail. "Objectification" was a consummate degree of "sincerity." If it was achieved, each part of the work of art would fully harmonize with other parts. Contemplating an object of this kind, the mind was referred from part to part within it, rather than being led out of it toward knowledge or action. Zukofsky called this "rest."

Zukofsky's collected short poems are entitled *All*. The poem "Hi, Kuh" will serve as an introduction. It seems simple, almost a doodle.

> Hi, Kuh
>
> those
> gold'n bees
> are I's,
>
> eyes,
>
> skyscrapers.

"Cummings!" we might think, for the puns (haiku; *Kuh* = German "cow"), metamorphoses (bees, be, is, letter I's, numeral I's, eyes, Hi, high skyscrapers) and attention to visual shapes on the page (the letter *I* looks like a skyscraper, and so does the columnar poem) put us into Cummings' world of playful gimmick and pastoral, where cows are friends and bees are egos. That this takes place amid skyscrapers may remind us also of Williams, who delighted to find his pastorals in an urban environment. Williams wanted to show the transforming power of mere observation, how things bloom for us if we eye them. But in "Hi, Kuh" Zukofsky's eye is not on anything. He is attending to words and syllables, especially to their fortuitous aspects—the homonyms, homophones, and visual shapes they bring to mind.

Thus or similarly a reader might take the poem, finding it pleasant. But about this poem we have more information. From a published interview with Zukofsky we learn that he observed Elsie, the Borden cow, on a signboard. The bees are B's. And we also gather that "Hi, Kuh" is epistemology, in fact, the poem does the "short way" what *Bottom: On Shakespeare* does the "long way." It "does away with" the theory of knowledge. Pursuing this clue, we may see that the poem goes round in a circle. It revolves from things predicated as external and objective (*Hi, those*) to things conceived as subjects (I's), each I being a way of seeing (eyes). We get similar results by playing with *be*ing and *eye*ing. On the one hand, the world is what it is; on the other hand, it is what we see—it varies with our subjective selves (I's). That the speaker observes not a cow but the sign of a cow, and transposes this into a verbal sign (*kuh*) which the reader must transpose into another verbal sign (*cow*), is not irrelevant to this nest of problems. No wonder the final line of the poem dismisses the issue. After all, there are objects out there: *skyscrapers*.

But this is not quite what Zukofsky meant. Or rather, in the interview he obtained the meaning another way. The point was, he is astigmatic, so if he eyes the B's without his glasses, they look like I's, in fact, like skyscrapers. "All right, the epistemological question? I see this? Yes. The eyes see it? But there's also an object out there. All right, whichever way you want." But, without this interview, we could hardly have read out of this poem what Zukofsky thought he put into it.

Zukofsky also composed relatively straightforward poems in well-established modern styles, and these are among his best. There are lovely quasi-Imagist poems, such as "Ferry" and "Passing tall" (numbers 5 and 10 in "29 Poems"). Number 42 in "Anew" and passages of "*A*" 12 speak of himself personally in a pleasantly relaxed style. "The" is an anecdotal, witty, rollicking, serious monologue, headlong in momentum, variable in style, and packed with literary quotations and allusions. In its combination of far-fetched comparison, social observation and protest, intricate form, and reflection upon the form "Mantis" may have affinities with Auden. "To My Washstand" celebrates the sensory pleasures of the ordinary—a theme out of William Carlos Williams—and also, as Williams might equally have done, finds in the washstand an occasion for reflecting upon poetry, though the sustained wit is unlike Williams. Illustrating its argument about the course modern poetry must take, the poem deploys the most ordinary diction in drab, featureless, musicless stanzas. They release their unobtrusive metaphors only to a reader who pays the close, meditating attention the speaker gives to his bathroom fixture.

"*A*" is a poem in twenty-four movements, which Zukofsky began in 1928 and completed in 1974. Different movements vary enormously from one another; moreover, Zukofsky's style changed over the years. In method the early movements resemble the *Cantos*. "*A*" 6 presents a trip across the United States. It is a panoramic indictment of the waste land of contemporary America. "*A*" 7 is a sequence of seven (the typically appropriate number) sonnets. *"A"* 8 begins by juxtaposing music, or Bach, with sociopolitical realities, or Marx, and struggles to unify them. This impulse seems lost in a long section that resembles in form the American history Cantos (62–71) Pound was turning out at the same time. But the two themes that opened *"A"* 8 are interwoven in the ballade that closes it, and the double canzone of *"A"* 9 is constructed in the first half out of the words and phrases of Marx. *"A"* 10, written in 1940, surveys the world in that bad year. *"A"* 11, in total contrast, is a highly formal, musical address to his song, telling it what to say to his son after his death.

By 1950, when *"A"* 11 was composed, the *"A"*s no longer much resembled the *Cantos*. Through its first eleven movements *"A"* interweaves a personal element, for history in the public world is recurrently juxtaposed with that in the private world of the family, where the child Paul was growing up. This personal theme emerges strongly in *"A"* 12 (1950–51), where passages presenting the life and character of Zukofsky's father have a direct human interest mostly lacking in Zukofsky's work. Their lucid, sustained, legato syntax was for him a new style. Writing no more *"A"*s for ten years, Zukofsky then composed *"A"* 13–21 between 1960 and 1967. *"A"* 15 meditates on the assassination of President Kennedy and the state and fate of the nation. *"A"* 16 consists of four words. In memory of William Carlos Williams *"A"* 17 makes a collage from Zukofsky's previous writings, using bits associated with his dead friend. *"A"* 21 translates Plautus' *Rudens*. *"A"* 24, which has 240 pages, recapitulates Zukofsky's work. Five parts are voiced simultaneously throughout. One part consists of harpsichord pieces by Handel; each of the other four, named Thought, Drama, Story, and Poem, speaks words taken from a different appropriate publication of Zukofsky's.

"A" is eccentric, experimental, impenetrable, boring, amusing, touching, distinguished, powerful; in short, it includes very diverse kinds and qualities of writing. But it is never of the highest intensity. The later *"A"*s, in fact, are much more likely to sound like this passage on the death of President Kennedy:

> the nation
> a world
> mourned
> three days in
> dark and in

> daylight
> glued to
> TV.

Even this brief extract shows the intention, shared with Williams, to exhibit the everyday language, its words, word-orders, junctures, and sentences. Within the discipline of this minimalist style, Zukofsky arranges and even slightly distorts ordinary speech for emotional effect. Thus in this passage the two opening lines, with the pronounced pause that follows each, build to a slight climax in "mourned," a line that both terminates the first emotional impulse and begins another.

I admire and enjoy Zukofsky's acute, concerned intelligence, his musical gift, and his surprising methods, but I am seldom deeply moved. But to this generalization there is one large exception. His poems convey a spiritual attitude so rare in modern literature that one might have thought it extinct. The angels in heaven contemplate goodness, praising and singing. So does Zukofsky. Many of his poems are images or renderings of childlike (not childish) good people or good states—purity, serenity, the simple, loving heart—as we see in the portrait of his father in "A" 12:

> He died certain—
> With such the angel of death does not wrestle—
> And alone,
> Not to let me see death:
> "Isn't visiting over?
> Go home,
> Celia must be anxious,
> Kiss Paul."

"Measure, tacit is," goes the next line, transposing a moral quality of the father into a principle for poetics also. Since Zukofsky's world of goodness is located within our world—it is not in New Jerusalem, so to speak, but in New York—it includes time, aging, grief, and death. When he speaks of these, his pathos is light, swift, and restrained—in short, measured.

Charles Reznikoff (1894–1976) summed up his own poetry as "'Objectivist,' images clear but the meaning not stated but suggested by the objective details and the music of the verse; words pithy and plain; without the artifice of regular meters; themes, chiefly Jewish, American, urban." The self-characterization is itself characteristic in its lucidity, terseness, accuracy, and objectivity. Reznikoff was born in Brooklyn of Jewish immigrant parents. He studied law and was admitted to the bar of New York, but soon ceased to practice. He made his living as a salesman, translator, editor, and writer for a law encyclopedia. Besides poetry he wrote family memoirs and two novels. Until the 1960s he had almost no recognition.

His style was formed on models and values that were avantgarde in the 1910s. Whitman and Imagism were the decisive influences, a combination of sources that was common at the time, as one sees in Sandburg. Simple Imagism appears in Reznikoff's

> About an excavation
> a flock of bright red lanterns
> has settled.

A great many similar poems record perceptions on the long walks he loved to take about New York City, where he lived most of his life. Whitman may be seen in "Ghetto Funeral":

> Followed by his lodge, shabby men stumbling over the
>   cobblestones,
> and his children, faces red and ugly with tears, eyes and eyelids
>   red,
> in the black coffin in the black hearse the old man.
>
> No longer secretly grieving
> that his children are not strong enough to go the way he wanted
>   to go
> and was not strong enough.

In *Uriel Acosta* (1921) and occasionally in later volumes brief life histories recall Masters' *Spoon River Anthology*. The lives and characters presented are sometimes shabby, morally speaking, and the satire implicit in such poems (for example, "The Deserter") is voiced openly in others, which have reminded some readers of Martial. Reznikoff writes, for example, of a movie director who is reluctant to shake hands:

> Why do you go to such trouble
> to teach me that you are great?
> I never doubted it until now.

"Poetry," Reznikoff said, "presents the thing in order to convey the feeling. It should be precise about the thing and reticent about the feeling." But if reticence is carried far enough, it becomes difficult to tell from apathy. One sees this in Reznikoff's two long poems, *Testimony* (2 volumes, 1965 and 1968) and *Holocaust* (1975). *Testimony* narrates, in a free verse Reznikoff calls "recitative," brief stories derived from legal cases in the United States between 1885 and 1915. It seemed to Reznikoff "that out of such material the century and a half during which the United States has been a nation could be written up, not from the standpoint of an individual . . . but from every standpoint—as many standpoints as were provided by the witnesses themselves." Much in this collection is harrowing, and everything is in *Holocaust*, which sets forth Nazi genocide with the same objective, case-by-case method. Before such material Reznikoff's factuality or mere objectivity has seemed to many readers a moral limitation. But no poet has yet managed to write well on this subject.

Carl Rakosi (b. 1903) is the pseudonym of Callman Rawley. He published only in magazines until New Directions brought out a small volume of *Selected Poems* in 1941. Most of these were reprinted, with occasional changes and with additional poems, in *Amulet* (1967). From 1941 to 1965 Rakosi wrote nothing at all, but he started composing again in the 1960s. The interplay of wit, sentiment, personal charm, and intelligence in his earlier poems make a livelier and to me more fetching texture than in Oppen or Reznikoff. And though he resembles William Carlos Williams more than he does any other poet, few of his poems seem especially "Objectivist." Some of his later ones are in stanzas and rhymes. "The Old Man's Hornpipe," from *Ere-Voice* (1971), returns to the Imagist-Objectivist style and illustrates the charm with which Rakosi infused it; with wistful understatement the old man regrets the lost Atlantis of hope and energy, which the puppy, the little girls, and the whippoorwill possess so fully and naturally:

This puppy jumping up
to reach the mouth
            of man

this running of little girls
            like sandpipers
to get there before their thoughts do

this whippoorwill at the tail end of winter

ah, Atlantis!

George Oppen (b. 1908) also urged that a poem must be sincere, but by this he meant plain, direct honesty. There are moments, he says, "when you believe something to be true, and you construct a meaning from these moments of conviction." We should not say more than we feel sure we know. Silence surrounds his words. As he puts it, the aim is "clarity," but

> Clarity
>
> In the sense of *transparence*,
> I don't mean that much can be explained.
>
> Clarity in the sense of silence.

Oppen's restraint is especially impressive when the poems arise, as often they do, out of his strong political concern, for wholehearted denunciation and protest might easily have seemed more appropriate, even to the poet, than the hesitations of sincerity.

Oppen's first volume, *Discrete Series* (1934), contained free-verse poems in a staccato style. In a brief introduction Pound described Oppen's style as an "adequate variation" on that of Williams. Oppen wrote no more poems for twenty-five years, but reemerged in the 1960s with *The Materials* (1962), which was followed by six other volumes, including *On Being Numerous* (1968), which won the Pulitzer Prize in 1969. His later poems turned to the animal world for images of the peace he could not find within the human.

PART THREE

POSTMODERNISM

14

THE POSTWAR PERIOD: INTRODUCTION

URING the 1950s poets in both England and the United States rejected the styles that were then established. In the continuity of poetry from generation to generation, there had been no comparably sharp break for forty years, since the advent of Modernist poetry just before and after the First World War. The beginning of this new period might be pinpointed in 1954, when Philip Larkin's *Poems* appeared and when, in a completely unrelated event, Allen Ginsberg gave the first public performance of his *Howl*. Other points of departure were Robert Lowell's *Life Studies* (1959) and Charles Olson's 1950 manifesto "Projective Verse," which voiced premises shared by many of the younger poets.

As a name for this period I adopt the term Postmodernism. It is not more satisfactory than similar terms in literary history, such as Modernism, Romanticism, and the Baroque, and I shall briefly discuss the word and the problems it creates. But it is better than other names that have been suggested, for it highlights a central fact about poetry since the 1950s, namely, that it is shaped by the poets' reception of Modernism.

The term "Modernism" derived from poets in the 1910s. It named the new style they hoped to create. In its current senses "Postmodernism" was invented by critics in the 1950s and 1960s.

So far as I know, Charles Olson, Robert Creeley, and Robert
Duncan are the only poets who often referred to contemporary
poetry as "Postmodern." They meant that they and their fellow
poets in the 1950s and 1960s were basing their work on the styles
of the 1910s and 1920s. Olson's influential essay "Projective
Verse" emphasized that this verse develops as a next step from
what Olson called the revolution of 1910. As Creeley put it in
1951, "Any movement poetry can now make beyond the achievement of Pound, Williams, et al. must make use of the fact of
their work and, further, of what each has stressed as the main
work now to be done." Olson also meant by the term that after
the Second World War a new human consciousness was developing. At present the term retains both these implications along
with many others, and has, as is normal with such terms, no
agreed meaning. It may refer, as it does for Olson, to a new
mentality, which is being formed, so the argument goes, by contemporary history and technology—by such influences as the
memory of concentration camps, Dresden, and Hiroshima, by
travel, cultural eclecticism, ecological activism, communes, the
use of drugs, television, computers, and the exploration of
space. Those who use the term in this sense believe that there
has been a radical break with the past in human sensibility, imagination, and morality. Or the term may be used to refer only to
a style in the arts. In the latter case, Postmodernism may be
thought to characterize all the arts or only some, and in any one
art, such as poetry, it may be applied to the contemporary period
as a whole or only to some tendencies within it. Critics variously
date the beginnings of Postmodernism from the 1950s, 1960s,
or 1970s. Some maintain that Postmodernism is a more radical
Modernism and others that it negates Modernism, and still others hold that Postmodernism is an altogether different style
which flourishes along with Modernism.

I use the term as a *pis aller*. If contemporary American poetry
can, as I believe, no longer be called Modernist, we need a name
for our different period. Postmodernism is a more or less accepted term, and highlights, to repeat, a central fact about contemporary poetry, namely, that the most strongly shaping factor
in it is the Modernist achievement from 1910 to 1950. Reasons
for thinking that our poetry should no longer be called Mod-

ernist have already been indicated, and this and future chapters will elaborate them. I shall also argue that contemporary poetry has a period style or styles of its own, and shall thus reject the interpretation of Postmodernism as a radical perspectivism. According to this interpretation, which derives from contemporary architecture, a Postmodernist artist is one who neither continues from Modernism nor negates it. Instead, he regards Modernism as one historical style among others; he may draw motifs and methods from it, but for him Modernism has no special prestige. If our poets were Postmodernist in this sense, their work might be eclectic, using and combining a variety of past styles, and would not be more closely related to Modernist styles than to others. This is not what we find.

Since the Second World War the prevailing style of poetry in Great Britain has been unlike that in the United States, yet it may equally be called Postmodern. For the term Modernism, like all such terms, covers many moments and tendencies, and, on the whole, the contemporary poetries of England and America have been formed in relation to different moments in the Modernist period. In England the new poetry of the 1950s was created in antagonism to the revived Romanticism of Dylan Thomas and of much poetry written during the Second World War, and it was equally created by a decisive rejection of the high Modernism of Eliot and Pound. (Yeats was repudiated more as a belated Romantic than as a Modernist, and Stevens and Williams were hardly known.) The values that inspired the new poetry from Larkin to Geoffrey Hill included rational thought and communication and introspective honesty, with the complexity of perception and attitude that inevitably attends the honesty of the intelligent. These values were associated with the "academic" New Criticism in the United States, but in England they were regarded as elements of native tradition to which English poetry should return.

In the United States, in contrast, the feeling of impasse and crisis, which so many poets experienced in the 1950s, was caused by the dominance of the New Criticism. As I said in Chapter 5, the New Criticism was established in university English departments, widespread as a method of instruction in classrooms, and reflected in a style of poetry. This style was exemplified in the

1950s by, among others, Allen Tate, Adrienne Rich, Robert Lowell, Randall Jarrell, Richard Wilbur, Melvin Tolson, and Howard Nemerov.

The literary values of the New Critics derived in important respects from the criticism of T. S. Eliot, and so did the canon of authors they admired. One of the reasons the New Criticism had achieved its great influence was that it provided criteria for the defense of Modernist poetry—of Eliot, Yeats, and, in lesser degree, Pound—from conservative attacks. Essentially the New Criticism was a rationalizing of the Modernist legacy. The New Critics retained basic Modernist values—economy, wit, irony, impersonality, scrupulous handling of form—but abandoned, without saying so, specific technical features of Modernist poetry, such as the extreme ellipsis, fragmentation, and discontinuity of *The Waste Land* and the *Cantos* and the density of symbolism and overlapping myth in *The Waste Land* and *The Bridge*. As a result the New Critical style was cautious and traditional in comparison with the high Modernism it descended from, and, unlike high Modernism, it did not seem in the least disorienting, grand, or revolutionary. To many of the younger poets the New Critical message was similar to that James Merrill later attributed to the batlike voices in his *Mirabell:* "ALL ENERGY SOURCES MUST BE KEPT COVERD/ THAT IS OUR PRINCIPAL TASK   THE DAM BURSTS AS IT ERODES." When they rebelled against the New Critical mode, American poets did not repudiate the high Modernism of the 1920s, but in fact returned to it, and especially to Pound, Williams, and Stevens, for sources of a breakthrough. As they rejected the New Criticism, American poets took many different paths from Whitmanian prophecy to the style of William Carlos Williams, pop, Surrealism, Dada, confession, and collage.

THE CONCEPT OF A PERIOD STYLE

In every age only a small number of the techniques and conventions that are possible in poetry are actually used. The others are not adopted because they would be inconsistent with those which are, or because they involve moral or metaphysical assumptions the poet does not share, or because (in ages that prize originality) they would remind readers of some past style or other poet and are thus suited only for allusion or parody. Our time is unusually open, tolerant, and eclectic, but even so a poet cannot now write "ere" or "hist!" except for comic purposes, cannot use Miltonic blank verse, as eighteenth-century poets could, cannot compose a panegyric, and so forth. And of course in every period much has not yet been conceived. Keats could not have deliberately violated grammar, created collages, or used free verse; if such techniques had occurred to him, they would not have seemed appropriate to poetry, in fact, they would have seemed uneducated and ludicrous.

What we mean by a "convention" in art ranges from an accepted distortion of reality, as when a character speaks in meter, to an expected system of feeling. Petrarchan love in the Renaissance and love of nature in the nineteenth century were conventions of the latter kind. Good poems violate convention in some respects, but all poems follow conventions more than they do not. Otherwise they would be too difficult for the poet to write and too disorienting for readers. In these considerations—that poetry is largely made out of conventions, that the number of conventions available for use at any particular time is limited, and that different conventions are available at different times— we have part of the explanation for a period style, for the fact that poems by different poets who lived in the same age and place are likely to resemble one another in style and content.

Why conventions of art change over time can be debated forever, but in the long run conventions reflect premises about reality and change because these do. Thus, for example, the "beauty" of imagery and sound in the poetry of the Romantic period was not merely pleasurable and escapist. It reflected Romantic Platonism and transcendentalism; beyond the veil of phenomenal experience there was, according to Romantic beliefs, the reality of Harmony and Love, to which poetry lifted the soul. The "happy ending," the closing note of uplift, consolation, reconciliation, or promise for the future, which in one form or another pervades nineteenth-century art, was related to this metaphysical and religious premise and also to Christian beliefs. As acceptance of the underlying ideas waned, the "beauty" of Romantic poetry lost much of its sanction, and it persisted in Tennyson, Rossetti, William Morris, and later poets as something unrelated to reality but expected of poetry. The Modernist movement involved, in part, an acceptance in poetry of a naturalistic view of reality which had long been present in novels. In this transition the more obviously conventional was replaced by the less obviously so. Thus meter, rhyme, stanza, archaic or otherwise "poetic" diction, "beauty" of sound and imagery, formal closure, and the figure of the poet as apart from ordinary life gave way to free verse, colloquial diction, images of everyday experience, open form, and, in one famous example, the figure of the poet as New Jersey doctor.

Conventions normally linger for a while in art even though the beliefs they once embodied are gone. Developments in philosophy and intellectual *Weltanschauung* are assimilated into emotion and imagination with a time lag. The audience, to the degree that the writer composes for an audience, is a conservative influence; the larger the audience intended, the more this is the case. But the main reason is the one I have stressed: literature resists change because it is made out of previous literature.

Sometimes the transformation of conventions is initiated by external events; the Romantic revolution in the arts is commonly associated, for example, with the French Revolution and the upheaval it caused in every realm of thought. Frequently, however, the moment of change seems to come just after the familiar conventions have been associated with an obviously weak literature. We see this in the poetry of the United States at the end of the nineteenth century, just prior to the Modernist period, and in the late Augustan poetry of England before the Romantic creativity. At such moments the distance between conventions and realities is either greater or more visible than usual, forcing a reconstruction. The argument presupposes that poets seek to disclose or convey "reality." The reality intended may be naturalistic, archetypal, unconscious, transcendent, or whatever; the means of rendering it may be relatively direct or by detour, as in fantasy; but "truth" is always the object.

Hegel is the main source for the assumption that every "period" has its own style, an ensemble of qualities that are coherent with one another because they reflect an underlying spirit of the age. But we may accept that period styles exist, and prefer more empirical explanations of them. Poets have worked with the same or similar conventions because they inherited them, were exposed to the same cultural and intellectual influences, lived through the same historical events, and imitated one another. Whether it is appropriate to speak of a period style that does not embrace all the important writers (or even all the arts) of a time and place, or whether the term may also apply to a style shared by many but not all, is a matter of definition; in practice, the term is used in either sense. And though I would not use the term unless the qualities I discerned were logically or psychologically integrated with one another, the extent to which this must be the case is open to dispute.

We would expect a period style of the present to seem less integrated than one in the past, if only because our culture is less coherent. Since there is no longer any authority or consensus to determine what languages, books, phonograph records, films, art reproductions, and so forth an educated person should know, and since all these media are available in overwhelming quantity, the cultural experience of different individuals has less in common than in the past. Especially in the United States, moreover, there are enormous differences in cultural experience that stem from race, ethnic background, region, and political allegiance to a cause, such as ecology, Black power, gay rights, or feminism. And though in any age since the Renaissance artists have been ambivalently motivated both to imitate one another, if only to be up-to-date, and also to depart from the currently fashionable, if only to attract notice, the latter motive urges more powerfully in the twentieth century than ever before.

Nevertheless, since the Second World War we can observe period styles in the poetry of both Great Britain and the United States. They are different styles, but in each country there is a nexus of interrelated tendencies. That their interrelation is often by opposition does not distinguish our time from others. Styles and periods are not usefully to be compared with persons, but they have one point in common with them: they are best understood by their tensions and polarities. Not only what we do or affirm, but also the inner doubt or opposite impulse our words and actions strive to silence, reveals who we are. In this chapter I shall describe the contemporary period style in American poetry and trace its historical development since the Second

World War. Except incidentally for purposes of comparison, I shall postpone characterizing the different period style in England until Chapters 18 and 19, which are devoted to that subject.

POETRY IN THE UNITED STATES

Since generalizations lie inert without examples, I may begin by citing verses from various poets. My point, for the moment, is only that they could not have been written in the 1940s and 1950s during the heyday of the New Criticism. Consider these quotations: from John Ashbery's "The Skaters" (1966), where he speaks of a political revolution

> in Argentina! Think of it! Bullets flying through the
> air, men on the move!

From John Berryman's *Love & Fame* (1970):

> I drink too much. My wife threatens separation.
> She won't "nurse" me. She feels "inadequate."
> We don't mix together.

From Sylvia Plath's "Lesbos" (1962):

> You say I should drown my kittens. Their smell!
> You say I should drown my girl.
> She'll cut her throat at ten if she's mad at two.

From Galway Kinnell's *The Book of Nightmares* (1971):

> learn to reach deeper
> into the sorrows
> to come—to touch
> the almost imaginary bones
> under the face, to hear under the laughter
> the wind crying across the black stones. Kiss
> the mouth
> which tells you, *here,*
> *here is the world.* This mouth. This laughter. These temple bones.
>
> The still undanced cadence of vanishing.

From James Merrill's *The Changing Light at Sandover* (1982), which I cite with the reminder that Merrill is a very sophisticated artist:

> NOW LET US BANISH GLOOMY DREAMS
> FOR HEAVEN ON EARTH MOST LIKELY SEEMS.

In later chapters I shall comment on most of these passages. I am not yet arguing that they have much relation to one another, and I am not asserting their worth as poetry. My point is merely that they are characteristic of our period, and could not have come from the 1940s and 1950s.

A comparison of these extracts to the earlier poetry of high Modernism, however, shows both continuities and differences. Stevens could never have written the lines from Ashbery, but he almost could have. The Berryman passage might have been one of the fragments quoted in *The Waste Land*. The bit from Merrill's parodic masque has distant precedents in Auden. The verses from Kinnell sound more like Rilke than like any predecessor in English, and Plath's style is too mannered and percussive to recall any other poet.

The salient characteristics of contemporary American poetry are, in general, that it is or seems spontaneous, personal, naturalistic, open in form and antagonistic to the idea of form, intellectually skeptical yet morally concerned and sometimes even righteous, and imbued with feelings of vulnerability, yet with the humor of resignation, acknowledging helplessness. These generalizations, which I shall soon elaborate, naturally require innumerable qualifications and exceptions, and the rest of this book will make them, but first I must, since I observe a period style, try to describe it plainly.

In comparison with most previous poetry, this characteristically seems directly spontaneous. Spontaneous utterance—or the illusion of it—descends to American poets from Whitman and Williams. It may seem easy and swift, as in Gary Snyder; or hysterical, as in Sylvia Plath; or impassioned, as in Allen Ginsberg. Most frequently it seems casual, relaxed, and conversational: "All the untidy activity continues," writes Elizabeth Bishop at the conclusion of "The Bight," "awful but cheerful." "I had a most marvelous piece of luck," says John Berryman in

Dream Song 26—"I died." "I could say it's the happiest period of my life," John Ashbery begins "The Ongoing Story"; "It hasn't got much competition!" Such speech attracts because it overcomes the sense of artifice produced by New Critical formality and compression. Its risk is dilution. Spontaneous talk may take too many words. The cost may be greater when the emotion is low-keyed; for the conversational and unexcited may seem dull.

This spontaneous speech has its theoretical justification in a prevalent concept of art in our period, one I mentioned in connection with William Carlos Williams and shall discuss again in Chapter 21, when I come to contemporary ideas of open form. In the 1890s "art" implied primarily the work as finished object—fictional, constructed, closed, perfected, and posed—and the term also referred to the mental powers and acts by which such an object is produced. The work of art was to be created laboriously through repeated revisions. But contemporary concepts of art may stress the process of creation, and may interpret this process as immediate mastery exhibited in appropriate motions. Art, in this sense, is less the painting than the sequence of touches and strokes, one balancing or completing another, by which the painting comes into being and of which it is the record. Analogies to express this sense of art usually involve a creature in action—a bird on the wing, a man diving into water, a shortstop fielding a grounder—and the art lies in the sequence of complexly integrated motions. At least in theory, revision is discouraged, and so is closure, for each particular act is part of an immediate, ongoing process.

Though the natural, spontaneous speech of contemporary poetry is often low-keyed, it need not be. Especially in the 1950s and 1960s, many poets eagerly wished to be directly and strongly emotive, if only to distance themselves further from the New Critical mode, which was intellectual and oblique. But in order to feel and express emotional fervor, a person must normally be in a relatively undivided state of mind, and since poets, like other reflective persons in our time, are alert to the Freudian ambivalence of emotion and prone to intellectual skepticism and perspectivism, they can seldom speak with fervent conviction. Of course, emotion may be intense yet still qualified, and usually we find this in the poetry of Robert Lowell, John Berryman, Allen Ginsberg, and Sylvia Plath, where ambivalence and humor are present amid remorse, disgust, or anguish. Emotions that are strong, direct, and also unqualified are voiced especially in connection with certain subjects, such as the unconscious and myth. In archetypal poetry and in Surrealism the poem is by convention to be read as an expression of the unconscious mind, and in this case the emotion may be complexly qualified at the unconscious level, but is not devitalized by the criticism of the intellect and ego awareness. Poetry of this kind has been written by Robert Bly, James Wright, W. S. Merwin, James Tate, Mark Strand, and many others; in fact, it was a vogue of the 1960s. Poetry about myth is not necessarily emotive, needless to say, but when a poet seeks to recapture and possess the myth-believing mind of ancient or primitive peoples or of the worshipper, he similarly escapes irony and intellectual inhibition. Such passages are frequent in, among others, Robert Duncan, Charles Olson, Allen Ginsberg, Gary Snyder, and Galway Kinnell. These poets may perceive lovers, enemies, parents, children, animals, and landscape in terms of myths, and in form their poems may be incantations based on mythical beliefs, such as spells, litanies, and mantras. In the poetry of Surrealism, archetype, and myth there is frequently a willed simplicity and even sentimentality. This too appeals as a relief from the sophisticated wit of the New Critical mode, but contemporary poets are not genuinely simple; they merely long to be and may write as though they were. James Wright's famous "A Blessing" offers one example. Here the sentimental view of nature is psychologically self-defensive. The poem represses the appalled awareness of modern urban reality that Wright articulates in other poems.

In poetry of social protest, which has been widespread since the 1960s, tentativeness, speculativeness, skepticism, and humor are frequently short-circuited. If the subject is race relations, atomic armaments, the war in Vietnam, environmental pollution, nuclear energy, patriarchy, or the like, the attitude may be morally certain, righteous, denunciatory, and prophetic. Genre offers one explanation; a poet writing to rally and inspire a political cause cannot express doubts. Often, moreover, the poets of protest—Bly, Merwin, Ginsberg, Rich, Levertov—are not the same ones who are otherwise most committed to a skeptical, open-minded way of thinking. To this generalization, however, there are notable exceptions. Robert Lowell was Hardyesque on religious questions but morally convinced on the Vietnam war; Robert Duncan is profoundly speculative, but not on the Vietnam war or environmental issues; James Merrill is eagerly open to diverse meanings in his experience, but closed and prophetic on ecological problems. For poets, like most intellectuals, are genuinely frightened by the dangers of war and environmental pollution, and they are also buoyed into certitude by the support of others, the heady sense of swimming with a political crowd. The opportunity to indulge in feelings of conviction tempts all the more because of the intellectual uncertainty in which we usually languish. And finally, to assail timber companies and nuclear power plants provides a cover and outlet for emotions that are less focused and more problematic. I am alluding to the way in which sensitive contemporaries are turning in disgust against what man is and does.

In his critical essays T. S. Eliot stressed that good poetry is always "impersonal," and the New Critics, elaborating this opinion, argued that in reading we must always distinguish between the speaker and the poet, since the poet has invented the speaker as the appropriate person to utter the poem. No matter how closely the speaker or "persona" seems to approximate the poet in character and biographical circumstances, there is, in principle, a difference, and a reader who ignores this is naive. Though the New Critics were surely right, their view emphasizes that a poem is art—fabricated, fictitious, and illusionistic—and thus distances poetry from "life." For this reason contemporary American poets have rejected it. Their repudiation of the "persona" is consistent with their general antagonism to art, in any sense of art except spontaneous rightness in action, and with their commitments to naturalism and immediacy.

In reading contemporary American poetry, therefore, the convention is usually that the poet is speaking. The so-called Confessional poetry of W. D. Snodgrass, Ginsberg, Lowell, Plath, Anne Sexton, and John Berryman established this convention in a dramatic way, but the grounds of it are wider. At the present time, a personal voice does not in the least imply a confessional subject or emotion. It is the voice of the poet, spontaneously uttering his or her thoughts or emotions. In Denise Levertov's "Triple Feature," for example, we are to suppose that Levertov is watching a poor Mexican family and trying to imagine their experiences in going to the movies. In Richard Wilbur's "Cottage Street, 1953" the poet looks back on an occasion when he had tea with Sylvia Plath. We are not, on reading this poem, to suppose that the "I" speaking is an invented character, a "persona." And so with poems of James Merrill, Gary Snyder, Adrienne Rich, James Wright, Frank O'Hara, James Schuyler, Robert Hayden, James Dickey, Elizabeth Bishop, and many others. Unless the poem indicates a different convention, as with dramatic monologues, parodies, and some collages, contemporary American poetry is, to repeat, to be read as though it were the immediate utterance or interior monologue of the poet; the circumstances narrated or implied are to be taken as autobiographical.

Contemporary American poetry is naturalistic primarily in this sense. Its subject is the emotions and experiences of the poet, and the poet presents himself as living much as other Americans do—making love, raising children, drinking with friends, camping out, getting sick. In Confessional poetry the subject matter is particularly intimate and harrowing. These poets describe aspects of their lives that most people would conceal, such as impulses to suicide, abject humiliations and lusts, and hatred of their families. The most frequent subject of Confessional poetry is the family interpreted in a Freudian perspective: the family is a nexus of rivalry and emotional ambivalence; parents and children view each other through distorting psychological projections. Even though contemporary poetry is naturalistic, the emphasis on the life of the poor, which was present in the naturalistic novel of the nineteenth century, is absent, and so is the attempt to report with a scientific precision that excludes subjectivity. Since few poets now believe in a transcendent reality, and since the post-Marxist, post-Freudian, post-Hitler vision of this world offers little consolation, the image of life is bleak, or would be except for the redeeming power most poets find in their own minds, in creativity, meditative energy, and memory. The spontaneous, colloquial language of most contemporary poetry is also naturalistic, needless to say, and is part of a more general antagonism to form, which I shall soon discuss. Modernist techniques such as fragmentation, ellipsis, and allusion are present in contemporary American poetry, and sometimes are used heavily, but bear an uneasy relation to its naturalistic tendency, and are seldom as prominent as they were in Eliot and Pound. Of course, much contemporary poetry is not naturalistic, particularly that which is formalist, Surrealist, Dada, archetypal, mythical, or collage.

In its image of life much of our poetry might be more suggestively described not as naturalistic but as "creatural." The term, which is usually employed in connection with the art and literature of the late Middle Ages, refers to an emphasis on man's vulnerable and suffering body and mortality as these unite all human beings. The iconography of the Dance of Death is one well-known example of "creatural" realism, but unlike such work in the fourteenth and fifteenth centuries, the stark, detailed presentation of bodily sufferings, aging, and death in modern poetry is seldom intended to disengage the emotions from earthly existence, since the poet can hope for no other, and is, therefore, seldom wholly unrelieved. John Berryman's "Homage to Mistress Bradstreet" is perhaps the most powerful modern poem of this "creatural" realism, but one thinks also of images of vomiting, hospital operations, sexual impotence, senility, and the like in, among others, Lowell, Plath, Sexton, Ginsberg, James Wright, and Frank Bidart. To which we may add the sense of man's psychological vulnerability and sickness, as in Ginsberg's "Kaddish." "Creatural" realism is especially associated with Confessional poetry, but spreads into other kinds as well, and was much less present in the high Modernist era.

The "creatural" vision of man in our poetry reflects the contemporary weakening of humanism and of religion. "Creatural" man has no greatness or even dignity. Of course this antihumanist vision of man coalesces with the revelations about human nature given in Freudian depth psychology, and the sense of bodily and psychological vulnerability intertwines with the revulsion from man motivated by images of concentration camps, bombings, torture chambers, and the holocaust—images imprinted on the imagination of every child in our time—and by instances of ecological pollution, exterminations of animal species, and fears of nuclear devastation. In sensitive persons, therefore, the human mind is turning in moral anguish and disgust against itself, against mankind, human nature, and what man has done and will do. That most poets, like most Americans, are living in relatively comfortable circumstances and are not immediately threatened does not mitigate feelings of vulnerability and disgust, and may intensify them. Whether the states of mind of intellectuals and writers reflect those of society at large is always doubtful, but ours is not the poetry of people who feel in control of their lives or hopeful about them. In some poets—for example, in Olson, Merwin, Snyder, Ginsberg, Merrill, and Wright, there is a compensatory assertion that nature is good. For these poets man is no longer primary, either in moral rank or as an object of emotional identification, but is an element in an ecological field that has no moral center apart from the whole.

The forms used in the contemporary poetry of the United States include traditional and free verse in narrative, dramatic monologue, long meditation, list, catalogue, and lyric, including sonnet, song, chant, litany, spell, and mantra. There is also collage, as in early poems by John Ashbery and some by Robert Duncan, and concrete poetry, of which the work of Michael Phillips offers witty examples. Different forms permeate one another in innumerable combinations. Since expectations associated with genres are now much less definite than they used to be, our poets tend to orient their readers by invoking analogies. The poem may resemble a prose essay, conversation, meditation, interior monologue, dream, prayer, primitive myth, diary, notebook, photograph album, film, painting, or musical composition. Such analogies help the reader to understand and accept the poem's tone, content, method of procedure, and purpose.

Generally speaking, our poets repudiate "closed" forms, and many of them are antagonistic to the idea of form. The period style of the present, then, is characterized less by the forms that are used than by the way they are handled, the techniques and procedures that keep form "open" or even abolish it in the same moment that it is being created. I discuss these techniques in Chapter 21, and the purpose here is merely to note their general, underlying motivations. The New Critical poem of the 1940s and 1950s was formally "closed," in other words, metrical, rhymed, and organized into stanzas, tightly integrated in images and figures, and completed in the "curve" or "plot" enacted. Eventually such poems seemed artificial, as I said, and were rejected for that reason. Spontaneous immediacy in expression was prized because of its "truth," "sincerity," or "naturalness," because it enacted a concept of art as motion or becoming rather than being, and because it seemed democratic. For since the New Critical poem was compressed and ironical, it was also difficult and implied an elite audience of especially qualified readers; to create an opposite style was a political gesture.

Poets, furthermore, have become uneasy with the very idea of form because of our modern awareness of the relativism, perspectivism, multiplicity, and swift transition of our mental experience. Such awareness also characterized the Modernist period, needless to say, and no poems more reflect it in their forms than *The Waste Land* and the *Cantos*. But *The Waste Land* and the *Cantos* were formally radical in their day, and they would not seem so now. To impose a form on an experience or a thought is to put it into a context and perspective, and thus to repress other contexts or perspectives that might be no less valid. From instant to instant our thoughts are innumerable, complex, and changing in their interrelations. We doubt that we have a continuing identity. Since experience is a deluge no form can contain, the poet's truth inheres in his stance, in his openness to whatever comes immediately as it comes, in his refusal to impose a form or his readiness to destroy whatever form he has imposed. Not all postwar poetry in the United States is shaped by such considerations. Wilbur, Bishop, Plath, Bly, Wright, Merwin, John Hollander, and Kinnell are generally little influenced by them. But such considerations underlie the notebook or diary poems of Lowell, Berryman, Creeley, Rich, and Levertov; the "I do this I do that" poems of Frank O'Hara; the poems Ginsberg dictated into a tape recorder while riding along the road; the open sequences of Olson in the Maximus Poems, of Duncan in "Passages," and of Gary Snyder, Ed Dorn, Jack Spicer, and many other poets; the collages of Robert Duncan and the "montage succession" of David Antin and Robert Kelly; and the continually changing onwardness of meditation in the long poems of A. R. Ammons and John Ashbery.

Our poets are, to repeat, deeply alienated from our imperialist, bureaucratic, consumerist, commercially manipulative civilization. "Moloch," as Allen Ginsberg calls it, is the vast, entrenched system of economic, political, and ideological power: the government, armed forces, police, business corporations, labor unions, and media. Disgust and fear of this and its manifestations are voiced by approximately half of our contemporary poets; the others are not of an opposite opinion, but are too urbane in style or too personal in subject matter to voice such emotions directly and strongly. But of course "Moloch" seems quite impervious to the fulminations of poets. As one of a huge population, caught like everyone else in the toils of history, of the bureaucratic state, and of the large institutions in which we work, shop, and amuse ourselves, the poet cannot feel that his or her ideas and desires make any difference. What we experience as our own ideas and desires may, in any case, have been instilled in us by propaganda and advertising.

Given the degree to which individuals in the modern world feel vulnerable and helpless, it is not surprising that humor is almost omnipresent in our poetry as a defense. The humor of contemporary American poetry is usually of a kind that acknowledges powerlessness. We find clowning, camp, Dada, parody, but seldom, except in Lowell, the savage disgust of Eliot, or the grand, satiric contempt of Yeats, or the unmitigated invective of Lawrence, or the fury of Pound's Hell Cantos. Even when our poets are prophetically denunciatory, they are also comic, and their comedy undermines their attack. The poet is a buffoon, as in camp humor; or is deliberately, wildly ineffective in his gestures of protest, as in Dada; or is amusing only to intellectuals, as in parody. That our poets do not think themselves a serious threat is one of the reasons why they often seem strangely good humored as well as humorous. In fact, the poet frequently characterizes himself as a more or less ineffectual person. (Significantly, women poets rarely adopt this pose.) He is the perplexed man of Robert Lowell's late sonnets, or the helpless, self-mocking compulsive of Berryman's Dream Songs, or the laconic worrier of Robert Creeley, or the politely self-deprecating Merrill, or Ginsberg, the crank and nonstop yammerer, or Ashbery, contemplating his can of worms and blandly, resignedly, even cheerfully making the best of it. Ours is a humor expressing the fatuity of our struggles in the very moment that we are struggling.

THE DEVELOPMENT OF CONTEMPORARY POETRY

The chapters that follow trace the history of contemporary poetry from the 1950s to the present. I begin with older poets such as Robert Penn Warren, Theodore Roethke, and Elizabeth Bishop. They were of the same generation as Auden, Spender, MacNeice, Dylan Thomas, and other British poets who were famous in the 1930s, but they developed more slowly and did not bring out their first important books until the 1940s. The chapter entitled "Breaking Through the New Criticism" expresses the dominance of the New Criticism in the United States at the end of the Second World War, and describes the careers of a number of poets, including John Berryman and Randall Jarrell, who began to write in this style and gradually rejected it. (One chapter cannot include all the poets whose careers followed this course, and many of them, such as Sylvia Plath, Adrienne Rich, and W. S. Merwin, are discussed elsewhere in other connections, while Robert Lowell is considered in a separate chapter.) In each poet much the same general ideas and influences motivated the transition. These were too complex to be summarized here, and later chapters go into them at length, but they ranged from metaphysical assumptions—that reality is open, multiple, in swift transition, and ungraspable—to considerations of morality and taste. The ethos of the New Criticism came, as I said, to seem repressive and elitist, and the dense, intellectual idiom and closure of New Critical poetry seemed artificial. These literary reactions were of course supported by developments in society at large, especially in the 1960s. Beatniks, drugs, communes, feminism, gay liberation, black pride and power, Zen, and other manifestations of cultural eclecticism, and the protest against the war in Vietnam had an impact on the subject matter and style or poetry, which generally rejected "high" culture, "closed" and therefore "strict" forms, tradition, and other embodiments of authority. But the most immediate reason for the reaction against the New Criticism was, I believe, its acceptance within the classroom. Once it was being taught to students as a dogma, it was doomed. Here, however, I should distinguish between poets such as Allen Ginsberg, Robert Duncan, and Frank O'Hara, who rejected the New Critical mode as students, and somewhat older poets, such as Robert Lowell, who had written brilliantly in it for years. As these older poets changed their styles, they did not abandon their rigorous artistry, but merely concealed it. This is one of the reasons why Lowell in *Life Studies* (1959), Berryman in his Dream Songs, and Elizabeth Bishop in

Poems (1955) and subsequent volumes are among the greatest poets of our time.

Meanwhile in England during the 1950s poets broke with the high Modernist tradition, and they also reacted strongly against Dylan Thomas, who was then at the height of his fame. They emphasized such values as clarity, realism, empirical honesty, and rationalism, and they looked with favor on past styles, such as that of the later eighteenth century and of Thomas Hardy and Georgian poetry in the early part of this century, to which such values could be attributed. The language of British poetry was sober, low-keyed, exact, and reflective. Philip Larkin is the great poet of this phase. He and several others were associated in the 1950s in a group called the Movement, but most English poets, whether numbered in the Movement or not, shared a similar ethos. They expressed a rather drab, painful sense of existence. Outwardly their eyes focused on weedy railroad embankments, littered back lots, hospital waiting rooms, and the like, and inwardly on boredom, envy, fear, and darker emotions. Moral self-scrutiny was common, though moral judgments were baffled by honesty. To what extent this poetry was shaped by postwar English history is a difficult question. Deflated emotions, anti-romantic ennui, and a questioning, as in Robert Frost's poem "The Oven Bird," of "what to make of a diminished thing" seem appropriate in the aftermath of the Second World War. They might also be related, as we shall see, to the Labourite social revolution in postwar England, which left many liberal intellectuals feeling that they must now accept what they had made.

In the 1960s the type of poetry associated with Larkin and the Movement began to be challenged in England, and poets again opened themselves to American and Continental examples. Robert Lowell had a vogue in England; Geoffrey Hill formed his style partly on the New Critical mode of the United States; Sylvia Plath learned from her husband, Ted Hughes; Thom Gunn from his teacher, Yvor Winters; Donald Davie was fascinated by the style of Ezra Pound; and Charles Tomlinson by that of Wallace Stevens. Poets also experimented with the Surrealism of central Europe and with Poundian discontinuity. Basil Bunting's *Briggflatts* (1966), though quintessentially English in its regional diction, is in form a *symboliste* poem, and the favorable reception it received would have been less probable in Great Britain ten years earlier. The poetry of Ireland, though quite different from that of Great Britain, resembles it much more than it does American poetry, and I shall describe it immediately after the poetry of England, though in a separate chapter.

Despite what I have just said, English and American poetry have, on the whole, developed independently of each other in the last forty years and are quite different in style. There has been nothing comparable to the transatlantic impact of Eliot, Yeats, and Auden during the first half of the century. The present difference between English and American poetry helps us to see each more clearly.

Since the three connected chapters on England and Ireland bring us to Geoffrey Hill and Seamus Heaney, I violate chronology by returning, in the chapter entitled "Open Form," to developments in the United States during the 1950s and 1960s. I also move without transition into a very different milieu and ethos. The remaining chapters are devoted to poetry in the United States. Thus the organization of Part Four of this history reflects the fact that English and American poetry have followed relatively separate, national lines during the postwar period.

The 1950s were the formative decade of postwar American poetry. As this new poetry was more widely read, appreciated, and imitated during the 1960s, it established itself as the dominant American style or nexus of styles. Though the social upheavals of the 1960s conduced to the favorable reception of this poetry, it was created during the Eisenhower era, when social protest and innovation were less widespread and less visible. During the 1950s William Carlos Williams first became an important influence on younger poets, teaching them his natural, American speech rooted in the immediate, local, and particular. In Ginsberg's *Howl* and Lowell's *Life Studies* the Beat and Confessional movements produced their respective masterpieces. The camp, pop poetry of Frank O'Hara and others dates originally from the 1950s, and Charles Olson and Robert Duncan began then to adopt and revise the methods of Pound's *Cantos* and to transmit them to younger poets. In the 1950s Olson also began to influence younger poets by the energy of his theorizing in manifestoes and personal letters. In the chapter "Open Form" I discuss his theories and those of others associated with him, especially Robert Duncan, Robert Creeley, and Denise Levertov, keeping in mind that although Olson expressed his theories in an extreme, provocative, and mannered way, the theories themselves were broadly representative. What Olson said, other American poets also assumed.

The perception of postwar American poetry was greatly influenced by Donald Allen's 1960 anthology, *The New American Poetry*. Allen intended to show that many of the younger American poets had been developing along similar lines. But gathering so many poets into his anthology, Allen was naturally under the necessity of dividing them into subgroups—Black Mountain Poets, New York Poets, Beat Poets, San Francisco Poets, and so forth. In literary conversations and critical essays thereafter these classifications enjoyed a great career. They were irresistibly tempting, not only because they organized a scene that seemed confused, but because they allowed readers to feel and seem *au courant*. Moreover, Allen's classifications reflected networks of personal acquaintance among his poets, and personal acquaintance had led in many cases to similarities in style. Anyone discussing the poets Allen presented is still likely to group them in similar ways, the more so since Allen's classifications are well known. Two of his classifications are adopted here in the chapter entitled "Poetry in New York and San Francisco," where the work of a New Yorker, Allen Ginsberg, who also lived in San Francisco, is used to represent the Beat poetry that flourished there, and Frank O'Hara exemplifies the quite different style of Allen's New York School. The poetry of John Ashbery, whom readers once associated with this school, now transcends this identification, and I discuss Ashbery in a later chapter with A. R. Ammons, the other important "meditative" poet of our period.

Though postwar American poetry is, on the whole, naturalistic and personal, opposing styles arose in the 1960s. One of these was Surrealist, and poets in this vein included Frank O'Hara, Robert Bly, James Wright, W. S. Merwin, Mark Strand, Gregory Orr, and James Tate. Most of these poets have been Surrealist only at times, and partly for this reason I have not dwelt on the American Surrealist movement in a separate chapter. Though it was a flourishing vogue, it was transient both in the careers of most of its adherents and in the poems it produced. Another style grounded itself in the presentation of myth and archetypal symbol. Bly, Merwin, Gary Snyder, Galway Kinnell, and Louise Glück are among the poets of this tendency. The poetry of myth and archetype shares with Surrealism an impulse to escape from the limitations of a personal voice and of naturalistic immediacy, to speak from a deeper, more universal level of feeling and experience. These different types of poetry naturally interfuse, and they also combine with the personal and naturalistic, as in poems of Charles Wright and Frank Bidart that include or center on dreams. The dreams reflect the poet's personality and experience, but they also have the disorienting, phantasmagorical qualities of Surrealist verse. The poems of Charles Simic are terse, disturbing metaphors, many of them drawn from memories of his childhood in wartime Europe, in which the personal and naturalistic becomes Surrealist or mythical. Many of these poets do not fall within our chronological limits, and therefore are not discussed at any length. The others are here grouped in the chapter entitled "Against Civilization." They voice hostility to our urban-militarist-industrialist society and a compensatory primitivism and sympathy with "nature."

The final chapters of the book deal at length with the most difficult, formally complex, intellectually sophisticated, and brilliant of contemporary American poets, John Ashbery and James Merrill. Before coming to them, however, I take up the poetry of women's experience and of blacks. These are distinct types of poetry because of their subject matter, and one of the characteristics of our period is the new freedom and boldness of self-expression in these groups. Poetic tradition and social convention obviously inhibited women poets more than men in the past, since the social conventions governing women were more restrictive. So far as postwar women poets have escaped these inhibitions, the personal, Confessional tendencies in American poetry have helped them to do so. These tendencies interacted with the feminist movement in American society, for both the Confessional style and feminism demanded the overthrow of inner censors, internalized representatives of social convention and authority. Feminism helped inspire the breakthrough of some women poets directly, as with Adrienne Rich, but for others who were not themselves feminists, such as Sylvia Plath and Anne Sexton, the feminist movement was nevertheless a strong, indirect support, both psychologically and in bringing them an audience. The audience feminism helped create was of women who no longer shrank from confronting their authentic emotions, even when these emotions were not what social convention dictated. In Rich, Plath, Sexton, Denise Levertov, Muriel Rukeyser, Diane Wakoski, and others, women readers especially welcomed the strong, direct truth to experience. These poets might voice hatred outweighing love for their fathers, resentment of their children, sexual lusts, and similar emotions that had, for the most part, previously been buried in silence. The Black poetry of America was liberated by a similar combination of a political cause, the Confessional movement in poetry, and the general, cultural revolt in the 1960s against authority, of which the Beats and Hipsters were the most visible symbol. In a poet such as Baraka the Beat ethos merges with modern avant-gardism.

15

ROBERT PENN WARREN, THEODORE ROETHKE, AND ELIZABETH BISHOP

I F in the 1930s one had asked who were the American contemporaries of Auden, Day-Lewis, MacNeice, Gascoyne,
Dylan Thomas, and the other English poets who, although
still young, were already well known, few names could have been
suggested. Not, at least, if by "contemporaries" were meant
poets of the same generation, poets born between 1900 and
1920. There were, of course, American poets of comparable
stature in this generation. But most of them did not publish their
first books until the 1940s, at a time when Auden and Thomas
were already near the height of their fame. Writing in 1945,
F. O. Matthiessen explained the dearth of new American talent
as a consequence of the Depression, which led "most of our new
writers . . . to prose, particularly to the novel of social protest."
From our later vantage point, it is clear that poets of this generation in the United States simply developed more slowly than
their English contemporaries.

Most of the poets who emerged in the United States during
the 1930s reacted against the ascendancy of T. S. Eliot. Speaking
both of his friend Roethke and of himself, Stanley Kunitz said
that "the Eliot school was our principal adversary. We fought for
a more passionate art." In an *Essay on Rime* (1945), Karl Shapiro
expressed his opposition to what he considered fashionable

over-intellectualism, which emanated, in his view, from Eliot and Pound, and was championed by the New Critics. "The crux of the problem for our generation," Karl Shapiro once explained, "was the Modernism which Eliot and Pound and Joyce represented."

Nevertheless, the protest of American poets against Eliot was half-hearted. Like their English contemporaries, they felt that poetry must go back to more traditional modes, yet also that the advances of Modernism must be preserved. To poets who sought to return to tradition, two traditions offered themselves. The critical essays of Eliot had proposed that the English tradition of poetry was to be found in the seventeenth century. In general Eliot had in mind the combination of Metaphysical wit with neoclassical elegance. We have seen that an enormously influential movement in criticism and poetry developed out of this from the late 1920s on; it touched most American poets from the 1930s to the 1960s. The other tradition was the Romantic one of nineteenth-century poetry, which the high Modernists had denounced. In the 1930s and 1940s few American poets yet dared to proclaim that they were Romantics, as many English poets did toward the end of the 1930s. The prestige of Eliot and the New Critics was too intimidating in the United States to be defied this openly. But Theodore Roethke's *The Lost Son* (1948) powerfully revived Romantic values, and so did volumes in the 1950s by Robert Penn Warren, James Wright, and W. S. Merwin. That Wright and Merwin were just starting their careers especially indicated a trend. Thus in the 1950s a poetry developed that fused essential principles of the Modernist revolution in style with the more directly emotional utterance of the Romantic mode. To represent this phase of modern poetry I concentrate on Robert Penn Warren and Theodore Roethke.

Elizabeth Bishop, who is the greatest poet discussed in this chapter, is placed here largely for chronological reasons. Usually she is associated either with Marianne Moore or with Lowell, Berryman, and Jarrell. But in a book on this scale she cannot be considered with Moore because she was born twenty-one years later and belonged to a different generation. Placing her with Lowell would also be unsatisfactory, for though the two poets were friends and influenced each other, their styles were quite different. Including Bishop in Chapter 16, with Jarrell, Berry-

man, and other poets who, like Lowell, broke through the formalism associated in the 1940s with the New Criticism, would be
misleading as well. Bishop differed from the other poets in that
chapter because the New Criticism was never strongly imprinted
upon her. Moreover, when she evolved a freer, more personal
style in the 1950s, she did not become a Confessional poet, as
Lowell and Berryman did. Her transition of style was made
under the auspices of Williams but not of Ginsberg. She was not
closely aligned with any school. But it is appropriate to discuss
her in this chapter, which begins to describe the transition from
Modernist to Postmodernist styles. In the context of the 1960s
and 1970s Bishop seemed stylistically conservative. Only since
her death in 1979 has the general reader begun adequately to
appreciate her superb artistry and intelligence.

ROBERT PENN WARREN

As a novelist, critic, biographer, teacher, and poet, Robert
Penn Warren (b. 1905) has attained immense distinction and influence. At Vanderbilt University in the early 1920s he was associated with John Crowe Ransom and Allen Tate (he roomed
with Tate one year) in the Fugitive group. After a Rhodes scholarship in England he taught at Vanderbilt and then at Louisiana
State University, where he founded *The Southern Review.* With
Cleanth Brooks, who was also on the faculty, he wrote *Understanding Poetry,* which appeared in 1938 and is still in print. No
textbook in our century has more influenced the way poetry is
taught. Few students in English classes now use *Understanding
Poetry,* but most of them still do assignments in "close reading."
If as they ponder their texts they trace the "organic" interrelations within them, they are doing what Brooks and Warren said
they should, for *Understanding Poetry* illustrated the methods of
the New Criticism before the term was current.

Warren had published two earlier volumes of poetry, but his
Selected Poems, 1923–1943 (1944) established him as a poet. The
poetry of Metaphysical wit (which I described in Chapter 5) was
now in favor, and many of Warren's lyrics illustrated this style.
"Love's Parable," "Bearded Oaks," and "The Garden" are examples. For a variety of reasons—the Second World War, the

neo-Romantic revival in England, the pervasive seventeenth-century influences—high rhetoric was acceptable in the United States at this time, and a poem such as "Terror," which now seems overwritten, appealed to the same taste as did Marianne Moore's "In Distrust of Merits" (1944) and Robert Lowell's "The Quaker Graveyard in Nantucket" (1946). Other poems showed influences of Eliot, Hardy, and Ransom, and in hindsight some poems indicate the main line of Warren's subsequent development. One sees this in the various syntheses of the descriptive, narrative, reflective, and regional in "Kentucky Mountain Farm," "Mexico Is a Foreign Country: Four Studies in Naturalism," and "The Ballad of Billie Potts" (1944). The latter poem was a new departure for Warren; it tells a story of frontier Kentucky in which a father unwittingly murders his son. Reviewing the poem favorably, F. O. Matthiessen spoke of the "blinding" discovery of "essential evil."

In this phrase Matthiessen's rhetoric resembles Warren's, and emotions of the period speak through both. There is no objective reason why awareness of man's evil nature should impress itself on one age more than on another, since every generation contemplates the same cruelties in the past and adds its own in the present. But in the United States during the 1940s the literary world was, on the whole, pessimistic. The image of man then accepted may be recalled merely by citing reviews of Warren's 1944 and 1953 volumes: "we must return to the old man, to an awareness of our roots in erring humanity"; Warren is imbued with the sense of "some nameless evil" or "curse"— "Original Sin"; "it is the nature of man which is in question . . . the actuality of human evil"; "Most of us know, now, that Rousseau was wrong: that man, when you knock his chains off, sets up the death camps." These are remarks by Matthiessen, John Crowe Ransom, Delmore Schwartz, and Randall Jarrell. So far as I know, no critic in those years debated Warren's grim portrait of human nature. It was the poets on the other side of the question—Whitman and Williams, for example—who were viewed dubiously and criticized for an inadequate awareness of evil. Hitler and the Second World War of course underlay this state of opinion, but other factors also entered in. The Southern writers who now became prominent generally shared a sense of tragedy suggested by the history of their region and the sense of sin

of its fundamentalist religion. Many intellectuals who had committed themselves to the radical hopes of the early 1930s experienced a swing of feeling in the late 1940s that was the more
violent because compensatory. Finally, we must again recall the
enormous prestige of T. S. Eliot. His religious and pessimistic
Weltanschauung answered to the mood of the literary world at
this time but also helped to create it.

This context must be kept in mind as we read Warren's *Brother
to Dragons* (1953, revised 1979). In this book-length poem various speakers—Thomas Jefferson, Warren himself, and the characters in the action—narrate and reflect upon the grisly murder
of a slave on a plantation in Kentucky in 1811. The killer was
Jefferson's nephew, and the deed forces Jefferson to repudiate
his former faith in humanity and its future. From him we hear
that the high-minded ideals both of the Enlightenment and, indirectly, of the early 1930s were illusions; in the poem Jefferson
speaks as one who, having believed too hopefully, now insists
almost too starkly and vehemently on the opposite point of view.
The role of the speaker named Warren is, in general, to articulate the intellectual effort embodied in the poem as a whole; he
strives to face up to life's evil directly and yet to affirm the "glory"
of existence despite it. Generally this is the theme of all Warren's
poetry henceforth, and the word "glory" indicates the basis of
whatever yea-saying he finds possible. The world he presents is
naturalistic—no religious purpose informs it—and existentially
somber, yet on this naturalism he mounts a Romantic hope, for
he finds that special moments of perception or experience are
ablaze with intensity and meaning and redeem the rest. Or if he
does not fully believe this, at least he wishes to do so, and the
speaker of his poems is on the watch, so to speak, for such moments or in quest of them. Often he searches back into memory.

After the 1944 *Selected Poems* Warren was for approximately
ten years unable to complete a lyric. He started many, but they
all "died on" him. His breakthrough in 1954 depended partly
on changed personal circumstances and partly on a new way of
conceiving poems. As he later explained to interviewers, he had
formerly "tended to start from a verbal and abstract place" or
from "an element of narrative." Now his poems originated more
directly in personal experience, in some event, observation, or
mood. Also, the "narrative genre began to enter the short poem"

in the sense that he composed in suites or sequences, planning individual lyrics as elements in larger structures. Since *Promises* (1957) he has produced a new volume of lyrics every two or three years.

Over this more than a quarter-century his style has naturally changed. Each volume, moreover, has much variety. Yet Warren's style is distinctive and can never be confused with that of someone else. To exhibit it I may refer to "The Dogwood" from *Promises*. The poem tells a story, typically, and Warren's veteran skills as a writer are evident in the speed and shapeliness of the narration, the vividness of the imagery and the clear, pithy idiom. To readers of poetry—and this also is typical of Warren— the story is of a familiar kind, in fact, it is a version of the archetypal Romantic quest. Entering a wood at night the protagonist is afraid; brambles, the lash of a bough, and the startling whoosh of an owl express the resistance of the woods to his penetration. As he presses on he comes to a place where formerly a dead cow had been left:

> The bones are long lost. In green grass the skull waits, has waited:
> A cathedral for ants, and at noon, under white dome and transept,
> They pass in green gloom, where sunlight's by leaf mitigated,
> For leaf of the love vine shuts eyehole, as though the eye slept.
>
> But now it's not noon, it is night, and ant-dark in that cow skull.
> And man-dark in the woods. But go on, that's how men survive.

The images presented here are reminders of time, change, and death in a completely naturalistic world. But before the speaker returns again to his ordinary, familiar milieu ("home"), he is granted a redeeming moment or symbol as he sees a dogwood blooming in the dark. Compared to the poem's wealth of implication, the summary I have just given is a travesty, but it highlights the degree to which the plot and emotions come out of Romantic tradition. Within this tradition Warren can write splendidly, but he seldom evokes feelings to which we are not already accustomed in poetry. That the quester wants to strike the dogwood is an unexpected reaction, though Warren is always mindful of the evil in the heart, but it is also one of the many details in the poem that recall Wordsworth's "Nutting."

Though "The Dogwood" is typical of Warren, its style is more artificial and even mannered than his later work. This poem does not much recall Hopkins, but Warren seems to have been under Hopkins' spell in the 1950s. Hence, perhaps, the strong rhythm, the heavy alliteration and assonance, the compounds ("man-dark"), repetition, and occasional parataxis. Warren had always mingled a colloquial idiom with a more elevated or rhetorical one, but such contrasts were especially evident in this period. So also were the short clauses, which required many verbs and thus further invigorated an already energetic style.

Around 1966 Warren's poetry entered another phase, and to most readers he seemed a greater poet in his sixties and seventies than ever before. It is not easy to say how his poetry was now different, however, for his themes and technical resources remained what they had been. Yet whatever had been rhetorical, mannered, and forced in his poetry gradually disappeared or diminished. That he abandoned meters and stanzas for free verse is typical of this general change. And while creating a more relaxed and natural way of speaking, he retained undiminished his clarity, vividness, speed, surprise, and density of expression, his narrative and constructive power, his psychological alertness and reflective tenacity. Perhaps the major change was simply the extent to which his poems now interrelated with one another. I am thinking not only of the cross-connections within particular sequences but of the way in which the whole of his previous work now formed a resonating, enriching background to new poems. The main reason for this lay in Warren's lifelong preoccupation with the same or closely similar themes and with the images, human situations, or plots which expressed them for him. To pursue and illustrate this point would require more space than can be afforded in a book concerned with so many poets. But the reader may wish to study especially "Notes on a Life to be Lived," "Red-tailed Hawk and Pyre of Youth," "Heart of Autumn," "Memory Forgotten," "Mountain Plateau," "Sunset Walk in Thaw-Time in Vermont," and "Reading Late at Night, Thermometer Falling."

MINOR AMERICAN POETS AND THE RETURN OF ROMANTIC VALUES

Despite his love for the English Romantics, Stanley Kunitz (b. 1905) did not follow them in specific details of style. For he naturally wished to be a poet of his own time, and to him this meant that he must master the idiom we associate with Modernism. Before the revival of the Metaphysical poets had become pronounced, Kunitz had already discovered them and sensed that "the way into the new poetry was through the doorway of the seventeenth century." He also studied the French *symbolistes,* particularly Baudelaire and Rimbaud. From such mingled sources and impulses he forged a style somewhat in the vein of Yeats, whom he thought "the great master of the poem in English in this century." Kunitz's poems were lyrical and personal but intellectually allusive, concentrated, and firmly controlled. Among his better poems are "Deciduous Branch," "Words for the Unknown Makers," on America's primitive artists, and "King of the River," which speaks of aging and death in the metaphor of the salmon returning upriver from the sea. The combination of values his style expressed is suggested by the remark of Blake, "a tear is an intellectual thing," from which Kunitz drew the title of his first volume, *Intellectual Things* (1930).

Richard Eberhart (b. 1904) graduated from Dartmouth and then studied at Cambridge University from 1927 to 1929. F. R. Leavis was his supervisor and I. A. Richards took a friendly interest in his work, but Eberhart was never their disciple. His first publication was a long poem, *A Bravery of Earth* (1930), which some reviewers compared favorably to Wordsworth's *Prelude.* Poems of his were included in *New Signatures* (1932), the influential anthology in which Michael Roberts first presented the younger generation of English poets as a group. Returning to the United States, Eberhart taught at St. Mark's School (Robert Lowell was among his pupils), and served in the navy during the Second World War. After a few years as a businessman he became a professor of English at Dartmouth, where he taught poetry and how to write it.

Throughout his career Eberhart has written essentially two kinds of poem. One is the lyric that assigns symbolic values to images and explores the implications thus activated. In "New Hampshire, February," for example, two frozen wasps are brought indoors. As the speaker breathes on them, they come to life. They "withdraw to ice" again when he stops. He feels like God, and recalls Michelangelo's scene of the creation of Adam in the Sistine Chapel. But one wasp blunders onto the kitchen floor and the speaker, equally by accident, steps on it:

And so the other is still my pet.
The moral of this is plain.
But I will shirk it.
You will not like it. And
God does not live to explain.

In "Seals, Terns, and Time" the seals are symbols of animal flesh,
the terns of mind, wit, or spirit. The speaker, "resting on the
oar," balances in this precarious moment of harmony and contemplates the almost equal pull and enticement of "the mammal
water" and "release of sky."

Eberhart's other kind of poem is straightforward meditation
or declamation. He awakens attention in such poems by the naked and passionate sincerity of his concern. Sometimes this is
enough, as in "The Fury of Aerial Bombardment." But in many
poems, such as "Meditation Two" and "Sanders Theater," the
importance of his subject and the intensity of his emotion make
his prosy expression seem anticlimactic:

Shall man destroy the face of the earth,
By universal hatred bomb himself to death,
Shall he still lust, erect evil
And shall madness overwhelm our reason?

Karl Shapiro (b. 1924) became prominent during the Second
World War through his long, blank-verse *Essay on Rime* (1945), a
poem he later seems to have disowned, since he excluded it from
his *Collected Poems* (1978). In it he advocated a "plainer art" than
that represented by Eliot and praised by the New Critics. Readers already apprehensive that the values of the New Criticism
(which was becoming a new orthodoxy in universities) would
restrict the range and accessibility of poetry warmed to a young
soldier poet ready to throw down the gauntlet. Hence they were
more friendly than they might otherwise have been to his
V-Letter and Other Poems, which had been published in 1944.
"Give me," he said in the title poem, "the free and poor inheri-
tance/ Of our own kind, not furniture/ Of education." He won
the Pulitzer Prize for 1945.

Shapiro returned from soldiering in the South Seas to become
Consultant in Poetry to the Library of Congress, and then, after
a few years of teaching at Johns Hopkins, served as editor of
Poetry magazine from 1950 to 1956. Thereafter he lived as a

university teacher. Between 1945 and 1964, his best period, Shapiro wrote poems that meditate or argue, poems structured on a metaphor, and many other kinds, but his most successful or at least his most interesting poems narrate or describe an experience. In his best poems the experience is one that naturally rouses strong emotions. For his responses are direct and passionate whatever their occasion, and often they seem excessive, as though he were trying to lift his subject by emotive intensity. His mind is partisan, and his feelings run toward either sympathy or denunciation. In both directions they would, if better controlled, be easy to share, for he assails social injustice and identifies with the victims of it. Much of his poetry might be described as a quarrel with the United States. For example, "The Dome of Sunday," the first poem in his *Collected Poems 1940–1978* (1978) and one of the best, observes the row houses of a city street and the people who live in them, and, in doing so, conveys the uniformity, narcissism, and retreat from life's realities of American middle-class existence, in which the speaker feels constricted. Perhaps Shapiro was right to assume that his unguarded warmth of feeling voiced a direct, natural humanity, and that this differentiated his work from the intellectualism and elitism of Eliot and the New Critics. Yet, on the whole, he preserved strict, closed verse forms, and he often tried to achieve a compressed idiom.

As early as *Trial of a Poet* (1947) Shapiro had published two experiments in the "prose poem," and he later used this form throughout *The Bourgeois Poet* (1964). Meanwhile, from the onset of his career he had written occasionally on themes connected with Jewish identity, and this interest culminated in *Poems of a Jew* (1958). When the Beat poets started publishing, Shapiro was sympathetic to them, especially to Ginsberg, as was natural, for in their anti-intellectualism, emotional directness, and indictment of society the Beats proclaimed in amplified voice much that Shapiro had asserted more cautiously. In welcoming them Shapiro resigned, as he put it, from his own generation, but he also admitted that this was impossible, and *White-Haired Lover* (1968) and *Adult Bookstore* (1976) blend his earlier styles with the newer ones of the 1960s.

In his last years Kenneth Patchen (1911–1972) was also viewed as a proto-Beat, but this identification, which he strongly resented, was somewhat misleading. For though Patchen shared the anticapitalist, antiwar, antimaterialist convictions of the Beat poets, he did not accept their hip morality. He derived from Whitman and Sandburg. Patchen grew up in Ohio industrial towns, where his father worked in the steel mills. In high school he cut a figure in football, track, the school newspaper, and the classroom, and two of his sonnets were published in the *New York Times*. When he graduated from high school, he worked in the steel mills to raise money for college. He was in college for a year and a half, and then, with the Depression at its height, he led a nomadic life, finding jobs here and there as a janitor, gardener, crop picker, and the like. He married in 1934 and moved into a one-room apartment in New York City. His first book of poems, *Before the Brave,* appeared in 1936 and was favorably received as the expression of a "proletarian" poet, a member of the working class who expressed its strength and protest. The next year he severely injured his spine. Thereafter he was compelled to struggle against pain, psychological depression, and physical incapacity. But he continued to wage "mental fight" (in Blake's appropriate phrase). His poetry pleaded for love, brotherhood, and faith, for beauty and wonder. During the Second World War he denounced America's participation. The moral issue was not problematic to him: we should stop killing people.

In 1950 fellow poets raised money through public readings to pay for an operation on his spine. A second operation in 1956 enabled him to move about. In the next couple of years he performed his poems in night clubs, colleges, and concert halls to the accompaniment of a jazz sextet. But in 1959, during a third operation on his back, he fell from the operating cart to the floor. His spine was now beyond surgical help, and he spent the remaining thirteen years of his life unable to stand, sit, lie on his back, or move without torturing pain. Yet he continued his work, and produced nine more books, some of them montages of poems with paintings.

Patchen was a moral prophet and liberator. His technique was designed to convey his urgent vision as forcefully and widely as possible. Not that he was always easy to understand, for as he battled against restrictive convention and soi-disant reason, he could be deliberately paradoxical, as Blake was for similar purposes. But in general Patchen aimed for instant communication, and he hoped to achieve this through spontaneous, emotional utterance, words spoken directly from him to us. Naturally, therefore, he was a poet of free verse, and his lines often accumulated in parallel rhythmic and syntactical patterns, like Whitman's. His poems of protest often included grisly images and anecdotes, but even such passages embodied his faith in man. They were written to shock and thus to activate man's inherent love and goodness. Patchen sounds, for example, like this (in "Delighted with Bluepink," a lyric written in 1954):

> Flowers! My friend, be delighted with what you like;
>   but with *something*.
> Be delighted with something. Yesterday for me it was
>   watching sun on stones; wet stones.
>   . . . .
> But today what delights me is thinking of bluepink
> flowers! Not that I've seen any . . .
> Actually there isn't a flower of any kind in the house—
>   except in my head.
> But, my friend, oh my friend! what wonderful bluepink
> flowers! Delight in my bluepink flowers!

Obviously Patchen's poems are sentimental, but they are also, in Patchen's circumstances, heroic.

As a young teacher at Vanderbilt Donald Davidson (1893–1968) contributed to the *Fugitive* and also did much of the editorial and administrative work for the magazine. In his poetry he pictured the typical modern individual somewhat as Eliot had—aimless, rootless, bereft of religious faith and social community—and argued that a Southerner might escape this condition by returning to traditional ways of life and habits of feeling. In poems such as "Lee in the Mountains" or *The Tall Men* Davidson drew moral inspiration from figures in Southern history. Davidson was a fluent poet, but far less so than Merrill Moore (1903–1957), another Fugitive, who became a Boston psychiatrist. Moore could compose two sonnets while waiting for a traffic light to change. Such facility was naturally unpromising, but a few of Moore's sonnets are readable. Mark Van Doren (1894–1972), one of the prominent teachers and men of letters of his generation, produced important works of many kinds incessantly. His mind was balanced, sane, humorous, and detached, and his poetry was low-keyed. Roethke described Van Doren accurately as a "careful craftsman with a sharp eye for the homely and a mind aware of the profound implications of the casual." Peter Viereck (b. 1916) is a critical foe of Romantic emotion who writes best when he surrenders to it, as in "Well Said, Old Mole." The thoughtful, academic verse of John Ciardi (b. 1916), John Frederick Nims (b. 1913), and Robert Fitzgerald (1910–85) also extends the Romantic reaction I am tracing in this chapter. The three last-named poets are also skilled translators.

Because of his direct methods, narrative skills, and use of Southern regional materials, James Dickey (b. 1923) has affinities with Robert Penn Warren, who has championed Dickey's poetry. Like Warren, Dickey is also a novelist and critic. After serving in the air force from 1942 to 1946, Dickey graduated from Vanderbilt University. Except for five years as a copywriter with an advertising firm, he has made his living as a college teacher; he is now Professor of English at the University of South Carolina. He started reading poetry while he was in the air force, and his first publications came in the 1950s. *Buckdancer's Choice* (1965), his finest volume thus far, was awarded a National Book Award. During the 1970s Dickey put his strength into prose. His novel *Deliverance* (1970) was made into a well-known film, but his reputation as a poet declined, partly because his later poems in longer lines and looser forms are less successful than his tighter, earlier ones in strong rhythms. Also, his affirmation of life began to seem too easy and uncritical, and his macho pose in many poems gave offense.

Byron was one of Dickey's favorites in childhood, and both his liking for Byron and his success as an advertising copywriter suggest some of Dickey's virtues as a poet. Whether they are ballads, visions, or dreamlike sequences, his poems are purposefully plotted with direct and accessible phrasing. His emotions are Romantically mystical; he reveres natural instinct and seeks communion with wild nature and regeneration through it. "Listening to Foxhounds," for example, expresses his empathy with animals and with hunting. "The Heaven of Animals," Dickey's finest poem, voices both the joy of the predatory animal as it leaps on its victim and the "acceptance, compliance" of the hunted animals. All that happens as a part of nature is good,

and there is no death: the torn prey "rise, they walk again."
Dickey is an important influence on many younger poets in the
South, such as Dave Smith.

Louise Bogan (1897–1970), Babette Deutsch (b. 1895), and
May Sarton (b. 1912) write reflective poems with careful craft-
manship. Deutsch often composes in modern forms, but with
the earnestness, dignity, and sadness of the late Victorian, elegiac imagination. She has translated German and Russian poets
and written comprehensive surveys of modern poetry (*Poetry in
Our Time*, 1952, revised 1956, 1963). Deutsch's poetry is emotionally reserved, and seems the more so if compared with Sarton's, which can be sentimental. Bogan, the best of these poets,
was poetry editor of *The New Yorker*. The poems she wrote toward
the end of her career are especially moving as they express the
difficulties of a woman facing old age alone.

For Muriel Rukeyser (1913–80) writing a poem was a process
of collecting "surfacings" from the unconscious. When "collected" these were criticized and revised, but these activities did
not essentially modify her product. Her poems are difficult if
one seeks intelligibility, but not at all for readers satisfied with
vague, intense, idealistic emotion. Her themes were frequently
political—the Depression, the Second World War, the war in
Vietnam, feminism. She combined an imprecise idiom with committed emotions. A Chinese proverb warns against whipping an
ox that is already running, but this is what Rukeyser does. Her
poems move persons who share her emotion before they read
the poems.

THEODORE ROETHKE

Theodore Roethke (1908–63) went to the University of Michigan and briefly as a graduate student to Harvard. He lived
thereafter the typical career of a contemporary American poet
as a teacher of "creative" writing and poet-in-residence at La-
fayette, Michigan State, Pennsylvania State, Bennington, and
the University of Washington. In addition to teaching he supported himself in later life by fees for public readings, fellowships, and poetry prizes with cash attached. His education and
information were almost entirely literary, although, beginning

in his forties, he also read religious writers, such as Tillich, Buber, and Kierkegaard, and he picked up psychoanalytic concepts during treatment for the mental breakdowns he recurrently suffered. He wrote constantly, for his manic-depressive illness left him manic most of the time and he had enormous energy. Moreover, he was intensely competitive with other poets and determined to be foremost. He kept notebooks into which he copied poems and passages he liked, remarks about poetry, drafts of his own poems, and innumerable lines, phrases, metaphors, images, and the like, bits that might someday be fitted into some poem, though only a very small percentage of them ever were. He would interrupt a conversation to jot down a phrase or rhythm that had just come to him. When a poem was finished and he knew it was good, he would, he said, weep for joy and kneel down, though as for kneeling, he never made up his mind about God and never stopped thinking about Him. In dry spells, when he couldn't write, he felt like a fraud, he didn't exist. When he was writing, "At last I was somebody again." Though his poetry sought God or Being, in a more immediate and psychological sense his salvation was to write.

In Roethke's first volume, *Open House* (1941), the title poem proclaimed, "I'm naked to the bone, / With nakedness my shield," but this was hardly the case, for he was clothed in predecessors. The volume included poems sounding like Auden, Frost, Dickinson, Elinor Wylie, Leonie Adams, Louise Bogan, the Metaphysical Poets, and Yeats; each of these styles was followed with proficiency. That the book makes a period rather than an individual impression did not harm it at the time, needless to say. In his review Yvor Winters singled out "The Adamant" for favorable analysis, and, given the date and the critic, the last stanza shows why:

> Compression cannot break
> A center so congealed;
> The tool can chip no flake:
> The core lies sealed.

But by 1938 Roethke was himself tired, he told his notebook, of the "well-made poem." "Modern poetry," he wrote, "has been cursed with too many 'well-written' poems: the tiny emotion expanded ludicrously beyond its own shape and size." He spoke at about the same time of "Elemental poems—when we are outside ourselves." His dissatisfaction resulted, ten years later, in a famous volume. *The Lost Son* (1948) begins with an extraordinary group of poems recollecting the greenhouses of his father, who was a nursery florist. Roethke empathizes with the plant cuttings and the effort involved in poking new nubs through the sand:

> I can hear, underground, that sucking and sobbing,
> In my veins, in my bones I feel it,—
> The small waters seeping upward,
> The tight grains parting at last.
> When sprouts break out,
> Slippery as fish . . .

In a 1945 letter Roethke said, "I am trying to avoid the sentimental and literary diction of the Georgians or the earlier *Floral Offerings* of the nineteenth century, and write a natural sensuous poetry with some symbolical reference in the more complex pieces." Since rejection of Georgians and Victorians had now been a critical routine for thirty years, the remark was out of date, provincial, but certainly Roethke's vegetation has qualities unknown in the seemlier poetic posies of the past. The passage quoted above uses orgasm as a metaphor. The "Root Cellar" has a grotesque vitality, fertile, erotic, stinking, and obscene. Plants in the moist heat of the "Forcing House" sweat, pulse, and swell. "Black hairy roots . . . hanging from drain holes" are "lewd monkey-tails" ("Weed Puller"). Not all the poems center on plants. "Moss-Gathering" and "Child on Top of a Greenhouse" recall childhood experiences in a Wordsworthian way; In "Old Florist" and "Frau Baumann, Frau Schmidt, and Frau Schwartze" (a poem added later to the group) the greenhouse workers become mythical presences to the child.

The five parts of the title poem, "The Lost Son," enact a psychological and spiritual pilgrimage from death-haunted paralysis to illumination and vision. The sequence ends with an injunction to wait in trust and serenity:

> A lively understandable spirit
> Once entertained you.

> It will come again.
> Be still.
> Wait.

The poem is also a journey back in memory, for in his "hard time" the speaker recollects his childhood relation to Being. In a way that is typical of Roethke he even recalls and imaginatively reenters an earlier phase of existence:

> I feel the slime of a wet nest.
> Beware Mother Mildew.
> Nibble again, fish nerves.

The parts of the poem deploy different styles and methods, and some parts contrast brief, stanzaic lyrics with passages in longer lines or freer verse. The ellipsis and parataxis of his writing in this poem characterized most of his poems from this time on, and so did his frequent shifts from statement to exclamation, question, command, or wish. He also made effective use in "The Lost Son" of forms and rhythms associated with childhood— question and answer, riddle, nonsense—and his next volume developed these possibilities more boldly.

The general conception of "The Lost Son"—a five-part sequence enacting a spritual quest—was taken from the *Four Quartets*. In fact the final movement may be read as a variation, in the musical sense, on portions of "East Coker" and "Little Gidding." But Roethke does not express himself within the vocabulary of Christian thought. Neither has he Eliot's allusiveness. Because Eliot's poem refers to St. John of the Cross, Dante, Juliana of Norwich, seventeenth-century poets and preachers, the Bhagavad-Gita, and so forth, the emotion seems not merely personal. What the protagonist voices has objectivity and authority from its recurrence in the experience of other men and women at other times. For better or worse, Roethke's protagonist has the authority only of his own experience and feeling. And Roethke lacks Eliot's reflective passages. We may recall that Auden, after meeting Roethke, remarked that he was totally bereft of general ideas, but we should add that Roethke deliberately rejected Eliot's method, thinking it ineffective. He aimed for "dramatic" poetry, "with the mood or the action on the page, not talked-about, not the meditative T. S. Eliot kind of thing."

Similar poems in three to five parts followed "The Lost Son" in that volume and the next, *Praise to the End!* (1951). The poems in the latter book were conceived as a single "sequence of dramatic pieces," Roethke said, "beginning with a small child and working up. A kind of tensed-up *Prelude,* maybe: no comment; everything in the mind of a kid." In referring to the *Prelude,* Roethke meant that his theme was Wordsworth's, "the spiritual history of a protagonist." "Tensed-up" because, among other things, childhood is not presented by recollection, description, narration, or discourse, as in Wordsworth, but by the child's speech or interior monologue. "Blest the infant Babe," says Wordsworth, and describes the babe in his mother's arms. "Sing me a sleep-song, please," writes Roethke, becoming the baby. His identification with a child permits uses of babble—"Mips and ma the mooly moo." From childhood he proceeds to sex-ridden adolescence ("I dream of nothing but boards; / I could love a duck") and on to later agitations of love, mindfulness of death, searching for Being. Each poem, Roethke said, "is a stage in a kind of struggle out of the slime; part of a slow spiritual progress; an effort to be born, and later, to become something more." But the stages are by no means easy to distinguish; the plot, if there is one, is involuted; and each poem in the sequence enacts its own movement toward illumination and affirmation. For these poems are also "tensed-up" Eliotic quartets. The themes come "alternately, as in music," Roethke said, "and usually" there is "a partial resolution in the end." As in Eliot's long work—and Wordsworth's—the imagery of *Praise to the End!* is incremental. Images of water and of creatures associated with it—otters, frogs, fishes—of light, seeds, bones, and so forth, recur in different contexts and thus develop through the work into symbols, nodes of complex association and suggestion.

Besides Wordsworth and Eliot, a third poet especially presides over both *The Lost Son* and *Praise to the End!* The fame of Dylan Thomas was rising to its height when these volumes were composed, and Thomas' quasi-mystical feeling of union with Life or Being helped evoke in Roethke a similar emotion. "Reason," Roethke snorts, that "hutch for grubby schoolboys!" "The hedgewren's song says something else." "The force that through the green fuse drives the flower," as Thomas phrased it (and that Wordsworth remembered in his childhood self and intuited in periwinkles, and Whitman in everything) sings for Roethke in

the hedgewren. Roethke's quest for oneness with this "force" led
him back in memory to childhood, down into the unconscious
and archetypal, and out into the world of natural things;
Thomas had already blazed these paths.

> Morning-fair, follow me further back
> Into that minnowy world of weeds and ditches,
> When the herons floated high over the white houses,
> And the little crabs slipped into silvery craters.
> When the sun for me glinted the sides of a sand grain.

The lines just quoted are from Roethke's "The Shape of the
Fire," but Roethke always risked sounding too much like other
poets, and these lines might almost have been written by
Thomas.

Acts of psychological identification asserted Roethke's oneness
with Being in its particular manifestations, and a sequence of
identifications was Roethke's mode of quest. Like Thomas, but
more effectively and clearly, he tried to imagine existence in its
more primitive modes. He represented, as I said, his state of
mind as a child. He entered imaginatively into a tree, a pond,
or even a pebble. A typical gesture was to descend the steps of
evolution, identifying his way back down through lambs, the "fat
lark," and "pulsing lizard," until he came to salmon, herring,
minnows, and more primitive watery forms—snails, worms,
scum—"With these I would be. / And with water: the waves coming forward . . ."

But these passages are not merely solemn, or not always so.
Roethke struck surprise and wit from his theme. "Bless me and
the maze I'm in," he said, detaching himself from himself with
good-humored irony. Even in a worm, he noted, the hind parts
are livelier, and "I've traced these words in sand with a vestigal
tail." To follow his discontinuities requires nimbleness of mind,
as in the passage from "I Cry, Love! Love!" I've been quoting:

> Reason? That dreary shed, that hutch for grubby schoolboys!
> The hedgewren's song says something else.
> I care for a cat's cry and the hugs, live as water.
> I've traced these words in sand with a vestigial tail;
> Now the gills are beginning to cry.
> Such a sweet noise: I can't sleep for it.

Bless me and the maze I'm in!
Hello, thingy spirit.

Like Thomas, in other words, Roethke incorporated some elements of the intellectual lyricism against which he also reacted. At this point Roethke changed again. He entered what is usually but much too simply called his Yeatsian period. The wet, sticky push of Being became less prominent, and he wrote more about aging and death. Probably the more traditional and firmer forms he used after 1953, the public voices, intellectual antitheses and generalizations were, as in Yeats, a retreat from the now less auspicious realm of nature and organic process. Probably his change of style was also motivated by a fear of descending too deeply into his own psyche, for by the end of the 1940s he had undergone three mental breakdowns. He now typically composed a poetry of abstraction:

> Wisdom, where is it found?—
> Those who embrace, believe.

He wrote memorable poems in which he invoked the predecessors he emulated, such as "Four for Sir John Davies," in which he alluded not only to the Elizabethan poet of the title but also to Dante and Yeats ("I take this cadence from a man named Yeats").

Roethke's final, posthumous volume, *The Far Field* (1964), included a "North American Sequence" of poems that returned in some ways to the mode of his earlier sequences. Now, however, he did not attempt to enter a child's mind or to retrace the stages of consciousness. Hence his language lacked the novelty of those earlier sequences. The beauty of these poems lies in their limpid diction, descriptive care, long, elegiac cadence, incremental symbolism, and moving significance. In one passage, for example, Roethke describes the edge of the sea:

Where the yellowish prongs of grass poke through the blackened ash,
And the bunched logs peel in the afternoon sunlight,
Where the fresh and salt waters meet,
And the sea-winds move through the pine trees,
A country of bays and inlets, and small streams flowing seaward.

The subject of these poems is the journey of the spirit out of frozen self-disgust, darkness, fragmentation, and isolation into vital wholeness and union with Being. They are written under the awareness of approaching death: "The self persists like a dying star"; "The dry scent of a dying garden in September,/ The wind fanning the ash of a low fire"; "I feel a weightless change, a moving forward." These poems, with their wealth of particular detail and changing mood, are a late, long look at what can be loved, a last effort to live.

> How slowly pleasure dies!—
> The dry bloom splitting in the wrinkled vale,
> The first snow of the year in the dark fir.
> Feeling, I still delight in my last fall.

ELIZABETH BISHOP

Elizabeth Bishop (1911–79) spent her early childhood on her grandparents' farm in Nova Scotia. Her father died when she was eight months old, and her mother, after repeated breakdowns, became incurably insane. At the age of six Bishop was taken from Nova Scotia and settled with other relatives in Massachusetts. A period of fearful ill-health followed—bronchitis, asthma, eczema, and other symptoms—and since she could not attend school regularly, she filled her life with books. At the age of sixteen she was able to go to boarding school and then to Vassar. She lived thereafter in various parts of the world and especially in Brazil (1951–67) until in 1974 she returned to the United States and taught at Harvard. She published only four small volumes of poetry (in 1946, 1955, 1965, and 1976).

Her work is brilliantly varied, and particular poems unify opposite qualities. She is plain, witty, realistic, imaginative, objective, dreamlike, idyllic, pessimistic, associative, intellectual, and extremely averse to making generalizations. Her assessment of life and its possibilities is clear-eyed to the utmost degree, both in general and on every particular occasion. Her mind is troubled, open, and exploratory.

Bishop, who was influenced by Marianne Moore, was famous for close, particular, and witty descriptions of objects: the "lines of pink cloud" in the sky at dawn like "wandering lines in marble"; the buzzards ("thirty or more") she sees floating down in the sky "like stirred-up flakes of sediment / Sinking through water"; and the irises of fish (in "The Fish"),

> backed and packed
> with tarnished tinfoil
> seen through the lenses
> of old scratched isinglass.

Despite her grip on existential reality, Bishop liked to imagine simple, innocent goodness. One thinks of her charming, almost idyllic depiction in "Manners" of her grandfather's rural courtesy; of "Cape Breton," where human life so little disturbs the natural environment; of the "Invitation to Miss Marianne Moore" in which Manhattan, to entice Moore, "is all awash with morals this fine morning"; and of "The Moose," in which everyone on the bus feels a "sweet/ sensation of joy" at the animal's unafraid nearness. "Jeronimo's House" is one of several poems in which the organization is partly that of a picture and frame. The picture is one of those idylls of coziness with which Bishop occasionally delights us; the furnishings and decor of the house are bright, pleasant, innocent, and comfortable, like similar interiors in Dickens. "The Map" pictures the earth with a similar feeling, and "Filling Station" both expresses and questions the emotion. Ultimately the idyllic element in these poems lies in the loving care, as in pastoral, that is implied. Somebody waters the hirsute begonia of the filling station. Yet Bishop never becomes sentimental and is sometimes satiric. In "Roosters," for example, she bristles at male assertion and perhaps even more at feminine admiration of it. "Cries galore" of the roosters

> come from the water-closet door,
> from the dropping-plastered henhouse floor,
>
> where in the blue blur
> their rustling wives admire,
> the roosters brace their cruel feet and glare . . .

In her poems there is usually an undernote of disappointment, depression, existential *Angst,* and psychological vulnerability, in short, of potential threat and horror. In "At the Fishhouses," for example, we find Bishop singing Baptist hymns to a seal in the harbor: "I also sang 'A Mighty Fortress Is Our God.'"

The scene is as pleasant in a pastoral way as can be imagined:
the seal

> stood up in the water and regarded me
> steadily, moving his head a little.
> Then he would disappear, then suddenly emerge
> almost in the same spot, with a sort of shrug
> as if it were against his better judgment.

No wonder the firs behind the harbor remind Bishop of Christmas! But the scene is described in order to be counterpointed, more exactly, to be overwhelmed by contrary symbolic suggestions. As a sea creature the seal is utterly alien from human beings. And the sea, "element bearable to no mortal," symbolizes ultimate reality much more probably and ominously than the Christmas story and "A Mighty Fortress Is Our God." So intent is Bishop in this poem on a metaphysical-religious statement that she concludes in emphatic rhetoric. Though this is uncharacteristic, the speculative, philosophizing intellectuality is not.

Bishop did not follow the neo-Metaphysical, Symbolist style of the 1930s—she was never a follower of anything—but many of her poems, such as "The Imaginary Iceberg," "The Gentleman of Shalott," "The Man-Moth," "A Miracle for Breakfast," "The Unbeliever," and "The Monument," especially pleased devotees of this style. For such poems presented a complex symbol and developed it with imaginative detail and intellectual ingenuity, forcing readers to puzzle out meanings. "The Monument," for example, describes a wood rubbing by Max Ernst. If we ask what the monument symbolizes, the general answers are art in its relations to reality, to the artist, and to itself; more particular suggestions are innumerable. "The Man-Moth" is a strange, moving poem that pictures man as a moth. Contemplating, perhaps, man's aspiring religious impulses, the poem pictures the moth's tropism toward the moon and the childlike wrongness of his cosmology. The moth thinks the moon "a small hole at the top of the sky" and hopes to squeeze through it. It climbs up the skyscraper facade toward the moon, "falls back scared," and returns to the horror of its subway world.

After her first volume, *North and South* (1946), Bishop became much more direct, plain, and circumstantial. More exactly, she became expert in using metonymic detail to define emotion, and she also exploited detail dramatically to delay and resist emotion and thus build to a climax. Her poems were subtly plotted, but the plot was often concealed beneath an appearance of casual description. These lines from "The Bight" are typical:

> There is a fence of chicken wire along the dock
> where, glinting like little plowshares,
> the blue-gray shark tails are hung up to dry
> for the Chinese-restaurant trade.

Such lines are in the world of William Carlos Williams more than of any other modern poet, though of course Bishop does not much resemble Williams. "A Cold Spring" offers a direct comparison, for its overt subject, the coming of spring, is the same as Williams' "Spring and All."

> A cold spring:
> the violet was flawed on the lawn.
> For two weeks or more the trees hesitated;
> the little leaves waited,
> carefully indicating their characteristics.
> Finally a grave green dust
> settled over your big and aimless hills.
> One day, in a chill white blast of sunshine,
> on the side of one a calf was born.
> The mother stopped lowing
> and took a long time eating the afterbirth,
> a wretched flag,
> but the calf got up promptly
> and seemed inclined to feel gay.

If we ask why Williams could not have written this, one answer is that Bishop gives the illusion of finding no symbolism or moral in her material. Williams' "Spring and All" is a metaphor of life thrusting up into a cold, bleak world. The energy and purpose he intuits in grass and bushes correspond to his own procedure as a poet. He organizes images to convey a meaning, and so, of course, do Warren, Roethke, and virtually every poet one thinks of, including Bishop. But if we can infer Bishop's attitudes from her technique, she felt that the selecting, coloring, ordering, unifying, and so forth, in which every poet must engage, are suspect. To her moral feelings this way of using materials was assertive and therefore repugnant. The word "using" itself suggests what might be troubling. Moreover, a poet who dominated his materials risked falsifying them, and also risked the obviousness from which Williams' "Spring and All" slightly suffers. The ideal to which Bishop aspired in many poems was a complete receptivity to whatever appeared, somewhat akin to that desiderated by Charles Olson and Robert Duncan in their theorizing about "open" form. Thus in the lines quoted we observe nature taking its course. Its manifestations are many, diverse, and only loosely coordinated. The "little leaves waited," and we approve their prudence, but the calf, though as newly born as the leaves, got up promptly. While they were "careful," the calf was "gay" (or seemed so, for of course Bishop could not know what the animal felt). Both births occur in spring, but in contrast to what happens in Williams' poem, no obvious imaginative theme links one to the other. For example, in a simpler poet the cow and the calf would make an imaginative unit, but this does not happen. Separate instincts lead the calf to get up and the cow to eat the afterbirth; the poem dwells on their disconnection as much as on the opposite.

If we ask why the hills in this poem are appropriately described as "aimless," one answer is that aimlessness is what Bishop perceives generally. In "Over 2000 Illustrations and a Complete Concordance" she explains that "Everything" is "only connected by 'and' and 'and.'" At the conclusion of "Little Exercise" she takes Shakespeare's "Another part of the field," the stage direction for the battle scenes in *Henry IV*, Part One, as her ordering principle, the point being that reality is a field on which very different things happen simultaneously. Describing the diverse goings on and litter of a harbor, "The Bight" sums up with the adjective "untidy": "All the untidy activity continues / awful but cheerful." The "aimless," "untidy," "'and' and 'and'" quality of Bishop's observation contributes to its realistic strength. She includes such diverse possibilities that we read her with confidence. Yet the aimlessness is more apparent than real. In "A Cold Spring" the season advances little by little, its motion carefully registered through the early dogwood and redbud to the later oak leaves, and so forth, until finally summer fireflies glow in the evening. There is an order in events that, at first, may seem almost random.

Many of Bishop's poems enact an archetypal Romantic experience. In such poems a special perfection of Bishop's art is the poetic tact or prudence with which she hides, so to speak, the traditional pattern within a slowly accumulating mass of realistic detail. "Roosters," for example, moves from dark to dawn. This progression is completely probable, since the roosters wake up while it is still night and keep on crowing, but it is also symbolic, and it is sustained and elaborated by other developments. At first the roosters are associated with male, assertive sexuality, stupid instinct, egotism, territoriality, aggression, and the like. Embodying all this, the roosters are reminders of reality; their crowings at dawn say, "Get up! Stop dreaming!" But toward the end of the poem Bishop recalls the biblical association of the rooster with St. Peter's denial of Christ; she describes a medieval sculpture in which the rooster stands in the scene with Christ and Peter. The cock-a-doodle may mean "forgiveness." Thus though the roosters symbolize a naturalistic or fallen world, they also bring to mind the possibility of its redemption. The final lines return from the description of this sculpture to the ordinary, real world, which now seems no longer dark, stupid, and beastly but delicately beautiful. The cocks are almost inaudible, and the light of dawn floats in the backyard, gilding everything it falls on. The light symbolizes a quasi-numinous blessing, and even "broccoli"—an image of ordinary actuality if ever there was one, both by its associations and its sound—is gilded "leaf by leaf." The poem, in short, has three phases: in the first we are in the world of everyday experience, which seems merely naturalistic, harsh, and dark; the sense of this deepens until suddenly, in the second essential moment of the poem, a concrete, redeeming vision or symbol is beheld; this is followed by a return to the everyday world, now viewed in a different way and accepted.

In "At the Fishhouses" this pattern is more complicated. The initial, ordinary reality is not here unpleasant; as the poem continues, however, the ordinary transmutes itself. While remaining completely real, objects become also visionary. They are pervaded with silver light from the sea, from the wet rocks, from the herring scales in the tubs, and even from the grass. Then, however, another movement begins, and this vision is challenged by a deeper one—the existential reality of the sea I mentioned earlier. "Over 2000 Illustrations and a Complete Concordance" inverts the usual Romantic plot, for the central symbolic image here is deeply pessimistic in its implications. "The Moose," to take a final instance, embodies the archetypal experience in a narrative. On a bus trip fog closes in, evening comes on, and finally the woods are entered. All this corresponds to the Romantic quest pattern, and from the start there are suggestions of eeriness, resistance, and danger, which the quester must encounter and pass through. Also there are anticipations of the visionary moment to come. Realistic description of sights and events modulates into a dreamy feeling of timelessness. Recollections of childhood come to mind, saturated with feelings of gentleness, peacefulness, acceptance, and reassurance. Rational, daylight consciousness is now suspended. In Romantic quest poems this is the moment or state of mind in which the central symbol or vision is given. Here, however, the relaxation of will also anticipates or preludes the vision in emotional content. The bus stops suddenly. A moose stands in the road. "Grand, otherworldly," it looks the bus over and sniffs at its hood. The bus then continues its journey—this is the return to ordinary reality—but for a while, as the bus drives away, the moose can still be seen, and its smell mingles with the "acrid/ smell of gasoline." The poem is ineffably delicate. Any interpretation will be hopelessly inadequate. Yet the poem questions with terrific emphasis,

> Why, why do we feel
> (we all feel) this sweet
> sensation of joy.

at the presence of the moose, and by asking this question, the poem forces us to try to answer.

> Towering, antlerless,
> high as a church,
> homely as a house,

the moose is peaceful, female, massively protective, and simply there, a maternal figure, apparitional yet plain, solid, familiar, and reassuring like a house. The sight of it makes the passengers whisper "childishly, softly." Nature does not here lastingly permeate or form the soul of man, as Wordsworth hoped it might; the last lines of the poem dwell on the "acrid/ smell of gasoline." But at least there is a brief moment in which the human and the animal in its natural environment stare peacefully at each other. In this moment the sight of the moose returns the bus passengers to gentleness and wonder.

16

BREAKING THROUGH THE NEW CRITICISM

ROBERT LOWELL, Richard Wilbur, Anthony Hecht, John Berryman, and virtually all other American poets who went to college in the 1940s were imprinted with the New Criticism. They began their careers as second-generation exemplars of this style. As it became prevalent, however, the New Critical type of poem gradually seemed too easy to produce. As Robert Lowell put it in a 1961 interview, "Any number of people are guilty of writing a complicated poem that has a certain amount of Symbolism in it and really difficult meaning, a wonderful poem to teach. Then you unwind it and you feel that the intelligence, the experience, whatever goes into it, is skin deep." Lowell's reference to the value of experience is typical of its time, and indicates that poets were finding the formalism of the New Critical poem not only too easy but also imprisoning. Impressed by the growing appreciation of William Carlos Williams and by the bold, direct methods and shocking frankness of the Beats, they sensed that in their complex, witty, symbolic, and metrical type of poetry their voice could not be natural. They could not be themselves in their poems but only personae, and their personae, moreover, were strangely lacking in ordinary human experiences and emotions. In pursuing art they had relinquished life, and they sought in the 1950s to write with a greater immediacy and reality. Robert Lowell published in *Life Studies* (1959) a sequence of painful, intimately autobiographical poems which were widely imitated. Critics described this type of poetry as Confessional, and the Confessional School was said to include Theodore Roethke, Allen Ginsberg, John Berryman, Sylvia Plath, Anne Sexton, Adrienne Rich, W. D. Snodgrass, and Diane Wakoski along with Lowell. Meanwhile in the 1960s followers of Charles Olson and Projective Verse further encouraged everyone to write with meterless spontaneity. And at more or less the same time the Surrealist revival in the United States freed poets to set down irrational images. In the Surrealist mode, moreover, the poet would not consciously know just which irrational suggestions the image might activate or why they might be appropriate.

In such manifestations American poetry was abandoning the New Critical values of impersonality, formality, intellectuality, and self-conscious control. But the poets I dwell on in this chapter and the next make a more complicated story. After they broke with the New Critical style, they concealed the rigor of their craftsmanship under the appearance of a more casual and immediate way of writing, but they never completely relinquished their former standards. Precisely this combination of the new vitality and reality of the 1960s with the formal intricacy and discipline of the 1940s contributes to the greatness of their achievement.

To present this transition in American poetry I here focus on only some of the poets who underwent it. Many others, discussed elsewhere in other connections, might have been included here, since their work changed in similar ways; among them are Robert Penn Warren, Theodore Roethke, W. S. Merwin, James Wright, Adrienne Rich, and Sylvia Plath. I begin with Richard Wilbur, who was in the 1940s the most elegant poet of his generation. If Lowell represented the new Academic style in its formidable difficulty and ambition, Wilbur showed its possibilities of charm and pleasantness. Many readers assumed that he would lead it in a quasi-popular direction. Wilbur still continues to argue for the New Critical values, and though he, like everyone, has modified his style, he has done so less than most of his contemporaries. Poets such as Anthony Hecht, David Ferry, and Reed Whittemore are also in the New Critical tradition, and no formalist of the 1940s was more rigorous than John Hollander still is. J. V. Cunningham was never a disciple of the New Critics generally, but he studied with Yvor Winters at Stanford and shared his ethos. Long after he had written the books that helped create the New Criticism, I. A. Richards became a poet—and a good one—in his old age, publishing his first volume of verse in 1958 at the age of sixty-five. Sometimes his poems reflected the imagination of the Georgian poets he had read in youth and continued to love, but they also sparkled with intellectual wit. I discuss these poets so far as space permits, but the chapter concentrates especially on Richard Wilbur and John Berryman. The career of Robert Lowell, who was central to this major transition in American poetry, is postponed for separate discussion in the following chapter.

RICHARD WILBUR

Wilbur published his first volume in 1947, at the age of twenty-six. It excited much admiration, and in order to see why (apart from its intrinsically good qualities) we must again think of the state of affairs in university English departments, of which Wilbur himself was first a child and than a member. The high Modernists had by now been absorbed into the curriculum; the first Ph.D. theses on Stevens were under way; above all, literary undergraduates were learning from the New Criticism its premises and methods of analysis. Wilbur captured this audience almost at once and held it for twenty years. He was kindlier than Stevens, and his meditations were much less urgent and difficult. Like the high Modernists and the New Critical poets of the 1920s and 1930s, he was formal, witty, and impersonal; he kept his subject at an emotional distance and activated very diverse attitudes toward it. But his texture was less dense than theirs. In other words, his work followed currently favored modes but generally revised them toward perspicuity and charm.

"Ceremony," the title poem of his second volume (1950), has his characteristic note, with its combination of sophisticated civilization—paintings, Europe, ballet—and decent affections, its playful yet serious wit, its fresh, apt, sympathetic descriptions, reflective intelligence and formal skill:

A striped blouse in a clearing by Bazille
Is, you may say, a patroness of boughs
Too queenly kind toward nature to be kin.
But ceremony never did conceal,
Save to the silly eye, which all allows,
How much we are the woods we wander in.

Let her be some Sabrina fresh from stream,
Lucent as shallows slowed by wading sun,
Bedded on fern, the flowers' cynosure:
Then nymph and wood must nod and strive to dream
That she is airy earth, the trees, undone,
Must ape her languor natural and pure.

Ho-Hum. I am for wit and wakefulness,
And love this feigning lady by Bazille.
What's lightly hid is deepest understood,
And when with social smile and formal dress
She teaches leaves to curtsey and quadrille,
I think there are most tigers in the wood.

The nymph Sabrina is one with nature, but the lady of Bazille's painting seems not to be. Doubtless Wilbur had a particular painting in mind, but the name Bazille sufficiently contributes the note of minor French Impressionism. The painter—or the speaker—sees the lady as a striped blouse, as clothing and pattern. She is further associated with social or societal forms (patroness, social smile), and the poem sprinkles these with courtly, old-world flavorings (quadrille, curtsey, queenly). All these associations are gathered into the term "ceremony," which is thus implicitly defined as a social form that stands over against nature and conceals it. But the pastoral or idyllic harmony of the second stanza is equally a ceremony, an artful feigning, and into its Marie Antoinetteing the poem appropriately introduces a naif ("the silly eye") in order to remind us that we sophisticates do not believe either the one perspective or the other. From us neither conceals that the woods are bestial (ape, tiger) and that we are the woods. So we come to the next refinement of sophistication, and choose our illusion. The speaker finds the illusion of harmony boring. Merely to think of it makes him yawn. But, he argues, if we pose ourselves as unlike nature and superior to it, this pretense will keep us witty and wakeful. Hence he loves the "feigning lady." What is she feigning? Well, of course, that she is not a tiger. But she is. Painting a striped blouse in the woods, Bazille has at the same time wittily painted a tiger. And Wilbur has neatly tied together the first and last lines of his poem. What kind of person is saying this poem? A connoisseur with, maybe, a taste for minor painters—Bazille—and a slightly old-fashioned diction ("silly eye, which all allows") and propriety, who apologizes discreetly ("you may say") for his bolder figures. He may seem a bit affected: to be bored ("Ho-hum") with natural harmony is a preciosity borrowed from the *fin de siècle*. With his meters, rhymes, and stanzas, puns, paradoxes, and balanced alliteration, he writes with the ceremony he praises. The pose of superior grace, disengaged and intelligent, is seductive, and though he likes subtlety and indirection, the speaker is not hard to follow; he is thoughtful, but has no unfamiliar thoughts. His tigers are not dangerous, but pleasurable, like everything else in the poem, suggesting at most an agreeable shudder.

This, then, was Wilbur's first style, which dazzled and fetched so many readers. If he did not subsequently change his way of writing as remarkably as Rich, Merrill, and other contemporaries, he nevertheless developed a plainer style and, in some poems, a greater emotional intensity. The considerations that motivated him were typical. "Most American poets of my generation," he says, recounting the same history that we have tried to bring into focus, "were taught to admire the English Metaphysical poets of the seventeenth century and such contemporary masters of irony as John Crowe Ransom. We were led by our teachers and by the critics whom we read to feel that the most adequate and convincing poetry is that which accommodates mixed feelings, clashing ideas, and incongruous images. Poetry could not be honest, we thought, unless it began by acknowledging the full discordancy of modern life and consciousness." But such poetry has limitations, for the "atmosphere of contradiction can stifle passion and conduce to a bland evasiveness." At the same time, poems spoken in a "dramatic" voice, that is, in some particular character and moment of feeling, can give "free expression to some one compelling mood or attitude . . . we are not always divided in spirit." Doubtless Wilbur was further prompted toward the dramatic lyric by his experience in translating Molière—his brilliant versions of *The Misanthrope* (1955) and *Tartuffe* (1963)—and in writing the libretto for the musical comedy *Candide* (1957). It was natural that for help in writing his dramatic lyrics he turned briefly to Yeats ("Talking to Himself," "Another Voice"). In his plainer style he can be nobly eloquent, as in his poem on the death of Dudley Fitts ("For Dudley"). And whether in his dramatic lyrics or his meditative utterance he is still a master of elegance and wit.

William Meredith (b. 1919), Hayden Carruth (b. 1921), and Philip Booth (b. 1926) continue to illustrate the conservative style forged in the 1940s and 1950s. They are all identified with New England. Meredith, who teaches at Connecticut College, published memorable poems of his war experience in his first volume (1944). To his own disadvantage Meredith often catches the voices of greater poets, such as Yeats and Frost. His work is thoughtful and studiously skilled, but somewhat lacking in individuality. Carruth lives in northern Vermont, and many of his poems take their metaphors from this rural world. He is not a "nature" poet, but expresses man's existential situation. *The Bloomingdale Papers*, for example, which were written in an asylum during a period of mental breakdown, represent, Carruth explains, "the inner condition of exile as the experience *par excellence* of the mid-twentieth century." A virtuoso stylist, Carruth also echoes the voices of great predecessors, such as Frost, Eliot, Stevens, Pound, and Yeats. His *Asphalt Georgics* (1985) present the milieu of highway shopping strips and malls in the United States. Booth traces his derivation from Thoreau, Emerson, and Frost. His locale is the Maine coastal region, and his poetry has many bleakly beautiful images of snow, tides, rocks, marshes, and beaches. His early poems were somewhat unadventurous, both emotionally and speculatively. Though Booth has since widened both his stylistic resources and his spiritual exploration, he remains essentially the same craftsmanlike, poised, sane poet. His note is terse, stoic, and elegiac.

Two other poets of New England are Donald Hall and Peter Davison, both born in 1928. In his first mature poetry Hall was a marvelous craftsman, completely in control of his medium and his meanings. In the later 1950s, however, he was somewhat persuaded by Surrealist theories of the "deep image," as were many poets at this time, and he sought to let his poems well up from the unconscious. The poems thus created consisted of juxtaposed fragments with obscure connections, and were sometimes mysteriously moving and beautiful. More recently Hall has written quiet narratives. Davison also began as a master of traditional forms, though he was less precocious than Hall. Many of his poems took for their subject his childhood relations with his parents, which seem to have been difficult in normal ways. In the 1970s he explored this subject in a verse biography of his father (*Dark Hours*, 1971) and a verse autobiography (*Half Remembered*, 1973); the latter especially was influenced in its frankness by the Confessional poetry of the 1960s. In subsequent volumes Davison has trusted to one of his first inspirations, Robert Frost, with whom he had a friendship in his youth, and has written about New England landscape and rural life with loving, Frostian craftsmanship, sensory vividness, and wit.

The early poetry of Thomas Merton (1915–68) and Donald Justice (b. 1925) was in the witty, neo-Metaphysical mode of the 1940s and 1950s. Justice, a professor of English literature, expressed a melancholy sense of life with formal spareness and control. "Ladies by Their Window" (in *The Summer Anniversaries*, 1960) is one of his best poems. More recently he has been influenced by Mark Strand. Merton, a Trappist monk, was better known for his prose writings than for his poetry. Though his verse is rather conventional, some lines are memorable, as, for example, when he observes that Greek women "Walk like reeds and talk like rivers." In the 1960s Merton's verse engaged social issues, and became satiric and declamatory.

Among the poets who, with Wilbur, maintain a civilized, sophisticated ethos are Howard Moss, David Ferry, J. V. Cunningham, Howard Nemerov, Anthony Hecht, and John Hollander. Moss (b. 1922) was for many years the poetry editor of the *New Yorker*, and his poetry is of the city both in its subject matter and its tone. His seriocomic verse may be represented in the final lines of "Horror Movie": "Make the blood flow, make the motive muddy:/ There's a little death in everybody." David Ferry (b. 1924) has published relatively few poems over the last twenty-five years. At his best he is a poet of subtle charm and perfectionist workmanship. His "The Unawkward Singers," for example, argues that man, unlike the birds, must sing clumsily, but itself sings like the birds for three stanzas until, in the final one, it deliberately stumbles—slightly and still gracefully—in order to prove its point. Forming his style especially out of Ransom and Stevens, Ferry gives short sketches and uses homemade myths of ironical simplicity. Many of his poems have an element of parody; more exactly, they imitate some sprightly, attractive type of poem of the Middle Ages or the Renaissance—pastoral, aubade, Petrarchan love lyric—while criticizing its emotional associations.

J. V. Cunningham (1911–85) was a university professor of English, versed in the literature of the Renaissance and in Latin. His poems are terse, formal, lucid, and definite. Their intelligence and skill are always admirable, but their power lies especially in their ruthlessness:

> After some years Bohemian came to this,
> This Maenad with hair down and gaping kiss
> Wild on the barren edge of under fifty
> She would finance his art if he were thrifty.

This is Roman satire and worthy of its models. The final lash—"if he were thrifty"—is typical.

Cunningham's poetry is, in one of its aspects, a protest against the age. Its attitudes are intended to be dramatic and exemplary, hard because the age is soft, unilluded because it is sentimental. It was with a somewhat similar intention, maybe, that Cunningham said he writes "verse" rather than poetry. He went on in this statement to locate his art within denotation, craftsmanship, shared experience, communicated meaning, and objective truth, as opposed, for example, to the spontaneous, private, vatic, or mystical. Because Yvor Winters championed Cunningham's work, and because also the two poets have similar values and repugnancies, readers have naturally associated them. Cunningham's fierce satire gives more joy from its intensity than anything in Winters, yet his moral definiteness, the indispensable base of his satire, is ultimately reductive. In his best poems, such as "Hymn in Adversity" and "To the Reader," he makes his more or less depressing observation and ends in questioning or in balanced ironies, not knowing what attitude to adopt.

Howard Nemerov (b. 1920) began his career under Modernist and New Critical influences. When like most of his contemporaries he changed his style in the 1960s, he adopted an ideal of relaxed, meditative speech and plain realism. The art of it lies in its clarity, subtle modulation, and unstressed suggestion, in short, in the combination of apparent ease and simplicity with depth of implication. "Vermeer" is an *ars poetica* for this phase of his career:

> Taking what is, and seeing it as it is,
> Pretending to no heroic stances or gestures
> Keeping it simple . . .

As a representative poem I may cite the well-known "A Day on the Big Branch." In this narrative some poker players drive north after an all-night game, and come in the morning to a "stream high in the hills." Symbolically they are returning to a source, seeking an oracle in the depths of nature, and they have to struggle toward it up "the giant stair of the stream," like Wordsworth climbing Mount Snowdon. Within the Romantic conventions the poem activates, a revelation is expected at the top. It comes and it doesn't. The middle-aged poker players are uncomfortable lying about on the rocks; the rocks are just "modern American rocks," and do not mean anything. But there are still sermons in stones, at least, there are vague intimations and examples. The stones endure, "weathering . . . being eroded, or broken," and they induce a stony peace in the poker players. They come to recognitions, inner settlements, resolves, which are that they will go on playing poker, and drinking, and smoking. Somehow they have accepted their lives as they are. Both the framework of Romantic convention and the stoic morality of endurance are typical of Nemerov.

Earlier in his career his poetry was more troubled and interesting. In *The Image and the Law* (1947) and *Guide to the Ruins* (1950) he was influenced by T. S. Eliot, and viewed the world as a waste land. By 1955, in *The Salt Garden*, Yeats had led him to a paradoxically positive ideal: the heroic, Romantic self rejoicing in its lonely strength to be ("A Song of Degree," "Phoenix"). Seagulls were powerful symbols of this ("The Lives of Gulls and Children," "The Gulls"). As natural creatures, the gulls were alien from the human and, though "majestic," they were also frighteningly cruel. Hence they could not be wholly positive symbols, yet in their strength of being they represented a hope against despair. *The Salt Garden* was Nemerov's finest book, for it expressed intense emotion and intellectual struggle.

Anthony Hecht was born in New York City in 1923, went to Bard College, and served in the army. He now teaches at the University of Rochester. In the complex stanzaic forms of his first book, *A Summoning of Stones* (1954), he leapt from rhyme to difficult rhyme like an acrobat. According to the convention of that time, such technical display was not for its own sake. Formal agility and control were outward symbols of the same qualities in intellect and feeling, as displayed in the rapid wit, for example, by which "La Condition Botanique" connects Finns in a sauna with plants in a hothouse, the hothouse with Eden, and its steam pipes with the snake. "The Gardens of the Villa d'Este" associates the "bounce/ Of sex" with a lark and with the famous fountains, for all are rising and aerated, as the erotic should be. Most of the other poems in this volume are similarly formal, musical, witty, and lightly serious.

Ten years later came *The Hard Hours* (1967). "Behold the Lilies of the Field" narrates torture. "Rites and Ceremonies" describes the persecutions of the Jews throughout history. These poems also explore the psychological effects of having watched or suffered such cruelties—the clinging horror and guilt, the broken will to live. In "It Out-Herods Herod. Pray You, Avoid It" the speaker's children view him as a hero. Yet at one time, he reflects, he could not have "saved them from the gas." The poems that lack such shocking materials are still somber.

> And between us there is—what?
> Love and constraint,
> conditions, conditions,
> and several hundred miles
> of billboards, filling stations,
> and little dripping gardens.

In this volume some poems still represented the mode of his first book, but for the most part his elaborations of form and wit were much subdued or avoided completely. His poems now relied on the facts they presented. The effort of his style was to make these vivid and precise. The book was a bitter, sustained indictment of God, man, and the world for being as the poems find them.

In its personal, emotional immediacy, moral intensity, and shock tactics *The Hard Hours* reflected general developments in American poetry in the 1960s. Hence the next book, *Millions of*

Strange Shadows (1977), was a surprise, for most of these poems returned to Hecht's first manner, though with a more controlled artistry. They are impersonal essays, with educated allusions, intricate stanzas, and cascades of witty comparison. *Venetian Vespers* (1979) is remarkable for its longish, narrative-meditative poems in blank verse. "The Short End" exhibits American life in its crass vulgarity, phoniness, and hopelessness. The title poem is also a depressing slice of American life, interesting for its story and its psychological insight. Apart from the painful facts they report, these poems are of a familiar, traditional kind.

John Hollander (b. 1929), an authority on English literature and prosody who teaches at Yale, also began as a poet of wit in the style of the 1950s. His skill in handling different meters and stanzas was dazzling, comparable to Auden's, and he proliferated learned puns. Such formality was not for its own sake, however, but expressed an ideal of cultivated civility ("Upon Apthorp House"). Here, again, Auden was perhaps an influence. Another strong influence came from Stevens, and both Auden and Stevens still appear occasionally in Hollander's work. "Green" (in *Spectral Emanations*, 1978), for example, alludes to both poets in its diction and to Stevens especially in its imagery. Yet Hollander's voice was distinctive, and may be described as rueful wit. He combined elegiac emotion with grace and poise, and his tone frequently bordered on the comic. As the years passed Hollander's formal skills did not increase, for he was already a master, but he extended his formal range and his thought and emotion deepened. Such poems as "Under Cancer" and "Kranich and Bach" meditatively elaborated a metaphor, Hollander managing the flowing modulation of his musing with rare delicacy. While retaining his artistic control, he has written in the last decade with new power. "After an Old Text," for example, a poem about jealousy, shocks with its emotional force, and *Spectral Emanations* is a long work of complex imaginative symbolism and prophecy.

With Hollander and Hecht we may associate Frederic Prokosch (b. 1908), Theodore Weiss (b. 1916), Richard Howard (b. 1929), X. J. Kennedy (b. 1929), and Frederick Seidel (b. 1936), learned poets of intricate formal skill. Weiss's long poems are his best. His subject is the plenitude and complexity of any object or moment of consciousness. Typical Weiss poems are "Caliban

Remembers" and *Gunsight* (1962), which presents the mentality of an etherized soldier. Howard has written witty and perfectly managed poems such as "The Return from Montauk" (in *Quantities*, 1962), recollections of childhood, occasional poems, and dramatic monologues, including one spoken by Robert Browning ("November, 1889" in *Findings*, 1971). He is also a wide-ranging critic of contemporary poetry. Many of his poems are connected with the theme of homosexuality. The formal control and impersonal distance of Seidel's poetry contrast chillingly with his subject matter of cruelty and madness, as in "The Heart Attack" and "The Sickness."

RANDALL JARRELL

The mature verse of Jarrell (1914–65) presents the lives and feelings of middle-class Americans by narratives, monologues, or other quasi-dramatic techniques. The style is plain, colloquial, and uncompressed, the states of awareness more moving than complex. As she looks into the mirror, the woman of "The Face" says,

> Not good any more, not beautiful—
> Not even young.
> This isn't mine.
> Where is the old one, the old ones?
> Those were mine.
>
> It's so: I have pictures . . .

"The monotone of these flat repetitive phrases," comments John Crowe Ransom, "makes for a powerful eloquence. The moment is so actual and prolonged, the theme so absolute and simple"; but, not surprisingly, Ransom prefers the earlier, denser "Death of the Ball Turret Gunner." (A ball turret, Jarrell explains in a note, was a "plexiglass sphere set into the belly" of a B-17 or B-24 bomber; it carried a "short, small man" who machine-gunned fighters attacking from below.)

> From my mother's sleep I fell into the State,
> And I hunched in its belly till my wet fur froze.
> Six miles from the earth, loosed from its dream of life,
> I woke to black flak and the nightmare fighters.
> When I died they washed me out of the turret with a hose.

A convention of war poetry—the vivid, shocking truth told to civilian readers—underlies the last line. Behind the rest of the poem, however, are Auden and Thomas and the period mode of concentration with complexity.

Like Tate and Warren, Jarrell came into the orbit of John Crowe Ransom as a student at Vanderbilt. Like Lowell, he followed Ransom to Kenyon College, where he taught English until moving to the University of Texas in Austin. During the war he served in the air force, though not as a pilot. By 1942 he had published two collections of poetry. The preface to the first (1940) confessed his wish and failure to replace Modernism with something else. At the air base he listened to the stories of pilots and read newspaper war reports, and out of these materials he composed, in *Little Friend, Little Friend* (1945) and *Losses* (1948), what remain for many readers the finest "war" poems of our time. They are vivid and moving incidents of combat, told with an exceptionally sensitive psychological insight and moral perplexity. And the emotions of Jarrell's pilots were in some ways unfamiliar in the literature of modern war. He expresses the pity and protest typical of the better poets in the First World War, the shock, horror, weary resignation, and sense of doom common in war poetry, but also a nexus of other feelings; they do not belong just to Jarrell (or to Auden, whose perceptions helped form Jarrell's in these poems), or just to the Second World War, but persist to the present moment. The planes have more reality, more identity than their crews ("A Front"). Enclosed in machines in remote sky, the pilots are psychologically detached from the deaths they distribute and fall toward. They are murderers who are likely themselves to be murdered, yet also passive, helpless, and innocent ("Eighth Air Force"). In short, in his pilots Jarrell expressed the feelings of alienation, helplessness, regression, irresponsibility, and vulnerability that our vastly unmanageable, bureaucratic, technological civilization seems to create.

With these poems Jarrell abandoned his former generalizing lyrics, and he never returned to them. When the war was no longer his theme, he more or less ceased to report vivid incidents, and his poetry henceforth tended to characterize people or to present them in dramatic monologues. His speakers, often women, have comfortable spouses, children, dogs, station wagons, electric toothbrushes, and safety deposit boxes, yet as they move in the supermarket "from Cheer to Joy, from Joy to All," anxieties assail them. Aging, death, and meaninglessness are not confronted, exactly, but vaguely acknowledged in a state of mind in which fears are partly faced and partly suppressed. Dramatic propriety compelled or at least tempted Jarrell to be a little prosy and verbose in these poems. But he had Auden's eye for the expressive, witty detail and some of Auden's gusto. He was full of insight and ironic fellow feeling, and in at least one of these portraits, "A Girl in a Library," he is witty and deeply moving.

He also wrote distinguished poems of dream, fantasy, and fairy tale, as may be seen in "Cinderella" or "The Black Swan." He learned German "durch Freud," as he punningly said, and made some splendid translations of Rilke and other German poets. Some of his poems based on works of art are·rather like Rilke's ("The Bronze David of Donatello"). Two nostalgic poems written toward the end of his life, "The Lost World" and "Thinking of the Lost World," explore memories of his childhood. Anxieties he had previously voiced in the monologues of invented characters were now confessed as his own.

> I hear a boy call, now that my beard's gray:
> "Santa Claus! Hi, Santa Claus!" It *is* miraculous
> To have the children call you Santa Claus.
> I wave back. When my hand drops to the wheel,
> It is brown and spotted, and its nails are ridged
> Like Mama's. Where's my own hand?

Meanwhile Jarrell had been publishing the brilliant reviews and essays that made him one of the most influential critics of his generation. He was far from the New Critics, however, for his essays lacked their theories and methods and his taste differed completely. Frost and Whitman were among his favorites. He spoke his likes and dislikes straight out freely from his liver, in the idiom of his beloved German, and the imaginative cruelty of his phrasing made him feared by other poets.

With Jarrell we may associate Delmore Schwartz (1913–66) and Louis Simpson (b. 1923). Schwartz is now remembered as much for his tragically self-destructive life as for his poetry. He brought out his first volume when he was twenty-five: *In Dreams Begin Responsibilities* (1938), a collection that included short stories as well as poems. In this work one sees already the virtues and limitations that continued through *Summer Knowledge* (1959). After this volume of selected poems Schwartz wrote little poetry, became increasingly dissatisfied with his work, wrestled with mental illness, drank heavily, and lived alone in a cheap New York hotel, where his body was found three days after his death from a heart attack. The causes of his tragic self-rejection are a subject for psychoanalysis rather than literary history, but difficulties in the historical situation, as Schwartz encountered it, may also be mentioned. Aspiring to be a great modern poet, he derived his interpretation of the modern world from literature. Inevitably, therefore, he found that his subject matter had already been represented by writers he greatly admired and could not hope to rival. Moreover, Schwartz believed that the "only life available to a man of culture" in our century is "the cultivation of his own sensibility, that is the only subject available to him." He later realized that this premise restricted his poetry, and tried through echo or parody (of Sir Edward Dyer, Christopher Marlowe, Wordsworth) to escape from the morass of subjectivity he feared. Influenced by Auden and other English contemporaries, Schwartz also sought to be a "thinking" poet; he hoped to present common experience with philosophical depth. Yet he was not a philosopher by natural talent, and his two years as a graduate student of philosophy instilled too high a standard, so that he lacked confidence in the quality of "thinking" he could express in poetry. Thus his poems were rejected by his own aspiring and self-divided conscience as a writer, and he became hesitant, now solemn and abstract, now conversational, too often merely flat. His stories, which he approached with less anxiety, are spritely and energetic in their satiric perception. They show us a Delmore Schwartz to whom his friends—however provoked by his paranoiac attacks in later years—have remained loyal. And a few lyrics—"In the Naked Bed, in Plato's Cave," for example, and "The Heavy Bear Who Goes with Me"—have entered the canon of modern poetry.

Louis Simpson grew up in Jamaica, served in the American army during the Second World War, took a Ph.D. in English at Columbia, and taught in universities in California and New York. His career took generally the same course as that of the other poets discussed in this chapter. In the 1950s he composed impersonal, detached poems in regular meters and stanzas. Among these a group of bitter poems on his war experience were especially memorable (for example, "Carentan O Carentan"). In the 1960s Simpson, like most poets, adopted free verse and a more personal voice, though he was not a Confessional poet. *At the End of the Open Road* (1963), which won the Pulitzer Prize, contrasted the urban, materialistic civilization of the United States with the ideal nation Whitman had prophesied. With the American involvement in Vietnam, Simpson's protest and critique became fiercer, like those of many other poets. Under the influence of Robert Bly, he shared the idealization of the primitive that was then common in American poetry (I describe it in Chapter 23 in connection with Bly, Galway Kinnell, and Gary Snyder), and he also flirted with Surrealism, though his statements in support of this style were more extreme than his practice. Since the 1970s Simpson's most interesting poems have depicted the ordinary lives of middle-class Americans, and may be compared with ones on the same subject by Jarrell and Reed Whittemore (b. 1919). Simpson's poems are narrative in form, but his purpose is not to generate suspense through story. Instead, he uses narrative form to organize incidents and characters that present a milieu and evoke an emotion. Chekhov, whose career and work are touched on in "Chocolates," may have helped Simpson to the conception of such poems. They are composed in quiet, unobtrusive language and verse, and depict their characters and settings with complete realism. The persons rendered have obvious spiritual limitations. They are routinely materialistic, plodding, vague in their thoughts, and somewhat apathetic in their emotions. Simpson's narrator sees all this and conveys it, yet generally his feeling seems less satiric than sympathetic or compassionate, as in Chekhov.

JOHN BERRYMAN

John Berryman (1914–72) was born in Oklahoma and grew up there and in Florida. He went to secondary school in Connecticut and then to Columbia, writing poems and reading voraciously. He devoured the Modernists; he liked the writers they liked, such as Pascal and Corbière; he bought all twenty-eight

back numbers of *Hound and Horn* to feast on the criticism of
Richard Blackmur; he hated Ruskin, Carlyle, and Wordsworth.
For a student in the middle of the 1930s all this was remarkably
au courant. Then and for the next ten years his poems were typical poems
of the young academic at the time—firm, packed, and carefully
finished, with meters, stanzas, correct diction, proper sentences,
meditated symbols, allusions, and generalizations. Without anything very vivid or individual, they conveyed by their styles an
emulative respect for predecessors and a loving craftsmanship.
The main single influence on him in these years was Yeats's poetry of reflective talk, which came upon him with a double impact because it was also picked up and transmitted by Auden,
whom Berryman greatly admired. Berryman's problem was, of
course, that

> I didn't want my next poem to be *exactly* like Yeats
> or exactly like Auden
> since in that case where the hell was *I*

—a question not to be answered for twenty-five years.

After Columbia Berryman studied at Clare College, Cambridge, where he didn't "do a damned thing but read and write."
He lived thenceforth by college teaching punctuated with years
on fellowships. By the 1950s he was an alcoholic. Seeking a cure,
he was in and out of psychoanalysis and sanitariums for the rest
of his life. He had three wives and many pre- and extra-marital
loves, of which at least one was important to the development of
his poetry.

By 1948 Berryman, having internalized the New Criticism as
a superego, was wearying of the self-examination and constriction he had imposed on himself. In a symposium on "The State
of American Writing" he said, "It is not clear that poetry *has*
benefitted from the intense concentration upon it of modern
criticism. There are things that you cannot see with a micro-
scope, for instance, you cannot see the sun." He was infatuated
in 1947 with an "excellent lady" his poems call "Lise," and he
proliferated sonnets. A sequence of love sonnets is the *ne plus
ultra* of the traditional and conventional. Moreover, as Berryman
described his joys, longings, guilts, and so forth, he invoked
Renaissance sonneteers. Petrarchan metaphors appear occa-

sionally; "Helen, and Isotta" are mere toys beside his girl. Yet the strong presence of a form and a tradition may have allowed Berryman to speak more intimately. That the poems were not written for publication may also have helped (they were not published until 1967 as *Berryman's Sonnets*). Whatever the explanations, the sonnets partially escaped from the academic style into life. Daiquiri-sloshing Lise, saying, "You'll give me ulcers if all this keeps up," is believable and present. The conscience throes of the homing poet, rehearsing more lies for his wife, are actual. Lise and her husband, Berryman and his wife, are "all four, marvelous friends—/ Some horse-shit here, eh?"; the comment is in the real world. As a poet Berryman was heading in the right direction for him. Writing in a talky style about his own immediate experience, he voiced stronger, more diverse and complicated emotions than he had previously, and he also presented character, episodes, and story.

HOMAGE TO MISTRESS BRADSTREET

In 1953 Berryman published another love poem, this one devoted to the first American poet, Anne Bradstreet (c. 1612–72). *Homage to Mistress Bradstreet*, which was republished as a book in 1956, includes dialogue between the modern poet and Bradstreet, but for the most part it is Bradstreet's monologue. Like the dramatic monologues of Browning, it is steeped in history, which it vividly recreates. The poem concentrates on the psychology of its protagonist—her repressions, ambivalences, fantasies, protests, and submissions—and conceives this also historically, that is, as a product and expression of her Puritan world. Its style is contorted, quirky, and mannered, but with vigor and strength.

Academic in style though it is, the poem has a resemblance to Ginsberg's *Howl* in that it explores psychological and spiritual states of an extreme kind. Anne's horrors and joys stun with their intensity; they are accompanied by grotesque upwellings of the unconscious in fantasies. The physical goings-on are no less vivid and unpleasant. Before the 1950s it was not common for poetry to mention such health problems as "vomitings, trots, rashes." The body is overwhelmingly present. Bradstreet reports her sensations in childbirth through sixteen lines; the catalogue of her smallpox symptoms goes on for five; Father "keeps his bed, / and threw a saffron scum Thursday . . . His stomach is cold." Sickness and starvation—"clams & acorns stomaching"—are dwelt on. Bradstreet ails, recovers to endure more hangnails and piles, ails again, and her "carcass" is eaten by worms. When Bradstreet bears her first baby, her touching pride centers in her body—"I did it with my body!" She is acutely conscious of her smallpox-"cratered" skin, silky breasts, and "ravendark" hair. "Brood I do on myself naked." The poem is so extremely mindful of the body partly because Berryman thought women are. (He studied *Anna Karenina* to learn how to portray a woman.)

The poem dramatizes the impact on Bradstreet of the repressive social and religious norms she internalized. But though it presents these and their workings in her psyche and life with credibility and power, the poem naturally does not share them. As a result we see Bradstreet as an unwitting victim of her Puritan world, her human potentialities in many ways suppressed and wasted. (But emphatically the poem does not think our world better.) The perspective of time in the poem suggests futility. Bradstreet's life, prototypical for everybody's, takes its course from youthful health and beauty, smallpox, marriage to her "so-much-older," unloved husband, settlement in America, householding, childrearing, loss of friends, illnesses, death. No pattern, meaning, or purpose emerges, and the end, of course, is a leaning headstone and then not even that. As the centuries run from hers to ours, she becomes all but lost in time, almost unknowable, irrecoverable. And the day will come, the poem concludes, when her world and ours will be equally "nothing." In her religion Bradstreet finds consolation and strength, yet the strength is mainly to renounce her desires, accepting suffering as punishment and submitting to the will of earthly and heavenly fathers. "Vanity & the follies of youth took hold of me," she remembers, and then, typically, "the pox blasted, when the Lord returned." The poem unsparingly shows her religious and moral fears expressing themselves in fantasies of hell:

> Father of lies,
> a male great pestle smashes
> small women swarming towards the mortar's rim in vain.

The lines come just after a brief, rebellious flirtation with sexual desire. Expressing her ambivalence, they associate Father with the Devil, yet the Devil with her brief temptation, a temptation immediately crushed and punished by the terror that rises from her unconscious. Along with all the other fears and fascinations it so obviously embodies, the image conveys her feelings about male power. "Torture me, Father, lest not I be thine!" she appallingly says. The futility and cruel waste is partly offset by Bradstreet's fulfillment in childrearing and by diffused emotions of achievement in surviving and making a home in the wilderness—the usual colonist theme.

But the portrait of the Founding Fathers flouts the popular myths of the last century. The poem does not dwell on their historical mission and meaning. Though Bradstreet mentions several friends, acquaintances, noted persons, events, and social changes over time, this larger, public world is just a blur in the background. The focus is so much on Bradstreet's feelings, psychology, and domestic doings that her life seems constricted, airless. The Indians are savage without being Romantically interesting. Pioneer heroism is not featured. There is no Thanksgiving turkey, for though this day of "glorious feasting" is once remembered, the poem does not develop feelings of bounty and gratitude. In accumulating details the poem builds a psychological portrait that seems intensely real, deep, original, and true. Yet if this were all, the poem despite its brilliance, would seem laborious and remote.

But in the central dialogue between the modern poet and Bradstreet the poem enters a different imaginative dimension. As the two talk across the centuries, we are in a scene that is no longer historical reconstruction but fantasy. We overhear a wooing, a strange, impossible, attempted seduction. Shy, tender, eager to reassure each other, the lovers approach, until the differences in their historical times and cultures prove too great and divide them.

Homage to Mistress Bradstreet was still an academic poem of the 1950s, but was striving to break away from this style. To write on the obscure, historical Bradstreet made the poem academic, and the formal versification, archaic diction, and contorted syntax supported this impression. But in identifying with a character, and in laboring to make her and her world seem real, Berryman was going beyond academic convention. His insistence on naturalistic physical details especially revealed his intention. He was not in pursuit of symbolisms but of life.

THE DREAM SONGS

In 1964 77 *Dream Songs* was published, and Berryman continued to write Dream Songs for the rest of his life. The final collection (1969) has 385 of these short poems; more are in manuscript. They are not especially dreamy or songlike, but just talk, sporadically rhymed, telling the thoughts and fantasies of a middle-aged "Henry." Each has three stanzas of six lines. Their topics are whatever suggested itself to Berryman that day, and the work as a whole has, as Berryman put it, "not a trace" of structure. The Dream Songs are emphatically a sequence in open form. The poems are composed out of recurrent materials—the same emotions, characters, memories—with which, after reading a bit, we familiarize ourselves. Gradually the world presented comes to seem more or less natural and one poem resonates to others. Their sequence builds long rhythms of emotions and rudiments of plot—plot especially toward the end, when Henry travels to Ireland. Otherwise there is no reason to start at the beginning or, except for pleasure, to read every poem.

The diction runs wild. No norm is preserved, and no generalization can be made except that Berryman uses any language that seems effective. Slang, archaisms, dialect (especially—with horrible taste—the black talk of the minstrel shows), poeticisms, lisps, baby talk, ampersands, illiteracies ("in all them time," "his baby borns"), laughs ("ha he"), ah's, O's, spoonerisms, and pig Latin intersperse in medley with ordinary colloquial or written English. Sometimes the highjinks have a particular function in their context; sometimes they merely signal a break-loose, slapdash state of mind. Many of the Dream Songs wholly lack such mannerisms.

Humor was not Bradstreet's forte, but the Dream Songs are comic. Henry is an antihero, feckless, vulnerable, guilt-ridden, and absurd:

> Henry rested, possessed of many pills
> & gin & whiskey. He put up his feet
> & switched on Schubert.
> His tranquillity lasted five minutes.

Even the indulged self-pity of the poems becomes acceptable as part of the comedy of our errors. The metaphors of Henry's trapped helplessness are appalling yet amusing—"He lay in the middle of the world, and twitcht." Energy of language and exuberance of imagination add to the comic effect throughout, and there are lots of gloomy jokes:

> What happen then, Mr. Bones?
> I had a most marvellous piece of luck. I died.

In other words, the mode is comic, but the substance, if abstracted, is woe. In poem after poem Henry inventories his state and finds it awful. We hear about his desperations, death wishes, sexual hungers, griefs, drunks, boredoms, follies, fractures, and so forth. The intimate disclosures of most people are depressing, but Henry's are more so. For Henry's are Berryman's. (To take Henry as Berryman is naive; not to do so would be more naive.) Moreover, the context of the Dream Songs is the Confessional utterance of the fifties and sixties. Like other Confessional speakers at this time—Ginsberg, Plath, Lowell, Sexton—Henry has food, shelter, and friends. His health is bad only from drinking. His pains are self-tormenting, the regrets, compulsions, reproaches with which we assail ourselves when nothing else assails us. Henry has a quarrel with God, also with the United States sometimes, but mainly his troubles are with his own psyche, tilted since childhood toward grief, guilt, and self-destruction. He sucks up occasions for these. (Hence, among other items, the numerous elegies on dead poets, including Frost, Roethke, Schwartz, and Jarrell.) For when Berryman (and Henry) was eleven, his father shot himself. The fact haunts him. As he contemplates his world, life, self, or spiritual state, he is implicitly or explicitly wrestling with suicide. "Mercy! my father," ends one poem,

> do not pull the trigger
> or all my life I'll suffer from your anger
> killing what you began.

The Dream Songs are uneven in quality, but mostly they have a texture of phrasing and bounce of imagination that reward reading. In the best, such as numbers 76 ("Nothing very bad happen to me lately") and 29 ("There sat down, once, a thing on Henry's heart") there is original fantasy, insight, compassion, and delicacy. These are Berryman's seldom-reached heights.

The poems in *Love and Fame* (1970) are autobiographical in form (but not, Berryman claimed, in fact) and sensationally explicit. Though they thus hold interest, they lack the wit and imagination of the Dream Songs, and represent ordinary life in an ordinary voice. Like much literature of our time, in other words, *Love and Fame* relies for its effect on the stark case it presents. The poet's mind does not act transformingly upon it, for that would be art, play, precisely what is being rejected as a betrayal of reality, a lie. And so the lines have impact without resonance. One could not get further away from the academic, metaphysical mode of Berryman's beginning.

Delusions, Etc. (1972) reflects Berryman's conversion in his last years; the poems wrestle with the Catholic God he had abandoned as a schoolboy. His last work (except for manuscripts culled and published by his executors) was *Recovery*, a prose account, fictionalized and unfinished, of his final struggle to overcome alcoholism and of his deep ambivalence in that struggle. The book is so insightful and articulate that it is appalling, wringing the heart with pity for the psychological trap he was in.

17

ROBERT LOWELL

ROBERT LOWELL (1917–77) came of the same Boston Brahmin family as Amy Lowell, who was his cousin—the relationship caused him some embarrassment. As a boy he nourished his imagination by reading the exploits of Napoleon and other conquerors, and these manic monsters, with their freedom from social controls and moral scruples, continued to fascinate him throughout his life. At St. Mark's School he acquired his lifelong nickname of "Cal." This was originally a shortened form of Caliban, a name his schoolmates gave him, but Lowell soon preferred to think of it as short for Caligula instead. In his final year at St. Mark's he resolved to become a poet. Harvard College, of which cousin A. Lawrence Lowell was president, was the inevitable choice, but after two years he transferred to Kenyon College in order to study under John Crowe Ransom.

In Lowell's first year at Kenyon he had Randall Jarrell as a roommate. The previous summer Lowell had descended as a vagabond student on Allen Tate, pitching a pup-tent on the Tates' lawn since there was no room in the house. After graduating from Kenyon College, he went for a year to Louisiana State University, where Robert Penn Warren and Cleanth Brooks were among his instructors. Thus by the time he was twenty-three,

Lowell had met and greatly impressed a number of persons—
Ransom, Tate, Jarrell, Warren, Brooks—who were or would be
prominent among the New Critics. He absorbed their values and
exemplified them in his poetry, and his reception was greatly
assisted by their influence on readers.

At Harvard Lowell had worked on an epic dealing with the
First Crusade, but Robert Frost, on reading it, had told him,
"You have no compression." He had studied Eliot, Pound, and
Williams, learning to produce vivid images in free verse. At Kenyon he took the advice of Ransom to major in Classics. He also
read Hart Crane, Dylan Thomas, Allen Tate, and William Empson's *Seven Types of Ambiguity*, and each poem he composed, as he
later recalled, "was more difficult than the one before, and had
more ambiguities." Ransom, who thought these undergraduate
poems clotted and forbidding, accepted only two of them for
the *Kenyon Review*.

In 1940 Lowell married the writer Jean Stafford. After their
year at Louisiana State the Lowells lived briefly in New York City,
and then spent the winter of 1942–43 with the Tates in Tennessee. Since Caroline Tate was also a writer, at least four books
were in progress in the house, and Lowell was additionally making notes for a biography of Jonathan Edwards. Both he and
Tate studied sixteenth- and seventeenth-century poetry. At this
time Lowell composed most of the poems in his first book, *Land
of Unlikeness* (1943). When the United States entered the Second
World War, Lowell tried to enlist, but by August 1943, when he
was called for induction, he was a conscientious objector. He
expressed his refusal to serve in a public statement, and was
sentenced to prison, where he served four months. In 1948 his
first marriage ended in mutual misery and divorce, and a year
later he married Elizabeth Hardwick.

Meanwhile in 1941 Lowell had converted to Roman Catholicism. In the next several years his poems were heavily charged
with Christian myth and symbol, and expressed a mind appalled
at the world's evil and in pursuit of the transcendent. To join the
church of Boston's immigrants was an act of family rebellion—
one of several such rebellions in his early life—and the clash of
proper Boston's Protestant ethos against that of the Irish Catholics became a theme of Lowell's poetry. Lowell's conversion followed upon hard reading and thinking, and his motivations

were not modish, yet a historian may note that both Lowell's vision of evil and his conversion were in keeping with a trend among intellectuals in the 1940s. Lowell's faith gradually waned, and in "Beyond the Alps," the first poem in *Life Studies*, he abjured. After roughly 1950 God no longer existed in Lowell's universe, though he sometimes mentioned Him unfavorably.

The publication of *Lord Weary's Castle* in 1946 forever established Lowell's reputation. The volume included such famous poems as "After the Surprising Conversions" and "The Quaker Graveyard in Nantucket." In the latter poem Lowell aspired to rival Milton's "Lycidas," and to many of his readers he seemed almost to have done so. After *Lord Weary's Castle* Lowell's eminence among American poets of his generation was acknowledged, though some readers in the rebellious 1960s associated him with the Establishment and rejected him accordingly.

In 1949 Lowell was placed in a mental institution, where he spent three months. The diagnosis was manic-depressive illness. It was the first episode in what was to become an almost annual occurrence, causing enormous anxiety and suffering to himself, his family, and his friends. He always eventually recovered from these attacks, but they were preceded by weeks or months of uneasiness as his behavior began to seem erratic, and the manic phases of breakdown could be dreadful. Even when Lowell was relatively well, he was subject to sudden rages, obsessions, and confusions of subjective fantasy with reality, and so was led into actions that subsequently caused him acute remorse, for his feeling of guilt was in proportion to his imagination and sensitivity. From his experience of manic egoism, obsessional craving, paranoia, and remorse his poetry derived much of its moral authority, for his insight into evil was clear and anguished, and he could not view it as merely external to himself.

Henceforth Lowell's life followed more or less the same course from year to year. He taught at Boston University and then at Harvard, had love affairs, traveled, and wrote. His reputation was increased further by *Life Studies* (1959), in which he created a new, more accessible style, and was sustained by two more brilliant volumes in the 1960s, *For the Union Dead* (1964) and *Near the Ocean* (1967). Lowell actively opposed the war in Vietnam, and supported Eugene McCarthy in his 1967–68 primary campaign for the Democratic presidential nomination. He made friends with McCarthy and speeches in his favor. Many of the poems in *Notebook 1967–68* (1969, revised 1970), a collection of fourteen-liners in a personal, relatively spontaneous style, expressed his political perceptions and experiences.

The notebook genre was much favored by American poets in the 1960s, and Lowell turned out three more such volumes. *History* (1973) rearranged and revised the poems in *Notebook* on public or historical subjects. *For Lizzie and Harriet* (1973), dedicated to his wife and daughter, contained similarly redone poems from *Notebook* dealing with Lowell's personal life, and *The Dolphin* (1973) reflected his affair in England with Caroline Blackwood, his divorce from Elizabeth Hardwick, whose letters to him are quoted in some of the poems, his marriage to Blackwood, and his waverings about these steps. His final volume, *Day by Day* (1977), is filled with memories, not always nostalgic, of his past life and with present thoughts of death. Death had always obsessed him, but now he contemplated it with a flat, moving weariness:

> Tortoise and hare
> cross the same finishing line—
> we learn the spirit is very willing to give up,
> but the body is not weak and will not die.

While returning from England to visit Hardwick, Lowell died of a heart attack in a taxi driving from Kennedy Airport.

STYLE AS "HARDSHIP"

Until the publication of *Life Studies* in 1959, Lowell was and saw himself as a strict formalist in the New Critical mode. As he later put it, speaking of himself and Allen Tate in 1942–43, poets of this type wanted their "formal patterns to seem a hardship." Lowell and Tate wove many "formal patterns" at once: logical statement, grammatical syntax, integrated and counterpointed strands of metaphor and symbol, shapely plot, emotional climax, strict meter and rhyme, and alliteration and assonance. They made their poems compressed, complex, and ironic. Influenced by the Metaphysical poets of the seventeenth century, they were witty, punning, and paradoxical. The speaker in their poetry was a "persona," and was not to be confused with the poet, and the subject matter did not reveal or necessarily arise from the poet's life. The "hardship" was felt by the poet in composing and by the reader in appreciating the poem, for the style imposed minute, conscious attention to nuances, and had to be achieved slowly with innumerable revisions. The style was, as John Berryman said in 1948, the "natural product of an elaborate, scrupulous and respected literary criticism." Lowell's poetry in *Land of Unlikeness* and *Lord Weary's Castle* illustrates this dominant American mode of the 1940s and 1950s. Though he rebelled against his parents, he was docile to his fathers in verse.

Nevertheless, a comparison of Lowell to other New Critical poets of this period, such as Hecht and Wilbur, reveals striking differences. Lowell had an ambitious grandeur of intention. His prophetic denunciations, wrestlings with God, and attempts at mystical vision were altogether foreign to the poised, elegant, quasi-popular style of Wilbur and Hecht. Lowell's verses had frequent spondees and caesuras yet were strongly enjambed, with an effect of energy blocking itself and suddenly exploding. His images were violent, telescoped, and bristling with ambivalent implications; transitions between them were sudden or seemingly nonexistent; meanings were difficult and sometimes impenetrable; yet in the clotted awkwardness there was intellectual strength. For many readers Lowell's intensity and force redeemed contemporary poetry. If he was a bull in a china shop, he was also a whale among minnows. And the sound and rhythm of his lines had sometimes, as in Part V of "The Quaker Graveyard in Nantucket," an old-fashioned elevation for which readers secretly yearned:

> When the whale's viscera go and the roll
> Of its corruption overruns this world
> Beyond tree-swept Nantucket and Wood's Hole
> And Martha's Vineyard, Sailor, will your sword
> Whistle and fall and sink into the fat?

Lowell created out of his native Boston a world of his own, visionary and damned. Eliot's *The Waste Land* had expressed the present and past life of a modern city and also Eliot's own despair, conflating a historical, sociological, and personal vision, and Lowell's poems had the same multiple dimensions. In Lowell's Boston the season is usually winter, the colors gray, white, and black. Cold grips the trees, the houses, and even the gravestones. Men and women prey on one another, and death preys on them. Love is adultery or incest, obsession and guilt. Mammon rules. Even the "bread-stuffed ducks" of the Public Garden are images of dull greed. Allusions to New England's Puritan past recur frequently, but the past was not better than the present, for it was a demon-ridden time of manic violence: "Our fathers . . . fenced their gardens with the Redman's bones." Though a Roman Catholic, Lowell expressed himself through the Calvinist theology of the Puritans, especially the Puritan insistence on the rooted evil of the heart and on God's incalculable will. Against God human beings are like spiders thrown into a fire or blown out to sea. The latter illustrations are taken from "Mr. Edwards and the Spider." Another remarkable poem spoken by Jonathan Edwards, "After the Surprising Conversions," tells of God withdrawing from the land: "At Jehovah's nod/ Satan seemed more let loose amongst us: God/ Abandoned us to Satan." Lowell also dwelled on Edwards' fascination with madness, torture, and death. Within or beyond Lowell's Boston there was a realm of transcendence, inhabited by fabulous beings of classical or Christian myth—God, Christ, Mary, Satan, Morpheus, Charon—and the poems shifted suddenly from the naturalistic to the mythical planes of reference. In Part IV of "In Memory of Arthur Winslow" (Lowell's grandfather) Trinity Church in Boston's Copley Square sinks like Atlantis and knocks "the Devil's teeth out by the roots." In the same poem the ghost of Jesus arrives walking the waves, and conducts Arthur Winslow "Beyond Charles River"(which runs through Boston) "to the Acheron." Thoughts of the Second Coming and the Last Judgment pervade the poems, but there is no apocalypse.

In later years Lowell's vision of the world did not change fundamentally, but the dimension of transcendence was largely absent from his poetry and so was the machinery of Christian myth. In some poems of the 1950s nuclear holocaust tended to fill the role formerly assigned to the Last Judgment, but as time passed Lowell increasingly rejected the idea that history could have any finality, much less teleology. *History*, Lowell's most extended statement on the subject, focused on mania, egoism, obsession, lust, conquest, dominance, violence, cruelty, servility,

greed, corruption, and suffering from the ancient world to the
present day. Throughout history no advance had taken place,
and Lowell hoped for none in the future. As Lowell wrote in the
conclusion to "Waking Early Sunday Morning," wars

> flicker, earth licks its open sores,
> fresh breakage, fresh promotions, chance
> assassinations, no advance.
> . . . .
> Pity the planet, all joy gone
> From this sweet volcanic cone;
> peace to our children when they fall
> in small war on the heels of small
> war—until the end of time.

The same vision of things interpreted personal and domestic
life. Lowell had and expressed much humor, tenderness, and
kindness, and he was grateful for these qualities in others. But
he also understood that human beings can be monsters even—
or especially—to their spouses, children, and friends. Dino-
saurs, newts, turtles, and the like are frequent in Lowell's poetry.
For him such stupid creatures, all egoism, appetite, and awkwardness, image much of human nature. A skunk is ambigu-
ously the hero in the final poem of Life Studies, "Skunk Hour."

LIFE STUDIES

With Life Studies (1959) Lowell created a style that was widely
influential on other poets. For poetry of this type the critic M. L.
Rosenthal found the epithet "Confessional"; it indicates a poetry
in which the expression is personal, or is conventionally accepted as personal, and reveals experiences or emotions that are
more or less shocking—hatred of one's parents, children,
spouse, or self, lust, voyeurism, suicidal fantasies, madness. Beat
poetry, such as Allen Ginsberg's Howl (1956), was Confessional
before Lowell, and had an impact on him. But the Beats intended to transvalue values; if a reader was shocked by their
writings, the Beats assumed that he or she was morally constricted. Lowell had also been impressed by the drab honesty of
Philip Larkin in personal poems about depressed spirits and sex-

ual apathy. Larkin presented himself and his experience as completely ordinary, and Lowell was struck by the same stance in *Heart's Needle* (1959) by William Snodgrass (b. 1926), which Lowell read in manuscript. The title sequence presented Snodgrass' feelings in his divorce and remarriage, and everyday incidents—for example, the parents lifting their small child over a puddle—were filled with complicated, painful tensions. Lowell especially admired Snodgrass' artistic control in handling this material. "Other poems that are direct that way are slack," Lowell said, "and have no vibrance. [Snodgrass'] experience wouldn't be so interesting and valid if it weren't for the whimsy, the music, the balance, everything revised and placed and pondered. All that gives light to those poems on agonizing subjects comes from the craft."

In *Life Studies* Lowell the rigorous formalist used free verse. According to Lowell, this change was motivated, in part, by reading his poems aloud. "I went on a trip to the West Coast [in 1957] and read at least once a day and sometimes twice for fourteen days, and more and more I found that I was simplifying my poems. If I had a Latin quotation I'd translate it into English. If adding a couple of syllables in a line made it clearer I'd add them, and I'd make little changes impromptu as I read." Moreover, in these poems on his personal life an illusion of sincerity was necessary. "If a poem is autobiographical," Lowell later explained, "you want the reader to say, this is true." He had started several of the poems in *Life Studies* "in very strict meter, and I found that . . . regularity just seemed to ruin the honesty of sentiment, and became rhetorical; it said, 'I'm a poem'"; "there was always that standard of truth which you wouldn't ordinarily have in poetry—the reader was to believe he was getting the *real* Robert Lowell."

Life Studies had still another inception in autobiographical prose Lowell began to write in 1955. Working on this, he developed the subject matter of his famous volume. Moreover, strengths we associate more with prose—narrative, description of milieu, characterization of persons—support his poetry in *Life Studies*. Yet Lowell owed these strengths partly to the poetry of Elizabeth Bishop, whose quiet flow of realistic, unobtrusive, metonymical detail he greatly admired.

Thus the boldly direct poetry of the Beats in California, the

vogue of William Carlos Williams, the dreary, personal truth of
Larkin and the Movement poets in England, and friendship with
Bishop all tended in the 1950s to shake Lowell's former allegiance to New Critical ideals of poetry. But also Lowell was sensitive to the widespread reaction against New Critical formalism
because he shared the feelings that motivated it. He had spent
fifteen years packing strict meters with symbolism and wit, and
he felt that such poetry had become academic, "Alexandrian,"
and too easy to write. "Poets of my generation," he said in 1961,
"and particularly younger ones have gotten terribly proficient"
at writing "a very musical, difficult poem with tremendous skill
. . . Yet the writing seems divorced from culture" and "can't
handle much experience. It's become a craft, purely a craft, and
there must be some breakthrough back into life." After the long
prevalence of a type of poem Lowell described as "a symbol on
a hatrack," he, like most American poets in 1959, was ready for
"human richness."

Nevertheless, Lowell thought the poetry of the Beats undisciplined. And though he spoke admiringly to and of William
Carlos Williams, he thought him "dangerous and difficult to imitate"; the poetry of his disciples was slack. In short, the winds
of poetic liberation carried Lowell toward the direct, personal,
and immediate, but he also maintained his former stylistic values, and whoever studies the poems in *Life Studies* will find that
beneath their accessible surface they are packed, witty, intellectually demanding, and rigorously crafted.

All the poems in this volume have a remarkable vitality, brilliance of phrase, and speed in presentation, and they all characterize, that is, they present characters. But the greatest impression was made by the poems in Part IV, itself subtitled "Life
Studies," in which Lowell wrote autobiographically and "confes-
sionally." These express horror and fascination with death, sexual restlessness, infantile regressions ("Grandpa! Have me, hold
me, cherish me!"), suicidal impulses, and fear of madness, and
they are often harrowing. One tragicomic poem, "Waking in the
Blue," presents Lowell in an insane asylum. Yet readers must
cherish views of human nature more ideal than my own if they
find these poems very shocking. They "confess" no grand crimes
or horrors. Instead, they illustrate the irrational, graceless, grotesque sides of the psyche and of life—how, for example, Lowell

liked to watch at night the lovers in their parked cars, or how when his mother died in Italy, her body was brought back to the United States wrapped in tinfoil like a cake. And though such passages are painful, others shade toward humor, as when Lowell remembers how in his adolescence he and his mother would sit up late at night "with unadulterated joy . . . rehashing Father's character" ("During Fever"); or how when he first met his future wife he was "too boiled and shy / and poker-faced to make a pass" ("Man and Wife"). The start of this poem, which describes the morning after a night passed in marital yammering, has superb comic energy:

> Tamed by *Miltown*, we lie on Mother's bed;
> the rising sun in war paint dyes us red;
> in broad daylight her gilded bed-posts shine,
> abandoned, almost Dionysian.

A political-historical theme runs through "Life Studies." One recurrent metaphor associates the world of Lowell's grandparents and parents with the *ancien régime*, formal, formidable, and gone, and the young Lowell with the revolutionary Napoleon. Another system of metaphors expresses within personal and family history the drift of American historical experience. Like Lowell's earlier lyrics these autobiographical poems are also sociological and historical in their themes. We see this most obviously in "Memories of West Street and Lepke." Here Lowell describes the jail in which he was briefly incarcerated during the Second World War, and the jail becomes an image of the United States in the 1950s. Abramowitz, a pacifist and intellectual prisoner, "so vegetarian,/ he wore rope shoes and preferred fallen fruit," represents the radical tradition of the United States become ineffectual. The "Hollywood pimps" Bioff and Brown correspond to the "suburban" middle class, and the pinnacle of society is occupied by the big businessman, Lepke, czar of *Murder Incorporated*. Lepke's "little segregated cell" is "full of things forbidden the common man." Awaiting execution, Lepke drifts "in a sheepish calm," and no "agonizing reappraisal" jars "his concentration on the electric chair." His existence is the more empty and aimless because of his fear of death, yet the electric chair is an "oasis in his air/ of lost connections." "Agonizing reappraisal" was John Foster Dulles' phrase in threatening as Secretary of

State to use nuclear bombs. The allusion suggests that American society is "lobotomized" like Lepke and waiting, even unconsciously wishing, for extinction. An "air/ of lost connections" hangs over all the characters in the poem. "The man/ scavenging filth in the back alley trash cans" is not poor but insane. He has a beach wagon, two children, and "a helpmate," and is a "young Republican." Lowell, as he presents himself in the poem, is, like Lepke, well-off and "tranquillized."

LOWELL'S LATER CAREER

A number of American poets took an initiative from *Life Studies*—Sylvia Plath, Anne Sexton, Adrienne Rich, and, among younger poets, Diane Wakoski, Louise Glück (in her first volume), Frank Bidart, Richard Tillinghast, and Alan Williamson. But Lowell himself did not continue in this style. The personal lyrics in *For the Union Dead* (1964) generally lack the full, circumstantial detail and the narration of *Life Studies*. The title poem, however, may be the supreme poem of Lowell's career. Composed between January and June in 1960, "For the Union Dead" meditates upon the statue of Colonel Robert Gould Shaw, who led a regiment of black infantry in the Civil War and died with his troops in South Carolina. The poem contrasts the twentieth and nineteenth centuries, and also interrelates historical with psychic realities. The nuclear bombing of Hiroshima, for example, expressed regressive and destructive impulses the speaker knows in himself. As a child his hand tingled to burst the bubbles and break the tanks of the fish in the Boston Aquarium, and he still longs for this. The poem closes with a memorable image of the contemporary United States:

> Everywhere,
> giant finned cars nose forward like fish;
> a savage servility
> slides by on grease.

A humanity so materialistic, regressive, cowed, and self-hating is riding on a bubble it will soon break.

Many of the poems in *For the Union Dead* were in short lines and stanzas, sometimes with rhymes. Lowell's return to formal meters continued in *Near the Ocean* (1967), where most of the poems were in rhymed, tetrameter stanzas. The great poems in this collection were "Waking Early Sunday Morning," from which I quoted earlier, and the translation of Juvenal's Tenth Satire, to which Lowell gave the title used by Samuel Johnson in his translation, "The Vanity of Human Wishes." In Lowell's translation Juvenal is less mournful and pious than in Johnson's, and life in Rome is much more corrupt, brutal, and cruel. Other translations and allusions in *Near the Ocean,* together with the neoclassic formality of style in this volume, further suggest a comparison of Lowell's to Roman poetry and of the contemporary United States to the Roman empire. Indeed, in *Lord Weary's Castle* Lowell had formed his style on the Roman classics as well as on Eliot, Crane, and Tate, and Roman poetry continued to influence him throughout his career. It supported both the harsh realism of his vision and the formal integrity and weight of his verse line.

In the 1960s the notebook genre flourished in the United States, as I mentioned earlier; the aesthetic theories that motivated these notebook poems are discussed in Chapter 21, "Open Form." That a former disciple of the New Criticism should have shared these theories shows the power of the *Zeitgeist,* but Lowell never accepted them completely. His *Notebook 1967–68* (1969) and the volumes that evolved out of it—the revised *Notebook* (1970), *History* (1973), *For Lizzie and Harriet* (1973), *The Dolphin* (1973)—are much less like genuine notebooks than are sequences written in the same period by Robert Creeley, Denise Levertov, A. R. Ammons, and Robert Duncan. The entries in Lowell's Notebooks are unrhymed sonnets, and the texture of Lowell's phrasing is packed, ambiguous, and difficult. Yet inspired partly by competitive alarm at John Berryman's Dream Songs (1964 and later years), Lowell wrote his sonnets rapidly. He knew that "breathing in/ my life" and "breathing out/ poems" (to quote Denise Levertov) is a recipe for the second-rate. He understood that in poetry "life" must be an illusion produced by art. Nevertheless, he thought a mass of unperfected writing might generate a greater cumulative power than a smaller, more unified volume of finer work. Like every creator of a poetic heap since Pound, he hoped that recurrent themes might transform the heap into a whole. And he trusted that to write more spontaneously would help him rival Berryman's random, unpredictable vigor of talk and his wide range and sudden shifts of emotion. "I wished," Lowell said, "to describe the immediate instant." Lowell's risks were not rewarded. His Notebook poems are less brilliantly sustained and finished than his earlier work, yet are too indirect to create a strong human interest. They are very uneven. Among the best—and they are wonderful—from *Notebook 1967–68* are "Long Summer" 1 and 3; "Mexico" 1 and 6; "Robert Frost"; the last six lines of "February and March: 12. First Spring"; "April 8, 1968: 3. The Petit Bourgeois"; "Power: 2. Attila"; "April's End: 2. Night-sweat"; and "April's End. 3. Caligula"; and from *The Dolphin*, "Mermaid" and "Flight to New York" 11 and 12, both entitled "Christmas."

When he revised and rearranged the poems in *Notebook 1967–68* in order to produce *History* and *For Lizzie and Harriet*, Lowell almost invariably improved. Moreoever, these volumes are more interesting because their subject matter is more unified, though they retreat in this respect from the Notebook concept. The personal poems in these volumes (and in *The Dolphin*) refer to circumstances they do not fully narrate, and it helps in reading them to know the details of Lowell's biography. With *The Dolphin*, in which Lowell's writing was even more relaxed than in *Notebook 1967–68*, his five-year experiment with sonnet sequences ended. From *Notebook 1967–68* on, even in his love poems, Lowell had maintained the unsparing, naturalistic vision that impressed him in the poets of ancient Rome. Prominent among his themes were aging sexuality, failing health, fear of death, politics and their psychological motivations, the horrors and ambivalent joys of the psychopathic, rueful shame and pride in leathery survival, memories of youth, and tributes to old friends and loves.

The poems in Lowell's final volume, *Day by Day*, continue these themes, but, as Helen Vendler has pointed out, his way of experiencing was now somewhat different. The lack of a teleological perspective, which had long characterized Lowell's view of history, was now carried over into his sense of personal life. Since early in the 1950s he had not related his experience to a final cause. But his earlier poems on personal life had assumed that the past leads to the present and the present to a future. *Life Studies* had traced the adult self back to the child; *The Dolphin* had shown Lowell wavering between different possible futures. In other words, events in Lowell's earlier volumes connected with one another; moreover, he assumed that he knew what the events were—what had happened. In Lowell's last volume he questioned these assumptions. Many of the poems are dramas of the poet trying to connect events with one another and understand them, but unable to do so. Hence also they show a wish to take experiences one at a time, to perceive each only for itself. The disconnected immediacy of the Notebook has, so to speak, ceased to be a literary form and become, instead, a way of living. In contrast to Lowell's poetry in the 1940s, in which the historical and the transcendent grandly impinged on the present moment, his final poems attempted, as he put it in "Epilogue," only to "say what happened" and

> to give
> each figure in the photograph
> his living name.

The poems of *Day by Day* are retrospective and elegiac, with vivid perceptions of life's swift transition. "We are things thrown in the air/ alive in flight"; we are "like ears of corn . . . green, sweet, golden, black." Lowell's marriage with Caroline Blackwood has failed:

> seven years, now nothing but a diverting smile,
> dalliance by a river, a speeding swan . . .
> the misleading promise
> to last with joy as long as our bodies,
> nostalgia pulverized by thought,
> nomadic as yesterday's whirling snow,
> all whiteness splotched.

Waiting for death, he is appalled by life but still hungry for it:

> Dividing the minute we cannot prolong,
> I stand swaying at the end of the party,
> a half-filled glass in each hand—
> I too swayed
> by the hard infatuate wind of love.

18

IN AND OUT OF THE MOVEMENT: THE
GENERATION OF THE 1950s IN ENGLAND

IN the 1950s contemporary English poetry reacted strongly against the neo-Romantic mode of the war years. Among the poets who first obtained recognition in this decade, a few—Dannie Abse, Thomas Blackburn, David Wright—seemed to continue the Romantic vein, but more and better poets, such as Roy Fuller, Philip Larkin, Donald Davie, and C. H. Sisson, were hostile to it. It is often said that the anti-Romantic developments in poetry expressed a fatigue and disillusion in the aftermath of the Second World War. The "post-war mood," Ted Hughes once explained, was

of having had enough . . . enough rhetoric, enough overweening push of any kind, enough of the dark gods, enough of the id, enough of the Angelic powers and the heroic efforts to make new worlds. They'd seen it all turn into death camps and atom bombs. All they wanted was to get back into civvies and get home to the wife and kids and for the rest of their lives not a thing was going to interfere with a nice cigarette and a nice view of the park. . . . It was an heroic position. They were like eskimos in their igloo . . . They'd had enough sleeping out.

This interpretation is attractively sympathetic to the poets and has some validity, but essentially it superimposes cultural memories of the First World War and its aftermath upon the more complicated attitudes that prevailed during the next war. The varieties of emotional and spiritual "push" Hughes mentions certainly flourished in poetry written during the Second World War, but from start to finish there was also a mood of realistic disenchantment, especially among the soldier poets. In the immediate postwar period Dachau and Hiroshima affected English poets strongly, yet the impact of these horrors on sensibility was less than that of the Labourite revolution. Poets favored this revolution, but the social transformation was too peaceful, many-sided, and far-reaching to evoke any simple attitude or emotion, and the frame of mind of most poets was critically reflective, not only with respect to the social changes but pervasively in personal life. They were morally concerned in an intense degree, examined their experience with striking honesty, and typically articulated judgments that were complex and empirical.

The 1950s were the heyday of the so-called Movement. The poets included in this group were Kingsley Amis, Donald Davie, Robert Conquest, Philip Larkin, John Wain, Elizabeth Jennings, John Holloway, D. J. Enright, and Thom Gunn; collectively they were said to represent English poetry and even the contemporary English soul. The critical invention of the Movement gave these poets instant prominence. It long influenced the way they were interpreted. And the effort to characterize the poetry of the Movement gave the poets involved a clearer sense of their own values and aims, the more so since many of them were also critics and provided the characterizations. For these reasons literary history cannot ignore the Movement. But as with many other such events in the arts, the grouping was half accidental. Whatever generalizations are true for the Movement poets are also true for most of the other emerging English poets of the 1950s, even though they happened not to be numbered in the Movement. For example, in 1957 Dannie Abse and Howard Sargeant, reacting against the Movement anthologies, tried to produce a rival anthology representing different poets and an alternative tendency, but no one saw much difference between the poetry in Abse's anthology, *Mavericks,* and that in the Movement ones.

A literary undergraduate at Cambridge or Oxford around 1950 concentrated on masterpieces of English literature from *Beowulf* through Chaucer and Shakespeare to the close of the nineteenth century; probably he also read in French and the classics. Modern poetry figured little in the curriculum, but a student might explore it on his own, rejoicing especially in Yeats. Except for Eliot and whatever was found in anthologies, modern American poetry was seldom read. In fact, the books of Wallace Stevens, Marianne Moore, and William Carlos Williams were still hard to obtain in England. When Pound's *Pisan Cantos* were published in England in 1949, their stature was not recognized and university students seldom encountered them. So far as the dons gave any guidance on how to write, the Metaphysical mode was recommended. Inevitably students were exposed to Dylan Thomas, whose readings resounded over the BBC. If they were at Cambridge, they attended the lectures of F. R. Leavis. Even if they did not become disciples, they were impressed by his conviction of the importance of literature and criticism, his attacks on Romanticism, and his close analysis of texts. When student poets imagined Leavis examining their own poems, they shuddered and revised.

On leaving the university and starting gradually to publish, review, and establish contacts with other poets, their attention was magnetized, as always happens, to the poets of just preceding generations, against whom they had to establish their own identities. In the early 1950s most phases of the modern movement in English poetry were not as yet merely history. Among those which had died out were the Impressionist-Symbolist-Formalist style of the 1890s and Imagism. The latter had been Anglo-American in its inception, but had made its impact and career chiefly in the United States. The high Modernist mode of Eliot and Pound was past and yet overwhelmingly present. It had seldom been closely imitated in England, but Eliot had enormous prestige. The rhythms, diction, and themes of his *Four Quartets,* just completed in 1942, were still echoed. Everyone was waiting for his next great poem.

More recent period styles were still thriving in the 1950s. Metaphysical "wit" was sometimes present in Thomas and was prominent in the newly appreciated Graves and Empson, though the looser, seemingly more casual verse Empson had published in 1940 appealed more at this time than his earlier work. The academic vogue of Donne continued. In the 1950s the "thirties" poets, such as Day-Lewis, MacNeice, Spender, John

Lehmann, and Ruthven Todd, were middle aged; they had modified or abandoned the period style of the 1930s, but most of them brought out a volume of poems every two or three years. To their contemporaries Eliot, Empson, Auden, and their respective followers had seemed dryly intellectual; readers delighted in their work, but also hungered for a more directly emotional utterance. They had found this in Yeats, and among living poets in the 1950s they still found it in Thomas, Edwin Muir, David Gascoyne, Kathleen Raine, Vernon Watkins, George Barker, and Edith Sitwell (in her poems written after 1942). All these poets presented dreams, visions, or archetypes and assumed the grand role of the poet as vates or seer. By the war years these poets were generally characterized as Romantic, and so were a number of other poets who wrote on the basis of nineteenth-century styles almost as though the modern movement had never taken place. These included older survivors, such as Andrew Young, poets now in midlife such as Roy Campbell, and such newer poets as John Heath-Stubbs. And Lawrence Durrell, Bernard Spencer, F. T. Prince, William Plomer, John Betjeman, and Stevie Smith were also highly visible and active in the 1950s.

With so many poets on the scene already, it might seem there was no need for a new generation. This was not the opinion, however, of the younger poets. Though they attacked mainly the "Romantics" in reviews and articles, in their hearts they might reject most of the modern styles, not only that of Thomas but also those of Eliot, Yeats, the Metaphysical revival, or Auden.

THE MOVEMENT

The term "The Movement" comes from an article written in 1954 by J. D. Scott, the literary editor of the *Spectator.* Scott described a new trend in contemporary English poetry, which, half-jokingly, he called The Movement. The sense of a new development was widely shared, and the name caught on. The neo-Romantic mode was giving way to something radically different. Remarks on this had previously been made in various journals, and illustrative readings had been broadcast over the BBC Third Programme. In 1955 an anthology edited by D. J.

Enright, *Poets of the 1950s*, contained work by Enright, Kingsley Amis, Robert Conquest, Donald Davie, John Holloway, Elizabeth Jennings, Philip Larkin, and John Wain. This was the first presentation of these poets as a group, but it was printed in Japan and had little impact in England. The next year, however, the same poets appeared with the addition of Thom Gunn in another anthology, *New Lines*, edited by Conquest. With this famous anthology the poetry of the Movement began to be viewed, both in Great Britain and abroad, as representing the typical feelings, thoughts, and spiritual conditions of men and women in postwar England. The Movement authors produced novels, literary criticism, and other types of prose as well as poetry, but I shall consider them only as poets. Admiration for them was far from universal, and as the Movement became prominent it provoked sharp attacks. What is more, as soon as they were established, the writers in the Movement began to repudiate it. Either they denied that it had ever been more than a "journalistic convenience," in Thom Gunn's phrase, or, especially in the case of Donald Davie, they questioned the literary values associated with it. Each former Movement author is now understandably concerned lest the group identification obscure individual achievement. Davie and Gunn, moreover, are now writing types of poetry that are quite remote from anything we associate with the Movement of the 1950s.

THE STYLE OF THE 1950s

The Movement poets were often accused of writing on the basis of attitudes that were essentially negative. The chief reason for this charge I have already mentioned: as critics they attacked kinds of poetry that were influential when they began their careers. If we assume that their positives were the opposite of what they assailed—the self-expressive, emotive, intuitive, prophetic, obscure, experimental, sentimental, undisciplined, and vaguely suggestive—we obtain a cluster of values that the Movement poets shared with Roy Fuller, C. H. Sisson, R. S. Thomas, and most of the other poets who first had their strong impact in the 1950s, and that even poets who seemed to start in an opposite camp, such as Dannie Abse and David Wright, eventually came to share: reason, skepticism, empiricism, clarity, tradition, realism, and formal control. The influence of Leavis and the New Criticism compelled them to seek a "logical *raison d'être*," as Amis put it, "for every word, image, and metaphor used."

The poets themselves discovered what they valued by exactly the negative method just followed: they consulted their misgivings about the poets they read, a common procedure. Amid the Socialism of the 1950s it was virtually impossible for an English poet to sympathize with the elitism of the high Modernist mode, in other words, with a mode few readers could enjoy or even understand. Empsonian packed metaphors might seem similarly undesirable. The direct, generalizing reflection in the poetry of the 1930s was more attractive, but the verse of the 1930s also seemed unacceptable as a model. It tended toward the slapdash, and it reflected a zest for life that seemed suspiciously euptic. (The same experiences—quietly toasting sausages with a friend, for example—that had seemed intensely happy in the 1930s, when war threatened to overwhelm them, were found to be dreary and meaningless in the safer 1950s.) Dylan Thomas was too relentlessly melodious and rhetorical, making the fifties poets all the more conscious of the morality of plainness. Moreover, they could not recognize their world in the sentimental cliches of Thomas' "Fern Hill" or *Under Milk Wood,* and thus they were motivated all the more toward an honest realism. That Thomas' archetypal symbols seemed vague and obscure to the point of self-indulgence impelled them with stronger conviction toward lucid, rational discourse.

In the process of discovering their values poets of the 1950s produced a new view of literary history; more exactly, they revised an old one. In the Modernist theory of literary history the sweep of poetry from the great Romantics to the Georgians was regarded as sentimental aberration. But from the 1920s on a feeling had persisted in England that the "American-Montparnasse" styles of Eliot and Pound were foreign intrusions that English poetry could not completely assimilate. Sharing this feeling, poets in the 1950s looked back with appreciation to twentieth-century poets, such as Housman, Hardy, and the Georgians, outside the Modernist development, most of whom (though not Hardy) the literary intelligentsia had ignored or dismissed for the last thirty years. A masterly presentation of their idea of

twentieth-century literary history may be found in John Holloway's "The Literary Scene" (in *The Modern Age,* edited by Boris
Ford, 1961). "Eliot and Pound," Holloway concluded, "now seem
to have constituted a highly distinctive *phase* of poetic history,
one which was at bottom a continental impact, rather than the
decisive restoration of a central English tradition; and recently,
the English traditions these writers displaced have been reas-
serting themselves." Philip Larkin's *Oxford Book of Twentieth-
Century English Verse* (1973) embodies this point of view. Poets
now also emphasized the virtues of eighteenth- and nineteenth-
century poetry. The critical writings of Donald Davie, for example, highlighted the exemplary continuous syntax and moral
sensitivity of Wordsworth, Gray, Cowper, and minor Augustans
such as John Langhorne, though Davie himself was already devoted to Pound as well. Poets newly admired will also be imitated. The Augustans loom large in the work of Davie, of
Charles Tomlinson, who was Davie's student, and of Thom
Gunn.

Dylan Thomas had intuited or, at least, asserted the existence
of an omnipresent life-force uniting him with the world. But for
such would-be mysticism the new poets had no sympathy. The
political faith of the thirties poets was equally unappealing. For
although poets now approved, on the whole, of the Welfare
State, they naturally did not feel impelled to campaign for it.
"The unions are as powerful as they could wish to be," as Thom
Gunn explained in 1957, "National Health has been around for
ten years, and the village squires are all dead." Their view of the
past and present corresponded somewhat to that of a sated revolutionary. Feelings of nostalgia were inhibited, for naturally the
present society was to be preferred. To regret the disfigurement
and pollution of the countryside through the spread of housing
estates was sentimental and reactionary, and it was right to feel
the same satisfaction in the proliferation of television and automobiles. But when a commitment to Socialist ideals manifests
itself chiefly in a lack of complaint against the changes Socialism
brings, the commitment is rather inactive. As compared with the
poetry of the 1930s, that of the 1950s reflected the enormous
difference between the inspiring visions that precede a revolution and the *triste* loss of emotional purpose that attends its success. The strongest desire of poets now was to state candidly

what they believed to be true, but since their truth was not accompanied by any strong faith, it was just truth for its own sake, and this is always depressing. What was true, when they came down to it, was meaninglessness, nothingness, and death.

At a less ultimate level poetry in the 1950s recorded the drab facts and emotions of ordinary life. You had sexual encounters, but if you were honest with yourself, you admitted that sex wasn't very compelling or pleasurable. You felt sometimes like protesting against gross injustice, but the impulse was weakened by a sense of futility. By the evidence of your own poetic imagery, present-day England was tawdry and spiritless, but you found it bearable. You felt guilty about moral and personal failures, but were they really failures and what did it matter? Of course you knew all about your own psychic twists and wounds, in fact, you might loathe yourself, but there was nothing to be done about it. These impressionistic generalizations can be contradicted by innumerable particular poems, needless to say, but may suggest the dominant collective tone. The reflective moralizing that abounded in this poetry was often a reflex of self-dislike, but it was fine and moving in its attempt at objectivity and justice.

Though this realistic, honest, deflated style flourishes chiefly in England, it also exists in the United States. Howard Nemerov is one distinguished example. Poetry of this type is delimited on one side by the neo-Metaphysical or New Critical mode, for in comparison with this it is plain, direct, and personal. Larkin, Fuller, and Enright reported their own experience and emotion; by their convention the "I" who speaks is the poet himself. What they tell of themselves we can usually recognize in ourselves also, but most readers would find it slightly painful to acknowledge these emotions of hurt, resentment, self-pity, apathy, fear, envy, boredom, grudge, narcissism, egomania, masochism, and the like. On another side this mode is delimited by poetry of the Confessional type, for although Larkin was among the poets whose work led Robert Lowell to write *Life Studies* (1959), the English mode of Larkin does not present such an intimate, sensational, and explosive subject matter as that of the Confessional poets. We do not read, for example, of alcoholism, suicidal urges, or madness as we may in John Berryman, Sylvia Plath, or Lowell. Or if we do, the subject is kept in lower key or at a greater distance.

ORIENTATIONS TO AN AUDIENCE

An English poet is more likely than an American one to be mindful of his audience as he writes; the different poetic traditions and sociology of the two countries ensure this. Moreover, the ideology of the Labourite state encouraged writers to accept society as a guide to their literary aims and as a source of discipline in their styles. If a poet were mindful of his readers, Enright explained, he would be more likely to "restrain his oddities." Socialist criteria for literature fused quite amazingly with the Augustan ideal of the polite *monde*, the homogeneous, educated, refined audience that would hold in check an individual writer's crankiness and obsession.

Of course there was no such audience in the modern world, and since in the 1950s the Beat poets had not yet enormously increased the audience for poetry, much of the actual readership in both England and the United States was associated with universities—teachers, students, and recent graduates. The English poets were completely aware of this: in fact they sometimes viewed their university audience as the equivalent of the Augustan *monde*. And several of them were dons themselves. Commentators have often suggested that traits of their style—objectivity, sobriety, logical sequence, restraint—were typical donnish virtues. Many of the poets shared the Leavisite premises and methods that were widespread among teachers at the time. The poets who participated in The Group, for example—Alan Brownjohn, George MacBeth, Peter Redgrove, and others—started gathering in London in 1955 for the purpose of criticizing one another's work. "The only principle to which we would all subscribe," Edward Lucie-Smith later explained in his introduction to *A Group Anthology* (1963), "is that poetry is discussable, or, to put it another way, that the process by which words work in poetry is something open to rational explanation." But whoever discusses poems by "rational explanation" tends to write them for such explanation, in other words, creates by scrutinizing. Just as poets in the United States were composing lyrics for New Critical explication, poets in England expected that their academic audience would subject poems to a somewhat similar analysis, and they wrote accordingly.

But they also struggled to break out from their small academic audience, and since the academic was within themselves also, their anti-academic poses and gestures were sometimes compensatory and excessive. Only if we keep in mind how deeply rooted and often mired many poets were in academic life, both psychologically and often professionally, can we understand the motivations behind their anti-intellectual and anticultural aggressions. But poets sought a wider, less academic audience for other reasons also—the ethos of the Socialist state, for example, or the poets' nostalgia for the nineteenth century. That the Modernists had been of a contrary tendency—the arts are not a "democratic beer garden," Pound had warned, and if you hunger for readers, you will "dilute" your style—confirmed them all the more in their opposite tendency. Perhaps their poetry would have sought perspicuity and human interest in any case, but hope for a large audience was also a motivation. Larkin is the extreme instance. He described how as he composed he was careful to "lead the reader by the hand." "This is the initial experience or object," he would indicate at the start of the poem, "and now you see that it makes me think of this, that and the other," and thus "gently" the poem would work up to a "big finish." James Whitcomb Riley might have used the same words. Larkin openly envied the sales of the Georgians formerly and of Sir John Betjeman in the present day.

ROY FULLER, C. H. SISSON, AND R. S. THOMAS

Entering now upon discussions of particular poets, I find myself in a dilemma. Each of the English poets who emerged in the 1950s is of course individually different, and their careers after the 1950s carried them still further apart. But in the 1950s they were of one school. There were no important rival programs or tendencies among them; this basis of classification, which can be used in most decades, is not available. Since, however, some ordering principle must be employed, I shall fall back on chronology, noticing the oldest poets first and the youngest last. We shall find that this ordering is significant.

Roy Fuller, C. H. Sisson, and R. S. Thomas were born just before the First World War. They lived through the 1930s as adults, when most of the others we take up in this chapter were

still in school, and Fuller reports that Auden was the "great influence" on him throughout his career. R. S. Thomas had fully
matured his distinctive and powerful vein by 1946, but his work
found little recognition until some years later. C. H. Sisson did
not even write much poetry until 1950. None of these older
poets was included in the Movement. With them we may associate Thomas Blackburn, who was born in 1916 but did not begin to publish until 1954, at first as a disciple to the Romantic
style. Whether he writes of the atom bomb or his dissolving marriage, Blackburn's poems are powerfully direct and painful.

Roy Fuller (b. 1912) was a solicitor and Director of the Wool-
wich Equitable Building Society. His time was given first to business, second to writing novels, and finally to poetry. He was Oxford Professor of Poetry from 1968–1973. He has sensitivity to
evil, suffering, and pain, and an unsleeping premonition of
them. This awareness and fear seem generally to numb more
positive emotions. Even his pity turns often into disgust. His first
memorable poem was a skillful Audenesque, "August, 1938."
During the war he served in the Navy, and his poems reported
with honesty his lust, anger, dread, and so forth, the war providing also a metaphor for his *Weltanschauung*. He was bored,
but waiting in suspense amid the boredom for horror and death.
In "Defending the Harbour" he described the scene—the cob-
blestone quays, the trawler, the familiar faces of his section—in
images and metaphors of grayness, dullness, and monotony:

> on the quay, in our imagination,
> The grass of starvation sprouts between the stones,
> And ruins are implicit in every structure.
> Gently we probe the kind and comic faces
> For the strength of heroes and for martyr's bones.

In *A Lost Season* (1944) the unfamiliar sights of Africa stimulated
some excellent descriptive-reflective poems, versions of the essay
poem that became common in the next decade ("The Green
Hills of Africa," "The Giraffes," "Sadness, Theory, Glass," "The
Coast"). The African animals were, for Fuller, no more admirable or fortunate than any other part of life, but his heart
warmed toward them more.

His poetry since the 1950s reflects the ordinary life of a cultivated professional man, with the phonograph after dinner, the

Times, gardens, rail journeys, medical examinations, and "amatory botherations." But a minus sign stands before whatever he does or considers. Though the nagging pain he has been feeling proved unmalignant this time, doubtless it will not the next. A "green and reasonably buried walnut" on his lawn has, he congratulates it, prepared itself for the "ice-age" and the "burning should it come." History is for him a dreary record of egotism, violence, and suffering, but he is also frightened that it may end. His apprehensions were suitable in 1939 ("End of a City") and continued to be so after Hiroshima, but they were also natural expressions of his temperament.

Perhaps he may find inward sources of resistance and strength? No, when he looks within himself, he only discovers much to blame. He is a man of half-measures, he says. He has timidly diluted his Marxist politics with prudence. He has led a half-life, evading experience. His lusts are painful to him, but he also dislikes himself for not acting on them. He thinks that his sensitivity to a suffering world is morbid. His money has

> supported a life I can't approve of:
> I've saved it for a life I shall never enjoy.

His "Obituary of R. Fuller" sums up his self-portrait:

> He passed his adult years of peace
> In safe unease, with thoughts of doom.

The fine Fullerian note lies in the unsparing truth—"safe unease"—abandoned, as it were, on the doorstep of the reader's attention. For apart from passive repugnance and hurt, Fuller has usually no response to the truths he presents. He does not protest, seek solace, or offer a remedy. Neither does he place his observations within a larger perspective—philosophical, religious, or imaginative.

"Men improve with the years," Yeats tried to believe, but Fuller naturally thought the opposite. Nevertheless, his poems got better, though good from the start, and in 1968 his *New Poems* registered a breakthrough in his career. He was now writing in syllabic verse (brilliantly discussed in his Oxford lectures, *Owls and Artificers,* 1971), and the form brought with it an easier, more varying flow of talk and a lightening of spirits. Some poems are even charming, even cautiously hopeful. These relaxations are, in part, infusions from the later Auden, but poets can borrow only what they already possess. I quote from "To an Unknown Reader" in his *Tiny Tears* (1973):

> Would you want me to end in such a forlorn
> Key? I think not, for the poet is disposed
> To believe the domestic bell will be rung
> At last by the understanding stranger—
>
> Quite against probability. And it's just
> That continuing expectation of words,
> Of opening portals, to promise more than they
> Really signify to which man's hope adheres.
>
> Alternatives to dead-ends of history
> Are what's conspiratorially offered;
> All verse threatening that, as the Yankee said:
> "The astonished Muse finds thousands at her side."

C. H. Sisson (b. 1914) had a career as a civil servant in the Ministry of Labour. His first volumes came out in 1955 and 1961. His discursive utterance, depressed realism, moral sensitivity, and satire are typical of many of the poets I am considering, but Sisson is more abstract, weighted, stark, and savage than most of them, and he draws on different sources. Though he says that his aim in style "is to make plain statements, and not more of them than is needed," one recognizes in his "statements" the power of the Roman poets—Catullus, Horace, Virgil, Ovid, Propertius—from whom Sisson finely translated. His taut, firm, frank lines surprise by their variation of tone and even more by their bald truth, as in "No Address":

> I am no man, Caesar, to stand by you,
> Nor have the whimsical humour of pre-war Oxford
> But my unrecognised style was made by sorrow.
>
> Inching towards death, let me go there quickly.
> Silently, in the night or in the day-time,
> Equally, I would take it like a Roman.

In Sisson a continually questioning intellect combines with the torment of a sensitive awareness of barrenness and evil in the world and within himself, and he strips off surfaces to reveal what festers underneath, which he takes for reality. His aphorisms are harsh: "Failure makes enemies as success friends"; "flowering" is "a matter of choking off others." His strength, like Larkin's, lies partly in his willingness to acknowledge truths about himself that are not in the least uncommon but are usually unmentioned:

> What am I?
> The man inclined to larceny
> Who stops at envy.

His self-undermining sometimes appalls. In the seventh poem of "In Insula Avalonia," on the myth of Proserpine, he reflects that his role in this myth is that neither of Dis nor or Orpheus but of Cerberus:

> I stand and roar and only shake my chain
> The river passes and gives others sleep
> I am the jaws nothing will pass between.

The image of gaping dissatisfaction and futile rage is one of many such in his poetry that locate him in hell. Yet this is one end of his spectrum; his satire also turns outward against others and can be funny, as in "The Spectre," an accurate account of a typical modern man and his career. One of his finest poems is "Catullus," of which the theme is lechery preluding religion. This development is seen in the Roman world just before the coming of Christ, and occurs also, the poems suggests, in the lives of individuals. The poem ends,

> Catullus my friend across twenty centuries,
> Anxious to complete your lechery before Christ came.

Within the last ten years Sisson's poetry has obtained some late recognition in England, but he deserves more and closer readers than he has had.

For the past twenty years most of the poems of Ronald Stuart Thomas (b. 1913), a Welsh country priest, have been reflective, often religious lyrics of sensitivity and intelligence. But in the 1940s and 1950s he also worked in a more distinctive vein of stark naturalism. Because his poems of this kind describe the Welsh hill farmers, he might be considered a regional poet, and a comparison might suggest itself with other regional and reli-

gious poets such as Norman Nicholson. But Thomas reaches a
different level of quality, and his poetic personality is remarkably
individual. A more illuminating comparison can be made to
Robert Frost, who also presents the lonely, impoverished life on
mountain farms in a realistic way. Both poets can be deeply
troubled by the harsh, alien life they describe, and cold toward
it, but Frost has also a humorous affection, sympathy, and sometimes even admiration for his characters, and deeply feels the
pathos of their lives. These emotions are not absent in Thomas,
but they are mingled with protest and even denunciation. Not
since that other country clergyman-poet, George Crabbe, has
there been a picture of rural life so ruthlessly and disturbingly
unsentimental. In "The Welsh Hill Country," for example, the
tourist, looking at the sheep "arranged romantically in the usual
manner," is blind to the sickness of man and beast:

> Too far for you to see
> The fluke and the foot-rot and the fat maggot
> Gnawing the skin from the small bones,
>
> . . . .
>
> Too far, too far to see
> The set of his eyes and the slow phthisis
> Wasting his frame under the ripped coat.

The protest and attack here lashes out against the "tourist" (a
surrogate for Thomas himself) and his false romantic idea of a
pastorally idyllic countryside, but the poem also seems to denounce the countryside for not living up to this vision. In some
poems Thomas gives up on his farmers; "Valediction" is an example, or "The Muck Farmer":

> Leave him, then, crazed and alone
> To pleach his dreams with his rough hands.
> Our ways have crossed and tend now apart;
> Ours to end in a field widely sown,
> His in the mixen of his warped heart.

In many poems Thomas insists on the full humanity of his Welsh
peasants, as in "Affinity," "The Labourer," or "The Hill Farmer
Speaks" ("Listen, listen, I am a man like you"). Or if he suggests
that they are almost animal, he argues that the circumstances of
their lives and the indifference of society have made these

people what they are. In some poems he tries to see them as possessing or symbolizing virtues such as patience and endurance. But these attempts to mitigate his repulsion are due, probably, to compunctions of conscience; at any rate, they are more impressive morally than poetically. They lack the convincing, Swiftian power of the disgust and anger with which Thomas reacts to the dullness, ignorance, hardness, and coarseness of his characters, even to their dirt and smell.

The individuality and power of his vision are the first things to praise in Thomas' poetry, and the second is his craftsmanship. Thomas admired Yeats, but seldom sounds like him or anyone else. His style is obviously not Modernist or Postmodernist, and it does not closely resemble any other period style of the twentieth century. Its virtues are those of good writing of any time— clarity, speed, force, compactness, depth of suggestion and significance. The changing texture sustains interest by its continual slight surprise. "A Peasant," for example, belongs to the Augustan genre of the portrait ("see him . . ."), and opens with Thomas replying to us in natural colloquial speech ("be it allowed,/ Just an ordinary man . . ."), as though we had been looking at the peasant and asking who he was.

> Iago Prytherch his name, though, be it allowed,
> Just an ordinary man of the bald Welsh hills,
> Who pens a few sheep in a gap of cloud.
> Docking mangels, chipping the green skin
> From the yellow bones with a half-witted grin
> Of satisfaction, or churning the crude earth
> To a stiff sea of clods that glint in the wind—
> So are his days spent, his spittled mirth
> Rarer than the sun that cracks the cheeks
> Of the gaunt sky perhaps once in a week.
> And then at night see him fixed in his chair
> Motionless, except when he leans to gob in the fire.
> There is something frightening in the vacancy of his mind.
> His clothes, sour with years of sweat
> And animal contact, shock the refined,
> But affected, sense with their stark naturalness.
> Yet this is your prototype, who, season by season
> Against siege of rain and the wind's attrition,
> Preserves his stock, an impregnable fortress

Not to be stormed even in death's confusion.
Remember him, then, for he, too, is a winner of wars,
Enduring like a tree under the curious stars.

The fresh, vivid metaphors—the hill farm a "gap of cloud"—
make us see the landscape. The bleak beauty in these images
interplays with the equally vivid but repulsive and ominous comparison of mangels to decomposing bodies ("green skin," "yellow
bones") at which Prytherch chops. The combination of unsparing naturalism and revulsion continues in "spittled mirth" and
in the picture of Prytherch at night, "Motionless, except when
he leans to gob in the fire." The images have a latent metaphysical dimension, and this emerges when Prytherch's face is compared to that of the sky. Many readers will make the traditional
association of the sky with the divine. No wonder that Thomas
backs off, so to speak. At line thirteen the poem shifts suddenly
into a reflective-discursive mode of speech. But the reflection—
"There is something frightening in the vacancy of his mind"—
is utterly inadequate to the suggestions that have been activated,
as though Thomas wished not to admit what was stirring in his
imagination. The rest of the poem presents one of Thomas' typical moments of compunction. He struggles for a way of imagining this peasant that will be more acceptable to his conscience.
The attack on the "refined" reader is typical of such moments,
and so also is the fact that the reader's guilt would lie only in
sharing the revulsion that overwhelmed Thomas in the first part
of the poem.

LARKIN AND HIS CONTEMPORARIES

Philip Larkin (1922–85) published his first volume of lyrics,
The North Ship, when he was just down from Oxford in 1945.
These were lyrics of quasi-personal, quasi-realistic experience
and emotion, with an inclination toward moodiness. Often they
sounded like Yeats. Twenty years later, in the introduction to the
1966 edition, Larkin said that *The North Ship* contained "not one
abandoned self but several—the ex-schoolboy, for whom Auden
was the only alternative to 'old-fashioned' poetry; the undergraduate whose work a friend affably characterized as 'Dylan

Thomas, but you've a sentimentality that's all your own'; and the immediately post-Oxford self, isolated in Shropshire with a complete Yeats stolen from the local girls' school."

But though *The North Ship* lacked the drab delineations and meditative acuity of Larkin's mature style, his characteristic vision was already present. Wan unhope—the Hardyesque phrase is appropriate—was the pervading emotional state; it might also be described as low-grade psychological depression. The young speaker of these lyrics is bored with youth's illusion and unrest. Love, he foresees, will subside after a few meetings, and his sense of this dampens love's brief moment. His perceptions are saturated with awareness of time, transience, and death. Such phrases as "snow everywhere," "dumb idleness," "pastime of a provincial winter" suggest the emotional tone.

By 1946, Larkin says, he had started to read Hardy. Larkin explains this as happenstance, but to his readers it seems a fated conjunction. After ten years, during which he published two novels, appeared his second volume of verse, *The Less Deceived* (1955). In this collection his work was fully developed, and subsequent ones—*The Whitsun Weddings* (1964) and *High Windows* (1974)—added excellent poems but made no significant advance. His poems are by convention to be taken as personal, autobiographical speech; his plain words erect no barrier to readers; his pose—direct, fair-minded, frank—is attractive. Ruefulness, wistfulness, patience, and resignation tame his melancholy into pathos. Read out of the Larkin context, some of his poems would seem slick and sentimental. "At Grass," for example, is an impression of former racehorses now out to pasture. *Ubi sunt* the silks, parasols, starting-gates, crowds, and so forth? "Do memories plague their ears like flies?" Yet in the Larkin context the poem pictures life's emptiness. Nothing is happening in the lives of the horses; nothing is going to happen except death.

At bottom Larkin's vision and emotion are not merely realistic and unsentimental but painful. In "Reasons for Attendance" he watches young people dancing and feels excluded from their "happiness." Or is it happiness, he asks himself:

> Sex, yes, but what
> Is sex? Surely to think the lion's share

Of happiness is found by couples—sheer
Inaccuracy, as far as I'm concerned.

One sees why Robert Lowell was impressed. Since most people would rather admit to suicidal urges than sexual apathy, Larkin's reflection is no less courageous than the more sensational intimacies of the Confessional school. The lines illustrate the thoughtful, empirical honesty that makes Larkin so powerful as a moralist. He adheres to what he individually feels and knows, and is original and liberating for that reason.

At the end of "Church Going" we see Larkin's feelings in rebellion against his sense of reality. The stanza treads the brink of sentimentalism—this is the drama of it—for he almost succumbs to his emotional wish, but he never quite does, and in the end he puts it aside. He knows that in the past the church, or faith in its teachings, gave coherence and significance to living; he senses that the church still reminds "serious" persons how desperately these are necessary but lacking in the present; whatever else it also implies, his traditional prosody expresses the tug of his emotion toward a past when the church was not just an empty building visited by sightseers. But the poem does not include Larkin among the "serious" persons "gravitating" to the church. The insight he comes to is merely that there will always be such persons. What blocks further "gravitation" is his mindfulness of death, the essential reality in which the poem ends. More than it brings anything else to mind, the church is a *memento mori*—"so many dead lie round."

> A serious house on serious earth it is,
> In whose blent air all our compulsions meet,
> Are recognised, and robed as destinies.
> And that much never can be obsolete,
> Since someone will forever be surprising
> A hunger in himself to be more serious,
> And gravitating with it to this ground,
> Which, he once heard, was proper to grow wise in,
> If only that so many dead lie round.

Though in form most of Larkin's poems are short, stanzaic lyrics, he was essentially a poet in the English descriptive-meditative tradition. Typically his poems describe some sight, object, place, or event and present his response or lack of response to it. As it is presented the response is thoughtfully appraised, other considerations are brought to bear, and the poem may end in a passage of memorable generalizing and moralizing. "Church Going" is typical. In "Dockery and Son," to take another example, he hears on a visit to his old college that the son of a former classmate is now a student. The news jolts him into reflecting on his own situation.

> To have no son, no wife,
> No house or land still seemed quite natural.
> Only a numbness registered the shock
> Of finding out how much had gone of life,
> How widely from the others.

He goes on to meditate on the different courses of life he and Dockery have followed and to speculate on their motivations. In the end, however, it makes no difference, for all lives follow the same course in general and end in the same way. (To American ears the rhythm of the last two lines recalls Robert Frost.)

> Life is first boredom, then fear.
> Whether or not we use it, it goes,
> And leaves what something hidden from us chose,
> And age, and then the only end of age.

Larkin's powers were extraordinary, but many of his poems do not convince. His dispiritedness seems too untested; apathy wins too easily. His images fall within a narrow register of emotional suggestion: the deserted church, the defaced poster, the littered back yard, the cheap hospital furniture, the "perms,/ The nylon gloves and jewellery-substitutes." Such items abound in other modern poets also, but in most others they are balanced or opposed by images in a different emotional tone. Even in *The Waste Land* the "Ionian white and gold" of the church of St. Magnus Martyr is still felt to be splendid, and on the patch of cinders in William Carlos Williams a broken bottle shines in complex refractions like a beautiful work of art. The compensating element in Larkin was only that he did not much mind the drabness he saw. Yet I am doing him an injustice, for his poems implicitly questioned their own vision of things. Was life "first boredom, then fear" for Dockery, whose "Innate assumptions" motivated him to have a son? In "The Whitsun Weddings" the bridal parties—fat mothers, smut-shouting uncles, and girls in "parodies of fashion"—are full of vitality, and though Larkin deflates and condescends, he also senses in them something vaguely positive. Such poems shade over into impressive ones in which he presents the world under his usual minus sign—dreary, empty, boring—and then turns back on himself, his subtle, honest reflection seeking the cause within his own psyche for what he sees without. In "Mr. Bleaney" we see Larkin replacing Bleaney as the tenant of a rented room. As he lies in bed stubbing cigarettes he is doubtless thinking that Mr. Bleaney is dead and he soon will be, so why in the meantime should he do anything. But he also wonders whether "how we live measures our own nature," thus tentatively locating the impairment or vacancy not in existence but in himself. And if "Church Going" gives a depressing view of human nature as Larkin meanly drops an Irish sixpence in the collection box, it affords more hopeful ones in his impulse to reverence and in the intelligence, sensitivity, and scrupulous honesty with which he meditates upon this feeling.

Several of Larkin's associates in the Movement are more important in other genres or literary connections than as poets. Robert Conquest (b. 1917) is best known for his anthologies introducing the Movement—*New Lines* I (1956) and *New Lines* II (1963). His poetry tends not to present the thing vividly but to reflect upon it. This is true whether he writes about persons (usually literary, as in "Byron's Sex-Life," "Reading Coleridge," "Keats in 1819," and his contemporary hero, "George Orwell"), places ("Near Corinth," "Birmingham"), or general subjects ("Art and Love," "The Virtues of Poetry"). He has written two novels and several books on the Soviet Union, and he spent ten years in the diplomatic service. John Wain (b. 1925), well known for his novels and other prose, is a poet of awkward sincerity and uncertain taste. In "Anniversary" he says that his thoughts are "solid as bricks./ And like bricks fearsome in their everyday squareness," and this seems about right. Kingsley Amis (b. 1922) published two volumes of poems (1947, 1953) before his first novel, *Lucky Jim* (1954), and has continued to write poetry amid his greater application to fiction. His poems are somewhat limited by their intention to clear the poetic air. Nobody, he said, "wants any more poems on the greater themes for a few years"; nobody wants poems about "philosophers or paintings or novelists or art galleries or mythologies." But neither do we much want poems that merely articulate or self-consciously exemplify these opinions. Yet many poems linger in the mind. "Against Romanticism" puts his poetic credo in positive as well as purgative terms. "An Ever-fixed Mark" manages through sheer neatness to give a novel twist to its hackneyed subject, steadiness in love as contrasted with the "momentary itch" of sex. "After Goliath" sharply raises the question whether the real enemies are the Philistines or the shrill hangers-on of culture. When Amis forgets his war against "rhetoric" he can be eloquent and moving, as in "Masters": "we are known/ Only as we are weak"—

> By yielding mastery the will is freed,
> For it is by surrender that we live,
> And we are taken if we wish to give,
> Are needed if we need.

Among the young poets of the 1950s who began and have continued in more traditional veins I may mention Elizabeth Jennings (b. 1926), who takes her themes from domestic circumstances. The life her poems describe is an ordinary one, but unusual intelligence and imagination are brought to bear in contemplating it. David Wright (b. 1920) spent his early years in South Africa and has lived since in England. An accident in childhood left him deaf. After his featureless first volume in 1947 his individual qualities asserted themselves with growing effectiveness. Though lacking in strong surprise or intense imagination, his poems win attention by irony, by continual slight variations of tone, and by their immediacy and directness. "Monologue of a Deaf Man" and "Grasmere Sonnets" are among his better poems. John Holloway (b. 1920) is a professor of English at Cambridge University. His poems reflect the Renaissance and nineteenth-century poetry in which he has a scholarly interest. His diction can be contemporary, but is most vital when old-fashioned. Elaborate prosody, melody, beauty of imagery, and reflectiveness tend to keep his subjects at a distance.

Dennis Joseph Enright (b. 1920) has spent much time abroad, teaching in universities in West Berlin, Egypt, Thailand, India, and Japan. His experiences as what he calls a "mendicant professor" appear most directly in his novels ("all really travel books," he says), but they have also widened his horizon and given objectivity to his poetry, to which, as a writer, he has been more committed than to prose fiction. In his own critical writing he strongly protests against the aestheticism that regards a poem as pure artifact and concentrates on technique apart from subject matter. His poems make a point, and very often their point is the obtuseness, crassness, hypocrisy, and so forth of human nature. But Enright avoids rhetoric and makes no overt denunciation. Instead, he offers bright, clear, rapid talk in a tone pitched between humor and seriousness. Though Enright is almost continuously ironic and often bitter, his irony is not satiric in the full sense of the term, for he has no hope of shaming the behavior he describes, much less of correcting it.

He has a journalist's gift for finding the telling detail, both realistic and typical, that evokes the moral atmosphere of a place or experience. Teaching literature in the Middle and Far East, he naturally focuses on the impossibility of transferring one culture to another, an especially rich illustration of the general hopelessness. As, for example, he explicates in class Hopkins' great lines, "God's most deep decree/ Bitter would have me taste: my taste was me," his Chinese students are thinking "how sweet they taste, like moon-cake." His personal memories, recounted in *The Terrible Shears: Scenes from a Twenties Childhood* (1973), are often gruesome.

Anthony Thwaite (b. 1930) presents ordinary experiences and emotions with honesty, subtlety, and unobtrusive formal skill. Many of his poems have historical subjects. In one of his poems in *Victorian Voices* (1980) George Meredith's wife replies to *Modern Love*, Meredith's sonnet sequence about their failed marriage. How strange, she says, to be remembered only because of these poems: "I was a wisp, a nothing, on my own." In its quiet pathos the line is typical of Thwaite.

Two of Donald Davie's (b. 1922) early books of criticism, *Purity of Diction in English Verse* (1952) and *Articulate Energy: An Enquiry into the Syntax of English Poetry* (1955), were read at first publication as expressions of the poetic values of Davie's generation. These books were not about the poetry of the eighteenth century only, but they dwelt with enthusiasm on it. In this poetry what Davie most admired was the sense of responsibility that shaped its style. The Augustan poet was committed not solely to the poem he was writing, as a Modernist poet was, but also to the audience and, more generally, to the traditions of civilized intelligence. Grammar and logic, for example, were not for Augustans any more than for modern Symbolists the specific disciplines of poetry. But for Augustan feeling they represented basic values that transcended poetry. Hence even those Augustan poets who associated the "poetic" with the "wild," primitive, imaginative, or sublime and pursued these qualities were also faithful to an ideal of rational intelligibility. But though Davie opposed the Modernist-Symbolist premises in poetry, he admired many Modernist poets, especially Pound. And with similar paradox he repeatedly conceded that Augustan poetry, despite or even because of its responsible virtue, was generally minor. He hoped his criticism might help contemporaries to write a poetry of "urbane and momentous statement," but the emphasis he attached to this was to some extent a relative and historical one. The moral attitude implied in Augustan style would always be valid, but was now especially necessary as a corrective of the present.

Davie's ideals as a critic did not describe his own poetry, but they provided a system of considerations that defended some aspects of it, transforming what might have seemed limitations into intentions. In "The Garden Party," for example, the speaker attends a wealthy party and feels envious; he wishes he could enjoy the party as he might have if invited when younger. The final stanza goes,

> My father, of a more submissive school,
> Remarks the rich themselves are always sad.
> There is that sort of equalizing rule;
> But theirs is all the youth we might have had.

The poem is without Romantic melody, emotional intensity, symbolism, or myth, and it equally lacks the puns, ambiguities, telescoped metaphors, and other forms of wit of the Empsonian or neo-Metaphysical style. Probably we would not have recognized the poem as "Augustan" either, but once the term is in mind, it evokes precedent. The sobriety, directness, and realism of the poem might be Augustan, and so might the regular, closed versification, the compact, lucid syntax, and the deliberate yet colloquial diction. Its moralizing is practical, that is, it applies to actualities of middle-class existence, and as in many passages of

Augustan verse, thinking—one might almost say, arguing—constitutes the "plot" of the stanza, which enacts the stepping of the mind amid concessions and qualifications. But the poem is as characteristic of the 1950s as of the eighteenth century. In it the upwardly mobile speaker voices feelings that rise directly out of his life; his personal honesty cuts through well-intentioned protest to express his slightly mean emotion as it actually is.

The poem is typical of Davie's earlier ones, yet in many of them intellectual wit animated the plain style, and some, such as "Rejoinder to a Critic," were ingenious arguments from metaphors. Poetry, poets, and styles were frequently his subject matter, and so also was England. Its places and ways of life were presented as symbols of its spiritual condition. On both poetry and England Davie's points of view were usually surprising and often hostile. His best moments came when his criticism turned into self-criticism and self-criticism into generous acknowledgment of others. In "Remembering the 'Thirties,'" for example, he notes weaknesses of the thirties poets with inspired malice— such as their "insistence on the quizzical," their "craze/ For showing Hector was a mother's boy"—but he adds,

A neutral tone is nowadays preferred.
And yet it may be better, if we must,
To praise a stance impressive and absurd
Than not to see the hero for the dust.

The Forests of Lithuania (1959), a long poem adapted from Mickiewicz, was presumably an effort at self-correction. The poem took him out of England, the Movement, and the contemporary world, and into Lithuania in 1811 and 1812, where there were impenetrable woods, picturesque customs, and romance. Though very readable, the poem is not important, yet it is moving as the moral effort of a contemporary writer to impel himself into warm, positive emotions and an uncramped world, escaping the "small and mean utilities" (as Davie called them in "Among Artisans' Houses") of English social life. Davie could not continue this vacation in the realm of Sir Walter Scott, but his best lyrics—"Bolyai, the Geometer," "The Hardness of Light," "July, 1964," "Pietà," "Ezra Pound in Pisa"—still keep something of Lithuania. They have the short, rhymeless lines and flowing, legato syntax he first developed in some sections of that long poem. They may suggest without stating; in other words, Davie now often relinquishes firmly uttered conclusion and point. And they are tender, appreciative, and admiring, with less of the criticism and self-criticism that had pervaded his earlier poems. In *Six Epistles to Eva Hesse* (1970) the former champion of Augustan virtues tried his hand at another Augustan form, the half-comic verse epistle that seems improvisation. The lightness, grace, and play that distinguish these epistles would not have been predicted of the young poet who wrote "The Garden Party." Probably they would not much have appealed to him. And to that young poet *The Shires* (1974) and subsequent poems might also have seemed undesirably relaxed.

In his teens Dannie Abse (b. 1923) wrote politically committed and rhetorical poems, their style influenced by the Spender and Lehmann anthology of *Poems for Spain* (1939) and by the verse he read in the *Left Review*. He studied medicine and became a doctor. After the Second World War his themes were no longer political. Hiroshima and Auschwitz, he suggests, were enormities that made rhetorical denunciation irrelevant. Many of the lyrics of *After Every Green Thing* (1949) and *Walking Under Water* (1952) were touched with the music and imagery of Dylan Thomas, though they were plainer and simpler than most of Thomas. In the 1950s Abse opposed the type of poetry attributed to the Movement. Some of the poems of his 1957 volume, *Tenants of the House*, described dreams and visions; most of them were more directly emotive than was typical of Movement poetry. Abse's talent reached its finest development up to now in *A Small Desperation* (1968) and *Funland and Other Poems* (1973). These poems told incidents from contemporary life with a sensitivity to its pain and horror, but from an oblique perspective. Auschwitz, for example, is a major theme of "A Night Out," but the focus of the poem is on seeing a movie with scenes from Auschwitz. In the cinema Abse lives vicariously in Auschwitz, but he cannot assimilate what he sees. In the coffee shop afterward he has nothing to say about it. He goes home to his usual routine. But he cannot forget Auschwitz either, and it continues vaguely to frighten, depress, and disgust him, while also making him feel guilty. The sensitivity of the poem is so complex that its emotion seems almost mute, and one must study the simple words closely to catch their notes. This is typical of Abse. Both Abse's sense of Jewish identity and his work as a doctor have been increasingly reflected in his themes and images as the years have passed, and they are prominent in *Way Out in the Centre* (1981).

19

ENGLISH POETRY IN THE 1960s AND 1970s

THE tendencies of English poetry since the 1960s are not unified but divided, as they have usually been in the modern period, and most poets are divided within themselves. But the opposite poles of this division are not now quite the same as they were in the immediate postwar years. Then a Romantic revival was dominant, and in the same moment most of the younger poets were strongly reacting against it. Dylan Thomas was the chief representative of the Romanticism of the war years, and Philip Larkin the central poet of the antagonist younger group, several members of which made up the Movement. But like the Romantic mode it supplanted, the poetry of the Movement was also a revival, and the styles on which it based itself had been created before or apart from the development of Modernism. In the early 1950s, then, the most important split in contemporary poetry was between different possibilities inherent in the English tradition. To characterize the style of the Movement in such phrases as late Augustan, Hardyesque, Georgian, or whatever is obviously inadequate, as any phrase would be, but may suggest the type of realistic, reflective, moralizing, empirical, personally honest, occasionally satirical poetry, suspicious of human nature and saturated with a sense of life's pain, that has been dominant in Britain for the past thirty years. One finds it, *mutatis mutandis,* not only in Larkin, Roy Fuller, Donald Davie, R. S. Thomas, and C. H. Sisson, but also in poets who started writing or attracted attention a little later, such as Geoffrey Hill, Jon Silkin, Alan Brownjohn, Peter Porter, Toni Harrison, Jon Stallworthy, James Fenton, and, in many poems, Ted Hughes, George MacBeth, and Thom Gunn.

With the partial exception of Davie, Hughes, Hill, and Gunn, none of these poets is Modernist or Postmodernist in style, not at least in ways that would be recognized as such in Europe or America. But the Movement poets of the 1950s had carried the anti-Modernist, insular reaction, which has been present in English poetry since the 1920s, to unusual lengths, and this, in turn, also generated opposition. By the early 1960s the Movement was under strong attack. In an introduction to a 1962 anthology of *The New Poetry* Alfred Alvarez argued, for example, that contemporary poetry in England was blinkered by "gentility." The English believe, said Alvarez, that "life is always more or less orderly . . . emotions and habits more or less decent or more or less controllable." Hence English poetry could not express the suffering and horror of modern experience. It was the age of Confessional poetry, and Alvarez began his anthology with selections from Robert Lowell and John Berryman. Controversy arose over his remarks, naturally, and persisted for at least ten years, for Alvarez had expressed misgivings many poets shared. Even poets who had been featured in the Movement anthologies were snipping at the "tame," "academic," "arid," "mean spirited" style and ethos the anthologies had promoted. English poetry, in other words, was again opening itself to influences from abroad. In the 1950s the work of David Jones and Basil Bunting, for example, would have been less readily included in the canon of significant modern poetry. The reception of Charles Tomlinson provides another brief illustration. Founding his art on Wallace Stevens and especially on William Carlos Williams, Tomlinson had little acceptance in England in the 1950s; in 1973 a poem of his that would earlier have been ignored was included in the *Oxford Anthology of English Literature.* Yet the controversy surrounding Ted Hughes's *Crow* (1970) shows that the English attitude to international styles is anything but uncritical.

That British poetry has now returned to its typical modern

self-division, which is its particular strength, appears clearly in
the four poets I concentrate on in this chapter: Charles Tomlinson, Ted Hughes, Geoffrey Hill, and Thom Gunn. Their work
is formed in tension between the strong, persisting appeal of
native English styles, on the one hand, and on the other hand,
the Modernist and Postmodernist styles of the United States and
of Europe. The interaction of opposed values shows itself not
only in particular volumes and poems but in a poet's reversals
of direction over the years. Works that reflect international or
transatlantic, Modernist or Postmodernist modes, such as Hughes's *Crow* and Hill's *Mercian Hymns*, are followed in the career of
the same poet by works of a very different character—for example, by the rural elegies and farm "diaries" of a relatively traditional kind in Hughes's *Moortown* and by the baroque poetry
of Hill's *Tenebrae*. A similar tension and interplay shapes the poetry of Jon Silkin (b. 1930), Alan Brownjohn (b. 1931), Peter
Redgrove (b. 1932) and Peter Porter (b. 1929).

Continuing a brief survey, I may mention Norman MacCaig
(b. 1910) and Charles Causley (b. 1917), poets of an older generation whose newly appreciated art is almost completely traditional. Four younger poets, James Fenton (b. 1949), Tony Harrison (b. 1937), Craig Raine (b. 1944), and John Stallworthy (b.
1935) slightly recall, though in different, completely individual
ways, the later Auden and Louis MacNeice. They are witty, perspicuous poets who write for the common reader. Their poems
are frequently humorous, sometimes satiric, and occasionally
light. They are virtuosos of form. Fenton and Harrison are poets
of intellectual point. Like many of the younger poets in the
United States, these English poets have recently explored the
possibilities of realistic narrative. Raine and Stallworthy have
been led toward this partly by Robert Lowell's *Life Studies*, and
have published narratives concerned with their own childhoods
and families. Interest in character and story again indicates the
desire of these poets to reach an audience. Nevertheless, though
they are taking poetry in quasi-popular directions, these poets
are themselves intellectuals, formidably erudite and brilliant.

Among these four poets, the generalizations just suggested
apply least to Stallworthy, whose work is more conventional than
that of the others. Now a professor of English at Cornell University in the United States, Stallworthy writes best of love and

family life, its tribulations, griefs, and cozinesses. Tony Harrison, a poor boy from Leeds, Yorkshire, obtained scholarships and majored in classics at the University of Leeds. His attitudes, or those of the characters through whom he speaks, tend to be insouciant and defiant. He writes movingly about the social transition he experienced in attending the university and about the complications this created in his relations with his parents. He is also a gifted translator, especially in creating acting versions of dramas. James Fenton writes frequently about war and politics. Some memorable poems draw on his first-hand experience in Cambodia. he also composes collages, assembling quotations of erudite prose for seriocomic effect. Craig Raine, like Seamus Heaney, excels at rendering objects through apt, unexpected metaphors. Fenton described Raine and Christopher Reid as "Martian" poets, meaning that they describe objects as would a visitor from that planet who would not know their character or purpose. Thus Raine's poem on a telephone views it as though it were a child being cuddled, tickled (in dialing), and so forth.

The work of George MacBeth (b. 1932) somewhat resembles that of the young George Barker in *Calamiterror* and *True Confessions*. MacBeth's poetry may perhaps be interpreted as a violent reaction against the careful craftsmanship and rationalist ethos of the Movement. "The important thing," MacBeth once said, "is to thrash out huge quantities of fairly well-written poetry." His poems are Surrealist nightmares of sex, violence, and cruelty; they are intended to shock, and are sometimes satiric.

Here also I may mention Derek Walcott (b. 1930), who grew up on the Caribbean island of St. Lucia. He is a poet in a modern international style, but very much influenced by twentieth-century English poets. So far as his subject matter reflects his Caribbean background, he dwells on the realities of life in the Caribbean as contrasted with the Romantic vision put forward by tourist agencies. The lack of an artistic tradition within his native country is one of his themes, and he perhaps reflects this in his readiness to adopt the voices of other poets.

Of the many poets who illustrate the possibility of a radically Modernist or Postmodernist British poetry, Christopher Middleton (b. 1926), I. H. Finley (b. 1925), and J. H. Prynne (b. 1936) are the most distinguished. Middleton, a professor of German at the University of Texas, published his first volumes in 1962.

Many of his experiments with poetic form have been suggested to him by European avant-garde movements. His work is almost continually discontinuous. When it can be understood, it may be fine and moving, as, for example, in "Night Blooming Cereus" and "Autobiography." Prynne has been influenced by the "projectivist" verse of the United States, as in Charles Olson, Robert Duncan, Robert Creeley, and Jack Spicer. Even persons who do not usually respond to concrete poetry are struck by the wit and beauty of I. H. Finley's poster poems and poem-objects in an environment; the latter are stones, sundials, and the like that bear brief texts and are placed in a setting conceived as part of the composition.

Yet when all these poets have been named, C. H. Sisson, Geoffrey Hill, and Thom Gunn remain the finest living English poets. Though the work of Ted Hughes appeals less to me, he has written impressively and innovatively at times, and is important. Charles Tomlinson, though not quite the equal of these others, is also extremely accomplished.

CHARLES TOMLINSON

In *Some Americans* (1981) Charles Tomlinson (b. 1927) gives a luminous account of the development of his work. Whitman "along with Nietzsche, formed the style of the earliest unfortunate poems" that he "wrote on going down" from Cambridge in 1948. Over the next three years he read "a lot of Augustan poetry"—he had been a student of Davie's—and in 1951 he brought out *Relations and Comforts,* a collection of lyrics he has since for the most part disowned. He had first encountered Pound, Wallace Stevens, and Marianne Moore in an anthology he bought while at grammar school. Around 1950 he read them more extensively, and Hart Crane's "Voyages" also "laid hold" of him. But Tomlinson kept his spiritual distance from the poetry of Crane. Reading Crane, he was "finding my way closer to my own basic theme," but his theme was "relationship" as opposed to merging: "the 'I' can only be responsible in relationship and not by dissolving itself away into ecstasy or the Oversoul." Certain fragments from Pound and Moore—for example, "Miss

Moore's penetration of the sea in 'The Fish' while refusing to merge with it"—were also "working" for him.

Between 1950 and 1953 he wrote the poems that appeared in *The Necklace* (1955). The *Harmonium* of Wallace Stevens was the main influence in this volume (see, for example, "Nine Variations in a Chinese Winter Setting" or "Suggestions for the Improvement of a Sunset"), but the book also carries one back to the poetic milieu out of which Stevens emerged, to the enthusiasms of the 1910s for poetic Impressionism, Imagism, French *symbolisme*, Chinoiserie, and Impressionist and Postimpressionist painting that produced, along with Stevens, such other manifestations as the "Color Symphonies" of John Gould Fletcher. For example, the fifth of Tomlinson's "Nine Variations in a Chinese Winter Setting" is a fine but strange poem to have been written in England during the 1950s:

> Pine-scent
> In snow-clearness
> Is not more exactly counterpointed
> Than the creak of trodden snow
> Against a flute.

Yet this and other poems in *The Necklace* had already the essential Tomlinson virtue of precise, sensory observation. The spare, somewhat astringent suggestions of the imagery are typical of the moral atmosphere of Tomlinson's poetry. Snow, flute, and pine-scent compose a world that is the opposite of warm and lush. The mental gestures the poem enacts—attending to the sensation, comparing it to another, finding a relationship—express Tomlinson's notion of how best to fill a world in which so much white space or emptiness surrounds the brief, muted manifestations of being. His suppression of emotion and of self in this poem—there is an observer and comparer, but no "I" and no response—are appropriate to its discipline of attention and enforce also Tomlinson's determination to keep his distance from an Oversoul which, in any case, does not exist.

The Necklace found no welcome in England but a warm one in the United States from Hugh Kenner. By 1956 Tomlinson had completed poems for another volume. These poems, to which I shall return, enforced the morality sketched above. American influences were again at work in them—Tomlinson had already begun his "inner emigration" from England—and he could find no English publisher, though he "tried most of them." *Seeing Is Believing* eventually came out in New York in 1958. Meanwhile, Tomlinson had started to read and admire William Carlos Williams, and as with so many poets, the virtues of Williams led to dilution in Tomlinson. He could not follow Williams very far, for Tomlinson's habits of moral insistence and reflective abstraction interfered, and so did a heaviness and turgidity in his diction and syntax. But if you take away from the style of Williams his remarkable freshness, lightness, speed, and imaginative sensitivity, it becomes merely casual and relaxed, with the attendant risk of dullness. From this Tomlinson was preserved by many things, including his intelligence, but he tended toward it, and his later volumes are less impressive than the earlier *Seeing Is Believing*. Apart from experiments with various types of line and subject matter, the main development in the more recent books is a partial return to the typically English poem of meditative landscape description, derived in Tomlinson's case from Augustan poetry and from Hardy. Tomlinson has also translated a good deal from Spanish poets, and he is a painter as well as a poet and critic.

A prototypical Tomlinson poem is "The Atlantic" from *Seeing Is Believing*. The poem might be described as an exercise in the disciplines of observation and description; the last line points the moral: subservient attention to "all we are not" replenishes us. The almost cranky insistence and firm, bristling specification ("in subservience") of the final lines are unfortunately also typical of Tomlinson:

> Launched into an opposing wind, hangs
> Grappled beneath the onrush,
> And there, lifts, curling in spume,
> Unlocks, drops from that hold
> Over and shoreward. The beach receives it,
> A whitening line, collapsing
> Powdering-off down its broken length;
> Then, curded, shallow, heavy
> With clustering bubbles, it nears
> In a slow sheet that must climb
> Relinquishing its power, upward
> Across tilted sand. Unravelled now
> And the shore, under its lucid pane,
> Clear to the sight, it is spent:
> The sun rocks there, as the netted ripple
> Into whose skeins the motion threads it

> Glances athwart a bed, honey-combed
> By heaving stones. Neither survives the instant
> But is caught back, and leaves, like the after-image
> Released from the floor of a now different mind,
> A quick gold, dyeing the uncovering beach
> With sunglaze. That which we were,
> Confronted by all that we are not,
> Grasps in subservience its replenishment.

The closeness of the description and the play of metaphor exact a concentration on the poem analogous to that of the poem on the wave, and so make the poem a spiritual exercise in Tomlinsonism. Yet while following the changing action of the wave in detail, the poem does not grasp it as a coherent whole. For these and other reasons the final effect of the poem is to confine rather than release imagination, and if this is appropriate to Tomlinson's moral idea, it also suggests that his moral idea limits the potentialities of his art.

TED HUGHES

Ted Hughes (b. 1930) grew up in Yorkshire. In his poetry the bleak moors and skies of that county, its wind, rain, and stony hills are images of a pitiless natural world; the landscape expresses grim truths it may have helped to implant. From childhood he was fascinated with animals and identified with them, and as predators and victims they too became symbols in his poems—"The Hawk in the Rain," "Hawk Roosting," "An Otter," "Pike," *Crow*—where they exhibit their oneness with nature, mindless instincts, and ferocity. They seem alien from the human, yet in a deeper perspective they ominously image the essence of man's nature and condition. Hughes's father, a carpenter and later a shopkeeper, had served in the First World War. Hence the war was vivid to Hughes's imagination, and as a child of four he would lie on the carpet "Among jawbones and blown-off boots, tree-stumps, shell-cases and craters, / Under rain that goes on drumming." The landscape of Flanders seemed superimposed on that of Yorkshire, so that even as an adult he could "never escape the impression that the whole region is in mourning for the first world war."

He spent two years in the National Service, and then entered Pembroke College, Cambridge, where he read first in English Literature and later in Archaeology and Anthropology. After graduating in 1954, he worked at various odd jobs in Cambridge and London. In 1956 he met Sylvia Plath, who was studying at Cambridge on a Fulbright scholarship, and within four months the two poets were married. In Plath's letters at this time we see Hughes through infatuated eyes. He was steeped in poetry. "We drink sherry in the garden and read poems; we quote on and on: he says a line of [Dylan] Thomas or Shakespeare and says: 'Finish.'" As for his appearance, he "wears always the same black sweater and corduroy jacket with pockets full of poems, fresh trout and horoscopes . . . He may shock you at first, unless you imagine a big, unruly Huckleberry Finn."

Hughes's pockets had not always been full of poems in recent years. After writing in school, he had ceased to do so at the university, numbed perhaps by the demands of the English tripos. Then, he recalls, "I read a Penguin of [contemporary] American poets that came out in about 1955." Among modern poets he had previously read Eliot, Dylan Thomas (whose 1946 *Deaths and Entrances* "was a holy book with me for quite a while when it first came out"), Lawrence, and "some Auden." And of course he was versed in older poets. Around the time he met Plath he was devoted to the poetry of John Crowe Ransom. Though the poets most evident in his early work were Yeats, Hopkins, and Thomas, it was Ransom and the other Americans—Shapiro, Lowell, Merwin, Wilbur—who somehow made it psychologically possible for him to write again, and by 1956 he was composing with utmost purposefulness and ambition. Plath entered a collection of his lyrics in a contest, the prize being publication by Harper, and the judges—Auden, Spender, and Marianne Moore—selected Hughes's manuscript. *The Hawk in the Rain* was published in London and New York in 1957 and was widely reviewed.

For the next two years Hughes and Plath lived in the United States, teaching and writing in or around Boston. In 1959, expecting a child, they returned to London. Hughes looked after the baby in the mornings while Plath wrote, retreating for that purpose to a room in W. S. Merwin's apartment; in the afternoon Plath cared for the baby and Hughes enjoyed the quiet of the writing room. They soon looked for a house, and found one in 1960 in a village in Devon. A second child was born, but marital strains developed, and Plath was "ditched," as she put it. They were living apart when Plath committed suicide in 1963. Hughes continued to work, turning out literature for children, translations, radio plays, and short stories as well as poems. Meanwhile a meeting in 1957 with the American artist Leonard Baskin led over the years to frequent collaboration. They produced broadsides and books of poems and paintings illustrating each other, such as *Cave Birds* (1975, revised 1978) and *Moon-Whales* (1976). Baskin's wish for poems to go with his drawings of crows led Hughes to start writing the *Crow* sequence in 1966. Hughes married for a second time in 1970.

Hughes's fluent productivity is partly to be explained by his creative method. His poems take their initiative from a concrete subject—an image, character or action—which is developed until the poem stands complete. Usually his poems tell a story or have narrative elements, and in his sequence poems, such as *Gaudette,* a continuing story binds the separate lyrics into a whole. "Poems come to you more naturally," Hughes explains, "and accumulate more life when they are part of a connected flow of real narrative that you've got yourself invovled in." Thus his poems direct attention to the event contemplated rather than to his personal life and emotion. These are of course reflected, but only indirectly, tacitly, and in the objective form of a symbol.

In Hughes's first volume formality prevailed. The poems were divided into stanzas, and these were sometimes in complicated forms; syntax was compact, contorted, and often elliptical; lines were patterned through assonance and alliteration—"Winds stampeding the fields under the window." The metaphor of "The Thought-Fox" resembled the extended, ingenious comparisons in the neo-Metaphysical style of the period. "The Man Seeking Experience Enquires His Way of a Drop of Water" was baroque artifice. There was much variety. "The Horses" was a Wordsworthian poem. Over the next ten years Hughes learned to use simpler, freer methods, and in many poems of *Wodwo* (1967) he relied on short, simple, declarative sentences, repetition, white space, and the varying line lengths of free verse. "The Green Wolf," "Full Moon and Little Frieda," "The Howling of Wolves," and the title poem of *Wodwo* are lyrics he could not have composed ten years before. *Crow* (1970) was to be a major turning point, but many of Hughes's technical procedures in that volume had been mastered by the time he completed *Wodwo*. Meanwhile his characteristic *Weltanschauung* had been present from the start. In "Pike" the two fish died trying to swallow each other. "The Martyrdom of Bishop Farrar," who was burned at the stake, was unlike Hughes in drawing a moral, but less so in picturing the oozings and bubblings of the burnt flesh. "Hawk Roosting," a hawk's monologue, expressed murderous instinct and manic egoism. "View of a Pig" contemplated the slaughtered animal. In the "Relic" a jawbone from some sea creature was a reminder of "that darkness" where "Nothing touches but, clutching, devours."

Some of the poems in *Crow* (1970) are like the myths of primitive peoples. In form they may have been influenced by the Yugoslav poet Vasko Popa. Hughes's 1978 introduction to Popa's *Collected Poems* suggests what he admired in this writer, whose "vision" is "of the struggle of animal cells and of the torment of the spirit in a world reduced" to this. Popa's lyrics are simultaneously "plain-statement and visionary. . . . It is in this favourite device of his, the little fable or visionary anecdote, that we see most clearly his shift from literary surrealism to the far older and deeper thing, the surrealism of folklore." Several critics also relate Hughes's Crow poems to the Trickster myths of the North American Indians, which have, in Paul Radin's summary, "a hero who is always wandering, who is always hungry, who is not guided by normal conceptions of good and evil, who is either playing tricks on people or having them played on him." Often the Trickster is a raven. In both the myths of the Indians and those of Hughes the events take place at the beginning or end of the cosmos or, alternatively, at no place or time. Several of the Crow poems, like the myths of the Trickster and countless other primitive myths, explain how a feature of existence originated. Thus "A Childish Prank" goes back to the time when Adam and Eve lay on the "flowers of Eden." God fell asleep, and Crow bit a worm "Into two writhing halves." The tail was stuffed into man "With the wounded end hanging out," and the half with the head was poked into woman, where it "crept in deeper and up/ To peer out through her eyes." It called its "tail-half to join up quickly," and

Man awoke being dragged across the grass.
Woman awoke to see him coming.
Neither knew what had happened.

God went on sleeping.

Crow went on laughing.

The poems in *Crow*, Hughes later said, originated in "an idea
of a style. . . . The idea was originally just to write . . . the songs
that a crow would sing. In other words, songs with no music
whatsoever, in a super-simple and a super-ugly language which
would in a way shed everything except just what he wanted to
say without any other consideration." Not all the poems adhered
to this idea; there was much music, loquacity, and formal artifice,
but in general the poems told stark anecdotes in direct, laconic,
declarative sentences. In content they were often grotesque, obscene, blasphemous, and cruel.

The poems address ultimate religious questions. Some readers have felt that in *Crow* Hughes produced an antagonist Bible,
a myth that parallels and denies the biblical one. Though this
goes too far—the parallels to the Bible are not sufficiently sys-
tematic—God, Adam, Eve, and Satan have a role in many of the
poems, and the myths are arranged in a sequence from the beginning to the end of things, from Genesis to Apocalypse. God
is well meaning but ineffective, and other powers have contributed to create a world that God Himself deplores. In this respect
Crow contemplates a Gnostic universe. Yet to say that the volume
pictures existence as evil would be too simple. The poems are
saturated with physical pain and suffering, but we cannot predicate moral evil where there is no choice, and choice seems
largely absent in Crow's world of harsh natural necessities and
instincts.

At public readings Hughes tells a story about Crow and God
and reads the poems as moments in this narrative. Obviously
the poems have implications in this context that they do not have
in the book, which lacks the connecting plot. When Hughes tells
the story, it is not always exactly the same, but the gist of it is that
God has a nightmare that questions the worth of the cosmos He
has created. Challenged by God to do better, the nightmare
brings forth Crow. In a kind of game God and Crow then involve
each other in various difficulties, and as Crow copes with these,

he begins to increase in intelligence. Hughes said in an interview that in the background story Crow is trying to become a man, and some readers have perceived this theme within the book. But in another interview Hughes remarked that "The story is not really relevant to the poems as they stand." That the Crow poems are part of a larger, continually changing imaginative work that exists only in Hughes' mind makes any interpretation doubtful, but it is just as doubtful if we ignore the larger story. As a symbol Crow is inconsistent. It is impossible to say what he represents in the volume as a whole.

In many of the poems, however, Crow is the Survivor; though he is frightened, stunned, scorched, chopped to pieces, and hung up by one claw, he is never quite killed, and he embodies tough qualities that enable life to persist. These are not lovable; they include egoism, suspicious alertness, aggressive violence, limited imagination, insensitivity, and low-minded practicality. In "That Moment" when

> the only face left in the world
> Lay broken
> Between hands that relaxed, being too late,

"Crow had to start searching for something to eat." The merit of this anecdote is not subtlety, needless to say, but realistic essentialism. In the midst of despair and guilt we eat; there is Crow in all of us. In "Crow Tyrannosaurus" even Crow was feeling a little guilty because he ate other creatures. But when "his eye saw a grub," his "head, trapsprung, stabbed." The grubs wept, and so did Crow himself in sympathy: "Weeping he walked and stabbed." In "Crow and the Birds" the other birds swoop, soar, preen, and generally behave as birds commonly do in poems; "Crow spraddled head-down in the beach-garbage, guzzling a dropped ice cream."

Because Crow is stupid, we laugh at him. We also laugh with him, somewhat maliciously, when he plays his tricks. David Lodge has pointed out that Hughes's conception of Crow is influenced by the animals in Disney cartoons. The poems also show the impact of Hughes's writing for children and for radio. One should hear them read aloud. But Crow is also a version of the traditional comic type of Sancho Panza. Though we hate the mean creature, we also see in him a symbol of the scavenging self that preserves us, and we harbor a certain affection for him. There is reassurance in his scrawny, sinewy body, his ability to digest anything, his unfeelingness, tenacity, and indestructibility.

Moortown (1979) is a major, somewhat retrospective collection. It includes several poetic sequences, some of them published previously, and it probably also contains poems written earlier and never published. No new phase or resource of Hughes's poetry showed itself for the first time in *Moortown*, but I have not yet discussed his quasi-realistic poems based on experience as a Devon farmer; Hughes describes these poems as "passages from a verse farming diary."

Like many poets who compose in a fluent, workmanlike way, Hughes is sometimes too directly purposeful. His plotting is skillful in the sense that it underscores implications and builds climaxes, but the evident intention can unrealize the emotion, making it seem somewhat worked up. When, for example, we read of the birth of a calf ("Birth of Rainbow" in *Moortown*) taking place on a 'snow-powdered" ridge in "razorish" wind and with a hail storm coming over the moor, we may feel that Hughes has rather loaded the dice against this poor calf. Two and a half lines are devoted to describing the "flag of bloody" afterbirth flapping from the cow's "back end . . . in the unsparing wind"; one line pictures the "blood-dangle" of the calf's "muddy birth cord"; the cow eats the afterbirth that "Spinnakered from her rear." These and other details exhibit animal instinct and the subjection of the flesh with heavy emphasis. At the conclusion of the poem, with the hail coming on, the human protectors head for shelter, leaving "to God the calf and his mother." The calf was presumably called "Rainbow" because during the birth its mother stood under the end of a rainbow. Since the rainbow in Genesis is a token of God's presence and covenant, Hughes doubtless stuffed it into this poem for irony: God is absent from this wholly natural and unprotected birth. Every detail of the poem might have been observed just as Hughes described it, but in a work of art such a biased plot creates disbelief. The language of the poem contributes to the sense of artifice. "Flooded ruts" of the road are words chosen for their assonance. The brightness of the morning is rendered not from nature but from Hopkins—"the low morning dazzling washed sun."

In Hughes, then, I find an insensitive artistry and an interpretation of life too aggressively and unquestioningly committed to its premises. Many readers would resist Hughes's vision of life in any case. But the criticism here put forward is not a protest of outraged liberal humanitarianism. It refers to the many poems in which the mere, harsh, suffering naturalness of existence is expressed with obvious manipulation, undermining the credibility of the experience and the reader's assent. But in Hughes's better poems the vision of a brutally harsh world is complicated (though not mitigated) by the strangeness and originality of the imaginative experience and by the humor of tough survival. And his later volumes admit somewhat hopeful possibilities in existence that were absent from his earlier ones. He still portrays a mindless, ruthless nature, but he seems to sympathize or identify with it less.

GEOFFREY HILL

In the poems of Geoffrey Hill (b. 1932) a troubled conscience arrests and weighs every impulse. For with his shocked awareness of the evil of the human heart, Hill naturally mistrusts his own propensities also. Not least he suspects the impulse to write poetry, for his theme is human suffering, and to express this in artful form seems to Hill an evasion, possibly even a perverse feasting. His suspicion of human nature supports his belief that a poem should be an impersonal, objective, well-made artifact. To vent emotions and sensations spontaneously would release what ought, instead, to be checked and disciplined. His style embodies his commitments to intellectual and artistic rigor, scruple, and labor. His laconic, sometimes disjunctive phrasing is packed with connotations, and since he doubts in all directions, his implications are many-sided and ambiguous. Merely because it is condensed his style seems Modernist to some readers. His prosodic forms are closed. Having no wish to suggest that poetry is natural speech, he is lavish with rhetorical figures—alliteration, assonance, parallelism, antithesis, repetition, paradox, oxymoron—and these interplay with colloquial phrases that, in his contexts, seem no less artificial. His formal, polysemous, ironic, emotionally intense utterance is completely his own, though in

his early poetry it somewhat resembled that of Allen Tate and
of the early Robert Lowell before *Life Studies.*

Because Hill dwells on pain, suffering, and evil, his vision of
things might be called tragic, but not if that term implies a grandeur in human nature. It might be thought religious, for though
Hill withholds religious assent, he contemplates the human condition in its ultimate aspects. Moreover, since the evils that haunt
his imagination are less sickness, accident, mortality, and other
so-called natural ills than the heart's blindness, treachery, and
cruelty in the self-betrayals of private life and in persecutions,
concentration camps, and wars, his theme, were he a Christian
poet, might be called Original Sin. Confronting the truths he
lays bare, he sometimes expresses no attitude; the case is presented and the poem ends in bitter silence. At times he is compassionate. But usually his attitude is somewhat harsh, sardonic,
and condemnatory, and he turns on himself also. "Of Commerce
and Society," for example, dwells on the complacency and spiritual obtuseness of Europe recovering after the Second World
War. The horrors undergone have been scoured from memory.
Nothing has been learned:

> Europe, the much-scarred, much-scoured terrain,
> Its attested liberties, home-produce,
> Labelled and looking up, invites use,
> Stuffed with artistry and substantial gain.

Hill could not have written "Stuffed with artistry" without thinking of his own craft. The phrase even describes reductively the
style of his poem while also repudiating it.

Among Hill's important poems in the 1960s were the eight
sonnets entitled "Funeral Music." Spoken by persons executed
during the medieval Wars of the Roses, the sonnets meditate
upon violence and suffering, upon the motives that impell to
self-sacrifice, upon God and what it means to believe or not believe in Him, and upon the situation of man in relation to the
transcendent. Hill says that "In this sequence I was attempting
a florid grim music broken by grunts and shrieks . . . [an] ornate
and heartless music punctuated by mutterings, blasphemies and
cries for help." The sonnets lack dramatic immediacy, however;
the "mutterings" and "cries" of these intellectuals are generalizations and aphorisms:

> When we chant
> "Ora, ora pro nobis" it is not
> Seraphs who descend to pity but ourselves;
> . . . .
> I believe in my
> Abandonment, since it is what I have.

The second sonnet gathers the despair that runs through the sequence into a memorable image. "For whom do we scrape our tribute of pain," the speaker asks, and answers with a recollection of Towton Field after the battle, the "trampled acres" blown by empty wind:

> some trampled
> Acres, parched, sodden or blanched by sleet,
> Stuck with strange-postured dead. Recall the wind's
> Flurrying, darkness over the human mire.

Hill's *Mercian Hymns* (1971) were a new departure. The poems refer to King Offa of Mercia (A.D. 757–96), though they tell little about him and do not amount to a historical portrait or narrative. Offa is conflated with someone—we may call him Hill—growing up in contemporary England. The imaginative resort to England's medieval past, the framing of it in local history, and the superimposing of it upon the present generally recall as a formula Basil Bunting's *Briggflatts* (1966). The *Mercian Hymns* also bring to mind the writings of David Jones. Affinities of style or phrasing are sometimes such that Jones might have composed the sentences. And both Hill and Jones exhibit their contemporary subject matter with realism and yet also lift it into myth; in both poets, as in Bunting, the mythical dimension comes from connecting the present with a half-legendary past. In these respects, as also in their disjunctive juxtaposition of sentences, the *Mercian Hymns* are part of the high Modernist revival of the 1960s that spread the fame of Jones and heartened Bunting to write *Briggflatts*.

But if we exclude the vistas of the past and the mythological dimension, the contemporary world reflected in *Mercian Hymns* does not much resemble that of either Bunting or Jones. We behold, instead, the drab scenes and souls that filled the Movement pages of Larkin and Davie. The landscape includes holly groves and "Frail ironworks rusting in the thorn-thicket"—bleak

but not disagreeable features one might find in Hardy or Auden—but emphasizes such items as the M5 highway, ironically
"desirable new estates," and meadows "scabbed with cow-dung";
children are similarly scabbed, not with dung but with impetigo
and "dried snot"; chestnut leaves are unhealthily "inflamed";
and the protagonist, visiting a medieval dungeon as a tourist,
finds his imagination also inflamed by seeing the instruments of
torture. Unlovely recollections from childhood are superimposed on the image of the egoistic and tyranical Offa; they include battering a ditchful of frogs and also a playmate who was
"sniggering with fright," the playmate having lost a toy airplane.
In Poem XIX children romp in a kitchen garden "riddled with
toy-shards." As they "shriek and scavenge" they create an impression of the primitive and savage. They "haul" and "launch"
a "sodden log, hung with soft shields of fungus," upon the
flames. The description of the log, making it seem inert, soft,
and helpless, touches this Viking funeral with suggestions of
pain and sadism:

> We have a kitchen-garden riddled with toy-shards, with splinters of
> habitation. The children shriek and scavenge, play havoc. They in-
> cinerate boxes, rags and old tyres. They haul a sodden log, hung with
> soft shields of fungus, and launch it upon the flames.

In *Tenebrae* (1978) Hill opened himself to altogether different
influences. Several of these lyrics are closely modeled on Spanish
poetry of the Renaissance. The themes of this volume are love
and religious invocation without faith, and they are intertwined.
In style the poems are brief, terse, and closed, with much paradox and baroque artifice—"I founder in desire for things un-
found." The strong, harsh, contending emotions they express,
though with personal reticence, are appropriate to their baroque style and also characteristic of Hill. In the litany of love
in the "Tenebrae" sequence, for example, the juxtaposed feelings range from disgust to "purest praise":

> This is the ash-pit of the lily-fire,
> this is the questioning at the long tables,
> this is true marriage of the self-in-self,
> this is a raging solitude of desire,

> this is the chorus of obscene content,
> this is a single voice of purest praise.

The extreme and scrupulous artifice of this poetry, which seems to exclude the "real cries" of lived experience, naturally caused Hill the gravest compunctions; at the end of the volume, when the emotional crisis has died despairingly away, he typically remarks that the "music" or poetry written during the crisis survives it—music that is created amid woe, rage, loss, longing, and yet that inevitably transforms and excludes such emotions:

> Music survives, composing her own sphere,
> Angel of Tones, Medusa, Queen of the Air,
> and when we would accost her with real cries
> silver on silver thrills itself to ice.

That "Music survives" the lines themselves evidence, but as they voice this fact they are far from triumphant. Yet Hill's attitude toward "music" is not merely ironic and rejecting. Instead, the lines typically embody an intense, complicated self-conflict, and knot into unresolvable ambivalence.

THOM GUNN

The poetry of Thom Gunn (b. 1929) shares, on the one hand, moral attitudes and stylistic modes that are typical of poets in the United States today and especially of poets in California. On the other hand, it bears the stamp of Gunn's early training in a different school, so that amid the hot tubs, LSD, sunny flesh, sleeping bags under the stars, and general quest for Adamic innocence and spontaneous wholeness of being Gunn preserves the strong discipline of such masters as William Empson, F. R. Leavis, and Yvor Winters. And he also shares, as no American poet does, historical traditions of English poetry, so that, for example, the firm, sober, delicate step of Augustan versification articulates flowing, obscure moments of feeling, and the rocky walls of a California canyon afford the minute, nature-watching perceptions of a Cowper in couplets:

Those walls are crammed with neighboring detail,
Small as an ocean rock-pool's, and no more frail:
Pigmy fern groves, a long web slung across
A perilous bush, an emerald fur of moss;
Wherever it is possible, some plant
Growing in crevices or up a slant.

The biographical basis for such amalgamations is simply that after growing up in England—he was in the British Army, spent some months in Paris trying to write, and went to Cambridge University—Gunn moved in 1954 to California. He was a graduate student at Stanford, taught for eight years (1958–66) at the University of California at Berkeley, and has lived in or near San Francisco most of the time since.

The opposed stylistic traditions reflect divided impulses of Gunn's nature. He hungers to live in the vital moment, the full, quick, unselfconscious instant of being. In the midst of such moments, however, he is impelled to reflect upon them. He observes the experience as he undergoes it, classifies it, questions its value, and draws forth its meaning. The stylistic exponents of this distancing may be the intellectual irony of the neo-Metaphysical school, or the Augustan contemplative mode, or both at once, or something else, but the effect is always of a rather cool withholding of himself, of a watching, considering, formal shaping, and intellection even amid experiences, such as sexual intercourse or LSD, that by convention are or ought to be intense and self-forgetting.

The terms of this self-division ramify into others. On the one hand, he values hard indifference, aggressive thrust, keeping people at a distance. On the other hand, he wistfully contemplates self-forgetfulness and surrender, touch and union, trust, gentleness, nakedness, and passive, open being. The terms take on different weights and permutations from poem to poem, but each poem relates to this central, continuing dialogue with himself, and thus each acquires resonance in the context of Gunn's work as a whole. And just as the same or closely similar moral tensions recur throughout his work and unify it, their expressive symbols do also—for example, the symbolisms of a uniform (or something analogous to it) and of movement. In "On the Move" Gunn describes the goalless but somehow splendid onrush of a motorcycle gang. The uniform in this poem consists of the goggles and black leather jacket by which the motorcyclists put on "impersonality" and escape doubt and guilt—or try to. In "Innocence" Gunn sets forth the somewhat similar case of another uniform-wearer. As the soldier grew up a sense of history and guilt were never deposited in his mind, which retained

> A compact innocence, childlike and clear,
> No doubt could penetrate, no act could harm.

When in the war a captured enemy is deliberately burned alive, he stands by untroubled. In a lyric written some seven years later ("Misanthropos" XI) a German soldier who "helped the Jews to get away" is "on the move" like the motorcyclists, except that his motion is a steady, purposeful walk in a "direction." And though in uniform,

> He never did mistake for bondage
> The military job, the chances,
> The limits; he did not submit
> To blackmail of his circumstances.
>
> I see him in the Polish snow,
> His muddy wrappings small protection,
> Breathing the cold air of his freedom
> And treading a distinct direction.

In the "Elegy on the Dust" ("Misanthropos" XII), from which I shall quote shortly, we see an imaginative transformation of the image of the motorcyclists. They have become specks of dust "hurled/ In endless hurry" by the wind.

The balance of Gunn's moral allegiance gradually shifts from his early volumes to his latest. In the 1950s his heroes (though still ambivalently regarded) might be the "Sad Captains" who spend "wasteful force" in "hot convulsions"; in the 1970s he affectionately remembers Thomas Bewick, author of *The History of British Birds,* who forgot himself watching the creatures on his walks:

> a selfless self as difficult
> to recover and hold as to
> capture the exact way
> a burly bluetit grips
> its branch (leaning forward)
> over this rock.

The course of Gunn's stylistic development has been generally
similar to that of Robert Lowell, John Berryman, and other
older poets or contemporaries who began in the formal mode
of the 1940s and 1950s and sought in the 1960s to break out
into immediacy and "life." During the 1950s Gunn was usually
described as an Empsonian or Metaphysical poet, and reading
"The Wound," "The Beach Head," "In Santa Maria del Populo,"
"The Byrnies," or "On the Move" one sees why. Though these
are not so packed, punning, or difficult as Empson's early
poems, they also elaborate and draw out the implications of a
central metaphor with serious wit. In "On the Move," to advert
again to that famous poem, the leather-jacketed "Boys" on their
motorcycles are a many-sided symbol of the poet or poetry, of
technological civilization divorced from nature, and of modern
man existentially declaring himself in a universe without values
or meaning. All these poems exhibit the regular, traditional versification, proper grammar, and closed, compact syntax that
were common in the 1950s. Their diction mingles the colloquial
with the indirect, elevated, and unnatural (for example, "Exact
conclusion of their hardiness/ Has no shape yet," in "On the
Move"). And they have the ambivalent, ironical detachment
from their subject that was also typical of the period.

When in 1954 Gunn came to the United States he studied with
Yvor Winters, and this first American influence reinforced earlier English ones. But a Romantic strain persisted in him. "In
gleaming jackets trophied with the dust," a line describing the
motorcyclists in "On the Move," might have been written by Hart
Crane but never by Larkin, partly because of its surging emotional rhythm and climax and especially because of the emotion
gathered in "gleaming," which presents the leather jackets as
though they were coats of mail of questing knights.

At Winters' insistence Gunn began to study William Carlos
Williams, who was then being felt like a spring wind in American
poetry, and Williams freed Gunn from the ice palace of the
Metaphysical mode. "Blackie, the Electric Rembrandt," from
Gunn's 1961 volume, observes a tattoo artist inscribing a cluster
of stars on a boy's "virginal arm." The versification—seven-
syllable couplets—is not that of Williams, but everything else is:
the conception of the poem; the spare, vivid particulars; the
swift, direct, natural language and syntax; the warm sympathy

with "ordinary" reality and characters; the immediacy, sensitivity, and complexity of the emotions; the counterpoint of metaphoric suggestion surrounding the apparently simple words; even the slight defiance in finding a poem in such materials. As the boy is tattooed his eyes

> follow the point
> that touches (quick, dark movement!)
>
> a virginal arm beneath
> his rolled sleeve: he holds his breath.
>
> . . . Now that it is finished, he
> hands a few bills to Blackie
>
> and leaves with a bandage on
> his arm, under which gleam ten
>
> stars, hanging in a blue thick
> cluster. Now he is starlike.

Gunn did not write many poems this close to Williams, and of course the influence did not come just from Williams but was refracted and diffused from many other poets, themselves also responding to Williams. But henceforth the emotional and stylistic resources of the Williams poem modified Gunn's work. "The Outdoor Concert," "Autobiography," "The Idea of Trust," "Bally *Power Play*," and many another of Gunn's poems in the last ten years have an intellectuality and philosophical implication that belong to Gunn much more than Williams, but they are formed in Williams' school.

The next significant development came in "Misanthropos," which was printed in *Touch* (1967) but had been written between 1963 and 1965. A sequence of seventeen lyrics, "Misanthropos" renders the experiences, emotions, and thoughts of a "last man," a survivor of global war, from his solitude at the start of the sequence to the approach of other survivors at the end. The emotional drama of the poem lies in his changing inner attitude to human contact, a theme that always had much resonance for Gunn and is central to other poems in *Touch*, as indeed the title indicates. Each of the poems in "Misanthropos" evokes comparisons with the others and enriches itself thereby; I mentioned that this happens in Gunn's poetry as a whole, but in "Misanthropos" it becomes a conscious artistic method. Even in isolation some passages have extraordinary power. "Elegy on the Dust" describes a sea of dust to which all human beings come, breaking down to powder and drifting with the mass. The vision is a stark *memento mori* of a traditional kind, and, at the same time, a metaphor of the psychological disintegration of mass man into featureless units. The intense emotion of the poem sustains itself amid intellection and formal rigor, the meter being Gunn's adaptation of the classical elegiac distich. The poem is bitter, ominous, grotesque, and harshly satiric.

> They have all come who sought distinction hard
> To this universal knacker's yard,
> Blood dried, flesh shriveled, and bone decimated:
> Motion of life is thus repeated,
> A process ultimately without pain
> As they are broken down again.
> The remnants of their guilt mix as they must
> And average out in grains of dust
> Too light to act, too small to harm, too fine
> To simper or betray or whine.
>
> Each colorless hard grain is now distinct,
> In no way to its neighbor linked,
> Yet from wind's unpremeditated labors
> It drifts in concord with its neighbors,
> Perfect community in its behaviour.
> It yields to what it sought, a saviour:
> Scattered and gathered, irregularly blown,
> Now sheltered by a ridge or stone,
> Now lifted on strong upper winds, and hurled
> In endless hurry round the world.

From "Misanthropos" to the present day I find much remarkable writing in Gunn but no definite development. *Moly* (1971), his next collection of poems after *Touch*, had for its general themes the transformation or metamorphosis of the self and the quest for oneness, but the oneness sought was not with other people so much as within the self and with the cosmos. "Almost all of the poems" in this volume, Gunn said, "have in some way however indirect to do with" LSD, which was of "utmost importance" to him as a source of "discovery." "And now that the great sweep of the acid years is over, I cannot unlearn the things that I learned during them. I cannot deny the vision of what the world might be like. Everything that we glimpsed—the trust, the brotherhood, the repossession of innocence, the nakedness of spirit—is still a possibility and will continue to be so." In the poems of these years drugs, sex, surfing, camping, outdoor nakedness, and the like may bring momentary feelings of oneness; at least they symbolize the quest and the values associated with it. Children, animals, plants, and landscape serve as metaphors of mystical unity and fullness of being. Of the many remarkable poems that could be cited, "From the Wave" may be selected because it makes a significant contrast to "On the Move." Here again we see black riders at a distance, but instead of the leather-jacketed motorcyclists of the earlier poem, they are surfers in rubber suits. The motorcyclists represented an aggressive thrust of will in independence from nature, but the surfers look like seals. They suggest the metamorphosis of the human into the animal, and as they ride the boards, they merge with the wave and its rhythm. The final image of the riders close inshore, the wave having carried them and dissolved, suggests an attitude to life altogether different from the restless, assertive ethos of "On the Move":

> They paddle in the shallows still;
> Two splash each other;
> Then all swim out to wait until
> The right waves gather.

But the metamorphosis and achieved oneness such poems enact is not primitivistic. The riders in "From the Wave" do not cease to be human in becoming like seals. Gunn envisions a fusion, not a regression. Though the surfers unite with the wave in a sense that suggests self-surrender, they also maintain their difficult balance with "learn'd skill." They participate in the motion of the wave through a precise timing that involves attention and control. Moreover, in the wave they become a metaphor of mind or consciousness within the "mindless heave." In these respects the poem is typical of the complex spiritual ideal Gunn now entertains, which unites or seeks to unite such seemingly opposed possibilities as quasi-mystical unity with nature with self-conscious awareness; spontaneity and immediacy of utterance with art; being with knowing. His most impressive though deeply flawed lyric of the last ten years is the first one in the sequence entitled "The Geysers." It describes a night spent camping out of doors. The last three lines seem to me especially fine. The lyric articulates some of the themes just dwelt on; the final lines mingle a sense of regret, difference, and loss on waking with a complex, wistful readiness for the day.

> Gentle as breathing
> down to us it spills
> From geysers heard but hidden in the hills.
> . . . .
> I lie an arm-length from the stream and watch
> Arcs fading between stars. There
> bright! faint! gone!
> More meteors than I've ever set eyes on:
> . . . .
> I must have been asleep when morning came.
> The v-sides of our shadowed valley frame
> The tall hill fair with sunshine opposite.
> Live-oaks are of it yet crest separate,
> In heavy festooned arches. Now it's day
> We get up naked as we intend to stay.
>
> Gentle as breathing
> Sleep by the hot stream, broken.
> Bright, faint, and gone. What I am now has woken.

20

THE POETRY OF IRELAND

THROUGHOUT this century the poetry written in English by Irish poets has maintained traditions of its own. Irish poetry has distinctive themes and styles, and of course it reflects a national history and a social reality that are quite different from those of either Great Britain or the United States. Perhaps the most persisting topic of Irish poetry has been the quest of Irish identity. This was prominent in the poetry of the Celtic Twilight, around the turn of the century, with its cultivation of ancient Irish legends and myths and of world-weary sorrow and other moods assumed to be characteristic of the Celtic race. The search for Irish identity equally motivated the "folk" movement in poetry exhibiting the imaginative lore and way of life of the peasantry—for the peasantry, and not the middle class, was felt to be the bearer of "Irishness." The plays of Synge were the most important literary works in this movement, but lyrics of Padraic Colum, Joseph Campbell, and F. R. Higgins shared the same tendencies. Another type of poem, such as Joseph Campbell's "The Gombean" or Seamus Heaney's "Docker," portrays representative Irish persons. Poems on events in Irish history are frequent, and though some of these are only commemorative, others have an intellectual intention. They recollect the past in order to explain Irish character and

life in the present; such poems remember the conquest, occu-
pation, oppression, and exploitation by England, the bond between the people and the Roman Catholic Church, the centuries
of fear and poverty, the famines and mass emigrations. Poetry
of earlier centuries in the Irish language naturally fascinates
readers in quest of Irish identity, and many modern poets, such
as Austin Clarke, Frank O'Connor, Thomas Kinsella, John Montague, and Tom MacIntyre, have translated from this literature.
There are also poems on Ireland in general, such as John Hewitt's "An Irishman in Coventry" and Seamus Heaney's splendid
"Bogland." Irish history, character, problems, and ways of life
have been so strongly preoccupying that personal poems that
lack this national reference, as in the work of Denis Devlin, Seamus Heaney, or Michael Longley, seem to challenge tradition.

The representation of Irish character in the poetry of this century has, on the whole, not been sentimental or self-congratu-
latory. In fact, the topic of national identity is frequently associated with harsh realism and satire. Austin Clarke is the chief
poet in this vein. Patrick Kavanagh, in *The Great Hunger* (1942),
gives a powerfully detailed picture of the emotional and spiritual
deprivations of rural poverty. And many other Irish poets have
also protested against psychological, moral, or imaginative limitations they have internalized, as they feel, in growing up in
Ireland. Drunkenness, violence, anti-intellectualism, sexual
repression, and religious bigotry are the chief notes of negative
Irish identity as the poets perceive it.

The Modernist revolution discouraged for a while the use of
rural incidents and imagery that, until then, had been routinely
expected in poetry, but in Ireland this inhibition was less felt.
One reason was that the Modernist poet who loomed largest in
Ireland was not Eliot but Yeats. Neither Eliot's imagery of the
metropolis nor his critical judgments ever commanded as much
attention in Ireland as they did in Great Britain and the United
States. Another reason was simply that to write about the life of
a large city is less plausible in an Irish context. Moreover, Kavanagh, Heaney, and other poets had direct experience of farm
life and wrote about it. The quality of their work gives this subject special importance in contemporary Irish poetry. There are
also bucolic poets, nature lovers such as John Hewitt. But Irish
landscape—or the poetic version of it—changed from the start

of the century to now. It was formerly wet, windy, heathery, stony, gray, and glimmering, and now tends rather to be flooded, muddy, boggy, and dungy—in short, it has become less Romantically beautiful and more earthy.

In its methods of presentation the poetry of Ireland is conservative. It has slowly assimilated the Modernist or Postmodernist styles of Europe and America, but when compared to contemporaries in England or the United States, no Irish poet seems radically experimental. Lyrics are generally orderly and logical, and there is much intellectual point and declarative statement. The disorienting grammar of Ashbery, for example, would be very unexpected in an Irish poet, and so would Dada or Surrealism, though there are some recent Irish poems in the latter vein. But Irish poetry also lacks, on the whole, the intellectual difficulty and compression of the American New Critical style or of poets such as Geoffrey Hill in Great Britain. Musically and rhythmically Irish poetry is self-consciously artful and pleasing. To an Irish poet the deluging lines of Ginsberg, for example, would feel uncontrolled. Moreover, the outspoken emotionality of Beat and other American poetry in the 1960s is alien to the poetry of Ireland, in which emotional expression, however strong, is restrained. Recent Irish poetry tends also to be morally troubled, with much sensitive searching of the conscience.

During the twentieth century, poetry in Ireland has continued without dramatic revolutions against earlier generations. The nearest approximation to such a break was the lessening appreciation of the poetry of the Irish Literary Revival, of such poets as George Russell (AE), Katherine Tynan, F. R. Higgins, James Stephens, and Padraic Colum. These poets, who were contemporaries of Yeats, Synge, Joyce, and O'Casey, were more or less admired until the death of Yeats in 1939. They were discussed in the first volume of this history, and will not be further noticed here. (Louis MacNeice, who was born in Belfast but lived most of his adult life out of Ireland, was included with the English poets of the 1930s in Chapter 6.) Generally the Revival poets are now said to have been Georgian or Romantic, the terms being used pejoratively. Whether these terms apply is a complex question. Katherine Tynan and Padraic Colum were very conventional poets, and except in his first volume, *Insurrections* (1909),

James Stephens was less realistic in method than Austin Clarke or Patrick Kavanagh, but Stephens was not a lesser poet than they. To me it seems that the reaction against the Revival has been excessive, while it also seems that subsequent poets have wished to break more sharply with the past than they have been able to do. Of course, this judgment depends on my perspective. If we view the poetry of modern Ireland in context with that of Great Britain and the United States, we notice the continuity of Irish poetry. Viewing it from within and attending to Irish poets primarily, we would observe a greater differentiation.

After the 1890s, when Yeats gradually withdrew as impresario of the new poetry and drama in Ireland, he influenced other Irish writers relatively little. The reasons were partly that his work seemed less relevant to Ireland's later preoccupations, and chiefly that his achievement and reputation were too great and too much in everyone's mind. He was too visible to be imitated. He was important in guiding some poets toward their subject matter in Irish history, legends, folktales, or the life of the peasantry. And he had a practical impact on careers, since he assisted some poets, such as F. R. Higgins, and ignored others, such as Austin Clarke, whom he excluded from his *Oxford Book of Modern Verse* (1936). In fact, his power of patronage, which he exercised through his connections with publishers, his role in the Abbey Theater, and his general prestige, was greatly resented, and led after his death to denigration of some of the poets he had favored. It also contributed to the reaction against the poetry of the Literary Revival, which was seen as Yeats's creation. The work of contemporary Irish poets frequently alludes to specific phrases of Yeats or to his attitudes and opinions, but it is not Yeatsian in style.

Aside from Yeats the greatest Irish writers who also wrote poetry were James Joyce and Samuel Beckett, but the poetry of Joyce and Beckett is minor. Joyce's verse is formally meticulous art but of slight interest. The *Collected Poems in English and French* (1977) of Beckett are eccentric, vital, and amusing. They convey the same dismal vision as his dramas and novels, and would be more important if the latter did not exist. "Whoroscope," the most interesting of Beckett's poems, is an obscure monologue spoken by the philosopher Descartes. Neither Joyce nor Beckett is within the traditions of Irish poetry. With them, as Irish poets who lived abroad and adopted international styles, I may mention Denis Devlin (1908–59), Desmond O'Grady (b. 1935), and Thomas MacGreevy (1893–1967). MacGreevy was associated with Joyce and Beckett in Paris during the 1930s. American readers will recollect the enthusiasm of Wallace Stevens for this poet. MacGreevy returned to Ireland in 1940, where he was an art critic and director of the National Gallery. His cultivated intelligence and disciplined style of free verse may be sampled in "Nocturne of the Self-Evident Presence," a poem that compares the skyey vistas in the Alps to the painted ones in the Vatican palace and the speaker to the Pope. Unlike the Pope, the speaker sees no angels and prophets when he looks up, but only

> alps, ice, stars and white sunlight
> In a dry, high silence.

AUSTIN CLARKE

Austin Clarke (1896–1974) received an M.A. from University College in Dublin and briefly lectured there. He then lived in England for sixteen years as a freelance writer, turning out editorials and reviews for newspapers. Clarke's early poems were narratives based on Irish sagas and history. *Night and Morning* (1938) abandoned these subjects. The volume contained troubled, spiritually questing poems, and it also attacked the Roman Catholic Church, to which Clarke attributed the intellectual and emotional impoverishment of the middle class. "Martha Blake" and the later "Martha Blake at Fifty-One" are grimly detailed, harrowing portraits of a pious Irish spinster. Clarke's satiric critique of Ireland continued in *Ancient Lights* (1966) and subsequent volumes until *Mnemosyne Lay in Dust* (1966), which is a realistic narrative of a mental breakdown. In his last volumes, such as *Tiresias* (1971), Clarke told stories for the pleasure of it, and the pleasure was frequently erotic. He was an embittered, defiant poet, and his strong integrity as a craftsman, laconic speech, and objective methods of presentation added weight and dignity to his protest. He had, moreover, an important subject, though the importance was especially for Ireland.

In many of his poems Clarke uses an assonance derived from poetry in Irish. As he explained this technique:

the tonic word at the end of the line is supported by an assonance in the middle of the next line. The use of internal patterns of assonance in English, though more limited in its possible range, changes the pivotal movement of the lyric stanza. In some forms of the early syllabic Gaelic metres only one part of a double syllable word is used in assonance . . . and this can be a guide to experiment in partial rhyming or assonance and muting. For example, rhyme or assonance on or off accent, stopped rhyme (e.g. *win*dow: thin; horn: *morn*ing), harmonic rhyme (e.g. her*o:* wind*ow*), cross-rhyme, in which the separate syllables are in assonance or rhyme. The use, therefore, of polysyllabic words at the end of the lyric makes capable a movement common in continental languages such as Italian or Spanish.

"The Young Woman of Beare," a poem on a folklore figure, illustrates many of these possibilities; it begins:

> Through lane or black archway,
> The praying people hurry,
> When shadows have been walled,
> At market hall and gate.
> By low fires after nightfall;
> The bright sodalites
> Are bannered in the churches.

PATRICK KAVANAGH

Patrick Kavanagh (1904–67) grew up on a small farm, where he lived as such farmers did, ploughing, planting, mending fences, buying and selling cattle and corn at fairs, and attending dances and races. But from adolescence he was also writing poetry, and in 1936 his first book, *Ploughman and Other Poems,* was published. These were apprentice poems, their art and themes caught from anthologies, and only a few of them, such as "Tinker's Wife" and "Inniskeen Road: July Evening," closely reflected his actual experience. But since Kavanagh was authentically a farmer, he awakened interest as a "peasant poet" and reviewers thought of Robert Burns. In 1937 he left the farm and settled first in London and then in Dublin, where he spent the rest of his life.

In 1942 Kavanagh's most important work, *The Great Hunger,* was published. A poem of some twenty pages, *The Great Hunger* portrays the grim side of Irish farm life, and might be compared with the poems on the Welsh hill farmers of R. S. Thomas. The title uses the name given to the terrible famines of the 1840s, but the setting is contemporary, and the "hunger" is sexual; sexuality in this poem symbolizes a vital and imaginative relation to the world. Timid and passively patient, Maguire, the main protagonist, shrinks fearfully from sexual love, and masturbates at night over the ashes in his kitchen. His life has been wasted by social respectabilities, submission to the Church, economic hoarding, and endless, plodding labor in his fields. Above all, he has been broken by the bitter tongue of his dominating mother, who "praised the man who made a field his bride."

At their best, as in "Shancoduff," "From *Tarry Flynn*," and "A Christmas Childhood," Kavanagh's lyrics appeal by fresh, concrete images and by the colloquial force and directness of their language. When they fail it is because of conventional sentiments, flat and cliched phrasing, and rhythmic collapse. "Stony Grey Soil," a complaint addressed to the farmland of Monaghan, may be quoted as a humorous sketch on the same themes as *The Great Hunger:*

> You perfumed my clothes with weasel itch,
> You fed me on swinish food.
>
> You flung a ditch on my vision
> Of beauty, love and truth.
>
> O stony grey soil of Monaghan
> You burgled my bank of youth!

After 1937 Kavanagh made his living by writing newspaper columns and reviews, and in these he assumed the role of a social critic. In 1955 he was found to have cancer, a lung was removed, and in convalescing he experienced an emotional upheaval, memorialized in the sonnet entitled "Canal Bank Walk," in which he felt the fullness and love present in "the habitual, the banal." He resumed his former occupations, but in both prose and verse he assumed a mellower tone. His "purpose in life" was now "to have no purpose." He was trying to greet the ordinary and even the distressing with a love motivated by vague mysticism.

Both Clarke and Kavanagh had rejected the style of the Irish

Literary Revival, but they had still found their subjects in Irish life and their language in the English spoken in Ireland. Many poets of the next generation deliberately adopted, instead, an international point of view and style. As Thomas Kinsella and John Montague put it, in editing the *Dolmen Miscellany of Irish Writing* (1962), they sought to avoid all the forms of "Irishism" that had been "so profitably exploited in the past." Later in their careers, however, both these poets—and especially Montague—were to return in imagination to Ireland, writing some of their finest poems on its landscape and history. Kinsella also translated into English the ancient Irish epic *The Tain* (1969).

THOMAS KINSELLA

Thomas Kinsella (b. 1928) has been an Irish civil servant and, since 1965, a professor of English in the United States. He started to publish in the 1950s, and had he been an English poet he would have been included in the Movement. His sober honesty somewhat resembles that of Larkin, except that it is more conscience-stricken and self-tormenting. His forms owed nothing to the Modernist revolution. English Augustan poetry ("A Country Walk") and Hardy ("In the Ringwood," "Mirror in February") are strong influences. Like Geoffrey Hill, he is exceptionally sensitive to the temptations to dishonesty that are present in poetic creation—"We fly into our risk, the spurious"; a work of art is "a private masterpiece / Of doctored recollections." "Clarence Mangan," a monologue spoken by a nineteenth-century poet, describes the self-analysis involved in writing as surgery practiced by and on himself:

> Out of the shadows behind my laughter surgical fingers
> Come and I am strapped to the table.
>
> Ultimate, pitiless, again I ply the knife.

Living much of the time since 1965 in the United States, Kinsella has been open to influences that are usually less accepted in Irish poetry. In some poems he has adopted a relatively private symbolism taken from dream ("Wormwood") or from moments of peculiarly charged vision ("Hen Woman"). He has also experimented with techniques of discontinuity, fragmentation, and juxtaposition, as in "Ritual of Departure," where moments of Irish history are expressed in a visionary way. In *A Technical Supplement* (1977) he used a relaxed, talky free verse in the mode of William Carlos Williams.

Kinsella's imagination is preoccupied with the dreadful in human nature and experience, as such titles as "Nightwalker" and "Notes from the Land of the Dead" would of themselves indicate. The history both of our own century and of Ireland supply him with documentation and objective justification for this emphasis, but he usually illustrates it in more private reaches of experience, and at times his dark vision seems automatic and compulsive. He is like the tree he describes in "Open this and you will see," a brief lyric that serves as a foreword to the volume entitled *Wormwood* (1966):

> Open this and you will see
> A waste, a nearly naked tree
> That will not rest till it is bare,
> But shivers, shivers in the air
> Scraping at its yellow leaves.
> Winter, when the tempest heaves,
> It riots in the heaven-sent
> Convulsions of self-punishment.

JOHN MONTAGUE AND MICHAEL LONGLEY

John Montague (b. 1929) was born in Brooklyn, New York, but moved to Ireland as a small child. He worked for the Irish tourist agency and as a journalist, and since 1961 has frequently taught in universities. He is a Catholic living in Northern Ireland. His poems are on love and its vicissitudes and on the history and present troubles of his land. His poetry chiefly expresses feelings of loss and pain. In writing about the hatred and strife in Northern Ireland, he does not denounce or support either side. His attitude is one of understanding—the feud is inevitable, given the history of the land—and of helpless suffering. He is gentle, meditative, and wistful. Most of his later poems are in short lines with occasional rhyme or off-rhyme. "What a View" (from *Tides*, 1970), though too long to quote, is a fine example of his political poetry; "Windharp" (in *A Slow Dance,* 1975), on the whispering, rustling sounds of the Irish landscape, is a lyric memorable for its sustained, flowing syntax:

> The sounds of Ireland,
> that restless whispering
> you never get away
> from, seeping out of
> low bushes and grass,
> heatherbells and fern,
> wrinkling bog pools . . .

In the introduction to his *No Continuing City* (1969), Michael Longley (b. 1939), who is also a poet of Northern Ireland, refers to his own "rather extreme formalism," meaning that he tends to pursue form for its own sake in poems that are otherwise not very exciting. Since then Longley's formal skill has served a deeper concern. In *An Exploded View* (1973) he confronts the political troubles in Northern Ireland directly, though reluctantly, but for the most part he has found his subjects in personal and domestic life and in the search for Irish identity. Many of his finer poems are monologues spoken by typical Irish characters. His "Mayo Monologues" might be compared with Kavanagh's *The Great Hunger* as a portrait of literal and spiritual poverty in farm life.

SEAMUS HEANEY

Seamus Heaney was born in 1939 in the townland of Mossbawn, County Derry, in Northern Ireland. His family belonged to the Roman Catholic minority. He went to Queen's University in Belfast, where he studied English language and literature. After graduating in 1961, he found jobs teaching English, eventually becoming a lecturer at Queen's University, and he also started composing and publishing poems. By the middle of the 1960s his work was appearing in London periodicals.

Heaney had grown up on a farm, and many of his earliest poems, published in *Death of a Naturalist* (1966) and *Door into the Dark* (1969), were recollections of farm life or of childhood experiences in the countryside. He was initially reviewed as a "bucolic" poet, and since his anecdotes were skillfully plotted, his phrasing wonderfully sensuous and vivid, and his poetic personality sympathetically humorous and decent, he quickly became popular—or at least he became as popular as any good poet can now be. English readers associated his "nature" poetry with that of Ted Hughes, because both Heaney and Hughes presented an unsentimentalized nature of alien, threatened, and threatening existences, and Heaney has since said that Hughes's *Lupercal* helped him to have confidence in his own background as a source of subject matter.

The nexus of critical assumptions influencing Heaney's early poetry was more or less Symbolist. He was, in other words, extremely sensitive to the obscure suggestions of emotion and meaning latent in sounds and in the juxtaposition of images. Feelings are activated, for example, by the sounds of the syllables in a line about making butter in "Churning Day"—"the pat and slap of small spades on wet lumps"—and overtones of meaning are conveyed in the images "pat and slap," "spade," and "wet lumps." Moreover, he did not discourse or generalize, but expressed himself implicitly and concretely. In these respects Heaney was unlike the Movement poets then dominant in England, and, since the Movement ethos could already seem drab and limiting, even to some of the poets who had originally promulgated it, Heaney's work appealed as an alternative. It could not have done so without Heaney's honesty, realism, and acute psychological and moral concern and intelligence, for in the wake of the Movement these virtues were expected in England of all serious, contemporary poetry; but given these qualities, Heaney's music, suggestivity, and concreteness were especially welcome in England in the 1960s.

In 1970–71 Heaney taught at the University of California at Berkeley. In the United States he appears to have read William Carlos Williams, Robert Creeley, and other poets then in vogue, and their impact modified his poetic line. Up till then he had usually composed in regular meters, frequently with rhyme or off-rhyme, but he now used short lines of free verse grouped into unrhymed stanzas. The effect was of an effortless flow of colloquial, minimal lines. His former wit, descriptive metaphor, and sound effects influenced by Hopkins were now less obvious, and the beauty of Heaney's poems subsisted in the imaginative

ensemble—the bearing of the different ideas on one another—
and in the delicacy with which these ideas were suggested. "Anahorish," for example, about the place where Heaney went to
primary school, envisions a pristine world. No phrase can be
quoted separately, for no phrase is remarkable except for its
rightness in its context, but the whole is fine:

> My 'place of clear water,'
> the first hill in the world
> where springs washed into
> the shiny grass
>
> and darkened cobbles
> in the bed of the lane.
> *Anahorish*, soft gradient
> of consonant, vowel-meadow,
>
> after-image of lamps
> swung through the yards
> on winter evenings.
> With pails and barrows
>
> those mound-dwellers
> go waist-deep in mist
> to break the light ice
> at wells and dunghills.

"Anahorish" appeared in Heaney's third volume, *Wintering
Out* (1972), and not all the poems in this volume were similarly
serene. The strife between Protestants and Roman Catholics in
Northern Ireland had broken out anew, and Heaney's response
was complexly troubled. Except in some poems that have not
been included in his books, he handled the subject only
obliquely and from a distance, but he reverted to it frequently.
So far as he indulged the "bucolic" aspect of his imagination, he
suggested that the hate and violence were anomalous. "The
Other Side," for example, describes a friendly Protestant neigh-
bor from Heaney's childhood. There seems to be no reason why
Heaney could not still

> go up and touch his shoulder
> and talk about the weather
>
> or the price of grass-seed.

Imagery of violence and horror in other poems, such as "A Northern Hoard," reflected the emotional shock of the bloodshed. In several poems Heaney articulated feelings of guilt, amounting almost to seeing himself as a traitor or deserter, because he was not participating more directly in the struggle of his people. But generally he viewed the strife from a distant vantage point in the past, whence the bloodshed and hatred of the present could be viewed with objectivity, understanding, and compassion. Heaney did not fail to accuse himself of an evasion as his imagination withdrew into the past, but his poetry was deepened. In the strife in Northern Ireland he saw the nature and condition of man, the universal tragedy of human life.

In *Wintering Out* and his next volume, *North* (1975), a number of poems on ancient bodies exhumed from bogs especially conveyed this vision. In P. V. Glob's *Bog People* (1969) he read about these archaeological discoveries in Denmark, and the photographs of the remarkably preserved bodies from the Iron Age fascinated him. The bodies were of naked persons who had been strangled or had their throats cut, perhaps in connection with a religious cult, and they spoke to Heaney's imagination of the layers on layers of human lives extending back unchanged into time and of vulnerable, creaturely humanity abandoned to death. In "The Tollund Man," "Bog Queen," "The Grauballe Man," "Punishment," and other remarkable poems he imagined these people in their graves or as they were in their lives, and spoke to or for them in compassion and guilt. "Punishment," for example, associates one of the women whose body was found in a bog with contemporary Irish girls who were tarred and feathered for dating English soldiers.

> Little adulteress,
> before they punished you
>
> you were flaxen-haired,
> undernourished, and your
> tar-black face was beautiful.
> My poor scapegoat,
>
> I almost love you
> but would have cast, I know,
> the stones of silence.

. . . .

> I who have stood dumb
> when your betraying sisters,
> cauled in tar,
> wept by the railings,
>
> who would connive
> in civilized outrage
> yet understand the exact
> and tribal, intimate revenge.

If Heaney had ever been a bucolic poet, with these poems he was far from the pasture, and in general *North* was pervaded with the grimness of Nordic history and geography. Presumably Heaney was reading Geoffrey Hill, since so many others were, and though his style is quite different from Hill's, Heaney's *North* may be compared with Hill's "Funeral Music" (1968) and *Mercian Hymns* (1971). Both poets juxtaposed harsh images from northern regional history with contemporary ones, blending a long historical perspective with personal, moral shock and anguish.

In 1972 Heaney resigned his job at Queen's University and moved to Glanmore, County Wicklow, in the Republic of Ireland. He was "determined," as he later explained, "to put the practice of poetry more deliberately at the center of my life. It was a kind of test." In Glanmore he composed the poems of *Field Work* (1979). Some of these poems deal with incidents of violence in Northern Ireland more directly than Heaney had in the past. In other poems, especially the "Glanmore Sonnets," he returned to the regular forms and rural subjects of his first volumes, handling them with a richer music than ever. One of these sonnets describes his ideal of poetic music as

> Vowels ploughed into other, opened ground,
> Each verse returning like the plough turned round.

A new power of aphorism, nourished by his study of Dante, lent its strength to the poems. And influenced, perhaps, by the later poems of Robert Lowell in *For Lizzie and Harriet* (1973) and *The Dolphin* (1973), Heaney composed a number of tender, humorous, passionate expressions of married love, such as "The Otter," "The Skunk," and "Homecomings."

After four years in Glanmore Heaney moved to Dublin, where he again taught on a part-time basis, at first in Dublin and later in the United States at Harvard University. Using prose and verse, he translated as *Sweeney Astray* (1983) the medieval Irish poem *Buile Suibhne,* and his next volume, *Station Island* (1984) began with a collection of miscellaneous poems and concluded with "glosses" to *Sweeney Astray* in which Sweeney is the imagined speaker.

The second part of *Station Island,* the title sequence, is the most ambitious and also the most directly personal work Heaney has published thus far. Station Island is a place of religious pilgrimage on Lough Derg in Ireland. Making this pilgrimage, Heaney encounters ghosts of dead persons from his own past or from Irish literary history. The encounters are partly modeled on the one with the ghost in Eliot's "Little Gidding" III and even more on Dante (the verse of some sections is a modified *terza rima*), and from Dante the concrete, direct phrasing acquires a weight that is new in Heaney:

> And then as if a shower were blackening
> already blackened stubble, the dark weather
> of his unspoken pain came over him.

Yet other passages are pleasantly swift, simple, and colloquial: "I met a young priest, glossy as a blackbird." Most themes that have been important in Heaney's poetry reappear in this sequence, but the general subject might be described as a confrontation with his Irish matrix, and his emotions are ambivalent. He is immersed in this matrix and loyal to it, yet he also strives to transcend it, and he condemns personal qualities that might prevent him from doing so. The ghosts warn him to cut loose. In the first poem of the sequence a lawless "old Sabbath-breaker" shouts, "Stay clear of all processions!" and in the last poem the ghost of James Joyce, who was prefigured in the "Sabbath-breaker," says essentially the same thing:

> Take off from here. And don't be so earnest,
>
> let others wear the sackcloth and the ashes.
> Let go, let fly, forget.
> You've listened long enough. Now strike your note.

21

OPEN FORM

AMONG contemporary poets Charles Olson and Robert
Duncan have been the leading theorists of "open form,"
and for this reason the pages that follow dwell on their
statements. The ideas of other poets are cited only in ancillary
ways. The reason for this restriction is partly the need for focus;
if the theoretical utterances of other poets were also taken into
account, the argument would fragment into qualifications and
exceptions of little essential importance. Moreover, Olson and
Duncan were among the earliest postwar advocates of "open"
form, Olson was influential, and the theories of Olson and Duncan were radical and therefore challenging. But their theories
were also representative; many other poets in the 1950s and
1960s were holding the same thoughts more cautiously.

Olson and Duncan exchanged ideas in letters, and for a short
period they both taught at Black Mountain College in North
Carolina. Founded in 1933, Black Mountain College was a typically American attempt to create an ideal community. Students
worked on the farm, had their say in running the college, and
lived in close association with the faculty. The college was democratic, egalitarian, small, and isolated. It gave the arts a central
place in the curriculum. After the Second World War a number
of American poets were there, of whom the first was Charles

Olson. Beginning in 1948, he was on the faculty of Black Mountain at first occasionally and then regularly, and he served as rector of the college from 1952 to 1956, when he closed and sold it. Robert Creeley was associated with the college as a teacher along with Duncan, and Ed Dorn, John Wieners, and Jonathan Williams were students. Denise Levertov and Paul Blackburn, who are also discussed in this chapter, were never actually at Black Mountain, but readers connected them with this group for other reasons, including statements they made.

A forceful personality, Olson was the central figure. Naturally his impact was strongest on those who knew him personally, but it is also true that they were receptive to his teachings because they already shared them to some degree. Olson and the other poets whose work I notice in this chapter were prolific of prose statements and taped interviews, and in these they were literary historians of their own careers, frequently recounting their origins, sources, and affinities, generally with favorable references to one another. They tended to publish in the same journals, such as the *Black Mountain Review* (seven issues, 1954–57), which Robert Creeley edited from Mallorca, and *Origin*, edited by Cid Corman (twenty issues, 1951–56). When Donald Allen recognized them as a group in his now famous anthology *The New American Poetry* (1960), he was following their own self-perception. Thereafter they were widely known as the Black Mountain Poets, and though the name conveys no precise idea, it is now traditional and cannot be displaced.

DERIVATION FROM POUND AND WILLIAMS

Both in their theories of poetry and in their actual style, these poets descended from Pound and Williams. At the start of Chapter 9, where I discussed the 1950s resurgence of Pound, Williams, and Stevens, I explained why these older poets were then especially available and appealing for younger ones to adopt as masters. But Pound's art differed widely from that of Williams, and both had changed over the years. The styles to be derived from them were various. Moreover, as with many cases of literary influence, the young poets read what they needed into the older ones, sometimes discovering what was not really there. In his composition courses at Black Mountain College Olson taught the stylistic methods of the *Cantos* as a model. He dwelt especially on the sudden juxtaposition of images. He was also fascinated by Pound's historiography, a point to which I shall return. Reading the *Cantos* in college, Robert Duncan tried to like the dryer parts that deal with government and economic theory. But what he loved were the "autohypnotic" passages that evoke "gods and elemental beings"—passages such as the magnificent "Gods float in the azure air, / Bright gods and Tuscan . . ." from Canto III. For Duncan Pound was the "carrier" of a tradition of "sublime and ecstatic" poetry out of Neoplatonic and occult sources. Around 1949 Duncan was conducting an informal Pound seminar in his home. Robert Creeley in college was not up to reading the "intimidating" *Cantos* at all. Nevertheless, in the earlier poetry and essays of Pound, who was not taught at Creeley's Harvard, he found the premises of a style more "sincere" than the "socially based use of irony" in Auden or the "devices" of Stevens. The poems of Creeley's first decade are in the world and language of Williams, but their artistic carefulness, their conscious, minute attention to each syllable, was instigated less by Williams than by Pound. Denise Levertov, in contrast, owed very little to Pound. She took Williams as her model of American poetry, and her poems in the 1950s are individual variations on the Williams lyric. But each of these poets found in Pound and Williams the formal procedure that they referred to as "open" or "organic" form, "projective verse," or the "poem as process." As Duncan later put it, "with the *Pisan Cantos* of Ezra Pound and *Paterson* of William Carlos Williams" he sensed a new possibility. "I was not alone, for other poets—Louis Zukofsky, Charles Olson, Denise Levertov, Robert Creeley—following seriously the work of Pound and Williams, became aware, as I was, that what they had mastered opened out upon a new art where they were the first ones working."

Before describing what Olson and Duncan meant by "open" form, I may note in a preliminary way some of the essential respects in which their stylistic theories develop from Williams and Pound. They shared premises of Williams' thinking to such a degree that Williams viewed them as members of his party. As I noted, he published extracts from Olson's essay on "Projective Verse" in his *Autobiography*. I discussed in Chapter 11 the familiar

Williams positions: that poetry, like life itself, must always make a "fresh beginning," subverting "the moment before"; that writing is an act of living and a poem as it proceeds must at every point be changing and spontaneous, since whatever is otherwise is dead; that the process of a poem is "transfused with the same forces which transfuse the earth"; and that a poem, like life, has no goal except the vividness of each instant moment and therefore is unselective and without closure. "Style is death," as Robert Kelly (b. 1935) put it, and

> Finding the measure is finding
> a freedom from that death, a way out, a movement
> forward.

How theories of "open" form could be derived from the actual methods of Williams' *Paterson* and Pound's *Cantos* (especially the *Pisan Cantos*) is easy to see. These poems had not been planned out before the act of writing, and in the process of writing a similar freedom had been preserved throughout. From any point in these poems the poet could proceed in innumerable different directions. The poems enact and thus dramatize the instant, unpredictable motions—leaps of comparison, turns of feeling, reversals of argument, associations—of the poet's mind in composing. I am not, needless to say, asserting that *Paterson* or the *Cantos* were actually created in this way. I am describing a formal procedure these poems could suggest. To what extent the young poets were justified in attributing "open" form to *Paterson* and the *Cantos* is another question. That its form must begin anew in every moment was progammatic in *Paterson*. As for the *Cantos*, Duncan recognized that if their form is "open," this was contrary to Pound's wish or intention, for his poem was in quest of a valid, comprehensive order. Just this form of "a creation creating itself . . . that drew us to Pound's Cantos," Duncan observes, "alienated its author," and Duncan goes on to speak shrewdly of Pound's "conflict and distress" at the "complexity and heterogeneity of his world." But in order to find "open" form in the local texture of the *Cantos*, as opposed to their overall structure or lack of it, Duncan speaks of this texture in a way Pound would not have sanctioned. Duncan describes the *Pisan Cantos*, for example, as "composition by phrase," meaning that the phrases are discontinuous entities within a "field." Pound would have said that these discontinuous phrases compose "ideograms," and an ideogram, as Pound conceived it, was a closely integrated unit of meaning; in other words, the phrases assembled to make a Poundian ideogram are much more tightly interconnected than Duncan's "composition by phrase" would imply.

THE THEORY OF OPEN FORM

Since the Second World War most American and many English poems have been in "open" form, but we cannot always say which, for the implications of the term are not exact. An example is Robert Lowell's *Notebook 1967–68*. Though the notebook is an open form, the poems that make up this one are unrhymed sonnets. Besides the mixed cases, there are the alternative versions. The rules of procedure Allen Ginsberg caught from Jack Kerouac and illustrated in *Howl* and thereafter are almost completely "open," but this "open form" differs in significant ways from that of Charles Olson and Robert Duncan, who also, of course, differ from each other. But we need not go round in Schleiermacher's hermeneutic circle, for as Edmund Burke once remarked, though no exact line separates day from night, yet light and darkness are tolerably distinguishable.

Both historically and psychologically, "open" form in the poetry of the last thirty years began as a reaction against New Critical "closure," and in order to obtain a preliminary notion of what is meant by "open" form, we need only recall some of the formal qualities advocated and exemplified within the New Critical mode: correct grammar, logic, regular meter, rhyme, stanzas, coherence, condensation, polysemy, and control. "Open" form, then, implies qualities opposite to these, such as immediacy, spontaneity, and freedom. The "closure" of the New Critical poem was associated with a pessimistic and rigorous ethos. Every perception was difficult, for it could not be valid unless it was precise, nuanced, and complex. Intelligence had to discipline impulse. A poet had to write with continual self-criticism and revision. But the "open" poets hated this atmosphere of pickyness and inhibition. Revision was self-repressive; moreover, it was false to the instantaneousness and uncertainty of life. They were influenced by jazz—its freedom, spontaneity, and ecstasy. The predecessors they identified with were not those in the New Critics' line of "wit" from Donne to Eliot, but Blake, Whitman, and Lawrence, along with Pound and Williams.

The poets of "open" form overthrew the sacred New Critical doctrine of the "persona"—the premise that the speaking voice or "I" of a lyric is never the poet himself but always an imagined character. "The revolution I am responsible for," Olson told his fellow poet and friend Cid Corman, "is this one, of the identity of a person and his expression." But the "person" here meant is not quite the autobiographical personality of the Confessional poets. The "open" poet speaks, at least in theory, from a level of his being where the self fuses with impersonal nature, with a life force in us as in all nature. This is perhaps what Olson meant when he said of his Maximus Poems, "no persona and no personality—VOICE."

In some respects the poets of open form carried further, though largely without knowing it, premises that had been developed in England and Germany during the Romantic period. Borrowing from Friedrich Schelling, Coleridge had pointed to the "difference between form as proceeding, and shape as superinduced;—the latter is either the death or the imprisonment of the thing;—the former is its self-witnessing and self-effected sphere of agency." "Form as proceeding" is "organic form." In the opposite conception, "shape as superinduced," the form—a Petrarchan sonnet, an eclogue—exists prior to the creative process, and the evolving work must fit into this form. The "organic form," shaping itself "as it develops itself from within," comes into existence, Coleridge said, like a naturally growing thing. The poet, in other words, proceeds in the same way as nature; nature works in and through the creative act of the poet. The possibility of this presupposes "a bond between nature . . . and the soul of man." Reading such words and thoughts in Schelling, Coleridge, Friedrich Schlegel, Goethe, and Herder—if they read them—Duncan, Olson, and Levertov whoud have agreed enthusiastically. But they did not derive their theories from these sources. And compared with the Romantics, they were more radical. Coming after a half-century of stylistic fragmentation and free verse, their poetry was much more "open" than even the Romantic irregular ode or blank-verse effusion.

Ideas about style or form involve premises concerning morality and reality, and unlike many poets, Olson and Duncan reflected on theirs. They assumed that reality cannot be known
except in limited and temporary aspects. Olson was much influenced by the metaphysics of Alfred North Whitehead, and
imagined, much of the time, that every event has infinite aspects
and relations, is in process, and organically prehends the whole
of reality. Duncan, a reader of occult lore and Neoplatonic philosophy, was similarly imbued with the infinitude and dynamic
process of reality, with the different aspects things could assume
and the contrasting interpretations that could be made of them.
The two poets accepted that in our perceptions reality must appear contingent, inconsistent, changing, and uninterpretable. A
poem reflecting this would necessarily be unpredicatble in its
movement from part to part. Moreover, in homage to the infinitude of reality, the whole "field" of a poem, the ensemble of all
the fragments that make it up, would present enormous divers-
ities, including a great variety of different events and also wide
contrasts of emotion and interpretation concerning the same
event. Keats once asked himself whether any philosopher ever
achieved his system without putting aside numerous objections,
without deliberately ignoring points he could not answer. Striving to be open to the whole of reality, the poets of open form
had a horror of such exclusion, and though they were not influenced by later ideas about Deconstruction, they freely questioned the age-old assumption that a poem must seem internally
self-consistent.

But these theorists also assumed that the process of reality is
organically one. Like the blind men encountering the elephant,
we know only fragmentary parts. But unlike the blind men,
Duncan and Olson assumed that the parts belong to a unified
system. If, changing the metaphor, we imagine the whole of reality as a sphere, and if we further imagine that on this sphere
points A and B more resemble each other than points A and Z,
a process of consciousness that moves from A to B has a much
greater chance of seeming interconnected and coherent than
one that moves with no intervening steps from A to Z. Yet the
leap from A to Z includes more of the whole. Thus poets of open
form have been ready to put into their poems the widely dissimilar; how these items are related may be problematical, but that

they are related is a matter of faith. Paradoxically, the extreme heterogeneity and contrast of their poems, and especially of Duncan's, are permitted by their organicist metaphysics. In these poets the impossibility of knowing did not cause the emotional distress it is said to have evoked in Victorian intellectuals. They preached, instead, that we should concentrate on the moment, on what is now experienced immediately in this split second. Each instant involves the whole of reality, but the reality is constantly changing, so we have only the instant in which to apprehend it. The ideal of life is to be wholly responsive to each moment as it comes, to possess continually what Olson called "point by point vividness." "Every moment of life," Olson said, "is an attempt to come to life," and life has no other purpose. The "end," as Olson put it in "Human Universe," is "you, this instant, in action."

At least in theory, writing a poem was for these poets not different from any spontaneous act of living. Like most modern artists, moreover, they were impressed by the formal differences between life and the traditional work of art. The work was organized for an aesthetic purpose, selective in its use of experience, delimited and meaningful. Life, on the other hand, is unselective, for it presents anything and everything. It flows on and on, and nothing within it is isolated, nothing exists as a completed entity.

Wishing to emulate life in its process, poets of open form are inclined to view their poems not as separate compositions but as moments in one ongoing composition, the serial poem they are writing over the years. And naturally they also write long poems in which there is continuity without overall structure. Olson's Maximus Poems and Duncan's "Passages" are examples. According to Jack Spicer, a minor poet of San Francisco, "the trick naturally is what Duncan learned years ago and tried to teach us— not to search for the perfect poem but to let your way of writing of the moment go along its own paths, explore and retreat but never be fully realized (confined) within the boundaries of one poem."

The versification of this poetry not only is free but tends to emphasize that it is free. Wide variations in the length of successive lines dramatize the absence of any norm. The theory of free verse promulgated by these poets descends more from Wil-

liams and Lawrence than from Pound, and is essentially Lawrence's doctrine that free verse is "direct utterance from the
instant whole man." These poets sought a physiological justification for their line breaks. Lineation follows, they argued, the
writer's natural breathing; where the voice pauses for breath,
the line breaks. The line, Olson says, "comes (I swear it) from
the breath, from the breathing of the man who writes it, at the
moment that he writes." Upon such lineation these poets bestowed a mystical sanction. Because it is determined by bodily
processes, they argued, breath rhythm is continuous with the
deep nature in man as in all organic existence. "Whoever has
rhythm," said Olson, "has the universe." Duncan, with more sophistication, compared the producing of a poetic line to walking,
a natural system that proceeds by complex, unconscious acts of
balancing and timing. And these poets also invoke larger natural
regularities, such as the round of night and day and the return
of the tides, as sources of poetic rhythms. Before Olson only
Lawrence, among significant modern poets, had gone so far to
give free verse a deep, natural, quasi-religious ground. But none
of these metaphors of breathing, walking, ebbing and flowing,
and the like, can actually tell a poet when to break his line, and
the "open" poet does it, as Olson says, by "ear." The "open" line
ends, as Duncan and Creeley put it, just whenever it "feels right."

The diction of these poets avoids any norm. It may be rhetorical, learned, or extremely colloquial—"what I meant, like"—or
anything, and the type of diction may vary widely within a few
lines. In one passage of "Idaho Out," for example, Ed Dorn
writes "do scurry," "gay youth was yours," "physiographic menace," and "peneplain of central america." Such changing diction
enacts a moral stance of living in the instant and staying open
to anything.

SYNTAX AS KINESIS

But poets of open form enact their principles most dramatically in their syntax. According to Olson and Duncan, a poem is
created syllable by syllable in a process that moves steadily from
the first to the last. Thus if a poem were coming into being, the

opening syllable might be "five," the next might be "years," and
so on until the poem, not yet completed, read,

> Five years have passed, five summers with the length
> Of five long winters, and again I

—the start of Wordsworth's "Tintern Abbey." According to the
convention of Olson and Duncan, the last syllable quoted, "I,"
was once the "going live present," the "instant moment" where
Wordsworth was as he was composing. Since the poem should
always be open to new impulse, the next syllable should have
been unpredictable, as of course it was more or less. But Wordsworth was constrained by both the rules of grammar and the
intention organizing his statement from the start. Rejecting
these restrictions, Olson and Duncan can move from syllable to
syllable with a freer sequence, a more radical spontaneity.

In actual practice "open" syntax sometimes resembles the detached bones flying in old paintings of the resurrection. Tenses
are "kicked around," as Olson put it, and pronouns are inconsistent with the verbs they govern. Incomplete clauses and dan-
gling phrases succeed one another in swift medley: predicates
without subjects, antitheses without the opposing terms, free-
floating prepositional phrases, interjections, and so forth. Olson's poetry uses the unclosed parenthesis (to mark the beginning of a new thought. As Duncan explains in his preface to
Bending the Bow, each part—"the phrase within its line, the adjoining pulse in silence, the new phrase—each part is a thing in
itself; the junctures not binding but freeing the elements of con-
figuration so that they participate in more than one figure." The
poet "strives not for a disintegration of syntax but for a compli-
cation within syntax, overlapping structures, so that words are
freed, having bounds out of bound."

For an example of "open" syntax, we may consider a line of
Olson's. Were it grammatical, it might read, "The bow-sprit is
like the beak of a bird, and goes in"—a coherent and completed
thought. But Olson actually wrote,

> in! in! the bow-sprit, bird, the beak.

In this line there are no conjunctions or prepositions to indicate
how the individual fragments are related. The fragments are
short and their arrangement makes them disjunctive. But the

line has momentum, since we seek its sense and are thus impelled to read on. "ONE PERCEPTION MUST IMMEDIATELY AND DIRECTLY LEAD TO A FURTHER PERCEPTION," Olson wrote in his essay "Projective Verse," and the line illustrates this maxim. "Get on with it," Olson continued in his essay, "keep moving, keep in, speed, the nerves, their speed, the perceptions, theirs, the acts, the split second acts, the whole business, keep it moving as fast as you can, citizen . . . one perception must must must MOVE, INSTANTER, ON ANOTHER!"

Within the line of verse just quoted there are relationships of sound and sense between the fragments. "Bird" goes with "beak," and "beak" with "bow-sprit." And generally in the theory of Olson and Duncan the moment-by-moment freedom or openness of the poem, though larger than in traditional poetry, was still not total. They would not, for example, have countenanced merely arbitrary or random syllables. The principles that would especially preclude these are those of the "field" and of composition as "listening."

In the metaphor of the poem as a "field" all the syllables that make it up are imagined as points in space, all bearing upon one another. "All the syllables and all the lines," Olson says, "must be managed in their relations to each other." Each point within the "field" is a node of intersecting vectors. "Listening" is a metaphor for the poet's attention to these vectors. The term implies, in other words, that the poet is passive as he composes, that he allows himself to be led by whatever suggestions arise.

At any point in the process of composing a poem the sounds and semantic associations of the words already written suggest more words. In this sense what has been written exerts a "push." The poet must be aware of these instigations present in his text, and the feedback from this "listening" influences what he writes next. The mind of the poet as he composes is not, Duncan explains, "to be diverted by what it wanted to say but to attend to what [is] happening in the poem." In Duncan's vivid metaphor, a poet "sits in the light of words like a cat in the mote-filled sunlight of a window. Where he is in the sentence is there. And he listens. His poetry pictures his listening." (I should explicitly note that among the instigations shaping the future course of a poetic line, many are whimsical or random from the semantic point of view. The poem can progress by homonyms, homophones, puns, assonance, and the like.) Attention and initiative go to the smallest unit of the text. To the syllable, Olson insists, to its sound, quantity, and root meanings. "The locus of form," Duncan says, "lies in the immediate minim of the work." One should focus, as Duncan sums up, "upon the sound and meaning present where one [is], and derive melody and story from impulse not from plan."

Everything in the last paragraph is theory, needless to say. Few "open" poems are composed literally in this way. The poems of Olson, Duncan, and the other poets discussed in this chapter make sense. They communicate. Which means that among the teeming suggestions that arose, some were selected and others not. There is, in other words, a will or initiative in the poet as well as in the poem. Yet there is much truth, also, in this account of the creative process. "Listening," attention to the "immediate minim of the work," and "openness" describe or partially describe the state of mind in which all good poems are written, and describe it in a valuably concrete and practical way. And of course the poets of "open form" compose by these methods more than most other poets do. An understanding of their theory illuminates their texts.

CHARLES OLSON

Charles Olson (1910–70) grew up in Worcester, Massachusetts, and in summers in the seacoast city of Gloucester. Though he lived his last twenty years in our mild American Bohemia of little magazines and cafe poetry readings, he started out as a candidate for the power elite. In high school he was captain of the debating team and class president, and at Wesleyan College he was goalie of the soccer team and Phi Beta Kappa. He failed to get a Rhodes Scholarship, but he tried. After some years as a graduate student in English and a teacher at Wesleyan and Harvard, he entered government service in Washington, D.C., and by 1945 was being sounded out for a job as Assistant Secretary of the Treasury. But he then quit politics for literature.

For the next few years he lectured here and there, and composed stories, poems, and *Call Me Ishmael* (1947), his intuitive, suggestive interpretation of Melville's *Moby-Dick*. In 1951 he lived several months in Yucatan, fascinated by the people and by the Mayan ruins and hieroglyphs. His letters at this time to Robert Creeley (subsequently published as *Mayan Letters*, 1954) show him forming or confirming in this adventure fundamental ideas he would later expound. In 1948 he moved to Black Mountain College.

A class with Olson was memorable. He would taunt, stamp about, argue, and shout. Read, he said, Alfred North Whitehead, Carl O. Sauer (the geographer), Frederick Merk (the historian); study Mayan hieroglyphics, Sumerian, and mathematical topology; ponder space, process, yourself—and what *use* are you making of your knowledge? of your body? Are you living every moment with "point by point sharpness"? His mind went round with enormous energy and noise. Many students were put off. For some, however, Olson's intensity more than compensated for his vagueness and confusion. They saw him groping to clarify intuitions that were, he felt, immensely significant. He exhorted them to join in and take the thoughts further. The nakedness and urgency of his moiling, the sense of participation, and the aura of large importance caught them up.

After the Black Mountain years Olson settled in Gloucester. By now he had published two volumes of short poems, and had been at work since 1950 on his sequence of "Maximus" poems. His time henceforth went into writing, poetry readings, and brief spells of college teaching. He married twice, but in 1964 his second wife died in an automobile accident, and his last years were lonely. In the 1950s Olson had hardly any audience beyond Black Mountain College and the few journals that would take his work. But around 1960 he began to reach a wider public, and gradually he became a large name in the little magazines, his sayings quoted as authority and his personality mythologized.

Olson's relationship to Pound and Williams was a source of tension for him. When Pound was incarcerated in St. Elizabeth's Hospital, Olson spoke up for him, visited him, and tried to help. But the strong egos clashed and he stopped visiting. Thereafter his attitude toward Pound was divided. On the one hand, he bravely and honestly stressed Pound's greatness as a poet, with a perception the more admirable as it was then rare. Moreover, he fully acknowledged Pound's influence on his own work. On the other hand, his praise of Pound usually ended in carping, with suggestions that Olson's "stance" was superior. He worried all his life whether he was cutting his own notch or merely deepening Pound's. Williams evoked similar anxieties, though less intensely. In a 1965 reading at Berkeley, Olson remarked, according to the tape recorder, "I mean, I wrote a—a flagrant autobiography of myself [the Maximus Poems], imitating Ezra Pound . . . But every imitation stinks . . . I'd be proud to have been the in—man in this century—And like, here I am dragging my ass after Ezra."

An ideologue, perhaps a would-be prophet, Olson pushed his ideas in letters, magazine essays, and other prose. *Call Me Ishmael* begins, "I take SPACE to be the central fact of man born in America, from Folsom cave to now." Space as opposed to time. To live in time is to be conditioned and limited by the past. But if you live in space, every moment or point is a new beginning from which you can move anywhere. The connection with "open form" is obvious. Reading the *Cantos,* Olson delighted in the way Pound "razzledazzled" history. Cutting freely from one point to another, Pound treated history as space.

At times Olson would proclaim that history is over; we live in a "post historical" age. Among his meanings were that Hiroshima was an apocalypse. Continuity with the past is broken, and we must begin again amid our ruins. He also meant that our intuitive sense of life is transforming itself. Western man has thought in terms of evolution, progress, and purpose; he must now live in the immediate present. He must go back beyond history to a prehistoric or primitive state of mind, to a bodily, timeless, immediate, mythical relation to the world. Olson's notions of the primitive derived from Lawrence, and, like Lawrence, he strove to recapture a sense of the world as sacred. To express the presence of the holy any primitive myth would do, and Olson variously invoked deities of the American Indians, Sumerians, Hittites, ancient Greeks, and Egyptians. He was against Humanism. A human being, in Olson's opinion, should regard himself as no more than one among nature's infinite objects. Humanity as a whole has no special status. Melville, Dostoyevski, Rimbaud, and Lawrence were, Olson said, "the modern men who projected what we are and what we are in . . . They put men forward into the post-modern, the post-humanist, the post-historic, the going live present."

An ahistorical historiography, so to speak, perhaps resembles the "mapping" Olson undertakes in the Maximus Poems. He explores the place where he is, Gloucester, Massachusetts. Its present reality includes its history, but its human history is set within a larger field. The natural context partly determines the character of life in this locality throughout time. Thus in the Maximus Poems we see the glaciers forming topography, which in turn influences where people live and what work they do. And throughout the history of this town, from the earliest settlement to now, the chief fact is fish. In other words, Olson shows human life formed by objective, environmental circumstances that do not themselves change. In some ways Olson's vision is analogous to that of the structuralist history of Fernand Braudel and his school, though Braudel was not a source.

The poems of Olson may be read in *Archaeologist of Morning* (1970), a selection from his nine earlier volumes of lyrics, and in the three volumes of the Maximus Poems: *The Maximus Poems* (1960), *Maximus Poems IV, V, VI* (1968), and the posthumously published *The Maximus Poems: Volume Three* (1975). On his style several reports can be made. Especially in important earlier poems, he follows the methods of Pound. To read "The King-fishers" or "In Cold Hell in Thicket" is somewhat like reading the *Cantos*. In many poems of lucid, ordinary speech and continuous syntax he does not follow Pound; these mostly came later in his career. His diction, syntax, and versification develop from Williams, though they are quite different from Williams. Despite these clear derivations, he does not sound like Pound, Williams, or any poet except himself; in fact, his style is highly mannered. Open syntax, rhetorical repetition, extreme fluctuation of line length, percussive rhythm, and heavy, almost constant emphasis make up his stylistic signature. A passage in the first of *The Maximus Poems* goes:

> the underpart is, though stemmed, uncertain
> is, as sex is, as moneys are, facts!
> facts, to be dealt with, as the sea is, the demand
> that they be played by, that they only can be, that they must

be played by, said he, coldly, the
ear!

In this texture of dental and explosive consonants and numerous caesuras, of syntactical suspensions and repetitions, of exclamations, urgencies ("must"), melodrama ("coldly"), and
climaxes ("facts!" "ear!"), almost every phrase takes terrific emphasis. The predominant characteristic is energy.

Since the poems in Olson's Maximus volumes do not differ in
style from his other ones, I may draw my samples of Olson from
this long work. It is less a sequence than a collection. When Olson started his "Maxies," as he called them, he had (in keeping
with his principles) no notion of a plot, subject, purpose, or
length for the major work he hoped to write. The poems
changed character somewhat as the years passed, but this was
only because Olson was changing. Most of the separate poems
are linked by their setting in and around Gloucester, Massachusetts, and by their use of the topography, urban and rural images, social types, commercial activity, and history of the region.
And Olson's vision and style naturally pervade and interconnect
the Maximus lyrics, though hardly more than would be the case
in collections by most writers. Yet Olson thought of these lyrics
as a sequence, and both he and his explainers put forward various ways of describing the supposed continuity.

Autobiography, for example; and certainly many of the poems
include autobiographical recollections from childhood on. Or
the poems are autobiography in a more automatic sense: since
they were composed at moments spread over ten years, they record the occasions and development of Olson's mind during this
period. The course of Olson's development is generally from a
preoccupation with the historical and the personal to a perception of the mythical. If we think the path of Olson's psyche a
desirable one, we may even read through the collection with a
sense of emerging climax and psychological victory.

There are recurrent themes. Throughout the history of
Gloucester, from the first settlement to the present, capitalist
proprietors are contrasted with the farmers and fishermen, who
have a direct, personal, and sensory involvement. In the latter
we find intensity of emotion, vital attention, whatever makes life
worth living from moment to moment. Or there is the theme of

Olson as historiographer: he must find out first hand by going back to original records. He reveres particular facts, for in them all truth or knowledge begins. The frequent and boring citations in these poems of compass bearings or of the measurements of early roads and fields are ruthless exercises in Olsonian epistemology. A moral intention runs through the whole. Maximus is Olson, but Olson composing poems. He is, in other words, Olson functioning as he or anybody ideally should. What, then, is Maximus doing? He is paying attention, and by acts of attention coming alive. He is moving about the place where he is, getting to know it, taking possession of it, "fronting" the whole of it, "mapping" it in space and history, and coming to feel at home in it. And in the later "Maxies" he is living in the here and now like a Mayan or an Egyptian in presence of his gods.

"Letter 72" in *Maximus Poems IV, V, VI* begins by juxtaposing fragments that refer to gardens and love—"of love & hand-holding sweet flowers & drinking / waters." The items assembled include seventeenth-century gardens of the first settlers in the "Dogtown" area of Gloucester (for example, Samuel Davis and his wife Ann), the garden of Eden, Olson's wife Elizabeth, a Persian commentator on the fall of angels, the words "get back to," and a sloping arrow:

> of love & hand-holding sweet flowers & drinking
> waters) Hilton's & Davis', Davis' the
> > garden of Ann
> ↘ get back to
> > & Elizabeth & Eden
> Nasir Tusi
> > & where I fall
> man is the fallen angel

The arrow represents the fall, presumably, and also emphasizes the words "get back to," which may be both optative and imperative, both nostalgic yearning and urgent command. Their object—get back to what?—is left open, but the context suggests many possibilities: Eden, pristine freshness, love, the seventeenth-century Dogtown of the first farmers and fishermen, the state of mind of Nasir Tusi (and the colonial settlers) for whom myths were realities, and the heaven from which the angels have fallen. The complex of references make an ideogram, the Poundian technique. The poem continues, however, by a different technique; it states in a factual way just where in Dogtown the first settlers located themselves:

> Bennett placed himself
> above 75'
> . . . .
> —& Sam'l Davis on the height of
> the next rise, inside 125'.

The prosaic register of such facts continues for fourteen lines; however, the facts express an imaginative conceit in which the topography of early Dogtown recreates the spiritual cosmography of the seventeenth century. In this humorous yet significant mapping the "'hills' or hogbacks" on which the settlers build are heaven, the swamp and lower road are the opposite place, and between is the Common, a "garden"—Eden. The poem ends in Dogtown Common, an area of seventeenth-century cellar holes outside Gloucester, and renders the flowers and shrubs there with sensitive, spare images, lovely sound and cadence:

> the Commons is
> garden, and manor, ground rose
> & candle
> shapes of spruce & bayberry garden.

The reference is no longer to the seventeenth century only, for the ground rose and candle shapes of spruce are on Dogtown Common now just as then, and can be seen by Olson just as the earliest settlers saw them.

"The Cow of Dogtown" from the same volume is a traditional type of Romantic poem on landscape and the divine. After geological observations on the formation of Dogtown Common, the poem presents Olson on top of the great moraine. He is "up into the sky," in space, light, and freedom. A Thoreauvian good moment follows. Picking and eating blueberries, he is alone in a wondrously bountiful place of nature, feeding and moving about like a bear. The passage resonates to Olson's ideas—being in nature as a part of it, direct responsiveness, first-hand relation to things. The mode of locomotion on "one's own behind" sums up, with typical humor, the natural, independent, self-reliant, down-to-earth values.

> One would sit here
> and eat off checker berries, and blue-
> berries in season—they are around
> the place, at this height,
> like cups and saucers, and one moves around to
> eat them, out of one's hands,
> not by getting up but going from
> place to place on one's own behind. Burning
> balsam, or the numerous bushes of bayberry
> one could stay here with the sky
> it feels like as long as one chose.

As the poem continues, passages of geological lore refer to the land rising as the glacier melted. In the concluding lines Olson alludes to an Egyptian myth of the creation of the world: as earth, the Primeval Hill, rose from the waters, the goddess Nut, the sky, arched over it. She is the cow of Dogtown. In evoking Nut, Olson wanted to tell us several things: that he senses in this moment an all-encompassing presence—

> her air
> is as her light
> as close
> one is not removed even in passing through;

that the goddess is a Jungian archetype; and that primitive consciousness and its living, mythical world can be restored.

The first of the Maximus Poems is equally ambitious and traditional, but the tradition in this case is that of the Modernist long poem—of *The Waste Land,* the *Cantos, The Bridge,* the *Four Quartets,* and *Paterson.* "Off-shore, by islands," it begins in suspended syntax, telling where Maximus speaks from, and then, blending the outer and inner worlds, adds that the voice comes also from deep within—"hidden in the blood." Taking a gull's viewpoint high above, it sees the city of Gloucester as a bowl or nest, and it also compares the writing of the poem to building a nest. "Feather to feather added . . . curling hair, string"—the miscellaneous materials—

> make bulk, these, in the end, are
> the sum.

("Rolling up the sum," Williams had written at the start of *Paterson,* deriving his method from the Passaic River.) Thus the city,

Gloucester, becomes both the subject of the poem and also the poem itself, just as the city of Paterson is also Williams' poem *Paterson*. A sudden sight of a gull is taken as an epiphany:

> the thing you're after
> may lie around the bend
> of the nest (second, time slain, the bird! the bird!

And the passage somewhat painfully, though only vaguely, reminds us of analogous but more carefully prepared moments in *The Bridge* and the *Four Quartets*. The bird then becomes Saint Antony of Padua, is urged to "sweep low" ("Unto us lowliest sometimes sweep," Crane wrote in his great Proem to *The Bridge*) and bless the roofs, ridge posts, and flake racks "of my city."

ROBERT CREELEY

Around 1950 Robert Creeley (b. 1926), then unknown, started mailing out his work. He sent his poems and thoughts about poetry to many poets, old and young, and some replied. He and Olson exchanged letters, sometimes daily, for four years before they met in 1954. Living on Mallorca in 1952, Creeley found that printing was cheap there. Hence the *Black Mountain Review* (1954–57), which he edited. He also started a press, which published himself along with, among others, Olson, Duncan, Larry Eigner, and Paul Blackburn. Thus Creeley made himself known to his own generation. He climbed the hierarchy of little magazines from *Goad* and *Gryphon* to *Poetry*, and of publishers to Scribner's. By 1962, when *For Love* collected the best lyrics from his seven previous volumes, his style was being imitated.

For indeed it was distinctive. Whatever one thought of his lyrics—many readers admired them intensely—they were an unusual type for the 1950s. While many poets in the United States were breaking out into protest, confession, and liberation, with turbulent emotions, lavish particulars, and many lines, and while many others followed the New Critical mode, Creeley did neither. He retrenched into the small and muted. His poems focused on a metaphor or complex of feeling, which planted itself in the mind. Often the sentences were illogical, elliptical, or suspended in the indefinite; they opened delicate, precisely calculated gaps, so to speak, from which suggestions of meaning were emitted. "I Know a Man" is deservedly famous:

> As I sd to my
> friend, because I am
> always talking,—John, I
>
> sd, which was not his
> name, the darkness sur-
> rounds us, what
>
> can we do against
> it, or else, shall we &
> why not, buy a goddam big car,
>
> drive, he sd, for
> christ's sake, look
> out where yr going.

In a general way such poems derived from Williams, for Cree-ley dwelt in Williams' ordinary world and talked a simple, Williams language. But his character was utterly unlike Williams'. He was nervous and passive. He had little interest in other people or the outside world. His isolated, interior lyrics observed his own feelings—mistrust, fluctuating love, angst, loneliness. Restless insecurity made him press honestly and hard into his emotions, trying to know the truth of them. The states of mind he compelled himself to acknowledge were morally painful, di-minished, and above all, uncertain, so that from line to line his poems undermined what they tried to assert. The means to this might be slight—an interrupting line break, a question mark where we expect a period—but doubt insinuated itself every-where. "The Business" was a typical reflection on love:

> To be in love is like going out-
> side to see what kind of day
>
> it is. Do not
> mistake me. If you love
>
> her how prove she
> loves also, except that it
>
> occurs, a remote chance on
> which you stake
>
> yourself? But barter for

the Indian was a means of sustenance.

There are records.

The focus of anxiety—is love returned? how to know for certain?—is the same as in Proust, but Proust's narrator, studying his Albertine for clues, cared intensely whether she loved him or not. To compare love to a weather check, as Creeley does, suggests a slightly bored nervousness. And though Proust knew in practice much about love as "barter," his views were more romantic. He would not have considered whether he preferred barter and the meager "sustenance" it provides. Creeley's poem would alarm a psychiatrist, for it is deeply "disturbed." More exactly, it is apathetic, mistrustful, bitter, and isolated. But a critic must find it a remarkably honest report.

His style was usually called "minimal," meaning that in many things in which poets may be abundant Creeley is sparse or barren. His poems have few or no descriptions, characterizations, or incidents. He builds his subtleties and resonances by juxtapositions of short, simple lines and phrases, by manipulation of syntax and rhythm, and by metaphor. As Creeley says, "You can't derail a train by standing directly in front of it, or, not quite. But, a tiny piece of steel, properly placed . . ."

His poems in the 1950s were "open" mainly in their uncertainties and elusiveness. Their moral atmosphere lacked altogether that readiness and trustful momentum we associate with the Olson group. But beginning in *Pieces* (1968), where elliptical fragments were presented as jottings in a continuing notebook or journal, he moved toward the open ethos. *A Day Book* (1972) and *Hello* (1976) went further in this direction. His writing was now much less worked over. Some readers find it more vital, as in "For my Mother," which is certainly one of Creeley's best achievements.

DENISE LEVERTOV, EDWARD DORN, AND PAUL BLACKBURN

Denise Levertov (b. 1923) grew up in England and published there her first book of poems, *The Double Image* (1945). The well-made, moody impressions in this volume reflect, as she says, the

Romantic influences in England at that time. She married an American and moved to New York City. "The early '50s were for me transitional," she later recalled, "and not very productive of poems; but I was reading a great deal and taking in at each breath the air of American life." From these years she emerged with a new style. Her poems now concentrated on ordinary life—"dailyness," she called it—and took the "earlier and shorter" poems of Williams for their chief models. Meanwhile, Kenneth Rexroth had noticed and liked her first book. His praise alerted others, and presently little magazines and presses devoted to poetry were inviting her to publish. Though readers associated her with the other poets noticed in this chapter, she lacked the bold ambition of Olson and Duncan. Instead of swooping through historical time and geographical space, her verses remained modestly centered in the personal and immediate. As she lived her life, she attended to her feelings, and her poems articulated them in sensitive images and metaphors.

In the 1960s her poetry changed again. Caught up in the antiwar movement, she protested and demonstrated. Ultimately she visited North Vietnam. (It was, she reported, a paradise filled with beautiful, sensitive people.) Her poetry of antiwar protest fell into loose rhetoric, sensational imagery, and violent emotions. For Levertov could not integrate the shock of war with her vision of human nature. She could not see that she and the friends she admired might under other circumstances also have been guilty of the cruelties, such as the use of napalm, that she attacked. As a result the intelligence of her earlier poetry was lost, and she described a simplified world of heroes, innocents, and demons.

When the war ended, she again found her poetic subject in her personal life, but she wrote of it with a new frankness and immediacy. Some of her poems in the 1970s were in the notebook genre. As compared with her earlier style, the new one was both better and worse. Better, because human character and story are more interesting than mood and metaphor, and direct realism has power. To tell, as she now would, her sexual fantasy of stroking "your body" from "neck-pulse" to "cock" makes a more striking impression, at least at first, then to speak of peeling a stick. But immediacy may lose in subtlety what it gains in decibels. Second thoughts are usually more and better than first ones. Levertov's notebook poems appeal if you enjoy reading other people's diaries.

Levertov has the dubious merit of being a completely representative poet. She illustrates poetic styles of the times and places in which she has lived, and is lacking, as a poet, in strong individuality. Her gift lies in the sensitivity of her responses, and yet, strangely, failure of sensitivity is her glaring weakness, for her taste and tact are uncertain. Her best type of poem remains the brief, Williams-like utterance, though I should also mention two sequences in which she explores human relationships more complexly than she can in short poems: the 1964 "Olga Poems," on the troubled life of her sister, and the poems on a dying mother and her daughter in *Life in the Forest* (1978). These sequences suggest that Levertov may have a potential for sustaining major work. Her usual style may be sampled in "Overland to the Islands," a poem on how to compose poetry, in which she elaborates Williams' comparison of the poet writing to a dog sniffing about:

> Under his feet
> rocks and mud, his imagination, sniffing,
> engaged in its perceptions—dancing
> edgeways, there's nothing
> the dog disdains on his way,
> nevertheless he
> keeps moving, changing
> pace and approach but
> not direction—"every step an arrival."

The latest book of Levertov that I have seen is the bittersweet, pastoral *Pig Dreams* (1981). Spoken by a pet pig, the lyrics make pleasant lunchtime reading, but are pallid beside the fierce wit of Robert Siegel's pig poems in his volume entitled *In a Pig's Eye* (1980).

Another poet made and marred by Williams is Philip Levine (b. 1928). His poetry presents an ordinary mind and life in ordinary words. In his early volumes Levine wrote with hard humor and sympathy about working-class existence in Detroit, where he grew up. Now he reports his personal life with similar directness. Except in some Surrealist poems, his style is straightforward and colloquial. An anarchist political protest runs through much of his work. But the anarchist protest of Levine is not nearly so extreme as that of Charles Bukowski (b. 1920). A dropout from society, Bukowski describes his experiences and voices his feelings in literal, formless verse. His world is that of the urban unemployed and of skid row. With Levertov I may also mention A. L. Purdy (b. 1918) and David Ray (b. 1932), both of whom were also influenced by Williams. Purdy, a Canadian, grew up in rural Ontario, served during the Second World War in the Royal Canadian Air Force, and became a scriptwriter for the Canadian Broadcasting Corporation. Like Williams, he celebrates things resisting amid adversity, as in "Trees at the Arctic Circle," but more usually he expresses his sense of transience and mortality. Sensitive, humorous, and engaging, Purdy is one of Canada's most widely read and admired poets. David Ray attracts by his unobtrusive skill and by his sensitivity, decency, humor, and sanity. *Dragging the Main and Other Poems* (1968) contains political protest; in other volumes his themes are usually personal. Many of his best poems are travel pieces.

Ramon Guthrie (1896–1973), a professor of French and Comparative Literature at Dartmouth College, was a progressively better poet in the volumes he published between 1959 and 1968, and "The Bear" was his best poem. The Cro-Magnon speaker of this blank-verse monologue tells how he painted a bear on the walls of a cave, where no one would ever see it in the dark. The poem suggests many things about the making of a work of art—the mystery of the motive, the affectionate intimacy with the subject, the absorption and isolation of the artist as he works. But Guthrie's poems are much more likely to be contemporary in setting and his speakers to be deliberately gabby. Expostulating and reminiscing, they have a picaresque charm, and resemble William Carlos Williams mixed with Ginsberg and a bit of François Villon. Beneath Guthrie's willed *joie de vivre* there is bitterness and hurt. "Montparnasse," "Boul Miche, May 1968," and "Mongoose" are among his more interesting poems, and "Marsyas in the Intensive Care Ward" affords satiric relief to whoever has suffered hospital "care."

Josephine Miles (b. 1911) also found poetry in familiar details of the modern American scene. "Speech," she said, "not images, not ideas, not music, but people talking," is "the material from which poetry is made." Miles was a university professor (she wrote authoritative analyses of English poetic vocabulary in different periods), and some of her poems touch on philosophical or scientific puzzles. "On Inhabiting an Orange," for example, is concerned with the paradox that parallel lines on a sphere always meet. But most of her poems consist of quick sketches of familiar occurrences ("Moonrise in a Lumber Yard," "The Lighting of the Street Lights") or are peopled with individuals shopping at stores, looking at signs, or concerned with rent control, housing developments, and farm legislation. The mere mention of titles may illustrate the direction in which she moves away from the poetically conventional: "Market Report on Cotton Gray Goods," "Committee Report on Smoke Abatement in Residential Area," and "Purchase of a Hat to Wear in the Sun."

Except that she is also Canadian, Margaret Atwood (b. 1939), who is known especially for her novels, has little in common with Purdy. She is not a disciple of Williams or anyone else, but has absorbed the essential Williams disciplines of natural speech, clear, precise images, and everyday subjects and tones of voice. To the extent that she is in the Williams tradition, however, she is remarkable for having stripped away much of the warm empathy we expect of it, and brought to it, instead, sharply critical intelligence. She is not usually a satiric poet, but she has a strong sense of reality, and cannot help puncturing conventional expectations and illusions. Often her work has an undernote of tartness or bitterness. Recent poems, however, have tended to be philosophical in theme and tenderer in feeling. "There Is Only One of Everything" achieves the difficult literary feat of conveying a moment of happiness without seeming sentimental.

Alan Dugan (b. 1923), John Logan (b. 1923), and Robert Mezey (b. 1935) are interesting poets of the second rank. Mezey began his career under the influence of Yvor Winters, but later deserted regular meters. "Touch It" exhibits his smooth craftsmanship. Logan articulates his spiritual quest in straightforward language. Earnest, thoughtful, but not witty, he is sometimes portentous about commonplaces. Dugan's first volume won both the Pulitzer Prize and the National Book Award in 1962. His work is frequently ironic and sometimes shocking. Introspection leads him to recognize morally bitter truths about himself (which are also truths about everybody), and he articulates these with a depressed absence of emotion.

Edward Dorn (b. 1929) shares Olson's grapple with large ideas as well as his open syntax. In poems such as "On the Debt My Mother Owed to Sears Roebuck," "The Prisoner of Bellefonte (Pa.)," "Like a Message on Sunday," "Obituary," and "Los Mineros," he has the sensitivity of Williams and Olson to the atmosphere of local, American places. The poem on the debt to Sears Roebuck is set on a midwestern farm in 1943. The mother waits through the day in her kitchen for her husband and her son to come home. The imagery suggests poverty and fatigue, eroded possibilities and apathy. If the poem were only this, it would be in the vein of Williams. Dorn's original note is that the family broods on the debt it owes to Sears Roebuck. That the debt figures so prominently in the poem is, in one sense, an aesthetic distortion, almost a comic exaggeration. Precisely for this reason it forces us to think. Sears Roebuck represents the economic system in which the family is enmeshed. Speaking ironically for the system, the final lines suggest that the function and duty of this family is to buy, owe, and pay by installment; "owing that debt" the family is part of the patriotic, "*stay at home army*" that keeps "things going." The juxtaposition of Sears Roebuck with the second World War assumes the Marxist connection of war with capitalism. It is also an aesthetic effect, for it widens the perspective, extending what is happening on this small farm to ultimate historical manifestations. But war is not the only cost. Sears Roebuck and its debt indeed keep this family "going," but the reduced life on this farm is far from what life could and should be.

This type of poem is Dorn's best, but he also writes lyrics with a more traditional content. "There Was a Change," "Time to Burn," "If It Should Ever Come," and several of his *Twenty-four Love Poems* (1969) and of his poems in *Hello, La Jolla* (1978) are subtle, suggestive, humorous, and philosophical. All his short poems are or seem immediately spontaneous. They enact the sudden discoveries, shifts, digressions, long leaps and lapses of the mind from moment to moment. Dramatizing spontaneity, they present sequence by apposition and subjects without predicates.

In the mid-1960s Dorn wrote long poems also, and in these he lost focus. In such poems as "The Problem of the Poem for My Daughter, Left Unsolved" and *The North Atlantic Turbine* (1967) the flow of wit cannot compensate for the loss of coherence. These are poems of satiric denunciation; more exactly, they voice a fierce rejection of every political and social manifestation. They are radical, but with the extreme, contemporary radicalism that despairs of reform, so entrenched and pervasive is the evil, and that therefore has no program except to demolish. The poems attack all countries and social systems but dwell especially on the United States. The state of mind they reflect was a response to the war in Vietnam, which the poems mention repeatedly, and Dorn's rage is of course the other side of his sentimental attachment to his country, at least to its people and geography.

From 1968 to 1977 Dorn worked sporadically on a long poem in four books. Though many critics have explained and evaluated *Slinger*, probably none has fully understood it, and neither do I. It is a philosophical, didactic, and sometimes allegorical poem. Thus, for example, in Book II a character named "I" expires and is not regretted. This death of the ego makes a moral point plainly, but in general the poem must be obscure if it is true to its premises. For one of its teachings is that nothing can be taught, especially in language. Language hides reality; to describe something is to kill it. Moreover, since reality exists only in this instant, we cannot know it. In the appropriate metaphor of the Slinger, it disappears before you can get the drop on it.

> What does the foregoing mean?
> I asked. Mean?
> my Gunslinger laughed
> *Mean?*
> Refugee, you got some strange
> obsessions, you want to know
> what something *means* after you've
> seen it, after you've *been* there.

Hence the Slinger must teach by indirection and disorientation, as in Zen. The poem means its paradoxes seriously but not trag-

ically, for it is a comic work. Its speed and illogicality contribute
to the comic effect, and so, more obviously, do parodies, allusive
and mimetic uses of comic strips and radio serials, and conventions from western movie, tall tale, and vaudeville patter.

The poems of Paul Blackburn (1926–71) develop in a leisurely way by accumulating details. As they describe a scene or
incident, they hold attention by their vividness and reality, humor and pathos, and also by their form—the easy yet unexpected motions of Blackburn's attention and the fine cadence of
his free verse. With references to footloose wandering, un-
washed clothes, bars, casual sex, and the like, the poems create
the impression of a somewhat vagabond or Bohemian personality ("I"), and Blackburn's apparently laid-back style contributes
appropriately to this. But like the Troubadours he translated, he
was a skillful artist. The seemingly casual details carry, as we
reflect on them, a weight of meaning and psychological insight,
and when we come to the end of his anecdotal poems, we find
that they have planted in our minds a sharply focused, unified,
and suggestive image. Perhaps his best single poem is "Sun-
flower Rock." A derelict is chased out of a bar. Though their
reactions are highly individual and differentiated, the persons
in the bar show, on the whole, a shallow inhumanity. Outside the
world is equally unsympathizing, as the poem suggests in bleak
images of night, rain, and "the evening traffic uptown." In the
concluding lines the narrator identifies himself with the derelict,
and the shock of this creates pathos and foreboding. "Soon," the
narrator says, "we" step into the traffic

> ourself, stop
> to buy a half-pint at the corner
> for the cold night, for the pocket.
> Already wet, we turn our back to the northwind,
> feel the whiskey burn.

Jonathan Williams (b. 1929) was at Black Mountain College
with Olson. His poems are champagne, sprightly and pellucid.
They move fast in open form, uncovering puns as they go. Some
of his poems are heard/found objects. Like William Carlos Williams, in other words, he listens to people talking and makes
uniquely American poems of what he hears. He lives in North

Carolina and mocks the racists, dancing on their pinheads. The title of "Lawless [George] Wallace Über Alles" suggests the lightness of his bite. Other poems are more personal, such as the thoughtful and moving "The Distances to the Friend." *An Ear in Bartram's Tree* (1969), a selection of his poems from 1957 to 1967, makes the best introduction. *Blue & Roots, Rue & Bluets* (1971) is for browsing; some of the speech heard in the Appalachian hollows is wonderful. Williams publishes Jargon Books, gives many public readings, and in other ways also plays an active, valuable role in support of poetry.

ROBERT DUNCAN

Robert Duncan was born in Oakland, California, in 1919, and was adopted at the age of six months. He began to write in adolescence. By the time he was eighteen he had recognized "in poetry my sole and ruling vocation." He sought "the idea of the modern" in Joyce, Eliot, Stravinski, Picasso, Gertrude Stein, and E. E. Cummings; Pound especially was his "mentor." He was now a freshman at the University of California at Berkeley; the next year, having fallen in love, he left college and followed his lover east. After brief service in the army he obtained a psychiatric discharge in 1941. At this time he changed his surname, dropping the adoptive Symmes and reverting to the Duncan of his birth.

His poems came out in little magazines. By the end of the 1940s he had a local reputation in San Francisco, where he was living. He met Charles Olson in 1947, and contributed to *Origin* and the *Black Mountain Review*. In 1956 he went as a teacher to Black Mountain College. He articulated his ideas about poetry in forcefully argued essays and introductions. (At the beginning of this chapter I set forth his theories with those of Olson; the single most revealing of Duncan's prose pieces for understanding his poetry is *The Truth & Life of Myth*, 1968.) Duncan knows three or four languages and is, in the famous phrase with which Coleridge described himself, a "library-cormorant." He could add with Coleridge that "Metaphysics, & Poetry, & 'Facts of Mind'—(i.e. Accounts of all the strange phantasms that ever possessed your philosophy-dreamers from Thoth the Egyptian to Taylor, the English Pagan,) are my darling Studies." Volumes of lyrics appeared regularly from 1947 on, and in the 1960s three volumes—*The Opening of the Field* (1960), *Roots and Branches* (1964), and *Bending the Bow* (1968)—made clear that Duncan is one of the major poets of his generation.

The upheavals in Duncan's personal life between the ages of eighteen and twenty must have been felt as an acute crisis, the more so since attitudes were much less tolerant forty years ago than they are today. Neither should memories of social opinion during the war in Vietnam mislead us about what was generally felt during the Second World War. To affirm oneself as a poet, homosexual, and nonparticipant in the war was to reject the social and moral world of most people in ways that would provoke extreme disapproval. As a son of the middle class Duncan had presumably internalized the values he now defied. The "mental strife" he must have waged within himself was undoubtedly a source of strength, but may also have exacted its psychological cost. That his psyche is, as he sees it, a field of conflicts—he hopes they may be only "contrasts" within an underlying unity—does not distinguish him from most other modern writers. That he tends, apparently, to react against whatever type of poetry he has been attracted toward is more suggestive. Space is lacking to elaborate this point: I am not thinking merely of his unusually different styles in every phase of his career, or of his openness to very diverse influences, but especially of his periodic retreats from styles that he has particularly identified as his own. One such moment came in the 1950s, when he wrote a great many dull poems (such as the "Imitations of Gertrude Stein") in an attempt, presumably, to deflate his "Romantic" imagination, of which he was then somewhat ashamed. Another such withdrawal from himself seems to have begun after 1968, when he went for inspiration to the conceited, Metaphysical style of the seventeenth century. Also, Duncan takes for granted that a huge gap yawns between his own feelings and beliefs and those of most readers and critics of poetry. He is not wrong to assume this. But the assumption is also a projection from his own self-division.

Criticism, he rightly says, ought "to raise a crisis in our consideration" of content; much modern criticism is written to "dismiss" it instead. The statement breathes anxiety. Duncan expects to be rejected. We will not, he thinks, be willing to experience the world as his poems do. His fear, to repeat, is not for his stylistic methods, though these would have raised a crisis indeed for earlier generations. The reaction of Robert Bridges, or John Crowe Ransom, or W. H. Auden on reading Duncan would be a theme for comedy. Duncan's states of mind and vision of things are the source of his misgivings, yet most readers will find that, though Duncan does not reflect the world they live in, he does so as much as Milton, for example, or as many another poet with whose work they engage themselves fully. His emotional world— for emotions and their interrelations are the "content" with which we chiefly engage ourselves in any poem—may be suggested if we imagine some ancient shrine where a believer attends at sacred rites, terrible yet reconciling. Or we may think of a worshipper alone before the image of his god.

The allusions in Duncan's poetry to esoteric cults and myths— Orpheus, Demeter, Osiris, and so forth—essentially reenact such scenes. In them the participant is subject to extreme emotions—horror, exaltation, despair, awe, ecstasy, peace—that shift suddenly and involve one another. Or changing the metaphor, we may imagine the psyche as a dark abyss in which demonic and divine powers are battling. From these depths manifestations rise, overwhelming the self. In such upwellings we are passive, for we cannot resist them and would not if we could. But behind or within the apparent disharmonies of existence and of the psyche, the demonic is one with the divine. Both poetic creation and sexual love may participate in the unified divine life. Presenting his theme of love's holiness, Duncan does not fig-leaf for shy readers. The sexual images are as explicit and vivid as their religious resonance is intense. His poetry in this aspect resembles the sacred prostitutes of Corinth.

Duncan characterizes his vision of things as Romantic, and the term, though imprecise, is appropriate. Brought up by Theosophists, he learned in childhood to read not only Greek and Germanic myth, the Bible and Plato, but all stories, dreams, and life itself for "messages" they contained and revealed, or would reveal if we could unlock the esoteric meaning. When, later, he first committed himself to poetry and eagerly explored the "idea of the modern," he was swept up by Milton's rhetoric and Hopkins', by St.-John Perse's visionary and dreamlike *Anabase*, by

Dylan Thomas, Pound, Blake, and most of all, for a while, by George Barker's *Calamiterror*. This was around 1940.

Such early poems as "Persephone," "Passage over Water," and "Toward the Shaman" had lush music, cadence, and haunting imagery. They were not cloudy, adolescent allegories, for the images were charged with sensitive meanings. "King Haydn of Miami Beach" showed that Duncan had been studying Laura Riding. "An African Elegy" arose from his strong response to Lorca's "Oda al Rey de Harlem." Though both these poems were written in 1942, they differ widely in tone and feeling. "The Years as Catches" ends magnificently:

> Catch from the years the line of joy,
> impatient & repeated day,
> my heart, break. Eye
> break open and set free
> His world, my ecstasy.

His early poems subsequently lost Duncan's favor, though in 1966 he reprinted them, having decided to "admit them as part of my life's work." "The Venice Poem" (1948) was a long, ambitious suite and was followed by another, "Medieval Scenes" (1950). All these and many others, such as "Strawberries under the Snow," were important poems. Yet he fell, as he put it, "under the wing of the Adversary." At times the Adversary incarnated itself in Laura Riding, for Duncan was haunted and depressed by "her doubt of the truth of poetry," and saw himself in her hostile descriptions of the Romantic type of poet. Thence came the dull period in the early 1950s, from which Duncan recovered in *Letters* (1958) and the three major volumes of the 1960s I mentioned. His work culminated in the *Passages* sequence, to which I shall turn, skipping for brevity many interesting poems. A list may be helpful: "Poetry, a Natural Thing," "Roots and Branches," "A Sequence of Poems for H.D.'s 73 Birthday," "Come, Let Me Free Myself," Sonnets 1, 2, and 3, "Variations on Two Dicta of William Blake," and the "Structure of Rime" poems.

Since I make a large claim for Duncan, I should acknowledge plainly that he can and often does write horribly. Many passages are hopelessly vague, inert, rhetorical, empty, or clichéd. Moreover, he has habits—the indefiniteness of open syntax is one—against which I feel no bias, but many readers do. We can assume that the Poundian methods of allusion, ellipsis, juxtaposition, and collage are by now acceptable to most readers. But whoever thinks (with the followers of Williams) that the language of poetry in the United States should be spoken American will be disappointed in Duncan, for (like Olson and Dorn) he writes a language that was never spoken anywhere. "News" that "larvae *do* feed upon" (my italics) is one of countless illustrative items that could be cited. Most readers may consider the symbol-cluster of Shelley and the Pre-Raphaelites to be now outworn, but Light, Beauty, Stars, Heaven, Shadow, Fire, Flames, Love, Night, Eternity, and so on appear lavishly in Duncan's lines. Readers who care about restraint, good taste, and the like have no business reading Duncan (or many contemporary poets), for such conceptions have no more relevance for him than they would for a bonfire. Fear of being sentimental is only, in his opinion, an internalized and repressive social norm. Even readers who do not find his *Weltanschauung* sentimental will look askance at some passages. He begins a poem dedicated to Robert Creeley ("Thank You for Love"), "A friend / 's a distant nearness"; Edgar Guest would hardly have put it differently. Duncan's poems have little narrative substance or characterization (except of himself), and for some readers therefore want human interest.

The *Passages* sequence contains Duncan's finest work thus far, but that is not the only reason for dwelling on it. Because the poems it includes are diverse, it illustrates the range of his art from his most obvious rhetoric to his most inward and difficult subtleties. And since his poems of the latter kind, like many of the *Cantos*, can hardly be read until at least some glosses are provided, any notice of them must be at some length.

The title implies discontinuity. Passages, we assume, are extracts from a large whole. And indeed these passages are, but the whole from which they are taken is not yet and never will be written, for it is the whole of reality in its evolving process. Of this we apprehend only fragmentary bits and inconsistent perspectives. Even the longest and most structured of poems, such as the *Divine Comedy*, is only a passage, a fragment or perspective within the unknowable whole. (The "open" form of *Passages* acknowledges this situation; the form of the *Divine Comedy* does not.) But at the same time a poet feels and responds to the underlying coherence that he cannot perceive, and in the faith of this, Duncan juxtaposes one passage with another. The form, in other words, presents drastic discontinuities, but with a faith in their intrinsic continuity or ultimate connection. That the poem will have such continuity is assured, in Duncan's opinion, by "projective" composition, utterance welling up immediately from the depths of the self or, more exactly, from the cosmos in the self. Of course the same formal principle works in every part of the poem. A Passage may itself be made up of passages, and these of briefer passages, and so forth, though Duncan rarely carries this out in practice to the extent that his theory would justify.

But passages are also corridors toward, transitions. As "extracts," the term implies discontinuity, but it also implies ongoingness. Duncan's *Passages*, we suppose, will have that "kinesis" Olson desiderated. They will be, like the universe, an "open" form, "a creation creating itself," as Duncan once put it. "Open" to the unknown. "Passages" may also remind us of Keats's great letter of May 1818, in which he envisions the "many open doors . . . but all dark—all leading to dark passages" to which we all come as we begin to feel the "burden of the Mystery" (Keats is in this phrase quoting Wordsworth). "Now if we live," adds Keats, we "shall explore them . . . make discoveries, and shed a light in them."

Conceptions of a form are not, needless to say, always carried out in the actual form. "Up Rising, *Passages* 25," is a visionary and prophetic poem of continuous utterance; its form reflects Duncan's theories less than it does Blake's *America*. It is a political poem, and Duncan's politics are anarchy. He believes in complete individual liberty and full human community, and he is sure that these are compatible, in fact, that each presupposes the other. Hence he is against the bureaucratic state and all that it does. He was violently opposed to the war in Vietnam, and this is the subject of "Up Rising" and of some other Passages as well. President Johnson is a Urizenic figure out of Blake, and the war is "a great potlatch" or "Texas barbecue / of Asia." These images, sustained and amplified throughout the poem, speak of greed, infantile destructiveness, and egoism in American life and character. The war, the poem asserts, is the bloated image or rising up of our inner selves and wishes. (The punning motif of rising up continues throughout the poem in images of airplanes, the American Eagle, ascending smoke and fire, rising digestive gases and diseased swellings, and upwelling repressed hatreds.) With its headlong syntax, rhetorical repetition, apocalyptic imagery, and sweeping, unqualified generalization, the poem shares the raging, swollen character it condemns, but like its prototype in Blake, the poem also thinks amid its vehemence, explaining through psychological and historical insight what it condemns.

"The Fire, *Passages* 13," begins with thirty-six disconnected words arranged in vertical and horizontal rows of six. They lack syntax and make no sense. Perhaps this part of the poem represents unorganized matter; or an inorganic arrangement of matter, as in crystal; or an early phase on the way to life, as in amino acids. At any rate, it is a first beginning, out of which a more organized being will evolve. Some short, doodling lines follow. They represent a second phase in which syntax is achieved. "Do you know the language of the old belief?" this prelude ends, and the "old belief" is then presented in a highly organized work: Piero di Cosimo's fifteenth-century painting of animals fleeing a forest fire. The theme connects later in the poem with that of man's ecological destructiveness and atomic war, but at first Duncan concentrates on the painting itself. (His way of "reading" it provides a model for approaching his own poems.) With its hazy outlines, esoteric symbols, and extreme and opposite emotions, the painting somewhat resembles a Duncan poem. It reflects a tradition of occult lore, which the poem traces back to Orpheus, that all things are ultimately harmonious, as in music. Thus even though it depicts panic, flight, and terror, the painting—this is its mystery—unites them with Edenic peace, stillness, and beauty. The painting is a "charmd field" of contrasts within a unified whole. Its Orphic vision of harmony emerges from the depths of the "Anima Mundi."

Against this painting the poem contrasts a terrible vision of hell by Hieronymus Bosch. As this "illumination" is described, the poem mingles details that make the vision also of our own time—"flaming automobiles, enraged lovers, wars against communism, heroin addicts, police raids, race riots." Quick allusions rehearse the course of the Second World War, and survey the apocalyptic evil of the present.

My name is Legion   and in every nation   I multiply,
   Over those who would be Great Nations   Great Evils.

They are burning the woods, the brushlands, the
      grassy fields razed;   their
         profitable suburbs spread.

In its final section the poem repeats in reverse order the
thirty-six words in rows and columns with which it began. If we
take the sequence of passages in the poem as a temporal one,
we see a world gradually created and then destroyed. Our age
is followed by total disintegration, a return to the beginning before organic life. References to atomic and hydrogen bombs reinforce this interpretation. Yet the two paintings with their opposed visions were done at more or less the same date. The
relation between them may be not so much chronological as
simply alternative. The details of the two paintings activate
many subtle parallels and contrasts, which the reader will wish
to explore, but using the lexicon of the poem, the opposed visions may be broadly characterized as southern and northern,
pagan and Christian. The pagan vision of Piero di Cosimo continues from a remote past and is, paradoxically, happier and
more hopeful. The Christian one of Bosch seems more accurate
to the present world and more prophetic of the future. Yet to
our lives and history in the present we could bring the Orphic
lore and vision; though the poem does not do this, it suggests
the possibility. If we followed this interpretation, we would read
the final thirty-six words not as an image of disintegration but
as a rearrangement.

"The Currents, *Passages* 16," shows Duncan at his most difficult
and mysterious. Keats's "Ode to a Nightingale," for example,
also descends into deep, murky, and subtle realms of human
psychology, yet it is naive daylight compared to Duncan's obscure, floating fragments. "Now more than ever seems it rich to
die," writes Keats, and considering the state of mind he expresses, the language is remarkably lucid and direct. Keats
understands what he feels, has (in this line) little ambivalence,
and advances with firm rhythm and syntactical momentum.
Duncan, by contrast, is indefinite, ambiguous, elliptical, allusive,
esoteric, Delphic; in short, his Romanticism makes even Keats
seem classical.

The poem juxtaposes seven separate passages. Each is dated (and is referred to hereafter by its date), and thus in sequence the passages present a lapse of time, a changing state of mind over a period of slightly less than two months, from August 9 to October 1, 1964. "No, Verlaine," the poem begins, addressing the French poet. For just before this poem in *The Bending of the Bow* Duncan placed two poems taken from Verlaine, both of which have for their theme the quest for the Holy Grail. Refusing this quest, Duncan elaborates in the first passage ("August 9") a complex image of his opposite quest or choice. He describes a shady, watery place. Lavish play of sounds (shade, shadow, shaken; down, drifting, dreaming, and so forth) enacts the pleasure of it; present participles make it timeless; repetitions of phrase suggest the lingering there; yet the "pouring" syntax and the enjambment with feminine endings make a flowing onwardness. The mysterious, streaming, indefinite place of wellings up, sinkings down, and chiaroscuro has an erotic allure or magic, the more so in that it is also "cold." Yet the erotic is only one element in the complex state evoked. The description brings to mind some of the qualities of Piero di Cosimo's paintings—mystery, shadow, depth, peace—just as the Verlaine poems on the Grail resonate to the Christian vision of Hieronymus Bosch. The "drifting, dreaming" of the seventh line refers syntactically to the "coins of light" falling into water, but also expresses a state of mind. When all this is juxtaposed at the end (after a dot, which indicates a timed rest as in music) to "words," we understand that an utterance has also been described. Along with whatever else it also images, the passage represents a poem of poetic state of mind, drifting and dreaming among words. The words, we note, are not being controlled or manipulated, but stream in their own current.

August 9, 64:

No, Verlaine, I thirst for cool water, for the
    cool of the shade tree,   I would

    drink in the green of the leafy shade,

for the sweet water that wells up from under
    the rock ledge,   the mossy shadows

the coins of light,   shaken down
    drifting, dreaming in the ever-running

stream of bright water pouring over
    rocks gleaming against the cold

    current,s   words

The "Sept 5" passage that follows is cryptic:

    Sept 5:   Sweet his mouth   bitter his mouth

If we associate "mouth" with "words" (mouth/myth is a favorite
pun with Olson and Duncan), "sweet" and "bitter" refer to
speech. The mouth could also be that of a lover. Uniting opposites, the paradoxical line might be voiced in the tone of a
Delphic fragment, oracular and spooky. But it might alternatively be the meditative stream-of-consciousness of the quietly
drifting mind.

"Sept 7" conflates a lover awakening at dawn with the coming
of a god into his shrine and image. The words in French are
quoted, as Duncan notes, from R. P. Festugière, *La Révélation
d'Hermes Trismegiste,* in a context where a worshipper addresses
the ancient god Mandoulis as the sun. The lover is also associated with the sun returning into its sanctuary and the landscape awakening into light and life at dawn. "Auras of the cool
line of hill-horizons" are presumably gleams of light behind the
eastern hills as the sun rises; "auras" recalls Aurora, the dawn.
The "hill-horizons" bring into the poem a suggestion, among
other things, of far distance from which the god comes.

    Sept. 7:   At dawn, your breath stirs   first light

                  auras of the cool line of hill-horizons

    ringing,   your eyes closed,   sweet smile

            bitter smile.   The first ones are awakening.

    You come early, à l'heure juste quand tu
        te lèves, morning your temple,
    donnant à ton image et à ton sanctuaire
        le souffle de la vie et une grande puissance.

"A current of air," the next passage ("Sept 22") begins, the
phrase detached from any sentence. We should think, perhaps,

of the dawn wind. But also the phrase refers back to "le souffle de la vie" in the line before, to "your breath stirs" in the first line of the "Sept 7" passage, and to the word "current" at the end of the first passage. "Night's seance" attempts to call back the dead, as happens in the next passage ("Sept 23"), where an old photograph of a former lover now stirs no recognition. The song of love—"the longing, the lingering tune of it"—has been forgotten, and darkness deepens above and below. The flow of consciousness in the poem has come to a blind place, which is the same place as at the start, but now darkened. Here the god does not come; the landscape of this passage contrasts strongly with the dawn scene of "Sept 7."

By association the thought enters of Jean Genet's film *Chant d'Amour*, which is set in a prison. Though in "Sept 23" the song of love has been forgotten, in Genet's film we "witness the continual song that runs through the walls." Speaking to Eros, the god, Duncan remembers his first experiences of love—

> I loved all the early announcements of you, the first falling
>   in love,
>   the first lovers

—and by contrast falls back immediately, in the "Oct 1" passage that concludes the poem, to the present. The shocking and terrible images are despairing, yet the lines are also ambiguous, partly because the word "mouthing," along with its sexual implication, continues the imagery of utterance. It suggests the possibility of a saving good within the despair.

In the final lines the imagery of isolation, darkness, and horror gathers into that of being within a "dark belly," yet even here love comes, striking "a light that illumines." (The images present a version of the myth of Orpheus descending into the underworld to free Eurydice.) Over this image a contemporary illustration is superimposed. Writing during the Vietnam war, Duncan speaks of a soldier "in a dirty corner of the war / finding his lover"—and not "his" only but "the lover," for every lover is ultimately the divine Eros. Against this, Duncan juxtaposes the image of an old man remembering love. The suddenness of that love, and much else also, is wonderfully suggested in the metaphor of "the bird's leap upward to flight towards the heart." The condensed, final line of the poem speaks of a fountain (the foun-

tain of the first passage) forcing "dewy lips" (dewy: wet, young,
innocent), an image both of sexual climax and poetic creation.

Sept 22:   a current of air.   This late in the year
     morning gets darker.

          And at the seance night holds at day's
          table

          I let sadness gather

(Sept 23)
     clear light and shadow on the moving water.

     Coming across an old photograph of him
          no recognition stirs,   his time
     that was forever has slipt away.

     The key of C minor no longer belongs to
          the song I have forgotten and will never
     sing · the longing, the lingering
          tune of it

                    · a heavy bough of darkness above

mirrord   depth-dark   below ·

     sparks of sun-light   There must be

breaks in the first-thought-solid shade

(Sept 27:)   Then Jean Genet's *Un Chant d'Amour*
     where we witness the continual song that runs thru the walls.

     I loved all the early announcements of you, the first falling
          in love,

                    the first lovers

                              (Oct 1)

          mouthing the stone thighs of the night,

     murmuring and crying out   hopeless   words of endearment.

     The soldier in a dirty corner of the war
          finding his lover,   the lover   sending roots of innocence
     into the criminal ground   striking   a light that illumines
          the dark belly,   the old man   recalling

the bird's leap upward to flight towards the heart

from his nest of hair,   his

mimesis song makes of the dewy lips the fountain forces.

To some readers this poem will seem sentimental. To most it will seem a jumble of broken hieroglyphs, or, at best, notes jotted toward a poem that was not written. In this brief commentary I have tried to show that such criticisms cannot be accepted. Space forbids a more extended account of this poem, but it could never be "explicated" adequately, for the connections it activates are much too irrational. Yet as we read it, we follow a subtle, suggestive transition of mind and feeling. The poem is written from deep within the tensions and contradictions of human psychology, experience, and interpretation of the world. It is utterly serious and bold in its attempt. The more readers ponder the poem, the more they will find that, using his own different methods, Duncan has created a Romantic ode in the grand style.

22

POETRY IN NEW YORK AND
SAN FRANCISCO

DURING the 1950s and 1960s distinctive styles of poetry developed in New York and San Francisco. In New York the more interesting of the young poets expressed the randomness of experience or consciousness. Their work was light, witty, sophisticated, and ebullient, and beneath their bright surfaces were serious implications. In San Francisco were emotional and mystical poets of countercultural protest. Naturally these generalizations oversimplify, and I shall soon qualify them. Moreover, though the poetry of the counterculture was centered in San Francisco, it spread throughout the United States; San Francisco was not its niche in the same sense that New York was of the other style. Needless to say, many good poets in both cities did not belong to either mode.

Poets of the two schools had some things in common. As a matter of moral and aesthetic faith, they composed with rapid spontaneity. They were Dadaist and Surrealist, though much more so New York than in San Francisco. And they shocked traditional readers by their dissolution of form, their subject matter, and their moral and philosophical attitudes, which could seem frivolously nihilistic. But despite these and other resemblances, the two styles were not closely similar; they were both versions of the general period style of the United States in the

1960s, which I described in Chapter 14, but they had no greater similarities with each other than they did with other types of poetry in the period, and I place them together in this chapter for convenience.

In discussing the poetry of the counterculture, I concentrate on Allen Ginsberg. Of the other poets with whom Ginsberg was linked, only Gary Snyder has comparable stature, and he is discussed in a different connection in Chapter 23. Among the poets of New York, I dwell in this chapter especially on Frank O'Hara rather than on John Ashbery, for though Ashbery was initially associated with this group, his achievement completely transcends this early identification. The major transition in Ashbery's style around 1970 and his immense productivity since then make him less representative of any group except that of himself and his numerous imitators, and he is the subject of a later chapter. The untimely death of O'Hara in 1966 led to the discovery of a great many poems by him that had never previously been printed. With the publication of these in the 1971 *Collected Poems*, O'Hara's work was noticed more widely and seriously than it had been during his lifetime, and readers in growing numbers turned to it with delight.

FRANK O'HARA AND THE "NEW YORK SCHOOL"

In the 1960s O'Hara, Ashbery, Kenneth Koch, James Schuyler, Ted Berrigan, and some others were viewed as a "New York School." The grouping dates from Donald Allen's 1960 anthology and was a natural one. These poets were friends, referred to one another in their poems, lived in New York City, and described or alluded in their verses to its sophisticated pleasures. Moreover, the sources from which they formed their poetry were somewhat different from those of most contemporary American poets. Quite as strongly as Olson, Duncan, or Ginsberg, these poets deplored the teachings of the New Critics and the formally closed poem. But few other American poets in the 1950s were equally intimate with avant-garde painters and their work; much in the styles of Ashbery, O'Hara, Schuyler, and Koch might be explained by reference to Abstract Expressionism and collage, and the work of Fairfield Porter was a strong influence on Schuyler. From Abstract Expressionism, Ashbery says, O'Hara caught his conception of art as process, of "the poem as the chronicle of the creative act that produces it." In New York they heard concerts of contemporary music and met the composers. "We were both tremendously impressed," Ashbery recalls, by a performance in 1952 of John Cage's "Music of Changes," "a piano work lasting over an hour and consisting . . . of isolated, autonomous tone-clusters struck seemingly at random all over the keyboard." The music illustrated "that chance elements could combine to produce" a "beautiful and cogent" work. "It was a further, perhaps for us ultimate proof not so much of 'Anything goes' but 'Anything can come out.'"

Much that preoccupied their contemporaries seemed not to concern these poets. Political and social themes—the controversy of their generation with the United States—rarely entered their poetry even during the war in Vietnam. When they alluded to such topics, it was often in a spirit of camp. The tones of political-moral prophecy in Ginsberg, Lowell, Duncan, Olson, Bly, Levertov, and so many others were not included on their register. They did not feel the religious longings that led Gary Snyder to study Zen Buddhism, Duncan to immerse himself in the hermetic tradition, and Ginsberg to pray to virtually every god, goddess, spirit, or spiritual power the human mind has conceived. Having rebelled against his Roman Catholic upbringing, O'Hara was antireligious in a conventional way, but he was also postreligious, and felt no need to relate his existence to transcendent being. Ashbery's feelings in this respect are now wistful, but in the 1960s they did not seem different from O'Hara's. "Old heavens," Ashbery wrote in "The Skaters," "you [who] used to tweak above us . . . Can you hear, there, what I am saying?"

> For it is you I am parodying,
> Your invisible denials.

For O'Hara's circle the primitive mythologies that Olson, Duncan, Ginsberg, and Snyder invoked with sacred enthusiasm were sources of humor. Mystical experiences were common as grass in San Francisco but absent in the New York School. If these poets took drugs, it was not in quest of the divine but of a "high." The way of life reflected in their poetry was bohemian but not hip.

O'Hara (1926–66) grew up in Massachusetts exurbia. He served two years in the navy during the Second World War and then attended Harvard College, where toward the end of his senior year he struck up a friendship with John Ashbery. He spent a year (1950–51) as a graduate student at the University of Michigan, and then took a job selling books and postcards at the Museum of Modern Art in New York City. By 1965 he was responsible for major exhibitions at the museum as Associate Curator. In a short life filled in every moment with work, parties, concerts, art galleries, movies, gay bars, and all-night conversations, he was able to compose a great many poems, which he did at incredible speed. Often he would turn out one or more during a lunch hour, writing while others were talking or even while participating in the conversation himself. He made little effort to publish his poems, and after his death Donald Allen, gathering the loose sheets for the collected volume, found them tucked between books and underwear. But by the time O'Hara died—he was killed in an automobile accident—he was well known to other poets, and younger ones were beginning to troop around him. His *Collected Poems* fill almost five hundred large pages.

When O'Hara moved to New York in 1951 he became briefly fascinated with Surrealism, and to some readers the poems he wrote in this phase, such as "Second Avenue," seem more imaginative than those composed later. With the collages of Ashbery in *The Tennis Court Oath* (1962) (which I discuss in Chapter 26) and the light Surrealist verses of Kenneth Koch (b. 1925) throughout the 1960s, the Surrealist poems of O'Hara contributed to an impression, which still persists, that the poets of the New York School were merely frivolous, witty demolishers of meaning. They were Dadaists, collagists, Surrealists—to many readers and critics these were all one—who, it was said, were amusing but not to be taken seriously. As time passed this generalization became steadily more dated and misleading. O'Hara and Koch dropped Surrealism, and Koch took to writing serio-comic, essayistic poems such as "The Boiling Water" and "The Problem of Anxiety." Ashbery quickly ceased his experiments with collage and became a discursive or meditative poet of a new kind, disorienting, comic, and profound. But even in poems that were Dadaist, Surrealist, or collage the effects could range from the light, bright impenetrability of which readers complained to moving wit and point.

A passage in Koch's *When the Sun Tries to Go On* (1969) may illustrate the weaker side of the New York School. It offers strings of puns, homophones, and other types of irrational connection; following them, we can trace the associations from rugs to dogs, and from dogs to cringe and shaggy, and a shaggy dog may remind us of stories in the gents' ("Ghents") room, and so forth, but the more effort we spend, the less we feel rewarded:

> He blankest of rugs
> Dens, toe, and "character nearest bells-hills"—
> Dogs. The soldiers wander him rum. Danai-
> Cringe-yellows. Shaggy Ghents!

If O'Hara's "Second Avenue" is Surrealist—

> a pus appears and lingers like a groan from the collar
> of a reproachful tree whose needles are tired of howling—

much of it is also wit:

> I scintillate like a glass of ice
> and it is all for you and the boa constrictors who entertain
> your doubts with a scarf dance called "Bronx Tambourine."

In his later verse, which is not at all Surrealist, O'Hara sounds like this:

> Khrushchev is coming on the right day!

This opening line (of "Poem") is ebullient gush, in fact, a parody of gush that is also sincerely gushing—a kind of camp. "Khrushchev is coming": even the heavy sounds (Khrush/crush) and alliteration express the portentousness we—most of us—associate with a state visit from the rival brandisher of atom bombs. But the chatty and personal end of the line ("the right day!") surprises by an entirely different tone of feeling hardly appropriate to Khrushchev. And even in the first half of the line the rhythm dances ($´ ` \times ´ \times$), anticipating the light joyousness of the poem. In this mood Khrushchev's visit is just one more excitement on a day when O'Hara is already delighted. Why? Because the wind is blowing, because he is in love, because last night, the poem goes on to explain, he went to the movies with "Vincent,"

and afterward had "blueberry blintzes" and talked about Ionesco and Beckett.

Ionesco is greater
than Beckett, Vincent said, that's what I think, blueberry blintzes
and Khrushchev was probably being carped at
in Washington, no *politesse.*

Or O'Hara sounds like this:

partly because of my love for you, partly because of your love for
yoghurt.

This is the fourth line of "Having a Coke With You," and answers
the question, why is having a coke with you "more fun than
going to San Sebastian, Irún, Hendaye, Biarritz," and Bayonne.
The line might have seemed sentimental, but the speed, surprise, and humor of the anticlimax ("yoghurt") save it.

In this line the yoghurt is of course the puzzling item. Since
"my love for you" fully explains why "Having a Coke with You"
is fun, "your love for yoghurt" seems an odd, additional fact of
little relevance. It stops us as we read and makes us consider.
Conventions of reading compel us to expect important meaning
and coherence in a poem, and we cast about for an interpretation that would produce these, but none is completely satisfactory. In this dilemma we move to a different order of interpretation, and find the significance of the phrase in precisely the
quality that makes it puzzling—its lack of consequence. "Having
a coke with you" is "fun" for no reason that can be known. Since
this interpretation fits in with O'Hara's *Weltanschauung* in general, it is easy to accept. But significance in lack of significance
is a paradox, and even after we have "explained" the phrase to
ourselves, we continue to seek a more definite and "organic"
meaning than can be found. These phases of bafflement, partial
understanding, and continuing frustration are typical in reading O'Hara. There is always a residue of incoherence and randomness that cannot be resolved, and which expresses O'Hara's
sense of existence.

The "I do this I do that" poem was O'Hara's name for one
specific type, which he more or less invented (though Williams
wrote somewhat similar poems) and which has proved influential. In these directly personal, anecdotal poems O'Hara tells in

a flatly factual voice his literal, small doings on an ordinary day. In the well-known "The Day Lady Died," for example, O'Hara reports that he gets a shoeshine, has a hamburger and a malted, buys a copy of *New World Writing*, goes to the bank, and shops for presents and cigarettes. Summary cannot convey the very unusual casualness and detail:

> and for Mike I just stroll into the PARK LANE
> Liquor Store and ask for a bottle of Strega
> and then I go back where I came from to 6th Avenue
> and the tobacconist in the Ziegfeld Theater.

Passages such as this illustrate Ashbery's remark, in his introduction to the *Collected Poems*, that O'Hara was "part of a modern tradition which is anti-literary and anti-artistic." The conclusion of the poem, however, explains why Ted Berrigan felt that in "The Day Lady Died" O'Hara "seemed to create a whole new kind of poetry." For as the poem continues, O'Hara buys a *New York Post*, sees on the first page that "Lady" (the singer Billie Holiday) has died, and, suddenly "sweating," remembers a moment when in the 5 Spot she "whispered a song along the keyboard / To Mel Waldron and everyone and I stopped breathing." Thus the casual details terminate in a moment of intense elegiac tribute. The effect is dramatic because unexpected, and convincing because of O'Hara's autobiographical factuality.

"Personal Poem," to take another example, tells how O'Hara walks to Moriarty's and waits for LeRoi. They have lunch and talk, and after lunch O'Hara, buying "a strap for my wristwatch," wonders "whether one person out of the 8,000,000 is / Thinking of me." He returns to the museum "happy at the thought possibly so." At first reading the poem seems pointless, yet with all its rambling and inconsequence the poem has a theme. Here is O'Hara's summary of the lunchtime conversation:

> we don't like Lionel Trilling
> we decide, we like Don Allen we don't like
> Henry James so much we like Herman Melville.

The flat tone of his summary conveys O'Hara's recognition that it is mere superficial chatter. But the point is that in their likes and dislikes the friends agreed; in fact, their lunchtime review of their tastes was a routine confirming or creating a feeling of friendship, like the triumph ceremony among geese, and this explains why the boring conversation seems also to have been pleasant.

The "I do this I do that" poem includes as one of its features a nonexplanatory mention of proper names. We hear about friends or lovers—Vincent, LeRoi, Mike—and they affect us as enigmas. For by assuming that we know all about them, O'Hara's familiar reference reminds us how little that is the case. When, for example, we read,

> and Peter is back not talking very much
> and Joe has a cold and is not coming to Kenneth's
> although he is coming to lunch with Norman,

our impression is of a complicated social circle about which we are blank. The title of this poem, "Adieu to Norman, Bon Jour to Joan and Jean-Paul," of itself produces something of this impression and has been much imitated (as for example in James Schuyler's "Dining Out with Doug and Frank" and Ted Berrigan's "Living with Chris"). In such poems the poet's direct, personal talk creates an effect of alienation.

"Il *faut* glisser la vie," the young Hugo von Hofmannsthal earnestly reminded himself in his diary, and no one's poetry—perhaps no one's life—has skimmed more resolutely on the surface than O'Hara's. At his most straightforward, earnest, and brooding, O'Hara is still typically rapid and apparently superficial. In "Joe's Jacket," for example, he is at a party and analyzes why he drinks:

> I drink to smother my sensitivity for a while so I won't stare away
> I drink to kill the fear of boredom, the mounting panic of it
> I drink to reduce my seriousness so a certain spurious charm
> can appear and win its flickering little victory over noise
> I drink to die a little . . .

These remarks build a surprising pattern. Qualities are suppressed (smothered, killed, reduced), he says, in order to release others, but the qualities suppressed seem more valuable than the ones released. By smothering "sensitivity" O'Hara lives more fully in the moment at this party; by reducing "seriousness" he increases a "certain spurious charm." These acts of the psyche are a kind of suicide, but to "die a little" is less terrible to him that the "mounting panic" of boredom. This "panic" and the reasons for it are not explored. Since his "fear" is being evaded rather than confronted, the passage, considered as an act of thinking, enacts the flight from seriousness that it also mentions. Yet by the dialectical reversal O'Hara's poetry forces upon us, superficiality conveys awareness of depths. O'Hara, the passage suggests, is subject to intensities of painful emotion from which he wishes to escape. He guesses truths about himself and about existence in general that he does not wish to confront. Digression and superficiality thus become deliberately chosen defenses. Precisely because he will not face the realities he is aware of, O'Hara indicates what such realities might be and how sensitive he is to them.

As well as poems, James Schuyler (b. 1923) has written plays and novels, including *A Nest of Ninnies* (1969) in collaboration with John Ashbery. He did not start to write until he was twenty-five or twenty-six years old, and his early efforts were encouraged by Ashbery and O'Hara. At first his poems were "inclined to be Dada or surreal," as he put it in an interview, and his style has changed over the years. In his finest book, *The Morning of the Poem* (1980), which won the Pulitzer Prize for poetry, the title poem is a reminiscent interior monologue, mixing memory and desire. As in much contemporary painting, his style combines apparent simplicity or even naïveté with artistic sophistication. Schuyler is always a poet of the concrete rather than of reflection upon it, and his poems deliberately lack depth. Moreover, he tends to look on himself in a rather detached way and with a striking lack of affect. As an example of his authentic note I may quote the conclusion of "Growing Dark," where the "racking sobs" are those of a suffering friend who is with him:

> When
> I was young I
> hurt others. Now,
> others have hurt
> me. In the night
> I thought I heard
> a dog bark.
> Racking sobs.

Poor guy. Yet,
I got my sleep.

MINOR POETS OF SAN FRANCISCO

In the 1950s San Francisco became a center of poetic creativity. Kenneth Rexroth had long been established as the city's senior poet, and Robert Duncan lived in or near the city most of the time. In 1951 Lawrence Ferlinghetti settled there, and soon opened with Peter Martin the City Lights bookstore, a gathering place for poets. Ferlinghetti also founded the City Lights publishing company, which brought out many volumes of counterculture poetry. Allen Ginsberg moved from New York to San Francisco in 1953, and Gary Snyder was pursuing his study of Oriental literature and Zen Buddhism at the University of California at Berkeley. Among others in San Francisco or associated with it were Thom Gunn, Helen Adams, Brother Antoninus, Gregory Corso, Philip Lamantia, Michael McClure, Jack Spicer, and Philip Whalen.

Owing especially to poetry readings and to regular gatherings in the homes of Rexroth and Duncan, poets in San Francisco were acquainted with one another. They found or developed intellectual interests in common, shared subjects and styles in poetry, and felt that they constituted a "school" or "movement." Their "school" was anything but isolated, however. They knew the theories of Charles Olson and his associates, for Duncan, as we noted, had been friendly with Olson and had eagerly exchanged ideas with him since 1947. They were influenced by the same predecessors—Whitman, Lawrence, Williams, Pound—as other American poets in their reaction against the New Criticism at this time. And their poetry was also shaped by the general misgiving and protest of poets in the United States at the tone of national life in the Eisenhower years.

The most important of these poets I discuss elsewhere—Ginsberg in the next section, Duncan with Olson in Chapter 21, Gunn with other British poets in Chapter 19, Snyder in Chapter 23—and I here notice some of the lesser figures in order to give an impression of the variety and vitality of poetry in San Francisco at this time. The poetry of Lawrence Ferlinghetti (b. 1919) has an easy, natural grace and humor. His idiom is completely accessible. In his later poems the anecdote the poem tells, or the extended metaphor it constructs, may open a range of suggested meanings. Many of his poems attack contemporary American civilization, either in outright denunciation or, more effectively, by focusing on case histories, as in the amusing and deadly accurate "Lost Parents." He also writes love lyrics of a traditional kind. Perhaps his most remarkable poem is "The Great Chinese Dragon."

Jack Spicer (1925–65) went to the University of California at Berkeley and lived most of his life in San Francisco. At Berkeley he struck up friendships with Robert Duncan and Robin Blaser, and they remained his chief poetic associates. He greatly admired Yeats, whose influence can be seen in his early poetry. Learned in linguistics, semiotics, and modern philosophy, Spicer had a strong sense of the difference between "reality" and anything that can be expressed in language, and in his mature verse he strove to overcome this difference by developing open, serial forms. Emotionally Spicer was self-thwarting and wounded; many of his poems quarrel with God and many others with lovers or with love. Because of their intellectuality and bitterness, his poems are rebarbative. *After Lorca* and "Imaginary Elegies" are the poems to read first.

Philip Whalen (b. 1923), a friend of Gary Snyder's, was a Zen Buddhist priest. His poems juxtapose fragments of simple speech, and sometimes reflect the style Pound created for his translations from Chinese in *Cathay*. Michael McClure (b. 1932) is superficially a very different poet. Yet if one ignores his Surrealist and pop verses, four-letter-word outspokenness, bathos as a would-be guru, and aggressive anti-intellectuality, one can appreciate his gift for fresh, simple lyric. His is a minor talent choked in pretensions.

Among these poets, Kenneth Rexroth (1905–82) was the finest. His parents died while he was young, and he lived with an aunt in Chicago until, at the age of sixteen, he traveled west, finding jobs along the way. Returning to Chicago, he threw himself into politics and the arts. He joined the Industrial Workers of the World, studied painting at the Chicago Art Institute, and pored over poets from Sappho and Tu Fu to those in the little magazines. A long poem, *The Homestead,* voiced his philosophy at the age of seventeen. He worked his way to Europe and then to Mexico. In 1927 he married and moved to San Francisco. There Rexroth's way of life assumed a pattern it kept henceforth. On the one hand, he was strenuously engaged both in politics and in a literary career. He organized and agitated on behalf of his leftist, anarchist beliefs. He reviewed, edited, gave public readings (sometimes to jazz accompaniment) and wrote wide-ranging essays. Taking sides in the wars of literature, he promoted poets such as Denise Levertov, Kenneth Patchen, and Gary Snyder, while attacking Eliot and the New Critics. He presided at the famous San Francisco reading where Allen Ginsberg first recited *Howl,* and he briefly thereafter championed the Beats, though later he assailed many of them. He translated Japanese, Chinese, ancient Greek, Latin, and Spanish poetry. Occasional teaching led in 1968 to an appointment at the University of California at Santa Barbara.

But, meanwhile, Rexroth also went to the mountains and nourished his spirit on rocks, pine smoke, quiet streams, stars, space, and emptiness. He found, like D. H. Lawrence, a sanctity in simple, universal things, such as bread, fire, and wine. In sexual experience and marriage he intuited a deep, quasi-religious communion with Being. He had mystical experiences. Love, creativity, the intuition of oneness with nature, and the sense of the transcendent in the familiar offered, he felt, possibilities through which life might be redeemed. But such redemption is transitory, for space and time swallow all our moments. In his last thirty years he was elegiac. He also studied Zen. He was a seeker of wisdom all his life.

In the 1920s Rexroth was a Modernist, in fact, a "Cubist" poet, and wrote such verses as,

> Rain falls on her glyptic eyelids
> Beauty of vectors dies young and fair.

In this early phase of his career he dedicated poems to William Carlos Williams and Louis Zukofsky, studied Gertrude Stein, and adapted techniques from the songs of Hottentots and Eskimos. Political emotions in the 1930s motivated a more accessible style, as in many other poets at this time. Auden influenced him in this period, and he shared Auden's vast perspectives of space and time, even though the melancholy they evoked was inconsistent with his revolutionary hopes. In "Requiem for the Spanish Dead" persons slain in the Spanish civil war merge in his mind with a child killed in San Francisco by a truck, and the voice of the parents mourning for their child joins a dirge rising from earth into the cosmos:

> Voice after voice adds itself to the singing.
> Orion moves westward across the meridian,
> Riegel, Bellatrix, Betelgeuse, marching in order,
> The great nebula glimmering in his loins.

"I have spent my life," Rexroth said in *An Autobiographical Novel* (1966), "striving to write the way I talk." His thoughts move at a legato pace over longish stretches without surprise or intensity. Even when he is describing erotic or mystical experience— "Time has had a stop. / Space is gone"—the simple, factual tone seems unexcited. Lines quoted out of context cannot adequately represent him, so I give a complete poem, "Andrée Rexroth," on his dead wife:

> Now once more gray mottled buckeye branches
> Explode their emerald stars,
> And alders smoulder in a rosy smoke
> Of innumerable buds.
> I know that spring again is splendid
> As ever, the hidden thrush
> As sweetly tongued, the sun as vital—
> But these are the forest trails we walked together,
> These paths, ten years together.
> We thought the years would last forever,
> They are all gone now, the days
> We thought would not come for us are here.
> Bright trout poised in the current—
> The raccoon's track at the water's edge—
> A bittern booming in the distance—
> Your ashes scattered on this mountain—
> Moving seaward on this stream.

Some of Rexroth's later poems are so simple and quiet that one must read them in the spirit of Zen in order to get much out of them. A line from *The Heart's Garden / The Garden Heart* (1967), "The mind rests in the clear void," more or less expresses the reader's feeling.

From Rexroth a connection runs back to Robinson Jeffers and forward to such younger poets as Gary Snyder and Robert Bly. The poetry of Jeffers planted in the imagination his version of the landscape of the California coast, a place, as Jeffers rendered it, of space, emptiness, vistas, and huge, silent forms of hill, cliff, and canyon. Their vast, perpetual being makes humanity seem unimportant and fugitive. Essential features of this landscape reappear, though changed, in Rexroth and Snyder. Along with the landscape itself, the younger poets caught Rexroth's and Jeffers' Romantic use of nature as an imaginative escape from the human and a primordial rebuke to urban, bureaucratic, technological man.

THE COUNTERCULTURAL ETHOS

In the 1950s poets of the counterculture perceived a prosperous, conservative, Communist-chasing, Cold Warring, imperial United States. The nation was, in their view, morally visionless and constrictive. The war in Vietnam, the atom bomb, and ecological pollution were later foci of protest, but such obvious events do not fully explain these poets' disaffection, which was also related to pervasive features of the social and economic order, such as bureaucratic impersonality, huge populations, material glut and waste, the feeling of being manipulated by advertising and publicity, alienation from work, rootlessness, existential aimlessness, and the sense of powerlessness vis-à-vis the large organizations within which a person typically works, votes, plays, and shops. To many poets it seemed that Western civilization and its cultural ideals were spiritually bankrupt.

In his *Cantos* Pound had celebrated bringers of a new civilization—Dionysus, the first Chinese emperors, even (alas!) Mussolini. He had hoped to play this role himself. The ethos of the counterculture assigned this role to every member and especially to poets. Controversy about values, about how to live, took place eagerly and constantly in the counterculture, and typically pushed into religious and metaphysical dimensions, seeking to relate moral ideals to something ultimate. The poet, a marginal figure within our society as a whole, was a central one within this alternative society, which looked to poets for leadership. A poet of the counterculture might speak as a sage and prophet, denouncing the evil of America, preaching a new way of life, and describing visions of eternity. But even more than poetry, the counterculture prized a way of life that expressed its values by enacting them. If a guru may be described as a moral and spiritual teacher who instructs both by his sayings and by the example of his life, everyone in the counter-culture both sought a guru and was one—or wished to be. When a poet's transvaluations dramatically challenged the accepted norms of society, and his way of life proved his sincerity by what it sacrificed, immense moral power accrued. Allen Ginsberg and Gary Snyder sometimes write very well, but their great influence has derived from the image we have of their lives in conjunction with their poems.

Meditating on the social or political impact of poetry, Auden concluded that it was zero. Poetry, as he said in his great elegy on Yeats, may bring healing to the heart, but in the public world it "makes nothing happen." Thomas Mann described his own *modus vivendi* as "outer conformity, inner rebellion"; his novels were "higher spiritual entertainment." Both Auden and Mann were committed politically, but in this commitment they saw almost no role for their art. The poets I am now considering held the opposite position. Their critique of American civilization and consciousness was voluminous, rhetorically forceful, sometimes profound, and documented in powerfully realistic images of American life. Yet both their protest and their positive social vision were sometimes expressed with zaniness or buffoonery, as if in implicit acknowledgement that the United States was unlikely to be revolutionized. Underlying their Whitmanian hope, in other words, was a characteristically modern fear that the existing social-ideological system was too big, too entrenched, and too all-pervasive for revolutionary overthrow. Confronting this, they protested while feeling that protest would be ineffective, and often they did not even protest but merely sought to "drop out" of the bourgeois order and to live, like Ginsberg, as a "city hermit" or to settle in rural communes. Yet we should also bear in mind the belief of the European avant-garde, which the American counterculture shared, that one radicalizes society by changing consciousness. This belief not only gives a revolutionary role to art but also bestows a political meaning on almost every defiance of social or moral convention; so long as what

Blake called "the mind-forged manacles" are assaulted, a revolutionary end is served. The more extreme the gesture is, the more it may shake the mind's entrenched assumptions, and the value of provocation partly explains the endorsement within the counterculture of much that to ordinary, middle-class Americans seemed irrational or criminal—Dada, drugs, madness, mysticism and orgiastic sex. But if members of the counterculture were fundamentally despondent about the possibility of any large, general change in society, at times they were Shelleyan. The revolution, to repeat, would be propagated not only by poetic texts but by personal example in living. "Outer conformity, inner rebellion" was not the way to create a new civilization.

These poets were "open" not only in form but about themselves personally. They reported what others would have hidden—sexual lusts and failures, masturbation fantasies, death fears, grandiose imaginations of power, rage, loneliness, self-hatred. They believed that candor is taboo-breaking, liberating. A reader would find that his personal shames are commonplace and can be discussed, are merely human, so to speak. Nakedness was a powerful symbol in the counterculture, and Ginsberg occasionally took off his clothes at poetry readings. In fact, the poets of the counterculture were essentially optimistic about the possibilities of human nature and life. Though battered and dusty, we are all sunflowers, aspiring and beautiful—or so Ginsberg maintained in a famous poem. Beyond our "ego-driven anxieties and aggressions," said Snyder, lies "the mind of love and clarity." Moreover, since these poets were transvaluing, much that would have been Confessional in other poets acquired a positive moral implication in them. And finally, like all Romantics, they hungered for intimacy and felt that social convention keeps us isolated. Poetry, Snyder typically said, "is to give access to persons—cutting away the fear and reserve and camping of social life." The impulse to nakedness was a yearning for love.

The social ideal of these poets might be described as communalism or tribalism. Few of them actually lived in communes or ashrams; they had houses or apartments, spouses or companions, much as most people do. But the middle-class family did not command their moral allegiance, and they sympathized with larger, more open groups of mutually supportive individuals.

Such groups were, in their eyes, good communities within the evil society of industrial-imperialist America. For the Beats and Hippies this community was scattered; it consisted of a few persons like themselves in every city, and the rootless, "on the road" motif of Beat literature reflected, in part, the effort of this dispersed elite to keep in touch. But normally the "tribal" community was located in a particular place, which it knew intimately, and the place was very often rural, for ecological ideals and reverence for life could be enacted in farming. The community was bound together by work shared in common but much more by its shared ethos. In such communities, or in the ideology that supported them, there was much primitivism, a desire to get back to a way of life that supposedly prevailed for eons until the rise of cities. The New Stone Age was extolled as man's happiest time. And there was also intense nostalgia for the mythological beliefs through which primitive man related himself to the world. In such respects the "tribal" ideal looked to the past, but if modern Western society was morally bankrupt and in disintegration, the tribal ideal might also claim the future. Hopeful speculations that a new consciousness was forming in the Western world were rife within the literature of the counterculture. Gary Snyder envisioned a "free, international, classless world . . . a totally integrated world culture with matrilineal descent, free-form marriage, natural credit communist economy, less industry," and far less population. The lifestyle of the coming age will, said Snyder, be "based on community houses, villages and ashrams; tribe-run farms or workshops or companies; large open families; pilgrimage and wanderings from center to center."

In such a world personal relationships of a romantic kind would be more relaxed than they now usually are. Sexuality would be uninhibited, for the tribe believed with Blake that "he who desires but acts not, breeds pestilence," and that "The nakedness of woman is the work of God." The attitude toward deviant sexuality could be expressed in another Blakean rule: "One Law for the Lion & Ox is Oppression." Each must follow his own nature. Lovers would separate easily, since fidelity would have little social support. The tribe frowned on jealousy and possessiveness, and insisted that the freedom of a person must be respected. Sexual intercourse was frequently viewed as a way to transcendence. In sex the human merged with nature and the divine. Orgiastic intercourse might especially conduce to religious-ecstatic emotions.

Because it is condemned by the bourgeois world, the use of marijuana, peyote, LSD, and other drugs dramatized defiance and freedom, and drugs were valued as symbols. Because they alter consciousness, they were said by their advocates to help decondition the psyche, ridding it of repressions, routines, and norms that were internalized within the middle-class world in which one was reared. Drugs, the argument continued, overthrow rational processes of thought which alienate us from reality, and they liberate intuition and vision. At the same time, however, they could leave a residue of guilt. For even if there was nothing wrong with taking drugs as such, as a way to truth drugs could seem dubiously easy.

In their search for wisdom the members of the counterculture were likely to turn especially to sources outside Western culture and to minority traditions within it. In poems quoted in the previous chapter, Charles Olson, needing a goddess, typically invoked the Egyptian goddess Nut, and Robert Duncan quoted from a prayer to Mandoulis. Hinduism, Buddhism (especially Zen), Shamanism, Amerindian religions, Gnosticism, alchemy, and the like were studied, and often their ritual practices were adopted. Thus it came about that contemporary American poetry abounds in sutras, Indian spells, mantras, and litanies to miscellaneous gods. Real efficacy was sometimes attributed to magic formulas, so intense was the revolt against rationalism. Even if spells lacked magical power, the chanting of them over and over might overwhelm consciousness and reason, opening the way to that which is beneath or beyond. The religiousness was usually eclectic. A litany in this poetry may assemble gods from all over the world. In "Wichita Vortex Sutra" Ginsberg prayed to various Hindu Lords, William Blake, the Sacred Heart, Allah, Christ, Yahweh, Seraphim, and Devas.

Within the counterculture Hart Crane was posthumously a cult hero, a status I think he would not have enjoyed. He was seen as a poet who had rejected middle-class values and had been persecuted for this. His homosexuality and drunkenness were interpreted as elements of a life lived at high risk in search of ecstasy and transcendence. *The Bridge* idealized prototypes of the hipster, such as hobos, pioneers, and sailors shipping out on the clippers, and saw them enacting the essential meaning of America as a transcendent quest. The religious experience imagined or created in *The Bridge* was analogous to that sought by members of the counterculture, for it took place without institutions, rituals, or dogmas, and was ecstatic, Dionysian, and mystical. The imagining of Amerindian religious emotions in *The Bridge,* as in Maquokeeta's dance in the section entitled "The River," corresponded to the counterculture's invocation of Amerindian and Shamanistic religions.

ALLEN GINSBERG

Allen Ginsberg (b. 1926) grew up in Paterson, New Jersey, where his father taught school. His feelings about his parents seem to have been unusually ambivalent and guiltridden. Within the family the father, Louis Ginsberg, pleaded for prudence, self-restraint, and acceptance of social norms. Naomi, his wife, was politically radical, idealistic, and emotional; gradually she became frighteningly hysterical and delusional, convinced that she was being persecuted by Roosevelt, the FBI, the CIA, and other demons of her private mythology, including her husband. When Ginsberg was twelve years old, she became completely insane, breaking down in a rest home to which the boy had accompanied her. He had, as he felt, abandoned her there, wishing that she might die. Many readers have surmised that Ginsberg's ideology and style embody an unconscious siding with his mother against his father. This motive might underlie his radical politics, for example, and also the personal nakedness of his utterance, which is so extreme that the reader experiences it as an assault. His poems are acts of political-moral aggression. Since Ginsberg's father was a poet whose timidly conventional verses were not much noticed by the literary world, he might also by this failure have represented a model to be rejected; the son displaced the father by writing the boldly unconventional poetry that made him famous.

At the age of seventeen Ginsberg entered Columbia University and studied economics, for he planned a career in the labor movement. Soon he was also writing poems. These early verses were in the academic style, much influenced by Renaissance models, which many young poets were then following, but personal experiences were already leading Ginsberg toward rebellion. He accepted the fact that he was homosexual. He struck up friendships with Jack Kerouac and William Burroughs, and through Burroughs was introduced both to the use of morphine and to drifters of the drug "scene"; in their amoral, reckless life Burroughs taught Ginsberg to see a Romantic pathos. Suspended from Columbia, Ginsberg shipped out as a sailor, interrupting his voyages for visits and amours. By the time he returned to the university, his literary program was partly formed. He would present his feelings and way of life with unflinching realism, while at the same time accusing the social order. But he had as yet no literary form in which he could express himself effectively, and he had no audience.

One day in the summer of 1948, Ginsberg tells us, he was lying in bed reading Blake's "Ah! Sun-Flower." Suddenly he heard a voice speak this and other lyrics of Blake, and at the same time he was aware of a vast, tranquil, vital presence. In this moment he knew "that there was this big god over all, who was completely aware and completely conscious of everybody, and that the whole purpose of being born was to wake up to Him." Whether Ginsberg had experienced such visions before I do not know, but henceforth he was in pursuit of them. Through drugs, orgiastic sex, and Buddhist chants he sought to transcend normal states of consciousness and achieve mystical ones.

Sheltering a drug addict for several months in 1949, Ginsberg became an accessory to thefts committed by the addict and his friends. Arrested, he pleaded psychological disability in order to avoid jail. After several months in the Columbia Psychiatric Institute he went to live with his father in Paterson. There he cultivated the acquaintance of William Carlos Williams, who was later to write the introduction to *Howl*. Talking with the older poet, Ginsberg absorbed Williams' belief that poetry must reflect contemporary social reality, present images rather than ideas, and base its idiom on immediate speech rather than the poetic tradition. He wrote "simple little poems like Williams," as he later described them, but they were not accepted for publication. (They appeared later in *Empty Mirror*, 1961). But Kerouac was already a stronger literary influence than Williams, and when in

1951 Kerouac composed *On the Road* in three weeks of spontaneous outpouring, Ginsberg felt he had discovered a new literary form expressing a new mode of consciousness.

Meanwhile, Ginsberg had been working in market research, wearing a business suit and carrying a briefcase. But he quit and went to Yucatán for several months and then to San Francisco. He met Peter Orlovsky, who was to be a companion over the years, and with Orlovsky he felt, at least at moments, an emotional intimacy and security he had not previously experienced. In sessions with a psychiatrist he gradually decided to drop market research, in which he was again employed, and follow his own ideal of life, which was to "do nothing but write poetry and have leisure . . . And cultivate my perceptions, cultivate the visionary thing in me. Just a literary and quiet city-hermit existence." In the fall of 1954 he wrote *Howl*. When it was published the next year, the publisher, Lawrence Ferlinghetti, was tried in San Francisco for disseminating "indecent writings." Controversy rose and so did sales. Attacked by most reviewers—"formless," "sentimental," "barbarian"—the poem did not go away, and by 1959 the Beat poets were a subject of discussion in popular magazines such as *Time*.

Even after thirty years *Howl* still impresses by its long, chanting rhythms, moral defiance, and boldly prophetic stance:

> I saw the best minds of my generation destroyed by madness,
> starving hysterical naked,
> dragging themselves through the negro streets at dawn looking
> for an angry fix,
> angelheaded hipsters burning for the ancient heavenly
> connection to the starry dynamo in the machinery of night,
> who poverty and tatters and hollow-eyed and high sat up
> smoking in the supernatural darkness of cold-water flats
> floating across the tops of cities contemplating jazz,
> who. . . .

Howl descends remotely from *The Waste Land*, and retains something of the compression and ellipsis of the high Modernist mode (in the lines quoted, for example, there is the unpunctuated jamming of adjectives—"starving hysterical naked"; the elision of "in"—"who [in] poverty"; the impressionistic adjectives—"negro streets"). But the fragmentary and allusive methods of *The Waste Land* have, on the whole, been replaced by continuous, relatively uncompressed utterance, and the impact of *Howl* depends mainly on poetic conventions and emotions of a traditionally Romantic kind. The poem celebrates heroes, and its heroes are versions of the Romantic figure of the outcast and quester. As in Wordsworth and Whitman, the poet speaks personally, providing someone for us to identify with. His emotions are straightforward and strong; in fact, he speaks in a poetically sublime role. The world he presents is exotic and Romantically interesting to middle-class readers, though hardly beautiful or agreeable as in Shelley. The drug-hipster idiom ("angry fix," "high") is colorful, and was fresh in poetry in 1954. Images that might seem surreal—"floating across the tops of cities"—may actually be realistic, for they may express the sensations of persons high on drugs.

Essentially, then, this is an accessible and popular style. Whatever difficulties readers may find in *Howl* derive from its vision of the world, which is not difficult to grasp but to sympathize with. The poem transvalues, since the heroes it celebrates are not types of persons traditionally viewed in that light. The emotions and experiences it presents are either ecstatic or extremely sordid and painful, or both at once. The in-between range—that of William Carlos Williams, for one example—is missing. Perhaps the hardest aspect of the poem to accept is, paradoxically, its humor. In the lines quoted, for example, the "angelheaded hipsters burning for the ancient heavenly connection" are compared to light bulbs, or to any machine that can be plugged in and operated by electricity. Even in relation to Ginsberg's conception of mystical experience (let alone Whitman's, Crane's, or Eliot's) the comparison is reductive, for it suggests that such experiences turn on, galvanize the instant, and wink off, having no significance beyond the momentary "kick" or "trip." For another example, consider the persons in *Howl* who "threw their watches off the roof to cast their ballot for Eternity outside of Time," and then "alarm clocks fell on their heads every day for the next decade." These Dadaists are typical Ginsberg questers, heroic and futile. He celebrates and ironizes. As he put it in a letter to Williams, he has "W. C. Fields on my left and Jehovah on my right." Though virtuous in other kinds of poems, in lament and prophecy this double perspective is a limitation. But Ginsberg's self-reducing humor helps to explain the remarkably good-natured acceptance bestowed on him. He is perceived more as a spiritual clown than as a threat. A psychoanalyst might suggest that Ginsberg is a child testing the father's love. His provocations are what Erik Erikson calls "teasing." They defy and disarm at the same time.

Behind Ginsberg's hipster figures lie such prototypes and sources as Nietzsche's Dionysian ecstatic, Rimbaud and the "dérèglement" of the senses, the alienated *poète maudit* of Baudelaire, Lawrence's mystique of sex and quest of the primitive-sacred, Dada, Henry Miller, and, most immediately, the addicts in William Burroughs' *Naked Lunch* and the character of Dean Moriarty in Kerouac's *On the Road*. The hipster also belongs in the American tradition of mystical religiosity and lonely, personal search for God that sweeps through Emerson, Melville, Whitman, and Crane. Superimposing such literary conceptions upon persons he actually knew, Ginsberg created a figure whose quest involves risk and suffering—poverty, illness, police brutality, incarceration, starvation, evil hallucinations, madness, and suicide.

Legally speaking, the hipster is criminal, for he traffics in drugs, though the poem shows him doing nothing worse and finds no wrong in what he does. He is also an intellectual, well read and volubly talking "about America and Eternity." A great copulator, he "sweetened the snatches of a million girls trembling in the sunset," and he is also homosexual. His sexual appetite—the hugest since Gargantua—and uninhibited modes of satisfaction express his vitality and freedom; ultimately sex, like everything in the poem, is at once suffering and ecstasy. The hipster lives wholly in the moment. Jobless, rootless, and without family, he is continually on the move, and he finds supportive fellow hipsters everywhere.

The hipster is also a victim, but of just what is obscure. Ginsberg calls it "Moloch," and Moloch is the economic system, urban-industrial milieu, government, police, war, atom bomb, everyone's mentality, America, and Time (as opposed to Eternity). Within Moloch our loves, visions, ecstasies, and epiphanies seem crazy, and the only escape from Moloch lies in suicide. Because of the power of Moloch no rebellion can hope for practical effect. Gestures of defiance are, as I said, merely expressions of feeling, and the more they are extreme and absurd, the greater the emotional satisfaction. When the hipsters "distributed Supercommunist pamphlets," they did not expect to persuade anyone, any more than when they "burned cigarette holes in their arms," or "threw potato salad at CCNY lecturers on Dadaism and subsequently presented themselves on the granite steps of the madhouse . . . demanding instantaneous lobotomy." In his feelings of bafflement, helplessness, constriction, and woe Ginsberg speaks for many readers, but by conjuring Moloch he also provides himself with less acceptable satisfactions, for he locates the evil outside himself and his fellow hipsters. Or if Moloch exists in them also, it is not, Ginsberg thinks, as an inherent part of their being but an invading infection. Viewing the enemy as wholly external, Ginsberg sentimentally transforms him into a demon and his victims into innocents.

It is often said that *Howl* influenced American poetry more than any poem since *The Waste Land*. The assertion may be true, but much that characterizes *Howl* is also typical of other poems by other poets written at the same time or earlier. In its direct emotion, versification by breath, agrammatical syntax, spontaneous composition, and unplanned development *Howl* participated in the larger contemporary movement I described as "open form." Its controversy with America dovetailed with a similar preoccupation (though differing interpretations) in Lawrence, Williams, Olson, Duncan, and many others. In some of its more individual and arresting features—the long rhythms, rhetorical repetitions, Dada gestures—the poem seems not to have been much imitated, even by Ginsberg himself. Its prophetic stance encouraged other poets to adopt a similar role, especially in the poetry of protest against the war in Vietnam, but for this poetry Whitman and Blake were more important predecessors than Ginsberg. Perhaps *Howl* was most original and instructive for other poets when it exploited the intimate, painful, sensational, and shocking. It represented psychological and physical states that to most readers seemed disgraceful: "finished the whiskey and threw up groaning into the bloody toilet"; "bit detectives in the neck and shrieked with delight in policecars for committing no crime but their own wild cooking pederasty and intoxication." Yet in *Howl* Ginsberg did not present such experiences as his own. He took this further step in *Kaddish* (1961).

Ginsberg was only twenty-nine when he wrote *Howl*. Since then he has been celebrated or notorious. Most of his poems since *Howl* contain effective lines and passages, but none is better than *Howl*, and we need not dwell on them. *Kaddish*, a long poem in memory of his mother, is harrowing. *Wichita Vortex Sutra* (1966) assails the war in Vietnam. I have never mentioned the title of this poem to anyone without their grinning, a point that again indicates the degree to which Ginsberg is enjoyed and dismissed as a buffoon. In this the "longhaired Crank," as Ginsberg calls himself, has increasingly cooperated. It is a kind of self-betrayal. By the mid-1960s Ginsberg's writing was deteriorating. He was turning out diary or journal poems—a favorite mode of the time—and he was traveling about the country in vans, planes, trains, and buses, dictating verses into a tape recorder. He described *Wichita Vortex Sutra* as "a collage of news radio paper optical phenomena observed & noted in a field of vision outside car window, at stops, etc. + fantasy" and other mental operations. Other such poems may be read in *Planet News* (1968), *The Fall of America* (1972), and *Iron Horse* (1973). A great many poems were written under the influence of one or another drug. He wrote too much, he mythologized rather than criticized himself, and he repeated himself like a dotard. His Vietnam invectives, dream horrors, sex memories, religious chantings, mystical ecstasies, middle-aged alarms over balding and impotence, and fascinated terror of death all become wearisome, and so do his doleful images—leaking toilets, black-spotted tomatoes, Two Billion Hamburgers, and garbage trucks uplifting "iron/buttocks," while "old meat gravy & tin cans sink to bottom." One wonders whether he is still a poet or has become a type of journalist. Yet the picaresque element in his writing continues to entertain, his psychological and autobiographical nakedness catches attention, and his expression may still seem accomplished when you share his feelings. At the end of "Wings Lifted over the Black Pit," for example, the play of sounds is admirable and so is the rhythm as it peters out in hopelessness: we Americans are

> Living like beasts,
>   befouling our own nests,
>   Smoke & Steam, broken glass & beer cans,
>   Auto exhaust.

23

AGAINST "CIVILIZATION"

T HE poets discussed in this chapter—Robert Bly, James Wright, Galway Kennell, W. S. Merwin, and Gary Snyder—articulate a feeling that probably every reader shares in some degree. Oppressed by crowds and noise in cities, by roads, wires, and houses everywhere in the landscape, by the glut and litter of material goods, by daily reports of ecological pollution through oil spills, strip mines, smokestacks, and pesticides, by guilt at the extinction or near extinction of animal species, by terror of war, and by contemplation of the possible end of life on earth, the mind is tempted to turn against the civilization Western man has created. There is no reason to believe that primitive man was (or is) morally, socially, or religiously in better case than ourselves, or that the unconscious is more the locus of the "self" than the conscious mind, or that what Freud called the *id* is wiser and more disposed to love than the *ego*, or that emotional urge is a better guide than rational thought, or, in short, that "nature" is superior to modern "civilization." But once we think in terms of this antithesis (in some senses a false one, but most of us accept it habitually), it is almost impossible not to sympathize with "nature." We live in "civilization" and are intimately familiar with its injuries. "Nature," which we do not know, inevitably becomes the realm onto which we project whatever wishes "civilization" evokes as its antithesis.

This reaction has been familiar since the Romantic age, but much has changed since then. With vastly more people and new machines from radios to snowmobiles, all that we negatively categorize as "civilization" has become more inescapable. If "nature" is farmland and wilderness, there is now less of it. Thoreau could find "nature" by Walden Pond, where now one finds a parking lot. Conceptually, also, "nature" may be less accessible than it was two hundred years ago. Intellectuals in the Romantic period thought they were able to study "nature" objectively in animals, children, African tribes, primitive poets such as Homer and "Ossian," and the like, and we now see that they created myths and mistook them for the concrete reality. We hope our present-day mammalogy, anthropology, and depth psychology are more reliable, but the errors of the Romantics make us (or should make us) suspect our own. Moreover, we see that the supposedly primitive tribes we study are actually thick with culture, and at what point can we draw the line between the culture that is still "natural" and that which is already remote from nature? But if it is now harder to make out just what "nature" is, we are generally readier to accept that we are animals and hence part of it. Poets of the Romantic age expressed an identification with all living creatures based, as in Schiller's ode "To Joy," on the pantheistic (or panentheistic) belief that one divine spirit dwells in all things. This indwelling divinity is now less frequently intuited, needless to say, and our own feelings of oneness with nature are less religiously and more existentially toned. In fact, they are imbued with the sense of mortality. To judge from contemporary poets, our sense of identification with other creatures rests on a conviction that we possess not the same soul but the same instincts as our fellow animals. Even more important, we see in them and in ourselves the same creaturely subjection to time, sickness, wounds, and death. Less confident of the guidance of a providential God, man feels responsible for the survival of life and hates "civilization" as its destroyer. That "civilization" might even end itself and everything else apocalyptically was rarely imagined in the Romantic period, and then only in art or literature, not in the calculations of physicists and military leaders. All the more, then, we are motivated to attribute to primitive man a better relation to "nature," a relation of closeness, harmony, fulfillment, and reverence, and to seek this as our ideal.

If we ask our poets where and what "nature" may be, their answers have already been suggested. Nature is wilderness, the central Alaska where John Haines homesteaded for most of twenty-two years and found himself "more in touch with an essence." "It was for me," he said, "the beginning of what I have come to understand as the myth-journey of humankind. This life of food gathering, of making for ourselves out of what we can find around us, this is what we have come from and will return to." Or nature is the coastal mountains of the West where Gary Snyder cut trails, worked as a fire lookout, and now lives by growing vegetables and hunting. Or it is the farm country of Minnesota where Bly lived and Wright visited on weekends. Or nature is the twelve-acre farm of Wendell Berry (b. 1934) in Kentucky, where he writes quiet pastoral verse conveying his passion for rural life and his belief that it can save us. Or nature is to be found in simple, essential experiences such as eating and sleeping, or in instinctive interactions between people—in bodily touch like the nuzzlings of animals, in sex, and in care of infants, the latter beautifully portrayed in poems by Snyder and Kinnell. "Birth, copulation, and death," says Sweeney in T. S. Eliot's "Sweeney Agonistes," "That's all the facts when you get to brass tacks." Eliot was exposing the vanity and emptiness of life, but the poets I am now considering invest these fundamental experiences (at least the first two, and the poets struggle to include the third) with goodness and profundity. Nature, in their opinion, pervades the small social unit of family or "tribe" and the work of such groups, such as baking bread and making clothes, that survival necessitates. Nature resides of course in animals and in the way of life of primitive peoples—the ancient Amerindians Snyder loves. Their myths and folklore are to be studied not out of anthropological curiosity but for the wisdom they embody, the states of mind to which they give access. In imagination we may try to reenter this state of mind, as Kinnell does through the Eskimo or Indian speaker of his well-known "The Bear." Nature is the unconscious as opposed to the conscious mind. And nature is to be discovered in the poetry and religious writing of the Orient, and in Buddhist meditative practices, which give access to the depth of the self where we are one with nature, with reality or being. "If you could keep going deeper and deeper," Kinnell says, "you'd finally not be a person ... you'd be an animal; and if you kept going deeper and deeper, you'd be a blade of grass or ultimately perhaps a stone. And if a stone could read, [poetry] would speak for it."

A SHARED STYLE

The poets I discuss in this chapter share essentially the same style. The moment one says this one needs to make qualifications and exceptions. Gary Snyder, for example, never accepted the Surrealist methods that were important in varying degrees to the other poets I consider here, and their knowledge of the religions and art of the Far East was superficial compared to his. The thoughts and feelings sketched in the preceding paragraphs are generally to be found in Merwin, but little that can be said about these poets collectively applies to Merwin with close particularity, and he is included in this chapter partly because he would be less appropriate in any other. But such qualifications and all the others I might add only make the familiar point that the classifications and generalizations of literary history can be valid only at a certain level of abstraction. If they activate the mind to explore their validity, that is not the least important of their uses.

With this cautionary preamble I may observe that the stylistic development of Bly, Wright, Merwin, Kinnell, and Snyder followed a somewhat similar course. In college most of them composed in the formal styles of the 1950s. This moment continued long beyond college in Wright and Merwin; it did not take place in the career of Snyder. Like other poets of their generation, Wright, Merwin, and Kinnell based their formal styles on the Metaphysical and Modernist poets advocated by the New Criticism. But among their contemporaries they were unusual because they also loved the styles of the later nineteenth century. In this respect they resembled many poets of the 1940s and 1950s in England, such as Sidney Keyes and Philip Larkin.

A second moment in their evolution came in the 1950s or early 1960s, when they committed themselves to open form.

With the partial exception of Snyder, they did not, like Olson and Duncan, break away from the then academic formalism by building on Pound's *Cantos*. Allusion, fragmentation, and sudden juxtaposition of dissimilars were never among their primary methods. Neither did they adopt the "projective" grammatical discontinuity and spontaneity we associate with Olson or, in a different form, with Ashbery. Yet the influence of Pound and Williams was inescapable in the 1950s, and their lyrics became "verse lessons," as John Haines put it, for himself, Bly, Wright, and Snyder. From the poems and critical statements of Pound's Imagist period they learned the virtues of direct presentation, economy, emotional reserve, and suggestion. Pound's *Cathay* led them to other translations of ancient Chinese poetry by Arthur Waley, Robert Payne, and Kenneth Rexroth (whose *100 Poems from the Chinese*, 1956, was an important book in its time), and as they studied these poems they assimilated a sensibility and ethos along with a style. Thus the principles of Imagism coalesced with Oriental influences again in the 1950s as they had in the 1910s and 1920s, and every reader of Bly, Wright, and Snyder has felt the resemblance between their mode and the earlier one.

In Bly's "The Loon," for example, there is Imagist presentation:

> A loon's cry rose from far out in the center
> Of the lake—
> It was the cry of someone who owned very little.

Though one of Pound's famous "A Few Don'ts by an Imagiste" was "don't be viewy," Bly rather spoils the suggestions of his first two lines by sermonizing in the third. Bly greatly admires ancient Chinese poetry and sometimes reproduces its effects. In "Driving towards the Lac Qui Parle River" the moon, river, boat, and human figures compose a scene typical of Bly's Chinese models—

> When I reach the river, the full moon covers it;
> A few people are talking low in a boat.

But I am speaking of a resemblance to Imagism, not a revival, for the poems of Bly, Wright, Snyder, and Haines that most recall the Imagist mode also reflect the tendencies of their own generation. In part this means that they are as much influenced by Williams as by Pound, as no poet was in the 1920s. In part there are generational differences that have other causes. Their poems are longer than Imagist ones typically were, are more personal, and include narrative elements. And though they usually present objects and sensations in preference to general ideas, they present them by stating rather than by Poundian complexes of interactive, concrete details. The difference is approximately that between "frost on the horse turds," which Snyder observes at dawn in a mountain camp, and Pound's

> Salmon-pink wings of the fish-hawk
> cast grey shadows in water.

Compared to Pound's exactness and multiplicity of notation, Snyder's image is simple and referential; it tells without saying so that the morning is cold. For Snyder's intention is not Pound's. Snyder aims to present things easily, casually, and naturally, and, like Williams, with a momentum that impels us through the poem quickly and thus makes us register it as a whole experience. To arrest attention by dense nodes of language, as Pound does, would violate this purpose.

In the 1950s and 1960s these poets were also influenced by a number of foreign ones who had hitherto been little read in the United States. Snyder was much too committed to the Orient to make discoveries in European literature, but Bly and Wright chanced independently to read the Austrian poet Georg Trakl (1887–1914), whose emotionally powerful utterance might seem Symbolist, Expressionist, or Surrealist. The Chilean poet Pablo Neruda (b. 1904) aroused intense enthusiasm, especially his *Alturas de Machu Picchu* (The Heights of Machu Picchu) from *Canto General* (1950). And I should also mention at least two Spanish poets, Federico Garcia Lorca (1898–1936) and Juan Ramon Jiménez (1881–1958), though others were also important. Merwin lived many years in France, and contemporary French poets also became sources for his style in the 1960s.

No nexus of shared qualities explains the appeal of this diverse group of foreign poets in the United States at this time. That they were relatively unfamiliar made them available, so to speak; a poet could acquire identity by championing them, and from them he could bring something new into American poetry. Enthusiasm for Rimbaud, for example, would have been no less justified, but could not have offered the same psychological and competitive advantages. But if these were the only motives, other poets in Europe and South America were also excellent and unfamiliar and might equally have been selected. Trakl, Neruda, Lorca, Jiménez, and Machado impressed by their emotional intensity or directness, qualities that were especially prized in the 1950s and 1960s by poets struggling to free themselves from New Critical influences. In many poems Lorca and Neruda evoked sympathies with the elemental or primitive, and Lorca's *Poeta en Nueva York* was a powerfully negative vision of civilization. Poems of Jiménez that sought to express an "absolute moment" had affinities with the rejection of historical context and autobiographical detail, with the "inwardness" and evocation of "absence," in much American Surrealism, and Lorca and Trakl were sometimes Surrealists.

None of the poets I dwell on in this chapter composed Surrealist poems only, but except for Snyder, all of them employed Surrealist technique as one element within many of their lyrics. In Merwin it was especially prominent. From these poets it descended to a younger generation and became a vogue. In its career in South America and central Europe Surrealism was associated with political protest; it was a style that reflected the violence both of a repressive social order and of the poet's emotional rejection of this order. It presented the verbally disintegrated and absurd to highlight the disintegration and absurdity in social and cultural reality. During the 1960s it seemed to many poets the only literary language in which it was possible to write of the war in Vietnam. But Surrealism also appealed as a way of evading the ego and making contact with a deeper self, sometimes identified as the unconscious. Or it allowed one, so the theory went, to get beyond the personal, social, and historical and to reach a more essential reality. But the appeal of Surrealism, in its American version, was also that it revived some of the pleasures of nineteenth-century Romanticism and made them seem modern. James Wright and W. S. Merwin began their careers by emulating styles of the nineteenth century. For them the transition to Surrealism, with its haunting cadences, its glamorous imagery (bones, light, fires, stars, and so forth), its vague emotions, and its suggestions of silence, absence, and chthonic depth, did not involve a major change in sensibility. Surrealist poetry also reflected the imprinting of twentieth-century history on the imagination, for it was filled with images of violence, wounds, detached parts of the body, and lurking death. But while it presented these images, it also muffled them in dreamy contemplation, and they were ominous without being sharply frightening. Surrealism also appealed to American poets as an alternative to the Confessional style—general where it was particular, cool where it was strident, impersonal and mythical where it was personal. It had a brief, intense vogue in the 1960s and 1970s, and might have been the main topic of this chapter. To have entitled this chapter "American Surrealism" would have more sharply identified the poets it includes (for most contemporary American poets are "Against Civilization," including poets such as Ginsberg and Rich whom I discuss in other chapters). But the identification would have been misleading. Virtually no American poet has been a Surrealist through the greater part of his career or in the majority of his better poems. By the end of the 1960s Surrealism in the United States had become, as Alan Williamson said in a 1975 protest, "easily the most formulaic style we have had since the 'academic' poetry of the 1950s." Even the better Surrealist poets, Williamson added, thinking of Mark Strand (b. 1934), Gregory Orr (b. 1947), and Charles Simic (b. 1938), could be hard to tell apart.

Prototypical volumes of American Surrealism were Strand's *Reasons for Moving* (1968) and Orr's *Gathering the Bones Together* (1975). Orr is warmer in feeling, and Strand is a better craftsman with a more original imagination—he conveys a chilling awareness of emptiness and isolation—but their poems could generally be described in similar terms. They used spare, simple words and images. Vague, dreadful things happened or seemed about to happen in their poetry, but these were described or suggested with a lack of affect. Their verse was abstract in the sense that it presented elemental symbols or archetypal fables, stripping away circumstantial details of setting, plot, and character. Later they moved away from Surrealism. Charles Simic writes brief, brilliant, disorienting parables. Often his narratives and imagery recall his experiences as a child in Yugoslavia during the Second World War. With these poets I may mention Michael Benedikt (b. 1935) and Robert Kelly (b. 1935). Benedikt is, at his best, a witty, fantastic poet whose metaphors develop and continue with a life of their own. Kelly combines some of the tenets of Olsonian open form with Surrealism. He has a flowing rhythm, graceful and strong, and simple, eloquent words, though his work suffers from the abstraction inherent in the Surrealist-archetypal style.

Though Louise Glück (b. 1943) is not a Surrealist, she shares the imaginative resort to myth and archetype that characterizes other poets in this chapter. In her first volume Glück was almost a Confessional poet, for though she did not tell shocking, personal histories, her subject was that of the Confessional school—family tensions observed from a post-Freudian perspective. Her sense of pain was unrelenting. Even flowers were sick: "The crocus spreads like cancer." When in later volumes she imagined in terms of myth and archetype, her subject was still the ambivalence and pain of close human relations, and her style, which had always been terse, was further reduced. She speaks in remarkably few, simple words and images. She is haunted by fears of illness, abandonment, and death, and is a poet of ominous psychological insight, which she expresses with stark objectivity and detachment, as though gazing from a distance like the moon.

Charles Wright (b. 1935) is a poet of stunning gifts who is haunted by Pound. In its use of personal memory, Italian setting, techniques of juxtaposition, molding of lines, and in some of its themes, "Southern Cross," the title poem of Wright's 1981 volume, is an individual variation or reprise of Pound's *Pisan Cantos,* though it suffers in the comparison. It is admirably less elliptical than Pound's poem, but it lacks Pound's emotional range, and one especially hungers for the toughly realistic aspects that enter the *Pisan Cantos* through their setting in a prison camp. (Harshly realistic materials are included in Wright's next volume, *The Other Side of the River,* 1984.) Wright's *China Trace* (1977) is one of several famous volumes of postwar American poetry, including Snyder's *Riprap* (1959) and Bly's *Silence in the Snowy Fields* (1962), that adapt the style Pound invented in *Cathay* for translating Chinese.

Wright's poetry is unusually difficult to characterize because the qualities one might discriminate separately do not convey the impression of the whole. He has a strong visual sense, and tends to render images as though describing a painting. Rhythm

and sound are managed with scrupulous care, as in these lines
from "The Southern Cross":

> Nightwind by now in the olive trees,
> No sound but the wind from anything.

Like Mark Strand, Wright lays down one declarative statement
after another, using clear, simple words, and creates with them
a moody, detached atmosphere. But he is also witty and aphoristic: "The subject of all poems is the clock . . . One day more is
one day less." Yet what most defines Wright are his omnipresent
mindfulness of death and eternity and his wan, dreamy, ominous feeling about them. Objects are seen under the aspect of
eternity—"Now the wisteria tendrils extend themselves like
swan's necks under Orion"—or death is seen in them. "Homage
to Paul Cezanne (in *The Southern Cross*), one of Wright's finest
poems, conveys a mythical awareness of the dead still silently
present:

> They shuttle their messengers through the oat grass.
> Their answers rise like rust on the stalks and the spidery leaves.
>
> We rub them off our hands.

Wright is a poet with a small range of mood and a powerful
technique and intelligence.

The period style this chapter describes was established primarily through the following volumes: Robert Bly's *Silence in the
Snowy Fields* (1962), James Wright's *The Branch Will Not Break*
(1963), W. S. Merwin's *The Moving Target* (1963), and Gary Snyder's *Riprap* (1959), *A Range of Poems* (1966), and *The Back Country*
(1968). It is further illustrated in many subsequent poems by
these poets and by others such as John Haines and Galway Kinnell. Poems in this style typically present the poet alone or perhaps with a lover, friend, or small human group. Nature in the
form of skies, mountains, woods, fields, animals, and so forth, is
also present, and the relation between the human and nature
(reality, being, the cosmos) is the general subject of the poem.
The relation presented or achieved in the poem is almost always
intended to be exemplary in some respect; often the poem enacts a moment of illumination or discovery.

The presentation of images in these poems may be impersonal

but usually is not. The voice speaking is by convention that of the poet himself—there are no personae—and the poem reports something the poet "really" did, saw, or thought. In these senses the poems are personal and autobiographical. But the events that take place are of a simple kind—lying in a hammock in summer, or seeing an accumulation of snow in winter—and even when they are not, they are rendered without the ample or particularizing details that would generate interest in plot or character. In short, the actions narrated in these poems are felt to be simple, natural, essential, primordial, elemental, or archetypal.

In the foregoing sentences "events" and "actions" refer to external happenings, not to the poet's thoughts and feelings. Inwardly there may be surprising excursions of association, dramatic climaxes and reversals of emotion, and sudden illuminations. Just how these inner transformations arise from the outward event or relate to it is often mysterious. A typical poem in this respect is James Wright's "Lying in a Hammock at William Duffy's Farm in Pine Island, Minnesota." The last line, "I have wasted my life," does not seem to follow from the images that come before. It has been attacked for this reason, and defended in many interpretations that link it with the rest of the poem but do not agree with one another. My point is merely that the line illustrates the extreme degree to which these poets activate and rely on suggestions. Poetic suggestion has its effect precisely because its indefiniteness can never be completely resolved. In this context the language of these poets has a special implication. The apparent casualness of their phrasing reminds us that language cannot incarnate the experience to be presented, that at most it can only point toward it. The ordinariness of the phrase expresses the defeat of language, so to speak; the poet has no motive to construct a more precisely or complexly meaningful phrase because the meaning would still inevitably be inadequate.

A MODAL POEM

An example of the style I am discussing here is Gary Snyder's "For the Boy Who Was Dodger Point Lookout Fifteen Years

Ago." In this poem Snyder describes a moment when he and his first wife, on a backpacking trip in the mountains, met the fire lookout, who hiked down from his hut two miles to their camp by a mountain pool.

> The thin blue smoke of our campfire
> down in the grassy, flowery,
> heather meadow
> two miles from your perch.
> The snowmelt pond, and Alison,
> half-stoopt bathing like
> Swan Maiden, lovely naked,
> ringed with Alpine fir and
> gleaming snowy peaks. We
> had come miles without trails,
> you had been long alone.
> We talked for half an hour up
> there above the foaming creeks
> and forest valleys, in our
> world of snow and flowers.
>
> I don't know where she is now;
> I never asked your name.
> In this burning, muddy, lying,
> blood-drenched world
> that quiet meeting in the mountains
> cool and gentle as the muzzles of
> three elk, helps keep me sane.

Reading this poem, we assume that the event actually took place. The convention activated is of literal speech, real experience. The heather meadow, snowmelt pond, Alpine fir, and gleaming snowy peaks make a scenic ensemble that would actually be observed in the Olympic mountains of Washington, where Snyder locates his poem. But most readers of poetry live in cities, and to them the naked bather, mountain peaks, and elks seem strange and wonderful. The situation is Edenic. The experience is secluded in space ("up / there," "miles without trails") and in the past. Except as a memory it has no connection with Snyder's present existence (he doesn't even know where his former wife now is; he never knew the name of the boy). In keeping with the theme of innocence, the image of the naked woman does not arouse erotic emotions, since these are repressed by the suggestions of purity (snow) and also by the casual acceptance of nakedness—they all "talked." More exactly, erotic suggestions are present, but only to enhance the emotions of wonder and strangeness. At this level the scenery of the high Olympics becomes a symbolic expression of the complex of feeling activated by the whole first paragraph of the poem—innocence, wonder, goodness—and the scenery lower down, the "foaming creeks" and "forest valleys," makes through its greater familiarity and hurrying energy a transition to the "muddy" world (the lowest stage of all) of the present in which the poet speaks. The release of such traditional and archetypal suggestions within a literal anecdote illustrates one means by which Snyder fulfills a cardinal point of his poetic, to find the form (meaning) in the actual.

But among the many traditional suggestions there is an especially Snyderian one: purity, innocence, and goodness are natural. The people in the scene are like animals. The woman is a swan, the boy a bird (from a mountain "perch"), the three together are like elks. The poem builds on a contrast between nature and innocent human beings like nature, on the one hand, and, on the other hand, the "burning . . . world" of the last paragraph. The "burning . . . world" is opposed to "our / world of snow and flowers," and "burning" also resonates to the opening line of the poem—"the thin blue smoke of our campfire." The "lying . . . world" corresponds negatively to their talk "up / there"; within Snyder's system of imagery "lying" would also be a contrast to "lovely naked." The "muddy . . . world" is the reverse echo of the "snowmelt pond," and "blood-drenched," the climactic term in the negative series, contrasts with the peace and friendliness of "that quiet meeting in the mountains." Yet in the emotional sequence that the poem enacts, at least some of the resentment Snyder directs against the "burning . . . world" seems to arise from the facts that his wife was lost in it and the boy never known. The same moment that keeps him "sane" in the world is also, as he remembers it, a source of grief and anger, making him hate the world more. Possibly there is even some resentment of the remembered meeting itself. It was impermanent and incomplete, and though momentariness and incompleteness are among the qualities the poem idealizes, they may also explain why the last line is anticlimactic, as though something in Snyder were begrudging the idealization he has bestowed.

ROBERT BLY

Robert Bly (b. 1926) grew up on a farm in Minnesota. Though he loved to read, he did not think of writing until after he had graduated from high school and enlisted in the navy, where he first met persons with literary inclinations. After a year at St. Olaf's college in Minnesota he transferred to Harvard. His poems and critical views as an undergraduate were typical of the academic formalism of that time and place. He received his B.A. in 1950 and then spent three years living in solitude, mostly in New York City. What the motives and psychic events of this self-chosen isolation may have been I do not know, but Bly has since argued that in learning to write a poet must seek loneliness and the "inwardness" it fosters.

In 1955 Bly married and enrolled in the Writer's Workshop at the University of Iowa. The next year he went to Norway, having received a Fulbright grant to translate Norwegian poetry into English. In Norway he discovered the work of Trakl and Neruda. Returning to Minnesota, he settled on a farm his father had purchased for him and founded a literary magazine. Originally entitled *The Fifties,* it became in due course *The Sixties, The Seventies,* and *The Eighties.* In this journal he translated and advocated poets of Europe and South America such as Trakl and Neruda, who were then little known in the United States. He also paid serious attention to young American poets, poets whose reputations were not yet established and who, therefore, would not ordinarily have been subjects of extended critical essays.

As the war in Vietnam developed Bly denounced it. He gave public readings of poetry in protest, helped found the society of "American Writers against the Vietnam War," and when his *The Light around the Body* won the National Book Award in 1968, he donated the cash prize to the war resistance. Many of Bly's antiwar poems made use of the stylistic resources of Surrealism. Despite his political commitment, he did not believe that poems on the war should be simply polemic. "As the war in Vietnam went on," he later explained, "I was interested in where it came from inside us." Doubtless thinking of a famous remark by Yeats, he added that "A true political poem is a quarrel with ourselves" and seeks to "deepen awareness." It must not become "rhetoric." Bly's own poems on the war did not live up to these wise intentions. He exposed the rage, racial hatred, and cruelty that found expression in the war, and he associated them with past episodes in American history. Doing so, he sought to explore dark regions of the national psyche, and, therefore, of his own as well. But the polemical mood, which inevitably animated these poems, militated against self-questioning. Bly's bitter hostility to the war made his states of mind perilously similar to the ones he reprobated. Too many lines were bereft of self-criticism. Righteous, reckless, and violent, they amounted to indiscriminate assaults, as one sees in *The Teeth Mother Naked at Last* (1970):

> The ministers lie, the professors lie, the television
>   lies, the priests lie. . . .
> These lies mean that the country wants to die.
> Lie after lie starts out into the prairie grass,
> like enormous trains of Conestoga wagons. . . .

As the passions of the Vietnam period receded, Bly became increasingly absorbed in a quest for enlightenment, which he sought in the writings of Jung, in Oriental wisdom, in the primitive mind, and in the unconscious. He studied "meditation," which he characterized as "sitting inside an interior space," with a Tibetan in Scotland. He was extraordinarily prolific, publishing eleven books of poetry in the 1970s, and he continued to tour universities, reading his poetry and teaching in writing workshops for three months a year.

In numerous prose pieces and interviews Bly urged his views on poetry and how to write it. The tentativeness and vagueness of his formulations reflected his moral stance. Such traditional virtues of the intellect as precision, qualification, sequence, and exhaustiveness were less prized by him, since they could be obtained only by forfeiting the greater values of spontaneity and emotional intuition. The essence of Bly's position was that poetry does not come from the "rational mind." It is not written with "craft," and, as he said in an interview, "all the traditional applications of the word craft" in reference to poetry "have to be dropped. American craft-talk has been connected with the idea of the poem as a dead object, as a dead object and constructed. But the whole genius of modern poetry lies in its grasp of flowing psychic energy." The poet, then, must escape from his rational self or "ego," and release the deeper, less conscious levels of the mind, where he is in touch with nature or being. In this connection Bly has talked much about poetic imagery. "To Pound an image meant 'petals on a wet, black bough.' To us an image is 'death on the wet deep roads of the guitar.'" Among Bly's followers imagery of the latter type is known as the "deep image." Bly supports or, at least, accompanies these points with observations on the three parts of the brain—reptile, mammal, and "neo-cortex"—on "inner space," Amerindians and shamans, mother consciousness, the "ancient memory," and the like, and his views are widely echoed. Gregory Orr, for example, follows the Bly line when he says, "What the act and art of poetics demands is a form of intense, naive enthusiasm. By naive, I simply mean that a poetics must be an unexamined intellectual and emotional energy flowing outward; as such it is opposed to logical analysis and critical thinking: . . . the notion of image which Bly repopularized [the "deep image"] is that of the crystallized intelligence of the unconscious mind." It would be profitless to ask Orr how one knows this "crystallized intelligence" is intelligence if one is not allowed to analyze or criticize it. One reader of Bly reports that "whenever I read Bly . . . [I feel] a slight 'unfolding' of the left side of my body." My objection, I should make clear, is both to Bly's ideas and especially to his expression of them. At best such views would represent half-truths, but they have been argued with profundity by others. In Bly's version they are vague and sentimental.

The best of Bly's poems are in *Silence in the Snowy Fields* (1962, revised 1967) and *This Tree Will Be Here for a Thousand Years* (1979). These two books represent the more traditional side of Bly's work, since in them his political preoccupations and Surrealist style are less prominent. Bly's poems of this kind are located in a bucolic world, generally that surrounding his Minnesota farm. Amid the fields, lakes, trees, domestic and wild animals, grass, weeds, moon, snow, and the like there may be no human beings. If anyone is present, he is the author. Sometimes there are also his wife, family, friends, or neighboring farmers, but there are no cities, suburbs, shopping centers, or crowded places of any kind. The stage is set for "inwardness," communion with nature, and metaphysical pathos. The emotions of Bly include a naive appreciativeness hardly seen since Rupert Brooke: "I feel joy seeing old boards scattered on the grass"; "There is a privacy I love in this snowy night"; "How beautiful to walk out at midnight in the moonlight / Dreaming of animals." Despite such enthusiasms, however, the underlying tone of Bly's "Snowy Fields poetry," as it is sometimes called, is melancholy; wide, empty fields, solitary human figures, oncoming twilight or snow, and the like, suggest man's metaphysical loneliness. Death obsesses Bly even more than it does most people; "'Living' means eating up particles of death"; even the voice of a cricket cries *memento mori* to him, for it is an autumnal sound. In "Amazed by an Accumulation of Snow" Bly tells how he works all day and observes, on pausing, that snow meanwhile has been piling up. The poem creates a typical Blyan (and Wordsworthian) effect in which the busy, self-absorbed mind is suddenly confronted with all the other life of the universe going on in the same moment. The last two lines—

> The horse's hoof kicks up a seashell, and the farmer
> finds an Indian stone with a hole all the way through

—bring to bear a moody perspective of infinite time and change; the stone sends the mind back to Indian days and the shell to an epoch when the farmland was ocean floor.

JAMES WRIGHT

James Wright (1927–80) was born in Martin's Ferry, Ohio, an industrial town where his father worked in a factory. Such towns, Wright believed, typify American civilization, and many of his poems dwell on the poverty, bleak experience, and wasted lives of their inhabitants. After graduating from high school, he served in the army for two years, and then went to Kenyon College in Ohio and, as a graduate student, to the University of Washington. He taught literature at the University of Minnesota and at Macalester College in St. Paul, and then found a permanent position at Hunter College in New York City.

In his first two volumes, *The Green Wall* (1957) and *Saint Judas* (1959), Wright sounded in some poems like Edwin Arlington Robinson, in others a bit like Frost, Yeats, Housman, Matthew Arnold, or some nineteenth-century poet one doesn't quite recognize, possibly a German. Wright's styles, in other words, were traditional. In "Eleutheria" (in *The Green Wall*), for example, the theme of love and its inevitable fading is couched in the nature symbolism that was omnipresent in the poetry of the nineteenth century, and the happily sad remembrance of love, of the moment of sympathy and beauty haunted with premonitions of loss, arouses elegiac emotion.

> We lay and heard the apples fall for hours,
> The stripping twilight plundered trees of boughs,
> The land dissolved beneath the rabbit's heels,
> And far away I heard a window close,
> A haying wagon heave and catch its wheels,
> Some water slide and stumble and be still.
> The dark began to climb the empty hill.

This was published a year after Ginsberg's *Howl* and four years after Olson's first Maximus Poems.

The poems of Wright that most struck his contemporaries in the 1950s did so because of their subjects and attitudes. In his foreword to *The Green Wall* Auden pointed out that the "persons who have stimulated Mr. Wright's imagination include a lunatic, a man who has failed to rescue a boy from drowning, a murderer, a lesbian, a prostitute, a police informer, and some children, one of them deaf." Auden had in mind such lyrics as "A Poem about George Doty in the Death House," Doty being a convicted murderer, and "To a Fugitive," on an escaping prisoner. *Saint Judas* added several more to this group of "social outsiders," as Auden called them, such as the subject of the title poem, Judas Iscariot, and Jimmy Leonard, a drunk ("A Note Left in Jimmy Leonard's Shack"). There was also "At the Executed Murderer's Grave," a second poem on George Doty. Wright identified with such figures, and if we ask with what he was identifying, the answer is helplessness, bewilderment, loneliness, creaturely suffering, defeat, the feeling of being an underdog and even a criminal. His poems on such figures are usually sentimental; on rare occasions his intense sympathies lead to statements so morally lopsided as to be perverse. Doty, for example, had picked up a girl in his car, made a pass at her, brained her when she resisted, and been arrested. "A Poem about George Doty in the Death House," an attack, among other things, on capital punishment, tells in Yeatsian verse how Doty sits in his cell, listening to complaining bums nearby, and ends,

> But I mourn no soul but his,
> Not even the bums who die,
> Nor the homely girl whose cry
> Crumbled his pleading kiss.

But whatever their weaknesses, such poems are never trivial. Wright was a serious man. "At the Executed Murderer's Grave" has power through its direct sincerity: "Doty . . . I confess I do not love you . . . I waste no pity on the dead that stink . . . I do not pity the dead, I pity the dying. / I pity myself, because a man is dead. . . . The hackles on my neck are fear, not grief."

In the poems of his next volume, *The Branch Will Not Break* (1963), Wright sought to utter his immediate feeling directly, escaping the distortions of impulse associated with a regular, strict form. The story of his stylistic transition, which he often told, begins with a crisis of despair after writing *Saint Judas*. He felt that he could not go on in that style, and the sense of a dead end in his work coincided with a similar emotion in his personal life. He had been reading Trakl and other poets who might be called either Expressionist or Surrealist, and must have glimpsed the possibility of a new departure based on their example. He was also impressed by Robert Bly's magazine, *The Fifties*, and the two poets became friends. Since Wright was teaching at this time at the University of Minnesota it was easy for him to visit Bly's farm near Madison, Minnesota, on weekends, and what he found there—"I'm a member of [Bly's] family too. I'm Mary's godfather. They love me"—and heard about poetry from Bly resulted in the remarkable lyrics of what remains Wright's finest single volume, *The Branch Will Not Break* (1963).

A sampling of Wright's mature poetry may start with "Autumn Begins in Martin's Ferry, Ohio":

> In the Shreve High football stadium,
> I think of Polacks nursing long beers in Tiltonsville,
> And gray faces of Negroes in the blast furnace at Benwood,

And the ruptured night watchman of Wheeling Steel,
Dreaming of heroes.

All the proud fathers are ashamed to go home.
Their women cluck like starved pullets,
Dying for love.

Therefore,
Their sons grow suicidally beautiful
At the beginning of October,
And gallop terribly against each other's bodies.

The poem interprets the emotions and culture of this American locale with an awareness that in the end becomes almost tragic. The football-playing sons (who themselves will in turn become just like their fathers) are fulfilling, to some extent, the fathers' heroic fantasies. The fantasies themselves are compensatory, rooted in the fathers' gray, defeated, and exploited lives, and there is a suggestion that industrial capitalism, represented by the steel company, is ultimately responsible for what the poem observes. Physical contact on the football field contrasts with the lack of it between the fathers and their wives. "Suicidally" implies the enormous waste of life's possibilities. The logically concluding term, "Therefore," comes with no apparent logic, yet conveys that what happens is inescapable; the term refers to the interconnectedness of the cultural-economic system, to all that lies behind and inevitably causes the manifestations the poem describes. The conjunction of the stadium with the idea of death vaguely brings to mind an autumnal ritual of sacrifice. Comparing the sons to horses, "gallop" evokes ideas of naturalness and innocence as well as speed. That they are galloping against each other, as horses would not normally do, suggests the violation of nature that is involved.

Passing over many fine poems (such as "Two Poems about President Harding," "Eisenhower's Visit to Franco," "Two Horses Playing in an Orchard," and "American Wedding") we may pause on "The Blessing," the most loved of Wright's lyrics. The poem tells how Wright and a friend stopped by the highway and two Indian ponies came "gladly out of the willows / To welcome" them. A moment of shy, intense emotion is expressed:

I would like to hold the slenderer one in my arms,
For she has walked over to me
And nuzzled my left hand.

She is black and white,
Her mane falls wild on her forehead,
And the light breeze moves me to caress her long ear
That is delicate as the skin over a girl's wrist.
Suddenly I realize
That if I stepped out of my body I would break
Into blossom.

The poem is of course sentimental. The horses were not filled with the "kindness" and "love" Wright attributed to them. Wright always had a tendency, as Robert Bly put it (thinking also of himself) "not to bite deeply enough into hard material, but to slide over it." Nevertheless, the poem is vivid and moving, and the final, Surrealist image conveys with freshness and depth of suggestion Wright's Romantic emotion, his longing to become part of Edenic nature.

In Wright's next volume, *Shall We Gather at the River* (1968) his technique was little changed but his mood more depressed. "I speak of flat defeat / In a flat voice," he said ("Speak"). "The Minneapolis Poem" roams the city and describes its brutality and dreariness. The poem begins in an almost suicidal state of mind, which is gradually relieved as Wright finds sustaining inward resources in humor and in his purpose as a poet. The poems in this volume evolve toward expressions of quiet happiness as they succeed one another, and thus repeat in a darker spirit the same emotional curve as *The Branch Will Not Break*. Wright's poetry henceforth reflected, on the whole, a resolve to be affirmative. In this he succeeded, but at a cost, for his imagination fed more characteristically on dreariness, loneliness, brutal violence, and death. In most of his later poems one appreciates his goodwill toward life and his capable invention and craftsmanship, but sympathy is less strongly stirred. His later volumes also contained many prose poems that evolved from notebook jottings; *Moments of an Italian Summer* makes pleasant reading. His achievement is important as it stands, but he died at a relatively young age, and one regrets both the poems he did not write and the influence he would have had. What was best in him recalls Thomas Hardy—sensitivity to the darker side of experience, direct honesty, seriousness, essentialism, compassion—and we remember that Hardy had published almost none of his poems at the age at which Wright died.

With Wright I may also mention Richard Hugo (1928–82)

and Dave Smith (b. 1942). The poverty of American life, both
spiritual and literal, that Wright described in river towns along
the Ohio, Hugo knew intimately in the Pacific Northwest, where
he lived. He wrote of bleak landscapes, polluted rivers, dying
towns, and empty, sometimes derelict lives in bars and stale
roominghouses. His ordinary words and declarative sentences
are straightforward and unadorned. His attitude is stoic. More
than survival cannot be hoped for. Compared with that of
Wright, Hugo's poetry is less imagined and more documentary,
and he was never Surrealist. His poetic vision recalls Wordsworth and Hardy in his feeling for perduring being in landscape
and for the minimal lives of people who, like landscape, are
mute, solitary, and enduring. But Hugo is much more hurt and
bitter than Wordsworth, and does not view his solitaries as sublime. His attitude is compassionate and elegiac.

In his first books Smith wrote about the watermen and their
families on the Virginia coast. He created character, described,
and narrated. His world was as bleak and circumstantially rendered as Hugo's, but his mood and style were different, for
Smith, a follower of Whitman, strove to hope and praise. In *Gos-
hawk Antelope* (1979) his scene was Utah and his perceptions
more darkly toned. His methods of presentation had changed
also, becoming less realistic and more archetypal and symbolic.
Smith abounds and flows like a river. His emotions are strong.
The world he presents is vivid and interesting. He is enormously
talented, but reading him, I feel stunned and finally numbed by
the volume, noise, and muscle.

GALWAY KINNELL

Galway Kinnell (b. 1927) grew up in Rhode Island. Like many
persons who will one day write poetry, he found in adolescence
that his "most intimate feelings were shared" in the poems he
read "more fully than in the relationships" he had "in the world."
But out of diffidence, perhaps, he did not start writing seriously
until he was an undergraduate at Princeton. Charles Bell, his
teacher and friend, recalls that these early poems used "a romantic and Miltonic pentameter almost totally remade under
impacts from Donne and the moderns." Among the moderns

Yeats was paramount. W. S. Merwin, a fellow undergraduate, had visited Kinnell "late one night, book in hand, and read Yeats to me until dawn." Thereafter for a while Yeats seemed to Kinnell "not only the greatest of all poets, but also . . . poetry itself. In everything I wrote I tried to reproduce his voice." A little later Kinnell read deeply in Whitman, and then the French Symbolists and post-Symbolists during a 1955–56 Fulbright year in France. He supported himself by teaching and, later, by odd jobs, "picking up my living as I could," but he had a wife and two children, and as he neared middle age the uncertainties of his livelihood increasingly alarmed him. So he went sporadically back to teaching, offering courses in the writing of poetry now at one college and now at another. Meanwhile, his reputation as a poet was growing.

In his early poems Kinnell wrote of erotic love, of the cold, vast, starry cosmos engulfing love's moment, and of the terror and allure of death. In apocalyptic vision he saw darkness enveloping a frozen earth and found the vision strangely comforting. He sympathized with the homeless poor in cities and with lonely persons "afraid in their beds" ("Night Song"). When a duck was shot over a marsh and its mate "flew on alone into winter," he brooded on the cruelty of life ("Winter Sky"). God was absent from his cosmos but not from his emotions, for he longed to merge with the transcendent. *Weltschmerz* was appropriate to his age and to the romantic tradition within which he was writing, but it had deeper sources in his own temperament, and he did not outgrow it as he modernized his style.

The latter process meant, for Kinnell, that he abandoned stanzas and meters for free verse and romantic diction for contemporary speech. William Carlos Williams was an inescapable example. But Kinnell, like many of his contemporaries, was willing to seem more loosely colloquial or prosy than Williams, and thus to dissolve further (more exactly, to produce the illusion of dissolving further) the boundaries between the poem and an ordinary, unpoetic state of mind. Williams, moreover, had usually maintained isochrony among the lines of a poem. By the late sixties Kinnell, perhaps influenced by Olson's "projective verse," might vary the length of his lines dramatically; a line of two syllables might be followed by one of twenty.

Behind Williams lay the greater figure of Whitman. He inspirited Kinnell in his preoccupation with ultimate concerns and doubtless also encouraged him to ignore considerations of finish and tact. Sincerity often led Kinnell into awkwardness, but also fostered his powerful directness of utterance. In "Freedom, New Hampshire," an elegy for his dead brother, he accepted Whitman's pantheism (there is no death, for the one spirit in all things "flowers" endlessly forth), but was too honest to find this consoling:

> But an incarnation is in particular flesh
> And the dust that is swirled into a shape
> And crumbles and is swirled again had but one shape
> That was this man. When he is dead the grass
> Heals what he suffered, but he remains dead,
> And the few who loved him know this until they die.

Most of Kinnell's more ambitious poems are sequences. They usually include narrative or narrative elements. People are characterized, human relationships sketched, doings reported; in short, though Kinnell is reflective and sometimes discursive, his meditations arise within or relate to particular, concrete events which are also presented. In many poems he interweaves images of pain, suffering, the crucifixion of Christ, concentration camps, and the butchering of animals, and identifies with both the victims and the killers. The natural necessity of killing in order to survive causes in him a deep emotional disturbance and metaphysical questioning. All this is vividly expressed in "The Avenue Bearing the Initial of Christ into the New World," the most important poem in Kinnell's first book, *What a Kingdom It Was* (1960). "The Porcupine" and "The Bear" in *Body Rags* (1968) are even more impressive. In "The Bear" the narrator, who is an Eskimo or Indian hunter, leaves a sharpened wolf's rib coiled in blubber for the bear to swallow. Starving as he follows the wounded animal, he eats the bear's bloody turd. The cunning of the hunter, his tenacious pursuit, ruthlessness, desperation, and identification with the bear are presented in the last line as a metaphor of poetry, which lives, like the hunter, under the compulsion of reality.

In *The Book of Nightmares* (1971) Kinnell wrote under the inspiration of Rilke's *Duino Elegies*. The ten poems, each with seven parts, make up a single work. The same or similar settings and images recur with incremental implication throughout the volume; their repetition is the main formal means through which the ten poems are linked together. Descriptions of butchering hens, icy skies, a fly in a spider web, and a drunk dying in a cheap hotel continue themes I have already touched on. Counterbalancing moments come in mystical intuitions of the unity of all life, but these are less convincing than Kinnell's middle-aged love for his wife and children. This material was new in Kinnell's poetry, and suggests a possibility in experience—we may call it "love"—that somewhat relieves suffering or gives it a meaning. The theme was continued in his next volume, *Mortal Acts, Mortal Words* (1980). In poems recalling his mother, brother, and childhood, his tone is elegiac as the past comes back in middle age to be understood and evaluated in a new way.

John Haines was born in 1924 in Norfolk, Virginia, the son of a naval officer. During the Second World War he served in the navy. In 1946 he moved to central Alaska, where he spent most of his time until 1969 homesteading in the wilderness. He and his wife lived on the vegetables he raised and the game he shot, and he earned a little money by trapping. Visits with friends and neighbors were infrequent. Much of his time was passed in reading and writing, thinking and dreaming. The impact of living off the land in this lonely place is reflected through all his poetry, not so much in the subject matter—after his first volume, *Winter News* (1966), Alaska is not usually the setting of his poems—but in more fundamental ways. He felt a resemblance between his way of life and that of primitive man. He knew the land that supported him with the intimacy survival necessitated. He identified with the animals he killed. Their rage, their fear in being hunted (Haines had fantasies in which they hunted him), and their bloody entrails were inescapable reminders of man's creaturely being. There was a mythical quality to his experience. He responded deeply to the space, silence, snow, and cold of Alaska. Typically in his poems three to five brief blocks of free verse foreground a scene, event, or object and surround it, so to speak, with blankness, muteness, and the omnipresent suggestion of death. His "Poem of the Forgotten" concludes:

> I made my bed under the shadow
> Of leaves, and awoke

in the first snow of autumn,
filled with silence.

The paradoxes of awakening to winter and of a poet "filled with silence" are typical.

With Haines I may mention two poets of the Pacific Northwest, William Stafford (b. 1914) and David Wagoner (b. 1926). Stafford expresses his mystical feeling for nature and his mistrust of civilization in limpid, conversational, uninsistent lyrics that listen for whatever truths may almost reveal themselves. He is gentle, nostalgic, and reverent. Wagoner's "Staying Alive" creates its metaphor by describing how to survive in the wilderness. Both Stafford and Wagoner are interested in the Amerindians, and in *Who Shall Be the Sun?* (1978) Wagoner expresses the consciousness of Amerindians by using their songs and myths. Haines, Stafford, and Wagoner are not as generally appreciated as they ought to be, and the reason lies, I believe, in the unobtrusiveness of their skills. To harried reviewers the clear can seem colorless and the unsensational uninteresting.

W. S. MERWIN

The son of a clergyman, W. S. Merwin (b. 1927) grew up in New Jersey and Pennsylvania. After taking a B.A. at Princeton, he attended graduate school for one year, but then listened to the advice of R. P. Blackmur, whom he revered, and left academic life. Moving to Europe, he supported himself by tutoring and translating. His inaugural book of poems, *A Mask of Janus*, appeared in 1952, having been chosen by Auden for publication in the Yale Younger Poets series.

In the course of his career Merwin's style has transformed itself many times, but his personality has not. His poetry is moody, suggestive, dreamy, contemplative, remote, and impersonal. In it the isolated mind beholds idealized or demonized symbols in a world of imagination. In "Anabasis," the first poem in his first book, the style is Tennysonian:

> One dreams fixed beasts that drowse or wonder,
> Not blinking; by the stream a few
> Poplars and white beeches where

Exhausted leaves, suspended through

The distant autumn do not fall.

Merwin would master other types of versification as time went on, and he would also battle, often successfully, against the more intrinsic qualities of his imagination. But he remains, on the whole, a poet in whom suggestions of dream, art, emptiness, oblivion, and death outweigh the fiercer, more adhesive or affirmative impulses that are also present. Even in the love poems of his latest volume, *The Compass Flower* (1977), where for the first time he speaks directly of erotic experience, the lovers seem from a Pre-Raphaelite painting. He falls to his knees and clasps her thighs ("Summer Doorway") and continues kneeling, the gesture becoming a pose and the emotion fading into contemplation and vague surmise.

In all his poems we sense a controlling and virtuoso artistry. The anthology piece "Leviathan" uses old English versification and bestiary form:

This is the black sea-brute bulling through wave-wrack,
Ancient as ocean's shifting hills, who in sea-toils
Travelling . . .

We appreciate that the diction and rhythm are not merely a *tour de force* but are appropriate in their massive power to the leviathan, and, moreover, that Merwin's leviathan is expressive as a symbol. Nevertheless, Merwin's self-conscious artistry has a special meaning in relation to his subjects, which are often charged with potentially intense, threatening emotions. A creature of overwhelming strength, leviathan evokes our feelings of terror and helplessness before the world's natural treachery and violence. Possibly he is even a figure of supernatural malice. But the archaic form of the poem sets this leviathan at a distance and frames him in irrelevance. He is exhibited in Merwin's poem, but he is also imprisoned within its naive charm, and cannot seem menacing.

"Dictum: For a Masque of Deluge" (in *A Mask for Janus*) has such tensions for its subject. The poem gives instructions for performing the deluge of Genesis as a masque. Scenes of suffering and destruction are to be represented, but the poem continually reminds us that these will be unreal, will be theatrical

illusions produced by technical means. Even the rainbow at the
end, the symbol of God's covenant, will be only colored paper.
Reducing apocalypse to theater, the poem keeps a distance from
human disaster, refusing to imagine it as real, present, and overwhelming. But the poem does not, as a Yeatsian poem might,
glorify art because it can do this. Art also is tacitly condemned
precisely because it is unreal. Art, the poem suggests, represents
reality only by miniaturing it, and though this gives art a cozy
charm, it is also an evasion. Merwin's poem, moreover, is not a
masque but only a monologue with directions for staging one.
The speaker describes both the reality to be represented (which
is only another work of imagination, the myth of the deluge)
and the artificial means to be employed, and remains emotionally disengaged from both.

"The Isaiah of Souillac" (in *Green with Beasts*, 1956) describes
the dancing figure of the prophet Isaiah that is carved in stone
on the medieval church. This poem dwells on the paradox that
motion (wind, dance, God's spirit) can be expressed in the mo-
tionlessness of stone. Once again the work of art invokes a
mighty reality—the breath of God in the prophet—and in doing
so miniatures and freezes it. As the poet meditates on the stone
figure he identifies with it:

> So there is terrible gentleness
> Unleashed in the stone of his eyes, so
> The words dance as a fire, as a clapping
> Of hands, as the stars dance, as the mountains
> Leap swelling, as the feet of the prophet, faithful
> Upon them, dance, dance, and still to the same song.

But the emotion enacted here belongs primarily to the stone
prophet and only in a derived or secondary sense to the speaker
of the poem identifying with the prophet. Merwin, in other
words, voices the emotion without committing himself to it *in
propria persona*. The emotion in which the poem ends is appropriate to the symbol it contemplates and to the religious vision
of the age that produced this symbol. That this emotion and
vision have any connection with what Merwin might himself feel
or believe is not implied.

The poems I have cited come from Merwin's first three volumes (1952–56), after which his style changed somewhat. The formality, contemplative detachment, impersonality, and irony of these volumes were typical of an American period style of the 1950s, but while Merwin was as much attracted to these qualities as were any of his contemporaries, he was also trying to break out of them. In "Song of the Mad Menagerie" (in *The Dancing Bears*, 1954), for example, he goes to Yeats (or possibly to Yeats via Roethke) for a more direct and passionate diction and syntax; he is emulating the hard, enigmatic, oracular style of Yeats's intellectual lyrics:

> On straw I lie down.
> Wise hand, be wary:
> My rage is uneven.

Among Merwin's contemporaries Wilbur was much more accomplished in his elegant, intellectual, and witty way and Lowell far surpassed Merwin in force and grandeur, but both these poets were somewhat older. Among poets of approximately the same age as Merwin—Ammons, Merrill, Creeley, Ginsberg, O'Hara, Bly, Ashbery, Wright—Merwin was at first the most conspicuous, and readers hailed him with hope for his future development.

The title poem of *The Drunk in the Furnace* (1960) promised a breakout from imprisoning decorum. Here Merwin chose as his symbol of the poet a drunk hammering within an abandoned furnace. Other poems in the volume did not sustain this assertion of rowdiness, but some of them nudged closer to contemporary reality. "John Otto" and "Grandmother Dying" were typical of a number of deliberately prosy poems on ordinary American life. To write these Merwin evidently studied Robert Frost. Open form was prominent in Merwin's next volume, *The Moving Target* (1963), and for this reason the book is now often considered as making a sharp break in his career. Merwin was now feeling the typical disaffection from contemporary America of poets in the 1960s. An economic order that sanctioned greed and promoted ecological pollution and war was headed for catastrophe, and Merwin voiced his protest with uncharacteristic harshness in *The Lice* (1967).

At the age of eighteen Merwin had briefly been fascinated by

Lorca and André Breton and had tried to write in their styles. Submerged for many years, Surrealist influences were again prominent in *The Lice.* In "An End in Spring," for example,

> The compatriots stupid as their tables
> Go on eating their packages
> Selling gloves to the clocks
> Doing alright.

The compatriots think they are (quoting them) "Doing alright," but while they are pursuing their greed and absurd commerce, time is ominously ticking. Many of the poems are Surrealist fables. In these poems, such as "The Last One," an attack on ecological pollution, the language is simple and straightforward in itself but the events are Surrealist. In all his Surrealist poetry Merwin does not attempt to release the unconscious through spontaneous or automatic writing. Instead, he interweaves connotations and juxtaposes statements or fragments of statement in an alogical but deliberate way.

After 1970 Merwin, like Wright, advanced (or retreated) toward naive affirmation. All the general reasons for "pessimism" were as much present as ever, he said, but he was no longer "floored" by them. He published many quasi-philosophical lyrics of a vague, musing, moody description. "At the Same Time" (in *Writings to an Unfinished Accompaniment,* 1973) was typical:

> While we talk
> thousands of languages are listening
> saying nothing
>
> while we close a door
> flocks of birds are flying through winters
> of endless light
>
> while we sign our names
> more of us
> lets go
>
> and will never answer.

Many of Merwin's poems now expressed sympathies with animals and nature. Others celebrated erotic love. Quasi-descriptive poems remembered a modestly good place or moment. The general mood was calm.

GARY SNYDER

Gary Snyder (b. 1930) grew up in the Pacific Northwest, where his father had "a little dairy farm, two acres in pasture, surrounded by woods." "From a very early age," he says, "I found myself standing in an undefinable awe before the natural world." His attitude toward it was one of "gratitude, wonder, and a sense of protection." At the age of nine or ten he liked to pretend he was an Indian, and would sleep nights in the forest alone. By the time he was thirteen he was backpacking and mountaineering in the high wilderness of the Cascade Mountains. In these mountains the loggers were gouging roads and strip-cutting, and by the time he entered Reed College Snyder was questioning an economic and social system that destroyed the natural environment. The political tradition of his family was radical, and he was briefly attracted to Marxism. But Snyder soon began to question basic cultural assumptions of the Western world, of which Marxism was a part, and at the same time he threw himself with a hope that amounted to faith into a study of the mythologies and cultures of the American Indians. In the same spirit he also pored over the writings of the Far East—translations of Pound and Arthur Waley from Chinese poetry, translations of *Tao Te Ching* and Confucius, the *Upanishads, Vedas,* and *Bhagavad-Gita.*

Thus his spiritual journey toward the East began in disaffection with the West, that is, with the society he observed all around him and of which he was part. The original cause of his alienation was his love of nature—the wilderness, the Indians—to which the capitalist-industrial civilization of the United States was inimical. But the feeling of disaffection soon nourished itself on many other grounds also, while his exploration of the ethos of the East became an absorbing interest, leading to identification and commitment. Already in college his still-experimental faith in the non-Western was so strong that he taught himself Buddhist meditation, deriving instruction from books. Meanwhile at college he was concentrating in anthropology and literature, and he was writing poems. On graduating from college, he planned to become an anthropologist, and he went for a semester as a graduate student in anthropology to Indiana University.

But at this point he decided instead to go to Japan and study Buddhism. He moved to San Francisco in order to prepare himself by learning Oriental languages. For the next four years (1952–56) he worked on them on his own and at the University of California at Berkeley. To earn money he occasionally held jobs as a fire lookout in the mountains, as a lumberman, and as a member of a crew clearing trails in the Yosemite. He met many writers in and around San Francisco, including Allen Ginsberg and Jack Kerouac, and shared a cabin with Kerouac for several months in 1955–56. (He is described as Japhy Ryder in Kerouac's *The Dharma Bums,* 1958.) Many people who met him were impressed by his cheerful and voluntary poverty, his inner freedom, and his motivation, seriousness, and integrity as a student and seeker of wisdom.

From 1956 to 1968 Snyder spent most of his time in Japan. He was a novice in a Zen monastery and in his last year a member of a small community (Banyan Ashram) living on an island. He mastered the languages, civilizations, and philosophies of the Far East with an intimacy few Americans have ever achieved, yet intimacy created uneasiness. Studying the mythology and thought of India, Snyder felt its profundity, yet he was chilled by its vision of ultimate destruction and nothingness, "the emptiness of a million universes appearing and disappearing . . . the enlightenment that can say 'these beings are dead already; go ahead and kill them, Arjuna.'" And though he believed that a person must raise and confront his psychological demons, India seems to have evoked these with a power that frightened him. Mahayana Buddhism addressed epistemological questions with enormous sophistication and, of course, instilled a morality, yet in Snyder's view its most valuable teaching was its technique of meditation. In their institutional embodiments both Hinduism and Buddhism were, he concluded, indifferent to social "inequalities and tyrannies."

Though Snyder did not lose his sympathy and identification with the culture of the Far East, he felt a renewed enthusiasm for primitive peoples—Cro-Magnon, Shamanistic, ancient Amerindian, Hottentot, and the like. Whether or not these peoples had actually possessed the virtues Snyder attributed to them, his descriptions of them propounded an ideal for modern man. We must, he argued, recapture their mentality and way of life—communal, peaceful, anarchistic, sexually whole and harmonious, and mystically and ecstatically religious. Primitive man, in Snyder's portrait, seeks psychological and spiritual wisdom rather than technological lore. Above all, he feels himself to be one with the animals, plants, and the earth. Returning in 1968 to the United States, Snyder soon moved with his Japanese wife—he had recently married for a third time—to a home in the California mountains. Here he lived a life of relative independence from civilization, cutting his own firewood, growing vegetables, hunting and gathering. In the winter months, when he was snowed in, he wrote. He became a spokesman and leader in the ecological movement. His way of life, knowledge of Zen, ecological philosophy, poetry, and acquaintance with poets gave him guru authority in the counterculture, and he acquired a following, especially among the young. His poetry has had a remarkably diverse reception. Some readers scorn it as *simpliste,* some experience it almost as a conversion, and a few admire its aesthetic performance.

Snyder has been publishing volumes of poetry since 1959, and though these are collections of lyrics, in each case the lyrics have been selected and arranged to make a somewhat unified work. The sequence of lyrics in *Myths & Texts* (1960) enacts a deepening intimacy with the wilderness and a recovery of the oneness with nature expressed in primitive myth. *Six Sections from Mountains and Rivers without End* (1965) was the first installment of a long poem in open form to which several other sections have since been added. Readers who find Snyder "simple" have presumably not encountered these two volumes, since in them his methods of presentation descend from Pound's *Cantos* and are difficult. *The Fudo Trilogy* (1973) couches pro-environment rhetoric in Oriental forms ("Spel against Demons," "Smokey the Bear Sutra"). These are didactic poems, and so are many in *Turtle Island* (1974). But these volumes are not the ones that enchant Snyder's followers and bore his critics. The enthusiasm and controversy refer, instead, to the poems in *Riprap* (1959), *A Range of Poems* (1966), *The Back Country* (1968), *Regarding Wave* (1970), and *Axe Handles* (1983). These volumes present Snyder's characteristic subject matter—backpacking, outdoor work, sexual encounters, the industrial-bureaucratic wasteland, Zen meditative moments, the Orient, and, after his 1967 marriage, family love and the identification of woman with nature—in a style that seems casual and natural.

I quoted one poem by Snyder in the introduction to this chapter, and as another example of his poetic art I may cite "Trail Crew Camp at Bear Valley, 9000 Feet. Northern Sierra—White Bone and Threads of Snowmelt Water." It describes a day spent working in Yosemite National Park with the crew that clears the trails.

> Cut branches back for a day—
> trail a thin line through willow
> up buckbrush meadows,
> creekbed for twenty yards
> winding in boulders
> zigzags the hill
> into timber, white pine.
>
> gooseberry bush on the turns.
> hooves clang on the riprap
> dust, brush, branches.
> a stone
> cairn at the pass—
> strippt mountains hundreds of miles.
>
> sundown went back
> the clean switchbacks to camp.
> bell on the gelding,
> stew in the cook tent,
> black coffee in a big tin can.

The day here described is typical, the poem implies, of many similarly ordinary days, and it has a rhythm. Effort is enacted in images of going uphill through bush and difficult places (creekbed and boulders) and leads to a culminating experience at the stone cairn—the view for hundreds of miles—which is followed by the subsiding rhythm of an easy return downhill to camp at sundown and to the peaceful, reassuring sensations with which the poem closes. The meaning of the poem lies essentially in the rhythm of the whole experience, an experience that moves through phases of difficulty, achievement, and satisfaction, a rhythm in which each phase has its goodness and gives meaning to the others. Apart from the concreteness, restraint, ellipsis, and suggestiveness of the Poundian-Chinese style, the Oriental element of the poem lies in its serious attention to the ordinary and everyday. More exactly, it lies in the assumption that ordinary and everyday experiences are related to a universal value. The universal value here might be called "nature."

Read superficially, this poem about a day's work of the trail crew may seem to be jottings, as in a diary, of which the poem makes little. The day is merely reported in a language that seems to lack density and resonance. Yet the poem conveys Snyder's primitivist essentialism, reverence for the natural, and Zen concentration. That it does so by enacting rather than by stating is intrinsic to its moral ideal. The work described is significantly physical—we relate to nature through our bodies—and of a kind men and women have always done. The crew ride horses, live in tents, and possess few things and no modern technology except a coffee pot. The poem uses natural, direct, unpoetic words—a diction that might come to mind immediately. The essential act of the poet is to focus wholly upon the experience, upon its contents from moment to moment and upon the rhythmic contour of the whole. The technical means to this include a rigorous avoidance of self-expression; the poem does not tell what the poet thinks or feels, but presents images, and the images render what was seen, heard, and smelled. When the subject of a clause is "we" or "I," the pronouns are elided. The experience is presented by selecting the images, ordering them into a sequence, eliding, and by using white space to indicate timing. Snyder would conceive these techniques as nonassertive; they do not change the experience, but merely allow the rhythmic contour naturally inherent in it to appear more plainly. Such techniques express a spiritual discipline—the abnegation of the ego in concentrating on the immediately given. Moreover, the poem detaches itself not only from the ego but from imagination, intellectuality, and cultural resonance. It does not compare or juxtapose this experience with anything else, criticize it, allude to other poems, or in any way poeticize, enrich, ironize, or deviate from the thing at hand. Unity with nature or reality is to be achieved by being wholly where you are. As Snyder explains his Zen ideal, if you are sweeping the floor and thinking of Hegel, your mind is not focused with your body. But if you are sweeping the floor and thinking of sweeping the floor, you are unified in the moment, and "Sweeping the floor becomes, then, the most important thing in the world. Which it is."

24

SYLVIA PLATH, ANNE SEXTON,
AND ADRIENNE RICH

OF the three writers treated in this chapter, Plath and Sexton are usually included with the Confessional poets of the United States. Adrienne Rich is not, though she has written intimately on personal emotions and experiences. Rich is the most important living poet of feminist ideology, and feminist readers have also been fascinated by Plath and Sexton, though in both poets they may find much with which they cannot sympathize—such as Plath's scorn of childless women. Feminist poetry can be in quite different styles, needless to say, and as rhetoric, argument, narrative, or commemoration it need not be personal. Rich's "Paula Becker to Clara Westhoff," for example, tells the story of two nineteenth-century artists and friends who found in their relationship with each other a support they could not find in their marriages.

Nevertheless, at the present time the finest poetry by feminists is likely to be in the Confessional style, and, conversely, Confessional poetry by women is of absorbing interest to feminist readers. For Confessional poetry renders personal experience or emotion as it actually is, regardless of social conventions. Moreover, Confessional poetry expresses truths and experience so painful that most people would suppress them. If, therefore, a woman resents her children, or feels victimized by a patriarchal society and revengeful toward it, the Confessional mode enables her to express such emotions directly, and, for readers, they have a documentary value. At this level the confession of women's experience reveals, at least as feminist readers interpret it, emotions that have persisted throughout history but have not hitherto been acknowledged. Once they are articulated, other women recognize them in themselves, and thus Confessional poetry tends to promote psychological liberation, the liberation that comes in freely seeing and talking about what had previously been repressed. Moreover, in all such confession there is an additional revolutionary impulse. The confessor is in effect including what she confesses within the realm of human nature. She is challenging moral or social assumptions by widening our notion of the "normal."

The subject of this chapter is neither feminist nor Confessional poetry as such, but their interfusion. Many other poets might also have been discussed, such as Muriel Rukeyser, Audre Lorde, Denise Levertov, and even Edna St. Vincent Millay, but most women poets of the twentieth century do not belong in this chapter because they have not written personally and intimately. Marianne Moore and Elizabeth Bishop are examples, and so also are Laura Riding, Hilda Doolittle, and Josephine Miles. Their experience as women can be extrapolated from their poetry, particularly with the help of biographies, but it is seldom directly their subject.

Most readers have taken the poems of Diane Wakoski (b. 1937) as expressions of her personal life and emotions. She, however, insists that the protagonists are invented, and that she is a "personal" but not a "confessional" poet. Most of her poems have characters and a story, but they also somewhat resemble dream sequences and musical progressions; they enact, Wakoski says, "the process of making an idea into music," of which the essence is "motion." She is fascinated by the structural uses of digression. She composes spontaneously, writing with long lines and lavish words, linking her thoughts by association. She has been influenced by the Confessional movement, contemporary open form, and Surrealism. The subjects of her poems are the woes of the family and the disappointments of romantic love.

Though the Confessional mode in poetry was a reaction against the New Criticism, it was, as I noted, largely created by poets who had first formed their style under New Critical influences, such as Robert Lowell, John Berryman, and Sylvia Plath. Moreover, these poets were unusually acute in introspection and knowledgeable about psychoanalysis. Because of their literary training and personal awareness, they took for granted the complexity of any emotional state. In creating the Confessional mode with its shock effects, they did not simplify their self-perceptions. Thus as it developed Confessional poetry presupposed that feelings are ambivalent—in fact, the ambivalence may be what is confessed—and within the Confessional mode to express a simple, integral state of mind would be implausible. For this reason also it is an appropriate mode for feminist poets. The temptation of all ideologically committed writers is rhetoric, that is, a poetry designed more to rally and persuade than to question and explore. But the Confessional style makes rhetoric impossible.

SYLVIA PLATH

Sylvia Plath (1932–63) grew up in Boston, Massachusetts, where her father, Otto, taught at Boston University. A German immigrant, Otto Plath was an entomologist who specialized in bumblebees. He was, Plath told a college roommate, "an autocrat . . . I adored and despised him, and I probably wished many times that he were dead. When he obliged me and died, I imagined that I had killed him." After his death in 1940 Plath, as she later said, was never happy again. But she led a life that was normal in every way except for its unusual success, as teenagers measure this in popularity and prizes. Psychologically she was seriously troubled, however, though she seems to have been largely unconscious of this, and at the end of her junior year at Smith College she attempted suicide. *The Bell Jar* (1963), an autobiographical novel, describes her experiences in this period of her life. Recovering, as it seemed, she graduated with highest honors from Smith and studied in Cambridge, England, on a Fulbright fellowship. There she met and married the English poet Ted Hughes. She and Hughes lived in Cambridge, and then in the United States in or near Boston, supporting themselves by fellowships and teaching. Returning to England at the end of 1959, they settled in London and then in rural Devon, where they bought a house. A volume of Plath's poems was published (*The Colossus*, 1960), and two children were born. In 1962, however, Hughes was seeing another woman, and he left Plath in September. Plath stayed on for a while in the Devon house, where since June 1962 she had been composing the poems that were to make her posthumously famous. In October poems came at the rate of almost one a day. "Writing like mad," she said on October 12. "Terrific stuff, as if domesticity had choked me." And on October 16, "I am writing the best poems of my life; they will make my name." In December she moved with her two children to a flat in London, and in February she committed suicide.

Many of the poems of Plath's last year appeared in *Ariel* (1965). Coming after Lowell's *Life Studies* (and with a lurid introduction to *Ariel* by Lowell), the poems were read under the Confessional convention that the speaker was Plath voicing her own emotions. These included murderous rage and headlong suicidalness, and readers were strongly moved to pity and horror. They assumed that the poems, or the states of mind they expressed, preluded her suicide. Biographical and psychoanalytic curiosity excited many readers, and the volume made a strong impact. Critics since have emphasized other ways of viewing these poems. They are read as expressions of women's emotions in a society that frustrates the self-fulfillment of women. From this point of view the states of mind they reveal are not particular to Plath, except that Plath, like every good poet, was exceptionally aware of her feelings and articulate about them. Or the poems are read as versions of myths, or as conflating the personal with the mythical. All Plath's late poems now seem more complexly ambivalent than they did at first. Even "Daddy," a poem of hatred of the father and husband, is now read as also expressing love. The poems are brilliant in imagination and craftsmanship, and would not otherwise have gripped readers as they did.

The themes of the *Ariel* poems had appeared in Plath's earlier work without much exciting anyone, including herself. She referred to these poems, or many of them, as "death-wishes," but their style was death to the emotion. Not that her writing before

1962 was inept. She was formal, careful, and symbolical in the American academic style of the 1950s. But her poems moved slowly. Her sentences were complexly structured. Her lines were often clotted with emphases and arty in play of sounds. "Suicide off Egg Rock," for example, describes how "spindrift / Raveled wind-ripped from the crest of the wave," framing "Raveled" by "sp*indr*ift . . . w*ind-ri*pped." With their echoing sounds and crowded accents (ˊ ˋ ˊ x ˊ ˋ), the words almost compose a tongue-twister. Plath's style was influenced by that of Hughes and sometimes by Auden, Dylan Thomas, and Robert Lowell. Roethke, whom she read in 1959, was important to her later poetry, since she learned from him to write short, almost gnomic sentences of fast-moving, freely irrational assertion, as in "Poem for a Birthday" (1959):

> Let me sit in a flowerpot,
> The spiders won't notice.
> My heart is a stopped geranium.

The generalizations take us to 1960, when *The Colossus* was published. The most important poems in this volume were the title poem and "The Beekeeper's Daughter," an intense, erotically troubled, mythically allusive poem which foreshadowed the greater work to come. The next two years are usually described as her "transitional" period. The best poems of this period are "Parliament Hill Fields" and "Elm," the former coming at the start of 1961 and the latter in April 1962. These and most of the poems written between them suggest a simmering irritability and psychological malaise. Several poems express feelings of being a demonic god. In "Blackberrying" the berries "love me . . . They accommodate themselves to my milkbottle, flattening their sides"; in "The Moon and the Yew Tree" the grasses "unload their griefs on my feet as if I were God, / Prickling my ankles and murmuring of their humility"; in her role as God the speaker's response is sardonic or indifferent. The metaphors of "Elm," the monologue of a tree, suggest violence, suffering, and murder. In one eerie passage the elm says,

> I am inhabited by a cry.
> Nightly it flaps out
> Looking, with its hooks, for something to love.

I am terrified by this dark thing.

As an image of love the owl grips with its claws and kills. It in-habits the elm yet is not within its control. At a deeper level "this dark thing" of which the elm is "terrified" may be Plath's sense of the psychological trap she was in.

As compared with Plath's final ones, these "transitional" poems (though not "Elm") are still generally slow and obvious. In her last nine months Plath speeded up her verse partly by shortening her lines and stanzas and partly by ellipsis and en-jambment. Her stronger impact depended partly on her rapid-ity and even more on her content and tone. She mocked, raged, threatened, and triumphed, sometimes demonically. She voiced fantasies of destroying the world. Violent emotion was conveyed in images of disgust, sickness, torture, and Nazi and nuclear hor-ror—"a stink of fat and baby crap," "cancerous pallors," "the rack and the screw," "Dachau," "Hiroshima." In her flat, direct, colloquial statements of emotion, repetition suggested frenzy or panic—"hate/ Up to my neck,/ Thick, thick"; "They will not smell my fear, my fear, my fear."

If this were all, we might read her poems once, and find that enough. But Plath was strikingly original and fertile in imagi-native invention, in metaphors and fables, and her lyrics, brief though they are, set many metaphors going at once. The feel-ings they articulate are as complicated as they are intense. In "Purdah" the speaker compares herself to a woman in India hid-den behind purdah screens, to a jade statue, to an "enigmatical" image of the Buddha, to the moon, and to a small jeweled doll. The overlapping metaphors suggest that her self is suppressed, that she merely reflects whatever light shines on her, and that she is a costly, glittering object in the possession of her "bride-groom . . . Lord of the mirrors!" In the course of her poem her self—or another self—emerges as a powerful, queenly figure intent on destruction. In the final lines she imagines herself as Clytemnestra, murdering Agamemnon in his bath by throwing a cloak over him and stabbing through it.

> I shall unloose—
> From the small jeweled
> Doll he guards like a heart—

The lioness,
The shriek in the bath,
The cloak of holes.

Another of Plath's strengths is that the same motifs recur and resonate from poem to poem. "The Applicant," a bitterly ironical lyric, may be read as a woman's reply to a proposal of marriage. She offers different selves, and all are false. One of her selves is a "living doll" which (in allusion to wedding anniversaries) will turn silver and gold. Thus the jeweled doll and statue images of "Purdah" are repeated. "Lady Lazarus" is a rebirth fantasy. At the same time, however, it is a poem on failed suicides, which it views with contempt. As in "Purdah" and "The Applicant" the speaker has been made—or has made herself—into an object and been put on exhibition. She compares herself to a circus performer whose stunt is to die and rise from the grave. Again her sense of victimization transforms itself into fantasies of power and revenge:

I rise with my red hair
And I eat men like air.

The speaker also compares herself to an *objet d'art,* "The pure gold baby/ That melts to a shriek." Here again she is something made, owned, and operated by someone else. In one aspect the "gold baby" is a contraption like a doll that cries. Its shriek is an exhibition to entertain a crowd. In another strand of metaphor it is a baby thrown into the furnace of a Nazi death camp. In still another implication its fiery shriek voices rage and threat.

The poems of Plath's last nine months make their effect through their combination of velocity and emotional force with density of implication and extreme ambivalence of feeling. Were her poetry less harrowing she might be viewed as witty. But she is not always harrowing, for her states of mind in her final months included resolve and hope. It is now known that Hughes, in putting together the *Ariel* volume after Plath's death, omitted some of the poems she had intended to include, added others, and rearranged the order of the poems. Had he followed Plath's intentions, the volume would have made a different impression. She had planned to conclude the *Ariel* volume with a sequence of five poems on bees ("The Bee Meeting," "The Arrival of the Bee Box," "Stings," "The Swarm," "Wintering"). "I/

Have a self to recover, a queen," the speaker says in "Stings," and if this queen turns out to be another Clytemnestra in a fantasy of revenge, in "Wintering" the identification with the bees implies survival:

> The bees are all women,
> Maids and the long royal lady.
> They have got rid of the men,
>
> The blunt, clumsy stumblers, the boors.
> Winter is for women—
> The woman, still at her knitting,
> At the cradle of Spanish walnut,
> Her body a bulb in the cold and too dumb to think.
>
> Will the hive survive, will the gladiolas
> Succeed in banking their fires
> To enter another year?
> What will they taste of, the Christmas roses?
> The bees are flying. They taste the spring.

ANNE SEXTON

Except for her poetry and madness, Anne Sexton (1928–74) née Harvey, lived as a suburban housewife. Symptoms of serious mental instability had shown themselves in adolescence or earlier, and in 1954 she attempted suicide. Two years later she was again placed in a mental hospital, again attempted suicide, and was thenceforth under constant psychiatric care. In December 1956, her psychiatrist encouraged her to start writing poetry, to which she devoted endless hours. Its inception in therapy formed her poetry from the start, for her aim as a poet was to uncover painful, repressed emotions. She admired poetry that "reaches down and touches the inmost part of the reader." A sentence from Kafka's letters, which she chose as an epigraph for her second volume, states her simple intention: "a book should serve as the ax for the frozen sea within us."

She had read almost no poetry until she started writing it. In *New Poets of England and America* (1957), edited by Donald Hall and others, she discovered William Snodgrass' "Heart's Needle," and the poem "held me and hurt me and made me cry." At Snodgrass' advice, she took a class with Robert Lowell. Sylvia Plath and George Starbuck were in the same class, and after school the three students regularly examined their lines over martinis at the Ritz. Sexton also formed a lifelong friendship with Maxine Kumin.

In 1960 Houghton Mifflin published Sexton's first volume, *To Bedlam and Part Way Back*. These poems dwelled on her struggle against madness, her stay in an insane asylum, and her gradual recovery. Reviewers immediately classified Sexton with the Confessional poets, and her next volume, *All My Pretty Ones* (1962), consolidated her position. Though these early poems in meters and stanzas were much more carefully worked and heavily revised than her later ones, which were in free verse, her control was nevertheless uncertain from the start and remained so. When her phrasing was flatly direct, it was often inert, and when she reached for "style," she fell into arty absurdities. Her emotions were interesting, but were impoverished by her expression of them. Moreover, though she was resolved to be unsparingly truthful, her truth was more dramatic than meditative. She articulated her emotion or emotional conflict as she felt it, but she did not criticize it. The humor and poise Lowell maintained even in *Life Studies* seemed to her evasions.

Yet Sexton deserved her fame. Her detailed, intimate, physical descriptions of illness, hospital routine, childbearing and nursing, surgical operations, and so forth were relatively new in poetry. Her strong emotions—resentments of her parents and psychiatrists, fears of cancer, suicidal and sexual yearnings— have the typical power of Confessional poetry; if they are exhibitionistic and shocking, they are also liberating. Thus in "The Operation" she remembers her mother dying of cancer and her "fear" while

> the snoring mouth gapes
> and is not dear.

The lines certainly express what many people besides Sexton have felt on such occasions. Yet Sexton must certainly have felt other emotions besides fear and antipathy as she watched her mother, and thus the truthful lines seem also naive.

Sexton captured the large, new readership in the 1960s of women who welcomed literature that addressed their own experience. She allowed readers to share her life vicariously, and it was a sensationally painful life. "She did what few did," as Robert Lowell put it, "cut a figure." Given her late start and difficulties, her career was a remarkable success. Through poetry she found self-fulfillment, self-respect, fame, friends, readers, and students—she taught writing at Boston University. Yet her mental illness continued, and after *Live or Die* (1966) the value of her poetry declined. She committed suicide in 1974.

ADRIENNE RICH

Adrienne Rich (b. 1929) graduated from Radcliffe College in 1951, married shortly thereafter, and had three children. In the 1960s she moved from Cambridge, Massachusetts, to New York City and began to teach. She was deeply committed and active in the protest against the war in Vietnam and in other radical political movements, including feminism and the black struggle for racial equality. She left her husband, and in 1976 she affirmed herself as lesbian in a sequence of twenty-one love sonnets and in other publications. She is the leading poet of the radical feminist movement in the United States. Her special gifts as a poet are the honesty and complexity of her emotions and perceptions, together with her power to articulate these in images and metaphors.

Rich started writing poems in her childhood. By the time she graduated from Radcliffe, she was astonishingly proficient for her age, as one sees in her first book, *A Change of World* (1951), which was chosen by Auden for publication in the Yale Younger Poets series. Her poems in this volume were in the formalist style of the period, and were modeled on Frost, Yeats, Stevens, Auden, and Richard Wilbur.

In aspiring to be a poet, Rich says, she at first suppressed her identity as a woman. She argues that a poet was assumed to be masculine. A woman, it was accepted, would be at best a minor poet. In several poems, even as late as 1963, she spoke of or through males when it would have been more natural for her to speak of women or of herself. Her early volumes, then, show the normal conformities of a beginning poet and also special compliances as a woman poet. These acts of submission did not

motivate her radical feminism in the 1970s, but they were resented. Eventually she rebelled against the male tradition of poetry.

By 1963, when her third volume appeared, Rich had abandoned formalism. Her poems were no longer in meters and
stanzas, and depended on lineation, juxtaposition, and metaphor. If her style was Confessional, her subjects were not in the
sensational register of Lowell, Berryman, Sexton, and Plath. In
her poems an "I" voiced painful, intimate feelings in circumstances readers assumed were Rich's own.

To judge from her poems, the next ten years were hard. We
read of restlessness in feminine roles ("Snapshots of a Daughter-
in-Law"), ambivalence and disillusion in marriage ("A Marriage
in the 'Sixties"), gloomy obsession with death ("5:30 A.M."), impulses to live in the moment and in sex ("Holding Out," "Abnegation," "Two Songs"), fantasies of absolute liberation ("November 1968"), and resolves to start over again ("Diving into the
Wreck"). She was—and is—acutely sensitive to the painfulness
of life ("Study of History," "From the Prison House") and to social oppression and injustice. By 1973 she was sharing the emotions of radical feminism ("Waking in the Dark," "Rape," "The
Ninth Symphony of Beethoven Understood at Last as a Sexual
Message").

A Richean emotional dialectic runs through this poetry. She
internalizes the expectations of others, feels that she is not being
herself, not leading her own life, and rebels. "Snapshots of a
Daughter-in-Law" shows her fulfilling the role of a housewife
but "glowering" as she wipes the teaspoons. "Necessities of Life,"
a spiritual autobiography, expresses her fear of being melted or
swallowed into lives that are not authentically hers. She compares herself to Jonah, who was swallowed and then vomited out
of the belly of the whale. The allusion expresses both Rich's fears
of being engulfed and her fantasies of violent deliverance. In
"Snapshots of a Daughter-in-Law" the speaker might have been
compared to Jonah, the whale being her kitchen, but she was
compared to Joan of Arc instead, and heard voices saying, "Have
no patience," "Be insatiable," "Save yourself; others you cannot
save."

After *Diving into the Wreck* (1973) Rich wrote less immediately
of her own circumstances, and devoted herself as a writer more

to other women as her subject matter and purpose. She portrayed women in order to rouse feminist consciousness in women readers. "Phantasia for Elvira Shatayev" (1978) is such a poem; it celebrates a group of women mountain climbers who died near the summit of Lenin Peak. Despite their death, the poem imagines their climb as a fulfillment in love, courage, power, and achievement. Frequently Rich presents nameless women of the past, as in "From an Old House in America," a beautiful poem that commemorates the lonely, stunted lives of immigrant or pioneer women in their patriarchal society.

25

BLACK POETS OF AMERICA

I N the first volume of this history I traced the work of black poets in the United States from the turn of the century into the 1930s. I described the poems in the black dialect of the minstrel shows by Paul Lawrence Dunbar and his followers and the effort of later poets, such as Langston Hughes and Sterling Brown, to express racial experience in a style that would speak to black people. To this end these poets used dialects far more authentically than had the previous generation of poets, and in form and content they alluded to the music of blacks—blues, jazz, spirituals, and work and folk songs. I discussed the Harlem Renaissance of the 1920s—the burst of creativity centered in Harlem, in New York City—and the debates among poets in that period. Should they, as Countee Cullen believed, write in the same styles and for the same audience as their white contemporaries? Or should their style, content, and audience be racially distinctive?

By the 1930s poetry by American blacks was shaped by factors that still strongly influence it today: exploitation of the distinctive speech and culture of blacks as a new basis for poetry and the use of poetry to promote the advance of black people. Since then there have been three phases. In the 1940s and 1950s poets such as Gwendolyn Brooks, Melvin Tolson, and Robert Hayden wrote on racial themes in Modernist styles. Hayden's fine "Middle Passage," for example, reflected the high Modernism of Eliot's *The Waste Land* and Crane's *The Bridge*. Hayden also went through a "Baroque period," as he called it, in which he was influenced by the New Critical style, as was Tolson. At this time most poets were integrationist. They felt that to write well in styles approved by the literary world and to be praised by white critics would contribute to the black racial cause. When in 1945 Gwendolyn Brooks had a collection of poems accepted by Harper and Brothers, she and her friends were jubilant. She had then no thought that she should not give her poems to a white publisher.

During the 1960s, however, many younger black poets espoused a separatist ideology. Black Pride, Black Power, Black Is Beautiful, Black Nationalism, and the Black Aesthetic were proclaimed as slogans of political, psychological, and cultural emancipation. Departments of Afro-American studies were set up in universities, courses in English departments also concentrated on literature by blacks, and courses in the history of the United States traced the experience of blacks with a greater truthfulness and realism. Many black writers felt that a sense of the exclusion of blacks was built into the English language, and they attempted to modify the language for the sake of transforming consciousness. Images of blackness, for example, were deliberately given positive associations, as in Amiri Baraka's poem "leroy." Conventions of American culture and especially of popular culture were similarly challenged. "The three white men in the film *Gunga Din* who kill off hundreds of Indians," as Baraka pointed out in a 1966 essay, "are part of the image of white men. The various black porters, gigglers, ghostchumps and punkish Indians" of the "public image the white man has fashioned to characterize the Black Men" are imposed on black people every day by "white magic, i.e., television, movies, radio, etc." Exorcising "whiteness" from themselves, Baraka and other poets at this time frankly voiced hatred and menace toward whites, and they also addressed political appeals to black readers or hearers. "Blackness" was a prized quality, and endless thought and discussion went into defining it. At the same time there was heightened interest in the Caribbean and Africa—their social customs, cultures, and arts—and a feeling of solidarity with blacks throughout the world. "The problem of the de-Americanization of black people," Addison Gayle explained in 1971, "lies at the heart" of the Black Aesthetic program." This militant, separatist phase, from approximately 1966 to 1974, justifies my discussing poetry by blacks in a chapter by itself, as opposed, for example, to dwelling on Tolson in connection with Allen Tate, or Michael Harper with Robert Lowell, or Baraka with Olson, Ginsberg, and O'Hara.

The new militance had profound effects on poetry written by blacks, but gradually the effects were paradoxical. In the 1960s poems were often judged by a political criterion—did they contribute to black liberation?—and most poets shared this point of view. Militance summoned a host of poets; more blacks wrote than ever before, and new publishers and magazines arose, so that it was easier than before for blacks to be published. Sociologically this militant, separatist phase of poetry by blacks in the 1960s had many characteristics of an avant-garde movement. It was anti-establishment, continually self-dividing into factions, preoccupied with defining itself and its aims, prolific of manifestos, and enormously confident of its own vitality and importance. One difference was that black poets could tell themselves they were speaking for a large community—black people. This claim was exaggerated, but white avant-garde poets cannot make it at all.

But this phase of black poetry died away, chiefly because of changes in the political mood of blacks. As an additional cause, the demand that poetry conform politically came gradually to seem to the poets to be a form of oppression. In solidarity with the "people" one risked losing the complexity and depth of the particular case. Even writers who were themselves militant could not allow black political and cultural leaders to prescribe their emotion or style. In fact, as black militance of the 1960s strengthened individual pride or self-respect, it undermined the authority of the militants. Liberated individuals would not conform.

In style the younger poets of the 1960s emphasized the black cultural heritage and the idiom of contemporary urban blacks in the Northern cities. The poetic ethos of the 1960s allowed unprecedented realism in rendering this speech. Many black poets also reflected the Postmodernist influences of the time—

William Carlos Williams, the Beats, Confessional verse, Surrealism and Dada, the Projectivist theories of Charles Olson, Black Mountain style, and pop art. Often these poets—Baraka is a typical case—were in the paradoxical situation of being avant-garde in style and populist in intention. Like the young English poets of the 1930s, they wished to express the "people" and voice their solidarity with them, but they also wished to employ Modernist technique. They could not do both successfully in the same poem, and hence wrote sometimes in an accessible, public style and sometimes with Modernist inwardness and complexity. This self-division is of course characteristic of literary intellectuals in the twentieth century. If their works are politically engaged and also technically complex, the second motive makes the first ineffective, since the "people" cannot read what is supposed to instruct, rally, or inspire them. Poets of the political right, such as Pound, are as much in this bind as those of the left.

Both the Confessional conventions of the time and the insistence on Black Pride encouraged black poets to write frankly and intimately of their personal lives—something few black poets had done earlier. By the middle of the 1970s the self and its concerns might be represented without political intention and even without self-consciousness about race or color. Many poems of Audre Lorde (b. 1934), for example, express experiences in sexual love, raising children, and other intimate aspects of a woman's life with no special emphasis that she is a black woman. Clarence Major (b. 1936) often pursues philosophical reflections that have no racial reference. Before his years of racial militance, Baraka could compose poems of existentialist awareness such as any New York intellectual, white or black, might have composed at the time—for example, "Preface to a Twenty Volume Suicide Note"—and his recent Socialist poems are similarly not racial. Most poetry by blacks does continue to express racial consciousness, race being, as James Weldon Johnson put it many years ago, "perforce the thing that the American Negro poet knows best." My point is merely that poetry by American blacks is now freer to adopt any contemporary style and is in subject matter more individualistic and ranging than in the past. In the poetry of blacks at present we find different writers following their own lines of development, not a distinct movement.

The great predecessor of all contemporary black poets is

Langston Hughes, whose career I discussed in the previous volume. In this chapter I concentrate particularly on the poetry of Margaret Walker, Gwendolyn Brooks, Melvin Tolson, and Robert Hayden. The work of a few younger poets—Baraka, Harper, and Lorde—is noticed more briefly at the end.

MELVIN TOLSON

Melvin B. Tolson (1900–66) worked occasionally as an organizer among poor sharecroppers and also served as mayor of his town, but by profession he was a college teacher. He found time for writing by getting up in the middle of the night. He received many awards and honors in the last two years of his life, but since then his work has been somewhat neglected. One reason lies in the general rejection of the New Critical mode. Another has to do with Tolson's ideas on racial issues, for his views were antipodal to those of most young black poets in the 1960s. That a black writer should, for example, allude as Tolson does to Greek mythology, calling the common people "Gaea's children" ("The *Hohere* of Gaea's children/ is beyond the *dérèglement de tous les sens*"), seemed to them strange and reprehensible. The praise Tolson had received from white critics also offended the younger black writers, since whites, they believed, could not be qualified readers of poetry by blacks, and they were embarrassed that Tolson had been pleased by such praise. Their view of Tolson was unjust, for it was unhistorical and estimated him by the ideals of their own period rather than of the earlier one in which he had matured. He had studied and learned from great poets since the time of Shakespeare, and he sought to make his poetry worthy to be included in an anthology with theirs.

The development of Tolson's style followed that of the Modernist movement in general but with a time lag, since his situation in Langston, Oklahoma, was provincial. His first important work, *A Gallery of Harlem Portraits*, which he composed in 1932 but which was not published until after his death, was in the tradition of Masters' *Spoon River Anthology*. In *Rendezvous with America* (1944) his style was still that of the period before Eliot and Pound. Especially it recalled the rhetorical, patriotic poetry of Sandburg, Lindsay, and the Benéts. But now Tolson began to model his work on high Modernist poets. In notes for a speech he gave in 1949 Tolson wrote, "the time has come for a New Negro Poetry for the New Negro . . . The standard of poetry has changed completely. Negroes must become aware of this. This is the age of T. S. Eliot . . . Imitation must be in technique only. We have a rich heritage of folk lore and history. . . . we must study the techniques of Robert Lowell, Dylan Thomas, Carlos Williams, Ezra Pound, Karl Shapiro, W. H. Auden." Around 1951 he sent his *Libretto for the Republic of Liberia* to Allen Tate. This poem of 769 lines was published with seventeen pages of notes in 1953. Tate's preface claimed that "for the first time . . . a Negro poet has assimilated completely the full poetic language of his time, and, by implication, the language of the Anglo-American poetic tradition." By the "poetic language of his time" Tate meant the New Critical mode, the formal, ironic, condensed, allusive, academic style of the period. Tolson used the same style in his final volume, *Harlem Gallery: Book I, The Curator* (1965), a reworking of his earlier *A Gallery of Harlem Portraits*.

The *Libretto for the Republic of Liberia* begins:

> *Liberia?*
> No micro-footnote in a bunioned book
> Homed by a pedant
> With a gelded look
> You are
> The ladder of survival dawn men saw
> In the quicksilver sparrow that slips
> The eagle's claw

If this seems packed and difficult, it is airy compared to later stanzas in the poem. The texture of the *Libretto* and the *Harlem Gallery* is woven of metaphors, phrases in foreign languages, erudite puns, poeticisms, high rhetoric, motifs from black spirituals and blues, slang, and literary and historical allusions. (Typically the last two lines quoted above are adapted, Tolson's notes tell us, from Dryden's *All For Love*, II,i. His style combines jazzy, driving, climaxing rhythms with intellectual argument, directness with obliquity, and intensity with complexity of emotion. It is impressive, sometimes powerful, at other times eccentric, and generally keeps readers at a distance. It would seem strangely artificial, except that it is so typical of its school.

The content of Tolson's poetry was racial in the sense that he wrote on black character, life, and history. Moreover, his poetry contributed to racial liberation through the emotions and attitudes he expressed. But Tolson did not believe that poetry could or should have a distinctively black style, and so far as his intention as an artist was influenced by racial considerations, he wished to show that a black could write as well as whites in the accepted style of the age. His vision of America was similarly integrationist. America, he said in *Rendezvous with America*, is "A magnificent cosmorama with myriad patterns of colors . . . A cosmopolitan orchestra with a thousand instruments playing." He valued the variety and diversity of an ethnically plural society, and he believed that whites and blacks must and will work together for the common good.

ROBERT HAYDEN

The story of Robert Hayden's (1913–80) career is a moving one of integrity amid difficulties. Born as Asa Sheffey in a black ghetto in Detroit and abandoned by his parents, he was brought up by neighbors, who renamed him. Though his eyesight was severely limited from birth, he haunted the public library, and by the age of sixteen he had resolved to become a poet. In spite of being poor, he was able to obtain a college education, and made his living as a college teacher, first at Fisk University (1946–69) and then at the University of Michigan. He received hardly any recognition until 1966, when a jury headed by Langston Hughes awarded him the prize for poetry at the Festival of Negro Arts in Dakar, Senegal. Henceforth his work was increasingly known, but recognition brought bitter attacks from militant black writers. For though most of Hayden's poetry deals with black experience in the United States, he also wrote on other subjects, and he frankly declared that black poets should not limit themselves to "racial utterance." He also believed that poetry by blacks should be judged by the same standards that were "applied to the work of other poets."

Hayden's poems characterize people and tell stories. His methods range from traditional narrative, as in "The Ballad of Sue Ellen Westerfield," to Modernist discontinuity, allusion, and

collage, as in "Middle Passage" and "Runagate Runagate."
Among his poems on personal themes, the childhood recollections ("Those Winter Sundays," "The Whipping") are especially
sensitive and moving. But generally his best poems are on black
historical subjects. In "Middle Passage" Hayden quotes fragments from diaries and speeches of slavers to render the crossing from Africa. "Runagate Runagate" is about the slaves escaping from the South: "when shall I reach," the fugitive asks, "that
somewhere/morning and keep on going and never turn back
and keep on going?" "The Dream" contrasts the black fantasies
of liberation during the Civil War with the realities of that experience. In such poems Hayden's themes and emotions were
those of a people, and except when the speakers were white, the
diction, syntax, rhythms, and allusions also reflected folk expe- 7
rience and expression. Even during his "Baroque period" of the
1940s and 1950s, Hayden's style was not as intellectualized as
Tolson's. Honest poems on the historical experience of blacks
can hardly be eupeptic, but Hayden always concluded on a note
of hope. "Runagate Runagate" ends with the slave not caught
and still heading north. The final section of "Middle Passage"
deals with Cinquez, the leader of the slaves who took over the
ship *Amistad*. The crossing from Africa was, the poem concludes,
a "Voyage through death to life upon these shores."

All that learning, intelligence, taste, sensitivity, and care can
do, Hayden accomplished. He rewrote constantly, and he
handled several different forms and styles superlatively. In addition to traditional narrative, personal lyric, and high Modernist montage, I should also mention his ballads and uses of ballad
techniques, as in "Mourning Poem for the Queen of Sunday,"
his remarkable sonnet "Frederick Douglass," couched in a flowing rhetoric akin to that of a political speech, and his lovely
songs, such as "O Daedalus, Fly Away Home":

> Drifting night in the windy pines;
> night is a laughing, night is a longing.
> Pretty Malinda, come to me.
>
> Night is a mourning juju man
> weaving a wish and a weariness together
> to make two wings.
>
> *O fly away home fly away.*

Margaret Walker (b. 1915) received an M.A. and later a Ph.D. in writing from the University of Iowa, and published novels as well as poems. She taught in a college in Jackson, Mississippi. Her first volume, *For My People* (1942), began with generalizing, declamatory poems on the history of her race. Couched in long free-verse lines, these rhetorical poems were perhaps influenced by the work of Carl Sandburg. For the 1940s they were un-usually militant. A second section of *For My People* presented characters from black folklore, such as "Bag-Man Stagolee" and "Poppa Chicken." In these poems Walker used dialect. Finally, there was a group of personal sonnets in standard English; in the most memorable of these, "Childhood," Walker recollected the impoverished miners and sharecroppers she had known as a child in a region

> where sentiment and hatred still held sway
> and only bitter land was washed away.

She published no more volumes of poetry until the 1970s. In *Prophets for a New Day* (1970) some of the poems dated from the 1930s and 1940s, but in others she was moved to utterance by the civil rights struggle of the 1960s. As part of her rhetorical strategy she conflated contemporary black leaders and civil rights fighters with the ancient Hebrew prophets. The volume included a moving elegy "For Andy Goodman—Michael Schwerner—and James Chaney," three civil rights workers who were murdered in Mississippi in 1964. As well as any other poem by her, this one shows the strengths and limitations of Walker's rhetoric. It is generalized and somewhat predictable—for ex-ample, in its images of "green Spring returning" and "golden Autumn leaves"—and in places it too closely imitates Whitman. Yet in total effect the poem is sensitive, passionate, and noble.

GWENDOLYN BROOKS

Gwendolyn Brooks (b. 1917) grew up in Chicago, where she still lives. The poems in her first volume, *A Street in Bronzeville* (1945), portrayed types of person and ways of life in the black areas of Chicago. That she took black urban life as her subject was not for programmatic reasons, but because it was what she

naturally knew, what roused her emotion. She has continued to
be the same type of poet. Her poems are personal responses to
particular events. The event may be something she saw across
the street or read about in the newspapers, but always there is
the integrity of a direct, personal emotion, and always there is
her interest in the world—the curiosity, humorous relish, sympathy, and caring that leads her to write, for example, about a
zoot-suiter named "Satin-Legs Smith," about old, impoverished
couples ("The Bean Eaters," "The Old-Marrieds"), street gangs
("The Blackstone Rangers," "We Real Cool"), whites visiting the
black ghettos ("The Lovers of the Poor," "I Love Those Little
Booths at Benvenuti's"), a "Boy Breaking Glass," "Malcolm X,"
"Martin Luther King Jr." and "Medgar Evers." She can satirize
and moralize, but usually she just realizes and presents.

In *Annie Allen* (1949) Brooks worked in the condensed, formal
style of the period, and the book won the Pulitzer Prize. She
believed that "The Negro poet's most urgent duty, at present, is
to polish his technique." By the 1960s she had become a rather
difficult poet, compact, elliptical, and sensitive to the multiple
connotations of words. In the late sixties she began to share the
militant and separatist feelings of younger black poets. Thereafter her impulses were divided. She believed a black poet
should try to reach ordinary blacks, and she voiced her emotions
of black pride and militance. In this sense she became a spokesman for the "people." But she never attempted to express the
"people" rather than herself, and she did not modify her style
to make it more accessible, a point that irritated militant critics.
Her poetry was and is realistic, shrewd, sensitive, empathetic,
and unsentimental.

AMIRI BARAKA (LEROI JONES)

Amiri Baraka (b. 1934) published under his given name,
LeRoi Jones, until 1968. He grew up in Newark, New Jersey,
graduated from Howard University, served in the U.S. Air
Force, and then, at the age of twenty-four, settled in Greenwich
Village in New York City, working in avant-garde bookstores and
editing little magazines. He made friends with fellow writers,
including Allen Ginsberg, Charles Olson, and Frank O'Hara,

and married a white woman, the marriage taking place in a Buddhist temple. His poems, essays, and especially his dramas (*The
Toilet*, 1963; *Dutchman* and *The Slave*, 1964) brought him fame.
At this time Baraka was living in a white Bohemian milieu,
and though his subject matter included race and tensions between the races, his ethos was not that of black separatism but
of the Beats. In other words, he assailed the false values, loveless
Puritanism, hypocrisy, and so forth, of the American middle
class, black and white, and wrote for himself and for fellow hipsters. If he hoped for revolution, it was not a revolution of or
for blacks only but a general liberation of consciousness, and he
tried to achieve this in himself. He was not sanguine, however.
In his first two volumes, which appeared in 1961 and 1964, his
utterance was often disillusioned and depressed. Death was both
dreaded and longed for as a refuge. Life seemed emotionally
dry, vacuous, and meaningless. He was living in the Waste Land,
and Eliot was a strong influence, as one sees in numerous echoes
and allusions—for example, to "Tiresias'/ weathered cock." He
had the clear insight of the depressed mind into the twisted
workings of the human psyche, and knew that

> Love is an evil word.
> Turn it backwards/ see, see what I mean?
> An evol word.

His style varied from poem to poem but was always that of the
anti-academic rebels of his generation. If there was a period
style based on William Carlos Williams, Charles Olson, Allen
Ginsberg and other Beats, and Frank O'Hara, Kenneth Koch,
and the New York School, Baraka exemplified it. "In Memory
of Radio," from which I just quoted, included references to pop
culture in the style of O'Hara, Ginsbergian word jamming—"I
cannot even order you to *gaschamber satori* like Hitler"—and various Projectivist mannerisms of Olson, such as eccentric typography and punctuation and extremely varied line lengths. The
wordplay of finding "evol" in "love" was itself typical of Olson,
Duncan, and Creeley.

Meanwhile, however, Baraka had visited Cuba in 1960. Seeing
a real revolution seems to have sharpened his anger against the
American "Moloch," and it also helped him to see that the Beat
stance was narcissistic and politically ineffective. Increasingly his

poems satirized his Bohemian friends and their way of life,
which was still also his own. Black militancy was growing, and
Baraka shared it. He was attacked for his marriage to a white
woman and his integrationist way of life, and these reproaches,
with other tensions, contributed to upheavals in his way of life.
In 1965 he obtained a divorce and moved to Harlem. Around
1967 he converted to the Muslim faith and took his new name.
He founded and supported black cultural institutions, devoted
himself to practical politics in his home city of Newark, and became a leading spokesman for the black separatist movement.
As Werner Sollors has shown, Baraka's black political militancy
retained elements of Bohemian ideology. He continued to assail
the black middle class, and he also evidently assumed that political change comes about not only through votes, demonstrations, and riots but also through a change in consciousness.

From approximately 1965 to 1974 his poems were of two
kinds. A great many aimed to change the consciousness of
blacks, and were in this sense political. In these poems Baraka
preached or supported racial pride, unity, and militancy. Sometimes he warned and threatened, as in the fine "We Own the
Night," where he indulged his frequent fantasy of magical
power: "Black arts," he said, are being brewed in "black labs of
the heart." Poems such as "SOS" and "It's Nation Time" summoned all blacks to rise and band together; their simple, rousing
style was wonderfully effective in public recitation. Often his
poems employed the street language of urban blacks and alluded in formal method to black music. Some were old-
fashioned rhetoric, as in his powerful utterance on the death of
Malcolm X, "A Poem for Black Hearts." Because of his political
purpose, his style gravitated toward the oral, that is, he wrote
poems that would be understood immediately when heard and
would move mass audiences.

But Baraka also continued to write poems that were not overt
expressions of "blackness," such as personal memories of childhood or philosophizing meditation. And even in his politically
motivated poems, his style might still reflect the artistic influences he had absorbed at the start of his career. Whatever he
thus lost in political effectiveness, he usually gained in poetic
interest. By 1974 he was disillusioned with racial politics, which
had, he believed, benefited only the black middle class. A Com-

munist revolution would rescue the poor, he believed, and he converted to Marxism. Henceforth his poems reflected his Socialist faith. Many of them were designed for recitation to the music of a band. In performance they could be stirring, but Baraka will be remembered as a poet for his work of the 1960s.

Audre Lorde (b. 1934) grew up in New York City, where she still lives, and many of her poems are about life in the city. Seeing a girl high on drugs in the subway ("To My Daughter the Junkie on a Train"), Lorde, herself a mother, both deplores and feels guilty:

> up and down across the aisle
> women avert their eyes
> as the other mothers who became useless
> curse our children who became junk.

In "One Year to Life on the Grand Central Shuttle" the subway becomes a symbol of the rush-hour, underground life that we all lead to some extent. Other poems reflect sensitively on her personal life—on erotic experience or childhood memories—and a number of especially fine poems express her feelings as she watches and reflects on her children growing up ("As I Grow Up Again," "Progress Report"). Still other poems speak bitterly of the contemporary experience of blacks in the United States. For example, "The Day They Eulogized Mahalia" juxtaposes the public eulogy of a famous black singer with the death on the same day of six black children in a fire in an underfunded day-care center.

Many of the poems of Michael Harper (b. 1938), a teacher at Brown University, allude in content and form to the music of blacks, especially blues and jazz. Poems such as "Dear John, Dear Coltrane" and "Effendi" read as though they were words passing through the mind while listening to music. In other poems Harper presents vignettes from American history, seen from the point of view of blacks. In *History Is Your Own Heartbeat* (1971) he interprets American history through metaphors of illness and gruesome hospital operations. Still other poems characterize particular persons, white and black, and many express emotions of personal life, particularly in relation to the poet's wife and children. Harper writes in a wide range of styles. At one extreme he is accessible, direct, and intense, as in "Reuben, Reuben," a lyric on the death of his infant son:

> a brown berry gone
> to rot just two days on the branch.

In other poems devices of Modernist and Postmodernist poetry—discontinuity, ellipsis, juxtaposition of fragments, ambiguous grammar, shifting reference—make Harper's work difficult. His emotions are complex and ambivalent, and typically they are also bitter, anguished, and accusatory.

26

MEDITATIONS OF THE SOLITARY MIND: JOHN ASHBERY AND A. R. AMMONS

ASHBERY and Ammons are our most important contemporary poets in the meditative mode. They do not render actions or characters, or write overtly about their experiences. Their poems are trains of thought, interior ruminations addressed to no audience. Ashbery enacts the mind's always baffled pursuit of reality; so does Ammons, but he also explores particular dilemmas and beliefs in epistemology and metaphysics. Neither poet is especially given to abstract terminology, but both convey philosophical *Weltanschauungen*. Ashbery represents the Impressionism of the 1880s and 1890s in a late, extreme form. In Ammons naturalistic premises conflict with the Romantic pantheism, transcendentalism, or organicism toward which he is also pulled.

The interior excursions of Ashbery and Ammons may be initiated by their doing or noticing something, but are in principle independent of the external world. The mind begins and continues on its own, as one idea, association, or memory evokes another in endless succession, and a poem, in their convention, is merely the written record of these mental acts. Both poets, in other words, could in theory and may in fact start writing with no preconception of the poem. To take Ammons, the simpler case, as an example, one may imagine him looking at puddles in his driveway, or walking along a tidal inlet, or watching a gold-finch in a cherry tree. He observes something, but it is an ordinary, familiar object, one that would not interest most persons. In it he sees motions, patterns, complex balances, details within details, and infinitely graduated transitions. Such, he tells himself, is reality. How, then, can the mind's paradigms ever correspond to it? The slightest thing, he reflects, is alive with particulars and processes; presumably they are infinite in number. Yet there is unity amid this multiplicity. Or is there? Is there something "underlying" that "weaves in and out" of all things ("Identity") or an "Overall" or "accounting" of the infinite particular accounts ("Corson's Inlet")? If there is a "center," can one ever be at it? Would one wish to be at the center, or, instead, at the circumference, the realm of the richly multiple and diverse? There is no reason except fatigue why such a meditation should ever end.

In Ashbery and Ammons the meditative mode coalesces with open form, which I described in Chapter 21, and much that was said in Chapter 21 is closely relevant to Ashbery and Ammons. The transformations of Ashbery's pronouns (an "I," for example, may become a "you" or a "they"), and the restriction of Ammons' punctuation to colons (an incomplete close indicating that more is to come) has naturally caused much comment, but such devices are widespread in contemporary poetry. Both Ashbery and Ammons tend to avoid climax, which they associate with closure. Ashbery produces grand effects and dissipates them in the same moment. Ammons usually prefers many phrases to one; a condensed phrase is a node, momentarily arresting our momentum through the poem, while many phrases, as in lists of objects or qualities, keep us moving onward at a steady pace. Ammons wants to flow "without flashing" like a brook in "abundant / tranquility" ("Easter Morning"). Both poets, then, subordinate climax to values of vital spontaneity and continual transition. Both tend to write longish to very long poems. Ashbery did not adopt the diary mode of the 1960s and 1970s, but Ammons did so egregiously. On December 6, 1963, he started jotting daily entries on an adding machine tape. By January 10, 1964, the tape was used up and the poem thus ended. He published it as *Tape for the Turn of the Year* (1965).

Yet though they share a meditative mode and have other fundamental features of style in common, Ashbery and Ammons cannot easily be discussed together. For as soon as we descend from general observations and seek to characterize them more particularly, we are confronted with their differences.

JOHN ASHBERY

John Ashbery (b. 1927) grew up on a fruit farm in upstate New York. At the age of fourteen he was a radio Quiz-Kid. He met Kenneth Koch and Frank O'Hara at Harvard, where he majored in English and wrote his senior honor's thesis on Auden. Living in New York as a graduate student at Columbia University, he caught O'Hara's enthusiasm for contemporary painting and music. Both arts influenced his technique in poetry. His first volume, *Turandot and Other Poems* (1953), was obscurely published by an art gallery and is now a collector's item. The poems of *Some Trees* (1956) are characteristic and charming, though Auden had some misgivings about them when he chose the volume for publication in the Yale Younger Poets series. In 1955 Ashbery went to France as a Fulbright scholar and stayed for ten years. He translated poems and other writings from French into English, supplied art criticism to the Paris edition of the New York *Herald Tribune* and to *Art News,* and of course he composed verse. A special interest at this time was the work of Raymond Roussel (1877–1933), an eccentric stylist who was then virtually unknown. "Europe" (1960) differed greatly from the poems in *Some Trees,* for it was a long collage with extreme fragmentation. Together with similar poems in *The Tennis Court Oath* (1962) it made a distinct phase in Ashbery's career, and some readers prefer it to the more discursive poems he wrote later. Ashbery told an interviewer that in composing "Europe" he "would sit down and cover pages without really knowing" what he had written. "I'd get American magazines like *Esquire,* open the pages, and get a phrase from it, and then start writing on my own. When I ran out, I'd go back to the magazine. It was pure experimentation." We must believe this account, but should not suppose that the collage of "Europe" was therefore random. It expressed, as we shall see, conscious artistic intentions and meanings.

In 1965 the death of his father brought Ashbery back to the

United States. He settled in New York City and worked as executive editor of *Art News*. Later, when the magazine was sold, he became a professor of English at Brooklyn College, where he teaches poetry and the writing of it. He also writes art criticism for *Newsweek* magazine. By 1965 his poetry was already known and admired by many young poets, but his reputation had not yet spread to university English departments and to the general public. *Rivers and Mountains* (1967) was remarkable especially for "The Skaters," a long poem of marvelous verve in which Ashbery's methods were as expansive as they had been the opposite in "Europe." In "The Skaters," he later said, he was trying "to see how many opinions I had about everything." In *The Double Dream of Spring* (1970) Ashbery first mastered the apparently discursive yet still disorienting style that has generally characterized his work since. I may quote as an example the conclusion of "Sunrise in Suburbia": as morning returns and the dreams of night are dispelled,

The thieves were not breaking in, the castle was not being stormed.
It was the holiness of the day that fed our notions
And released them, sly breath of Eros,
Anniversary on the woven city lament, that assures our arriving
In hours, seconds, breath, watching our salary
In the morning holocaust become one vast furnace, engaging all tears.

What the lines mean is a puzzle, but they have the air and form of traditional poetic meditation, somewhat resembling both Stevens and Auden, with legato syntax, seemingly mellow, affirmative attitudes, and emotional climax and finale. Typically the longest poem of this volume was entitled "Fragment." Ashbery continued the formal methods of *The Double Dream of Spring* in his next book, *Three Poems* (1972), except that these poems were in prose. He then went as far as he has yet gone toward straightforward reflective utterance in the title poem of *Self-Portrait in a Convex Mirror* (1975). The book won several prizes, including the Pulitzer. As if in compensation for this relatively traditional and earnest poem Ashbery amused himself in *The Vermont Notebook* (1975) with collages and parodies. The poems of *Houseboat Days* (1977) mainly continued along lines familiar to Ashbery's readers since *The Double Dream of Spring*, but *As We Know* (1979) began with a "Litany" of almost seventy pages composed in two separate columns. The columns are theoretically to be read simultaneously. Since this is impossible, a reader may at any point read down the column or across the page. Each time you go through "Litany," you do it in a different order. Reading down one column, you are aware at every moment that the text is incomplete, since there is also the other side of the page. To read across from one column to the other violates the syntax of Ashbery's sentences, which flow down each column. If you leap from a sentence or paragraph to another in the facing column, the text is discontinuous and disorienting, though in many passages there are parallels or contrasts of theme and imagery. A poem could hardly be more indeterminate and "open." *Shadow Train* (1981) swung in an opposite direction; the fifty poems, each with sixteen lines in four stanzas, resemble a collection of sonnets. In this volume the novelty and challenge to Ashbery lay in repeating the same form, which he had never done before.

Since Ashbery's poems often seem obscure at first reading, something must motivate us to the second and later readings in which the difficulties of his texts gradually clarify themselves. At this point, therefore, some *trouvailles* may be quoted as a type of writing that attracts immediately: a poet who is like a "lewd/ Cloud placed on the horizon"; pleasure that persists "like a dear friend / Walking toward one in a dream"; music as "innocent and monstrous / As the ocean's bright display of teeth." Many a single line could be detached from its context and exhibited as though it were a poem in itself. "Our star was brightest perhaps when it had water in it" expresses lifeless dryness, belatedness, and nostalgia with incertitude ("perhaps"). "The winter does what it can for its children" wistfully assesses our limited possibilities. Typically these phrases are touched with rueful fantasy: "You have slept in the sun / Longer than the sphinx, and are none the wiser for it." Often Ashbery startles us into thought by reversing a cliché. That what we know does not necessarily modify our feelings or behavior is a stock observation from antiquity to the present: "I know all this/ But can't seem to keep it from affecting me."

Ashbery's mind percolates continually, surprising us with apt insights: "the loveliest feelings must soon find words, and these, yes, / Displace them." Why do diary keepers note the weather and the time of day in their entries? "Surely it is," he suggests in "Grand Galop,"

> because the ray of light
> Or gloom striking you this moment is hope
> In all its mature, matronly form.

For the most part Ashbery keeps to a middle range of feeling, flowing in a colloquial, freely varying tone of voice, but at times he is capable of grandeur, as at the conclusion of "Evening in the Country":

> We may perhaps remain here, cautious yet free
> On the edge, as it rolls its unblinking chariot
> Into the vast open, the incredible violence and yielding
> Turmoil that is to be our route.

THE NATURE OF THE REAL

Ashbery's subject matter is similar to that of his favorite poet, Wallace Stevens. Both poets write of the mind forming hypotheses about reality in general, about the ultimate truth or nature of things. Stevens, as I said earlier, took for granted that we cannot know reality in itself. Whether we conceive of it as a colorless, featureless continuum, like a gray haze on a winter afternoon, or as a "jostling festival" of concrete, particular identities, like a morning in June full of birdsongs, we are in either case forming an imagination of reality. We have no ground for believing that either the wintry realist (to use Stevens' metaphors) or the Romantic sentimentalist—or anyone else—is closer to the truth. And in the course of time whatever imagination of reality establishes itself will inevitably be dispelled and replaced by a new one. In metaphors, fables, and meditative commentary Stevens dramatized and reflected upon these acts of the mind, these structurings and restructurings of reality. Unlike Yeats, Eliot, and Pound, Stevens did not himself attempt to imagine or propose a particular structure of reality. He was a metacritic of such "fictions," and thought about the qualities they must possess if they are to be "credible" and about the human needs they serve. And he rendered the differing emotions and moral conditions of the psyche that might accompany different versions of reality, from the imagination of a "great disorder" to that of a totally structured reality or "supreme fiction." One should keep in mind that, though for Stevens a "supreme fiction" could not be ultimately true, it would seem "credible" in its epoch, and he pondered what characteristics might confer credibility in the present.

This question has no relevance for Ashbery. He dwells on the impossibility of credibility imagining any reality. Putting it another way, we might say that for both Stevens and Ashbery the imagination creates, destroys, and immediately creates another vision of reality, but that in Ashbery the process is enormously speeded up. His envisionings of reality are not merely provisional; they transform themselves and disappear in the very process of being proposed, leaving, as he puts it, "Nothing but a bitter impression of absence." His readers often explain this by supposing that the "grand march of intellect," as Keats called it, has advanced further into skepticism since Stevens' time, but from one point of view Ashbery's notions about the nature of reality are firmer than those of Stevens. For though neither poet believes that reality can be known, Ashbery is much more committed than Stevens to postulates that explain why it cannot be known.

Ashbery's ideas on this subject are typical for contemporary intellectuals, but since they underlie his poetic forms, a brief sketch of them may be useful. For Ashbery is attempting to resolve a formal dilemma that has been implicit in some modes of Modernism from the start. If reality is either incoherent or entirely unknowable, any form—so far as it is form—must be inauthentic. But a poem that corresponded to reality by being itself incoherent would produce no aesthetic effect, would not be a poem. Hence Ashbery has used procedures which produce neither formlessness nor form but a continual expectation of form that is continually frustrated.

"With the approach of the holidays," Ashbery writes in a deliberately zany passage, "the present is clearly here to stay." This, of course, is exactly what the present either never or always (by definition) is; the logical disconnection between the first half of the sentence and the second makes the point that we must always be moving on to a new beginning. Flux, the *glissade* of "everchanging minute adjustments," is fundamental to our experi-

ence as Ashbery conceives it. We try, of course, to orient ourselves to these "adjustments" as they are taking place, but are
always too late: "No use charging the barriers of that other:/ It
no longer exists." We may attempt to perceive an object, but since
it is always in motion, always forming and reforming itself, we
can never say what it is. Our attempts to describe it may resemble
the dialogue of Polonius and Hamlet watching a cloud: "By the
mass, and 'tis like a camel . . . a weasel . . . Very like a whale." No
principle—neither of cause and effect nor any other—governs
the flux of experience, which is merely random. Even to speak
of a flow implies a higher degree of organization than Ashbery
intends. His metaphors often picture reality or experience as a
blank, colorless continuum without phase, direction, or differentiation, like the sea or the sky. A stubble field and endless falling snow are among his alternative metaphors.

Even if we could focus on a present moment, it would contain
more than we could apprehend. Any instant of experience is
multiple, diverse, swarming with aspects. We cannot take it in.
Since we cannot grasp the whole, our expression must falsify
through its selectivity. But precisely the definiteness of this conclusion violates Ashbery's sense of truth, and he typically undermines it by a contrary premise. Thus in *Three Poems* he posits
that details, "no matter how complete, can give no adequate idea
of the whole," and can "easily become fetishes," yet adds that
"any detail is a microcosm of the whole." Such writing is not
argument but a sophisticated parody of it. Brought into contact,
the opposed premises explode and vanish, and so does any hope
we might have harbored that reasoning will take us anywhere.

At times Ashbery thinks that if he takes many separate views
of the object and superimposes them, he may build up a description that corresponds to the reality. But he rejects this project,
for such a portrait would be painted over time. Hence it would
be a generalized representation, and would not reflect the reality
of any particular moment.

What abides amid the flux, multiplicity, and contradiction of
our experience is *Angst*. Finding ourselves without any grasp of
the real, we are, Ashbery assumes, morally and emotionally
adrift. In one of the many extended, almost allegorical metaphors in *Three Poems* Ashbery speaks as someone suddenly aware
that he is lost. "The landscape isn't making sense any more; it is

not merely that you have misapplied certain principles not meant for the situation in which you find yourself, which is always a new one that cannot be decoded with reference to the existing corpus of moral principle, but there is even a doubt as to our own existence." We have, he suggests repeatedly, no basis for judging what is important and what unimportant. We are unsure what we ought to feel or even, in fact, what we do feel. "This severed hand," as Ashbery puts it in "Worsening Situation,"

> Stands for life, and wander as it will,
> East or west, north or south, it is ever
> A stranger who walks beside me.

We become spectators of our own lives, and watch from a distance the kaleidoscope of selves within us, the many "I's" or, worse, the "they" into which we are fragmented. In our uncertainty and self-alienation we feel uneasily guilty. "One day a man called while I was out," Ashbery writes in the poem just quoted,

> And left this message: "You got the whole thing wrong
> From start to finish. Luckily, there's still time
> To correct the situation, but you must act fast."

We feel that we ought to be not spectators of our lives but actors filled with passion and purpose. Or better still, we ought not to be in the theater at all, but should live naively, as in the "world of Schubert's lieder." And while we are not living, time is passing and death is approaching; we are always aware of it as "The background, dark vine at the edge of the porch." The conclusion of "Grand Gallop" is:

> But now we are at Cape Fear and the overland trail
> Is impassable, and a dense curtain of mist hangs over the sea.

As we read Ashbery we sense that he views all this as truism, a cluster of assumptions he takes for granted. He is a postnihilist, post-Existentialist writer, and the questions he addresses are: Where are you when you have gone through these and arrived nowhere? How do you feel when you are not sure what, if anything, you feel? What seems worth doing when you have no ground or motive for doing anything? Ashbery's position can only be described in paradoxes. If he negates everything, as he said to an interviewer, it is in order to "get on to what is left." As he put it in his "Variations, Calypso and Fugue on a Theme of Ella Wheeler Wilcox," "one must move forward/ Into the space left by one's conclusions." His poetry strangely fills this "space" with hopefulness. Ashbery has, of course, no "reason" for this disposition. So far as his hopefulness is not merely pose and parody—a point I am coming to—it can only be explained by lucky glands. But, he tells himself, if reality has no structure, we are free! To "ride" on the rapid flux is exhilarating. "These sails are life itself to me," he writes in "The Skaters," and elaborates in gush that pokes fun at gush: "Here I am then,"

> continuing but ever beginning
> My perennial voyage, into new memories, new hope and flowers
> The way the coasts glide past you.

Naturally there are mentions of pain, grief, repulsion, and despair, but Ashbery touches on such states only from a distance. The general tone of his feeling is mildly positive—interest, curiosity, amusement, vivacity, happy inventiveness.

UNSAYING WHAT YOU SAY WHILE YOU ARE SAYING IT

In the preceding few pages I described Ashbery as holding certain ideas and conveying a recognizable tone of feeling. Yet I might have argued that no ideas or feelings can be attributed to him at all. To accept this view would finally be false to the experience of reading Ashbery, but the reasons for it help suggest why his poetry is intriguing and problematic. One cluster of problems centers around his use of what we might provisionally call "parody." In interviews Ashbery denies that he parodies, and if by the term we mean the echoing of a voice for the sake of ridiculing it, we may concede that his phrasing is seldom merely parodic. Like Eliot in *The Waste Land* and Pound in the *Cantos* he adopts or alludes to a style in order to invoke the tone of feeling associated with it, and in comparison with Eliot and Pound, he is less likely to bring to bear literary styles of the past, though he draws on these also. But more frequently he exhibits the modern colloquial voices of different types of people and the styles of contemporary journalism, advertising, bureaucracy, business memos, scientific reports, newspapers, psychology textbooks, and the like. Since these styles are relatively graceless and inactive, we sense a certain irony as we encounter them in one of Ashbery's poems. The irony intensifies when the text shifts quickly from one style to another, exhibiting each in contrast while committing itself to none.

A similar irony is present in Ashbery's deliberate use of stock ideas and phrases. This pervasive technique conveys, among other things, his fear that in all our thought and speech we are helplessly trapped in the ready-made. Our minds cannot get beyond the systems of convention that fill them, and these codes divorce us from reality. Hence every utterance must be spoken with recognition and apology that the words and concepts are to some degree clichés, and this is what we find in Ashbery's texts. But the degree of this irony varies enormously. Some phrases are obviously exhibited as inadequate; at the other extreme the irony is scarcely detectable. "Definition of Blue" begins:

> The rise of capitalism parallels the advance of romanticism
> And the individual is dominant until the close of the nineteenth century.
> In our own time, mass practices have sought to submerge the personality. . . .

These are not serious historical generalizations but ironic mockeries of such generalizations. They are not false, of course. They are truisms. They say what every textbook says in the inert way ("rise of capitalism," "advance of romanticism") a textbook might put it. But the lines are not written to score satirically against textbooks. Ashbery is much too intelligent and serious to seek so easy a victory. The passage samples the intellectual counters ("romanticism," "capitalism") we use and must use, having no others, and thus it creates, among other things, a depressing feeling of the inescapability of the cliché. Later in the poem Ashbery refers to such generalization as "packaging" and adds that there is "no remedy" for it. A different example is "Syringa": Orpheus

> *didn't mind so much* about his *reward being in heaven*
> After the Bacchantes had torn him apart, driven
> *Half out of their minds* by his music, *what it was doing to them.*

Here the language does not enact the emotions it refers to but expresses, instead, the rather bored, unfocused state of mind of the narrator, who tells what happened in such a way as to deprive it of significance.

But the main single difficulty in interpreting Ashbery is that his texts simultaneously deny what they predicate. A paradox can usually be read by understanding one or both of its terms in special contexts or senses. Thus in *Ash Wednesday* Eliot writes, "Teach us to care and not to care," and we assume that the prayer is to care for some objects, such as God, or in some ways, such as caritas, but not for oneself anxiously. Of course, no paradox can be completely resolved; the contradiction continues to activate the mind to discover new meaning. But when in "Everyman's Library" Ashbery writes, "there is no freedom, and no freedom from freedom," the figure is not paradoxical. It is an oxymoron; opposite assertions, each possibly true, are brought into conjunction and cancel each other. So also with the intriguing message (in "The One Thing That Can Save America") whose "truth is timeless, but its time has still/ Not arrived." But such glaring self-contradictions are less typical. A subtler, more representative example may be found in the final lines of "As You Came from the Holy Land." If, somewhat simplifying, we say that in this passage "it" refers to a present moment, "it" can never come about. When we ask "what time it is," "that time is already past." "Today" is only a "gap . . . filling itself with emptiness":

> it can never come about
> not here not yesterday in the past
> only in the gap of today filling itself
> an emptiness is distributed
> in the idea of what time it is
> when that time is already past.

The contradiction comes in the third line of the quotation. The word "only" must mean, "it can never come about . . . only in . . ."; in other words, it can come about. The weight of Ashbery's assertion is clear—it "can never come about"—but as he expresses it, the opposite is said also. The text asserts what it denies, denies what it asserts, and thus leaves itself semantically open—and this within a passage of which the rhythm and feeling powerfully suggest resolution and closure.

Continually in reading Ashbery we lose the thread of his meanings. What distinguishes Ashbery from most other poets who are also discontinuous is that, at least in his work after "Europe," he leads one to expect continuous sense. Because the expectation is disappointed, we feel the absence all the more, and the creation of expectation is as important to his effects as the frustration of it. Encountering conventional grammar, for example, we anticipate no deformation at the semantic level. A sentence such as "Meanwhile the whole history of probabilities is coming to life, starting in the upper left-hand corner, like a sail," is startling as no agrammatical juxtaposition of fragments would be. In the sentence, "no hope of completing the magnitude which surrounds us/ Is permitted us," the disorienting moment comes at the word "magnitude." The context of it is so conversationally bland that the word almost slips past us and we do a double take. Logical or chronological sequence also generates expectation: when a passage begins in one of these, we assume the sequence will continue, but in Ashbery this is seldom the case. Chronology is violated. "The Skaters" concludes,

> The constellations are rising
> In perfect order: Taurus, Leo, Gemini.

But this is not the order in which these constellations arise. So also the logical next step seldom comes. "Thus" and "hence" are usually false markers. I cannot leave the subject of false logic without remarking what fine confusions Ashbery creates by predicating logical impossibilities: the two faces of a wall "were separated by a third"; "each house/ is noticeably a little nicer than the rest."

Or Ashbery's sentences may begin in correct grammar that suddenly lapses. A verb arrives in the wrong person, tense, or number. Or the wrong pronoun sends us back to the start of the sentence to see where we went astray. In "And *Ut Pictura Poesis* Is Her Name" a passage addressed to "you" concludes, "so much for self-analysis." Through the course of a poem "it" is especially likely to refer indefinitely and variably. Grammar also becomes confusing through omission of punctuation and through the piling up of relative clauses, appositions, and parentheses. Analogous misroutings and branchings out as in a delta take place in larger structures of narrative and argument.

Ashbery's metaphors similarly transform themselves as we read. We must keep forming new hypotheses as we follow them. For example, night brings "doubts/ That swarm about the sleeper's head." This figure from "Spring Day" seems almost too obvious: doubts that trouble us at night are like mosquitoes, or maybe like gnats or no-see-ums. Yet the next line narrates that the swarming doubts "are fended off with clubs and knives," which seem an improbable defense against mosquitoes, though possibly effective against harpies. In "Fragment" we read of a "hole, towering secret." Since a hole cannot tower, we attempt to resolve the contradiction, hypothesizing, perhaps, that this hole is like a tower in that it is large, visible, and impressive. This interpretation is far-fetched and unsatisfactory, so Ashbery's phrase continues to tease us until we come, two lines later, to the adjective "square"; since this adjective would not apply to a hole, it compels us to recognize that the hole is also a tower; it is one or the other depending on circumstances. When first poked into, in the uncertain light of the present, it is a hollow; when you see it behind you in reflection it has become a definite, looming shape:

> That hole, towering secret, familiar
> If one is poking among the evening rubbish, yet how
> Square behind you in the mirror . . .

At the conclusion of "Pyrography," to take a final example, Ashbery speaks of a "vast unravelling/ Out"; this "unravelling" becomes a journey toward "junctions," places of intersection and of new departures in different directions, and from "junctions" toward darkness and bare fields. Since there are no buildings on them the fields are metaphors of open potentiality, yet in a typical contradiction the final phrase affirms that they are "built;"

> only a vast unravelling
> Out toward the junctions and to the darkness beyond
> To these bare fields, built at today's expense.

To explain such apparent contradictions we could say that Ashbery keeps opposing points of view in mind simultaneously, or, alternatively, that his mind changes at high speed, so that what appears to be a contradiction is actually an ellipsis.

Ashbery's long poems tend, as I noted, to avoid climax. The

thoughts, images, and illustrations that replace one another seriatim may keep to much the same level of significance and emotion. The effect is rather like the garden and speech of "Scheherazade" in *Self-Portrait in a Convex Mirror:*

> In all this springing up was no hint
> Of a tide, only a pleasant wavering of the air
> In which all things seemed present, whether
> Just past or soon to come. It was all invitation.

There are innumerable good passages, but in comparison with most poets Ashbery shuns epiphanies, catastrophes, or other peaks of intensity.

The nonarrival of such privileged moments provides one of the richest themes of Ashbery's comedy. In "Grand Galop"

> Someone is coming to get you:
> The mailman, or a butler enters with a letter on a tray
> Whose message is to change everything, but in the meantime
> One is to worry about one's smell or dandruff or lost glasses—
> If only the curtain-raiser would end, but it is interminable.

In "Silhouette" we are in the ambience of a detective story, except that the murder will not out (Ashbery here also alludes to the familiar metaphor of Henry James that compares the plot of a novel to the pattern in a carpet):

> The catastrophe
> Buried in the stair carpet stayed there
> And never corrupted anybody.

Sometimes the revelation may actually be taking place but cannot be seen, as in the passage noticed earlier from "As You Came from the Holy Land":

> the time is ripe now and the adage
> is hatching as the seasons change and tremble
> it is finally as though that thing of monstrous interest
> were happening in the sky
> but the sun is setting and prevents you from seeing it.

READING ASHBERY

Since Ashbery's poems are difficult, it may be helpful to exemplify in a couple of passages the procedures by which he is read. "Europe" belongs to the group of collages he created around 1960, and though at first these poems seem harder to read than the quasi-discursive ones that soon succeeded them, yet within the Modernist tradition "Europe" represents a more familiar type of poetry. By 1960 discontinuous, heterogeneous juxtaposition had been an accepted poetic method for almost forty years. The fragmentation and disconnection of modern consciousness had repeatedly been displayed from *The Waste Land* on. *Paterson* had been composed from fragments of the most familiar and ordinary materials, and the *Pisan Cantos* had shown how brief the fragmentary units of meaning might be. Ashbery was somewhat interested in Surrealism in the 1950s, and he caught suggestions toward formal procedures in poetry from modern painting, including collage, and from the music of such composers as Schönberg, Webern, and Cage.

Section 35 of "Europe" begins with four lines that might have been assembled by scissoring and pasting from a newspaper:

> The sheiks protest use of
> aims. In the past
> coal has protected their
> O long, watchful hour.

However Ashbery produced these phrases, their significance and effect could not have been obtained by random selection. And yet, any number of quite different phrases might have been collected without changing the meaning in general. The controversies surrounding *The Waste Land* long since taught readers that such verses are to be understood as presenting the heterogeneity, fragmentation, and incoherence that characterize their subject—in this case Europe—a scene of newspaper headlines ("sheiks protest . . ."), of appeals to a nonexistent or irrelevant past ("In the past"), and of economic and sentimental clichés ("coal has . . ."; "O long . . .") in which nothing connects with anything else and banality is all-pervading. The verbal scraps joined together are individually inert, drab, and dry (except for "O long" in the last line), and appear to come from types of writing, such as journalism, to which everyone is boringly accustomed. The literary convention of this passage is the familiar Modernist one that stylistic features of the text—syntactical discontinuity, fragmentation, juxtaposition of the heterogeneous, banality—represent similar qualities in experience.

The other tradition from which Ashbery derives is that of the later Stevens and Auden, of Stevens after *Harmonium* and Auden after the 1930s, when both became major meditative poets. Ashbery's work after "Europe" fuses meditative discourse with discontinuity. In a passage from "No Way of Knowing," for example, he posits that as we seek to interpret reality or experience, we have

> No common vantage point, no point of view
> Like the "I" in a novel. And in truth
> No one never saw the point of any.

The second sentence is of course highly questionable, and its pert, dismissive phrasing may suggest role-playing. The speaker seems a somewhat petulant Modernist on the defensive. "This stubble-field," the next sentence begins, picturing experience as an already-harvested field,

> Of witnessings and silent lowering of the lids
> On angry screen-door moment rushing back
> To the edge of the woods was always alive with its own
> Rigid binary system of inducing truths
> From starved knowledge of them. It has worked
> And will go on working. All attempts to influence
> The working are parallelism, undulating, writhing
> Sometimes but kept to the domain of metaphor.

"Screen-door moment" refers to someone banging the screen door angrily as he leaves a country house and rushes to the edge of the woods; it is a metaphor of any moment receding into the past. A stubble-field looks somewhat like a computer grid and this one has, it turns out, a capacity of inducing "truths." The word is used ironically, and the proliferating metaphors—"rigid binary system," inductive logic, "starved knowledge"—suggest that the "truths" turned out by the "system" do not correspond to the complexity and swift transition of the real. Nevertheless the system "has worked"—the cliché again suggests that Ashbery is role-playing—and will continue to operate. Attempts to make its results ("influence the working") less mechanical and more adequately complex ("writhing" includes a pun on writing) produce no effect. Among other things Ashbery alludes here to the fact that in actual living we assume a much simpler, more knowable world than we posit intellectually. As epistemological inquirers we cannot be sure just who the figures we see on a morning may be; in actual practice we greet them as neighbors. But the fact that we drawl "hallo" to them does not mean that they are neighbors. We cannot know who or what they are, and whatever they are, they may change. Our "hallo" does not inaugurate a persisting manner or "style."

> There is no way of knowing whether these are
> Our neighbors or friendly savages trapped in the distance
> By the red tape of a mirage. The fact that
> We drawled "hallo" to them just lazily enough this morning
> Doesn't mean that a style was inaugurated.

Winding toward a close, or the illusion of it, Ashbery again speaks in an assumed voice, one that suggests mental slackness and complacency ("Kind of"): "Anyway evening/ Kind of changes things," but, of course, it does not change "things" at all. It—the sense that time is running out and that our possibility of "witnessing" will soon be at an end—merely changes us by stimulating "a general anxiety to get everything all added up." This is impossible, and the "vehicular madness"—our too rapid ride along the constantly changing—"Goes on." But in wish and imagination we entertain a different relation to experience or reality, one in which we are spectators from a fixed "vantage point," from a balcony. In the last lines we are, in typical contradiction to what has gone before, actually on the balcony, or almost ("one *may*"), and the sunset, instead of obscuring "things," is "just starting to light up."

> Anyway evening
> Kind of changes things. Not the color,
> The quality of a handshake, the edge of someone's breath,
> So much as a general anxiety to get everything all added up,
> Flowers arranged and out of sight. The vehicular madness
> Goes on, crashing, thrashing away, but
> For many this is near enough to the end: one may
> Draw up a chair close to the balcony railing.
> The sunset is just starting to light up.

In its ironic use of ready-made diction, its rapid slide from diction of one kind to another, its phrases that are implicitly acknowledged to be banal and inadequate formulas, its discursive ongoingness with self-contradiction, distraction, logical impasse, and double take, and its continuous transformations of story, speaker, grammatical structure, and metaphor, Ashbery's form enacts his vision of experience. He pictures consciousness responding to the flying penumbra of ungraspable events, the fast "ride" of our own lives in which we sit as spectators. Naturally poems so difficult must be read many times. And even so there is always some "strangeness in the proportion," to adopt a phrase from Bacon's essay "Of Beauty," and the poem is not completely interpretable. But Ashbery is not more difficult to read than great Modernist predecessors such as Yeats and Pound; the difference is merely that there is not yet a critical tradition attached to his work. There is no pleasure in remarking limitations in work of such brilliance, but if one were to be named, it is not obscurity but tedium. Through all his volumes Ashbery elaborates the same fundamental insights. That his subject, moreover, is not doings in the world but in the mind means that his poetry, like that of Stevens, largely forgoes the interest that attaches to human character and fate. He grips us by the profundity of his premises and by the brio of his expression, but when his skill as a stylist fails, he is boring. But when Ashbery writes well, no living poet in English can rival him in fresh, apt, surprising phrases. His attitudes and emotions are indescribably gallant as he mingles humor with pathos, resignation and elegy with hope, and maintains his relaxed, equable, fluent, wonderfully imaginative speech despite premises that might have led to despair.

At this point I may mention two other poets who have each published one excellent book. Amy Clampitt had published fugitively before *The Kingfishers* (1983), but she had attracted little notice, and thus her public career began in middle age. She has a virtuoso power of description and astonishing wealth of thought, metaphor, illustration, and association. She is not a poet of penetrating single insights but of lavish ongoingness; one thing leads her to another, or, more exactly, she has several things in mind at once and they all evolve simultaneously. She is a poet of wit, fecundity, and rich ornament, and her chief defect is the excess of her virtue, for she can overburden her syntax, losing momentum in amplification and decoration. Her meditations begin in her personal experience, and are, in a sense, about it, but they are discreet, and move from the personal and experienced to the general and intellectual.

Douglas Crase (b. 1944) published his first book, *The Revisionist*, in 1981. Certain features of his poetry suggest that he has absorbed Ashbery. I am thinking of Crase's bland tone, his occasional deliberate vagueness as to who is addressed or what is referred to, the clear, even intelligence of his writing, which is continually observant, thoughtfully generalizing, mildly witty, and at the same time comfortable, friendly, and low-keyed. No one else writes quite like Crase in these respects, but if I had to name predecessors, they would be Ashbery and Auden. The resemblances are not close, for the outward world is less present in Ashbery's poetry, while Crase describes it abundantly, vividly, and delicately. Moreover, Crase's subject matter—American history as it is reflected in particular places—is not Ashbery's. In fact one might argue that Crase takes more from Whitman than from any other poet, that he is trying to gather as much of Whitman's hope for America as can still be gathered in our time. Yet to me it seems that America and its history are only formally his subject matter, that the deeper meaning of his poetry lies in his vision of process, of unresting, somehow orderly change in natural things and also in buildings, cities, or "history." This sense of omnipresent process allies him with both Ashbery and Ammons. Crase and Clampitt are meditative poets in the sense I defined in my discussion of Stevens and in this chapter: they are very different poets, but both enact in their poetry the continual transition of thought, the inherent power of the mind to proceed on its own momentum.

A. R. AMMONS

A. R. Ammons (b. 1926) grew up on a farm in North Carolina. Some of his poems recall his childhood—his mule Silver, his hog, the unfortunate Nellie who lives with his family. He served in the navy at the end of the Second World War, took a B.S. degree at Wake Forest College, and then became principal of a small elementary school in the coastal town of Hatteras, North Carolina. While in the navy he had started writing poetry, and

probably his interest in poetry was what now led him to study
for two years at the University of California at Berkeley. His first
collection of poems, *Ommateum* (the word refers to the compound eyes of insects), was published in 1955. Biblical and Whitmanian sublimities are frequent in this volume: "The pieces of
my voice have been thrown/ away I said turning to the hedge-
rows . . . for I am broken over the earth" ("The Pieces of My
Voice"). Some of the poems are brief, philosophic parables resembling those of Stephen Crane. *Ommateum* contained a few
lyrics, such as "So I Said I Am Ezra" and "Bees Stopped," which
are frequently anthologized, but Ammons had not yet found his
characteristic style. Meanwhile he had moved from California to
southern New Jersey, where he worked as a business executive.
A second volume, *Expressions of Sea Level,* was not published until
1964, nine years after *Ommateum.* In the same year he accepted
a job at Cornell University teaching classes in the composition
of poetry.

Along with meditative poems, his major genre, Ammons has
continued to compose lyric parables. "Mountain Talk" may be
quoted in illustration, together with Ammons' interpretation
of it.

> I was going along a dusty highroad
> when the mountain
> across the way
> turned me to its silence:
> oh I said how come
> I don't know your
> massive symmetry and rest:
> nevertheless, said the mountain,
> would you want
> to be
> lodged here with
> a changeless prospect, risen
> to an unalterable view:
> so I went on
> counting my numberless fingers.

The poem, Ammons explained to an interviewer, tells

a very simple story. . . . A person is walking along a dusty highroad.
What does a dusty highroad mean? It's almost in a religious realm—
you know, *dust, height, abstraction, separation* from the landscape, in a

sense of perhaps being lost in it. And then, the moment of recognition when the person who is walking along becomes aware of a presence near him and he turns and it is not something that is wandering at all. It's a mountain that is always there. It occupies a single position and, as the poem says, it retains a single prospect. So the narrative then becomes the play of these two possibilities, of being stable and of occupying a massive view about things that is unalterable; or being tiny enough to go up and down pathways, to become lost. And the speaker finally prefers that mobility, that changeability, to occupying a single space.

Ammons' meditative poems vary enormously in length, quality, and style. Some take just a few lines; others are book length (*Tape for the Turn of the Year*, 1965; *Sphere: The Form of a Motion*, 1974). Many passages are eloquent and vital; others are extremely uninteresting. Ammons' descriptions of nature are delicate and vivid. His humor is sly, charming, witty, and often astringent, and he is fetching in folk modes of humor, in tall tales and extravagant metaphors, as in "Cut the Grass":

> I'm nervous: my morality's intricate: if
> a squash blossom dies, I feel withered.

Ammons can write with the polysemous wit and intricate interrelation of images that was typical of the New Critical mode, and he can be directly rhetorical and prophetic, as in "The City Limits." In a typical meditative passage he sounds like this:

> oh, it's spring, and I'm more transparent than ever:
> I heard the white-breasted nuthatch gurble over the trunk
> bark today, and tonight everything is so clear it's
>
> going down to zero: my idealism's as thin as the sprinkled
> sky and nearly as expansive: I don't love anybody much:
> that accounts for my width and most of my height: but
>
> I love as much as I can and that keeps me here but light.

In his poetry Ammons pursues philosophical intuitions inherited from the Romantic tradition, especially from Wordsworth, Emerson, and Whitman. He has also, he says, "read a good deal" in Emerson's sources in "Indian and Chinese philosophy." He does not share the social preoccupations and faiths of the great Romantic writers but does share their dialogue with the universe. Moments of belief—in man's power of transcendent intuition, in our oneness with nature and the cosmos—were already fugitive and precarious in those writers. In Ammons, who is also wedded to scientific naturalism, disillusion has gone further. In other words, though he addresses Romantic premises, hopes, visions, and quandaries, he lacks the Romantic afflatus. Yet he remains drawn to it, and permits himself as much as he honestly can.

"Mechanism" is a typical Ammons poem both in its theme and its method. Taking a slight subject—a goldfinch in cherry bushes—Ammons applies mind to it reflectively, and continues volubly through forty-eight lines. The poem involves a quasi-philosophical issue, the opposition of aesthetic and scientific perspectives, but does not pose the issue in general terms. On the one hand, the bird is beautiful; in hyperbolic defiance of scientific naturalism Ammons even affirms that the beauty of the goldfinch startles a hawk. On the other hand, the goldfinch is a system of chemical reactions. As he considers the goldfinch, Ammons perceives it as a process organizing an infinite number of more particular and local processes. The catalogue of natural processes in the goldfinch, which the poem gives, is introduced and governed by the imperative verb "honor" ("honor the chemistries, platelets . . . honor the unique genes"). Though the poem suggests no reason to honor this mechanism except that it is "working right," "honor" is not voiced ironically. Ammons is not asserting a humanist criticism of science. He is not suggesting, for example, that mechanistic fact—for example, that living things are chemical systems—is irrelevant to value judgment and emotion. Instead, he is attempting to synthesize the opposed points of view.

"Corson's Inlet" is a landscape poem in the Romantic tradition. Walking along this tidal inlet, Ammons observes its "flowing bends and blends," "disorderly orders," transitions without demarcations, and gradual, continual change through the whole system as the tide rises and falls. The landscape is a "'field' of action/ with moving, incalculable center," a "working in and out, together/ and against, of millions of events" simultaneously. As such it is, like the goldfinch in "Mechanism," both an instance and a symbol of nature or reality and also a symbol of the structure and process of the human mind.

A poem itself is also such a field of myriad processes. As an open form it receives "the becoming/ thought," stakes "off no beginnings or ends," spreads out "sharpness" and allows it "to occur over a wider range," and is at no point predictable or forced. In a poem as in nature every event exists in a context of infinitely numerous other events, and these are simultaneous and impinging. And, finally, every event is inexhaustible in the sense that it involves processes within processes; it repeats in its organization the organic form of the whole in which it is a part. Elaborating these principles implicitly as he describes the landscape, Ammons prescribes how a poem should be. More effectively than any other single poem, "Corson's Inlet" is the *Ars Poetica* of Olsonian open form. Its fundamental assumptions are that there is an ontological continuity between reality or nature and the human mind and that the poem is a spontaneous act of mind.

"Corson's Inlet" includes images of Darwinian strife: a

> gull, squawking possession, cracked a crab,
> picked out the entrails, swallowed the soft-shelled legs, a ruddy
> turnstone running in to snatch leftover bits.

"Terror pervades," the poem acknowledges, but adds that the terror

> is not arranged, all possibilities
> of escape open: no route shut, except in
> the sudden loss of all routes.

These passages illustrate how Ammons conceives the darker aspects of existence. If everything is part of an infinitely manifold context, evil cannot occupy the eye exclusively. The lines just quoted from "Corson's Inlet" are unblinking, but are part of a diverse "field." In general Ammons does not foreground suffering and death, as so many modern writers do, but he does not deny them either. He perceives them as elements of larger orders; they are present to his mind but not dominant for his emotion.

THE ACHIEVEMENT OF JAMES MERRILL

THE trilogy Merrill published in the 1970s, *The Changing Light at Sandover*, revealed him to be one of the most moving, imaginative, and ambitious of living poets. This long poem combines mythopoeic power and metaphysical themes with human intimacy and appeal. It questions whether "yes" or "no," being or negativity, is the ultimate truth, and it also presents, like Goethe's *Tasso*, an ideally affectionate, civilized circle of friends, who create, as the peacock Mirabell puts it, a "WORLD OF COURTESY." The intimate and cosmic dimensions are complexly interrelated. The kindness of these friends to one another is motivated, in part, by horror; their "WORLD OF COURTESY" is a defense, a protective "greenhouse," like the atmosphere of the earth, against encompassing cold, dark, and death. Being itself is, the poem suggests, a "resistance" against or within nothingness. Black fingers of nothingness, as the poem elaborates the metaphor, creep on the greenhouse panes, trying to get in, and though in fancy or speculation the threat is to existence in general, as an immediate, practical matter it is to our goodwill toward life. Imbued with the reality of the void, we may cease to feel that the fates of ourselves or of other persons matter, or even those of mankind or of nature as a whole.

Merrill's poem dwells on lore that impels the mind toward this "black hole"—the space-time of astronomy, in which life becomes infinitesimal, or the teachings of biochemistry, in which it becomes chemical processes, or those of physics, reducing existence to particles in motion. When the Ouija board commanded Merrill to write "POEMS OF SCIENCE," what was meant, to judge from the result, was a poem wrestling with the impact of science on moral faith.

The poem also contemplates science and technology as potential causes of the literal ruin of the world. Yet what negates and undermines, in Merrill's poem, is not only the intellectual perspectives of science and the prospect of a poisoned planet and nuclear apocalypse. Even without these, death is everybody's terrifying "black hole," and it threatens to swallow, as he reflects upon it, the desire to live. Merrill's poem is a massive, prolonged response to the sense of mortality. Against this permeating awareness the humor of the poem—light, ebullient, witty, campy—has pathos and gallantry.

In genre the first part of the trilogy, "The Book of Ephraim," is sharply different from the rest, for it is a *nouveau roman* in verse. The remaining books, which are much longer, continue themes and some threads of plot from the first part, but are a cosmic fantasia. They belong to the same Romantic genre as Shelley's *Prometheus Unbound* and the Second Part of Goethe's *Faust*. Before he published the trilogy Merrill was a poet of large and growing powers. But *The Changing Light at Sandover* is so much more imaginative and original than his earlier work that this chapter must dwell on it, and I must gain space for it by passing too quickly over Merrill's other writing. Even in style the trilogy has a variety and in many passages a mastery that transcends Merrill's previous and subsequent accomplishment.

Merrill grew up in privileged circumstances, the son of Charles E. Merrill, chief founder of the brokerage firm of Merrill, Lynch, Pierce, Fenner and Smith. When he was twelve years old his parents were divorced, and on the evidence of his poetry, which often alludes to this event, their separation was traumatic for him. As a schoolboy at Lawrenceville, a private school in New Jersey, he began to write poetry. At this time he could turn out, he says, "a poem a day. My very first efforts were sonnets which

I wrote as much with French models as with English—the melodic, empty headed fin de siècle sort of thing." At the age of fifteen or sixteen he "worshipped" Elinor Wylie. Rilke was also a favorite writer in adolescence. What then appealed to him in Rilke, Merrill suggests, was the sense of "loneliness and hopeless passions," the "*acceptance*" that "pain and suffering" are inevitable. Though many sensitive adolescents feel this *Weltschmerz,* Merrill's had special causes, for to judge from scattered passages in his poetry, he had already recognized that he was homosexual. In his sophomore and junior years at Amherst he started reading modern poetry. Wallace Stevens, a favorite of the Amherst English department, appealed to him strongly. He wrote his senior essay on Proust. If we ask what attracted him to Proust, the answer probably involves Proust's rendering of wealthy and cultivated life, his preoccupation with love and analysis of it, the theme of homosexuality, the idealization of art, and the elaborate, sensuous sensitivity of the narrator.

Merrill had his first collection of lyrics privately printed in 1946, just after a brief period of service in the army. Except for occasional college teaching, he has lived quietly in New York City and, after 1954, in the seaside town of Stonington, Connecticut, though traveling frequently. Between 1959 and the late 1970s he spent much of each year in Greece. Most of the time since 1953 he has lived with David Jackson, the DJ or "Hand" of Merrill's trilogy (in which Merrill is JM or the "Scribe"). In 1955 the two friends began to receive the messages from the Ouija board that resulted in *The Changing Light at Sandover.* On some assumptions Jackson is a joint creator of the poem. Books by Merrill have appeared every two or three years, and with the exception of two novels (*The Seraglio,* 1957, and *The Diblos Notebook,* 1965), these have been collections of shorter poems or, from 1978 to 1982, installments of the trilogy.

In the last analysis, Merrill believes, art is form. Experiences, emotions, ideas, *Weltanschauungen,* or whatever else we may consider to be the "content" of art may or may not be valuable in themselves, but they are not the object of art. At least this was Merrill's view until he wrote the trilogy. Throughout his work Merrill has been a virtuoso in meters and stanzas, writing sonnet sequences, double sestinas, terza rima, blank verse, syllabic verse, ballad stanzas, odes, and other patterns. He also writes free verse. Often the versification is wittily chosen, as when in "Lost in Translation" a painting of Arabian life is described in the stanza of Edward Fitzgerald's *Rubáiyát of Omar Khayyám*. The always brilliant versification is the most obvious but hardly the most important indication of Merrill's formalism.

Merrill's notion of form is that of the New Critics. He has never accepted open form. Neither does he believe that poems should be written spontaneously. Conscious deliberation and revision are central to his creative process. In these respects Merrill counters the dominant, though now receding, trend in American poetry since the 1960s. Despite the strange circumstances of its creation, to which I shall return, Merrill's trilogy is not an exception. However it came into being, the trilogy is a work of formal intricacy and skill.

In genre Merrill's shorter poems divide roughly into two types. Many are witty, impersonal poems that contemplate a symbol, such as "The Octopus," "The Lovers," "In Nine Sleep Valley," and "The Victor Dog." Others, no less witty and symbolic, are autobiographical, and present some incident in Merrill's own life. As he says in "A Tenancy,"

> If I am host at last
> It is of little more than my own past.
> May others be at home in it.

Usually the autobiographical poems have a narrative interest. Many of Merrill's poems do not belong to either type—"The Summer People," for example, is a ballad—and many are both impersonal and autobiographical. "Yánnina," for example, describes the Albanian town, and though the impressions are Merrill's as a tourist, the poem is not strongly personal in formal convention. But as the image of the formidable yet charming tyrant Ali Pasha is developed, he coalesces with Charles Merrill, and the poem in fact expresses perceptions and feelings about Merrill's father.

Poems of impersonal symbolism were in vogue when Merrill began as a poet, and he still writes them. He did not compose overtly autobiographical poems until the 1960s, and "An Urban Convalescence" in *Water Street* (1962) was the breakthrough. Already in this poem the personal subject modifed his voice toward colloquial directness. Speaking as himself, moreover, he had to create a convincing character and setting. Realism, the grit of particular fact, was required. And the "plot" of the poem became self-dialogic, like a dramatic monologue. Memories suddenly returned to the speaker, new doubts and considerations came to mind, feelings shifted.

Merrill's impersonal poems are accomplished, but the ones in his autobiographical mode appeal more powerfully. In addition to their greater drama and tension, they have human interest; they present a character and a life. Merrill often writes at different times about the same autobiographical event. Though they are composed from different perspectives, we associate these poems on the same episode as we read. Poems about his parents and their divorce form one such cluster—"Scenes of Childhood," "The World and the Child," "The Broken Home," "Days of 1935," "Lost in Translation." Another, less significant cluster of poems centers around the vicissitudes of his feelings for his Greek lover, Strato, as in "After the Fire," "Days of 1964," "Strato in Plaster," "To My Greek," "Flying from Byzantium," "Another August," and "Days of 1971." It is hardly accidental that these clusters include some of Merrill's finest poems. That he writes about these passages of his life so frequently indicates that they are psychologically charged for him. But also we read them with a more comprehensive response. We are curious to piece together the story they collectively tell, and, more important, the context of the whole associated group of poems enriches each, partly by alerting us to nuances of feeling and implication, and partly by setting each within a larger perspective, an emotional development that extends beyond the boundaries of the particular poem. The disenchantment expressed in "Strato in Plaster" is both more witty and more moving because we have also read "To My Greek" and "Flying from Byzantium."

Wit permeates virtually all that Merrill writes. In general, it is the sort of wit I noticed in discussing the Metaphysical revival of the 1930s and 1940s, and expresses quickness of mind with complex feeling and awareness. Typically wit makes the texture of Merrill's phrasing relatively packed, conveying multiple implications simultaneously. In "The Kimono," for example, a poem about falling in love over and over, Merrill writes,

> Times out of mind, the bubble-gleam
> To our charred level drew
> April back.

"Bubble" suggests love's brief, fragile iridescence; "level" an equable state of the psyche without depression or elevation. "Charred" adds that former flames, now cooled, have left the speaker *usé*. Like a burnt-over field, he is less likely to catch fire. Nevertheless, new love has the same springlike freshness.

In their resigned, bittersweet tone and rhythmic swing the lines are fine, yet they also illustrate that Merrill loves puns and overtones more than he does directly communicative terms. "Level" and "bubble" refer to a carpenter's level, but Merrill makes little use of the image. His "bubble" is not a gauge. He focuses less on the immediate sense of his words than on their suggestions.

Merrill is much given to wordplay: "scentless violets, / Senseless violence"; "Full of unfulfillment life goes on"; "The lapse that tides us over, hither, yon;/ Tide that laps us home away from home." One of his favorite *jeux d'esprit* is that of transforming clichés: in one example (from "Verse for Urania") the age of *Götterdämmerung,* the twilight of the gods, becomes the different, modern era of the "twilight of the worldly goods." Such figures usually please in context, but at a cost, for they attract attention, and when we have attended, we may find only a minor amusement or embellishment. Samuel Johnson remarked that a pun was Shakespeare's "fatal Cleopatra for which he lost the world, and was content to lose it." Thus Merrill has glorious precedent, but his excess of wit and verbal play clogs his style. His thoughts progress (to borrow a metaphor from Coleridge) like Surinam toads, sprouting little toads from back, side, and belly as they go. The proliferation is fascinating but distracting, and is especially undesirable in the trilogy, since a long poem must have a stride in its style.

Merrill is a spectator of life, *haud particeps* as Coleridge said of Wordsworth. In the world of his poetry other people—his father, for example, or his Greek friends—are the ones engaged in living; he observes them. In "The Book of Ephraim" the dead have this position. They watch the living but cannot "intervene."

Romantic love, a recurrent subject in Merrill, paradoxically confirms, as in Proust, his isolation. The protagonist in Merrill's lyrics is a person who has already lived through many love affairs. Waiting for the next love to rise above the horizon, he knows in advance that it too will seem a star at first and prove, in the end, a bubble. (The companionship of DJ and JM, movingly depicted in the trilogy, is not an exception, for Eros withdraws from it.) This is not, in Merrill, a theme for despair; it may leave him half-humorously resigned. Nevertheless, the rhythm of falling in and out of love creates its pessimism; while most in love, he may know it is illusion. Certainly he knows it afterward, and most of his poems are written in retrospection.

No contemporary poet is more practiced, moving, and inveterate than Merrill in Prospero-tones of valediction. His revels are always ended, and he looks back on them with gratitude, but also with disenchantment. Characteristically he is ready to relinquish, as in the lyric at the end of "McKane's Falls":

> Get me by heart, my friend,
> And then forget. Forgive . . .

Looking back on what was, he feels that it had its limited reality or value, but was also smoke. As people, experiences, emotions recede from him, they are transformed into themes for art.

Because Merrill's stance is retrospective, it is also contemplative. What was, must now be understood. This, however, is impossible, if only because our information, even about what we ourselves experienced, is always full of gaps. Merrill's situation in Greece, hearing a language he imperfectly understands, is characteristic. In other poems he receives telephone calls on bad connections or postcards that are half illegible. Moreover, when he tries to interpret, too many interpretations come to mind. Merrill moons and pores over events, memories, images, words, detecting always more possible meanings. His syntax extends horizontally, packing thought within thought, and loses thrust or momentum. He spreads metaphors like nets to see what they will catch. To make any particular interpretation of an experience is always, to some degree, willful, and Merrill finds this assertion difficult. One typically finds him as he describes himself in "The Will":

> wondering as always what it means

And what else I'm forgetting,
On my cold way.

Many of these themes are central to his poem "Lost in Translation." Here Merrill remembers a summer from his childhood in which his parents were absent and he waited for them to send a jigsaw puzzle. When this arrived and was pieced together, it showed a painting by a follower of Gérôme, and pictured a sheik, a veiled woman, and a "small backward-looking slave or page boy." For Merrill the scene expressed family tensions at a time when his father was taking a new wife. The past—that summer, his parents, and what was going on between them—is similarly a puzzle ("A summer without parents is the puzzle"), and solving it is impossible. A piece is missing, in fact, has been willfully secreted. Moreover, to recall the past is inevitably to transform it creatively, as the painting both reflected and transformed the family crisis, or as Merrill does in writing the poem. The governing metaphor of the poem is translation, a process in which the original is both reconstituted and lost:

Lost, is it, buried? One more missing piece?

But nothing's lost. Or else: all is translation
And every bit of us is lost in it
(Or found . . .

Like many artists Merrill feels guilty toward life. He suspects that he views his experience primarily as material for poetry and that to him the poetry is more significant and absorbing than the experience itself. Merrill even suggests that his emotions are theatrical, that he has arranged for his "passions and betrayals . . . Chiefly in order to make song of them." Yet he also suspects that in comparison with actual life art lacks seriousness. At the end of Merrill's trilogy the real and intense grief of a friend for his dead wife comes shatteringly into the poem of ouija board conversations, and for the moment makes them seem appallingly artificial. "The Broken Home" opens with a strange but characteristic prayer of the poet to be "as real/ At least as the people upstairs." And, like Tonio Kröger, Merrill is attracted to characters—his cat Maisie, his lover Strato, the Greek "Kostas Tympakianákis," the farmers in "David's Night in Veliès"—who are naive and unreflecting. As "The Book of Ephraim" puts it in doggerel verse,

> However seldom in my line to feel,
> I most love those for whom the world is real.

Recurrently this guilt toward life expresses itself in anxieties about childlessness. "The little feet that patter" in Merrill's life "are metrical," and the fact obsesses him. In Merrill's first novel, *The Seraglio*, Francis castrates himself, and is thereafter thrilled to suppose, wrongly, that he had previously sired a child. In his poetry Merrill produces children one way or another. He is a godfather in "Verse for Urania." In the trilogy he and DJ father children by "psycho insemination." At the end of the trilogy the four archangels and Nature herself attend the birth of a child like gushing grandparents. Naturally Merrill connects his excited reaction to childlessness, his anxieties and compensatory imaginations, with guilt about his sexual orientation. But the complex of guilts centered around childlessness and homosexuality feeds into those relating to art. Childlessness symbolizes, in the most urgent, charged way, the artist's problematic relation to life.

Yet Merrill also assumes that a detached, merely reflective, childless relation to life is intimately connected with intellectual and creative achievement. Works of art are conscience money, so to speak, by which the artist hopes to redeem the guilt of a childless life, and yet the childless life conduces to art. The "CHILDLESSNESS WE SHARE," the batlike 741 declares in *Mirabell*, "TURNS US / OUTWARD TO THE LESSONS & THE MYSTERIES." 741 continues, with typical punning,

> THE TYPE U SET JM, INVERTED & BACKWARD,
> IS YET READ RIGHTSIDE UP ON THE BIOLOGICAL PAGE
> . . . .
>   FOR THE LOVE
> U EXPERIENCE IS NOT THE STRAIGHTFORWARD FRONTAL LOVE
> MANY READERS INFER & YET OUR V WORK [art, intellectual
>   creativity] MUST SING OUT
> PAEANS TO THE GREENHOUSE THO WE OURSELVES ARE . . .
>   TONE DEAF.

THE CHANGING LIGHT AT SANDOVER

Merrill's poem of 560 pages has three books and a coda. The three books are apportioned into sections according to the plan of the Ouija board. "The Book of Ephraim" (1976), with ninety-two pages, is divided into twenty-eight sections, each beginning with a letter of the alphabet from A to Z. In the second book of the trilogy, *Mirabell's Books of Number* (1978), which runs to 183 pages, the separate sections are numbered from 0 to 9, and within each there are subdivisions, as 0.1, 0.2, and so forth. Number is important in *Mirabell* because the book playfully adopts a scientific view of reality. The communicator, corresponding to Ephraim in the first book of the trilogy, is 741, a batlike creature who thinks in mathematics and rattles off formulae. 741 contemplates the laws of science that determine what we experience, and these are, for him, ultimately mathematical. (As an indication of the degree to which Merrill loves word games, I may mention that in each major section of *Mirabell* the first syllable of the text names its number in some language: section 0 begins "Oh"; section 1, "I"; section 4, "Fear," punning on the German "Vier," and so on.) *Scripts for the Pageant* (1980), the third book of the trilogy, has only three major parts, entitled "Yes," "&," and "No." These are appropriate titles because this book, the longest of the poem, especially questions whether mankind will survive and whether God or the cosmos is on man's side in this struggle. As "Yes & No" suggests, no definite answer is given. A brief *Coda* of forty-one pages, *The Higher Keys* (1982), concludes the enormous poem with a gala in the ballroom at Sandover, Merrill's boyhood home. Here Merrill is to read his poem to illustrious guests from the other world, including Jane Austen, T. S. Eliot, Goethe, Gertrude Stein, Dante, and Proust. The poem ends as he enunciates its opening word.

While Merrill was writing "The Book of Ephraim," he did not know more was to follow. Within the completed trilogy, however, "The Book of Ephraim" serves as a preface, telling how Merrill and Jackson became absorbed in operating a Ouija board, and how their doubts about the credibility and significance of the messages they transcribed gradually disappeared. The narrative may be autobiographically truthful, but rhetorically it aims to create faith in the reader—at least to erode skepticism—by showing that Merrill and Jackson did not themselves believe without a struggle, and that they were finally converted by impressive evidence. Eventually, then, they accepted that through the Ouija board they were in contact with a reality they could not otherwise have reached—we may call it the "beyond"—and that the doctrines transmitted to them from this source were true. Just what their "beyond" may consist of—whether it is the dead (plus fabulous beasts, archangels, muses, Nature, and God) or their own unconscious—and whether its doctrines are "true" literally or symbolically, are questions to which I shall return.

In versification the trilogy includes odes, sonnets, sestinas, and other stanzaic forms, but generally the narration is given in blank verse; DJ and JM also speak in this measure, and so, usually, do the human dead, including Ephraim. 741 (later, Mirabell) speaks in syllabic verse of fourteen syllables to the line. The archangels speak free verse, and the voice of God falls into ten-syllable syllabics. The words dictated via the Ouija board are printed in capitals.

The different parts of the trilogy have different relations to the Ouija-board transcripts on which they are based. As the trilogy proceeds, the transcripts become, if we believe Merrill, progressively less "edited." In composing "The Book of Ephraim," Merrill was using material from the previous nineteen years of his life. "Many of the transcripts I had made from Ouija board sessions," Merrill explained in an interview, "had vanished, except for the high points which I'd copied out over the years into a special notebook." Since relatively much less transcription could be cited directly, the poem contains a higher proportion of narrative than the later parts of the trilogy, and Ephraim's teachings are summarized rather than quoted, with advantages to the speed of presentation. For *Mirabell* enormous amounts of transcript had piled up; "What you see in the poem might be half, or two-fifths, of the original." The problem in composing was to sift through this mass of material, to select, shape, and edit. Except for deciding about line breaks and other minute points, *Scripts for the Pageant* was transmitted just as it is. At least this is true of the "Lessons," which make up roughly two-fifths of the text; "in between the Lessons . . . I still felt free to pick and choose; but even there, the design of the book just swept me along." David Jackson adds that the "beyond" also supplied schedules, specifying when the sessions at the Ouija board were to take place and when the poem was to be completed and published.

Some readers will be interested in the chronology of dictation and composition. As the trilogy tells it, "The Book of Ephraim" was composed between January and December of 1974. In the summer of 1975 Jackson and Merrill were informed by Ephraim that they were to be the "VEHICLE" of a "BREAKTHRU." "POEMS OF SCIENCE" were required. Through the winter of 1975–76 Merrill read in science (of a relatively popular kind, needless to say), and the Ouija-board transcripts that resulted in *Mirabell* were obtained in the summer of 1976. Beginning in the fall of 1976, Merrill composed or "edited" *Mirabell,* and during the transmission of *Scripts for the Pageant,* which seems to have taken place largely between May and September of 1977, Merrill was still working on *Mirabell.* The action of the *Coda* takes place in the summer of 1978. Roughly two years earlier Merrill had been informed by 741 that after *Scripts* no more poems would be dictated.

ONE POEM BEYOND THIS IN CYCLE   AFTER WHICH
U WILL BE RETURND TO YR CHRONICLES OF LOVE & LOSS.

MERRILL'S TRILOGY IN LITERARY HISTORY

In terms of literary history *The Changing Light at Sandover* synthesizes different modes of contemporary poetry in the United States since the Second World War. Its stylistic ground is the New Critical or "academic" formalism with which Merrill, like most American poets of his generation, was imprinted in college. From this derive such elements of the trilogy as its mastery and display of strict, traditional meters and stanzas, its intricate organization of motifs, and its "wit." The persistent allusions in the poem to literature, art, and music of the past, to a painting of Georgione, to "The Rake's Progress" of Stravinski, to Dante, Pope, Wagner, Proust, and so forth, are also a legacy from the Modernist academic style of the 1940s and 1950s.

Like most American poets Merrill modified his style in the 1960s and 1970s in response to the new conventions of Beat,

Projectivist, Confessional, and Surrealist poetry. *The Changing Light at Sandover* is not a Confessional poem. Yet the directly autobiographical and intimate passages in it would not have been written without the Confessional movement in poetry and without the postwar changes in social mores that allowed poets, like everyone else, to speak more frankly about their personal lives.

In the 1960s poetry in the United States entered a phase in which the utmost earnestness could be combined with clowning. Eccentricity—what is out of the center—was welcome, if only because it manifested rejection of the established cultural and moral order. Dada gestures, Tibetan chants—Om! Om!—Surrealist dissociations, and epiphanies of Mayan and Egyptian deities and of Jungian archetypes explored new possibilities of spiritual experience. Sincere and meaningful as they were, these novelties were often also deliberately comic. The Ouija board in Merrill's trilogy is a similar eccentricity. Moreover, it puts responsibility for the poem on something other than the conscious intelligence of the author. Since he must be faithful to his sources, Merrill can be excused from imposing greater coherence on his work than they support. Thus changing perspectives become plausible, and so do different versions of the same event, unexpected interpolations, indeterminate relations between parts, inconsistencies, and other usual features of Modernist and Postmodernist art as it expresses our intellectual uncertainty and emotional ambivalence. And as Merrill said in an interview, "The mechanics of the board—this absurd, flimsy contraption, creaking along—serves wonderfully as hedge against inflation"— against pomposity, overseriousness. He himself is noticing that the Ouija board is a comic device. The tone of camp, which is prominent throughout the trilogy, is another humorous and eccentric novelty. Thirty years ago the Ouija board and camp would not have been acceptable in a major work, no more so than passages of personal autobiography.

READERS VERSUS THE OUIJA BOARD

If Merrill's trilogy had been composed by the same creative processes as his other poems, his imitation of Ouija-board transcripts would be regarded as a triumph of imaginative inventiveness. But that the transcripts, however edited, were actually produced via the board is a problem for readers. In an interview David Jackson feared that readers "would never quite suspend [their] disbelief and allow JM's poetry its own excuse for being." He argued that the source of the poem makes no difference; we must read it as we would any other poem. But this is impossible because the poem activates an autobiographical convention. We must, in other words, identify JM, the character in the poem, with James Merrill, the author, and therefore we must raise questions that, probably, we would rather not. Does Merrill believe, for example, that the dead continue to exist and communicate with him through the Ouija board? And that there are, as the Ouija board states, nine stages of life after death? As elements in an imaginative work, such propositions need cause no difficulty; as beliefs of the author, they are incredible, and undermine our faith in his intelligence. In Shelley's *Prometheus Unbound* Asia descends to the cave of Demogorgon, and we readily share her awe before this supernatural figure. But if at the Ouija board in their dining room Merrill and Jackson believe they confront the angel Gabriel, their fear and awe are ridiculous. The autobiographical level of the poem makes their credulity troubling.

How, then, do Merrill and Jackson, in their proper persons, understand their Ouija board experiences? They have waffled somewhat on this question. When Helen Vendler asked Merrill whether he believed the doctrines transmitted through the Ouija board, such as spiritualism and reincarnation, he replied, "when you are caught up in it you believe it wholeheartedly; when you cool off you see it as a stylization of various things in your experience." Jackson holds, to judge from published interviews, that the words they transcribed came from their "unconscious." In an interview for the *Paris Review* Merrill suggested that "if it's still *yourself*" that you reach via the Ouija board, "then that self is much stranger and freer and more far-seeing than the one you thought you knew."

Within the poem JM and DJ do not always take their experience literally and credulously. In section "I" of "The Book of Ephraim" JM's psychiatrist also suggests that the words of the Ouija board come from the unconscious, and at least in that moment JM thinks he has a point. At the end of "The Book of Ephraim" JM again adopts the view that the source of the poem was in themselves, not in the beyond: "We, all we knew, dreamed, felt and had forgotten . . . became through [Ephraim] a set of/ Quasi-grammatical constructions." In fact, the rhetorical strategy of the poem is to present JM and DJ as initially incredulous and finally persuaded by evidence impossible to explain away. Eventually they forget, most of the time, to question the source or reality of their experience, and simply accept it for its interest and beauty. Obviously Merrill hopes readers will do the same.

"THE BOOK OF EPHRAIM"

Compared with "The Book of Ephraim," other long poems of our time are structurally primitive. One strand in the complicated, triple plot is the friendship of JM and DJ over a period of twenty-five years, a moving story of love changing into affectionate companionship. In this aspect "The Book of Ephraim" is the most extended, circumstantial, and sympathetic portrait of a gay relationship that has yet been written by an American poet. The contacts of DJ and JM with Ephraim at the Ouija board and their developing relationship with him are very much a part of their story, for their experiences at the Ouija board reinforce the bond between them. They pursue this absorbing interest together, and share it with no one else. The "beyond" disclosed through the Ouija board becomes a world in which they live as much as they do in this one—or finally more. It tends to isolate them from ordinary life and society, and provides them with friends among the dead—an alternative society—sympathetic to their relationship and delightful in every other way also—witty, sophisticated, kind, affectionate, supportive. Ephraim himself, who was in life a favorite of the emperor Tiberius in his Capri orgies (the poem calls them "CAPRICES"), is an original and beguiling character.

A second strand of the plot concerns the novel JM had intended to write instead of the poem. Some characters and episodes within the novel are described—enough, in fact, so that we can reconstruct the plot, though not completely. We get a double perspective: the poem tells the story as (supposedly) it happened, and the novel represents the fictional version Merrill intended to create, partly on the basis of the "real" story, though with invented elements added. Characters in the poem are reflected in characters of the novel—Ephraim, for example, becomes Eros in the novel—and the plot of the novel counterpoints with that of the poem in an intricate way. Because the "story" exists in two forms, both are deconstructed; at the same time, though it seems a contradiction, the "real" version seems more real because it is contrasted with an admittedly "fictional" one. The poem's report also seems more "real" because the plot of the novel includes obviously melodramatic, Romantic, and conventional elements. There is much joking in the poem about the fictionality of fiction. Both the poem and the novel interconnect with Merrill's earlier life and poetry. Thus Matt Prentis in the novel is Matt Jackson in the poem, David Jackson's father, but is also a negative version of Charles Merrill. Joanna in the novel is the "other woman" who caused the divorce of Merrill's parents, though in the novel the wiles of this dragon-witch are defeated.

A third strand of the plot traces when and why the novel was abandoned and the poem written. As we read the poem, we can follow the chronology of its composition. For example, "A" is written in January 1974, "L" in the summer, "O" in August, "W" in the fall, "Z" in December. Thus we are always conscious of two times, that of the past and that of the present in which the past is being recollected and described. Events that happened long ago are counterpointed with others taking place in the year of composition. What occurs in the year of composition alters JM's understanding of the past.

During the year of composition, the most dramatic single event was the intervention (narrated in "U," though it actually took place in June 1974 and thus prior to the writing of the poem from "L" on) of a power higher than Ephraim. It commanded JM to finish the poem within six months—"MYND YOUR WEORK SIX MOONES REMAIN." The mysterious power reinforced its command by stamping on DJ's hand, leaving it "creased, red, sore." This event seems to have frightened DJ and JM, for thereafter they did not communicate with Ephraim for a year. Thus a time of tedium in their relationship coincides with a temporary loss of contact with Ephraim, and in the novel Ephraim is Eros.

That in the wake of this JM presumably devotes himself to composition is also a point of psychological and thematic meaning. The personal life becomes the work.

The theme of the DJ-JM-Ephraim plot is the "incarnation and withdrawal of a god." The god is Ephraim, a spirit from beyond, and Ephraim, to repeat, is Eros. The waning of erotic intensity in the relationship of JM and DJ is ruefully but firmly acknowledged, and the emotion left behind, in the aftermath, is the typically Merrillean one I characterized earlier, compounded of valediction and regret, yet also of gratitude for what was and for the intimacy and affection that still survive. In section "G" of the poem JM contemplates the remains of a heart that, long ago, a friend embossed on the threshold of their house. Drawn in flour, it was then sprinkled with rum and set on fire, and was thus baked to the floor.

> Heart once intricate as birdsong, it
> Hardened on the spot. Much come-and-go
> Has blackened, pared the scabby curlicue
> Down to smatterings which, even so,
> Promise to last this lifetime. That will do.

But in the theme of the "incarnation and withdrawal of a god," the god is also Hermes, the messenger of heaven and conductor of souls between this world and the other. The god of lucky finds and hence of interpretations, Hermes also lends his name to the type of occult writing to which Merrill's poem belongs because of its esoteric doctrines. According to the doctrines taught by Ephraim, every living person is the "representative" of a "patron" in the world of the dead. Patrons anxiously observe the lives of their representatives, but theirs "IS A SILENT LOVE"; they cannot intervene. The representatives are reincarnated over and over, however, and between lives they are instructed by their patrons in "savoir vivre." This teaching may not take hold, and there is "NO PUNISHMENT LIKE THAT OF BEING GIVEN/ A GROSS OR SLUGGISH REPRESENTATIVE," but if the representative learns "savoir vivre," he or she ceases to be reincarnated. This soul has now reached the first of the nine stages of the afterworld, where it becomes itself a patron, and its own patron also moves up a stage.

Just what is comprised in "savoir vivre" we much wish to know, but like other ancient sages, Ephraim conveys his ethical lore in aphoristic fragments, such as,

USE USE USE
YR BODIES & YR MINDS;

take

FROM SENSUAL PLEASURE ONLY WHAT WILL NOT
DURING IT BE EVEN PARTLY SPOILED
BY FEAR OF LOSING TOO MUCH.

We also note that as souls ascend in the afterworld, their sensory life revives, and that Hans Lodeizen, a dead friend of JM's, might now be at higher stage if he had "BEEN LESS VIRTUOUS THAT SPRING NIGHT." Clearly Ephraim's "savoir vivre" is not ascetic, but neither is it coarsely hedonistic, for it stresses the intellectual as well as the sensual. His awareness of life's vicissitudes and of death evokes an attitude of carpe diem, but this is balanced by a fear of clutching too strongly at what inevitably will be lost. During his life in the Roman imperial court, Ephraim probably read Epicurus.

On October 26, 1961, however, Ephraim communicates ethical teachings (quoted in "Q") of an altogether different tendency. These remarks anticipate later books of the trilogy. The "MAIN IMPETUS" of the whole system of representatives and patrons, of the relations between the living and the dead, is "DEVOTION": "DEVOTION TO EACH OTHER TO WORK TO REPRODUCTION TO AN IDEAL." Ultimately such devotion has God for its object, but God is here understood to mean "THE CONTINUUM." Our devotion, in other words, is to the continued existence of life, to the earthly greenhouse and the creation in it of Eden. History is approaching a crisis, Ephraim feels, when life will be transformed, "INTO WELL EITHER A GREAT GLORY OR A GREAT PUDDLE."

MIRABELL AND SCRIPTS FOR THE PAGEANT

The two latter books of the trilogy make essentially one didactic poem. Swatches of instruction are transmitted via the Ouija board, and the audience, which consists of JM, DJ, WHA (Wystan Auden), and MM (Maria Mitsotáki, a Greek friend of

Merrill and Jackson), and others as well, reacts emotionally and also tries to interpret what they have been told. They relate the latest communication to previous ones, guess at the motives of the "beyond" in its revelations, and speculate on the hierarchical relations among the various communicators. These exchanges of reaction and commentary also take place through the Ouija board, of course, since WHA and MM are dead. Only the dead can see what is happening in the beyond, and they tell the living pair what the communicators look like and describe the stages on which they speak. Much of the humor and charm of the poem comes in these interpolated conversations, though eventually some of the didactic passages also become fascinating.

As narratives *Mirabell* and *Scripts for the Pageant* are less interesting than "The Book of Ephraim," but we are motivated to read by the brilliance of many passages. Furthermore, like virtually all long poems since *The Waste Land,* Merrill's trilogy interweaves the same or similar images as leitmotifs throughout the poem. Imagery of mirrors, fires, streams, waterfalls, black, light, gardens, and much else recurs with increasing meaning and emotion. So also do themes, such as that of the "broken home." (In some passages the cosmology and planetary history set forth in the poem seem to be a transposition of this trauma in Merrill's childhood.) The more we read the poem, the richer in implication and association every passage becomes.

The parts of the poem are also bound together by two devices of plot. One of these, which I may call retrospective revelation, is to disclose something new about the past. Events, characters, and information given earlier in the poem are seen, later on, not to have been what they were initially said to be. The campy Ephraim, for example, turns out in the *Coda* at the very end to have been all along the archangel Michael. This discovery rewrites the character of Ephraim, giving, as the poem puts it, a "RESONANCE ... [a] HIDDEN 4TH DIMENSION" to his speeches from the start. Maria Mitsotáki is similarly revealed to be Plato. Merrill probably owes this device to Proust. The poem is also constructed, like Dante's, to create a progressive revelation. Merrill's "beyond" has a hierarchical structure, and as the poem unfolds, we mount with growing suspense from lower instructors to higher ones, ascending from 741 to Michael and other archangels and finally to God.

A great many separate stories and myths are set going in the last books of the trilogy, and some of them are deeply moving. One, for example, tells of the transformation of the batlike 741 into the peacock Mirabell, a metamorphosis engendered by contact with the "psychic atom" of JM, DJ, WHA, and MM—by the attraction, in other words, of the affectionate, sensory life of human beings. Another myth narrates the history of Atlantis. In another the voice of God, at least, the God of our galaxy, is heard as a radio transmission in outer space. He is broadcasting not to earth but into the extragalactic cosmos, from which no answer comes. These myths are not presented all at once; instead, a bit comes in one passage and a bit more in a later one. The reader must piece them together. Something similar happens at the level of doctrine. We try to make a coherent system out of patches of information the poem does not convey systematically.

The teachings from "beyond" fascinate only to the extent that we need not read them literally. As in Yeats's *A Vision*, a great deal is simply tedious. To learn, for example, that there are five "V" or elite souls through whom, in various reincarnations, cultural advance has taken place, and that these are Ahknaton, Homer, Montezuma, Nefertiti, and Plato, may be mildly entertaining, but the fantasy lacks beauty or significance. And to work out, as we must, the correspondence of each of these souls to a sense, season, color, archangel, and element (in Heraclitus' table of elements) is much labor for small reward. These correspondences enrich particular passages in the poem but have no bearing on any reality outside it. But when we read that because of the population explosion more souls are born than there are dead to be reincarnated, and that therefore the "lab," as it produces human souls, has been increasingly forced to use animal souls as raw material, we feel that this doctrine has much point, especially since the "lab" is worried about "ATOMIC/ WEAPONRY NOW FALLING INTO HANDS OF ANIMAL SOULS."

The doctrine of the nine stages of the afterworld illustrates how the esoteric lore of the poem may both bore and fascinate. To master the doctrine takes some effort, and literally it has no significance; obviously we do not read it as a revelation of what lies beyond the grave. But the poem hints at allegorical interpretations. The successive stages of the afterworld represent, for example, an increasing distance from life and, at the same time, a reconstituting of life into art. They also symbolize aging, in other words, dying conceived as gradual, continuing, and progressive. As the slow disintegration and vanishing of the self, this death is horrible, but in it the self is used to create something other and larger, as has happened to JM himself in the course of writing "The Book of Ephraim." "Here was I, or what was left of me," he reflects at the end; "Already I take up/ Less emotional space than a snowdrop":

> I used to
> Ask how on earth one got sufficiently
> Imbued with otherness. And now I see.

The nine stages also reflect a desire to escape from the confusions of life, a guilty desire, perhaps, through which one shows oneself "less noble" than those "untamed dead," such as JM's father and Mozart, who reject the nine stages and fiercely clutch at more lives. The text of the poem does not allow us to elaborate these suggestions into allegorical readings. But neither, usually, does it permit us to reject its doctrines as merely literal. Instead, it throws about them a penumbra of possible further meaning.

The poem describes mankind as a fresh start on the part of "God B" ("B" for Biology). Previously there was a civilization in China and then another in Atlantis, but both were destroyed in nuclear catastrophes. "V work" (the work of the five elite souls and also of life—French "vie") contributes to rebuild Eden, which is God B's aim. Thus the poem reflects a characteristic contemporary mentality in which the potentiality for destroying life on earth has produced a revulsion against technology. Science, which makes this possible, is felt to be problematic. The poem expresses a sense of human responsibility for the "greenhouse" on which all life depends, and, as one component of this, a hierarchical affection for animals, helpless passengers in our planetary lifeboat. As I just noted, the population explosion makes graver the menaces of ecological pollution and nuclear war.

The terrible side of the cosmos is personified in Gabriel, the angel of death. Yet the poem is ambivalent about death, for only through it can "V work" progress. Moreover, anxieties about overpopulation lead to a certain sympathy, chilling to the reader, with the impatience of Agatha or Nature, who is eager to get on with the earthquakes, droughts, and other natural disasters that will thin her garden. Such contemporary cultural manifestations as the pill, feminism, unisex fashions, and so forth are new rules emanating from the laboratory. In them God B is attempting to correct the signal, once proper but now false: "REPRODUCE!" *Scripts for the Pageant* culminates in a charming masque, written in a deliberately naive style, in which Nature, refusing to wear her glasses in public, either deliberately or inadvertently misreads her lines, and thus she does not say lines that had been written for her:

> NOW LET US BANISH GLOOMY DREAMS
> FOR HEAVEN ON EARTH MOST LIKELY SEEMS.

When at the end God is overheard, He draws a diagram and interprets it as a symbol of "MY UPRIGHT MAN," who is struggling to "CREATE FOR ME A PARADISE." Whether man will do this is finally up to man himself. *Scripts for the Pageant* ends with DJ and JM breaking off contact with the "beyond," as they have been instructed to do. Before this moment, God has commanded the poet to "MAKE A V WORK" out of the communications he has received.

Merrill's trilogy is an enormous achievement with enormous limitations. In grand themes, scale and complexity of design, mythopoeic power, human intimacy, wit, charm, sensory vividness, and metrical brilliance, the trilogy surpasses any long poem written in English since the Second World War. At the same time, however, its vision of things is ultimately incoherent, it suffers from the limitations of the fantastic as a genre and from the embarrassments of the Ouija board, and its polished, richly implicative phrasing lacks the speed, force, and sudden illumination of major poetry. Unlike *Leaves of Grass* or its great antagonist poem in American literature, *The Waste Land*, Merrill's trilogy cannot cause a revoluton in sensibility. It lacks the intensity of *The Bridge*, and it does not represent so wide and various a world as Crane's poem does. It is seldom so profound as the *Four Quartets*, and it cannot rival in pathos and sheer beauty the finest moments in the *Cantos*. But aside from these, no other long poem written by any American poet since Whitman can be ranked above Merrill's.

ACKNOWLEDGMENTS

Grateful acknowledgment is made for the use of material from the following:

Kenneth Allott, *The Ventriloquist's Doll,* The Crosset Press, 1943.

Kingsley Amis, *Collected Poems, 1944–1979,* Hutchinson & Co, Ltd., 1979. Copyright 1956 by Kingsley Amis. Extract of "Masters" reprinted by permission of Jonathan Clowes Ltd., London, on behalf of Kingsley Amis.

A. R. Ammons, *Collected Poems 1951–1971,* W. W. Norton, Inc., 1972; *Sphere,* W. W. Norton, Inc., 1977. Reprinted by permission of W. W. Norton & Company, Inc.

John Ashbery, *Rivers and Mountains,* Holt, Rinehart & Winston, 1966. Copyright © 1966 by John Ashbery; reprinted by permission of The Sterling Lord Agency, Inc. *Houseboat Days,* Penguin Books. Copyright © 1975, 1976, 1977 by John Ashbery; reprinted by permission of Viking Penguin, Inc., and Georges Borchardt, Inc. *The Tennis Court Oath,* Wesleyan University Press: excerpt from "Europe." Copyright © 1960 by John Ashbery; reprinted by permission of Wesleyan University Press. *As We Know,* Penguin Books, 1979. Copyright © 1979 by John Ashbery; reprinted by permission of Viking Penguin, Inc., and of Carcanet Press Limited. *Self-Portrait in a Convex Mirror,* Penguin Books, 1976. Copyright © 1972, 1973, 1974, 1975 by John Ashbery; reprinted by permission of Viking Penguin, Inc., and of Carcanet Press. *Some Trees,* The Ecco Press, 1978. By permission of Georges Borchardt, Inc. *The Double Dream of Spring,* The Ecco Press, 1976. By permission of Georges Borchardt, Inc.

W. H. Auden, *The English Auden: Poems, Essays and Dramatic Writings,* ed. Edward Mendelson, Random House, 1977; *Collected Poems of W. H. Auden,* ed. Edward Mendelson, Random House, 1976. Excerpts reprinted by permission of Random House, Inc., and of Faber and Faber Ltd.

Amiri Baraka, *Selected Poetry of Amiri Baraka / LeRoi Jones:* excerpt from "In Memory of Radio." Copyright © 1979 by Amiri Baraka; reprinted by permission of William Morrow & Company.

George Barker, *Collected Poems, 1930–1955,* Faber and Faber, 1957. Reprinted by permission of Faber and Faber Ltd. *The True Confession of George Barker,* New American Library, 1964. By permission of George Barker.

John Berryman, *His Toy, His Dream, His Rest,* Farrar, Straus and Giroux, 1968: excerpts from #235, #256. Copyright © 1964, 1965, 1966, 1967, 1968 by John Berryman; reprinted by permission of Farrar, Straus and Giroux, Inc., and of Faber and Faber Publishers. *77 Dream Songs,* Farrar, Straus and Giroux, 1964; excerpt from Dream Song #26. Copyright © 1959, 1962, 1963, 1964 by John Berryman; reprinted by permission of Farrar, Straus and Giroux, Inc., and of Faber and Faber Publishers. *Homage to Mistress Bradstreet,* Farrar, Straus and Cudahy, 1956. Copyright © 1956 by John Berryman; copyright renewed © 1984 by Kate Berryman; reprinted by permission of Farrar, Straus and Giroux, Inc., and of Faber and Faber Publishers. *Love and Fame,* Farrar, Straus and Giroux, 1970: excerpts from "Two Organs" and "Of Suicide." Copyright © 1970 by John Berryman; reprinted by permission of Farrar, Straus and Giroux, Inc., and of Faber and Faber Publishers.

Elizabeth Bishop, *The Complete Poems, 1927–1979,* Farrar, Straus and Giroux: excerpts from "The Fish," "Roosters," "At the Fishhouses," "The Bight," "A Cold Spring," and "The Moose." Copyright 1940, 1941, 1947, 1949, 1952 by Elizabeth Bishop; copyright renewed © 1968, 1974, 1976 by Elizabeth Bishop; copyright renewed © 1980 by Alice Helen Methfessel; copyright © 1983 by Alice Helen Methfessel. "At the Fishhouses," "The Bight," and "A Cold Spring" originally appeared in *The New Yorker.* Reprinted by permission of Farrar, Straus and Giroux, Inc.

Paul Blackburn, *In. On. Or About the Premises,* Cape Goliard Press, 1968. Reprinted by permission of Cape Goliard Press.

Robert Bly, *The Teeth Mother Naked at Last,* City Lights Bookstore, © 1970. Reprinted by permission of City Lights Bookstore and of Robert Bly. *This Tree Will Be Here for a Thousand Years,* © 1979: excerpt from "Amazed by an Accumulation of Snow." Copyright © 1978 by Robert Bly; reprinted by permission of Harper & Row, Publishers, Inc. *Silence in the Snowy Fields and Other Poems,* Jonathan Cape, 1967. Reprinted by permission of Robert Bly and of Jonathan Cape Ltd.

Basil Bunting, *Collected Poems,* Oxford University Press, 1978. Copyright © 1978 by Basil Bunting; reprinted by permission of Oxford University Press.

Roy Campbell, *Collected Poems,* The Bodley Head Ltd., 3rd impression, 1959. Reprinted by permission of Fransisco Campbell Custódio and Ad. Donker (Pty) Ltd.

Austin Clarke, *Collected Poems,* The Dolmen Press in association with Oxford University Press, 1974. Reprinted by permission of The Dolmen Press.

Hart Crane, *The Complete Poems and Selected Letters and Prose of Hart Crane,* ed. Brom Weber, © 1933, 1958, 1966 by Liveright Publishing Corporation. Reprinted by permission of the publisher.

Robert Creeley, *For Love: Poems, 1950–1965*, Calder and Boyars, 1966: "I Know A Man" and "The Business." Copyright © 1962 by Robert Creeley; reprinted by permission of Charles Scribner's Sons and Marion Boyars Publishers Ltd.

E. E. Cummings, *The Complete Poems 1913–1962*: excerpts from "Tumbling hair," "ta," "i thank you God for most this amazing," "a connotation of infinity," "raise the shade," "in the exquisite," "i will be," and "yoozwidduh" from *Tulips and Chimneys* (1923, 1976); "twi-/is-light" from *ViVa* (1931, 1979). Reprinted by permission of the Liveright Publishing Corporation and of Grafton Books, a division of the Collins Publishing Group. Excerpt from "this little bride & groom" reprinted by permission of the publishers listed above and of Harcourt Brace Jovanovich, Inc.

J. V. Cunningham, *Collected Poems and Epigrams*, The Swallow Press, 1972. Reprinted by permission of Ohio University Press, Athens.

Donald Davie, *Collected Poems, 1950–1970*, Routledge & Kegan Paul, 1972. Reprinted by permission of Donald Davie.

Cecil Day-Lewis, *Collected Poems*, Jonathan Cape with the Hogarth Press, 1954. Reprinted by permission of the Executors of the Estate of C. Day-Lewis, Jonathan Cape Ltd, the Hogarth Press, and A. D. Peters & Co Ltd.

Edward Dorn, *Gunslinger*, Black Sparrow Press, 1969.

Keith Douglas, *The Complete Poems of Keith Douglas*, ed. Desmond Graham, Oxford University Press, 1978. Reprinted by permission of the Oxford University Press.

Robert Duncan, *The Years as Catches*, Oyez, 1966. Reprinted by permission of Robert Duncan. *Bending the Bow*, New Directions, 1968. Copyright © 1965, 1968 by Robert Duncan: "The Fire" was first published in *Poetry*. Reprinted by permission of New Directions Publishing Corporation.

Richard Eberhart, *Collected Poems, 1930–1976*, Oxford University Press, New York, 1976. Reprinted by permission of Oxford University Press.

T. S. Eliot, *Collected Poems 1909–1962*, Harcourt, Brace and World, 1968. Reprinted by permission of Harcourt Brace Jovanovich Inc. and Faber and Faber Publishers. *Four Quartets*. Reprinted by permission of Harcourt Brace Jovanovich Inc. and Faber and Faber Publishers.

William Empson, *Collected Poems*, Harcourt, Brace & Co., 1949. Reprinted by permission of the Estate of William Empson, Chatto & Windus, and Harcourt Brace Jovanovich Inc.

Gavin Ewart, *Poems and Songs*, The Fortune Press, London, 1939. Reprinted by permission of Gavin Ewart.

Roy Fuller, *Collected Poems*, Andre Deutsch Ltd., 1962. Reprinted by permission of Andre Deutsch.

mission of Harper & Row, Publishers, Inc.; the same material reprinted by permission of Faber & Faber Ltd from *Crow.*

David Ignatow, *Rescue the Dead,* Wesleyan University Press, 1975: excerpt from "Rescue the Dead." Copyright © 1966 by David Ignatow; reprinted by permission of Wesleyan University Press. "Rescue the Dead" first appeared in *Poetry.*

Randall Jarrell, *The Lost World,* Macmillan, 1964. Copyright © Randall Jarrell 1963, 1965; reprinted by permission of Macmillan Publishing Company. *Little Friend, Little Friend,* Dial Press, 1945. Reprinted by permission of Mary Jarrell. *The Seven League Crutches,* Harcourt, Brace, 1951. Reprinted by permission of Mary Jarrell.

Robinson Jeffers, *The Selected Poetry of Robinson Jeffers,* Random House, 1937. Reprinted by permission of Random House.

David Jones, *In Parenthesis,* Chilmark Press. *Anathemata,* Chilmark Press. Reprinted by permission of Faber and Faber Ltd.

Patrick Kavanagh, *Collected Poems,* W. W. Norton & Co. Reprinted by permission of Mrs. Katherine Kavanagh and Devin-Adair Publishers.

Robert Kelly, *Finding the Measure,* 1968. Reprinted by permission of Black Sparrow Press.

Sidney Keyes, *Collected Poems,* Henry Holt & Co., 1947. Reprinted by permission of Routledge and Kegan Paul Ltd.

Galway Kinnell, *Flower Herding on Mount Monadnock.* Copyright © 1964 by Galway Kinnell. *What a Kingdom It Was.* Copyright © 1960 by Galway Kinnell. *The Book of Nightmares.* Copyright © 1971 by Galway Kinnell. Reprinted by permission of Houghton Mifflin Company and Andre Deutsch Ltd.

Thomas Kinsella, *Poems 1956–1973,* The Dolmen Press, 1980. Reprinted by permission of The Dolmen Press.

Kenneth Koch, *When the Sun Tries to Go On,* Black Sparrow Press, 1969. Reprinted by permission of Black Sparrow Press.

Philip Larkin, *The Less Deceived,* The Marvell Press: excerpts from "Reasons for Attendance" and "Church Going." Reprinted by permission of The Marvell Press. *The Whitsun Weddings,* Faber and Faber, 1964. Reprinted by permission of Faber and Faber Ltd.

John Lehmann, *Collected Poems, 1930–1963,* Eyre & Spottiswoode, 1963: excerpts from "Midsummer" and "Letter." Reprinted by permission of David Higham Associates Limited.

Denise Levertov, *Collected Earlier Poems: 1940–1960,* 1979. Copyright © 1955 by Denise Levertov. *Relearning the Alphabet,* New Directions. Copyright © 1968 by Denise Levertov Goodman. Reprinted by permission of New Directions Publishing Corporation.

Audre Lorde, *Chosen Poems Old and New,* W. W. Norton & Co., 1982. Reprinted by permission of W. W. Norton & Co.

Robert Lowell, *Day by Day*, Farrar, Straus and Giroux, 1977: excerpts from "Jean Stafford, a Letter," "Epilogue," "Last Walk," and "Seventh Year." Copyright © 1975, 1976, 1977 by Robert Lowell. *For the Union Dead:* excerpt from "For the Union Dead." Copyright © 1960 by Robert Lowell. *Life Studies*, Farrar, Straus and Cudahy, 1959: excerpt from "Man and Wife." Copyright © 1956, 1959 by Robert Lowell. *Near the Ocean*, Farrar, Straus and Giroux, 1967: excerpt from "Waking Early Sunday Morning." Copyright © 1963, 1965, 1966, 1967 by Robert Lowell. *Imitations*, Farrar, Straus and Cudahy, 1961: excerpt from "The Cadet Picture of My Father." Copyright (©) 1958, 1959, 1960, 1961 by Robert Lowell. All of the above are reprinted by permission of Farrar, Straus and Giroux and Faber and Faber Ltd. *Poems, 1938–1949*, Faber and Faber, 1950: excerpts from "The Quaker Graveyard in Nantucket." Reprinted by permission of Harcourt Brace Jovanovich, Inc. and Faber and Faber Ltd.

Thomas MacGreevy, in *Contemporary Irish Poetry*, ed. Anthony Bradley, University of California Press, 1980.

Archibald MacLeish, *New & Collected Poems, 1917–1976*, Houghton Mifflin, 1976. Copyright © 1976 by Archibald MacLeish; reprinted by permission of Houghton Mifflin Company.

Louis MacNeice, *Collected Poems*, ed. E. R. Dodds, Faber and Faber, 1966. Reprinted by permission of Faber and Faber Ltd.

Charles Madge, in *New Country: Prose and Poetry by the Authors of New Signatures*, ed. Michael Roberts, The Hogarth Press, 1933. Reprinted by permission of Faber and Faber Publishers and Charles Madge.

James Merrill, *Divine Comedies*, Atheneum, 1980: excerpts from "The Kimono," "McKane's Falls," "The Will," "Lost in Translation," and "The Book of Ephraim." Copyright © 1976 by James Merrill; reprinted by permission of Atheneum Publishers, Inc., and Oxford University Press. *The Changing Light at Sandover*, Atheneum, 1982. Copyright © 1982 by James Merrill; reprinted by permission of Atheneum Publishers, Inc. *Mirabell: Books of Number*, Atheneum, 1979: excerpts from "Mirabell: Book 1," "Mirabell: Book 4," and "Mirabell: Book 6." Copyright © 1978 by James Merrill; reprinted by permission of Atheneum Publishers, Inc., and Oxford University Press. *Water Street:* excerpts from "A Tenancy." Copyright © 1962 by James Merrill; reprinted by permission of Atheneum Publishers, Inc.

W. S. Merwin, *The First Four Books of Poems*, Atheneum, 1980. Copyright © 1975 by W. S. Merwin. *The Dancing Bears.* Copyright © 1954 by Yale University Press; copyright renewed 1982 by W. S. Merwin. *The Lice*, Atheneum, 1967: excerpt from "An End in Spring." Copyright © 1967 by W. S. Merwin. *Writings to an Unfinished Accompaniment*, Atheneum, 1973. Reprinted by permission of Atheneum Publishers, Inc., and David Higham Associates Limited.

John Montague, *A Slow Dance*, The Dolmen Press, 1975. Reprinted by permission of John Montague and The Dolmen Press.

Edwin Muir, *Collected Poems*, Oxford University Press, 1965. Reprinted by permission of Oxford University Press and Faber and Faber Publishers.

Howard Nemerov, *Collected Poems*, The University of Chicago Press, 1977. Reprinted by permission of Howard Nemerov.

Frank O'Hara, *Collected Poems*, ed. Donald Allen, 1972. Reprinted by permission of Random House, Inc. Excerpts from "The Day Lady Died," "Personal Poem," and "Poem" are also reprinted by permission of City Lights from *Lunch Poems*.

Charles Olson, *The Maximus Poems*, ed. George F. Butterick. Reprinted by permission of the University of California Press.

George Oppen, *Collected Poems*, Fulcrum Press. Copyright © 1962, 1965 by George Oppen; reprinted by permission of New Directions Publishing Corporation.

Kenneth Patchen, *Collected Poems*, New Directions, 1967. Copyright 1954 by New Directions Publishing Corporation; reprinted by permission of New Directions.

Sylvia Plath, *The Collected Poems of Sylvia Plath*, ed. Ted Hughes, Faber and Faber, 1981: excerpts from "Lesbos," "Poem for a Birthday," "Elm," "Purdah," "Lady Lazarus," and "Wintering." Copyright © Ted Hughes 1981, 1965; reprinted by permission of Olwyn Hughes and Harper & Row, Publishers, Inc.

Ezra Pound, *The Cantos of Ezra Pound*, New Directions, 6th printing, 1977. Copyright © 1934, 1937, 1940, 1956, 1959, 1962 by Ezra Pound, 1972 by The Estate of Ezra Pound; reprinted by permission of New Directions Publishing Corporation and Faber and Faber Ltd.

Kathleen Raine, *Collected Poems*, Random House, 1956. *The Hollow Hill*, Hamish Hamilton, 1965. Reprinted by permission of Allen & Unwin and Kathleen Raine.

Carl Rakosi, *Amulet*, New Directions, 1967. Reprinted by permission of Carl Rakosi.

John Crowe Ransom, *Poems and Essays*, Vintage Books, 1955. Reprinted by permission of Random House, Inc., and Laurence Pollinger Limited.

Kenneth Rexroth, *The Collected Shorter Poems*, New Directions, 1966. Copyright © 1940, 1944 by Kenneth Rexroth; reprinted by permission of New Directions Publishing Corporation.

Charles Reznikoff, *Poems 1918–1936*, vol. I of *The Complete Poems*, ed. Seamus Cooney, Black Sparrow Press, 1976. *By the Well of Living & Seeing*, Black Sparrow Press, 1974.

Theodore Roethke, *The Collected Poems of Theodore Roethke*, Doubleday & Co., 1966: excerpts from "The Adamant," copyright 1938 by Theodore Roethke; "Cuttings (Later)," copyright 1948 by Theodore Roethke; "The Lost Son," copyright 1947 by Theodore Roethke; "The

Shape of the Fire," copyright 1947 by Theodore Roethke; "Words for the Wind," copyright 1955 by Theodore Roethke; "The Long Waters," copyright © 1962 by Beatrice Roethke as Administratrix of the Estate of Theodore Roethke; "I Cry, Love! Love!," copyright 1951 by Theodore Roethke. Reprinted by permission of Doubleday & Company, Inc.

James Schuyler, *The Morning of the Poem*, Farrar, Straus and Giroux, 1980: excerpt from "Growing Dark." Copyright © 1976, 1978, 1980 by James Schuyler; reprinted by permission of Farrar, Straus and Giroux, Inc.

Anne Sexton, *All My Pretty Ones*. Copyright © by Anne Sexton; reprinted by permission of Houghton Mifflin Company.

C. H. Sisson, *In the Trojan Ditch: Collected Poems & Selected Translations*, Dufour Editions, Inc., 1975. Reprinted by permission of Dufour Editions, Inc., Chester Springs, Pennsylvania, and Carcanet Press Limited.

Gary Snyder, *The Back Country*, New Directions, 1968. Copyright © 1968 by Gary Snyder; reprinted by permission of New Directions Publishing Corporation.

Bernard Spencer, *Collected Poems*, Alan Ross Ltd., London, 1965. Reprinted by permission of London Magazine Editions.

Stephen Spender, *Collected Poems, 1928–53*, Random House, 1955. Reprinted by permission of Random House and Faber and Faber Ltd.

Wallace Stevens, *Collected Poems*, Alfred Knopf, 1955. Reprinted by permission of Random House, Inc., and Faber and Faber Ltd.

Allen Tate, *Collected Poems, 1919–1976*: excerpts from "Ode to the Confederate Dead" and "The Paradigm." Copyright © 1952, 1953, 1970, 1977 by Allen Tate; copyright 1931, 1932, 1937, 1948 by Charles Scribner's Sons; copyright renewed © 1959, 1960, 1965.

Dylan Thomas, *Poems of Dylan Thomas*. Copyright © 1938 by New Directions Publishing Corporation, 1952 by Dylan Thomas. Reprinted by permission of New Directions Publishing Corporation and David Higham Associates Limited.

R. S. Thomas, *Poetry for Supper*, Rupert Hart-Davis, 1958. *Song at the Year's Turning: Poems 1942–1954*, Rupert Hart-Davis, 1956. Excerpts reprinted by permission of Grafton Books, a division of the Collins Publishing Group.

Melvin Tolson, *Libretto for the Republic of Liberia*, Collier Books, 1970. Copyright 1953 by Twayne Publishers, a division of G. K. Hall & Co., Boston. Reprinted by permission of the publishers.

Charles Tomlinson, *Collected Poems*, 1985. Copyright © Charles Tomlinson 1985; reprinted by permission of Oxford University Press.

Margaret Walker, *For My People*, Yale University Press, 1942.

Robert Penn Warren, *Selected Poems: New and Old 1923–1966*, Random House. Reprinted by permission of Random House, Inc.

Vernon Watkins, *The Death Bell,* Faber and Faber, 1954.

Richard Wilbur, *Ceremony and Other Poems.* Copyright 1950, 1978 by Richard Wilbur. Reprinted by permission of Harcourt Brace Jovanovich, Inc., and of Faber and Faber Ltd from *Poems 1943–54.*

William Carlos Williams, *Collected Earlier Poems.* Copyright 1938 by New Directions Publishing Corporation; reprinted by permission of New Directions. *Paterson.* Copyright © 1946, 1948, 1949, 1951, 1958, by William Carlos Williams; copyright © 1963 by Florence Williams; reprinted by permission of New Directions Publishing Corporation and Penguin Books Ltd. *Pictures from Brueghel.* Copyright © 1954, 1955, 1959, 1962 by William Carlos Williams; reprinted by permission of New Directions Publishing Corporation.

Yvor Winters, *Collected Poems,* The Swallow Press, 1978. Reprinted by permission of The Ohio University Press, Athens.

Charles Wright, *The Southern Cross,* Random House, 1981. Reprinted by permission of Random House, Inc.

James Wright, *Collected Poems,* Wesleyan University Press, 1971: excerpts from "Eleutheria," copyright © 1971 by James Wright; "A Poem about George Doty," copyright © 1971 by James Wright. *The Branch Will Not Break:* excerpts from "Autumn Begins in Martin's Ferry, Ohio," copyright © 1962 by James Wright; "A Blessing," copyright © 1961 by James Wright. Reprinted by permission of Wesleyan University Press.

W. B. Yeats, *Collected Poems,* Macmillan, 1951. Reprinted by permission of Macmillan Publishing Company, New York; Macmillan, London Ltd; A. P. Watt Ltd; and Michael B. Yeats.

Louis Zukofsky, *"A,"* University of California Press, 1978. Reprinted by permission of University of California Press. *All: The Collected Short Poems 1954–1964,* W. W. Norton & Co., 1966. Reprinted by permission of W. W. Norton & Co.

INDEX